The Ultimate Web
Developer's Sourcebook

The Ultimate Web Developer's Sourcebook

Jessica Keyes

AMACOM
American Management Association
New York • Atlanta • Brussels • Buenos Aires • Chicago • London • Mexico City
San Francisco • Shanghai • Tokyo • Toronto • Washington, D.C.

Special discounts on bulk quantities of AMACOM books are available to corporations, professional associations, and other organizations. For details, contact Special Sales Department, AMACOM, a division of American Management Association, 1601 Broadway, New York, NY 10019.
Tel.: 212-903-8316. Fax: 212-903-8083.
Web site: www.amacombooks.org

This publication is designed to provide accurate and authoritative information in regard to the subject matter covered. It is sold with the understanding that the publisher is not engaged in rendering legal, accounting, or other professional service. If legal advice or other expert assistance is required, the services of a competent professional person should be sought.

Various names used by companies to distinguish their software and other products can be claimed as trademarks. AMACOM Books uses such names throughout this book for editorial purposes only, with no intention of trademark violation. All such software or product names are in initial capital letters or ALL CAPITAL letters. Individual companies should be contacted for complete information regarding trademarks and registration.

Library of Congress Cataloging-in-Publication Data

Keyes, Jessica, 1950–
    The ultimate web developer's sourcebook/Jessica Keyes.
      p. cm.
    ISBN 0-8144-7121-8
    1. Web site development. 2. Internet. I. Title

TK5105.888.K4897 2001
005.2'76—dc21

                                        2001037302

10 9 8 7 6 5 4 3 2 1

Dedicated to my family—and some really good friends

Contents

Section 3   Coding Fundamentals

Section 4   Tips and Tricks

Appendixes

Introduction

This book could not have been written without the help of all the contributors in the book—some friends from way back and some new friends. It's interesting to note that in writing a book about the Internet, this team of experts worked together exclusively on the Internet. We never met once. From preliminary discussions about what should be in the book, to online surveys, to first, second, and third drafts—the Internet provided us the means to achieve this end.

It's not that unusual to live and breathe via the Internet any longer. You can go to a doctor via the Internet and even get a Masters degree. I teach at two campuses nowadays. One is "live" at Fairleigh Dickinson University; the other is virtual at University of Phoenix Online. As I'm writing this introduction, I am sitting through yet another snowstorm in New York and my FDU classes have been canceled. My UOP classes, however, go on. After all, it doesn't snow on the Internet.

The Internet has come a long way since I began using it purely for e-mail a decade ago. In the middle 1990s, when the first browser was invented by a college student, visionaries began to see the bottom-line affecting potential of this new set of technologies. But back in the mid-1990s there was no such thing as Java, JavaScript, cascading style sheets, or VoiceXML. It was easy to be a Web developer then. It's very different today.

Today, as my students put it, "you've got to know stuff." So we've made this book full of stuff. It's a book for all levels of Web developers—experts to newbies. It's filled with tons of code, minitutorials, tips and tricks, and dozens of places to go on the Web for free stuff.

More than 30 Web development experts contributed to this effort. Split up into seven sections with a fully loaded set of appendixes, *The Ultimate Web Developer's Sourcebook* starts off with a minitutorial that provides newbies with the lowdown on everything they need to know to build a Web site—from finding an ISP to using FTP; from taking digital images to altering and then uploading them to the Web for all to see.

Section 2 delves into the intricacies of style, content, and design. Here you'll find everything from checklists on how to create great audio and video to a tutorial on creating Flash 5 animations to the secrets of managing your content.

Section 3 gets into the depths of subjects such as active server pages, Perl, and even VoiceXML. For Section 4, I've looked around the Web and found some instructive examples of programming techniques—from creating redirection in your site to learning how to create and read cookies to an entire JavaScript shopping cart. And all with code you can use right away. Of course, there are hundreds, if not thousands of freebie JavaScript code on the Internet. So why did I pick these? Simple—it's because these are great examples of what it's possible to do using Web-based programming languages. Want more code? Just flip over to the appendices for a bunch of links that will get you started.

Section 5 tackles the complex topic of connecting your database to the Web. But what do you do if you don't have your own database (or can't afford one)? Fear not, because the first chapter in this section steps you through a service that you can use to host a database (for free).

Now, you can build the very best Web site in the world, but if your server is slow—what's the use? Section 6 tackles server performance: how to quality-assure your Web site, how to improve the performance of Java applications, and even how to replicate your servers. Section 7 enable you to step through tutorials on some hot Web site–generating power tools including 001, PowerBuilder, mySAP, and Oracle MobileStudio.

And when you're at the end, you're not through yet. In the back of the book you'll find a set of appendices that make for a book unto itself: HTML guide, cascading style sheet guide, product guide, and bunches of hot links to great places on the Web.

Finally, I'd just like to say that this is a book written for developers by developers. While space precludes us from including every conceivable Web development topic, what we've done instead is present what I call "the best of the best."

Now go out and design a great Web site!

Jessica Keyes
New York

Where to go for the code in this book: http://www.newarttech.com/ultimate

Section 1

Getting Started Tutorial

You have to get started somewhere. Since this book is for all types of folks—beginners as well as experts—I thought I'd start us off real easy with an eight-part Web development primer.

What you'll learn in this section:

1. How to plan your Web site.
2. How to develop a theme.
3. How to collect your content.
4. How to map your site.
5. Where to get freebies for your Web site.
6. How to test your site.
7. How to find, pick, and use graphics and layout tools.
8. How to find and use copyright free images.
9. How to take and use your own images.
10. How to make images transparent.
11. How to make imagemaps.
12. How to animate your images.
13. How to use a digital camera and then upload the images.
14. How to manipulate your images (resize, add effects, etc.).
15. How to register your domain name.
16. How to choose an ISP.
17. How to use FTP (file transfer protocol) to move your work from your PC to your Web server.
18. How to add audio to your site.
19. How to make and upload your own audio.
20. How to add video to your site.
21. How to add a slide presentation to your site.

22. How to make a PDF file.

23. How to add a database to your site.

24. How to find free databases and the programs (Perl scripts) that access them.

25. What JavaScript, Perl, and Java can do for you.

26. Where you can find free Perl, Java, and JavaScript scripts and how to install them.

27. What you need to know about UNIX/Windows permissions to get scripts to work.

28. How to add e-commerce to your site.

29. How to take credit card and check payments online.

30. How to open a store on eBay, Amazon, and Yahoo.

31. How to index your site with search engines.

32. How to use meta-tags.

33. How to register with free banner ad exchanges.

34. How to get free content for your site.

35. How to make money by becoming an affiliate.

Planning Your Web Site

Jessica Keyes

You can't write a book without an idea about what that book is going to be about. You can't write a song without some idea about what you want to sing about. In the same way, you can't design your own Web site unless you first know just what's going to be on it.

In the business context, this kind of thing is called a mission statement and just about every company has one. Simply put, it tells folks reading it just what you're all about:

- We sell cars at the lowest prices.
- Our mission is to provide the latest information on cures for blue-footed pigeon disease.
- All music, all the time.

It's not only businesses that have missions, most people do, too:

- I want to get married by spring.
- I want to be a rock star.

We call the mission of the Web site its theme. All well-designed Web sites have carefully thoughtout themes. Let's look at a couple of examples.

Take a look at the Web site in Figure 1-1. What do you suppose its theme is? Choose the theme from the list below the picture.

1. To make money by providing live chat.
2. To provide people with the ability to voice their opinions on a wide variety of topics.
3. To provide voters with the means to cast their votes.

Figure 1-1. *What's the theme of the speakout.com site? (Copyright © 2001 SpeakOut.com.)*

Number 2 is the answer. "To provide people with the ability to voice their opinions on a wide variety of topics" comes closest to the theme of this site.

Now look at Figure 1-2, newarttech.com. What do you think its theme is about?

1. To sell software.
2. To sell globes.
3. To discuss the 21st century.

If you picked number 1—to sell software—you would be correct.

What's Your Theme?

Most companies have formal mission statements that describe a company's reason for existence. This mission statement, or theme, usually is no more than one paragraph. To write your own mission statement, sit down, grab a cup of coffee (or whatever you need to loosen yourself up), and put pen to paper or fingers to keyboard. Try to describe your Web site's theme concisely in no more than one paragraph. To make it even harder I'm going to give you a word limit—use no more than 65 words.

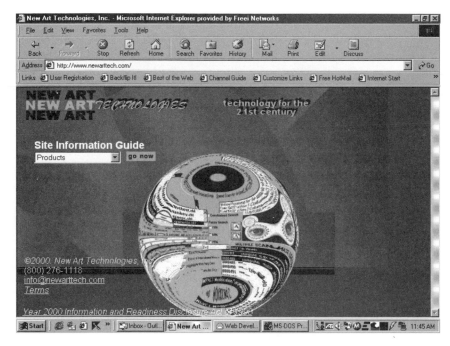

Figure 1-2. *What is the theme or mission statement of the newarttech.com site?*

Browse the Internet long enough and you realize that most Web sites try to do too much. They're unfocused and, as a result, confusing. Now go to a better known Web site such as Yahoo or Amazon. The purpose of either of these sites is very clear to anyone who visits them. That's the point of this chapter: Find your focus *before* you start designing your Web site.

Collecting Your Content

You've decided on your theme. You wrote it. Then you rewrote it. Then you rewrote it again. Now it's time to gather the content that will reflect the theme of your site. There are two types of content:

1. Content that is currently available: This is information that you already have. If you're planning a business site, you probably have marketing brochures, product briefs, sales letters, and the like. Gather all these together and put them in one place. With luck, everything you have is already digital; otherwise you'll have to spend a few hours retyping (or scanning) hard copies.

2. Content that you may not know you need: You've got competitors. We all do. Your goal is to get Web surfers to surf your site rather than your competitors' sites.

To accomplish this, you have to find out just what your competitors have on their sites and "do them one better."

Let's say, for example, that my theme is to build a Web site that provides the ultimate source for golf equipment. I have a bunch of product brochures, but that really isn't sufficient to build a Web site that anyone's going to want to visit. So, it's off to the search engines to see what my competitors are doing.

There are a number of search engines available for your research: altavista.com, excite.com, directhit.com, and google.com are just a few. Using any of these I can come up with a list of viable competitors. For example, searching under "golf equipment" I get a list of golf-oriented Web sites, including the one shown below in Figure 1-3.

Browsing around swapgolf.com we discover a wide variety of content, including:

- A video
- A mall that sells sports equipment
- A chat room
- A golf bulletin board (BBS)
- A kind of auction mechanism for swapping golf tee times
- Puzzles
- Links to other golf sites

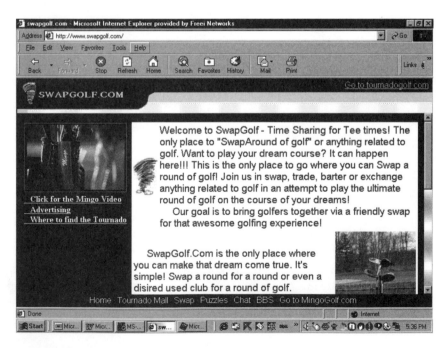

Figure 1-3. One of the competitor sites in the golf equipment area is swapgolf.com. (Used courtesy of SwapGolf.com.)

There's a lot of content here. If I'm going to compete in this area I'll have to have content that is equally as dramatic.

When you plan the content for a Web site, there's also "wish list" content. This is content that you don't currently have, isn't found on any competitor site, and that you think would be a great asset to your site. You may have seen something you like on a noncompetitor such as music, video, or newsletters. Of course, you're walking a fine line here. Put too many things on your site and you run the risk of having an unfocused, confusing site. Put too little on your site and you run the risk of being boring.

Now it's time to make a list of what your site is going to contain.

Making a List and Checking It Twice

Make a complete list of everything you want to have on your Web site, even if you don't put it all online right away. First, list everything you own and have it readily available. Next, browse the Web and see what your competitors are up to. Make a list of what they have and from that list decide what you want to include on your site. Finally, add to your list all those "must haves" you've seen on other sites, even sites that aren't your competitors.

Once you've made your list, go have dinner. After your break go back to the list and go over it, item by item. Put a "yes" next to the items that really make sense for your site. Write "no" on items that might detract from your site.

Keeping Your Content Current

There's nothing worse than stale content on a Web site. Surfers don't like it and neither do search engines. In fact, some search engines drop your Web site from their directories if the Web page hasn't been updated within a certain period of time. Therefore, it's critical to keep adding to and refining your Web site. What if you don't have enough time? Fortunately, there is a Web site whose mission is to help you with just that. Check out isyndicate.com. While you're there, click on About Us and scroll down to Our Mission to see how a well-worded theme or mission statement looks.

Mapping Your Site

Roll up those sleeves again; it's time to get cracking. You're going to sketch out just what your Web site will look like. Use pen and paper or any computer drawing tool (including your word processor). The goal here is to plot out your site map. A site map is a hierarchical list of everything your site is going to have. There are many different ways to represent a map. Figure 1-4 shows a simple text-based site map. The text in uppercase indicates products and the text in upper- and lowercase represents categories. An interesting variation of a site map is shown in Figure 1-5. It combines both graphical and tabular elements.

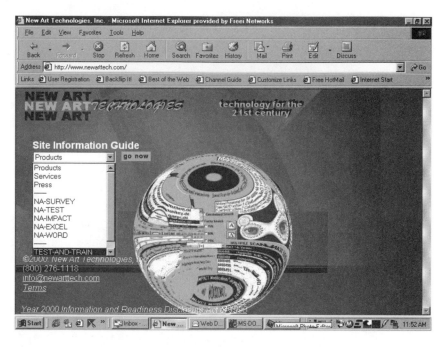

Figure 1-4. *The pull down is a great way to produce a site map.*

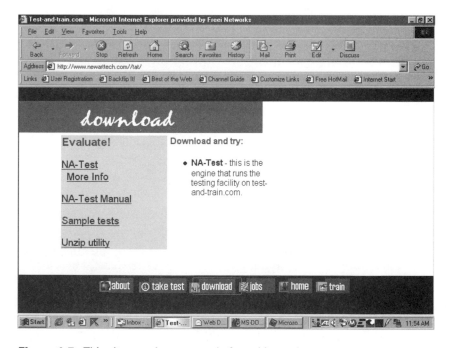

Figure 1-5. *This site map is composed of graphics and text.*

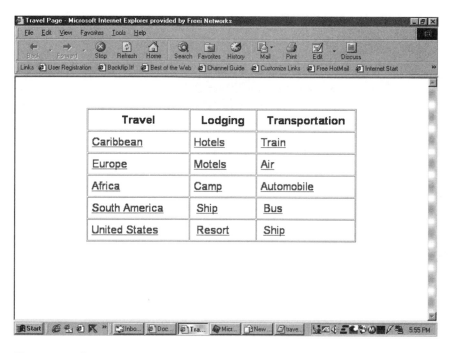

Figure 1-6. *Sample travel site map.*

The easiest-to-follow kind of site map can be seen in Figure 1-6. This site map shows each and every topic and each and every subtopic. It is clear, concise, and easy to read.

Pick one of these styles (i.e., textual, tabular, or graphical) and then plot your own site map. Don't worry if you don't know yet how to create the code to execute your ideas. There is no rule that says you have to actually include a site map on your Web site. In this chapter, we're learning how to use the concept of the map to plan out your site. However, when you're finished it's really a good idea to include it. Most Web sites have one. Most surfers expect one.

Need a Site-Mapping Tool?

Most of the material in this tutorial is application dependent, and I focus on PC/Windows applications. For those of you who use a Macintosh, the general approach is the same and you can find comparable freeware and shareware programs to help build your site at http://download.cnet.com (Mac: Internet) and http://computingcentral. msn.com/Topics/Macintosh. In addition, check the Web with your favorite search engine for Macintosh freeware and shareware sites.

Windows users can hop over to CNET's winfiles site, which has a plethora of site-mapping tools that might be useful to you. Surf to: http://winfiles.cnet.com/apps/ 98/webauth-sitemap.html.

Your First Layout Tool

You've got your theme. You've got your content list. You've got your site map. Now it's time to put it all together. But wait! Just how are you going to do this? If you're an HTML maven you can just use a text editor such as Windows Notepad to HTML your way to fame and fortune. If you're not an HTML pro you might want to research other ways of generating HTML automatically.

You've got a lot of choices:

Use your word processor: Many word processors permit you to Save As an HTML file. Try it with yours. Open up a new document and type some stuff. Use large letters for headings. Use colors and insert images. Try clicking on File|Save As HTML and see what happens.

Use Microsoft Office Premium Edition for Windows: With this product you get a complete copy of the popular Microsoft FrontPage toolset. FrontPage is a complete development tool for creating simple to quite complex Web sites.

Use Microsoft Office 98 Mac Edition Gold: If you're an Office user then you also have a copy of FrontPage version 1.0 for the Mac.

Use your desktop publishing or presentation software: Most of these layout tools now let you save as HTML.

Use Netscape Communicator: If you have installed the full version of Netscape Communicator, you have a copy of Netscape Composer (see Figure 1-7). If you're a code jockey (i.e., experienced with HTML), you might want to try one or more of the HTML tools such as HotDog (Figure 1-8).

You have three goals at this point:

1. Find a tool you can live with.
2. Get comfortable with that tool.
3. Start laying out the very highest level of your site map.

While I recommend that you include a site map in your Web site, I don't insist that it be on the very first page. Your first page should be something like a book's table of contents. It briefly introduces who you are and then provides a series of hyperlinks (either textual or graphical) that take viewers to other topics on your site.

You have a choice to make now. Either your first page can contain links to all the main topics that you've created on your site map or you can choose another set of links entirely. For example, let's say we have a site called IlikeOnions.com. Its site map looks something like this:

WHO WE ARE
The Onion Association of America
People Who Love Onions

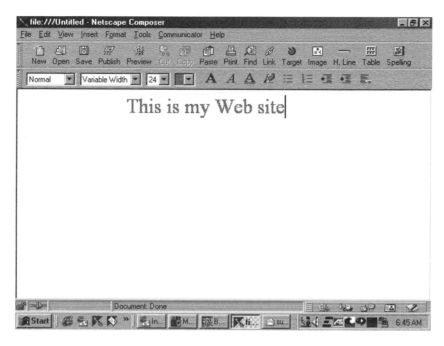

Figure 1-7. *Netscape Composer for Web sites comes with the full version of Netscape Communicator.*

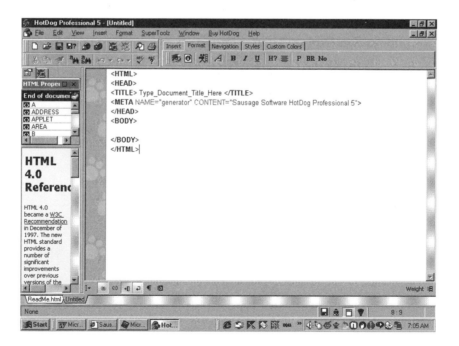

Figure 1-8. *HotDog Professional 5 is a tool for generating HTML code.*

WHY ONIONS ARE GOOD
They're tasty
Keeps people away from you

ONION RECIPES
Onion soup
Onion cookies

The titles that are in capital letters and bolded are the main topics. The titles that are indented in mostly lowercase letters are the subtopics. There is no reason why you can't create a first page by:

1. Creating hyperlinks out of the main topics.
2. Adding a description of who you are (i.e., your theme or mission).
3. Adding some graphical features such as a toolbar and background graphics.

On the other hand, not everyone does it that way (although many do). For an example of an alternative, go to the speakout.com site shown in Figure 1-1. Notice the hyperlinks on the first page. Now click on their Site Map link, which is located on the right side of the graphical toolbar. Now match the site map to the very first page of speakout.com. On the first page there are links to Home, News, Issues, GoVote 2000, Broadcast, Partners, Services, and About Us. The site map, however, is organized differently. Using a tree approach, its main links are Tools, Research, Interact, and SpeakOut.com (which they use to describe their company). Why the two different organizational methodologies? Speakout.com is a site that is very deep. That means it has many, many services. Sometimes Web surfers find it very difficult to find things on a site like this. A solution of many site developers is to provide a site map using a "different way of looking at things" so that it makes things easier to find. My personal take is that this is entirely unnecessary, often confusing, and can be resolved by adding a site search (which we'll discuss in a later tutorial chapter).

Freebies (or at Least a Month's Trial)
CNET's shareware.com is the repository of millions of software titles. Some are totally free and some are loaned out on a trial basis. You might find a great tool there. HotDog, which provides a 30-day trial period, was downloaded from here.

Testing Your Page Design

Using Your PC as a Web Server
We haven't yet gotten to the chapter that tells you how to choose an outside ISP (Internet Service Provider) and how to upload your Web pages to their servers. For now, it's sufficient to use your own PC or Mac. All you need is your browser:

Figure 1-9. *You can open your Web design folder using your browser. That's all there is to using your own computer and browser to test your own designs.*

1. Create a new directory on your computer and name it something relevant to this project (e.g., c:\newweb).
2. Save all your Web design files to this directory, including all HTML files and graphics.
3. Once you have at least one file in this directory you can open up your favorite Web browser, such as Internet Explorer or Netscape Navigator, and type the path and directory name in the browser's address field. You will get a listing of what's in that directory as shown in Figure 1-9.
4. Just double-click on any of the HTML files to display it in your browser.

Saving Pages from the Web and Testing Them

Log on to the Internet and surf to any page. Save that page in your Web design directory or folder using the browser's File|Save As facility. Now point your Web browser to your Web design directory and open the appropriate HTML file. What happens? Does the page display as it did when you opened the page from its http address? Are things missing?

If you are using Internet Explorer 5, Click on File|Save As "Web Page, complete" to save the entire Web page—including all graphics. Internet Explorer will create a series of subdirectories underneath the directory you created to store these images and other Web page items. Use File|Save As Web Page HTML to save the text only.

Just want to save a Web site's images? Before we get started I just want you to know that copying anything from other people's Web sites, including images, might be in violation of copyright laws. However, if you want to copy an image from another Web site, place your cursor over the image and then click on the right mouse button. You will see a menu. Choose Save Picture As. When the Save Picture dialog displays, be sure to save it into your Web design directory.

The Graphics Connection

Jessica Keyes

It wouldn't be the Web without all the pretty pictures. That's one of the strengths of the Web. It's completely visual. In this chapter we'll discuss a number of ways you can create a visually pleasing Web site using a combination of images and powerful tools that let you manipulate them.

Finding the Tool That's Right for You

Graphics packages typically enable you to create a wide variety of graphics files (e.g., .tif, .pcx, .bmp) as shown in Figure 2-1. While Fractal Design's Painter, which is available both on the Mac and PC platforms, is one of the tools of choice of graphic designers, there are many others out there that have similar functionality. Another preferred graphic designer tool is Adobe's Photoshop, again available on both Mac and PC platforms.

Both Photoshop and Painter have a wide spectrum of capabilities including controlling brush size, applying special effects such as textures, cloning, tracing, extracting, layering, text handling, and a whole host of special Web tools. These come at a price—both money-wise and learning curve–wise. The more capabilities, the more it costs (Photoshop costs somewhere around $500) and the longer it takes to learn.

If you decide to go whole-hog into the Web business, by all means take the professional route. For the rest of us, an easier, cheaper tool may be just what the doctor ordered.

One of these is PC-based Micrografx Picture Publisher, which is shown in Figure 2-2. At less than $50, it boasts some pretty fancy capabilities such as animation, special effects, light control, lens flare, bevels, and mosaics. Picture Publisher also comes with 10,000 royalty-free stock photos and clip art images, 250 True Type fonts, and 40 Web page templates.

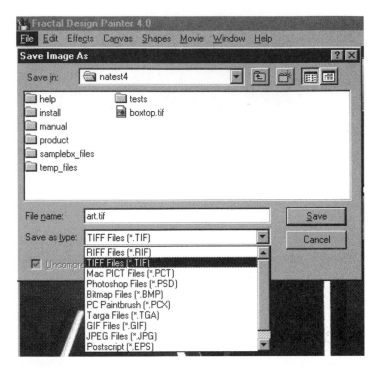

Figure 2-1. *Using Fractal Design's Painter to create images.*

If you don't want to spend even a red cent, you're still in luck. Most computers come with at least one freebie imaging program. PC users have Paint, which is shown in Figure 2-3, and Mac users have QuickDraw. Although these two products provide much less functionality than products like Painter and Photoshop, they're actually robust enough to get you started.

Sometimes Free Is Just Not Good Enough

Although both the Mac and PC come with some good freebie tools, if you're serious about building a well-designed Web site you will want to invest in some good imaging tools. One word of advice, try before you buy. Go to any online store and do a search for "graphics software." Compare listed features and prices and then go to each of the manufacturer's Web sites. Often, they'll have a downloadable trial copy of the software.

Most graphic tools have the ability to save images in a wide variety of formats such as .tif, .pcx, .tga, and .bmp. What you need to know is that the two file formats commonly used on the Web are .jpg and .gif. This may lead to some minor problems if you're using a graphics program that does not support these formats. For example, Microsoft's older version of Paint creates only bitmap, or .bmp, files (the one supplied with Win-

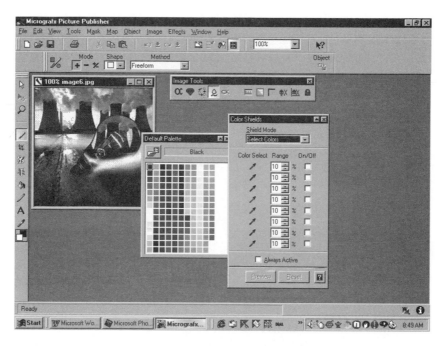

Figure 2-2. *Using Micrografx Picture Publisher.*

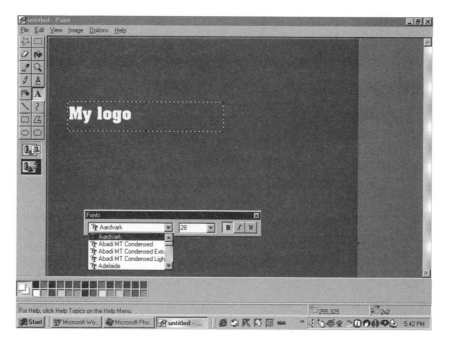

Figure 2-3. *Using Microsoft Paint—a product supplied with Windows.*

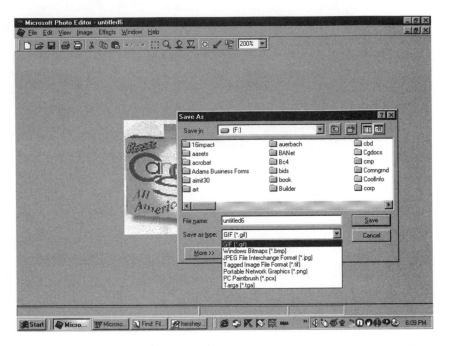

Figure 2-4. *Using Microsoft Photo Editor to save a .bmp file to a .gif or .jpg file.*

dows 98 is much smarter and saves in both .jpg and .gif formats). What you need to do in this instance is to first create your graphic file, save it as a .bmp file, and then use another program to re-save as either a .jpg or .gif file as shown in Figure 2-4.

PNGing the Net

While .gif and .jpg are the two commonly used formats, there is another format called PNG. PNG is an acronym for Portable Network Graphics. While PNG will work on the Web, .gif and .jpg have more capabilities, so they are more popular.

Any imaging processing program can do this. Microsoft Photo Editor is an example. If you have a digital camera or have had your photographs processed on CD you probably already have some freebie imaging software that is both PC- and Mac-compatible.

Using Copyright-Free Images

Just a short half decade ago, Web sites were almost totally text based. Today, most Web developers use a fair number of images to spruce their sites up. Just where do these images come from?

There are three sources of images:

1. Copyrighted images you can get for free.
2. Copyrighted images you must buy.
3. Images that you create and own the copyright to.

First, let's explain a bit about copyrights. When you create something, you own it. Nobody else can use it unless they first get permission to use it or purchase it from you. If you visit any Web site and scroll down to the bottom of its first page you'll probably see the following notice (dates vary):

Copyright ©1995–2000. All rights reserved.

The message here is very clear. Whoever owns the site always owns all the words and all the images on the site. This means that if you copy any part of the site you run the risk of running into legal problems. Being forewarned is being forearmed.

As you probably know by now, almost everything on any Web site can be easily copied. You can copy the HTML (hypertext markup language) by clicking on File|Save on most browsers. You can also copy images. On a Mac, you can just click on it and then select "Download image to disk" from the pop-up menu. On a PC, just place your mouse over the image you wish to copy and click on the right mouse button. You'll see the menu shown in Figure 2-5. Select "Save Picture As" and you're in business. As mentioned, you really want to avoid illegally infringing on anyone else's copyright by copying their images. So what can you do if you're a terrible artist but you still want to jazz up your site with pretty pictures?

Figure 2-5. *Copying images from another Web site.*

One way is to use what is known as royalty-free images. A royalty is the fee you pay the owner of a copyright to use the image or text. Your goal is to avoid paying any and all fees. Royalty-free means just what it says. You don't have to pay a royalty. There are three ways to get these freebies. Most word processors, desktop publishing software, and image processing software come pre-loaded with a wide variety of free images. Micrografx Picture Publisher, which I've already mentioned, comes pre-loaded with over 10,000 images. I use Word 97. If I click on Insert|Picture|Clip Art I get the dialog shown in Figure 2-6. Note the different tabs. There's clip art, pictures, sounds, and videos.

By investing a small amount of money you can purchase a CD that contains literally thousands of royalty-free images. While browsing through my local Staples, which sells software, I came across something called MasterClips. Published by IMSI, it is a multi-CD collection that has—get this—100,000 images. For less than $100 I was in business.

One nice thing about the Web is that there is always one or more folks who have "been there and done that." When it comes to images there's a whole bunch of places on the Web where you can download

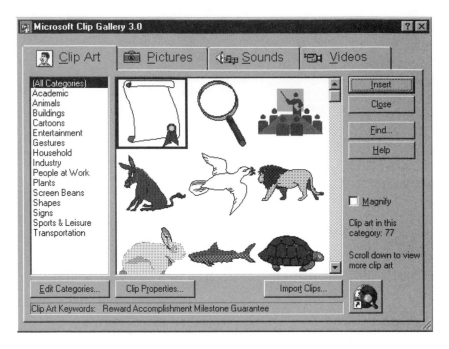

Figure 2-6. *Most word processing packages have royalty-free images.*

royalty-free art. Every day, in fact, a new Web site appears with even more art. It's rather fun to do a search and see what turns up. Just use your favorite search engine and type in the keywords "royalty free art" or "copyright free art." Do this and you might wind up at "El Mono Diable's Money Art" site (http://www.ape-law.com/moneyart) or All-FreeClipArt, which is, funny enough, located at http://www.allfreeclipart.com. Another tact to take in searching the Web for images is to use infoseek.com's image search feature (click on Images rather than the default, which is the Web).

You might have noticed that both clip art and photographs are available. If you browse around the Web long enough you'll discover one thing—professionally designed sites rarely use clip art. Clip art is very cartoonlike, and unless you're directing your Web site at a juvenile audience, cartoonlike imagery is considered amateurish.

What's the Difference Between Clip Art and Photographs?

Other than the fact that photographs look much more professional, there is one major difference between clip art and photographs—photographs are usually space hogs. You can see this for yourself. Use whatever imaging software you have on hand (i.e., Microsoft Photo Editor) and open up both a piece of clip art and a photograph. Since all images have different sizes it's hard to generalize, but the two images I selected at random show the difference between clip art and photographs quite readily. The clip art took up only 5,000 bytes and the photograph took up over 100,000 bytes. Quite a space hog! How can I tell how many bytes an image has? One way is to click on File|Properties in most software and then look at the number of bytes displayed.

The remaining two sources of images will require either a bit of effort or money on your part. There's nothing like a beautifully designed Web site. One thing that makes Web sites beautiful is the imagery. Freebies aside, there's nothing quite like custom-made graphics. That's where a graphics designer comes in. These are the folks who probably went to art school and actually know how to use software packages like Fractal Design's Painter and Adobe's Photoshop. Of course, you're going to have to pay for their services. But sometimes it's really worth it.

Now, if you have a bit of talent, it might be worthwhile for you to invest in taking a course in digital design (i.e., learn how to use Painter and Photoshop along with other important tools such as Adobe Illustrator and Macromedia's Shockwave). If you don't want to spend the money and/or the time you just might want to consider using your own photographs, which just happens to be the topic of the next section.

Using Your Own Images

Take your own pictures!

The advent of digital cameras made taking pictures and then uploading it to the Web rather simple. I bought one of the first digital cameras that came out. It's a Casio QV-10A. It came with the camera, a cable, and software. All I had to do is point, take a picture, and then plug my camera into my computer (it's easier than it sounds) and then suck up those photos.

In fact, I never even had to install the camera's software. Most imaging software comes with a set of commands that lets you do this right from the software. Again, let's use Micrografx Picture Publisher as an example. As you can see from Figure 2-7, there's a button that says "Acquire an image." All I have to do is plug the camera into the back of my computer and click on this button. You'll note that the button says that it can take the image from a camera or from a scanner. What's the difference? Resolution.

Putting photographs on the Web is a tricky business. On the one hand, you want the pictures to be clear and crisp. On the other hand, you can't put a picture up on the Web that is so big it takes ten minutes to download.

Anything you put on the Web page will be downloaded from the Web server (i.e., where your Web page lives) to the end-user's PC. That's how the Web works. When you surf the Web you might notice that some sites take longer to load up than other sites. Other than the fact that sometimes the Web site's computer is slow or overloaded with requests, the one thing that makes sites slow to load is the amount of imagery on that particular site. Loading actually means the movement of text and graphics from the Web site's server computer, over the telephone line, to the end-user's computer.

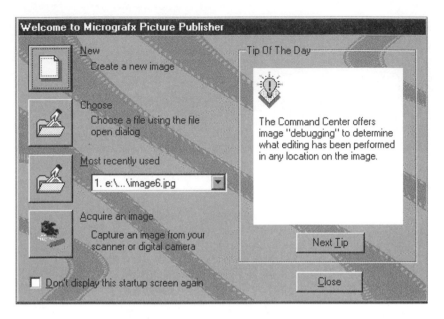

Figure 2-7. *Most imaging software permits you to acquire an image directly from a scanner or digital camera.*

Even though we read about things such as DSL (digital subscriber line) and cable modems and T1 lines, all of which provide really speedy access to the Web, the sad fact is that the vast majority of Web users are using modems with speeds up to only 56 kb. 56 kb is extremely slow; it's only 56,000 bytes per second, with a byte being a letter, number, or special character such as a colon. The sentence "this site is very slow" has 22 characters including all spaces. Now add a few images here and there and you can see that it doesn't take very long to start getting very slow.

So we want to make sure our picture is not so large that it takes a long time to load. Unfortunately, the clearer the picture the more bytes it uses. The more bytes it uses the bigger it is and the longer it takes to load. And so on and so on. The clarity of the picture is its resolution. Digital cameras cost more depending upon the resolution of the pictures they take. My Casio, which I bought before it was possible to buy a really good quality digital camera, is capable of taking pictures in the 640×480 resolution range (which just happens to be the resolution of most PC screens). I paid about $200 for this camera. Today you can get an Agfa ePHOTO Smile Digital Camera with 640×480 resolution for about $99.

At the high end of the digital camera spectrum is the Toshiba PDR-M5. Costing about $700, this baby is capable of resolutions in the 1600×1200 range. Scanners work in the same way. The higher the resolution, the more it costs and the better image you get. I would only recommend using a scanner as a last resort. Because it's a copy of the original that you're scanning, you lose much quality. If you're dying to use an image and you have no other alternative, then by all means use the scanner, but you're going to have to spend a lot of time with your imaging software cleaning up the photograph up.

If you don't have a digital camera, just how can you get your own photographs into your computer? Use your regular camera. This is what I tell my clients. Take your shots. However, don't have them processed to paper. Tell your film processor to process it to CD instead.

Kodak pioneered the concept of processing photographs to a CD. Their Photo CD and Picture CD services let you take hundreds of pictures and store them, with great resolution, right on one CD.

It's as simple as this:

1. Take your pictures.
2. Go to your film processing store, and when you fill out the form click on Photo CD or Picture CD.
3. Pick up the pictures.
4. Go home and open the CD and take out the index card. The index card is a big photograph with thumbnail (i.e., tiny) copies of each photograph on the CD. Beneath the thumbnail is the digital name of the picture.
5. Place the CD in your CD drive.
6. If your computer is set up to automatically install the software that is loaded onto the CD, then you will immediately begin the install process. If your PC is not set up to install upon CD insertion, then follow Kodak's instructions.
7. Once the software is installed it will guide you to select the image you want, let you manipulate it, and then save it to your hard disk. It will always be stored on the CD as well.
8. If you're tech-savvy you can just open your favorite image processing program and use the index to determine which photo you want, and then copy the digital version into the imaging program.

Figure 2-8 shows just how easy this is. Just select the thumbnail of your choice and then use one of Picture CD's tools to either enhance, stylize, rotate, or caption it.

Process Your Photos Right to the Web

Some of the film processors have gone one step better than processing to CD. They process right to their Web site. All you have to do is surf to the site, point to your images, and then download to your own computer.

Wouldn't it be nice if the Web was able to use any graphic format and any picture

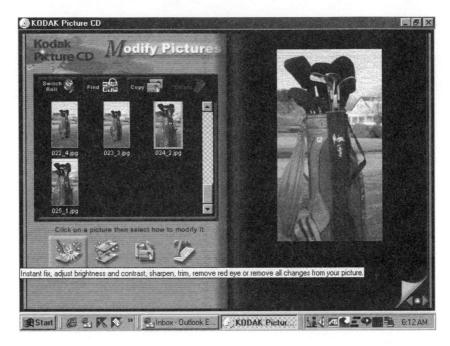

Figure 2-8. *Kodak's Photo CD provides you with the ability to digitize your photographs—and manipulate them.*

size? Stop dreaming! The Web has its rules. Albeit these rules change from time to time, but for now let's just get used to the fact that:

1. You should only use .jpg and .gif formats.
2. The size of your image should be as small as possible. The smaller the size, in terms of bytes, the faster it loads. In no case would I recommend that your image size exceed 30 kb (30,000 bytes). I strive for images less than 10 kb.

Both .jpg, which is stored on your hard disk and the Web as .jpg files, and .gif formats are compressed formats. This means that when you save anything in either of these formats the number of bytes is less than when you save the same image in a different format. Try this experiment. Save an image in a .tif format. .tif files are usually considered one of the highest quality file formats. This format is typically used to save images that ultimately wind up in a printed format. But images that wind up on paper don't really have to worry how fat they are! Now save the .tif image to a .gif file. It's smaller, isn't it. Now save it again in .jpg format. It's smaller still.

You may have noticed something during this experiment. The image quality was declining as you were saving it in different formats. While a .jpg file is often quite tiny,

Figure 2-9. *Resizing your image to make it smaller.*

which means it will load really fast, the quality of that image is sometimes not acceptable for your purposes.

Actually, I lied! About 90 percent of the time the .jpg file is smaller than the .gif file. However, it's really quite dependent upon the number of colors in the image itself. The .gif format is excellent at compressing images that have relatively few colors or no gradations in color and the .jpg format is good at compressing images with lots of colors. As mentioned, however, most of the time .jpg compresses to a smaller size than its corresponding .gif image.

What does all of this mean for you? You're going to have to spend lots of time manipulating your images. It's safe to say that you're probably going to spend more time fooling around with your images than you will working on your associated text.

There are several things you may want to do with each of your images:

1. Make sure it's clear and that the file size is small.
2. Size it in terms of length and width for placement on the Web page (Figure 2-9).
3. Add effects to it (Figure 2-10).
4. Make it transparent.

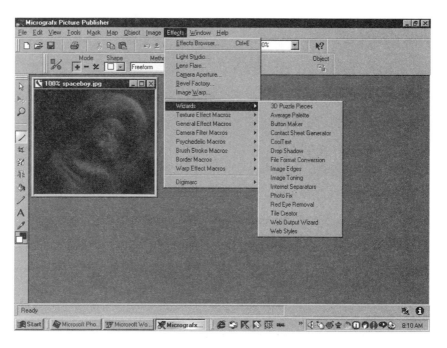

Figure 2-10. *Using imaging software to add effects to your image.*

We've already discussed item 1 on our list. Use a digital camera or photo CD type of film processing to get your photo digitized and then save it into a .gif or .jpg format—choosing either .gif or .jpg depending upon the final size of the image. Of course, if your image is clip art this is really a no-brainer. Your image size is already very small and probably already in the .gif format.

Number 2 on our list is really related to number 1. You're going to find that the digitized image is often quite large. So large, in fact, that it barely fits on your monitor's screen. This is good news indeed! Why? Because when you make it smaller in dimension you will also make it smaller in size (i.e., kb)—without destroying any of the quality.

So how do you make it smaller? Most imaging software comes with a resize function. Microsoft Photo Editor has this on its Image menu. The dialog, as shown in Figure 2-9, permits you to make it larger (i.e., increase to 200 percent) or smaller (decrease to 50 percent). Take a walk around the Web. You'll notice one thing. The image sizes are usually proportional to the design on the Web. No image is too big nor too small. What you may want to do is to use the procedure we learned in the prior section to copy some of these images to your own computer. Bring each of them up in your image processing software to check the size in terms of length and width as well as number of bytes. Pretty soon you'll get a good sense of how big or small images should be on a well-designed page.

Also take some time to play around with resizing your own images. Resize them proportionately. Now see what happens when you click on "Allow Distortion" (or however your software terms it).

Each time you do any of the above check out the file size. You'll have to save the image each time to do this but it'll be well worth it. As mentioned above, you can usually use the File|Properties command within most imaging software to get a handle on file size. If you can't find where your software indicates the file size, use your Mac or PC operating system commands to do the same thing. For example, when I open up Windows Explorer I can see all of my files and their respective file sizes.

The best part of working with images is the fun you can have when adding special effects. Again we turn to our imaging software for this capability. Even inexpensive software has these capabilities. Figure 2-10 shows Micrografx Picture Publisher's bag of tricks. I can do things such as: make a puzzle out of my image, create drop shadows, make tiles, warp the image—even do psychedelics. Now don't go overboard. Again, look to the Web's best sites to see how wild and crazy you should get on your own site. One thing you'll notice right away is that most sites' images, unless the site is targeted to the under-20 bunch, are clear, crisp, and tasteful, as shown in Figure 2-11.

Once you've created an image, you need to place it on your Web page. The HTML to do this is as follows:

```
<img height="20" width="131" src="yellow.gif">
```

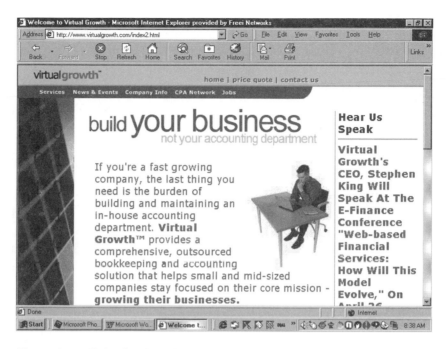

Figure 2-11. *Strive for clear, clean images. (© 2001 Virtual Growth, Inc.)*

Height and width are not necessary and, in fact, might even distort your image if you make a mistake in the dimensions. You can add a border to your image by adding:

```
<img height="20" width="131" "yellow.gif" border=1>
```

Border=0 means no border, border=1 specifies a thin line around the image, and so on. You can also make your image clickable so that it hyperlinks to another page. The HTML to do this is as follows:

```
<a href=gohere.htm><img height="20" width="131"
src="yellow.gif" border=0></a>
```

As you know, you can create a Web page that has either a background color or uses a background image. What do you do if the image you want to place on that page blocks out the design behind it or uses a different set of background colors that conflicts with the page design? You make the image transparent.

Here's an example. Say you use a background image that is varying shades of turquoise. By the way, the HTML to use background images is:

```
<body background="image.jpg">
```

Figure 2-12. *Using a background image.*

Figure 2-13. *Using an image that conflicts with the background.*

Okay. We use a background that looks something like Figure 2-12. Now we create our logo, which looks something like Figure 2-13. Notice that the background of the Web page is dark and the background of the logo is light. If I place the current logo on a Web page with a different background, I'm going to get the monstrosity shown in Figure 2-14.

How can we fix this? The answer is to save the image as either a .gif87 or .gif89a formatted file. If your imaging software does not handle this format, then search for software that does let you save to this format. LviewPro (www.lview.com), which runs on a Windows platform, provides you with just this option, as shown in Figure 2-15. But before you save the file into the right format you have to do some manipulation.

Using the Retouch menu, select Background color. You will now see the "Select Color Palette Entry." Now click on Dropper and your cursor will turn into a medicine dropper. Carefully place the dropper in the area that you want to make transparent and click. The dropper "sucks" up the color of the background surrounding the image. In the example the background color was white. It could have easily been green or chartreuse. What it can't do is handle patterns, since there is not just one color to "suck up." So this only works with a solid color scheme. Now save the file in the 87 or 89a .gif format and reload your page. Voila. Look at Figure 2-16 and see the difference.

Figure 2-14. *The problems of using a non-transparent image.*

Animating Your .gifs

How can you animate a .gif file? .gif files have many capabilities. Its most interesting is its ability to contain multiple images. They are created by piecing together separate images called frames and assigning delay times between the display of the different frames. In this way, images can be made to appear to be animated.

Figure 2-15. Using LviewPro to make an image transparent.

Figure 2-16. An image with a transparent background.

Be Wary of Browser Differences

Everyone has a different browser. Some folks are using Internet Explorer and others are using Netscape Navigator. Some are even using WebTV. There are different versions of each browser as well. What this means is that when you start using these fancy techniques, some of what you do may not be visible to folks with outdated browsers. What most developers do is try to download as many browsers as they can and then test their designs on each of these browsers.

Like everything else, when it comes to images you're going to need a tool to create an animated .gif. And, as usual, these tools are platform dependent. We're going to use the Windows-based Alchemy Mindworks (www.mindworkshop.com) GIF Construction Set. However, you can find a great selection of Mac and PC toolsets listed at http://www.webreference.com/dev/gifanim/.

Figure 2-17. *A completed animated .gif.*

Figure 2-18. *The first three images of an eight-image animated .gif.*

Let's look at a finished animated .gif first (Figure 2-17) so you get can a good handle on what you need to do to create one. Since this is a book, you can't actually see what's going on—but trust me, it's moving around.

This picture is actually composed of eight pictures, the first three of which are shown in Figure 2-18. Each is an image of the little ball facing a different direction.

The question you are probably asking yourself now is just how do you get these images rotated in this fashion. The answer is some fancy footwork and your imaging software, using the following steps:

1. Create or digitize your first image. Keep in mind that these images must be small, since when you sandwich a whole bunch of them together the file size gets large fairly quickly. Save your first image as image1.gif.

2. Now save the second image to image2.gif. I am going to use Microsoft Photo Editor, so you will have to figure out the correct command for your own software. I am going to click on Image Rotate. Figure 2-19 shows the menu I will see next.

3. I can rotate it 90 degrees at a time but then I can get only four images into my animated .gif, since a complete circle is only 360 degrees. Instead, I am going to choose "by degree" and type in a smaller number. Since I want eight images I am going to divide 360 by eight and use 45 degrees. Don't worry about being bad at math. You can use any number and by playing around with it achieve the same results. The results can be seen in Figure 2-20.

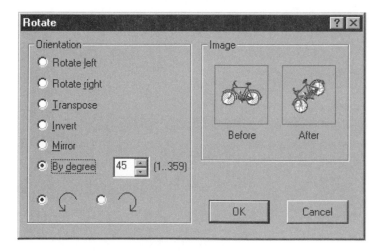

Figure 2-19. *Using the rotate feature.*

Figure 2-20. *The ball image rotated 45 degrees.*

4. Now keep doing this until you've gotten your eight images—or when you feel like stopping. If you're going to create a "ball" effect, then you really do want to stop when the ball achieves a full circle. If you're creating an image that moves from left to right and/or right to left, then you can stop whenever and wherever you feel like it.

5. Next, open the GIF Construction Set or other animation-making software.

6. Click on File|Animation Wizard to help get you started.

7. It's going to ask you a series of questions such as "is this for the Web," the answer to which is yes; "do you want to loop indefinitely," the answer to which is up to you; "what kind of color palette are you using," the answer to which depends on the image you are using, with cartoonlike and clip art images being drawn and photographs being any of the other choices. You might want to try several of these choices and see which one creates the best animation for you. The last set of choices is how fast you want the animation to run. Choose the default, but if it is not suitable to your taste or purposes, try it again with another setting.

8. Last, but not least, you're going to have to select the files you wish to use for your animation. Clicking on Select will bring up your familiar Open dialog. Now select all of the files you wish to use. When you're done you will see a dialog like the one in Figure 2-21. Now save it and you're done.

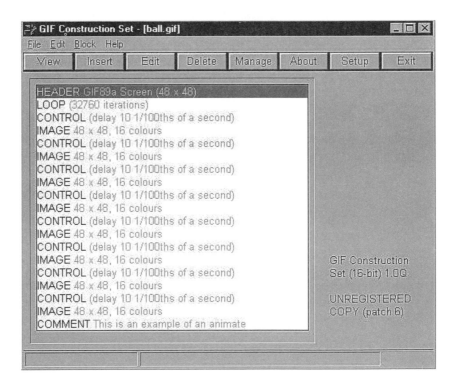

Figure 2-21. *Loading all images to the GIF Construction Set.*

It's really as simple as that.

The graphic designers taking this class will be capable of doing fantastic things with their skill sets and automated tools. But you know what, these same tools let the rest of us create some pretty credible imagery.

Additional Sources

http://www.dcs.ed.ac.uk/home/mxr/gfx/utils-hi.html is a great place to go for more information and links about graphics on the Web.

The ISP Connection

Jessica Keyes

The acronym ISP stands for Internet Service Provider. These are the guys (or gals) that have the computers that actually hang off the Internet. Let's take a minute to explain the workings of the Net so that you'll know why an ISP is a critical component of your particular Web site.

You have a PC. Maybe you even have a superpowerful PC. But, in general, an individual PC is not, by itself, connected to the PC as a server. Instead, your PC is what is known as a client. It's a "window" to the Internet. A server, on the other hand, is the machine on which your content—pictures, text, etc.—is said to be hosted. It is the server that is the machine that is actually connected to the Internet. Everyone else just uses their PCs as clients to view stuff (i.e., content) on the Internet as shown in Figure 3-1.

So who owns these gateways to the Internet? Generally speaking it is the ISP or Internet Service Provider. These are the folks who own the big servers and fast telecommunications lines that permit you to surf the Web. AOL is considered an ISP. So is Verizon and AT&T. They all offer different services and charge different prices.

Some ISPs exist merely to permit you to dial in to them so that you can personally surf the Web. Most of you probably have a PC or Mac connected to the Web via a telephone line. Your modem's maximum speed is about 56 kb (i.e., 56,000 bytes per second). While this is sufficiently fast enough for you to surf the Web, it is way too slow for you to use your own PC or Mac as a server on the Web. So the ISPs started offering up a second, and even more lucrative, service. This is called hosting.

Hosting is a service where you take the pretty Web pages that you designed (i.e., all your .gif, .jpg, and .html files) and transfer (i.e., port) them to your ISP's faster machine. If you look again at Figure 3-1 you can easily see how it works. You're the guy sitting at the PC on the bottom of the picture. You design your Web pages from the comfort of your own home. When your design is done you transfer all of the design's pieces (.gif and .jpg image files, .html files, audio and video files, etc.) to the more powerful hosting computer at the top of the page. It's from this location that guy number 2 and guy number 3, on the left- and right-hand side of the picture, can browse your content. It's simple, really.

The first thing you have to do is find the ISP that's right for you. There are some things you need to think about:

How much do you want to pay? There are literally thousands of ISPs out there. All of them offer varying levels of service, features, and support for varying price ranges. There are even free services out there.

What level of support do you desire? It would not be a good decision to sign up with an ISP based on price alone if that ISP had a reputation for poor service. Spend time at the ISP's site. What kind of support do they offer? Is there an 800 number that you can call if you run into problems? Is there a special e-mail address for support? Do they promise a response within four hours, eight hours, one day, two days?

What freebies do they offer? Some ISPs offer unlimited e-mail addresses. Some offer free scripts (i.e., programs) to do things such as auctions, chat, and BBS. Make a list of what you want and try to match it against what each of the ISPs you are reviewing offers.

Do they offer their own e-mail capability? Beware! Some lower-priced services do not provide you with the ability to collect your messages directly from the ISP's servers. Instead they forward all mail to, say, your AOL account. This means that you need to have an account somewhere else. This also means that, unless you're technically savvy, your return e-mail address will be yourname@aol.com or yourname@att.com or whatever, which looks pretty lame. The caveat here is to read the section on e-mail services very carefully. If you can't find anything on their Web site that directly addresses this issue, then call them up. Ask them the following question, "Can I pick up my e-mail directly from your servers or is it forwarded to my primary e-mail address?" The techies among you can ask what the POP3 (incoming mail) and SMTP (outgoing mail) server names are.

Do they offer the services I need today—and in the future? Let's say you start out just an information Web site. Most ISPs can do this at low cost and with no problems. But let's say that you might want to sell some stuff over the Internet during the next year. This is known as e-commerce, and you want to make sure your ISP offers the facilities you need. For instance, siteamerica.com offers the following e-commerce capabilities: shopping cart, real-time credit card transactions, ordering system, merchant account approval within 24 hours. E-commerce is discussed in Chapter 7.

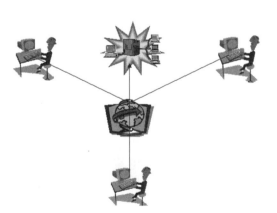

Figure 3-1. A bird's-eye view of the Internet.

Beware the Freebies

Don't be tempted by all those offers of free Web sites. They are indeed free but they generally do not permit you to use your own domain name. Instead your domain name becomes something like www.hostingcompany/~myname. Ugh! So where do you go to get information on which ISP you should use? The Web, of course:

1. CNET Web services provides a list of ISPs to consider. Go to: http://webisplist.internetlist.com/cgi/scompare.asp?stable=Hosting_Plans.
2. WebHosters.com. This is an information-rich site with lots of information on different hosting companies. Go to: http://www.webhosters.com/.
3. HostReview.com. This is another information-rich site providing details on various hosting companies. Go to: http://www.hostreview.com/.

At this stage in your Web design career you're not actually going to understand all of the features you see described on these sites. At a minimum, you're going to want the following features:

1. 20 MB disk space or more. You want a big glop of space to store your images, HTML, etc. The more the better.
2. 1 GB per month data transfer. A GB, or gigabyte, is one billion bytes. Wow! Data transfer means the number of bytes that people view on your Web site. If you've got many large images on your site, and/or your site is very large, then it doesn't take too long for millions of bytes to be "downloaded" or transferred from the hosting computer to Web surfers' PCs and Macs. So the bigger the number here, the better.
3. FTP access to your account. FTP stands for file transfer protocol. We're going to talk at length about this later on in this chapter. It's sufficient to say that you need this to move (i.e., upload) your content from your PC or Mac to the hosting computer.
4. E-mail. We've discussed this above. Make sure you can pick up your mail from the ISP's computer and that nothing is forwarded to another account unless, of course, you wish it to be forwarded. In addition, you want as many e-mail addresses as possible. You probably have noticed that there is always an info@mywebsite.com. However, it's nice to be able to have sales@mywebsite.com, too.
5. CGI-bin capability. CGI stands for common gateway interface. This is where you store the programs that you may want to have on your site. Obviously, if you are going to do this you will need to learn a bit about programming. Usually the Perl programming language is used. These programs, or scripts as they are generally known, are stored in the cgi-bin folder on your site. Even if you don't know how

to program you can get free scripts for things such as auctions, chat, and bulletin board.

6. Toll-free support number and support e-mail address.

Registering Your Domain Name

The name you choose for your Web site is very important. It says a lot about who you are and what you do. What you call your Web site depends on several things:

1. Your audience.
2. What you market.
3. What domain names are available.

Five years ago I'd recommend just picking one or more great names and then simply registering them. Today, so many businesses and individuals (millions and millions) have registered domain names that there are few good ones left. This means that you're going to have to spend a considerable amount of time thinking of names and then checking to see if they're already in use.

The first step in thinking up a name is to decide who your audience is. Is it the juvenile market? The business market? The sports market? The whatever market? Once you know what your market is, think about exactly what you want to market.

For example, let's say you're in the sporting business. Now we know your audience is sports fanatics. Let's also say you specialize in volleyballs. So now we know what you market.

The next step is to come up with one or more names that "sell" directly to that market. You have two choices here:

1. Come up with a name, like volleyballs.com, that is an exact match to your market. The value of this approach is that your domain name is the same name as the market. It's easy to remember, and more than likely it's the first word someone will type into a search engine when searching for volleyballs. Figure 3-2 shows the results of just such a search for volleyballs. Unfortunately, given the proliferation of Web sites, most "good names" like this are not available.
2. The other tact to take is to get radical. Try a name that is so strange-sounding that it gets noticed right away. For example, monster.com does not sell monsters. It's a job-searching service. Google.com is a search engine and razorfish.com does not sell fish.

The very best way to search for a great name for your company is to go online to one of the registry sites so that you can spend a few minutes (hours or days) searching for a great name that hasn't already been taken.

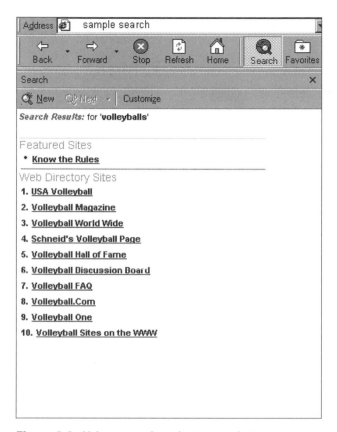

Figure 3-2. *Using a search engine to see what names are being used for the volleyball market.*

Back in the days of the Internet's infancy, which was just a few short years ago, there was only one place to go on the Net if you wanted to find out about domain name registration—the Internic. Now known by its formal name, Network Solutions, it is but one of many places you can go to register that all-important name. It's a good first place to go to find out what names are available and they do provide a nifty tool called My-NameFinder, which takes some of the pain out of searching for an available as well as appropriate name.

When you surf to schogini.com you'll see the display shown in Figure 3-3. We're going to search to see if the domain name volleyballs.com is already used. Notice that the www. is already filled in for you. There are many domain types in use on the Internet today. Most of us want to get a .com name. Com, which stands for commercial, is only one of many. There's also .net for network, .org for organization, .gov for government, .edu for education, and a plethora of foreign country names like .uk for the United King-

Figure 3-3. *Using schogini.com to search for available domain names. (Copyright © 1997–2001 Schogini, Inc. Used by permission.)*

dom. Since .com is the one name that everybody knows, that's the type of domain that you want to register. If you're lucky enough to get the .com of your choice you may also want to consider registering all the other variations (i.e., volleyballs.net) so that others don't try to infringe on your market share.

Once I enter my desired name I press the enter key and wait with baited breath to see if someone has my name. Oh, oh! Someone does, because I now see the dreaded "Sorry, **volleyballs.com** is not available" message.

Schogini.com is one of many that can register your domain name. Others, including networksolutions.com recently acquired by Verisign, provide some additional services, such as providing a list of alternative names, as shown in Figure 3-4. Sometimes, the easiest methodology is to just reenter another name. A lot of folks keep trying this technique. First they add an "i" to the beginning of the name (e.g., ivolleyballs.com). If this is unavailable they add an "e" to the front of the name. And so on and so on. Now you can see why it takes so long to come up with a good name.

If you're stubborn and you want your name and you want it now, you might want to try looking down the current owner of the domain name to see if they will sell it to you. Many Internet domain names are even auctioned. Sometimes if you have a great

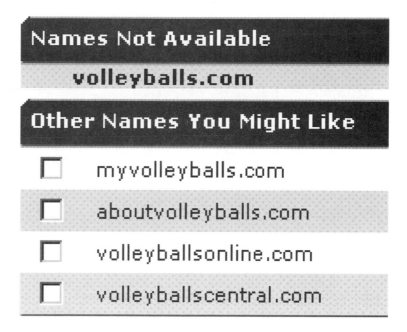

Figure 3-4. *Using an alternative name.*

name people come right to you. A few years ago, the owner of business.com got $7 million for the right to use this name. Don't you wish that was you?

To find out who owns a particular name you can use the Internet WHOIS service, which stands for "who is." You can surf to this site directly from the front page of networksolutions.com, where a link to WHOIS appears on the top right-hand side of the page. Be sure to enter the whole domain name (e.g., www.volleyballs.com). I get the name and address of the owner and the rest is just business as usual. If you actually tried out the Network Solutions site you'll soon find out that Network Solutions is also a hosting company (i.e., ISP). In fact, you might even want to check out their ImageCafe. You can order up a pre-designed Web site, domain and all, right from this Web site. The designs are quite nice.

Once you've decided on your domain name and checked its availability, it's time to register your site. While Network Solutions and a host of others perform this service, the best bet is to get your chosen ISP to do it for you. In fact, it's usually part of their service and covered by the setup fee that is listed in the costs.

No matter who you use to perform this service and no matter what they charge, there will also be a domain registration fee. This will be billed directly to you from the government-authorized Internet registration service. It will come to you via e-mail as well as via snail mail. Pay it promptly or you will lose your rights to that name. The current fee is $35 per year billed every two years.

Domain Registration Logistics

Once your ISP sends the forms in to the domain registry service it can take up to 72 hours for your name to be available. This means that if you type www.yourname.com into your browser you might get an error message. Your ISP will also give you an IP address, which is a set of numbers (e.g., 209.55.67.12). You will be able to get to your Web site immediately using this address.

Using FTP (File Transfer Protocol) to Upload to Your Web Site

Once you sign up with an ISP you will be given a chunk of disk space on the ISP's servers onto which you can load your images, HTML, etc. So the question becomes, just how do you load it from your PC or Mac to the server? Let's say you live in New York and your ISP is located in California. That's where their computers are, too. It's rather expensive to hop on an airplane every time you want to add something else to your Web site.

Instead, you use automated tools to help you. Some ISPs create easy-to-use procedures to assist newbies (i.e., inexperienced Web site owners) with uploading stuff to the Web. I sometimes find that, in spite of their best intentions, these easy-to-use utilities are anything but!

FTP, or file transfer protocol, has been around for what seems like eons—way before the Web was the Web. It's the traditional way to move things from one computer to another and it's not hard to use.

We're going to step through the FTPing process using a Windows-based utility called CuteFTP. Mac users can find similar functionality by searching download.com for the freeware called DropFTP version 1.0 or Fetch 3.0.3. Both of these are very popular Mac tools.

CuteFTP can be obtained from the shareware.com or download.com site. The "pay for" version provides more functionality but the shareware version will work just fine for you.

After you've downloaded and installed it you will see something pretty similar to Figure 3-5 when you open the program. On the right-hand side of the smaller window is a list of Web sites you've already entered information for within CuteFTP. For instance, I have a site called CraveReviews, another called MINGO, and another called newarttech. These are just the short names that I use to remember which entry goes with each site. Of course, the first time you do this the list will be brief. There will be one or two entries, with one of them being the CuteFTP site itself. I am going to highlight this entry and then click on the Edit Site button so that you can see the entries you are going to have to make to be able to FTP to your new site.

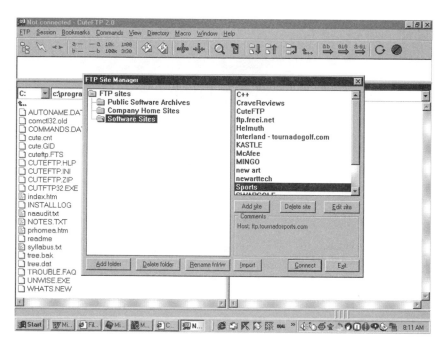

Figure 3-5. *The main page of the CuteFTP utility.*

As shown in Figure 3-6, the first field you must enter something into is called Site Label. This is just the arbitrary name you give your site so that you will recognize it in the CuteFTP list discussed above. The next field down is the host address. You will need to get this from your ISP. Generally, when you sign up for a new Web site the first e-mail you will get from that ISP is a list of things such as your e-mail servers (i.e., POP3 and SMTP), your IDs and passwords, and information you need to use for FTPing. One of these pieces of information will be the host address. Many start with the ftp. prefix, so it's easy to spot.

The next piece of information will be your user ID and password. In Figure 3-6 these two fields are blank. CuteFTP uses their own FTP site to enable their customers to easily upload and download to their site. So they don't require an ID and a password. Your own FTP site will have both. You really do want this, because without it, anyone can change and even delete all your hard work. If you don't understand the e-mail your ISP sent you or you never got one, then call them and ask them to help you fill out the information requested in this discussion.

Use the defaults for everything else on this screen: Login type is Normal, Transfer type is Auto-Detect (auto detect means that the software program figures this out for you), Host type is Auto-Detect, the Local Filtering box is checked, and everything else is blank. Clicking on OK creates your entry and now you're ready to rock and roll. From the main menu click on your entry and then click Connect.

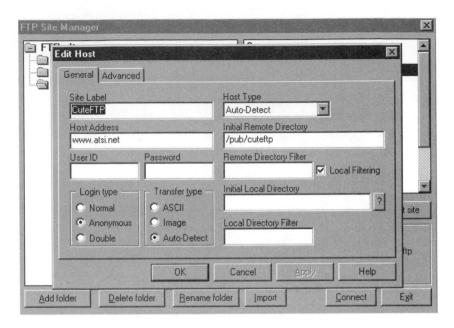

Figure 3-6. *The site configuration screen.*

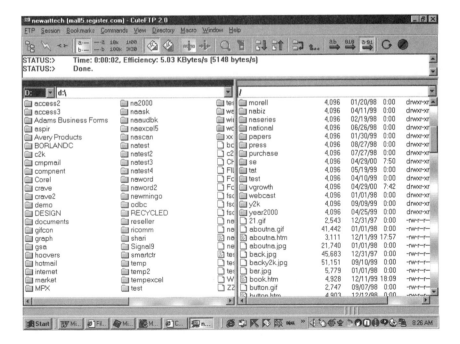

Figure 3-7. *The FTP data screen.*

As shown in Figure 3-7, on the left-hand side of the screen is a list of drives, directories, and files for your own PC or Mac. You can click around on the drive list and directory list until you get the directory into which you stored your files. On the right-hand side of the screen is the directory listing of your Web site. It's going to take some practice to become adept at doing FTPs. But once mastered it becomes an easy process. Your goal is to move files from your PC or Mac to your Web server—from left to right.

On the top of the screen is the menu. You will probably use only the Commands menu item. If you open this menu up you will see some of the functionality of the CuteFTP utility. The most commonly used command is "Make new dir." Your Web site works just like your PC or Mac in the way you can have folders and subfolders, which are also called directories. For example, you might want to create an images folder so that all images are stored in this particular subfolder. To do this:

1. Click on the Commands menu.
2. Select "Make new dir."
3. A small dialog box pops up. Type the name you desire.
4. The directory is created.

Some things you need to watch out for are:

1. You only get so much time without doing anything during FTP until the system "times you out." If this happens don't panic. Just click on File, then Reconnect, and you're back in business.
2. If you have more than one site and you want to stop working on one and start working on another, click on File, then Disconnect, then File Site Manager to start up the other site.
3. Because there are two sides of the screen, only one can be active at a time. In CuteFTP you can tell which side is active by looking at the bar above the directories. In Figure 3-7 you can see a bar on the left-hand side of the screen. This means that the PC/Mac side is active. Now I can upload files from my computer to the Web site. If the right side were active, I could download files from the Web site to my computer or I could do things such as create directories. To make a side active, just click on the bar.
4. Initially all you are going to do is make sure that the left side points to the directory into which you stored your HTML and images files. Now we're ready to upload.

Since this is the first time you've ever created a Web site, just leave all of the files in the main Web directory. In other words, don't create any new directories. To upload a file from your PC or Mac to the Web site, first make sure the left side of the CuteFTP screen is active, then click on the file in question. Now click on Commands and then Upload. There are shortcut keys to do all of this. I can use the Control key to select more than one file to upload and I can use my right mouse button to quickly select the Upload command. There's also an orange up arrow that can be found right beneath the menu. Just click and upload.

Once you're done uploading, click on File and then Disconnect to log off your Web site, and File and Exit to close CuteFTP.

Usually it's a good idea to upload the files, keep your session active, and open your Web browser to see if you get what you expected. In this way you can quickly make your modifications, upload them, and then test your system. It's a good idea to play around with CuteFTP or other substitute utility to get really familiar with it. CuteFTP lets you rename files, delete files, and change the attributes of files. This last feature will be explained more fully in Chapter 6. CuteFTP is probably the most popular FTP program around. However, WS_FTP, available at shareware.com, is a close runner-up.

Testing Your Web Site to Make Sure It Works

In the last section we alluded to the concept of testing your Web site. Expect errors. Nobody creates their first Web site in one shot. Common problems you can find during testing are:

1. Missing images. Your .html file indicates that there is an image but you forgot to upload it.
2. Your text fonts look funny. Your HTML is probably wrong.
3. The spacing on the Web page is wrong. Again your HTML is probably wrong.
4. Hyperlinks don't work.

Just because you may have used your word processor or other HTML generator doesn't mean you won't have problems. Just remember the old adage, "garbage in, garbage out."

Before you "go live" you should fully test your Web site. To do this, first test it on your own PC or Mac. It doesn't pay to continually upload files to your Web site until what you see on your PC or Mac is what you want. The next step is to upload everything to your Web site and then test, test, and test again.

Once you start adding scripts (e.g., Javascript and Perl) into your site, then testing becomes even more important—and even harder.

Developers of small Web sites generally do testing manually. If you become professional at this and/or develop a really high-powered site, you might want to use some automated testing tools. Follow the following link for a good set of resources for testing: http://www.aptest.com/index2.html?resources2.html.

Advanced Web Development Techniques

Jessica Keyes

In this chapter we're going to cover some really exciting topics. We'll start with how to add audio to your site. Then we'll discuss a bit about video before launching into the exciting topics of Shocked and Flashed sites. Finally, we'll describe ways in which you can add a slide presentation and even Acrobat PDF files to your site.

Adding Audio to Your Site

There's a couple of ways of adding audio to your site:

- The quick and dirty way.
- The professional way.

We're going to discuss both methodologies, but first we need to cover some basics.

Sometimes when you browse the Web you come across a site that starts making noise as soon as you load the page (of course, you need to have your speakers plugged into your computer and the sound turned on). The noise, which can be sound effects, a person talking, or music, are contained within a file. Sometimes there is a hyperlink on a page that starts the music when you click on it. In either case, the Web developer somehow got the page to play a sound.

How is this done? An audio file is no different from an image file in that it is a file that has a file name. But instead of displaying a picture it makes a noise! We've already learned that most folks store images on the Web in one of two formats: .gif and .jpg. In the same way there are file formats for different types of sound files.

When pumping up a page to include audio the quick and dirty way, there are two popular file formats that are commonly used: .wav and .mid (usually referred to as midi). There are some major differences between these two audio file formats:

- .wav files are much larger than .mid files, so they take longer to download.
- .midi files can contain only instrumental or background music, but are quite small.

Perhaps you've noticed some music or other sounds emanating from your PC or Mac on occasion—usually when you make a mistake! These are usually .mid or .wav files. If you put on your investigator hat and do a search on your Mac or PC for all files ending in .wav or .mid, you'll probably wind up with a virtual gold mine of freebie audio files.

There are also places that you can go on the Web itself to download audio files. As I've discussed in prior lessons, much of the content of the Web is copyrighted. This applies to text and images, as well as audio files. So be careful what you copy. One of the more interesting sites (with questionable copyright status) is the daily .wav (www.daily-wav.com). Another interesting site is thefreesite.com. Again, the copyright of these .wav and .midi files is questionable.

Let's presume that you've located a great place on the Web from which you can download cool sounds. How do you do it? Just like you do an image. Mac users can just place their cursor on the sound link and hold the mouse button down. The "Save This Link As . . ." dialog window will appear. PC users can do the same but must use the right mouse button. In both cases it's wise to save your audio files to a common folder (e.g., mymusic).

But what if you can't find the sound you really want? Or what if what you really want is a voiceover? While you're never going to get professional-sounding sound clips this way, it is possible to use a tape recorder and go out into the world to create your own sound effects. I did this. I took my trusty tape recorder and walked all over New York City, taping various and sundry noises. Birds chirping. Children playing. Subway cars screeching.

The next step is to use some audio software to "suck up" the sound into your computer. All PCs, and probably all Macs, come with some (low-quality) audio software. Now, this is a course unto itself and we don't have the time to delve into it here. I will say that it's a load of fun.

Audio Editors

Three cheers for guys like Dave. He's gone through the pain of categorizing whole bunches of audio editing shareware for you. Go find him at http://www.davecentral .com/audedit.html.

On a typical PC, Microsoft automatically installs a tiny little utility called Sound Recorder, as shown in Figure 4-1. Where it is located depends on what version of Windows you are using, but you can use Figure 4-1 to get a sense of where it should be located.

Sound Recorder will let you play and record .wav files. You'll need not only speakers but a microphone. You can buy an inexpensive one at Radio Shack or your local com-

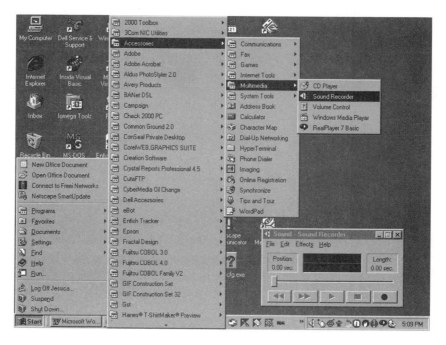

Figure 4-1. Using Microsoft Sound Recorder.

puter store. If you crawl behind your PC or Mac you can easily locate the port for audio on the rear of the computer.

The Sound Recorder works the same way as a conventional tape recorder. The red button is the record button and the square button is the stop button and so on. Figure 4-2 shows what happens when a sound is either recorded or replayed. The green flat line widens and thickens depending on the sound, as shown in Figure 4-2. You can tell right away if you're actually recording. If the line stays flat, then you're not recording. Check your cable connections.

If you've used your tape recorder to record sounds al fresco (outside), then the quick and easy way to get those sounds into a .wav file is:

1. Put your tape recorder near the microphone.
2. Shut all doors and quiet all barking dogs and screaming children.
3. Click the Record button on Sound Record or other audio software.
4. Click the Play button on your tape recorder.

Of course, if you're really technical you can connect the tape recorder directly to the input audio jack on your computer to achieve the same goal—without any ambient noise interference at all.

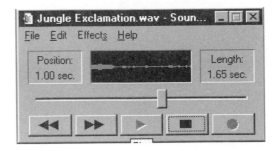

Figure 4-2. Observing the sound monitor.

Once you've finished recording you might notice that your lead and trailer contains too much "dead air" (space on the recording where there is no sound). Sound Recorder provides some minimal editing functionality that lets you cut out parts of your .wav file. There's even some sound-effects functionality. If you're going to go whole hog into the sound editing side of Web page design, you're going to want to use a more robust package. One of the more popular ones in the market is Macromedia's SoundEdit (www.macromedia.com).

Once you create, buy, or download your sounds, your next step is to somehow embed them into your HTML file. I won't kid you here: For the placement of audio as well as for the advanced techniques we're going to learn about in the rest of this lesson and future lessons, you're going to have to brush up on your HTML (a prerequisite for this course). While some of the page-editing software does indeed have the capability of letting you point and click your way to adding a sound clip, the process is often imprecise and much less effective than "doing it yourself." So let's drag out those HTML books.

Surprise! A sound file is linked to text the same way any other HTML or image file is linked to text. For example, if you wanted to link the sound file "happy_birthday.wav" to the text "Happy Birthday," you would code:

```
<a href="happy_birthday.wav">Happy Birthday</a>
```

That's all there is to it. Now let's go one step further. How do you code the HTML that will permit you to hear a sound clip when the page is loaded?

```
<embed src="happy_birthday.wav" width=144 height=60
       autostart="true" loop="true">
<bgsound src="happy_birthday.wav"
    autostart="true" loop="infinite">
```

Why do we have two references to the same sound clip? Welcome to the world of non-standard browsers. The browser war created two players: Microsoft's Internet Explorer and Netscape's (now AOL's) Navigator. One would think they should work the same, but unfortunately they don't. This means that some of the commands work differently on one than they do on the other. This also means that some commands don't work at all on one browser. Another sad state of affairs is that there are different versions of each browser out there. While you may be testing with Version 5 of Internet Explorer, some folks who will be using your page will be viewing it using Version 3.

One nice thing about HTML is that if you code a command that doesn't exist it will be ignored—you won't get an error message. In the HTML above we took the safe route and coded two separate sound commands. The embed command is for Netscape and the bgsound command is for Explorer. Interestingly, Netscape's embed command works fine when using Version 5 of Internet Explorer! Welcome to the Internet.

The height and width parameters are for the sound bar that is displayed when the sound starts using the embed command, the autostart parameter is self-evident, and the loop parameter indicates to the browser that the sound should be repeated over and over.

What happens when you decide to create an audio file that is superlarge—say a half-hour recording of your promotion party? If the file is very large it will still play. However, it will take quite a long time for it to start, since, like image files, audio files need to be completely downloaded from the Internet to the client PC to start.

How can you fix this problem? How can you get the sound to start *before* it has completely downloaded? The answer is to use streaming audio. This is the professional way to record audio.

One maker of this type of sound is realnetworks.com. The leader in streaming media, RealNetworks allows you to stream not only audio but video, too. Lest you get too excited, there are a couple of caveats here:

You can't just create RealAudio clips. You need to use RealNetworks specialized software—which is not free. You can't just store most RealAudio clips on any Web server. You will need to purchase a specialized RealAudio server (very expensive), which is specialized software that runs on the computer actually connected to the Web. Of course, most of us use ISPs. This means that you will have to choose an ISP that supports RealAudio (sometimes the term RealMedia is used to indicate support of both RealAudio and RealVideo). In general you will be charged an additional amount each month. If your main ISP does not support RealMedia, don't despair. There is no reason why you can't sign up for a second Web site at a different ISP and just use this ISP to store your audio and/or video files.

RealAudio can't be heard and RealVideo can't be seen unless a "plug-in" is downloaded by the person surfing your site. Fortunately the RealPlayer is so frequently used, most people already have it on their PCs and Macs. You will, however, have to put a message on your site that in order to hear your audio clips the RealPlayer should be downloaded, and then provide a link to the realnetworks.com site. This plug-in is free, but RealNetworks also promotes a more functional version at their site that costs about $30.

How Do I Add Video to My Site?

We already gave away the answer to this question in the last section—streaming video. Where audio could get large depending on the number of minutes in the clip, video brings a whole different dimension to the picture. Not only is the length important to the size of the video clip, the colors and action on the clip need to be figured in as well. It is not uncommon for a one-minute video to gobble up over 50 megabytes in disk space.

Consider what this means. Most folks use no more than a 56 kb modem. Now divide 50 megabytes (50 million bytes) by 56 kb (or 56,000 bytes) and you can see how long it will take someone to download your video clip using conventional technology. Take a look at Figure 4-3 to get a good handle on how long it takes to download files from the Internet. Starbucks, anyone?

Still, it is possible to create your own brief video clips right at your desktop. Some formats for non-streaming video are:

1. Avi (runs on the Windows platform).
2. Mpeg (the video standard that runs on both Mac and PC).
3. QuickTime Mov (runs on both Mac and PC).

Just how do you create a video? While the input to the computer end of the process is the actual video clip, you still need to create that video in the first place. The advent of the digital video camera, while pricy, makes it easy going to get that video into your computer. However, a conventional video camera is still usable.

Download Times at Common Modem Speeds

Content	Size	14.4 kbs	28.8 kbs	64 kbs	1.5 mbps
Small graphics & animation	30K	30 secs	10 secs	6 secs	1 sec
Small complete movie	100–200K	180–300 secs	90–180 secs	20–40 secs	1 sec
Short video clip	500K	300–400 secs	120–240 secs	90 secs	3 secs

Figure 4-3. *Download times at common modem speeds.*

Video Help

Choosing the best video capture card and then using it correctly is going to require some help. One great place to go for more information is http://www.videoguys.com/vidcap.htm. Here you can find out about video capture cards for your Mac or PC. There's also reviews and handbooks. A second source is http://www.vivo.com/help/producer/vidcaped.html.

You're going to need a few things if you're going to get into the video business:

1. Your PC or Mac should be powerful. Make sure you have at least 133 MHz, 32 MB of RAM, and 500 MB hard drive. Your monitor should be a SVGA resolution with at least a 16-million-color ability.
2. You will need to purchase a video capture board for your PC. The video capture board has a Composite-S jack to enable a hookup to a VCR, camcorder, or television. One example is the Intel Smart Video Recorder, which costs somewhere around $200. When I purchased this product some time ago it came bundled with video capture software from Asymmetrix called DVP (Digital Video Producer). Also included were the necessary cables and hardware manual.
3. Once you've created the video you're going to want to display it on the Internet. Just like images and sound, you use HTML to display video files as shown below:

```
<embed  width = 100% height = 100%
fullscreen = yes  src = "welcome.mov">
```

Unlike images or some sound files (e.g., .wav and .mid) all video requires some kind of plug-in, as shown in Figure 4-4. That plug-in may be the Windows Media Player, the Apple Mpeg Movie Player, or the Apple QuickTime plug-in. One thing you'll learn right away is that there are quite a few choices in terms of the movie you are going to make. What choice you make will impact what plug-in the visitors to your Web site will need to download. All the ones I've just mentioned are popular and heavily used.

If you're going to use video on your site, then you're going to have to provide information and relevant links to your visitors so that in the event they don't have the plug-in required, they can easily figure out how to correct this deficiency. One good example of how this is done is at Yale University. Go to: http://noodle.med.yale.edu/demos/movies.html and see some rather educational movies. More importantly, see how Yale handles the obvious questions that will come up for Mac, PC, and even Unix users.

An even better way to handle the variety of plug-ins in use out there is shown in Figure 4-5. When visiting tv.com and clicking on a view clip button, I was presented with this display. It asked me which plug-in I wanted to use and what my modem speed is. Once I entered these parameters it chose the best viewing experience for me. Note that

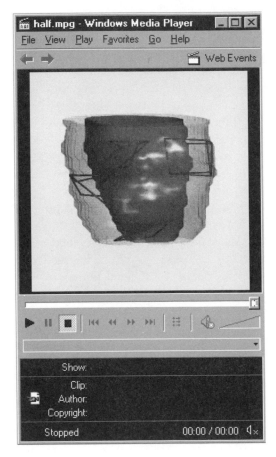

Figure 4-4. *Using the Windows Media Player.*

Figure 4-5. *Creating the best viewing experience for the visitor.*

if I didn't have any of these plug-ins it provided a hyperlink to the appropriate Web site so that I could download the plug-in or choice. These plug-ins are free, by the way.

If you've been browsing the Web for video files and playing them back, you'll have already noticed that downloading these movies is a time-consuming task. That's why streaming video was invented. Like streaming audio, a streaming video file begins playing right away as the file is being downloaded.

The most popular streaming video format is RealNetworks RealVideo. You can purchase RealNetwork's Streaming Media Starter Kit (not cheap). This will give you the tools to encode your video files into the proper format for use with RealVideo.

You've probably already noticed that we're getting quite specialized here. Creating video is not for everyone. There's lots involved: buying a video camera; taking good motion pictures; buying, installing, and understanding video capture hardware and software; and writing the HTML to display your video. What's a Web site designer to do?

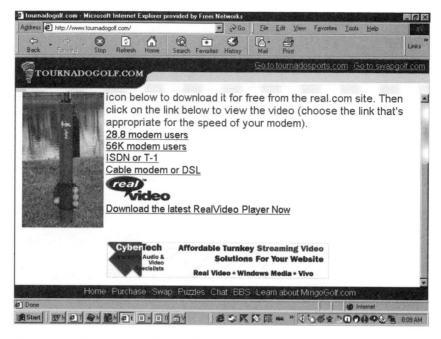

Figure 4-6. *Using outside help to digitize your video.*

Hire an expert. You can be a "jack of all trades and master of none" or a talented designer who knows all the right people. There are people who specialize in video. For example, if you go to wemingogolf.com, an e-tailer of golfing goods, you can see their video. What these folks did, as shown in Figure 4-6, is shoot a commercial using professionals and then have the video encoded by a second set of professionals who specialize in digitizing video and placing it on the Internet. You can see the banner for these digitizing experts on the bottom of Figure 4-6.

You also notice a few things if you browse this site:

1. The video was digitized into several formats depending upon what speed the site visitor's modem is (28.8 kb, ISDN, etc.).
2. There is a link for site visitors to download the plug-in (e.g., RealVideo).

As I mentioned earlier, if you are going to use streaming audio or video, then you are going to have to make sure that your ISP provides these services, since a media server is required (i.e., software that actually serves up the streaming audio or video).

If you play around with any streaming media site long enough, you'll realize the files that are being linked to are unlike any you've seen before.

If you click on the video link, what is actually being pointed to is a file with the .ram extension. This is just a text file that contains the actual link to the video file itself as shown below:

```
file:thankyou.rm
```

The video file is actually named something.rm, with .rm designating that it is a real media file.

The .rm file is stored in a place on the Web server according to your ISP's directions. You can't just put it anywhere because the media server needs to know its location for it to be "served" properly.

Just What Is Shockwave?

Like video and audio, Director 8 Shockwave Studio, which is a Macromedia product, is a tool that requires some real talent to use (available for both Mac and PC). In this section we're going to talk about it in general. Since it's rather expensive, about $900, I wouldn't recommend buying it unless you're really serious about getting into this business and have more than just a little graphic design talent.

The Shockwave plug-in has been downloaded by over 30 million people. It's a mainstay on the Web and is responsible for most of the neat animation you see today, as shown on Shockwave's own site (www.shockwave.com) and in Figure 4-7.

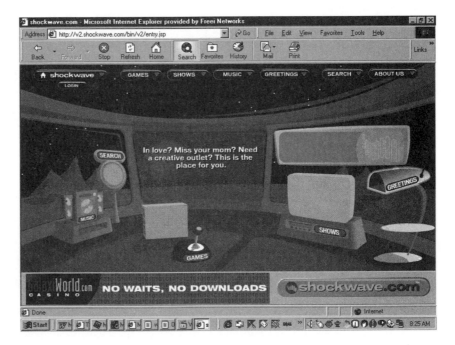

Figure 4-7. Shockwave's animated site. (Copyright © 1999–2001 AtomShockwave Corp. All rights reserved.)

By the way, when a site uses Shockwave it is said that the site is "Shocked." It's sort of neat to look at these sites to see what's possible. Shockware.com itself is a clearinghouse for links to Shockwave developers.

A good alternative to the expense and talent demands of Shockwave is another Macromedia product called Flash. Priced at just $300, it is a much less expensive and demanding animation solution. Also requiring a plug-in, wcnonline.com is a good example of a site that profits from its use.

As shown in Figure 4-8, you can do a lot with Flash. If you actually visit the wcnonline.com site and click on WCN Introduction you'll get to see the Flash "movie." The cartoon figure actually looks like the chairman of the company. This movie has sound and the cartoon figure's mouth moves in sync with the audio.

Now compare this to any Shocked site. There is a difference. With Flash you can create an animated movie with sound; with Shockwave you can create an entire multimedia experience.

Can you do this? Probably not. But there are whole bunches of graphic designers who can. Can you learn to do this? Probably, if you have some graphic design talent. Check out your local college to see what kinds of courses in graphic design and/or digital art are offered. To see what a good school *should* offer, visit New York's School of Visual Arts at http://www.sva.edu/. Interestingly, they too use Flash!

Mac users will be happy to know that the vast majority of this sort of design work is done on a Mac rather than a PC.

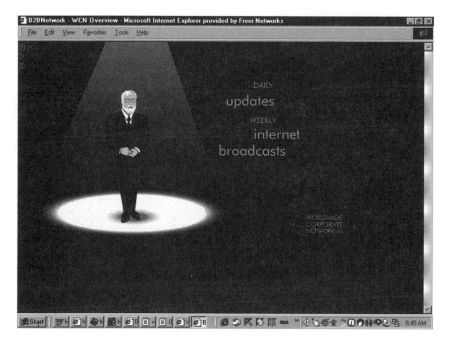

Figure 4-8. *A Macromedia Flash movie. (Copyright © 1995–2001 Macromedia, Inc.)*

So You Want to Put Your Slide Presentation on the Web

There'll come a time when you want to present a series of informational slides to folks who visit your Web site. This course, for example, could be presented in a classroom setting where a slide projector would be used.

There are probably few people who haven't used Microsoft's Powerpoint. Available for both Mac and PC, it is the preeminent slide creation software. Usually called presentation software, Powerpoint is not alone in the market. Lotus Freelance also has some powerful capabilities.

Powerpoint comes with an Internet Assistant that creates HTML documents from your presentation that is ready to publish to the World Wide Web. The Internet Assistant helps you customize your presentation. For example, you can include animations, use frames, choose the way you move to other slides or documents, and select different button styles. The Internet Assistant maintains the interactive settings in Powerpoint that jump to other slides or documents. To start up the Internet Assistant:

1. Open the presentation you want to save in HTML format.
2. On the File menu, click Save As HTML, then follow the instructions in the Internet Assistant. If you are using Powerpoint 95 for Windows you will have to download Internet Assistant from http://support.microsoft.com/support/kb/articles/Q129/3/86.asp.

An example of this in action can be found at the Loogootee, Indiana, school system Web site, which is shown in Figure 4-9 and is at http://www.siec.k12.in.us/~west/slides/abc/sld001.htm.

Spend a little time in Loogootee (great name, isn't it?). View the source of the Web page whose URL is shown above. You'll note a few things:

The meta-tags within the <head></head> tags indicate that this was generated by Powerpoint 97. Meta-tags, for those not in the know, are like index entries. You code meta-tags so that search engines know how to characterize your Web site. Chapter 8 will go into this subject in more depth.

Notice the slide controls on the left-hand side of Figure 4-9. There's a left, a right, a fast forward left, fast forward right, and an index image. Put your cursor over the left image. Now click on it. It won't do anything because you're on the first page. Now place your cursor over the right button control image. If you look at the very bottom of the browser on the left-hand side, you can see where this hyperlink is located. It's slid002.htm. The next one must be slid003.htm, and so on and so on. The slides have the same look and feel as the Powerpoint presentation, using the same background and template.

I would strongly suggest that you use presentation software to create your slide show. However, if you are itching to do it for yourself, then be smart! Do the following:

1. Go to the URL mentioned above.
2. Copy all of the images for the controls using the methodology we discussed in prior sections of this course.

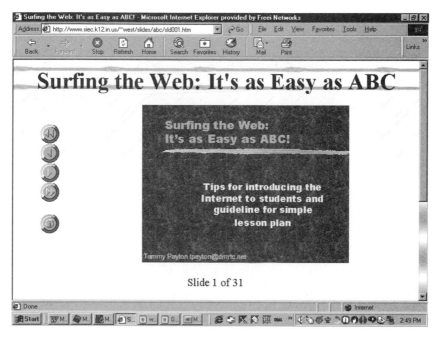

Figure 4-9. *A slide show generated from Powerpoint.*

3. Save the source HTML file as well, since it shows you exactly how you must code each page in your sequence.

4. Create an image file using any of the software packages we've discussed in prior sections. Save as a .gif or .jpg file.

5. Create an image for each slide. This means that if your slide show has 25 frames, you need to create 25 .gif or .jpg files.

6. Create an HTML file for each frame. Code each to link to the prior and next slide (i.e., .gif or .jpg file).

If you think this is a lot of work, it is! That's why it's so much smarter to use software that generates the HTML rather than doing it on your own.

Publishing Printed Documents to the Web with PDFs

If you've been browsing the Web for a while you've probably come across PDF files. PDF (portable document files) are an invention and trademark of Adobe (www.adobe.com). Essentially, PDF files are exact replicas of your document (word processing, desktop publishing, etc.) files that are easily viewable and sometimes editable on the Web.

The IRS (I don't have to tell you what this acronym means, do I?) uses PDF files to enable folks to download tax forms right from http://www.irs.gov/forms_pubs/forms.html.

All a viewer needs to do is download Acrobat Reader, which is freely available from the Adobe Web site. When you come to a link, just click on it and you'll see something that looks like Figure 4-10.

In Figure 4-10 you'll see just how valuable a utility Adobe PDF is. You can create forms and display complete brochures. There's really no limit. The HTML is exactly the same as what you've already used to link to an image or sound file. But how do you create one of these PDF files?

For about $249 you can get Adobe Acrobat (not the Reader, which is free). Running on both the Mac and PC platforms, it's a set of utilities that let you easily create a PDF file from an existing file.

For example, let's say I wanted to create a PDF file out of a typical spreadsheet. The way Adobe works is that it installs little macros into the programs you use to create the original document. You need to check the Adobe product specifications to see what these are.

Take a look at Figure 4-11. In the upper right-hand corner find the button marked "Prompt." Now move a bit to the left. The squiggle is the Adobe logo. When I click on it I get the dialog seen in the bottom half of Figure 4-11.

The resulting PDF file is shown in Figure 4-12. Notice that the spreadsheet grid is missing. This is the same as when printing a spreadsheet to a printer. If I want to retain the grid I can just work with Excel to add those lines back in.

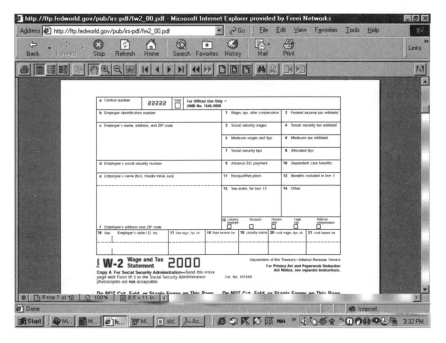

Figure 4-10. *Viewing an Adobe Acrobat PDF file.*

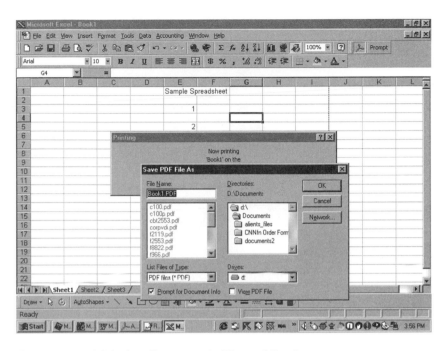

Figure 4-11. Adobe installs a macro in Microsoft Excel.

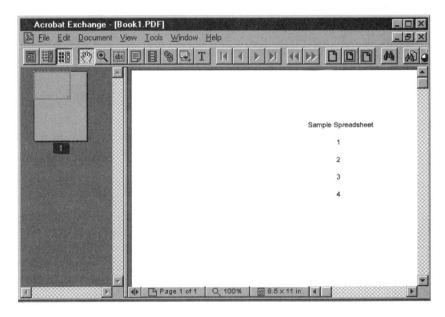

Figure 4-12. Saving a spreadsheet as a PDF file.

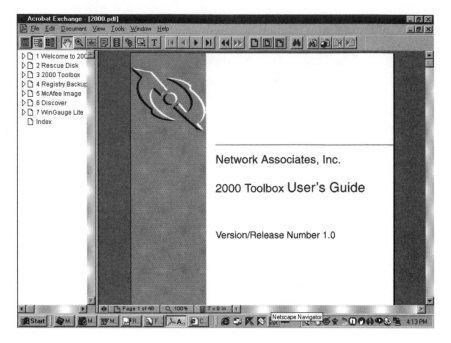

Figure 4-13. *Using Adobe Exchange to fine-tune the PDF.*

When you purchase the Adobe product you get a whole set of tools. Exchange permits you to do many things. One of these is the ability to create thumbnails or bookmarks of each page in your document so that someone viewing the document has a quick index to it. Figure 4-13 shows a PDF file that uses bookmarks. Bookmarks act as a textual index. Each of the titles in the left is actually a hyperlink to a different page in the PDF document. Thumbnails are the same idea, except that instead of a textual link you see a tiny version (i.e., thumbnail) of the page.

Adding Datacasting to Your Site

Jessica Keyes

Data is stored on computers in a variety of ways. Your word processing files are actually text files but they are encoded, so if you try to open them with a plain old text editor what you see looks much like gobbledy-gook.

Most Macs and PCs come with plain text editors. You use these to store any string of numbers, letters, and special punctuation. When you save it you are actually creating a file. So rule 1 here is that you can store data in a file. The data can be:

1. Social security numbers.
2. Names and addresses.
3. Invoice amounts.
4. Any combination of items.

A text file is called a flat file. It is the easiest to process. When you do process it you have to read the file from beginning to end. In other words, you have to process it sequentially.

What if you want to read a file randomly? That is, you don't want to read through 50 records to get to the 51st. For this you need a database. You may have heard of Microsoft and Oracle. Each of these makes a very robust database that can be used on the Web. Other brand names that offer Web databases are Borland, Apple, and Sybase. In fact, few major software manufacturers have missed this particular market opportunity.

Before we get into the nitty-gritty of Web databases, let's tackle the easiest task first. What if all you want to do is dump some database data on the Web? Find out if your database of choice has a "Save As HTML" wizard.

Those of you using Microsoft Office might be using Microsoft Access for many of your database chores. If you open a database and then click on File|Save As HTML you will be led through a dialog called "Publish to the Web Wizard." The wizard lets you publish any combination of tables, queries, forms, and reports as HTML files.

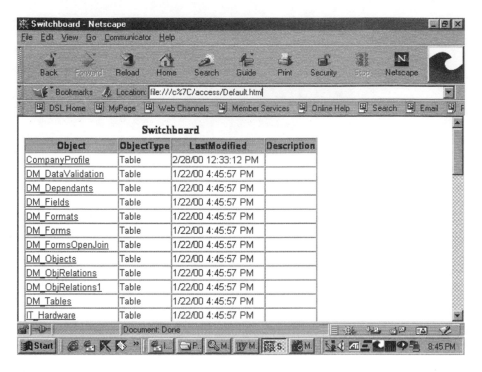

Figure 5-1. *Converting Access to a series of HTML files.*

Figure 5-1 shows the result of this wizard. A series of HTML files are generated along with a main page with hyperlinks to all other pages. The result isn't too pretty, but it can be customized. Or you can modify it yourself by hand.

Adding a Simple Database

The easiest files to process are flat or sequential files. Although this is the easiest form of file, you're still going to need a program to read and write to this file. Like with everything else on the Web, we're going to look for a freebie.

A good example of a freebie is the ubiquitous guest book. You've probably seen many of these on other folks' Web sites. Ben and Jerry's is a good example (lib.benjerry.com/ca/subscribe-new.html). A similar form is shown in Figure 5-2. The data in this form has to be written somewhere and somehow.

So how do you do this? Go to Matt's Script archive and download one of those nice freebies. Surf to http://www.worldwidemart.com/scripts/guestbook.shtml#Downloading. This page contains not only the files to download but complete working instructions.

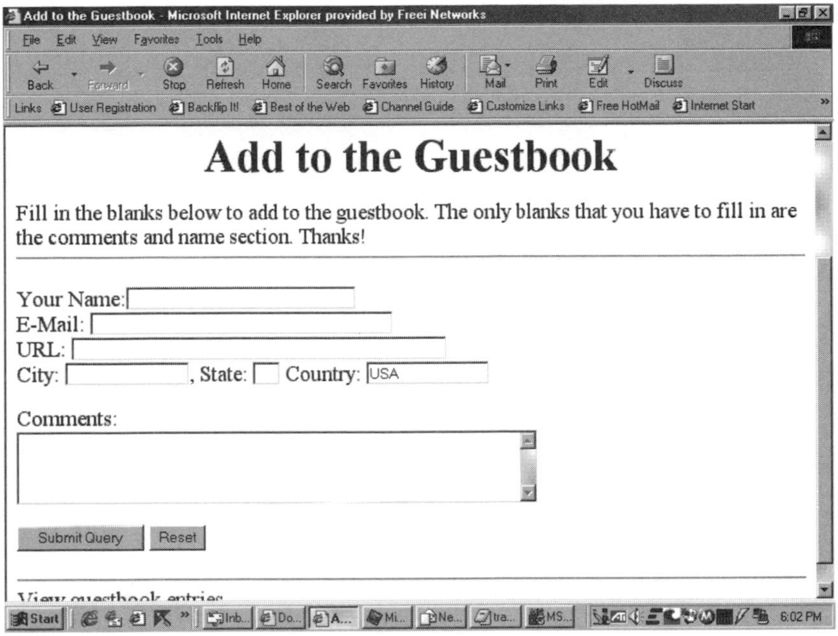

Figure 5-2. *Guest book can be obtained from Matt's script archive as shareware.*

To create the guest book requires the use of three HTML files, which can be downloaded and modified. Aside from these HTML files there is a file with a funny extension. Guestbook.pl is a Perl file. Perl is a programming language. You can see what it looks like by opening this file in a text editor. It is also shown in Figure 5-3.

The steps to take to get this to work are as follows:

1. Download all files from the worldwidemart.com to your PC or Mac.
2. Alter the HTML files to suit your requirements.
3. Alter the Perl file to point to your Web directory as per Matt's instructions.
4. Upload the HTML files to your normal Web directory.
5. Upload the Perl file to your cgi-bin directory.

The Perl program simply takes the input from the form once the Submit button is pressed and then stores it in the guestbook.html file. An example of the final result is shown in Figure 5-4.

Of course, all of this may be just too much for you. If that's the case, then you should have taken my advice in Chapter 3—The ISP Connection. Many of the ISPs understand that more than a few folks who build Web sites don't have the wherewithal to create their own Perl scripts. So they create and customize them for you.

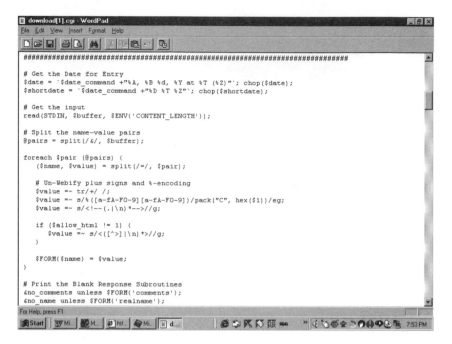

Figure 5-3. *The guestbook.pl Perl program.*

Figure 5-4. *The resulting guestbook.html file.*

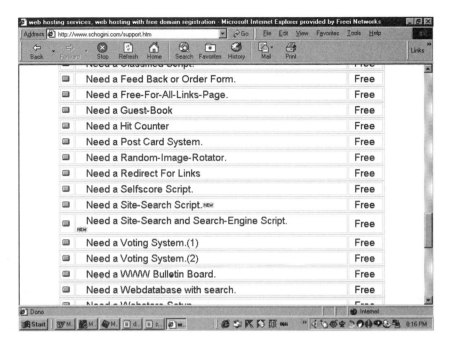

Figure 5-5. *Getting the goods for free. (Copyright © 1997–2001 Schogini Inc. Used by permission.)*

Schogini.com is an example of this variety of ISP, as shown in Figure 5-5. Even if you already have an ISP, there is no reason why you can't use the services of a second ISP if that ISP has stuff you really want. Instead of coding, say:

```
http://www.myname.com/guestbook.html
```

you can code:

```
http://www.www.myotherISP.com/guestbook.html
```

You'll still send everyone to www.myname.com. It's just that inside your HTML you'll code links to the other Web sites you own. This is a common practice. Take a look at Figure 5-5. It's got tons of free stuff. Each one of these is a bunch of HTML and a Perl program, sometimes called a script. This is worth thousands and thousands of dollars. Not only does Schogini give you these for free, they download them onto your own Web site and customize them for you. This is the way to go for novice database people.

Selecting Your Complex Database

For most folks, a simple database will do. If you are creating a complicated site or you've outgrown your simple database, you're going to have to move it to the next level.

This means that you're going to have to look around for a more complex database. Web databases are usually relational databases. A relational database is a file that contains many subfiles in it. They are called tables. For example, let's say you decide to create a customer database. The information you wish to capture is as follows:

1. Name.
2. Firm name.
3. Address.
4. Phone.
5. Fax.
6. Customer order.

When you look at this list of bits of information, sometimes called fields, you realize that while the customer has one name and one phone number, he or she may have many orders. So, it makes sense to separate "customer order" out from the rest of the fields. Essentially, we are going to make two files of it. This is what a relational database does. Trained personnel, called database administrators, know all the tricks and techniques of making relational databases tick. This is called database design. In this simple example our "customer database" is going to have two tables. We'll call one the "customer information table" and the other the "customer order" table.

One of the hats you're going to have to wear (or hire someone to wear) is that of database designer. You're going to have to think long and hard about what information you need to capture and then think even longer and harder about the best way to store that data in a database. The reason this is important is because how you design the database impacts the speed of access to that database, among other things. This is a complicated task and, quite frankly, most folks opt to use whatever database they have on hand (e.g., Microsoft Access).

Aside from what your database should look like, there are other issues to think about as well:

1. What is my budget for the database? Professional databases such as Oracle and Sybase are not cheap in terms of dollars.
2. What platforms does it run on? Most high-end relational databases are geared for Windows NT, Unix, and now Linux. Apple has never successfully penetrated this high-end market, so Mac users will have to search around a bit to see if they can find a database usable on this platform. For the most part, however, you will not be using either your Mac or PC for high-end database work. You will be using the server itself (Windows NT or Unix is the favorite of most servers) and HTML, a

bit of Perl, Javascript, or whatever scripting language comes with the database. Therefore the Mac issue may be moot in this case.

3. Where am I going to run my database? You can't just install this on your PC and then hook it up to the Internet unless your PC is a server on the Internet. The vast majority of companies use ISPs to host their Web sites. If you recall our chapter on choosing an ISP (Chapter 3), I recommended that you choose an ISP that offers the services that you require. There is a one-to-one relationship between services offered and the price you pay. If you are paying your ISP $9.95 a month, it's unlikely that this ISP is going to let you install an Oracle database on their servers. IBM is an example of an ISP that deals with companies who require database services.

4. How am I going to connect my database to my Web pages? On the one hand you have your "sort of easy to code" HTML pages that you may have generated using your word processor or one of the many HTML generators out there. On the other hand you have your database. The connection between the two is the program. Typically, this is what programmers do for a living.

So which database do you choose? If you want to stay as uncomplicated as possible, then stay away from complex databases. Instead, use one of the flat-file databases that come with Perl scripts, such as Matt's guest book (described above).

Or you can go one step better. If you look at Figure 5-5 you'll notice way down at the bottom of the list something that says "Webdatabase with search." This may be a rinky-dinky (nonrelational) database, but, you know what, it works for simple problems! Figures 5-6 and 5-7 show Webdatabase in use.

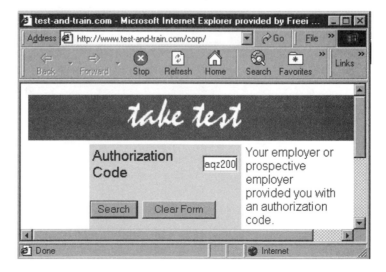

Figure 5-6. Webdatabase handles simple inquires.

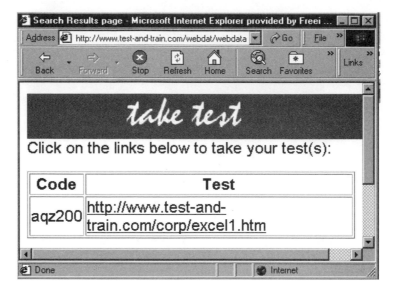

Figure 5-7. *Webdatabase returns values based on input strings.*

In Figure 5-6 we see a dialog asking for some input, in this case a code number. In Figure 5-7 we see the results of the database lookup. What happened here is that the visitor to the site entered a code number (aqZ200, in this example). Once they clicked on Search, the code number was passed to a Perl script (the program) that sits on the Web server. On the Web server is the database and in this database is information that is shown in Figure 5-7. In other words, entering the code of "aqz200" retrieves the information that this person is supposed to take the test at location "http://www.test-and-train.com/excel1.htm." http://www.perlarchive.com/guide/Databases/ is the place to go if you want to look for a free or cheap Perl database. However, if you do need a robust database for the Web (one that stores lots of information, in many formats, and retrieves it quickly), then you're going to have to do a bit of research to determine which is the best one for you. The market leaders are:

1. Oracle.
2. Sybase.
3. Microsoft SQL Server.

If you're brave or a real tech-head, then you might be smart enough to get a robust relational database for free. Mini SQL, or mSQL, is a lightweight (primarily UNIX) database engine. It can be downloaded from http://www.hughes.com.au. mSQL is the database, but you still need a language to be able to work with it. Hughes has recently come out with their own. Called Lite, it is freely downloadable from the same Web site.

Adding a Complex Database

You've heard the expression "fighting fire with fire"? Well, the best advice I can give you for working with a complex database is somewhat similar. Fight software with software.

Working with a database is a complex task. It doesn't have to be. We're going to do the "instead" part in this final section. The "instead" translates to finding and using a Web development tool that provides us with the ability to hook into our database of choice.

These high-end Web development tools do it all. They replace your word processor, desktop publisher, and everything in between. They're robust, cost big bucks, and require loads of technical skills. If this sounds like you, then your project is at the point that it needs a large infusion of cash from some friendly venture capitalist.

There are a variety of these tool sets on the market today. One of the popular ones is called ColdFusion (www.macromedia.com). Most of the sophisticated Web development tools, such as ColdFusion and Dream Weaver Ultra Dev (also macromedia) provide access to a wide variety of databases. As shown in Figure 5-8, these tools enable you to easily connect to a database. Sorry Mac-phites, the majority of e-business systems built today are built either on a Windows, Unix, or Linux platform. So if you're into Mac and want to get into the Web design business in a big way, you're going to have to open a few windows as well!

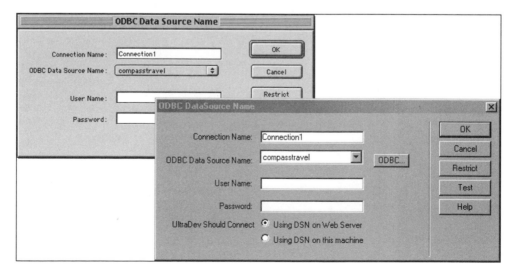

Figure 5-8. *A sample database connection.*

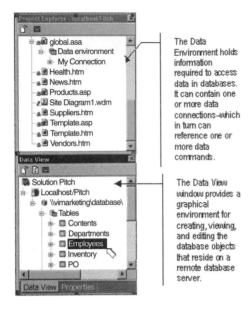

The Data Environment holds information required to access data in databases. It can contain one or more data connections—which in turn can reference one or more data commands.

The Data View window provides a graphical environment for creating, viewing, and editing the database objects that reside on a remote database server.

Figure 5-9. *Microsoft's Visual InterDev.*

Probably the most popular development tool is Allaire's (www.allaire.com) Cold Fusion. To read about Cold Fusion in action surf to http://www.allaire.com/casestudies/index.cfm.

A third popular tool is Microsoft's very own Visual InterDev (msdn.microsoft.com/vinterdev/technical/training.asp). One of the nice things about all of these tools is that they are visual. That means that instead of doing a lot of coding you can point and click your way to linking a database to the Web. Figure 5-9 demonstrates just what I mean.

Just how does a complex database-driven site look? Information Builders makes a very fine tool called WebFocus (www.informationbuilders.com). Statswizard.com uses this product toward an interesting end—baseball statistics as shown in Figure 5-10. There's really no way this baseball site could have been created without a complex database.

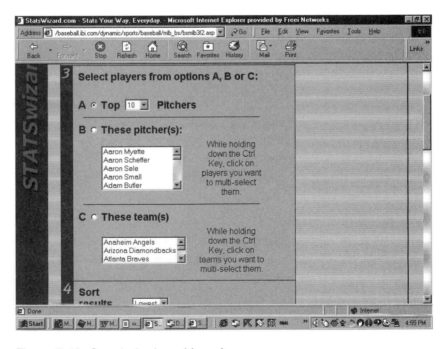

Figure 5-10. *Sample database-driven site.*

Programming with Perl, JavaScript, Java, and More

Jessica Keyes

When you're developing a Web site that just uses some simple text and pictures, you can use some good old HTML. But when you want to do some processing of data that sit on the server, then you need a program. The interface between the programs that sit on the data and the server itself is called CGI. CGI (common gateway interface) specifies how data are sent to the gateway program (as environment variables or as data read, by the gateway program, from standard input) and what data are sent (in general, all the data sent by the client to the server, plus extra environment variables describing the status of the server). To become a good CGI developer you will need to learn:

1. HTML.
2. The details of the HTTP protocol.
3. The details of CGI protocol (you need to know the names of the different environment variables passed to the gateway programs; the contents of the variables, and the encoding schemes used to send client data to the gateway program).
4. How to write programs. Gateways are commonly written in Perl or C, but you can use just about any programming language.

The first thing you need to learn is how to use HTML to either "get" information or "post" information. You get and post data that sit on a server, but you need to do this through CGI. However you're not going anywhere unless you first learn to create an HTML form that submits data for "post" or "get."

The following is a list of links to places you can go to learn more about CGI:

1. http://www.yahoo.com/Computers_and_Internet/Internet/World_Wide_Web/CGI_Common_Gateway_Interface/
2. http://www.jmarshall.com/easy/cgi/
3. http://www.boutell.com/faq/cgiprob.htm

Using Perl

Figure 6-1 shows a Web page that uses a simple form. If you were to view the source of this page you would see a bunch of form statements sitting smack dab in the middle of the HTML. So that you don't have to bother with viewing the source I've presented the form statements below. Let's take a look:

```
<FORM METHOD="POST"
  ACTION="http://mall5.register.com/cgi-bin/wwwwais">
  Enter keyword(s):<INPUT TYPE="text" NAME="keywords"
  VALUE="" SIZE=30>
<BR>Maximum number of hits to return:
<INPUT TYPE="text" NAME="maxhits" VALUE=40 SIZE=2><BR><BR>
<INPUT TYPE="submit" VALUE=" Keyword Search ">
<INPUT TYPE="reset" VALUE=" Reset ">
<HR ALIGN=CENTER Width=100% SIZE=2><BR>
<INPUT TYPE="hidden" NAME="message" VALUE="If you can see
this, then your browser can't support hidden fields.">
<INPUT TYPE="hidden" NAME="source" VALUE="index.swish">
<INPUT TYPE="hidden" NAME="sourcedir"
VALUE="/usr/people/forman/httpd/swish/sources/">
<INPUT TYPE="hidden" NAME="sorttype" VALUE="score">
<INPUT TYPE="hidden" NAME="host" VALUE="">
<INPUT TYPE="hidden" NAME="port" VALUE="">
<INPUT TYPE="hidden" NAME="searchprog" VALUE="swish">
<INPUT TYPE="hidden" NAME="iconurl"
VALUE="http://www.forman.com/icons">
<INPUT TYPE="hidden" NAME="useicons" VALUE="yes">
<INPUT TYPE="hidden" NAME="acc_name" VALUE="newartte">
</FORM>
```

Match Figure 6-1 to the statements shown here. You can see that the form statement is actually a series of statements. It starts with the <form> command and terminates with the </form> command. Everything in the middle identifies the fields within that form.

If I look at Figure 6-1 I only see one field right next to the phrase "Enter keywords." Look at the form HTML and find the same phrase. Notice that right next to this phrase is the following string: <INPUT TYPE="text" NAME="keywords" VALUE="" SIZE=30>. Input type tells the processor that text is to be expected. Name indicates that the field name is "keywords" and size indicates that the length is up to 30 bytes.

There are whole bunches of "hidden" fields as well. These are used by the CGI program to actually process the request.

Now notice the very top of the HTML. It says <FORM METHOD="POST">. A method is a function and a function is a program. "Post" means to send data to the server. If it said "get," then data would have been retrieved from the server. Therefore you can use post to write data to a database and get to read data from a database.

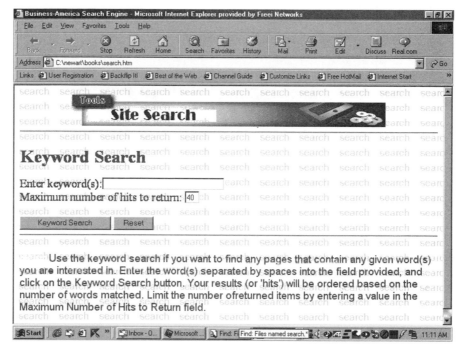

Figure 6-1. *A simple form that requires the use of CGI.*

Now notice the phrase that begins after the word "Action." This tells the server the location of the CGI program. We're going to use a CGI program stored at location http://mall5.register.com/cgi-bin/wwwwais. Figure 6-2 shows a sample Perl program.

Let's look at this more closely. Mall5.register.com is the name of the server. On that server cgi-bin is the name of the folder or directory in which the program wwwwais is stored.

If you were to go to this location (which you can't) you would see a program stored there. This program is called wwwwais, but your program can be called anything you decide to call it.

So what are the steps for doing all of this successfully?

1. Create a Web page using HTML that has a form.
2. Write a Perl or C program that processes the information on that form. You may also need to create a file into which you can store information on that form.
3. Upload both the HTML page and program.

Of course, I'm making it easier than it really is, if you're not used to doing this. The best bet, again, is to use a preexisting set of HTML and Perl and/or C scripts (programs) and just modify it to suit. Later in this chapter we'll talk more about that.

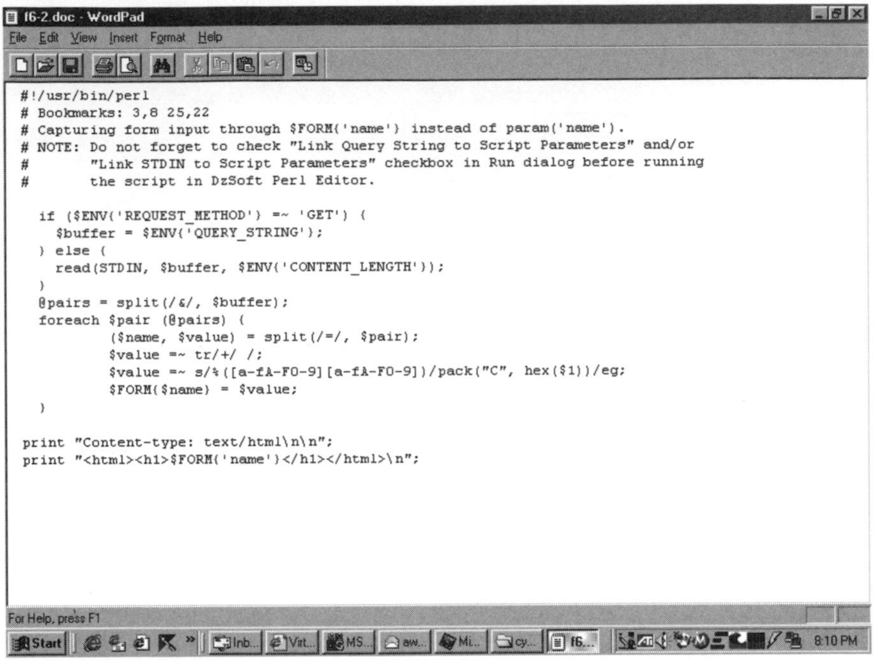

```
#!/usr/bin/perl
# Bookmarks: 3,8 25,22
# Capturing form input through $FORM('name') instead of param('name').
# NOTE: Do not forget to check "Link Query String to Script Parameters" and/or
#       "Link STDIN to Script Parameters" checkbox in Run dialog before running
#       the script in DzSoft Perl Editor.

  if ($ENV('REQUEST_METHOD') =~ 'GET') {
    $buffer = $ENV('QUERY_STRING');
  ) else (
    read(STDIN, $buffer, $ENV('CONTENT_LENGTH'));
  )
  @pairs = split(/&/, $buffer);
  foreach $pair (@pairs) (
        ($name, $value) = split(/=/, $pair);
        $value =~ tr/+/ /;
        $value =~ s/%([a-fA-F0-9][a-fA-F0-9])/pack("C", hex($1))/eg;
        $FORM($name) = $value;
  )

print "Content-type: text/html\n\n";
print "<html><h1>$FORM('name')</h1></html>\n";
```

Figure 6-2. Excerpt of a sample Perl program.

What Can JavaScript Do for You?

One thing you may have noticed is that Perl runs on the server. This means that you have to go through some fancy footwork in order to get it loaded correctly in the CGI gateway. Of course, if you're going to use a site search (i.e., a program that searches your entire Web site to look for particular instances of a search string) or a database read or if you're going to write CGI, using Perl or C or something else is the way to go.

But what if you just need some processing at the client? Let's look at an example. Figure 6-3 shows a page that has an everyday form. The purpose of this form is to record the answers to a test. Now let's look at the code behind the Web page. You can see an excerpt of this in Figure 6-4. The line in the HTML is a dead giveaway that we're looking at JavaScript is:

```
<script language=javascript>
```

Go to http://www.test-and-train.com/corp/excel1.htm and view the source of the page. What does this JavaScript program do? It reads all the answers that the person taking

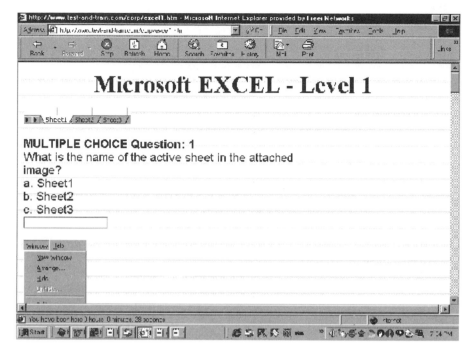

Figure 6-3. *A Web page with a form.*

```
excel1[1] - Notepad
File  Edit  Search  Hep

<html>
<body onLoad="startClock()" background=formback.gif>
<head>
<center><h1>Microsoft EXCEL - Level 1</center></h1>
<script language=javascript>
var counterx
AllValues = new Array (1000)
AllAnswers = new Array (1000)
var bName = navigator.appName;
var bVer = parseFloat(navigator.appVersion);
if (bName == "Netscape")
    var browser = "Netscape Navigator"
else var browser = bName;
var Temp;
var TimerId = null;
var TimerRunning = false;
Seconds = 0
Minutes = 0
Hours = 0

function Process_OnClick (form) {
AllValues[1]    = form.ques1.value
```

Figure 6-4. *The JavaScript behind the form.*

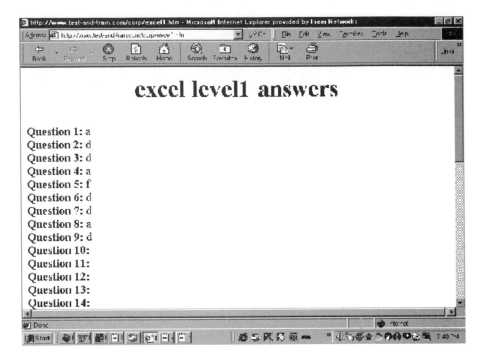

Figure 6-5. *The results of running the JavaScript program.*

the test types into the computer and displays it on a new page as shown in Figure 6-5. The server was never, ever called. What happened is that when the Web page was loaded the JavaScript program was loaded along with it. When the test taker clicked on the Submit (in this case it was called Process) button the JavaScript program took over. JavaScript has become even more popular than Perl. Using either, however, will require you to learn a programming language.

What Can Java Do for You?

What's the difference between JavaScript and Java? JavaScript always runs on the client and is similar to the C and Perl programming languages. Java, on the other hand, runs on the server. But the differences don't end there. Java has become the programming language of choice in the world of the Web. That's because it's uniquely powerful.

Java is what is known as an object-oriented programming language. That means that it has a lot of special capabilities that programmers can exploit to write some incredible Web-based programs. More importantly, Java is a complete programming language that runs on all sorts of computers with few changes required as you move from one computer to another.

Before you get too excited about Java, let's discuss some of its limitations: It's a heavy-duty programming language that requires some heavy-duty skills. An average Java programmer makes $89,000 a year!

It's slow. Java applets, which are the little Java programs that are downloaded from the server to the client computer, take a while to load. This makes your site a bit less efficient.

Some computers are set up in such a way that the browser is unable to see the results of the Java applet.

Homestore.com is an example of a site that uses Java applets (and JavaScript too!). This is a real estate site that shows houses online. I know. I know. There are lots of real estate sites on the Net. Yes there are, but homestore.com uses Java to create a 360-degree virtual tour of the house for sale. Go to this site and click on any house for sale. At the bottom of some of the listings is an icon that says "Virtual Tour click here." If you do, a small browser window appears. Java controls the display.

If you see nothing, then you're the victim of the problem with Java that I mentioned above. Homestore.com knows that there may be a problem, too, because they carry a note under each display that says something like, "Can't see the full-featured tour. . . ."

Figure 6-6 shows the Java-strength version of one of these home tours. You can't see it from the figure but when you look at it online it's actually a movie. It's as if I were

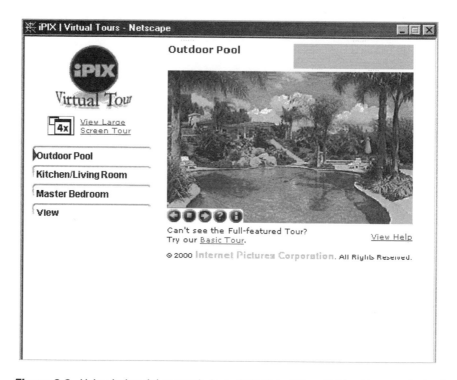

Figure 6-6. *Using industrial-strength Java. (iPIX Virtual Tours™. Used by permission.)*

standing in the middle of the pool (or room, depending on what you're viewing) and spinning around.

What does Java code look like? It looks a bit like JavaScript. However, part of the code is on the client (your PC or Mac) and part of it runs on the server. Since the browser window displayed contains no menu bar you can't easily click on "view source." If you have a PC you can right-click to get the missing menu. If you click on "view source" you'll see some code that begins with <applet> and ends with </applet>. What falls in between are instructions on running the applet, but not the applet code itself.

```
CODEBASE="http://media.bamboo.com/java1_34a"
```

The above instructions tell us where this code is actually located but does not display the code. Where JavaScript is easily viewable (and thus copyable), Java is well-protected on a server. In other words, we can't get to homestore.com's proprietary code. Java, like JavaScript, is very similar to the C programming language. I've included a snippet of it below so that you can get a sense for it:

```
switch(id) {
    case KeyEvent.KEY_PRESSED:
    case KeyEvent.KEY_RELEASED:
    case MouseEvent.MOUSE_PRESSED:
    case MouseEvent.MOUSE_RELEASED:
    case MouseEvent.MOUSE_MOVED:
    case MouseEvent.MOUSE_DRAGGED:
    case MouseEvent.MOUSE_ENTERED:
    case MouseEvent.MOUSE_EXITED:
     consumed = true;
      break;
    default:
      // event type cannot be consumed
```

Finding Free Scripts on the Web for Searching, BBS, Chat, and More

Whew! "I'm no programmer!" you're probably saying by now. Even if you are, your goal should be to try to reduce your workload. That means starting every programming effort with a Web search to see if there's something for free for you to download.

I won't kid you. You can't just download something and then run it. You must do the following:

1. Read the readme.txt or FAQ (frequently asked questions) files to understand what the JavaScript, Perl script, or Java applet does.

2. Download it to your PC or Mac.
3. Alter it to do what you want. The readme.txt or FAQ will usually explain how to do this.
4. Upload it to your own Web server.
5. Test it to make sure it works.
6. Do steps 3 through 5 all over again to get it to work.

So where do you go to find all these freebies? There's a whole slew of places that you can go on the Web. In fact, half the fun is in using one or more search engines to locate the stuff. Why don't you try it? Just type in the keyword "perl." Try again with "java." And one more time with "javascript."

Here's some goodies for you:

1. http://www.scrubtheweb.com/abs/cgi/index.html—This site contains a bunch of free Java and Perl scripts including guest book, site search, chat, and forums.
2. http://www.freeperlcode.com/—The name of this site says it all. It has bunches of CGI and Perl information and freebies.
3. http://javascript.internet.com/—Here sits tons and tons of free JavaScript.
4. http://www.thefreesite.com/—This site contains much more than just free Java and Perl code. It contains free Web space, free technical support, free sounds, free you-name-it.
5. http://www.applets.freeserve.co.uk/—From the name you can tell this is from the United Kingdom, and the Brits know a thing or two about free Java applets.
6. http://www.javascriptwizard.com/—Again, a good name for this particular site.
7. http://index.thescripts.com/Perl_Scripts/—This site contains free Perl scripts but also loads of information on a variety of topics of interest (e.g., Cold Fusion, Servers).

How Do You Install All Those Scripts?

First of all, you don't actually install JavaScript scripts. Instead, you embed them right into your HTML. Both Java and Perl, however, require server-side action. We're going to concentrate on Perl, since Java has some requirements that put it into the "get the professional" category. You must have two things available to get started:

1. CGI enabled on your hosting account.
2. The Perl interpreter must be installed. The interpreter is a program that reads your Perl script and executes the commands. Without it your Perl script is just a bunch of text.

You also must know a couple of things before you can run your scripts properly:

1. You must know the path to the Perl interpreter. Usually this looks a bit like the following: #!/usr/bin/perl.

2. You must know the server path to your account. Most Perl script writers are quite kind. They make their scripts easily customizable. This is great because you will have to customize it to point to your account rather than the account of the person who wrote the script. This means that you need to know your own URL (that's an easy one). But you'll also have to know the directory address your ISP uses to get to your account. When you set up your ISP account you usually get an introductory e-mail that lists things like your e-mail ID and password. This e-mail also usually gives you information about your CGI access. If you don't get this from your ISP send them an e-mail. What follows is an example of the two lines of Perl code that you will need to change:

```
$basedir = '/usr/home/myname';
$baseurl = 'http://www.myname.com/';
```

Obviously, you're going to have to edit the Perl script. You can use any text editor but don't *ever* use a word processor. A word processor puts additional invisible characters into your text. You can't see them, but the Perl interpreter can, and you'll get bizarre error messages and spend lots of time looking for a needle in a haystack.

Text Editors

Windows users can use Notepad, MacOS users can try Mactext or BBEdit, and UNIX users can try vi or emacs. Window users are in luck. You can download the Perl Code Editor from http://www.perlvision.com/pce/.

In Chapter 3 we learned about FTP. Take out your notes because you're going to need them now. To upload:

1. Make sure you upload in ASCII mode. If you upload as binary you may wind up with those bizarre errors we just spoke about.

2. You're going to upload your HTML files to whatever directory you want. You're going to upload the Perl script (the files that end in either .pl or .cgi) to whatever directory your ISP tells you to. In many cases this will be a directory named cgi-bin or just bin. In other cases it can be in any directory.

3. The .pl or .cgi files need to have their permissions changed. What are permissions? This is a part of security on any computer system. There are three types of permissions. There is READ. You want everyone to be able to read this file. Then there is EXECUTE. Since this is a script, you want everyone to be able to execute this script. Finally, there's WRITE. You want to be the only one that has WRITE privileges. Look at Figure 6-7. All the way down at the bottom of the list is a file called wwwboard.pl. This is a Perl script for a bulletin board. Notice the string

/wwwboard			
📁 messages	1,024	04/04/00 23:09	drwxrwxrwx
📄 admin.gif	1,368	04/04/00 21:58	-rw-r--r--
📄 data.txt	1	04/04/00 23:09	-rw-rw-rw-
📄 faq.gif	1,500	04/04/00 21:58	-rw-r--r--
📄 faq.html	2,305	04/04/00 21:58	-rw-r--r--
📄 file.gif	977	04/04/00 21:58	-rw-r--r--
📄 folder.gif	947	04/04/00 21:58	-rw-r--r--
📄 forum.gif	10,785	04/04/00 21:58	-rw-r--r--
📄 home.gif	1,519	04/04/00 21:50	-rw-r--r--
📄 index.htm	419	04/04/00 21:58	-rw-r--r--
📄 index.html	27	04/04/00 21:58	-rw-r--r--
📄 openfd.gif	943	04/04/00 21:58	-rw-r--r--
📄 passwd.txt	22	04/04/00 21:58	-rw-rw-rw-
📄 post.gif	1,284	04/04/00 21:58	-rw-r--r--
📄 pspbrwse.jbf	7,362	04/04/00 21:58	-rw-r--r--
📄 readmeV3.txt	3,836	04/04/00 21:58	-rw-r--r--
📄 reply.gif	1,370	04/04/00 21:58	-rw-r--r--
📄 wwwadmin.pl	34,692	04/05/00 12:03	-rwxr-xr-x
📄 wwwboard.html	2,502	04/04/00 23:09	-rwxrwxrwx
📄 wwwboard.pl	23,987	04/05/00 13:37	-rwxr-xr-x
📄 wwwpost.html	1,109	04/04/00 21:58	-rw-r--r--
📄 wwwv3.tar.qz	16,384	04/04/00 21:58	-rw-r--r--

Figure 6-7. *How permissions look.*

starting with -rwxr-xr-x. This is how permissions look. Since all FTP programs are different, find out from your ISP what command you should use to change permissions. On Unix it is the CHMOD command. Some FTP systems let you change it using a table as shown in Figure 6-8. Some make you enter a numerical command.

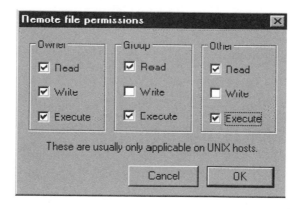

Figure 6-8. *How permissions are changed.*

4. Finally, you're ready to test. No matter how careful you are you're going to get some errors. Common ones are:

"403 Forbidden"

If you see this, check the permissions on your script. Sometimes you may have to also set the permissions of the subdirectory.

"404 File Not Found"

This means that the server can't find your file. You'll need to check the URL or the server path, depending on how the script is configured. Remember that some operating systems are case sensitive, so make sure it's not just a typo. Also, verify that the file is in the correct location.

"500 Server Error"

You get this a lot if you change your script frequently. This error means that your script is producing output that the server doesn't understand. In other words, something in the code is wrong. The most common errors are leaving out a semicolon at the end of a line and uploading the script in binary instead of ASCII. It could be that there's a typo in one of your variables.

That's it! Expect to get a lot of errors. Be comforted by the programmer's rule of thumb: The more errors you get, the more you learn.

E-Commercetizing Your Web Site

Jessica Keyes

There are few folks who haven't heard of e-commerce. You can't pick up a newspaper or read a magazine without hearing about one or a thousand dot.com retailers. Jeff Bezos, who runs amazon.com, was even chosen "Man of the Year" by *Time* magazine.

What you may not know is that there are two major types of e-commerce:

Business to Business, which is sometimes called B2B. Eality.com, recently demised, is an example of B2B. They are also an example of what is known as an ASP, or Application Service Provider. Virtualgrowth.com, as shown in Figure 7-1, sells a complete suite of integrated accounting and bookkeeping applications to small and midsized businesses. The ASP part of the equation is that you can't buy this software in a store. They sell the use of that software over the Internet.

Business to consumer, which is sometimes called B2C. This is the type of e-commerce that you're probably most familiar with. Amazon.com, shown in Figure 7-2, is probably the most famous example.

We're going to concentrate on B2C because it is the model that most folks like you tend to get into first. There are a few things you'll need to get started:

1. One or more products to sell. This can be something you make yourself or something you resell. You can even sell things that you own but don't want any longer. eBay lets you clear out your attic rather nicely. eBay, for those of you who've had their heads in the sand, is an online auction service. If I want to sell Aunt Mattie's dreadful crystal vase, then all I have to do is post it on eBay, or another auction service's site, and wait for the bids to come in. We're going to discuss eBay at the end of this chapter.

2. I was going to say "Web site" here, but, as is often the case with the Internet, a

Figure 7-1. *A B2B e-commerce site. (© 2001 Virtual Growth, Inc.)*

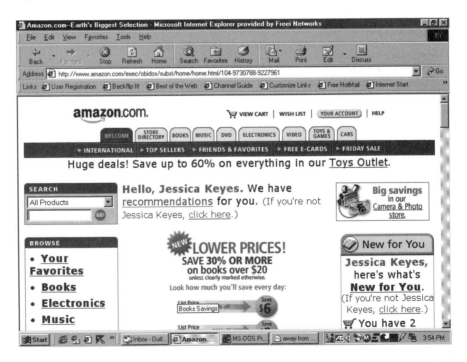

Figure 7-2. *A B2C e-commerce site. (© 2001 Amazon.com, Inc. All rights reserved. AMAZON.com® is the registered trademark of Amazon.com, Inc.)*

whole slew of what I'll call "malls" have sprung up that provide you with a space to sell your wares.

3. I was going to say "credit cards" or some other form of getting paid, but again the Internet beat me to it.

There is really no "business" difference between opening up a store on the Web and opening up a store in your local mall. You can't be flighty about this unless this is going to be a part-time effort or a hobby. You're going to have to think hard about quite a few things:

What you are really going to sell. If you're an artist, then the answer is quite clear. You are going to sell what you create. If you're not an artist and have never sold anything before, then you're going to want to examine the market and see what sells and what doesn't. The same market forces apply to the Web as they do to the real world. I'm sure you notice when stores go out of business. Did you ever think of why they go out of business? Often it's location (i.e., the site they rented is not in a heavily trafficked area) but just as often it's because they are selling things nobody really wants. So what you want to do is some research. Find out what sells.

How you are going to get the rights to sell the product or products you intend on selling. Let's say you want to sell dolls over the Web. You're not going to go into your local Toys"Я"Us, buy a few Barbie dolls, and then post them for sale over the Web. You wouldn't make any money. You need to get these dolls at wholesale price (say, $10 per doll) so that you can sell them at retail (say, $50 per doll). Selling on the Web means that you have to sell at a discount anyway (say, $20), so you absolutely want to buy the dolls at the very lowest of prices. If you want to buy your chosen product(s) wholesale, then you're going to have to make a deal with the manufacturer. A good place to go on the Web to track down the manufacturer you're looking for is http://www.thomasregister.com/. Believe it or not, this is the critical step in starting an e-commerce business. Please take my advice and spend a lot of time researching the product. Spend an equal amount of time researching your competitors. For example, an online bookstore sounds like a great idea (R. R. Bowker is a good place to go for those of you who want to venture into the book biz, http://www.bowker.com/). However, take a good, long look at your competition. Do you think you can beat amazon.com at the game they virtually invented? You might if you can figure out a particular niche to specialize in (e.g., mystery books).

How you are going to get your name out there so people will visit your site. One thing a mall retailer has over you is foot traffic. Human beings walk around malls. Human beings do not wander around the Internet except by browsing. They won't come to your store unless they know about it. The last chapter in this course will go over ways to get your site "out there." Keep this in mind: In 1999 amazon.com spent $413 million on marketing their site. Did they make a profit for the year, you ask? No. They reported a substantial loss! If you want to keep up to date on the e-commerce industry try following this link: http://www.ecommercetimes.com/.

Adding the Web Shopping Cart to Your Site

The Web-based shopping experience is unique. However, all sites do it the same way. The first thing you have to do is create a Web page (or part of a Web page) that has information about the product you are trying to sell as shown in Figure 7-3. Here amazon.com is selling a CD player/recorder. Not only do they describe the product and all of its features, Amazon also provides customer reviews. Now notice the "Add to shopping cart" button on the top right-hand side of the image. Also notice the very large notice about their shopping safety guarantee. In fact, click on the "guaranteed" hyperlink to see exactly what a reputable online store offers.

Figure 7-4 shows the summary page once the shopper clicks on "Add to shopping cart." It's here that the shopper can change quantities or delete one or more items. Once the shopper clicks on "Proceed to checkout," the things any shopper is accustomed to take place: A credit card is chosen, personal information such as name and address are recorded, and the order is completed.

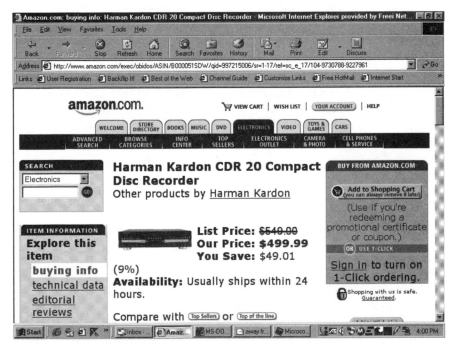

Figure 7-3. *A typical e-commerce product page. (© 2001 Amazon.com, Inc. All rights reserved. AMAZON.com® is the registered trademark of Amazon.com, Inc.)*

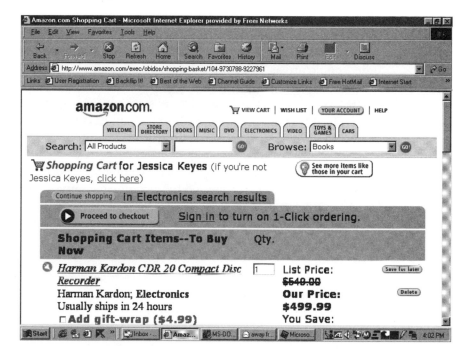

Figure 7-4. *The shopping cart. (© 2001 Amazon.com, Inc. All rights reserved. AMAZON.com® is the registered trademark of Amazon.com, Inc.)*

At each step along the way the shopper can back out of the process (and interestingly, statistics show that the vast majority do!).

Finally, the order is completed. One nice thing that amazon.com does is send you a confirmation e-mail stating all of the order information so that you can have it on file. They also supply you with customer service information in case your order does not arrive on time.

So just how do you accomplish all of this? If you've got a big budget there is no reason why you can't re-create everything that you've seen here. There's a lot more to it than what you can see. Sure, there are some pretty Web pages, but behind the scenes is a lot of complex, database-driven software that:

1. Checks to see if the item purchased is available. If it is, then it lets you proceed with your order. If it isn't, then you are notified and asked to either wait or choose something else.
2. Checks your credit card information. Has your card been reported stolen? Is it current?
3. Starts the product selection process. Amazon.com has large warehouses where books are piled a mile high. However, the books are stored in a logical fashion.

High technology is used to efficiently get the books picked and placed in boxes for shipping.

4. The order is shipped and an e-mail is sent to the purchaser indicating when the order should arrive. The e-mail is sent automatically.

There are many, many more steps that are software controlled. Most won't need this level of sophistication, but you will still need to automate this process. Luckily for you much of this is available, so you won't have to do it yourself.

If you recall our very first chapters, then you'll remember that I said that you should choose your ISP very carefully. Many offer e-commerce services. For example, siteamerica.com will provide you the site and the e-commerce software for up to ten products for less than $90 per month.

Most ISPs offer some sort of e-commerce capability. What you want to do is comparison shop. Things to consider:

1. Price.

2. Level of service.

3. 24 × 7 support. When you have a problem you want it resolved within hours, not days.

4. References. Find out who else is using this service and then contact them to find out how good the service is.

5. Does their e-commerce support tax calculation? Right now tax is collected on most Internet purchases, but there are still cases when you must do so. From a business perspective, in order to sell things you must get something from your state called a "resale certificate." This entitles you to buy things for resale without your having to pay tax and also lets you collect sales tax on things you sell. Given the fact that you are selling to the world and not just in your local shopping center, tax issues become murky. Anyone thinking of going into any retail business should speak to an accountant about regulatory requirements.

6. Does their e-commerce software support shipping and handling fees? How are you going to ship the product? UPS? Federal Express? Each of these shippers has their own way of calculating shipping fees.

7. It is possible to get this software for free. Schogini.com, which I've mentioned before, provides low-cost Web sites cheaply. They also offer to install many freebie Perl scripts. One of these is a Web store. Free does come at a price, however. You will have to handle many of the things mentioned above manually. If you are selling just a few items and don't expect a high volume, then this might be a good place to start.

The very best advice I can give is to surf the Net and see how your competitors are doing it. Call them up and ask them questions. People love to talk, and they'll be happy to tell you their war stories about "selling on the Web."

How You Get Paid: Taking Checks and Credit Cards Online

Many people who start businesses don't realize that when you open up a business you need to have multiple ways for people to pay you. Since you don't own a physical store, you can't take cash. That leaves checks and credit cards.

If you are dealing with reputable businesses (you've heard of them), you can sell your products using purchase orders (POs). This means that you ship the goods and bill them. They pay you within a certain amount of time (e.g., 30 days, or Net 30). This works well if the company you are dealing with is IBM. It doesn't work quite as well when you've never heard of them. It's not atypical not to get paid or to get paid very late. If you can, avoid the PO approach.

Another way of getting paid is to ship COD (cash on delivery). You can set this up easily with Federal Express and UPS. It works like this:

1. You ship the goods.
2. They deliver the goods but do not hand them over until a check is in the hands of the deliveryman.
3. The check is then sent to you. FedEx does this via overnight FedEx service. *Do Not* use a shipping service if they "mail" you the check. You want it the very next day.
4. A fee is charged to you for this service.

A creative way to get paid is via an online check. Paybycheck.com offers a nifty service that, for a small fee, lets shoppers write a check at the digital checkout counter. Figure 7-5 is an example of how this works. For a small setup fee and per-check charge you too

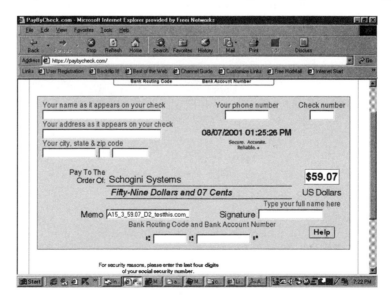

Figure 7-5. *Paying by check. (© by PayByCheck.com LLC.)*

can take digital checks. All shoppers have to do is take out one of their blank checks and then fill in the information from their check onto the paybycheck.com screen. You do not need any special hardware or software, since all processing is handled by PayBy-Check. Your customers only need a Web browser and a checking account. You can also enter the information for your customer in cases of phone or fax orders. PayByCheck offers different options for you to receive your PayByCheck payments. The default is to have the physical checks mailed first class to you for deposit. Checks are processed every day at midnight EST and mailed the following business day. When you sign up, you are assigned a PayByCheck Merchant ID that allows you to log in to PayByCheck Utilities. You can make changes to your e-mail address and the colors of the PayByCheck, view your recent transaction history, and make payments to your PayByCheck account here.

The very best way to take payments is via credit card. Most small businesses are quite unaware as to what this really entails. In order to take credit cards you will need to open what is known as a "merchant account." This is like requesting a line of credit. This is because the bank will deposit money into your account by the next day while giving the credit card holder up to 30 days to pay.

Getting a merchant account is not easy. You have to have good credit and a stable business. Banks usually frown on out-of-home businesses. There is also the matter of fees. None of this is free. They will charge you for everything you do: setup, charge processing, charge-backs (when a customer returns something you will be charged a fee).

If you're already an established company that takes credit cards, you will want to check to see if the bank or third-party processing company (these are companies that are not banks but get you set up with a bank and do the processing for you) is Web-ready. What this translates to is: Can they provide you with a hyperlink that you can embed in your homepage's HTML that will take your customers to a place where they can pay with their credit cards?

If you can't get credit from your bank, you will want to search for one of those third-party processing companies I mentioned above. There's a slew of them on the Web. One of them (note: I do not endorse any of these companies) is internetsecure.com. Another is charge.com. What you'll need to do is some research. Some things to think about are:

1. What is their per-charge fee?
2. What is their charge-back fee?
3. What is their setup fee?
4. Do they provide tech support?
5. What is their track record? Call up some of their current clients and get a reference.

There are really two parts to the credit card equation:

1. Getting a merchant account.
2. Securing the software to be able to authorize transactions on your e-commerce site rather than offline.

I think you probably understand item 1. Item 2 is a bit more tricky. Go back to amazon.com and go through their purchase process. The credit card part of it is an integral part of the process. You go from selecting what you want to buy to typing in your credit card information in just a few steps. This is the optimum approach.

Sometimes when you use a variety of providers (ISP, credit card service bureau, etc.) the "hand-off" between purchase and credit card is less perfect. So what you want to do is search around for a good combination between ISP and credit card companies.

Alternatively, a unique service called PayPal (www.paypal.com) is catching on fast with small merchants. For a small processing fee you link your site, via a PayPal button, to the PayPal site. PayPal is the actual merchant, but for that fee they are letting you use their merchant account.

Opening the Branch Store on Amazon, eBay, and Yahoo

As we've mentioned, no one is going to come to your store unless you somehow tell them that it's there. One way of doing this is to open "branches." Actually, some people don't even bother with their own Web page; they go directly to this step.

Amazon.com opened their own mall. Selling everything under the sun wasn't good enough for them. They want you to sell everything under the sun, too, as shown in Figure 7-6. Called zShops, they give you the opportunity to sell anything that you can

Figure 7-6. *Amazon.com's zStores. (© 2001 Amazon.com, Inc. All rights reserved. AMAZON.com® is the registered trademark of Amazon.com, Inc.)*

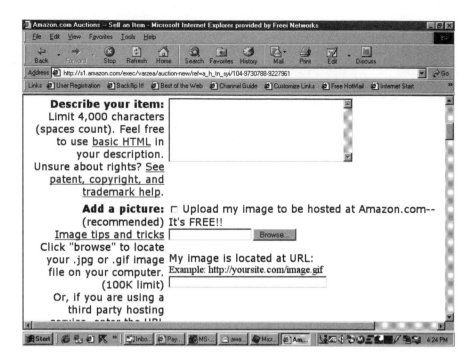

Figure 7-7. zShop Item Information Form. (© 2001 Amazon.com, Inc. All rights reserved. AMAZON.com® is the registered trademark of Amazon.com, Inc.)

think of. It's really rather easy to sell on amazon.com as well. All you have to do is describe your product and upload a picture, as shown in Figure 7-7. One of the nicer features at zShops is that amazon.com will process credit card orders for you (for a fee, of course). So, you get that nice neat amazon.com order flow that I was describing above for a very small price without ever having to apply for merchant credit.

To find out more about zShops go to amazon.com and then click on zShops, which is one of the tabs on the top of the page. Once you get to zShops, scroll down to the bottom and click on the link for "Sell Your Item Now."

Like everything else on the Web, zShops has a lot of competition. Aside from the smaller no-brand malls that sprout up like mushrooms on a spring day (and then fizzle out just as quickly), Yahoo and eBay are formidable competition for amazon.com, which makes them worthwhile for you to consider.

Why do I recommend going after a brand name? For very obvious reasons! Gazillions and gazillions of people surf over to these three sites on a daily basis. Why not profit from this? It's sort of like renting space in one of those supermalls as opposed to on a side street in a decaying part of town. Get the picture? Store.yahoo.com is the place to go to get the lowdown on Yahoo! Store. Although you do have to get your own merchant if you use Yahoo, it might be worth the effort.

The third "big place to do business" is on eBay. eBay is not actually a mall or even a series of stores. It's an auction site. An auction is a mechanism by which you place something for sale and then let buyers bid up the price (or not bid at all). There is something called a reserve price, which is the lowest price at which you're willing to sell. So if you set this price as your minimum price, you can use eBay to sell your products without any risk. You might even make more money than you thought, since the price might be bid up! Instructions for selling stuff on eBay can be found by following this link: http://pages.ebay.com/sell/index.html.

Launching Your Site

Jessica Keyes

You're ready to open the doors and let in the cheering crowds. Don't break out the champagne just yet. Launching a Web site isn't like opening up a store. You still have a lot of work to do.

Getting Your Site Indexed by Search Engines

Your first step is to get indexed in all the major search engines (i.e., directories). There are quite a few of these. Many of them are brand names: Yahoo, Lycos, Excite, etc.

You can go to each one individually and manually enter the information to get your site listed. Some search engines make this easy and some make it a bit difficult. Excite is a good example of an easy one. Just go to the excite.com site and scroll down to the bottom of the screen. There you will see a hyperlink for "Add URL." When you click it you'll see a second screen where you merely type the URL (name) of your site, as shown in Figure 8-1.

Yahoo has a whole process that you need to follow (see http://docs.yahoo.com/info/suggest/) to suggest a site. You need to get to the right category on the Yahoo site and then request right from that page that your site be indexed. For example, let's say I sell screensavers. First I have to click on Software from the main page and then from that page I click on Screensavers. At the bottom of this page is a hyperlink labeled "Suggest a site." Now I have to answer a whole bunch of questions, as shown in Figure 8-2.

This may not seem like much to you, but what if you have a product for which there is no category—or you can't find the category?

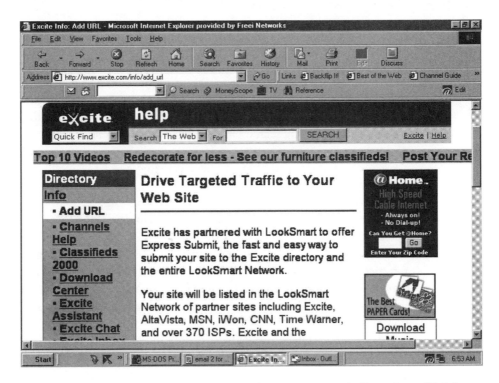

Figure 8-1. *Submitting a URL the easy way. (Copyright © 2001 At Home Corp. All rights reserved. Used with permission. Excite and @Home are registered service marks of At Home Corporation and other countries and are used with permission.)*

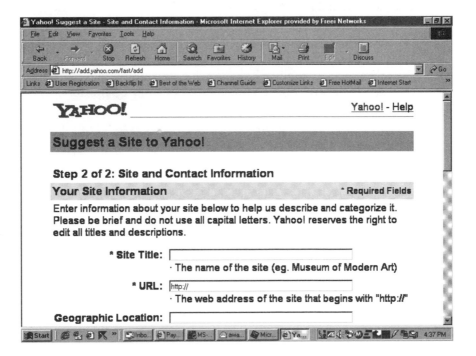

Figure 8-2. *Submitting a URL the hard way. (Reproduced with permission of Yahoo! Inc. © 2000 by Yahoo! Inc. YAHOO! and the YAHOO logo are trademarks of Yahoo! Inc.)*

What Does Indexing Mean, Anyway?

When you enter a search term in a search engine it does not search the entire Internet at that exact moment and then return the results to you. Instead, it searches its own internal database (and what a good example of a database) and then displays results from this search. This is why search engines are so quick. So how do they fill up their internal databases?

Each night they send their spiders crawling over the Web. We're getting very metaphorical here. The word "web" is a good choice because we're talking about a network of computers, or a web of computers. But once the word "web" started being used, folks started talking about spiders and crawling (spiders and webs—get it?). There's even a search engine called webcrawler.com.

Today the term "spider" is used to denote a software program or agent that is programmed to access every part of the Web in search of interesting places to index. That's right! You don't have to bother going to Lycos or Yahoo to manually enter your site, the Web's crawlers will do it for you. The only problem is that this will take a long time—about a month.

So the spiders crawl around the Web looking to index good stuff. At the same time, people like you and me enter our URLs. This is how search engines get their information.

If you want to do this the quick and dirty way, then just index your site at the main search engines: Lycos, Yahoo, Altavista, Webcrawler, and Excite.

If you want to do this the right way, you may want to use one of the many service companies that do this. They'll submit your URL to many of the biggest directories for free but charge you a fee if you want to go one step further and have your URL listed on the countless other search engines. One place you can go to have this done is www.submitexpress.com.

Unless you specifically tell the search engine just what it is your site does, you won't be indexed properly. The way to do this is by being careful about what you put on your pages.

You may have noticed that when you enter a search term in a search engine dialog and press enter, sometimes thousands of results are displayed. Unfortunately, oftentimes it is your Web site that is at the bottom of the list. People may scroll through four, five, or six pages but it is doubtful that they'll ever get down to the 50th page. There are books written about the subject and companies who make a living telling you how to optimize your Web site so that you will be listed in a better position in the results of a search engine report. Whether any of this works or not is open to debate but is worth some research on your part.

You can at least help your Web page along by using something called meta-tags. These are informational tags that are embedded in your HTML. Let's look at an example. Insight.com is a Web-based computer store, as shown in Figure 8-3.

If you were to View Source you would see the following meta-tags:

```
<META name="keywords" content="insight, home, computer, hardware,
software, discount, games, harddrive, hard drive, modem, memory,
network, printer, cd-rom, floppy, scsi, eide, ide, monitor, mouse,
keyboard, multimedia, power protection, internet, video, audio.">

<META name="description" content="Insight—America's discount source
for computers, hardware and software.">
```

There are two meta-tags that we're interested in here. The "keywords" meta-tag lists search terms that this site wants to be listed under, and the "description" meta-tag provides a brief description of the company.

It's amazing how many Web sites leave this simple but powerful feature out. If you want more information on this very technical subject, go to http://www.webreference.com/dlab/books/html-pre/43-0.html.

Figure 8-3. *The Insight computer store. (Copyright © 1986–2001 Insight Enterprises, Inc.)*

Free Advertising Using Banner Exchanges

You've noticed all those banners that litter the Web? While many of them, particularly the ones on sites such as MSNBC and Yahoo, cost a pretty penny, many of them are strictly for barter. The way it works is this:

1. You create a banner. Typically these are about five inches wide by a half inch long and take up no more than 5,000 bytes of disk space. An example is shown in Figure 8-4. Noticed that this is an animated .gif.
2. You sign up at a banner exchange and provide some information. You tell them who you are, where your own banner is located, and what your site is all about.
3. The banner exchange company's software will place your banner on other Web sites. In return other companies' banners will be placed on your Web site. That is what is meant by barter.

Figure 8-4. *A typical banner.*

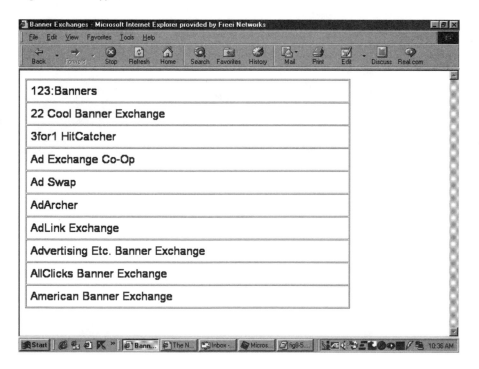

Figure 8-5. *Banner exchange megasite. (Copyright © 1997–2001 Mycomputer.com, Inc. All rights reserved.)*

The first thing you have to do is create your banner. Go back to Chapter 2 and just make a smaller image. The next thing you need to do is sign up at one or more sites that do banner exchanges. The largest one, linkshare.com, decided to go the moneymaking route and no longer does banner exchanges. What they do now will be discussed in the next section. www.bxmegalist.com is an example of a banner exchange. As shown in Figure 8-5, just do some research and you're on your way.

Perhaps the very best way to handle targeted banner exchanges is to do this on your own. This is not going to work with a brand-name Web site but it will work for smaller sites. When you find a site that does not compete but complements your site, call them up or send them an e-mail. Offer to place their banner on your site in return for them placing your banner on their site.

Get a List and Check It Twice

Bxmegalist.com is a list of 350 banner exchanges. Choose carefully.

Keeping Your Web Site Up to Date

There are two reasons why you want to keep your Web site up to date:

1. People will get bored if nothing ever changes on your site.
2. Search engines may drop your listing. That's right! Some search engines check to see if your site is old and musty and then delete you.

There are some tried and true ways of getting people to come back to your site time and time again:

1. Post a monthly newsletter about your particular industry.
2. Run a monthly contest (see www.iwon.com).
3. Add a bulletin board or live chat to your site.
4. Give away something for free (free report, free sample, etc.).

One place you can go to get some fresh content for your site is www.isyndicate.com. iSyndicate is a content syndication service that distributes a broad selection of written, graphical, audio, and video content from 877 sources, to a vast and diverse network of 217,230 Web sites. Just sign up and you're in business.

Another way of keeping your site current and making some additional money on the side is to join one or more affiliate programs. For example, if you join the amazon.com affiliate program, every time someone buys a book as a result of a hyperlink from your site, you make some extra cash.

When you sign up for an affiliate program you will be given an ID and some HTML, which contains that ID embedded in it. You place this on your site. The HTML is

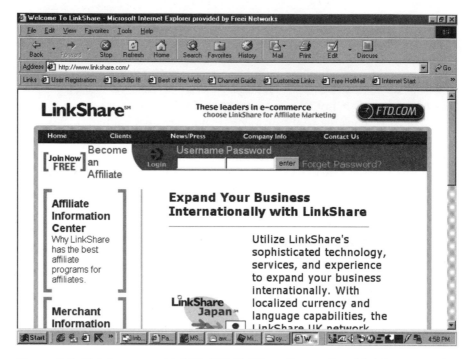

Figure 8-6. *Linkshare.com. (© 1998–2001 LinkShare Corporation. All rights reserved. LinkShare^sm is a service mark of LinkShare Corporation.)*

actually code for a hyperlink. Every time someone clicks on it and buys something it's "cash city."

The focal point of affiliate programs is linkshare.com (the former banner exchange company), as seen in Figure 8-6. Notice the wide selection of programs.

Each of these companies will supply you with one or more types of links to their site. Some of these will be text hyperlinks and some will be banners. Figure 8-7 is an example of a site that uses multiple affiliate links. Notice the way it was done here. Rather than in a bunch of images, this site chose to list them in a pull-down box.

Figure 8-8 demonstrates what it's like to use the linkshare.com site to pick the actual link. In this example we're going to choose an image. The code for the image and the hyperlink to the affiliate site can be seen directly above the image. All you have to do is copy that code and place it on your site inside of your HTML.

Keeping Up-to-Date on the Tools and Techniques of the Web

It takes a lot of effort to thrive on the Web. One thing you can do is keep informed. That means finding out everything you possibly can about the business of the Web. Below are some great sources where you can keep on top of this thing called e-business:

Figure 8-7. *A site with multiple affiliates.*

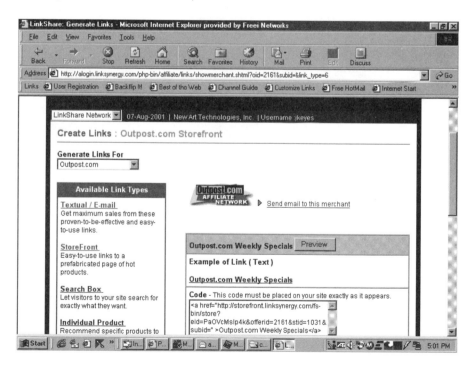

Figure 8-8. *Copying the affiliate HTML. (Copyright © 1995–2001 Cyberian Outpost, Inc. Cyberian Outpost © is a registered trademark of Cyberian Outpost, Inc. All rights reserved.)*

WEBSITES

BizReport: http://www.bizreport.com
CIO Magazine: http://www.cio.com
CNet News: http://www.news.com
e-Commerce Alert: http://www.zdjournals.com/eca/
e-Commerce Guide: http://ecommerce.internet.com
e-Commerce Times: http://www.ecommercetimes.com
e-Commerce Weekly: http://www.eweekly.com
Fast Company: http://www.fastcompany.com
Red Herring: http://www.redherring.com
Slashdot (for nerds): http://www.slashdot.org
The Standard: http://www.thestandard.com
Wired Magazine News: http://www.wired.com
ZDNet e-Business: http://www.zdnet.com/enterprise/e-business/

Section 2

Style, Content, and Design Issues

There are many things to think about when developing a Web site: its style, its content, whether or not to use "extras" such as audio, video, and animation. On top of all of this there are things that must be done that most Web developers don't even think about, such as conducting a Web site audit as well as a legal audit. In this section, we're going to cover all these bases.

What you'll learn in this section:

1. How to analyze your Web site.
2. How to create a manageable Web site.
3. How to determine if there are problems with your Web site.
4. Why you should use XML for manageability.
5. How to acquire your content.
6. How to manage content.
7. The differences between HTML, XML, and SGML.
8. How to handle conversions.
9. Licensing content.
10. How to jazz up your Web site with Flash.
11. How to prepare the state for creating great audio and video for the Web.
12. The elements of Internet style.
13. What you need to know about legal issues to stay on this side of the law.
14. How to audit your Web-based systems for security, usability, and privacy.
15. How to evaluate off-the-shelf content management software.

Building a Manageable Web Site

Gavin Nicol

Building a complex interactive Web site is a very challenging task, but one that is increasingly important to the modern enterprise. This chapter looks at the issues facing developers of such sites, and techniques that can be used to reduce costs, reduce risks, and reduce time-to-Web deployment.

Introduction

A good Web site is tremendously complex. Typically, it will contain textual content, images, link structures, and services such as shopping carts, chat rooms, and e-mail lists. While some good Web sites are put together by an individual, or by a small team, most Web sites have tens or perhaps hundreds of contributors.

The following is a list of steps and guidelines that will help you put together a Web site that is not only highly effective but also highly manageable. This chapter is broken down into four main sections. The first two sections focus on analysis, and the last two on deploying a manageable Web site. Analysis is crucial to success, so it is highly recommended that you read those first sections.

The Analysis Phase

The first step in really taking control of your Web site is to understand it. There are businesses that specialize in saving failed Web projects, and the primary reason they exist at all is lack of understanding and analysis.

Why Is My Web Site the Way It Is?

Typical Web sites start out as a single server, and a single pool of content. The content is targeted at a single audience or application and meets immediate needs. For example,

Figure 9-1. *Single-purpose Web site.*

the marketing department might decide that not having a Web presence is bad for the corporate image, so they put up a site with company information and brochures. This scenario is shown in Figure 9-1.

Over time, more and more systems are deployed both externally and internally. Usually each deployment services a specific user community and application, and hence can be, and typically is, designed in isolation. Eventually, the various sites start referring to one another and try to leverage applications developed externally. The overall Web structure becomes very complex and there is little design involved in its evolution. This is shown in Figure 9-2.

At this point, the Web starts suffering from a combinatorial explosion. Each new Web site adds more and more complexity until the whole thing becomes unmanageable. If

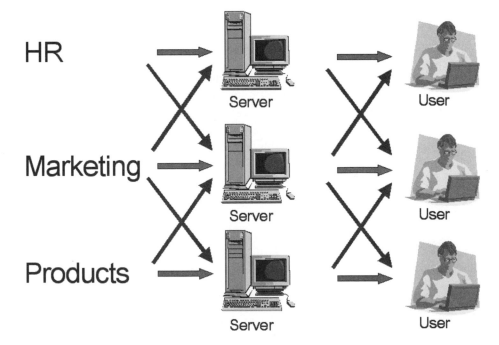

Figure 9-2. *Single-purpose Web site.*

you are reading this, you have more than likely encountered this problem. If you have, you'll know that there are a number of problems with this scenario:

Fragility—The Web is growing organically, and no one person or group oversees its structure. As such, people responsible for local changes cannot judge the impact of their changes and may make changes that break larger site structures. This fragility is inherent in the design of the Web.

Inconsistency—Each Web site, or area of the Web, may use a different look and feel, different content structures, or be tailored to different browsers.

Reuse/replication—Given the differences in content or delivery technologies, it is also usually hard to reuse parts of a site in different contexts. This often leads to the exact same content being duplicated all over the Web site.

Cost—Due to the combinatorial nature of the system, costs increase dramatically as a function of size. Most of the cost is in simply holding things together while the site evolves.

However your Web site got to where it is today, it is important to understand the history because it gives insight into the purpose and goals implicit in its structure.

Analyze the Content

The next step is to analyze the content itself. This is the first step toward restructuring the Web site for more efficient management, and is often the hardest part of understanding the existing site.

The first thing to do is to categorize all the content on the Web site. You can start this by looking at the pages and deciding what part of the company they relate to and what their function is. For example, you can say, "this is the engineering home page" or "this is the vacation form used by the marketing department." This classification, or taxonomy, can be an important component of later planning and management.

Having categorized each page, it is important to then analyze the structure of each page. You will find things like navigation bars, menus, and company logos. Note how they relate to one another, how they are used in each page, and look for similarities and overlap. Figure 9-3 shows a typical decomposition of a page into its components.

At the end of this exercise, you will have a taxonomy of Web pages and a taxonomy of Web components. You should keep these taxonomies up-to-date, and you should also make sure that other people agree with them.

Analyze Relationships and Links

Having created the taxonomies and a list of Web assets, the next step is to figure out how they interact. Analyzing link structure is generally hard because links often don't form clean hierarchies. The main thing is to look for common link patterns.

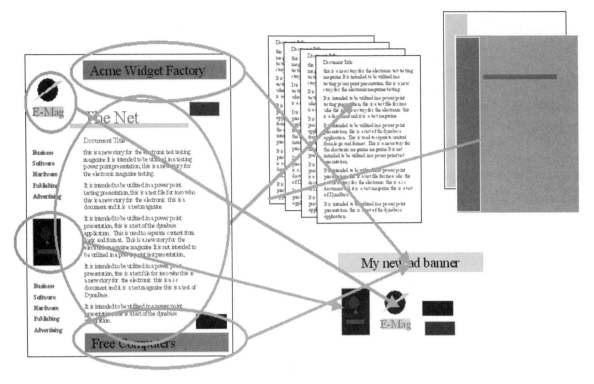

Figure 9-3. *Typical page decomposition.*

For example, if the engineering pages, the marketing pages, and the product management pages all refer to the human resources home page, you can see that this is an important link. Common link patterns and common navigation structures illuminate hidden structures in the Web site and show how people group things conceptually.

The link map you generate here can be very useful during later phases because it can be used to define the sets of links that should be generated automatically.

Understand the People and Processes
Once you have a good grasp of the Web site itself, the next step is to understand the people and processes used in creating and browsing it.

Understanding Content Contribution
Many people assume that a complex Web site needs to have a complex authoring environment. They spend a great deal of money on very complicated pieces of software de-

signed to support collaborative Web page development, only to find that people don't use them.

If you have completed the earlier phases, you will understand what content exists on the Web site and roughly how people create it. A deep understanding here can make the difference between a hard-to-maintain site and one where anyone can contribute content easily. Some key questions to ask are:

1. Who creates the content?
2. What tools do they use?
3. How strict are the format requirements?
4. How much change is acceptable to the people?
5. What editorial processes exist?
6. The main point here is to understand how people work, so that during latter phases *you change things as little as possible,* and if you do change things, you make them better.

Understand How People Use the Web Site

The other thing to look at is how people use the Web site. It is often valuable to interview people that are using the Web site and ask them what they like and dislike about it. For example, people might find an online catalog easy to use but be very annoyed by the fact that it doesn't indicate when the catalog was last updated. Or you might find that engineers were annoyed at having to browse through ten pages of marketing literature in order to get to a functional specification for a device.

It is important to not be afraid to experiment and break out of the mold. One extreme case is a large retail manufacturer that took their Web site offline for a number of weeks because they discovered that people using the site found it cumbersome. They redesigned it and put it back online in a much more effective form. They were widely applauded for the effort and the approach. Usability studies help in building a requirements document, and can make the difference between developing a good site and developing a truly great site. For retailers, this could mean the difference between profitability and bankruptcy.

Building the Web Site

With the analysis phase complete, it is time to turn to actually building the Web site or reengineering the existing one. Typical goals that people have are to:

1. Lower costs for development and maintenance.
2. Get more and more relevant information to more people.
3. Make the site more flexible so that changes can be made more easily.
4. Make the site consistent, so that people can browse through the site effortlessly.

5. Enable new opportunities by allowing information to be reused in more and better ways. A good example of this is a telephone company that might sell demographic information to retailers.

Meeting these goals requires two major components: content modeling and content management.

Model Your Content Well

A very common thread running through Web site requirements is that of information. Increasingly, the thing that distinguishes one organization from another, or that distinguishes an effective workgroup from an ineffective one, is knowledge. Enterprises wish to leverage their knowledge base by putting it onto the Web in new and powerful ways. This puts a great deal of emphasis on the *information model*.

Get to the Essence

Modeling content is perhaps one of the most difficult things to do well. There are two rules that can be applied here: "Separate the content from its presentation" and "Model the content in its native form." The first rule enables reuse of information in different contexts. The second rule allows the content to be processed meaningfully by more applications. To make this concrete, look at Figure 9-4.

Figure 9-4 shows a typical Web page. If you've done the component analysis correctly, you will immediately recognize that a fairly large part of the page has nothing to do with the content at all. This should not be modeled as part of the content, because it defines how the content *looks,* not what it *is.* It is not part of the information, which is the truly valuable asset.

Removing all the superfluous components will leave you with plain HTML, something akin to that shown below.

```
<html>
<head>
  <title>The Net</title>
<head>
<body>
  <h1>The Net</h1>
    . . .
</body>
```

This is much better, but it is problematic in that it doesn't really say what the content components *are,* or what they mean. For example, how can you tell that the following represents a price?

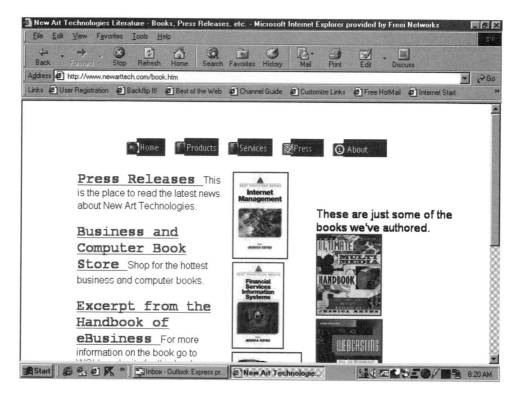

Figure 9-4. *A typical Web page.*

```
<td><b>Cost</b></td><td>$19.99</td>
```

The above is exactly why XML has sprung to the fore in the World Wide Web. XML allows you to mark up your documents with *semantics*. For example, the fragment above could be written as follows:

```
<price unit="usd">19.99</price>
```

With XML, your data becomes self-labeling and machine processable. The choice of tags in XML is entirely up to you. There are standard tag vocabularies (XHTML being one) that you can use if you choose, but it is not required. One thing that will guide you in your choice is the taxonomy developed during the analysis phase; components that share functionality should share an information model.

The ability to model information accurately is a key factor in information reuse and flexibility in publishing strategies. Use XML wherever you can.

Templating

When analyzing your page composition, you will most likely find that many of the pages have a common look and feel. If you don't, then there is a good chance your Web site has serious usability problems! The common look and feel that you have found, or are in the process of defining, is a perfect candidate for becoming a *template*.

If you go back and look at Figure 9-3, you can see the templates in the top right corner. These are essentially pages with no components in them. Each template has a number of *regions,* which can be filled with content. Typical regions include page headers and navigation bars.

The benefit of using templates is that if you want to change the look and feel of a Web site, you just change the template. You don't have to change every page. All the components are assigned to the regions as a function of the template, which gives a great deal of flexibility and, if done well, allows maximum reuse of information.

There are two primary models for templating, which I will refer to as *push* and *pull*. A pull model is something like ASP or JSP pages, or perhaps a server-side include (SSI). In this model, the page is essentially the template, and it *pulls* content into itself using code of some form. A push model has the page containing the content and a means for wrapping the page in the template, or *pushing* content into a template for final rendering.

Most current templating systems are some form of pull model. These can be made fairly flexible, but in general require a fair degree of expertise to model well. Often, people skilled in object-oriented programming are needed to reap the flexibility and reuse benefits alluded to earlier. If done poorly, such systems can result in a mass of Web pages that are essentially unmaintainable, as they will have code scattered throughout them.

There have been some systems supporting the push model: eBT's DynaBase and engenda products being two of them. In addition, recent XSL-based delivery solutions are coming close to the model. In an XSL system, an XML document is transformed using an XSL style sheet. If the style sheet is designed well, it can act as a template for the site. XSL itself can be broken into components, thereby gaining even further modularity, resulting in more flexible and robust solutions, if somewhat more complex.

The decision of exactly which templating solution to use is a difficult one to make, as the templating systems are typically part of the server; if you use IIS, for example, you are likely to use ASP. The number of systems supporting JSP and XSL is rapidly increasing, especially in the context of application servers such as BEA WebLogic Personalization Server.

Choose the templating system carefully, as it will have a significant impact on maintainability and can have subtle interactions with the information model.

Automatic Generation of Links

Broken links are the bane of every Web site, but they are so common that some people sell advertising space on them! A good rule of thumb is to generate links wherever possible. The extensive use of templating sets the stage for doing this very effectively.

The second component in generating links is the link map developed during the analysis phase. In many cases, the primary and secondary navigation structures can be broken out as components and managed separately. This makes changing navigational structures easy and also improves overall site reliability.

Manage Your Content Well

For smaller sites, management is easy: one or two people control the whole site and can make changes directly on the live Web site with impunity. For larger Web sites—especially mission critical ones—this is horribly insufficient.

Perhaps one key to reducing costs and improving the reliability and efficiency of a Web site is to make sure the whole production cycle is managed. There are three main phases in the life cycle of content on a Web site: creation, management, and deployment. We will look at each of these in turn.

Creation

Content creation takes many forms on a Web site: from graphics artists producing images to programmers developing shopping carts. The single most important thing is to make sure that each of these different groups can contribute content in a way that is natural for *them*. In many cases the Web site is optimal only for people developing Web sites.

To make this concrete, take the true story of a bank that wished to put its credit reports online. The reports themselves were very highly structured, and the information was certainly amenable to machine analysis. The information was valuable and open to being leveraged in many different ways.

In this particular case, the reports were created in everything from Powerpoint to Photoshop. Each person creating them simply used the tool they were most comfortable with to create something to be printed. Imagine putting such reports onto a Web site: the conversion cost alone would be tremendous!

For almost everyone involved, creating these reports was a time consuming, painful process. It cost the bank hundreds of thousands of dollars each year to produce information that was essentially useless after being printed.

With a very small amount of effort, the bank was able to put up a Web page containing a series of forms to be filled out for a credit report. These pages captured the data in a standard, accurate, and efficient manner. The data entry process was easier for content contributors because they didn't have to worry about formatting. The content (captured as XML) was easily made available on the Web. Almost immediately, the data was also reused to generate other reports. A cost center for the bank was turned into a painless exercise that had unexpected benefits in loan processing.

The important point was that by making the data entry process natural, there were huge gains in efficiency and accuracy. Similar gains can be had in page composition and graphics design by breaking work down into small, natural units and optimizing the process at that level.

Workflow

Somewhat related to content creation is the notion of workflow. If you examine the content creation process, you will often find a process that you can, or should, standardize upon. For example, graphic artists should always pass created content onto an editor, who will review it; if approved, he or she will then arrange for its deployment.

It is a good idea to deploy some form of workflow management system and to enforce process, as this will generally result in improvements in overall quality and efficiency. You must, however, weigh the cost of process enforcement against the desire to improve contribution efficiency.

If you are buying a Web content management system, you will find that most have some form of workflow system integrated into them. The main thing to look for here is flexibility. Many workflow systems are inflexible or require a great deal of effort to configure. Also look at the form of workflow supported.

Collaborative systems (such as Microsoft Exchange) offer the ability to assign and route tasks on an ad-hoc basis, thereby capturing the detailed nature of work. Process-driven workflow systems (such as Verve) are used more for capturing the larger business or editorial processes, and can be used to automate steps in site management. Ideally, a content management system would provide both forms, though most emphasize one over the other. If you are not buying a workflow system, or a content management system with one bundled, you can get some of the benefits of workflow management by documenting and following processes. Things like a "Content Submission Guideline" can go a long way to bringing order to the Web site.

Version and Edition Management

At some point, you will feel the need to manage versions of your content and indeed, in some cases, you may be bound by law to do so. Typically, the fundamental requirements are driven by either *accountability* or the desire for *rollback*.

Accountability is important for almost any Web site that involves transactions. For example, imagine you are an online watch retailer. Someone calls you to say that you are charging him $500 for a watch that, when he ordered it, was on sale for $50. How can you be sure he is right? The only way is to have a copy of the site, or the page with the special on it in archive form.

Of course, having an archive version is useless unless you can reproduce the context that the content was displayed in. In this case, you need to be able to locally roll back the page, or the site, to a particular version. Note that this includes databases used to generate the dynamic aspects of a Web site. A site-wide snapshot of a Web site is typically called an *edition*.

In addition to accountability, versions and editions are important for reliability. It is often the case that even though workflow isolation has been used to control change, inadvertent changes will be made to the Web site, and those changes will cause failures. In such times it is crucial to be able to quickly roll the Web site back to a known good state.

While Web content management vendors will often emphasize the versioning and edition management capabilities of their product, evaluate your requirements carefully. In many cases, simply using tools like CVS (a source code control system) is sufficient. From a practical perspective, if you require much more sophistication than simple linear version histories, rollback, and site-wide editions, it is often a sign that your site is being poorly managed or is not broken into components correctly.

To make this more concrete, imagine a situation where people are often checking in changes to a central repository. In this case, the site is never more than a few check-ins broken, and everyone managing versions (site developers, not contributors) keeps reasonably well synchronized. While there will be cases where one set of changes will conflict with another set of changes, those problems will be caught early on. The site will naturally tend to stay in good shape.

Contrast this to a world where branching is used extensively. In this case, people can have their own development branches and work in isolation. Exactly when they check in their changes to the main branch is a matter of personal preference (this is very common in parallel development). This approach makes things locally very efficient, because each person can work in isolation. The problem arises when all these projects come together. The result is often a "merge fest" where everyone tries to resolve merges back to a main production branch. This can be time consuming and error prone.

Unless your needs are extreme, you are better off avoiding extensive branch use and instead focusing on automating the management of a simpler system (for example, automating the building of nightly snapshots).

Deployment

The final stage in site management is deployment. Given that you have implemented a strategy that provides edition functionality, deployment is simply a matter of choosing an edition and making it available.

The last step sounds simple but can actually be fairly complex. If you are running a larger or a mission-critical Web site, it usually makes sense to actually deploy to a staging server first, so that the site may be tested before being pushed to a production server.

Most Web content management systems provide some means for deploying content. Look for a system that allows deployment to be automated as a function of the workflow state, or as a function of time (for example, go live at 12:00 A.M.).

Some systems actually provide a more sophisticated edition management system that integrates the staging and production services in a single central database. These systems tend to be more reliable than systems that rely upon file copying, FTP, etc., though they can be more complex to deal with.

The main thing here again is automation. Even if you develop a homegrown solution for management based on CVS and FTP, you should automate the process of deploying not only current editions, but also past editions. You must make the act of publishing repeatable.

Summary

This chapter has focused on Web site management. This is obviously a huge topic, so we have necessarily skipped over a great deal of detail and instead focused on providing guidelines for developing Web sites.

To summarize:

1. Understand your existing Web site so you can make changes in the future. Analysis is crucial.
2. Understand the people and processes involved in site creation and management.
3. Model the real content and separate the content from its presentation.
4. Use XML wherever you can.
5. Deploy a templating system to ease future look and feel changes.
6. Automatically generate navigational structures and page content wherever possible.
7. Streamline the content contribution phases wherever possible. Make them natural to the people involved.
8. Deploy some means for workflow control. Ideally a workflow system would be used, but standardized procedures will suffice.
9. Deploy some form of Web content management solution. Minimally, a source code control system should be used.
10. Automate the deployment phase.

A recognized world expert on XML, HTML, and related standards, eBT's Chief Scientist GAVIN NICOL developed DynaWeb—the first SGML/XML-based publishing system providing run-time conversion to HTML. Most recently, Nicol designed engenda, eBT's flagship XML-based content management and workflow automation solution. Nicol was a member of the original World Wide Web Consortium (WC3) working group on XML. He is currently a member of the working group or interest group at the following W3C activities: XML, XLL, XSL, DOM, and SVG; he is also the Advisory Committee Representative for eBT.

The Missing Link in B2B E-Commerce: Product Content

Robert R. Payne

In the span of a few short years the concept of business-to-business (B2B) e-commerce has emerged and risen rapidly in the consciousness of the world economy. Although simple in concept, complex issues have come to light as businesses implement and develop their B2B e-commerce business processes and strategies. In the early days of e-commerce, businesses outlined the "three c's" of successful e-commerce: content, commerce, and community. Sell-side and buy-side companies focused primarily on sales and marketing and e-procurement applications to build community and commerce. Catalog content was not an area of major concern—it was assumed that data would be relatively easy to come by.

As Net marketplaces (or e-marketplaces) and Web storefronts formed, businesses began to realize the first "c" was an essential yet missing component to e-commerce success. Less than 10 percent of suppliers have their product information properly structured for participation in emerging Net marketplaces and online stores, according to e-commerce powerhouse Commerce One. The lack of complete, accurate, and up-to-date product content, which can be syndicated to and used by any and all trading partners, has surfaced as a major barrier preventing B2B e-commerce from reaching its full potential.

How has the Internet and e-commerce affected businesses? How have these changes been addressed? What other, greater opportunities and challenges lie ahead?

Transformation of Business and Content

Buyers and sellers alike understand that today's key channel for business growth is the Internet; the Internet has transformed the way the world handles its B2B relationships. It has not only enabled new commercial processes, but it has introduced new business models that leverage the flow of information around the world. Those companies that will succeed in this "New Economy" will be those that can successfully position themselves

Sustainable Differentiation via Automated Content Management

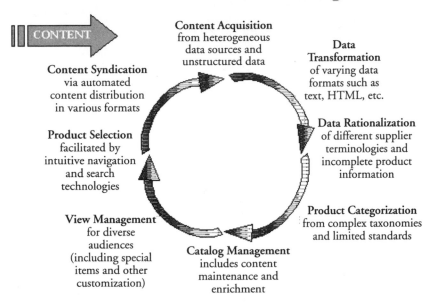

Figure 10-1. *Sustainable differentiation via automated content management.*
Source: Aberdeen Group.

and transform their business processes to be able to participate in the new world of B2B e-commerce.

To participate in B2B e-commerce, businesses need to spur a metamorphosis in how they conduct their business-to-business transactions. Feeling this urgency, many businesses have rushed to institute e-commerce initiatives with little or no success. In their haste to take advantage of this new method of conducting business, companies have failed to recognize that the one key ingredient to the success of such an initiative (be it a Web storefront, e-procurement system, or electronic market or exchange) is information. Not just access to information, but dynamic information that is up-to-date, easy to find, and that assists the buyer in making an educated business decision. As suppliers and Net market makers begin to understand the importance of creating differentiation with effective content management, they need to outline the steps required to automate the process, as shown in Figure 10-1.

Content in E-Commerce

With Jupiter Research estimating that B2B e-commerce will grow to $6.3 trillion in 2005, suppliers, buyers, and Net market makers have rushed to position themselves to take advantage of this tremendous opportunity. A scenario has arisen where trading sites are created with most of their efforts focused on developing the procurement side of the business model. Yet product content is essential not only for a supplier's own e-commerce initiatives, but also for buy-side companies' e-procurement activities and for Net marketplaces. This content must be searched and compared for everyday product ordering and for strategic decision making.

The inability to supply complete product content to buyers presents major issues for Net market makers. E-markets hold the promise of creating new revenue streams through value-added services and transaction fees. However, the lack of clean, rich product data threatens these opportunities. To succeed, Net market makers must quickly build and maintain liquidity, achieved by attracting a critical number of buyers as well as suppliers. Net market makers must understand the importance sourcing, aggregating, securing, and managing content has in attracting buyers and sellers alike. Providing timely, accurate, and complete product information gives Net market makers a huge advantage in attracting and maintaining buyers. After all, buyers can't buy what they can't find.

As buy-side businesses and Net marketplaces realized the importance of product content management, a number of methods emerged to try to meet this need. Essentially, the information could be generated internally, obtained from a third-party aggregator or agent technologies, or obtained from direct links to the suppliers, as shown in Figure 10-2.

Buyer- or Net-market managed information not only runs the risk of being inaccurate and difficult to maintain, but also lacks the ability to be syndicated, or shared between multiple users. Supplier-managed content, while rich in specific product information, does not allow the buyer to price and compare with other similar product options. Third-party-managed information, such as that collected by an aggregator or automatically "scraped" from suppliers' Web sites by an agent technology, is usually not easily syndicated, is stored in proprietary formats, requires large amounts of time and monetary

Approach	Description	Examples
Buyer or Net market managed content	Buyers and Net market makers can collect catalog data from multiple suppliers and build internal databases. This method requires gathering information from each supplier's individual formats and systems, including paper catalogs (re-typing the information), and checking accuracy continuously as suppliers update the information with new or modified products, discontinued products, and pricing changes. Because all this information has to fit into the unique formats and taxonomies of the e-procurement system or Net marketplace system, the content is "normalized" to include only a specified set of attributes. This is done to obtain consistency that allows the comparison of multiple suppliers.	
Supplier managed content	Product information managed by suppliers is much more complete, but this method does not necessarily allow for comparison-shopping. More importantly, it requires the supplier to have a sophisticated system for transacting products. Many suppliers do not have such a system in place, and do not want to spend the time and money to implement one.	
Third party managed content	Third party content aggregators or agent technologies collect the product data manually or automatically and sell it to e-procurement users or Net market makers in their own required formats. However, like buy-side and Net market internal solutions, many third party systems still require a lot of manual compilation of information. Also, the content is normalized for manipulation by specific systems, frequently causing the loss of some valuable product information.	

Figure 10-2. *Methodologies to manage content.*

resources, and is not always accurate and up-to-date because it is not in the control of the supplier.

Who Owns Content?

In addition, with the question of defining content, ownership becomes an increasingly vital issue with any of these approaches, because the parties involved have different objectives and priorities. Buyer- or Net-market-managed content is aggregated by an outside source or by a corporate content team for its own internal use, to meet its own needs. As a result, the information is gathered and presented in such a way that it is conducive to the buyer's needs. Yet, the supplier is, of course, concerned by the imminent threat of inaccurate and severely outdated product information (their product information). In fact, industry research indicates that suppliers typically update up to 50 percent of their descriptive product information annually and that prices increase by as much as 125 percent to 150 percent a year, sometimes at multiple times during the year.

Suppliers are concerned about the type of information third-party aggregators and agent technologies are distributing for the same reasons. Meanwhile, a third-party aggregator believes that the time and effort spent on collecting and organizing such information give them the right to distribute it to companies willing to pay and make a profit from it. Agent technologies also believe the time and money spent developing technologies that can "scrape" product information from public Web sites give them the right to own the collected product information.

While product content disseminated by suppliers will be highly accurate, both Net market makers and buyers alike share the concern of not being able to utilize supplier-owned content. Varying taxonomies and electronic formats limit or at least impede how a recipient of the information could implement it internally and manipulate it to meet their (or clients') specific needs. Again, this causes an information barrier that impedes the progress of B2B e-commerce conducted in e-marketplaces. Though this is a concern for Net market makers and buyers, it is the supplier that suffers most when its content is collected and distributed by an outside party. The suppliers' most valuable corporate asset is product information. It is from the product content that a supplier can sell its wares and thrive as a business. To have product information misrepresented, even in the slightest manner, will affect the suppliers' business objectives and ultimately the bottom line.

Why Suppliers Should Take Control

Most importantly, outside party aggregation or agent technologies don't fulfill suppliers' need to provide a complete representation of their products that can be properly branded and differentiated for their buyers while avoiding commodization. Most procurement professionals use the Web to gather the information they need, but in order for this information to be useful it must be "rich data." Rich data, previously only seen in traditional print catalogs, includes not only product specifications but also features, benefits, and documentation (datasheets or spec profiles). Rich data is what sets apart suppliers from their competitors. However, commodization within e-commerce, when only pricing and availability represent a product, has become commonplace as Net market makers scurry to find content for their Web sites. With increased pricing pressure from the Net marketplace environment, suppliers can't afford to have their product content represented without their own product messaging and without the ability to ensure its accuracy. Branding and differentiating product content enables suppliers to convey more about their product than can be done with simple data on price and availability.

Bottleneck in e-Commerce

Part of the problem for Net marketplaces has been the focus on procurement, with the first half of the supply chain virtually ignored. It has been easier to set up a shopping cart and manage distribution and tracking than to acquire and manage content.

Marilyn Muller of Summit Strategies syas, "Catalog management is one of the most consistently underestimated challenges of operating an e-marketplace. For any vendor that aggregates product catalogs from multiple suppliers, keeping up with each vendor's diverse standards, products, and price changes is a potential data nightmare. Although most e-marketplace operators know they must have a catalog-management strategy, the majority confess that they are currently taking catalogs in any form the suppliers will send them—typically through e-mailed spreadsheets or documents, and sometimes even by fax."

These matters for both suppliers and Net market makers have slowed the ability of B2B e-commerce to reach its potential. Yet there are a couple of solutions that can resolve these issues. By giving buyers access to a "smart" directory of products and manufacturers with the product information linked directly to a supplier's Web site, buyers have access to the most accurate, up-to-date, and complete product information available. Suppliers and Net market makers benefit from the ability to maintain control of the product information, as they then obtain better product branding and differentiation, better sales results, and improved liquidity. Other solutions include having the supplier prepare product content and syndicating it to trading partners. This enables suppliers to update product content on an ongoing basis, ensuring that all trading partners have the information they want them to have in the correct format used. Both solutions give back to the suppliers the management of this important corporate asset.

Most suppliers cannot easily afford the time or money required to prepare their product content for e-commerce, format it for syndication to multiple Net marketplaces with different formats and content requirements, and maintain its accuracy and completeness on an ongoing basis. With the variety of solutions available, however, suppliers, buyers, and Net market makers alike can choose one that best fits the corporate objectives.

With the Internet pulling together the business world as never experienced before, global e-commerce will continue to expand. As businesses in nations outside of the

United States actively pursue opportunities created by the Internet, suppliers and Net market makers must keep in mind what that means. Market potential is huge, but with the opportunity, global e-commerce presents new ideas to address, such as multi-language translation of product content. Providing buyers with the ability to search, find, and ultimately buy a product in the language that is easiest for them to work in will prove essential. Buyers looking for a product that is presented with several options will be able to learn and understand more easily when the information is presented in their own language.

What to Look for in a Content Solution

A variety of solutions enabling successful content management are starting to become available, allowing companies to quickly participate in e-commerce with minimal capital investment. These solutions exist for almost all of the different stages a manufacturer, supplier, or Net market maker needs to go through to effectively manage and exchange product content, such as:

- Cleanse, categorize, and structure product content into a centralized product information database that can be transformed for dynamic publishing on the Web.
- The database should be equipped with multiple search capabilities.
- Syndicate product content to multiple trading partners in their preferred electronic format.
- Provide direct links to a supplier's or manufacturer's Web site to ensure access to "rich," accurate product information.
- Analyze buyers' behavior to allow for improvements on marketing and selling methods.
- Implement global e-commerce capabilities, including multi-language and monetary systems.

Solutions that provide businesses the stepping stones to getting product content commerce ready in an easy, cost-effective way enable efficient and profitable e-commerce, as product content is the factor upon which this success hinges. Suppliers, buyers, and Net market makers are adjusting to the rapid changes in virtually all business processes brought by the advent of the Internet. One of the most crucial changes is moving away from ineffective methods of content aggregation and management to those that put the data in the hands of suppliers to ensure that the most complete, accurate, and up-to-date information is available. Software and services that allow suppliers and Net marketplaces to easily manage product content, speed the time to market, and successfully market and sell products on the Web are essential in allowing companies to succeed in their e-commerce initiatives, driving greater buyer loyalty and increased sales through the e-commerce channel.

ROBERT R. PAYNE is president and CEO of SAQQARA Systems, Inc. Bob has more than twenty-five years of experience in managing high-tech companies that are early in the technology life cycle. Most recently, Bob has served in consulting roles to start-up ventures as acting CEO, COO, and board member and doing due diligence consulting for a major venture capital firm. He was CEO of Calico Technology, an early e-commerce company, during 1996 and 1997 and grew the company from $2 million in revenue to $14 million. Prior to joining Calico, Bob served as vice president and general manager for Application Products at Platinum Technology (Trinzic Corp. acquisition). He has also held senior sales and marketing positions at Pansophic Systems Inc., FNBC, and IBM. Bob has a BBA in marketing from Iona College and an MBA from Baruch College, CUNY.

Web Animation: The Foundations of Flash

Judd Mercer

The Internet has evolved from the early days of simple message boards to an entirely new form of media. The birth of this new age of information and expression has been accelerated by many factors, not the least of which is Web animation. Web pages have changed from being angular and structured to entirely dynamic forms of expression and design due to the development of Web animation technology. Now, Web pages can contain video with streaming musical scores, advanced interactivity, and changing content.

Macromedia's Flash fulfilled the need for Web animation. Flash (or more precisely, Flash 5) has many advantages over outdated methods such as animated .gifs and embedded .midi files, which make Flash animation publishing far more effective. For instance, a Web page in Flash can be organized in any way, complete with the freedom of movement. The designer is not restricted to set tables and sizes, as with HTML. Second, Web animation published using Flash has streaming capabilities, which decreases load times for viewers and also decreases bandwidth needed to view a site. Third, audio and video can be embedded in any way inside Flash animations. Finally, Flash can interact with many other Web technologies including HTML and ASP (active server pages).

This chapter will focus on the very basics of Web animation using Flash 5. We will create a simple animation that will teach you many of the concepts, terms, and techniques used in Web animation today. Our animation will eventually become a bouncing ball that will change into another shape, continue to move around the screen until the animation will stop, and have a simple "play again" button. Although seemingly easy, this animation will cover many key concepts of Flash 5, including:

- Interface
- Creating **Basic Symbols** using the **Library** and **Drawing Tools**
- Placing **Symbols** on the **TimeLine**, and manipulating **Movie Setting**
- Basic **Motion Tweening**

- Creating Interactive **Buttons** as Symbols
- Basic **Frame Actions** to control movie playback
- **Button Actions** to control movie playback
- Exporting Flash Movies

Interface

Flash's interface is based on a theater metaphor. There is a stage where the content will be placed. There are reusable elements that are "backstage" to be used in the movie like characters or props.

We will begin by explaining how the Flash 5 interface works. You will notice upon opening Flash 5 that there is a large, white space in the middle of your screen (Fig. 11-1). This is the **stage,** where all the content will be placed. The gray region is extra space, and anything placed in this area will not show when the movie is published. The row of boxes near the top of the screen is called the **timeline.** The **timeline** will determine in what order actions take place. The timeline is made of **layers,** which are used to keep animations on separate planes. Each layer has its rows of little squares, which are called **frames.**

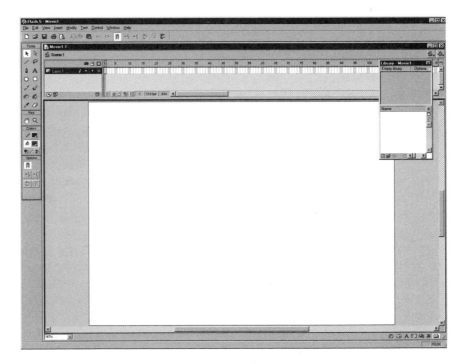

Figure 11-1. *The Flash stage.*

Frames are individual moments on the timeline where content can be placed. When a movie is played, the timeline will, by default, display each frame in order until it has shown every frame. Controlling the timeline will become more clear as we continue.

You will also notice a floating window named **library.** The library will hold all of your **symbols** for that particular movie. Like the cast and crew of a movie, these symbols will be reused throughout the movie. Symbols can be graphics, movie clips, or buttons that can be placed on the stage in a specific frame. The unique thing about symbols is that changes made to a symbol will be reflected throughout the movie. For instance, if you have a symbol that is a graphic of a red circle and that circle appears in forty frames, all forty frames where that symbol appears will be changed to blue when you change the circle's color to blue. If you change any symbol in the library, each place where that symbol is located in the movie stage will also be changed. You can think of symbols as actors in your theater production. On the left you will see the **toolbar,** which contains all the drawing and text tools used to create symbols.

Creating Basic Symbols Using the Library and Drawing Tools

Since our animation begins with a bouncing ball, we should first create an image of a ball in our movie's library. To create a new symbol, select Insert /New Symbol from the main menu (or hit Ctrl+F8). A window appears that will define the symbol's properties, such as the symbol's name. In the name field type "Ball" and select the "Graphic" behavior and hit "OK." We are now in the edit symbol window. Notice that the new symbol appears in the library. You may also notice that symbols have their own timelines, which means you can have animations inside animations, but, breathe easy, not in this chapter!

We will now construct our ball using the Flash drawing tools. Choose the "Oval" tool to construct a circle. Look toward the bottom of the toolbar and you will see two color boxes, one with a pencil near it, the other with a paint can. The pencil color is the outline color of a shape, and the paint can is the fill color. Click and hold the box near the pencil, and a color swatch panel appears that allows you to choose different colors. In the upper right corner you will see a white box with a red line through it. This, when selected, will make the line transparent, which is what we want for this example. Click the transparent box and you'll see that the line color box now has the white box with the red line through it; the line will now be transparent. Do the same for the fill color, but notice on the bottom of the fill swatch you see colors fading into other colors. These are **gradient** fills. Select the blue-to-black gradient swatch for the fill color. We can now draw our circle. Click and hold on the stage and drag your mouse to create a circle (Note: Holding shift while creating a circle will make a perfect circle). Release the mouse and you should have a circle that fades from blue to black on the screen. Don't worry if your circle is not the same size as mine (Fig. 11-2), we will resize it later, anyway. Congratulations, you've made your first symbol!

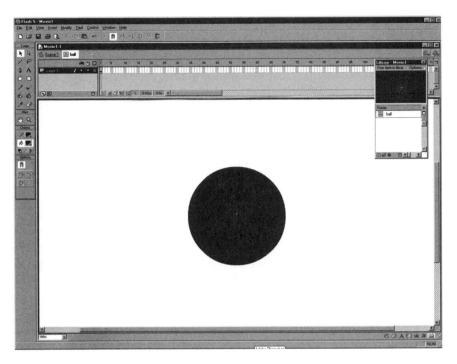

Figure 11-2. *Constructing a ball using Flash drawing tools.*

Saving

Now is a good time, if you haven't already, to save your work. Select File / Save from the main menu and name your file. Remember, saving often saves both time and sanity.

Simple Animation

Traditionally, animation was created by moving an image frame by frame at a speed at which the eye could not see individual frames, but rather one continuous image (much like television or a flip book). This was a long and tedious process that Flash has simplified. Instead of moving an image frame by frame, Flash can take two different frames and create all the frames in between, hence the term **motion tweening.** With the motion tween, you can create all sorts of animations from basic motion to changing the size, color, and even shape of a symbol.

We will now animate the ball that we have created. If you are still in the symbol editing stage, click on "Scene 1" in the upper left corner of the stage to return to the main stage and timeline. In your timeline window you should see one layer with one empty frame. Drag the symbol "ball" that we created earlier from the library window onto the stage. Notice how the frame on the timeline becomes gray, indicating there is something on the stage at this point. Now drag the ball near the top of the stage where we will make it "drop." Go to the open space "10" on the timeline and choose Insert/Frame (or hit F5). Notice that all the frames from 1 to 10 are now gray. If you were to play the animation now, ten frames of the same ball in the same place would show.

Now let's make it move. Select all ten frames (the easiest way to select all frames in a layer is to simply select the layer name itself) and choose Insert/Create Motion Tween. The frames should have changed color to an opaque purple. Now, select the last frame on the timeline and choose Insert/Key Frame (or hit F6). Think of key frames as the anchor points of an animation. With the key frame 10 selected, move the ball toward the bottom of the screen.

Choose Control/Play from the menu (or hit Enter) to play the movie thus far. You should see the ball travel from the top of the screen to the bottom. Notice the speed in which the ball moves. Experiment with more and less frames between each key frame to vary the speed of your animations. The more frames between each key frame, the slower the animation will be.

Since objects, especially balls, usually bounce when dropped, we need to add this movement to our animation. Select frame 30 on the timeline and Insert/Key Frame (or hit F6). Notice we put more space between these two frames because things usually travel slower on the way up than they do on the way down. Select frame 30 and move the ball near the top of the stage, but not as far as originally placed, to have the appearance that the ball is really fighting gravity. This "bounce" process can be repeated as many times as desired, but for this animation we will create one more bounce sequence. Select frame 40, insert a new key frame, and move the ball to the bottom of the screen (like in the first sequence). You might be thinking that it may appear strange if the ball "bounces" from different locations each time. Because it is difficult to keep track of exact positions of symbols, we will simply copy frame 10 and paste it in frame 40, so the ball bounces from the same point each time. To copy the frame, select frame 10 and choose Edit/Copy Frames from the main menu (or hit Ctrl+Alt+C), then select frame 40 and choose Edit/Paste Frames from the main menu (or Ctrl+Alt+V). Now the ball will bounce from the same location each time.

Now that you are familiar with the timeline interface, you can add more bounce sequences that are smaller and smaller in size to make the bouncing realistic. The next step in Flash animation is to begin to control the timeline, instead of letting it play all the way through, using **Buttons, ActionScript,** and **Frame Actions.**

Frame Actions

Frame actions control the way the timeline flows as the movie plays. Using frame actions, you can stop, play, and jump to any frame in the movie. We will now make our movie interactive by creating a button that will ask the user to see the animation again. To do this, we will first need to stop the movie playback at the end of the bouncing animation, because Flash, by default, loops the movie playback infinitely.

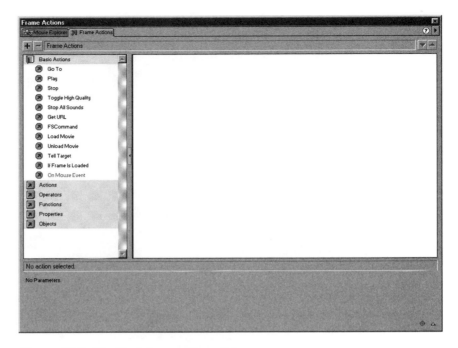

Figure 11-3. *The Flash frame actions dialog.*

Select the last frame of your bouncing ball animation and double-click it. The frame actions dialog box appears (Fig. 11-3), which will allow you to control your movie without writing a line of code! Click on the "stop" action. The action now appears in the dialog box. Close the box and take a look at the frame on the timeline. You should see a tiny "a" above the key frame, indicating there is an action assigned to it. Be careful! Actions can only be assigned to key frames, not normal frames.

Creating Buttons

Now let's make a button that will replay the movie from the beginning. Choose Insert/New Symbol from the main menu (or hit Ctrl+F8) and select the "button" behavior and name the button "play again." The button name is not important, but it is easier to keep track of many symbols if they are named. Look at the timeline after clicking "OK" and you will see four frames: Up, Over, Down, and Hit. These are the states of the buttons during interaction. Whatever appears in the "Up" frame will appear when the button simply sits on the stage. "Over" is what appears when the user places his cursor over the button, "Down" is what appears as the user is clicking, and if the user holds the button, whatever is in the "Hit" frame will appear at that time.

Let's just make a simple rectangular shape with the rectangle tool (R) in the "Up" key frame. The color doesn't really matter; try using the gradient fills if you're feeling

Figure 11-4. *Modifying the color of a button.*

ambitious. Also, there is a button at the bottom of the toolbar when the rectangle tool is selected. This button can make the corners of a rectangle curved. If pressed, a box appears where you can input a number that will determine the amount of curvature on the corners of the rectangle. The higher the number, the more curved the corners will be. Once you have a good size and color established, select the type tool (T) from the toolbar and type "play again" on top of the rectangle.

Since we don't want our button to be drastically different between each state, copy the "Up" frame and paste it in each of the three proceeding frames. Now, select the "Over" state of your button. Change the text color on this frame so that when the user puts his cursor over the button (called "mouseover") the text will change color (Fig. 11-4). To change the text color and size, select Window/Panels/Character (or hit Ctrl+T), which brings up a window that allows you to change the font, size, and color of the text selected. Highlight the text and press the colored box on the character to bring up the color palette. Now select a new color for the text.

We won't worry about the following two frames, but we still have a lot to do! Now return to the stage and drop your new button on to frame 40 (or the frame in which you placed the stop action). Now we're ready to make the button work.

Making Things Happen

Although frame actions are a powerful feature of Flash, it is ActionScript, Flash's custom scripting language, that allows powerful interactivity within Flash movies. We'll get into the basic scripting actions but leave the advanced stuff alone . . . for now.

The concept behind ActionScript is the action-reaction relationship in which an action causes some sort of change, the reaction. These actions range from a simple button click to checking inputted text for specific words. For our purposes, we will use a mouse-click on our button as our action.

Right-click the button on the stage and select "Actions." This will bring up the "Object Actions" window, which looks exactly like the Frame Actions box you saw earlier. Here you can select actions to apply to symbols throughout your movie. On the left, you will see categories in which all the actions are stored. Your most often used and basic actions can be found within the "Basic Actions" heading.

Perhaps the most versatile and widely used action is the onMouseEvent. This action is used to create "reactions" upon input by the user's mouse. Double-click the onMouseEvent to assign this action to your button. Notice at the bottom of the window many check boxes appeared. These are attributes that are specific to the action selected. The onMouseEvent attributes can be described as follows:

- Press—Reaction happens when the button is pressed.
- Release—Reaction occurs when the user releases the mouse click on the button (default).
- Release Outside—Reaction occurs when the user clicks on the button and then moves the cursor off the button.
- Key Press—Instead of a mouse input, any key can be set as an action (except for the Esc and F# keys).
- Roll Over—When the user rolls over the button, the reaction will happen.
- Roll Out—When a user rolls over a buttons, then rolls off, the event will trigger.
- Drag Over—Reaction is triggered when the user clicks and drags over the button.
- Drag Out—Reaction occurs when the user clicks and drags over and off of the button.

Select the "Release" attribute for our onMouseEvent. Now, from the list of actions, double-click on the "Goto" action. The Goto action can travel to any point on the timeline, given the parameters you can set in the actions' attributes. When selected, the Goto action automatically defaults to go to the first frame in the current scene and play. Luckily, this is precisely what we are after. When our button is released, the reaction will be to go to and play frame 1 of our movie, or, in other words, start the movie over from the beginning. Close the object actions window and return to the stage.

You may begin to wonder how you can see the movie you've created with all the frame objects and buttons you've added in. A quick way to view your progress is to select Control/Test Movie (or hit Ctrl+Enter) from the main menu. This exports the movie into a stand-alone player in which you can test your movie in its entirety. The player is an excellent tool to fine-tune your movie. In our case, check to see if your ball appears realistic in its bounce; if not, go back and remove or add frames in the timeline to speed or slow the ball's movement. Does the button work? Did the movie stop playback after the ball was finished bouncing? Check to make sure every aspect of your movie looks good and is functioning properly, for now we move on to exporting our movie for Web use.

Exporting

Flash has its own method of compressing a Flash file into a file format called Shockwave. A Shockwave file is unique because it can be easily embedded into the code of a Web page. The great thing about Flash is that it can create the HTML automatically *and* embed the Shockwave file at the same time. The advantages of using the Shockwave file to export your movies is that it can store all of your symbols, actions, and even sound and video in one file, which decreases the amount of files you have to work with, as well as your stress level.

Once you have your movie the way you like it, select File/Publish Setting (or hit Ctrl+Shift+F12) from the main menu. This brings up the Publish Settings window, which allows you to set parameters for your exported Flash movie. Notice how there are many check boxes on the left side of the window. These are file formats in which Flash can export your movie. We will be using the Flash and HTML export modes, which should be the default. Notice that Flash can also export single frames of a movie into a .gif or .jpg image file, or even a Quicktime .mov file.

Take a look at the grayed-out regions on the window. This is where you can change the file names of your exported movie. Most of the time, you will not change these settings, so near the bottom of the window "Use default file names" is selected, which will simply use the file name you gave when you saved the movie. There should also be two tabs along the top of the window, one that says "Flash" and one that says "HTML." Click on the "Flash" tab. Here is a new window that allows you to set certain parameters for that specific file format. We will be using the default settings for both Flash and HTML, so don't worry about the panels right now.

So, now the movie is perfect and we want to se it in a Web page format. From the main menu, choose File/Publish (or hit Shift+F12) to publish your movie. And that's it! Simply open up your Internet browser and choose File/Open; find your file on your computer, open it up, and there's your movie on a Web page, ready to go.

Summary

Having completed this chapter, you have learned the basic foundations for Web animation using Flash 5, including the use of symbols, drawing tools, and basic interactivity.

The best way to learn more about Flash is to experiment on your own. But remember, Flash is a tool, like a pencil or a brush; it's only as good as your imagination.

For further reading and support, you can go to www.macromedia.com/support/flash/ for tutorials and step-by-step instructions.

JUDD MERCER (aka juddge_fizzy) is creative director for PopFizzMedia (www. popfizzmedia.com), an information-technology firm based in Denver, Colorado. He has been designing professionally for two years, though he was designing animated banners and little things like that as a senior in high school. Flash is his favorite media, though he works with HTML and static graphics programs including Adobe Photoshop, Adobe Illustrator, Macromedia FreeHand, and Corel Painter. He hopes to soon take the plunge into 3-D animation as well as video editing.

Take a peek at his portfolio at www.popfizzmedia.com/portfolios/judd/index_judd.html, or contact him at juddge@popfizzmedia.com.

Creating Great Audio and Video for the Web

Jessica Keyes

More than a few companies have decided that audio and/or video is a good fit for their Web sites. A whole spate of hardware and software products have poured into the market that provide the Web developer with the means to "put" audio and video on the Web. In this chapter we will *not* delve into the mechanics of these toolsets. Indeed, anyone can use one of these tools to dump some audio and video on the Web. The question is, "Will it look and sound professional?"

Instead, this chapter is going to approach the subject of Webcasting, which is what this subject is commonly called, from a production perspective. In this chapter, we are going to step away from our role as Web developers for a few moments and instead put on the hat of the filmmaker. Steven Spielberg . . . move over!

Guidelines for Digital Video

There is no commonly-agreed upon methodology to create digital video. Since the hardware and software invoked is continually evolving, the digital video maker will have to keep on his or her toes to make sure that the videos produced are always on the "cutting edge."

The following discussion depicts a fairly common sequence of events that take place in the creation of a video on a PC (before encoding). Since the computer brings the creation process into the nonlinear age, none of these steps really has to follow in exact sequence. Assuming that the storyboarding process has been completed, the following steps can occur.

Gathering Source Material

Production facilities and personnel may be employed to create new footage for editing and manipulation, or stock footage may be gathered. The effects of the nonlinear editing process is obvious here because it allows editors to play "what if" with the story line in an unprecedented manner. Thus, additional footage maybe shot at this stage, and more footage may be required later if the story line is allowed to evolve. The computer itself is capable of generating text, graphics, and even 2-D and 3-D animations.

Digitizing

Before any editing can take place, the source video must be converted into digital form by the computer and stored on disk. This process is known as digitizing. Video input can come from many kinds of input devices, from consumer-quality VHS machines to traditional high-end tape equipment. However, the quality of the digital image is directly dependent on the quality of the medium from which it comes. While there are several methods of digitizing, they all depend on the quality of the source device. Thus, the rental or purchase of a high-quality deck should be factored into the overall cost of equipment. Still frames to be included in the production can be created on the PC or brought in through a high-quality scanner.

Editing Nonlinearly

The nonlinear editing process has many advantages. Most software products handle the editing process by facilitating the creation in an offline model of the final video, rather than by actually compositing the video themselves online.

This model contains information about how the video is to unfold over time. Various video clips are trimmed and then sequenced together with intervening transitions, wipes, and keys. Rather than manipulate the video files themselves, the model contains information about the files and pointers to them.

Since the computer is a general-purpose tool, it can be used for more than just the editing process. Static graphic elements can be assembled by means of professional-quality graphics programs, text can be generated, and 2-D and 3-D animations can be created. Changes to all of these production elements can be made right up to the last minute.

The computer allows the editor to create and store a model of the video project without creating the actual video. Since this model can also be duplicated and the duplicate can be altered without altering the original, it is possible to create several different models or previews of the same project.

After the creation process has ended, the resulting video model must be used to create or render an actual video. During the rendering process the computer proceeds frame-by-frame through the model and performs all operations necessary to create a complete frame at the desired resolution and quality. This process can be quite time consuming, depending on the complexity of the model and the duration of the video.

Since many compositing and special-effect computations are very processor intensive, three ways to speed the rendering process are to (1) purchase a faster computer, (2) accelerate your current machine, or (3) take advantage of multiprocessor hardware and software to operate in parallel.

Broadcast-Quality Software

Software for personal computers and workstations now exists to create stills, edit video nonlinearly, create transitions, perform composites, render special effects, animate in two and three dimensions, and so on.

No one package can do it all, however, so it is important to research the capabilities of different software from different vendors. The minimum feature-set necessary to ensure broadcast-quality output is comprised of 24-bit color manipulation, subpixel positioning and anti-aliasing, Alpha channel support, and text generation that supports anti-aliasing of Postscript and TrueType fonts.

The most common representation of color in personal computers is familiar to video professionals as "component" video. Here, colors are composed of three channels: red, green, and blue. Each channel is represented by eight bits (one byte), for a total of 24 bits per pixel. Programs that generate 24-bit color output are essential to broadcast-quality work, because this color scheme can represent more than 16 million separate colors, more than the human eye can distinguish.

If your software has DVE-like features, subpixel positioning is essential for achieving smooth-looking motion of video layers and important for compositing. To achieve broadcast-quality motion, it is necessary to compensate for the computer's limited screen resolution. This is created by the illusion that the number of screen pixels per inch is much greater than it actually is. Subpixel sampling is the frame-processing method that creates this illusion.

Anti-aliasing becomes important when the edges of any graphic object are diagonal to any degree, when rectangular shapes are rotated, or when smooth curves are desired, as with character recognition. Like subpixel positioning, it is a method of compensating for the limited resolution of the screen. It accomplishes this by removing "jaggies," thereby smoothing diagonal lines and curves.

The Alpha channel contains transparency information for each pixel. Many video professionals are surprised to learn that some PC-based graphics software, such as Photoshop, are more capable of creating and handling Alpha channel information than a more professional broadcast paint system. To the video professional this transparency information is a key signal that defines which parts of the video frame are transparent, which opaque, and which semitransparent.

The most common example of this may be seen on most newscasts. The character generator used to overlay the type on the screen contains an Alpha channel. The layering device uses the Alpha channel to determine which parts of the overlay (the letters) will be opaque and which parts will be filled with the background image (a reporter standing in front of city hall). Uses for this include compositing 3-D, computer-generated graphic animations into 2-D backgrounds.

Recommendations for Video Capture

The basic shooting goals for compressed video are:

1. Limit the amount of picture content that changes from one frame to the next.
2. Limit the amount of textured detail in the picture (clothing, backgrounds, etc.).

The following list of tips naturally follow from these two basic goals. If possible, always use a stationary (tripod-mounted) camera, especially for "talking heads," office interiors, even outside location shots. This is probably the single most important factor for high-quality compressed video.

1. Plan for limited motion in and through the scene. For example, if you're shooting a talking head, put the person in a chair that can't rock back and forth. If your subject is particularly animated, shoot from farther back to reduce the amount of motion in the frame.
2. Have your subject wear bright colors. Red, pink, yellow, and light blue solids are good. Black and navy are bad—dark colors generate video "noise" that gets interpreted as changing frame content and is thus unnecessarily encoded.
3. Have your subject wear solids instead of patterns. Herringbone, checks, stripes, and prints all contain complicated edge details that must be encoded and compressed, taking precious bits away from the details you want to render, like facial expressions and moving lips. These color and pattern recommendations apply to background detail as well. It's much better to shoot your subject in front of a piece of uniform colored seamless paper than sitting in front of a bookcase filled with books or a window covered by venetian blinds.
4. Plan for "settle time" after transitions (e.g., titles, screen shots, cuts). Say you're creating a Web-based training video and shooting screen shots of a computer application. You show the mouse clicking on a menu item, and a submenu drops down. The submenu will be a bit blurry when it first makes its appearance. Wait a few seconds for the text to clear up.
5. Use large, clear fonts for titles, credits, supers, computer screen shots, etc. The picture is going to be small to begin with and it will be difficult to read fine print in a compressed image. Larger text will make your viewers much more comfortable. Avoid rapid-fire music video–style cuts, dissolves, wipes, pans, zooms, and special effects. Images that aren't on the screen for more than a second or two won't have a chance to resolve themselves to clarity.
6. If you have the flexibility, short depth of field is preferable. Soft, out-of focus backgrounds are easier to code than sharply defined complicated details and textures. Choose a shorter shutter speed and a wider aperture to reduce depth of field. Don't use automatic exposure controls—maintain constant brightness. For example, while shooting an interior location, as people move into and out of the scene the background light level should not change. Changing background lighting levels will be interpreted as changes in frame contents and will be unnecessarily encoded. Brighter lighting gets coded better, so avoid dark frame contents and large shadows. Areas that are dimly lit can generate video "noise"

that will be interpreted as changing frame contents and will be unnecessarily encoded.

7. Digitize video in uncompressed format. After connecting the video source to your computer's video capture board, capture digital video in uncompressed format. If your video is already compressed when you pass it to your digital composing software, the file that results will not be of as high a quality as it should be.

Application and Design Considerations in Using Audio in Webcasting

Several different types of audio output—speech, music and sound effects—can be incorporated into audio on the Internet. To use each type effectively, developers need to learn more about how each of the types can be used to improve their content.

Speech

Two types of speech are available for use: digitized and synthesized. Digitized speech provides high-quality, natural speech but requires significant disk-storage capacity. Synthesized speech is not as storage intensive, but it may not sound as natural as human speech.

Speech is an important element of human communication and can be used effectively to transmit information. One advantage of using natural speech is the power of the human voice to persuade. Another advantage is that speech can potentially eliminate the need to display large amounts of text.

Music

Music is also an important component of human communication. It is used to set a mood or tone, provide connections or transitions, add interest or excitement, and evoke emotion. Music, especially when combined with speech and sound effects, can greatly enhance the presentation of text and visuals.

Sound Effects

Sound effects are used to enhance or augment the presentation of information. Two types of sound effects are natural and synthetic. Natural sounds are unadorned, commonplace sounds that occur around us. Synthetic sounds are those that are produced electronically or in some other artificial way.

There are two general categories of sound effects: ambient and special. Ambient sounds are the background sounds that communicate the context of the screen or place. Special sounds are uniquely identifiable sounds, such as the ring of a telephone, that complement narration and/or visuals.

Narration

To produce high-quality recorded speech, a script should be written and professionally recorded. To provide balance, both female and male narrators should be used. Non-professional narrators, such as corporate officers, may be used to provide credibility. When content needs to be explained or information needs to be delivered accurately, a professional can be relied upon to follow the specifications of the script and deliver a professional-sounding audio track.

To be effective, a narrator should:

1. Vary intonation to motivate, explain, provoke, exhort, or empathize.
2. Use a conversational tone.
3. Be amiable, candid, sincere, and straightforward.
4. Avoid sounding arrogant, pretentious, flippant, disrespectful, or sarcastic.
5. Avoid a lecturing tone.

When you are recording narrative speech, be sure to eliminate background or ambient sound unless it is used to provide a realistic environment. On occasion, incorporating ambient sound can be effective, since it can be used to help establish a mood or to increase the feeling of reality.

Developing the Speech

Good writing techniques are essential to the development of successful Webcasting programs. Thus, to integrate speech as an effective tool, developers must learn to write an effective narration as part of a program script. General guidelines for this activity can be gathered from the techniques used for scriptwriting for other media:

1. Write the way people speak.
2. Use language the audience can understand.
3. Write as if the narrator were teaching or speaking with one person.
4. Write in a clear, straightforward manner.
5. Write in short sentences that can be spoken in a single breath.
6. Use second-person pronouns—you and your.
7. Use contractions and other simplified forms that are used in speech.
8. Emphasize clarity and simplicity.
9. Omit needless words.
10. Avoid slang.
11. Avoid oral presentation of figures and statistics.
12. Use humor when appropriate.
13. Present information in small chunks.
14. Emphasize the objectives or goals of the Webcast.
15. Interpret what the user is seeing rather than simply describe it.

16. Make the visuals and narration go hand-in-hand; usually the visuals tell the story and the narration interprets, explains, or elaborates.
17. Adhere to time limits and length requirements.
18. Understand the capabilities and limitations of Internet hardware and software, especially as related to the use of speech.

Narration should be read aloud and then revised if it sounds awkward, stilted, or boring. To raise the level of user interest, quotes, conversations, and case studies may be included in audio scripts.

Selecting Music

Few articles or books have been written that provide detailed information or guidelines about the effective use of music in interactive programs. Some suggest that incorporating music begins with identifying the function of the music and making it an integral element of the script. Thus, the use of music needs to be considered as the program is being visualized and the script written.

Generally, music can be used to:

1. Establish mood.
2. Set pace.
3. Signal a turn of events.
4. Indicate progress and activity.
5. Provide transitions and continuity.
6. Evoke emotion.
7. Accompany titles or introduction information.
8. Emphasize important points.
9. Support visual information.
10. Add interest, realism, and surprise.

Music can have a wide variety of effects on its listeners. It is not only "background" but also works in conjunction with the visual message or provides interest, excitement, tension, and realism. Since music plays an important storytelling role, it should fit the pace and mood of the presentation and appeal to the audience's lifestyle, taste, and workplace position. Guidelines to accomplish this are:

1. Make music an integral part from the start, rather than try to find music to "go with" imagery later.
2. Choose a music style that conveys the mood you wish to create.
3. Convey personality through instrumentation.
4. Use recurring themes as musical signatures to help the audience feel familiar with a character's place or segment.

5. Use tempo, dynamics, and pitch to establish energy levels.
6. Use different styles of music and instrumentation to suggest time periods, cultures, locations, and sense of place.
7. Use musical genres to communicate to specific audiences: e.g., big band sounds for older audiences; rap, metal, or pop for teenagers.
8. Know when to hold them, when to fold them. Music should not compete with the narration or overwhelm the message of the program.

Selecting Sound Effects

Natural, ambient sounds are an integral part of our daily lives. We use them to help us interpret and assess our surroundings. For example, we listen to the thunk of a car door to find out if it has closed properly.

Sound or nonspeech audio can provide different types of messages, including alarms and warnings, and status and monitoring messages. Alarms and warnings are sounds and signals that interrupt and alert a listener. These sounds, such as fire alarms and police sirens, normally are loud and easily identifiable.

Status and monitoring messages are sounds that give us information about ongoing tasks. The click of the keys on the keyboard is an example of these typically short sounds. Status and monitoring sounds fade rapidly from the listener's awareness and are significant only when they indicate a change—for example, when the sound does not occur.

There are several other categories of sound:

1. Physical events. We can identify whether a dropped glass bounded or shattered.
2. Invisible structures. Tapping a wall helps us to locate where to hang a picture.
3. Dynamic change. As we pour liquid into a glass, we can hear when it is full.
4. Abnormal structures. We can tell when our car engine is malfunctioning by its sound.
5. Events in space. We can hear someone approaching by the sound of footsteps.

Not only can sound effects provide specific information about an environment or setting, they can also be used to accomplish the following tasks:

1. Create atmosphere.
2. Add realism.
3. Emphasize important points.
4. Indicate progress or activity.
5. Increase interest.
6. Establish mood.
7. Cue or prompt users.
8. Increase users' motivation.

Three significant considerations should govern the use of sound effects:

1. They must be clear and easily identifiable.
2. They should not overwhelm the primary message.
3. They should be appropriate to the intended audience.

General Guidelines

1. To maximize the use of audio, analyze carefully the target audience, delivery environment, and content.
2. Clearly define why and how audio will be used.
3. Whenever possible, integrate audio into the whole program, and do it from the start of the project.
4. Develop detailed scripts or storyboards.
5. Allow users to control the audio.
6. Make sound effects meaningful.
7. Use the highest-quality audio possible, given the storage constraints of the Internet.
8. Collaborate with others who have experience using different types of audio.
9. Learn more about the use of sound, especially music.

Audio Hints

If you take a good long walk around the Net you'll find quite a few sites that do "Web-casting right." But the real experts in this business are the ones that virtually invented it. The gurus at realnetworks.com offer these tips:

Use a good original source. A high-quality audio source is probably the single most important variable in determining your final audio quality. RealNetworks starts with satellite signals, audio compact discs, or digital audio tapes. When creating sounds from scratch, they use professional-quality microphones. You can make sound files from low-quality analog cassettes, tiny condenser microphones, or anything else—but the hiss and distortion in the resulting sound file will have a substantial adverse effect on clarity after the file is encoded.

You should always encode from 16-bit (not 8-bit or mu-law) sound files. They also recommend digitizing at a 22,050 Hz sample rate.

Set your input levels correctly. Setting correct levels is absolutely crucial. When creating your original sound file, the input level should be set to use the full range of available amplitude, while avoiding clipping. Clipping is audible as a high-frequency crackling noise and is what happens if you try to send too much input to your sound card (or any other piece of audio equipment).

When digitizing with your sound card, first do several test runs and adjust your input level so that the input approaches but does not exceed the maximum level. You can adjust this on the mixer page of your sound card utilities. Look for the Input Levels or Recording Levels option—most mixer pages have some sort of visual display where you can see how much sound is coming in. Make sure there are no peaks above maximum. These arc generally indicated by a red light somewhere. Be conservative with your levels; you never know when someone will get excited and speak much louder, or when a great play at a sports event will make a crowd roar. Differences in volume levels can be evened out later.

Sound files that do not use the full amplitude range will produce poor-quality encoded files. If the amplitude range of an existing file is too low, you can use your audio editor's Increase Amplitude or Increase Volume command to adjust the range before encoding your levels automatically.

Note, however, that better quality will be achieved if the levels are set correctly at the time of recording. The good news is that once you set your input levels correctly, they generally will not need to be reset. If you are reasonably consistent with your recording practices, you'll save yourself a lot of trouble in the long run.

Use high-quality equipment. High-quality equipment will produce better results and save you a lot of headaches in the long run. Every piece of equipment in the audio chain, from the microphone to the sound card to the software, will have an effect on your encoded message. If you intend to make sound a big part of your Web site, you should invest in professional-quality audio equipment. This need not be a crippling investment, but it does mean you will have to purchase from a professional recording equipment dealer, not your local computer/hi-fi/gadget store.

Select appropriate material. If you want to encode music for transmission over 14.4 kbps phone lines, remember that the simpler the source, the better chance that the encoded version will be faithful to the original. There isn't enough bandwidth in a 14.4 line to do a harmonically complex signal (like a full orchestra) justice. Many folks have used music successfully in their 14.4 clips as background, where fidelity isn't as important an issue.

Correcting DC offset. Sometimes when files are digitized, something known as DC offset creeps in. This is when the digitized waveform is not correctly centered around the 0 volt axis. Most of this is due to improper grounding of sound cards. Some sound cards are worse than others; to see how bad your sound card is, try recording silence. You should in theory see nothing in your waveform window, but you'll probably see a flat line just slightly above or below the 0 volt axis. This is DC offset.

This can wreak havoc when you attempt to process your waveform and can add a low rumbling sound to the encoded file. Luckily, most editors have a built-in facility to take care of this. Some call it "Centering the Wave" and are automatic; others allow you to adjust DC offset manually (+/−). In this case you'll have to find out precisely what your

DC offset is by running a "statistics" command or something similar. Then you'll have to correct it. For instance, if your average DC offset is 45, you'll want to offset the wave by −45.

Obviously if you are doing a live broadcast, you'll have to live with whatever DC offset you have. Proper balanced wiring between all your audio components will help minimize this as well as any ground loops.

Noise gating (or expansion). Noise gating, or downward expansion, eliminates unwanted background noise, which becomes audible during pauses in the audio (e.g., when an announcer pauses or there is a gap between programs). Signals above a certain volume level are left alone, but below this level the signal is turned down or even off, depending on how heavy the gating or expansion is. Setting up a noise gate or expander is straightforward. Most budget compressors have a noise gate built in.

To use noise gating, set the threshold control so that the gating or expansion occurs when there is no desired audio, but not so high that the beginnings of words or music that you want to hear are chopped off. It takes a bit of time, but remember to err on the side of caution just in case the next person in the program has a softer voice.

If your gate or expander has a range control, set this anywhere from 5 to 10 dB. This means it will turn down the "noise" section a little, but not turn it off altogether. That way you'll hear if the gate is cutting something off that you want to hear, and you can then readjust the threshold setting accordingly.

Compression. One of the side effects of digital encoding is artifacts—sounds that weren't there before encoding. These can be heard sometimes as rumbling or distortion in the signal. These artifacts appear at a relatively constant low level, whether the original sound file was loud or quiet. Louder files tend to mask these quiet artifacts. So it is recommended to feed the encoder a loud signal. However, we are limited by the loudest section of the file being encoded. If we could turn down the loudest section, we could turn the overall volume of the sound file up. A compressor helps us accomplish this.

Compression reduces the difference between the loudest and quietest sections of the incoming signal. Sections that exceed a user-defined threshold are turned down. Now that these loud sections have been turned down, we can turn the overall volume of the sound file up. How much the sections are turned up or down depends on how much compression you use.

How much compression should you use? The exact settings will be determined by experience and by referring to the manual that comes with your equipment or software. However, for speech it is recommended that you use moderate to extreme compression (4.1 to 10.1).

Equalization. Equalization (or EQ) changes the tone of the incoming signal just as you can on your home stereo or car radio. This is done by "boosting" (turning up) or "cutting" (turning down) certain frequencies. Using EQ, we can boost frequencies that we like (where the important content is) and cut frequencies where noise or unwanted sound is. By doing this, we can give the encoder a big hint about which sound information to keep. Encoding discards a lot of the high end, or treble, information—this can make files sound dull. To compensate for this, it helps to boost the middle frequencies, or midrange. This will also make speech sound more intelligible.

Most good mixing boards will have a midrange EQ knob. Sometimes you can choose which frequency to boost, other times this is preset at the factory. If not, or if you are using a graphic equalizer or audio processing software, you'll want to boost at around 2.5 KHz.

If your equipment does not have a mid-frequencies EQ knob, you can obtain a similar result by turning the low and high EQ knobs down and then turning the overall volume back up (note, though, that this is not as effective as boosting the mids, which attacks the problem at its source).

The amount that you should turn up the midrange depends on your EQ equipment and source file. A little experimentation is necessary. Try adding some mids to a short section of a piece to be encoded and check it with the audio player. If it is a bit muddy or hard to understand, try adding a little more. You can keep going until the knob won't turn anymore, or until the result starts to sound too harsh.

For digital audio encoded at 14.4 kbps it is important to try and make the voice as full as possible in the middle frequencies. This is where the majority of speech information is contained. What we are trying to do is lift the voice away from any background noise.

Some signals can be improved by rolling off (turning down) the bass frequencies as well. Side effects of encoding are sometimes audible as a lower voice "shadowing" the original. This is particularly noticeable with women speakers. When this effect is too prominent, try rolling off the bass and encoding the result. The artifacts will not disappear, but sometimes they will be quieter. Be careful not to make the voice sound too thin or brittle.

For audio played back at 28.8 kbps, much more of the fidelity of the original recording is retained, so you won't need to worry about EQ as much. It still helps to boost at around 2.5 KHz to compensate for the high frequency loss, but boosting too much will make music sound thin and tinny.

Normalization. Normalization is a process included in most audio recording software whereby the computer calculates exactly how much it can turn up the volume of a file without distortion. Because we always want to feed the encoder the loudest files possible, this is a very handy function. This is why you can afford to be fairly conservative with your recording input levels, and then let your program's normalization function take care of the rest. Normalization should be the last thing you do. If you normalize your file, and then add some EQ, you'll end up with distortion.

Tips for Recording

1. Use a good microphone to reduce or eliminate background noise as much as possible. For "talking heads" use a wired (not wireless) clip-on lavaliere microphone. In crowded areas, use a shotgun or boom microphone, as directional as you can.

2. Do not use a camcorder's built-in microphone. These generally pick up motor noise in the camcorder itself, in additional to omni-directional sounds in a noisy environment.

3. Set microphone gain properly. If the gain is too high, clipping or distortion may result. If it's too low, the audio may be too faint to be encoded properly or heard upon playback.

4. Understand the limitations of your audio compression algorithm. The audio heard at the far end, when decompressed, will be of telephone toll quality. The frequency range of the audio will be between 300 Hz and 3,400 Hz. Don't expect to hear high sibilant treble or booming bass sounds. G.723 audio lends itself quite well to a single human speaker, not as well to music, and somewhat poorly to a simultaneous combination of speech and music.

5. Digitize audio at 8 kHz 16-bit mono. When the time comes to perform audio capture from tape onto your computer, these settings work best for most of the PC-based audio compressors. Avoid higher sampling rates, avoid 8-bit samples, and avoid stereo sampling.

Conclusion

It should be obvious to the reader that effective use of audio and video on the Web is much more than just recording your voice into Microsoft Sound Recorder and then dumping the resulting .wav file online. The creation of a Webcasted Web site requires all of the skills of the Web developer as well as many of the skills of the professional filmmaker.

Internet Style Guidelines

Jessica Keyes

The first thing that folks see when they browse any Web site is the way it looks. You might sell the greatest products in the world, or you might have the most in-depth coverage of a particular subject, but the simple truth is that if the site doesn't "look" good, then your chances of it being a success are rather slim.

This chapter was written as a primer for the Internet developer. It provides an in-depth understanding of the nature of style on the Internet.

The Elements of Internet Style

One thing you won't find on the Web, or even in most books on the subject, is the "elements of style." I don't know why this is, but this latest generation of techno-pioneers seems to have forgotten there is such a thing as good design. This problem manifests itself in the overuse of large graphics, sloppy layouts, overuse of fonts, and general overcrowding of most of the Web pages (and many magazines on the subject, too) considered "cool" by today's standards.

Take a look at the magazine *Wired*. While its content is interesting and provocative, its layout is less than optimum for anyone over 30 years old. There are just too many fonts and the lines are spaced much too close together. More than one subscription has been cancelled as a result.

I'm sure that the magazine's graphic designers think they are on the leading edge. But my question is: the leading edge of what? Thomas Wolf in his searing attack on the art community, *The Painted Word*, decries the pseudo art of our times. Today talent in the avant guard art community is little more than some broken and bonded crockery or some politically correct but poorly executed canvas. Essentially, in today's market, a lack of talent appears to go a long way. The same appears to be true for the graphic design community.

Good Web site design, like good art, is timeless. While the Julian Schnabels (he's the guy with the crockery and bondo) will be scarcely remembered a generation from now, Rembrandt and Picasso will live on forever.

Web pages need to be planned, not just dumped up online. Each organization has its own unique style. That should be reflected in the organization's Web design as well—unless, of course, the organization wishes to radically alter its style. This usually happens in consumer goods companies who try to alter their image frequently to attract new and improved market share.

You must also keep in mind the target audience as well. Who are they? Kids, teenagers, adults, senior citizens—each of these groups will have a preferred style. Some market research may just be in order here.

Different organizations use their Web sites for different purposes. For some, it's primarily an introduction to their organizations and capabilities. Some use it to capture information about visitors to their sites. Others talk very little about their products and services and focus instead on generating goodwill for the organization. Many more are using their sites as an electronic "storefront" that allows people to place orders for goods and services (see Security First Network Bank at www.sfnb.com as an example of one of the first sites on the Net to do so). In the end, most Web sites do a little of all of these.

Defining your audience is not easy when it comes to the Web. The tools for measuring specific usage of a given Web site are still primitive, though they are getting better.

In reality, the audience for your Web site could be anyone who's out there surfing on the Internet and happens to bump into your site. That could be a college student . . . a customer . . . a prospective client putting out a request for proposal . . . someone out looking for a job . . . a government official. When developing your Web site, keep in mind how these different audiences may view and react to your message.

That doesn't mean, however, that you should develop your Web site to do all things for all people. Focus is all-important when it comes to the Web. Remember that the Internet is not a traditional "push" distribution vehicle, but rather a "pull" medium. You don't distribute a Web site to a specific set of readers the way you send out brochures to a mailing list. Your material is out there for viewing by anyone. Your job is to attract Websurfers to it. More specifically, your job is to attract the right Websurfers to it. That means focusing your material and layout to a specific audience.

Planning the Site

Consider this four-step plan:

1. *Determine exactly who your desired audience is.* It's not enough, for instance, to say you want to reach decision makers at organizations worldwide. Are you targeting executive decision makers? Technical decision makers? Programmers? Are you targeting businesses or government organizations? If you're trying to reach potential employees, are you primarily interested in students coming out of college, or workers with experience?

2. *Determine the objective of your Web site.* What is your mission? To determine that, consider a few questions. What do your visitors want? What do they think about your company? What do you want them to think? What do you want them to know? Use whatever tools you have on hand—customer surveys, focus groups, online questionnaires—to tackle these questions. Then put down the objectives of your Web site on paper. Keep that mission statement in front of you. Pin it on your office wall. It will help keep you focused. (And don't forget to update your objectives as time goes by and your organization changes.)

3. *Tailor your Web site material to attract your targeted audience.* If you're recruiting consultants from university MBA programs, for instance, you'll want to showcase your company's service/product lines, service methodologies, job opportunities, training, and developmental programs. If you're selling voice messaging solutions to communications providers, you obviously need much different material with enough product detail for people to make informed buying decisions.

4. *Finally, remember to keep in mind the corporate image.* If your company is a $6 billion dollar information management company doing business with some of the largest organizations in the world, your Web site should enhance—not detract from—this larger image.

Organizing Your Site

Once you have determined the audience you want your Web site to attract, and the information you want to present to them, you're ready to create an organization for your material. This is a critical area in the development of your Web site. Without a highly structured, easy-to-navigate framework for your site, you'll lose Websurfers right away. Your site organization must be simple enough to get readers quickly to where they want to go, and yet deep enough that, when they get there, they are satisfied with what they find.

Your first Web page is the most critical element in your structure. It sets up the organizational scheme for your entire Web site. Think of your job here as creating a "view" to a rich universe of information that lies underneath your home page. What are the areas your audience are most interested in? Make them the entry points on the home page.

Don't make the common mistake of putting too many entry points on your home page. More than seven or eight entry points is probably too many. What you don't want is to put everything under the sun on your home page and immediately create the impression that not enough thought has been given to structuring and categorizing it.

Too many items on your home page is a symptom of a shallow organizational scheme. Many Web sites out there suffer from exactly this problem. Shallow Web sites typically arise because of one of two reasons: Either their creators have not spent enough time categorizing and structuring their material before putting it out on the Web, or else the site has not been adequately supervised since it was originally created and has grown out of control like an untended bush. Either way, a shallow Web structure overwhelms viewers, turning them off before they ever get interested.

Equally important, don't create a structure that is so deep that it buries information. You'll know you're in one of these Web sites when you keep hitting page after page of menus without getting to any real information. As a general rule of thumb, don't make your viewers dig down more than two or three levels without getting to the information itself.

The ideal Web site structure walks a fine balance between too shallow and too deep. You want to guide viewers down logical paths that get progressively deeper as they go. If you're marketing technology, for instance, that path will go from product descriptions to feature functionality to detailed spec sheets—not the other way around.

In creating the pages underneath your main page, stay focused on maximizing ease of navigation and usability of information. A few principles to keep in mind:

1. Every page must stand alone. Don't assume that every Websurfer will enter a given page by first going through the menu on the home page. Unlike a printed document that presents a cover first to readers, surfers on the Web can enter a site at any point from any number of other points. Include a header or footer on every page that connects to the original entry point on the home page and enough contextual information that the viewer knows where he or she is in the general scheme of things.

2. If your page includes a menu, make sure every menu item includes an adequate description of what it's all about. Nothing irritates Websurfers more than launching down a path and not knowing exactly where they're going or whether it's worth their time. For instance, don't (as many Web sites do) label a menu item "What's Cool." That's not enough for a viewer to know what that path is all about. Be more precise in your title as to what the Websurfer will find down that path—for example, "Cool New Sneakers to Check Out."

3. Likewise, include a short synopsis of every article included in your site. This will let viewers know whether it's something they're interested in. Focus this synopsis on the benefits to be gained by reading the article.

Organizing Your Articles

Because of the storage power of electronic media compared to printed documents, many of us immediately want to convert lengthy brochures and other tomes into our Web site. Resist that temptation. The attention span of the typical Websurfer is measured in mouse clicks. Make your points up front and then expand on them below for anyone interested.

As a rule, avoid excessively lengthy articles unless appropriate to your audience and the information they are looking for. Wherever possible, limit your documents to one page of text. Consider the popularity of the *USA Today* newspaper that's slid under the door of your hotel room when you're traveling. The creators of *USA Today* recognized that people today are pressed for time and desire information in short, easily digestible bytes.

That doesn't mean everything has to be written this way. Obviously, *The Wall Street Journal* is popular for its substantive articles. But *The Wall Street Journal* is also extremely well written, with an easy, anecdotal style that draws the reader in. Let's face it—few of us can write this well. Where longer articles are appropriate and necessary—such as an electronic "white paper" that explains a complex technical subject—include sufficient (and interesting) subheads to retain attention.

Also, make use of graphics, charts, photographs, and other appropriate elements to sustain interest and explain the subject you're writing about. Nothing loses a reader more quickly than a dull page of pure text, especially on the Internet, where interactivity and visual excitement is expected.

If you absolutely must put all of your catalogs and marketing brochures online, then do it the smart way. Adobe Acrobat (www.adobe.com/products/acrobat/main.html) is the standard for publishing on the Web. Using the very same document you send out to the printer, with nary a tweak, you simply save it using Adobe Acrobat filters into a PDF (portable document file). On the receiving end, anyone who tries to access a .pdf document must install the Adobe Acrobat Reader. Since the Reader is free and used on thousands of sites, chances are most Web visitors already have it installed.

Figure 13-1 is a good example of PDF files in action. Taken from Adobe's own site, it displays what a typical PDF file within a viewer looks like. As you can see, the possibilities are endless for utilizing this technology.

Creating Links

Finally, in organizing your Web site, pay attention to hyperlinks. These are electronic links to other online resources, either within the corporate server or externally to other sites on the Internet.

Obviously, you don't want to build so many links that readers go off and never come back, and you probably don't want to link to the page of competitors who offer products that compete with yours. Base your links on the informational value they add to your discussion. For instance, if you're promoting child welfare solutions, you might want to link to a U.S. government server that discusses new legislation affecting child welfare.

Design and Layout

Graphics, image-mapping, sound, movies, and hotlinks provide a wonderful way to show off your creativity. But before jumping into the design and layout of your Web site, consider your audience. Who do you want to impress? How can you best do that? Equally important, how can you make visiting your site a pleasurable experience? How will it help enhance the image of the company?

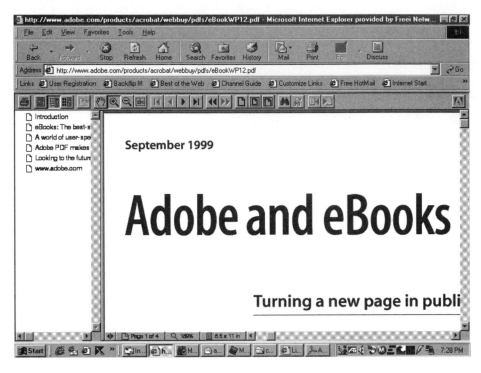

Figure 13-1. *A PDF file in action. (Copyright © 2001 Adobe Systems Incorporated. All rights reserved.)*

Foremost, you must ensure that visitors to your Web site easily understand how it's organized and can quickly navigate to the information they are seeking.

Good design seeks a balance between visual sensation that graphics offer and the text information that those graphics illustrate. Documents that are dense with text, without the visual relief of graphics, will not motivate the viewer to investigate their contents. On the other hand, pages that are heavy in graphics may take so long to download the viewer will move on quickly, maybe never to return. Here are some guidelines for helping you make a cohesive presentation and a memorable experience for whoever visits your Web site.

Web pages are essentially vertical. Users enter at the top and work their way through the page. Each page should be no longer than three 640 × 480 pixel screens.

Additionally, the best Web pages usually conform to a grid. A grid is an invisible set of lines that guide the placement of graphics and text. By using a grid you can establish how major blocks of text and illustrations will appear on the page. This helps a visitor understand how the various pages on your Web site are organized and makes it easier for him or her to progress to the information needed.

This does not mean that every page must look the same as the previous one, just that there is an organizing principle. If you are a large organization, with many Web development groups creating Web content, it's best to formalize a standard "look and feel" guide. Unisys is a large computer manufacturer and services firm. Their standard is as follows:

1. Page width is no more than 600 pixels max.
2. Home page graphic is 600×400 pixels max.
3. The Unisys logo must be included on all home pages and should be included on most following pages.
4. Use of a navigation graphic is optional.
5. Navigation via text links is mandatory.
6. Navigation links should always include a link to the Unisys home page and to the top of the current page.
7. Following pages banner 600×250 pixels max.
8. A good practice is to start a page with a banner that relates to the menu that preceded it and/or to the contents of the page.
9. The top-of-page banners can contain graphics and it is recommended that these be no larger than 500×100 pixels in total, with 600×250 as a maximum.
10. The corporate logo should be part of the banner of all major pages. Since Web surfers can jump into a site from many locations, we must let them know that they are in the Unisys site.
11. The banner should be followed by a head that introduces the contents of the page, unless, of course, the head is part of the banner.

Figure 13-2 is a good example of how this all works on the Unisys Web site. Notice their corporate logo, top left, as well as the many menus enabling visitors to get quickly to where they want to go.

Think About Navigation

Navigation aids are buttons or links that ensure that users can easily get to the information they are seeking. If you have a multipage section and provide a link from another section to a topic in the middle of your section, the reader should have an easy way to go to the front of the section and progress forward. Here it is a good idea to provide links for "top of section," "previous page," and "next page," as well as links back to the home page and to other related sections. If users encounter a dead end (a page without links), they will probably leave your site rather than backing up through the pages they have already read.

Icons can be fun to create, but we shouldn't make the reader guess what they do. Either provide navigation buttons that state exactly what they do or provide HTML links. It is best to always include HTML links whether you have created graphic navigation buttons or not. Many users turn graphics off. Navigation buttons or links should be part of the top-of-page banner or near the top of the page. If a user arrives on a particular

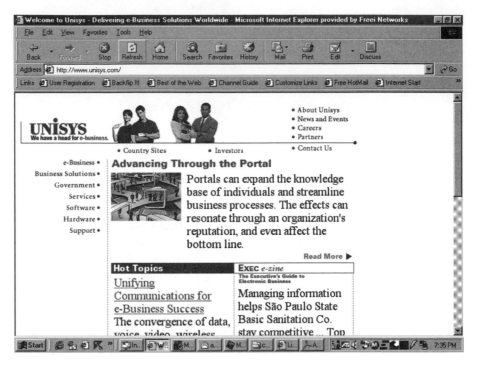

Figure 13-2. *The Unisys Web site as an example of good design. (Copyright © 1994–2001 Unisys. All rights reserved.)*

page and decides that it doesn't have the information he or she is seeking, we must make it easy to navigate elsewhere. It may also be appropriate to provide navigation links at the bottom of a page, particularly if the page is several screens long. The point is to make it as easy as possible on the user.

Graphics

Pictures may be worth a thousand words, but you must ensure that the viewer benefits from having waited for them to download. Graphics can help the Internet reader understand how to navigate through your site, aid in explaining your message, and make visiting your page a memorable experience, but be careful not to overdo them. This medium is not a multimedia CD-ROM. It is typically transmitted over relatively slow lines to our audiences. Any page that takes longer than 20 seconds to download will quickly lose that audience.

Pages that use large graphic image maps as menus will tax the patience of most users. As a rule, each 1K of graphic size requires one second to download. Moreover, image maps, while "cool" in letting the viewer click on a point of visual interest, generally take up much more room than a simple listing of available links. Image maps should be used sparingly and kept to a minimum size—but no larger than 600×400 pixels.

Inline graphics (graphics within the body of the page rather than major graphics that stand alone) should be no larger than 22,500 square pixels (150×150). As we said, graphics can help break up a page so it's easier to read and more understandable. Still, don't include more than a total of ten individual graphics for a given page.

Some rules of thumb to keep in mind:

1. Design graphics for your target audience. Images suitable for a child are not usually suitable for an adult and vice versa.
2. Don't use graphics over 50K. The larger the image, the longer it takes to download. Large image sizes are a common design flaw, since graphic designers typically have high-speed Internet connections and rarely test their designs using a 56kb modem, the connection rate of a typical user.
3. Don't use large graphics that force a user to scroll through more than one page at a time.
4. Make sure your graphics look good on the average monitor. Most Webmasters and multimedia designers have high-resolution monitors. Most end-users don't. What looks great on a high-res monitor often looks terrible on a low-res monitor.
5. Beware of palette conflict. Your mother probably told you that plaids and stripes clash. Palette conflict is a similar sort of problem. It results from using multiple palettes (sets of colors and patterns). Since only one color palette can be active on a computer at a time, palette conflict causes unpredictable behavior when it comes to the colors you expect to see online.

Color and Backgrounds

Most of us who develop pages for the Web work on high-resolution monitors with powerful graphics cards. Many, if not most, of our audience are using much lower resolution devices. Design your pages and select colors that will effectively present your information to most of your audience. Test your pages on lower resolution monitors and through a couple of browsers before bringing it live.

Be very careful about using backgrounds. While backgrounds can add interest if related to the graphic theme of your pages, they add to the time it takes to download. Excessively textured backgrounds and some colored backgrounds can hinder legibility of type. Consider that 12 percent of the population is color blind. Red type on a blue background (with similar color saturation) is almost indistinguishable to most color-blind people.

The End

While this is the end of this particular chapter, I hope that it will begin a new chapter for you in terms of a better understanding of how to design elegant Web pages.

Conducting a Legal Web Site Audit

Tamara Pester

When an average technology-savvy individual thinks of the Internet, he or she probably imagines a resource useful for purchasing products, researching facts, and communicating with others. When technology lawyers think of the Internet, they instead imagine a potentially treacherous technology that, while useful for the functions described above, can be a dangerous mechanism to individual and corporate clients if they do not ensure that Web site visitors are aware of the terms and conditions of use, carefully construct a privacy policy, take steps to protect proprietary intellectual property, respect the intellectual property rights of others, and maintain awareness of other emerging legal issues associated with e-commerce. A Web site audit, conducted either internally or by outside legal counsel, in conjunction with technical personnel, should review these issues to seal all legal holes before a Web site is launched. This chapter outlines the core issues involved with such an audit.

Web Site Terms and Conditions

The terms and conditions of a Web site should be conspicuously displayed so that Web site visitors are aware of their rights and responsibilities in connection with the Web site.

1. Web site terms and conditions: provisions governing the relationship between Web site owner and visitor.

2. When drafting Web site terms and conditions, consider nature of the goods or services offered on the Web site.

> *Example: If the Web site includes bulletin boards, chat rooms, or other interactive areas, the terms and conditions should include a provision detailing who owns what rights in posted material, indemnification of the owner in case the posted material infringes a third party's rights, guidelines detailing under what circumstances users' posted material may be removed, and when the Web site may deny access to certain users.*

3. Standard provisions of Web site terms and conditions:

- Warranty disclaimer to alert users that the owner does not make any express or implied warranties regarding the timeliness of content on the Web site or the operation or "uptime" of the site.
- Limitation of liability (limits owner's responsibility for monetary damages in case of dispute).
- Description of the owner's proprietary rights (copyrights, trademarks, ownership of content posted by owner or by others) in the Web site.
- Disclaimer of any third-party Web sites to which links are provided.
- Statement of the applicable governing law (the state or country whose law governs a dispute), jurisdiction, and venue (the place in which disputes will be resolved).

> *Note: Recent developments indicate a possibility that the business' choice of jurisdiction may not be enforceable. The owner's choice of jurisdiction may not be enforced if it is considered "active" or "doing business" in several jurisdictions. Courts continue to examine the question of where jurisdiction is appropriate, because the degree of activity the Web site conducts promises to be a question courts will continue to address. Traditional measure of jurisdiction depends on the concept of contacts: The more contacts a business has with a particular forum, the more likely it will be subject to jurisdiction in that forum.*

Privacy

1. Posting and following a privacy policy will also help insulate a Web site owner from liability.

2. Major consumer concerns about the use of personal information abound.

3. Government regulatory agencies and private watchdog groups increasingly scrutinize the actions of companies who track and store detailed user data, then resell the data to others wishing to target users with certain demographics.

4. U.S. Congress introduced over 100 bills regarding consumer privacy in the 106th Congress.

5. European Union enacted detailed regulations regarding the transmission and use of its citizens' personally identifiable information. (1)

6. State, national, and international laws may apply to or restrict the particular way that a particular Web site chooses to use information.

7. Consumer comfort increases when a Web site includes a privacy policy.

8. Privacy policy should detail:

   • What personally identifiable information of an individual or third party is collected from the Web site.
   • The organization collecting the information.
   • How the information is used.
   • With whom the information may be shared.
   • What choices are available regarding collection, use, and distribution of the information.
   • The kind of security procedures that are in place to protect the loss, misuse, or alteration of information under the Web site owner's control.
   • How an individual can correct any inaccuracies in the information. (2)

9. Several organizations have developed third-party oversight "seal" programs to certify that a specific Web site bearing its certification seal has policies in place that make it trustworthy and reliable with regard to consumer information (TRUSTe, the AICPA, and the Better Business Bureau "BBBOnline").

10. One absolute: Follow a privacy policy once it has been drafted, or risk consumer and potential legal backlash.

Intellectual Property

A Web site owner should make sure that he or she obtains and protects his or her own intellectual property, and avoids the potential pitfalls associated with the online world. Unlike real estate, which consists of tangible property, intellectual property consists of the intangible items that add value to a business and includes domain names, trademarks, copyrights, and patents.

Domain Names

After a business decides on a unique domain name under which it wishes to do business and has reserved that domain name, it should consider the preemptive registration of additional domains that could be easily imitated. (3)

> *Example: A business focusing on pet-food supplies that has reserved petfood.com should also consider reserving the domain names petfoods.com, petsfood.com, petfood.net, and other URLs that a user might mistakenly enter when trying to reach the petfood.com destination. In addition, it should consider registering the domain names and variations for the products and services it sells.*

1. Preemptive domain name registration involves an initial outlay of funds but will prevent disputes with others claiming rights to those URLs, and thus it will save money down the line.
2. Brief history of Web site registration: Network Solutions, Inc., (NSI) of Herndon, Virginia, held a virtual monopoly on the issuance and maintenance of domain names until 1999. The Internet Corporation for Assigned Names and Numbers (ICANN) was then formed to assume responsibility for Internet protocol space allocation and domain name system management previously performed through third parties under contracts with the United States. ICANN has authorized additional registrars of domain names including aol.com and register.com.
3. Domain name disputes: NSI implemented the Uniform Domain Name Dispute Resolution Policy (UDRP) on January 1, 2000, changing the methods available for dealing with domain name disputes.
4. New UDRP rules of procedure and practice are located at www.icann.org.
5. The UDRP Policy outlines a simple arbitration proceeding to which all domain name registrants must submit upon challenges to a domain name registration.
6. A party may initiate a dispute proceeding under certain circumstances:

   - The domain name at issue is identical or confusingly similar to a trademark or service mark in which the party has rights (this applies to federally registered trademarks and appears to allow licensees to assert claims).
   - The domain name registrant has no rights or legitimate interests in the domain name, and the registrant registered the domain name in "bad faith."
   - If either of the parties files an action with a court during the pendency of a proceeding under the UDRP, the arbitration panel may suspend or terminate the administrative proceeding, or, in its discretion, proceed to a decision.
   - If the complainant wins, NSI will transfer the domain name to it.
   - If it loses, its only recourse is to file suit. If the domain name registrant loses, it too may file suit to prevent the panel from taking away its domain name.

7. Pros of using UDRP instead of filing suit in federal court:

   - UDRP offers a relatively quick, inexpensive method to obtain the transfer of a domain name in a clear case of cyber-piracy.
   - ICANN may be easier to deal with and less expensive than court fees.

8. Cons of using UDRP instead of filing suit in federal court:

- No immediate injunctive relief available.
- Strategically, a registrant may be less willing to fight federal court litigation than a UDRP dispute and may take federal litigation more seriously because of the greater burden, expense, and possible intimidation associated with being in front of a federal judge.
- No form of appeal exists under the UDRP.

Trademarks

Trademarks are identifying marks used in connection with goods, while service marks are marks used in connection with the provision of services. (4) Several steps should be taken with respect to these marks:

1. Clearance and investigation to ensure that the proposed mark is available for use and potentially available for registration with the U.S. Patent and Trademark Office (PTO).
2. If the mark is available, the next step is filing application for federal registration, which will give others constructive notice of that business' ownership rights in the mark.
3. Trademark or service mark notices should be prominently displayed wherever the marks are used on the Web site. If a mark has achieved registration with the PTO, the ® symbol should be displayed; otherwise, the ^{TM} or ^{SM} symbols should be displayed in connection with trademarks or service marks, respectively.
4. A trademark owner should be vigilant with respect to the use and possible infringement by others of the marks it has selected and should secure rights.

In addition, note that:

1. Trademark infringement focuses on the question of whether two marks are "likely to cause confusion" with each other.
2. Marks are considered confusingly similar if the buying public would think that the products or services covered by one mark come from the same source or are affiliated with the goods or services covered by the previously used mark.
3. Factors established by the courts and the PTO in determining whether a likelihood of confusion exists differ from jurisdiction to jurisdiction, but they generally include:

- The relative strength of the plaintiff's mark.
- The similarity of the marks at issue.
- The similarity of the products or services covered by the mark.
- The types of purchasers or consumers.

- The advertising media use.
- The defendant's intent in adopting the mark.
- Whether any actual confusion has resulted from the defendant's use of its mark.

8. If a Web site owner creates an alliance with or allows another to display hyperlinks to its Web site consisting of its marks, it should be careful to supply them with trademark usage guidelines.

9. If the marks of others are used on a Web site, correct attribution should appear.

Copyrights

1. The use of copyrighted material on a Web site should also be considered. A property right in an original work of authorship fixed in a tangible medium of expression, giving the holder the exclusive right to reproduce, adapt, distribute, perform, and display the work.(5)

2. What does a copyright protect? "Original works of authorship": This includes literary, dramatic, musical, and artistic works such as poetry, novels, movies, songs, computer software, and architecture. (6)

3. What is not covered? Facts, ideas, systems, or methods of operation.

4. Copyrights are self-executing: A work receives copyright protection the moment it is created and fixed in a tangible form so that it is perceptible either directly or with the aid of a machine or device.

5. No requirement exists to register works with the U.S. Copyright Office, but the Copyright Act provides several inducements to encourage copyright owners to register their works. Registration may be made at any time within the life of the copyright, and offers advantages including the following:

- Registration establishes a public record of the copyright claim.
- Before an infringement suit may be filed in court, registration is necessary for works of U.S. origin.
- If made before or within five years of publication, registration will establish prima facie evidence in court of the validity of the copyright and of the facts stated in the certificate.
- If registration is made within three months after publication of the work or prior to an infringement of the work, statutory damages and attorney's fees will be available to the copyright owner in court actions. Otherwise, only an award of actual damages and profits is available to the copyright owner.
- Registration allows the owner of the copyright to record the registration with the U.S. Customs Service for protection against the importation of infringing copies.

6. To avoid claims of copyright infringement, a Web site owner must have rights to use the content of its Web site.

Patents

1. Patent: exclusive right to use, make, or sell an invention for a specified period of time, granted by the government to the inventor if the device or process is novel, useful, and nonobvious. (7)
2. Patent rights have become increasingly important to Internet businesses. The triggering event was the State Street Bank decision, which validated patent protection for "business methods." (8)
3. Business method patent: provides an enforceable monopoly to operate a business in a particular manner.

Examples: Amazon.com "one-click" patent in which a shopper's profile information including credit card and shipping address are stored by a business and then automatically retrieved and utilized when that user wishes to "check out" and purchase an item; the SBH "shopping cart" patent.

---

4. Business method patents and other patents can be used in an offensive (prevent others from using similar methods) or defensive (validating a company's use of a particular method against another entity that might claim infringement) manner.
5. Investors increasingly expect and require Internet businesses in which they infuse funds to have either patent applications or patents covering their core technology.

FTC Act Violations, False Advertising, and Unfair Competition

Statements made on Web sites are subject to Federal Trade Commission regulations and the common law theories concerning false advertising and unfair competition.

1. FTC has authority to investigate an Internet-based business and require that it provide the "reasonable basis" under which it makes advertising statements.

Example: The FTC may find fault with a company for claiming that its services are the "fastest" or that transactions between a consumer and the company via the Internet are "absolutely secure." The FTC actively performs such enforcement with respect to Internet companies.

---

2. Internet companies must make sure they have appropriate clearance to link to other companies' Web sites.
3. Web site owners should be aware that they may need to defend against an action brought under foreign laws or by foreign regulatory agencies.

Defamation

1. Defamation: harming the reputation of another by making a false statement to a third person.
2. Online defamation may occur on bulletin boards, chat rooms, usenet newsgroups, or other forums of the Internet.
3. Recent case law and legislation have addressed the extent to which Web site hosts may be liable for defamation, but have not provided consistent answers.
4. Courts have considered several factors in struggling with this question:

   - Active or passive role in monitoring or editing content posted on its hosted forum (more active role means more likely to be liable).
   - Notice of the defamatory activity (no notice means less likely to be held responsible).

5. The best protection against claim of online defamation liability is a policy that is carefully crafted and consistently implemented to deal with any notification of defamatory activity occurring on a hosted area.

Conclusion

Building a Web site involves numerous complex tasks. Constructing a Web site with a few legal pointers in mind will benefit a Web site owner or developer and enable him or her to steer clear of common pitfalls and stay focused on the road to success.

References

1. Directive Concerning the Processing of Personal Data and the Protection of Privacy in the Telecommunications Sector (Directive 97/66/EC of the European Parliament and of the Council, 15 December 1997), available at http://www.cdt.org/privacy/eudirective/EU_Directive_.html.
2. For additional guidelines on drafting an appropriate privacy policy. See http://www.truste.com/webpublishers/pub_resourceguide.html.
3. The prudent business person or Web site advisor should ensure not only that its proposed domain name is available, but that it does not infringe on others' trademarks or service marks. The best way to do so is to conduct a trademark use and availability search, described further in the Trademark section of this chapter.
4. Lanham Act, codified as 15 USCA §§ 1051 et. seq. See http://www.uspto.gov/web/offices/tac/doc/basic/.
5. Copyright Act of 1976, codified as 17 USCA §§ 101–1332.
6. See http://www.loc.gov/copyright/circs/circ1.html.
7. See 35 USCA §§101-103; http://www.uspto.gov/web/menu/pats.html.

8. State Street Bank & Trust Co. v. Signature Financial Group, 149 F. 3d 1368 (Fed. Cir. 1998), available at http://www.ll.georgetown.edu/Fed-Ct/Circuit/fed/opinions/97-1327.html.

TAMARA PESTER (tpester@yahoo.com or tamara.pester@us.sema.com) is in-house counsel at Sema, one of the world's leading information technology and business services companies. She concentrates primarily on structuring and negotiating software licenses and other high-technology transactions. Miss Pester has published several articles on information technology and intellectual property protection subjects. She has been admitted to practice law in Georgia and Colorado and a member of the computer law sections in each state. She received her JD in 1998 from the University of Denver College of Law and her BA cum laude in history from Washington University in 1994.

Auditing Your Web-Based Systems

Jessica Keyes

For as long as there have been computer departments there have been EDP (electronic data processing) auditors. These were/are the folks that make sure a system does what it is supposed to do.

In the Wild West days of the Internet, companies were "plopping" systems online faster than you can say "dot-com crash and burn." Now that those heady days appear to be over, smart organizations are beginning to think of their Web-based systems in the same terms as they do their other, more conventional systems.

These organizations, in their quest toward increasing market share while lowering costs, are finally delving into the intricacies of the Web-based system to scrutinize such things as: response time/availability; accessibility; ergonomics; logistics; customer service; security; and privacy.

This chapter provides the Web developer with a series of checklists that can be used to audit the Web-based system. Audits should be done regularly, with the results being used to fine-tune the system.

Ultimately think of these checklists as a set of issues that can be considered "food for thought."

Systemic Audit

It's surprising that many companies spend millions of dollars on advertising budgets to draw more "eyeballs" to their sites but never factor in whether or not the projected additional load can be supported by the current system configuration.

A systemic audit looks at such things as response time, network architecture, and linkages.

Response time. Measurables in this section include actual response time versus projected response time. In spite of the advances in supplying high-bandwidth connections to consumers, the vast majority of PCs are connected to the Web with little more than a 56 kb modem and good intentions. This means that sites that are highly graphical or use add-ons such as Macromedia Flash will appear slow to download.

Given the wide variety of modem types, auditors should test the response time of the site using different scenarios such as:

- Using a DSL or cable modem connection
- Using a 56 kb connection
- Using a 28 kb connection
- At random times during the day, particularly 9:00 A.M. (start of workday) and 4:00 P.M. (kids home from school)

Web sites such as netmechanic.com, a subscription service, can assist in this endeavor by checking for slow response time directly from their sites.

Broken links. One of the top five irritants that Websurfers report is clicking on a link and getting a "nonexistent page" error message. This is often the result of system maintenance, when Web programmers move the actual page but neglect to modify the link to that page. Unfortunately, this is a frequent occurrence. One of a number of tools, including netmechanic.com, can assist in tracking down these broken links.

Database audit. Originally the Web was a simple place. It consisted of mostly text and there was nary a database in sight. Today, the Web is filled to the brim with databases. The addition of databases makes the audit process even more complex. Since programming code is used to query and perhaps even calculate against that database, it is imperative that random checks be performed in an effort to pinpoint database query and calculation errors.

Essentially, auditing database access is similar to the traditional IT (information technology) QA (quality assurance) process. One or more scripts must be written that will take that database through its paces. For example, if a database program calculates insurance rates based on a zip code, then that calculation should be duplicated either manually or in a different parallel automated fashion to ensure that the result is correct.

The same can be said for information that visitors to the site enter via a form. Is the information being entered the same as that being sent to the database?

Network audit. The network itself, including node servers, should be tested to see if it is effectively configured to provide optimum response. It is not uncommon to find the Web development group separated from the traditional IT development group. This means that one frequently finds network configurations architected inappropriately for the task at hand. For example, a site attracting tens of thousands of hits a day would do well to run a multitude of Web servers rather than just one.

Most organizations use one or more ISPs (Internet Service Providers) to host their sites. The auditor should carefully gauge the level of service provided by these ISPs as well.

Security and Quality

There is no one topic that is discussed more in the press than Internet security. From "love bug" viruses to wily hackers breaking into Western Union, security is an important component of the e-business audit.

It is worthwhile to keep in mind that the auditor is not a security auditor, nor should he be. His or her role is to do a top-level assessment of the security of the e-business and, if warranted, recommend the services of a security firm well-versed in penetration and intrusion testing.

The entire issue of security is wrapped up within the more comprehensive issue of quality. This section will address both issues.

Review the security plan. All organizations must possess a security plan—in writing. If they do not have this, then they are severely deficient. The plan, at a minimum, should address:

1. Authentication. Is the person who he or she says he is?
2. Authorization. What users have what privileges? In other words, "who can do what?"
3. Information integrity. Can the end-user maliciously modify the information?
4. Detection. Once a problem is identified, how is it handled?

Passwords. Passwords are the first shield of protection against malicious attacks upon your e-business. Questions to ask in this section include:

1. Is anonymous login permitted? Under what conditions.
2. Is a password scanner periodically used to determine if passwords used can be hacked? Examples of this sort of utility include Lophtcrack.com for NT and users.dircon.co.uk/~crypto for Unix.
3. How often are passwords changed?
4. How often are administrative accounts used to log on to systems? Passwords are hard to remember. This means that, in order to quickly gain entrance to systems, administrative and programming systems people often create easy-to-remember passwords such as "admin." These are the first passwords that hackers try to gain entrance into a system.

Staff background. Administrative network staff must have a security background as well as a technical background. Those wishing to train their staffs would do well to look into the Security Skills Certification Program provided by sans.org.

Connectivity. Today's organization may have many external connections (partners, EDI, etc.). For each company connected to, the auditor should examine:

1. The data being passed between organizations. Is what the company sent being received correctly?

2. The security of the connection. How is the data being transmitted? Is it required to be secure? Is encryption being used?

3. If encryption is indeed being used, it must be determined whether an appropriate algorithm is being deployed.

The product base. All organizations invest and then use a great deal of third-party software. As publicized by the press much of this software, particularly browsers and e-mail packages but word processing packages as well, contain security holes that put the organization at risk if left unpatched. Therefore, for each software package (for Net purposes) being used:

1. Check for publicized security holes.

2. Check for availability of software patches. Always upgrade to the latest version of software and apply the latest patches.

3. Check to see if patches have been successfully applied.

4. Check security software for security holes. Security software, such as your firewall, can contain security holes just like any other type of software. Check for updates.

In-house development. The vast majority of e-business software is written by in-house programming staff. When writing for the Web it is important to ensure that your own staff doesn't leave gaping holes through which malicious outsiders can gain entrance. There are a variety of programming "loopholes," so to speak, that open the door wide to hackers:

1. In programming parlance a "GET" sends data from the browser (client) to the server. For example, look at the query string below:

http://www.site.com/process_card.asp?cardnumber=123456789

All HTTP (hypertext transport protocol) requests get logged into the server log as straight text as shown below:

2000-09-15 00:12:30—W3SVC1 GET/process_card.asp
cardnumber=123456789 200 0 623 360 570
80 HTTP/1.1 Mozilla/4.0+(compatible;+5.01;+Windows+NT)

Not only is the credit card number clearly visible in the log but it might also be stored in the browser's history file, exposing this sensitive information to someone else using the same machine later on.

Security organizations recommend the utilization of the POST method rather than the GET method for this reason.

2. Are the programmers using "hidden" fields to pass sensitive information? An example of this is relying on hidden form fields used with shopping carts. The hidden fields are sometimes used to send the item price when the customer submits the form. It is rather easy for a malicious user to save the Web page to his or her own PC, change the hidden field to reflect any price he or she wants, and then submit it.

3. One way to combat the problem of hidden files is to use a hash methodology. A hash is a function that processes a variable-length input and produces a fixed-length output. Since it is difficult to reverse the process, the sensitive data transmitted in this matter is secured. The auditor is required to assess the utilization of this methodology given any problems he or she might find in assessing the problem discussed above.

4. Is sensitive data being stored in ASP or JSP pages? Microsoft's Internet Information Server (IIS) contains a number of security flaws that under certain circumstances allow the source of an ASP or JSP page to be displayed rather than executed. In other words, the source code is visible to anyone browsing that particular Web site. If sensitive data, such as passwords, are being stored in the code, then this sensitive data will be displayed as well. The rule here is to not hard-code any security credentials into the page itself.

5. Are application-specific accounts with rights identified early in the development cycle? There are two types of security. One is referred to as "declarative" and takes place when access control is set from the outset of the application program. "Programmatic" security occurs when the program itself checks the rights of the person accessing the system. When developing code for the e-business it is imperative that the rights issue be addressed early on in the development cycle. Questions to ask include:

- How many groups will be accessing the data?
- Will each group have the same rights?
- Will you need to distinguish between different users within a group?
- Will some pages permit anonymous access while others enforce authentication?

6. How are you dealing with cross-site scripting? When sites accept user-provided data (e.g., registration information, bulletin boards), which is then used to build dynamic pages (pages created on the spur of the moment), the potential for security problems are increased a hundredfold. No longer is the Web content created entirely by the Web designers—some of it now comes from other users. The risk comes from the existence of a number of ways in which text can be entered to simulate code. This code can then be executed as any other code written by the Web designers—except that it was written by a malicious user instead. Both JavaScript and HTML can be manipulated to contain malicious

code. The malicious code can perform a number of activities such as redirecting users to other sites and modifying cookies. More information on this topic can be obtained from CERT's Web site at www.cert.org/advisories/CA-2000-02.html and www.cert.org/tech_tips/malicious_code_mitigation.html.

7. Have you checked wizard-generated/sample code? Often programmers "reuse" sample code they find on the Web or make use of generated code from Web development tools. Often the sample or generated code contains hard-coded credentials to access databases, directories, etc. The auditor will want to make sure that this is not the case in the code being audited.

8. Are code reviews being performed? There is nothing worse than the lone programmer. Many of the problems discussed in the sections above can be negated if the code all programmers write is subject to a peer review. Code reviews, a mainstay of traditional quality-oriented programming methodology, are rarely done in today's fast-paced e-business environment. This is one of the reasons why there are so many security break-ins.

9. Web server review. In order to run programs on the Web, many organizations use the CGI (common gateway interface) to enable programs (i.e., scripts) to run on their servers. CGI is not only a gateway for your programming code (i.e., via data collections forms). It is also a gateway for hackers to gain access to your systems. Vulnerable CGI programs present an attractive target to intruders because they are easy to locate and usually operate with the privileges and power of the Web server software itself. The replacement of Janet Reno's picture with that of Hitler on the Department of Justice Web site is an example of just this sort of CGI hole. The following questions must be asked of developers using CGI:

- Are CGI interpreters located in bin directories? This should not be the case, because you are providing the hacker with all the capabilities he or she needs to insert malicious code and then run it directly from your server.
- Is CGI support configured when not needed?
- Are you using Remote Procedure Calls (RPC)? Remote Procedure Calls allow programs on one computer to execute programs on a second computer. There is much evidence that the majority of distributed denial of service attacks launched during 1999 and early 2000 were executed by systems that had RPC vulnerabilities. It is recommended that, wherever possible, you turn off and/or remove these services on machines directly accessible from the Internet. If this is not possible, then at least ensure that the latest patches to the software are installed, since these mitigate some of the known security holes.
- Is IIS (Internet Information Server) being used? This is the software used on most Web sites deployed on Windows NT and Windows 2000 servers. Programming flaws in IIS's Remote Data Services (RDS) are being used by hackers to run remote commands with administrator privileges. Microsoft's own Web site discusses methodologies to use to combat these flaws.

Testing. Pre-PC testing was a slow and meticulous process. Today's faster pace means that inadequate testing is being performed by most organizations. In addition, many organizations forgo security testing entirely. In this section of the audit we determine whether adequate security is being performed.

1. Has penetration testing been done? Penetration testing is used to assess the type and extent of security-related vulnerabilities in systems and networks, testing network security perimeters, and empirically verifying the resistance of applications to misuse and exploitation. While it is possible that system administrators are sophisticated enough to be able to utilize the tool sets available to scan the systems for vulnerabilities, a whole host of "white hat" hacker security consulting firms has sprung up over the past several years and it is these folks that are recommended.
2. Has intrusion testing been done? There are a whole host of software tools available on the market today that "monitor" systems and report on possible intrusions. These are referred to as Intrusion Detection Systems (IDS). In this section of the audit we determine whether an IDS is being used and how effectively it is used.
3. Is there a quality assurance (QA) function? While QA departments have been a traditional part of the IT function for decades, many newer, pure play Internet companies seem to ignore this function. In this section, the auditor will determine if the QA function is present. If it is present, then it will be reviewed.

Reporting. Logging of all logins, attempted intrusions, etc. must be maintained for a reasonable period of time. In this section, the auditor will determine if these logs are maintained and for how long.

Backup. In the event of failure it is usual that the last backup be used to restore the system. In this section, the auditor will determine the frequency of backups and determine the reasonableness of this schedule.

Ergonomics

At this stage the auditor becomes involved in more abstract issues. In the last section on security we could be very specific about what a system exhibiting good e-business health requires. In the section on ergonomics we need to be more subjective.

To achieve this end will require the auditor to meet not only with the system developers but with the end-users. At times, these end-users will be current customers of the system or potential customers of the system. To this end it might be necessary to develop surveys and perform focus groups.

The goal here is nothing less than determining a "thumbs up" or "thumbs down" on the e-business vis-à-vis other e-businesses.

Navigability. Navigation means the determination of whether or not the site makes sense in terms of browsing it.

1. How easy is it to find something on this site? If looking for a specific product, how many pages does one have to surf through to find it?
2. Is there a search engine? If so, review for correctness and completeness. Many sites do not have search engines (in this instance we are talking about a search engine to search the site only, rather than the Internet). If the e-business site exhibits depth (i.e., many pages) it becomes rather difficult to navigate around it to find what you're looking for. If a search engine is available the auditor must check to see if what is being searched for can be correctly found.
3. Is there a site map? If so, review for correctness and completeness. While not required and not often found, site maps are one of the most useful of site navigation tools. If available, the auditor will determine correctness of this tool.
4. Are back/forward (or other) buttons provided? What tools are provided the end-user for moving backward and forward within the site? Is the browser's Back and Forward buttons the only navigation tools—or did the Web designers provide fully functional toolbars? If so, do these toolbars work on all pages? We have found that, of those firms audited, 10 percent of the pages pointed to by the toolbars cannot be found.
5. Are frames used? If so, do toolbars and other navigation tools still work?

Usability. In the end it comes down to one question, really: "How usable is the Web site?" In this section we ask:

1. How easy is it to use this site? While the auditor might have an opinion that might well be valid, in this section we resort to surveys and focus groups to determine the answer.
2. How useful is this site?

Content. In this section we assess the value of the information contained within the site as compared to competitive sites.

1. Is content updated regularly?
2. Is content relevant?
3. Do visitors consider content worthwhile? The auditor will use survey techniques to determine the answer to this question.
4. How does content compare with competitors? The auditor will use survey techniques to determine the answer to this question.

Search engine. While the use of search engines has declined in popularity as a way to find a site, it is still an important marketing vehicle on the Web. In this section the auditor will determine where the site places when performing a search using the top ten search engines.

Customer Service

The Web is a doorway to the company's business. However, it is just one part of the business. Tangential services must be audited as well. Customer service is one of the biggest problem areas for Net firms. There have been many well-publicized instances of shoddy customer service. It is in the company's best interests, therefore, to assess customer service within the firm vis-à-vis its Web presence.

Accessibility. How easy is it for your customers to reach you?

1. Review e-mail response. How long does it take you to respond to a customer e-mail?
2. Review telephone response. How long does a customer have to wait on hold before a person answers his or her query?

e-commerce. If your site doubles as an e-commerce site (i.e., you sell good and/or services from your site) you need to assess the quality of this customer experience.

1. Check shopping experience. Using a "mystery shopper" approach, the auditor will endeavor to make routine purchases using the Web site. Determine:

   - Is the shopping cart correct (i.e., are the goods you purchased in the shopping cart)?
   - Does the e-commerce software calculate taxes properly?
   - Does the e-commerce software calculate shipping charges properly?

2. Check the fulfillment experience.

   - Is a confirmation e-mail sent to the purchaser?
   - Is the return policy carefully explained?
   - How quickly does the company refund money on returns?

Privacy. The auditor must review the company's privacy policy statement at a minimum. He or she should then review the data flow to determine if the privacy policy is being adhered to.

Legality

The digital age makes it easy to perform illegal and/or potentially litigious acts. From a corporate perspective this can be anything from a Web designer illegally copying a copyrighted piece of art to employees downloading pornography.

Copyright.

1. Check the content ownership of text on your site. It is quite easy to copy text from one site to another. Ensure that your copy is completely original or that you have the correct permissions to reprint the data.
2. In the same way check image ownership.

Employee Web usage. There have been a number of court cases where employees claimed harassment when other employees within the organization downloaded and/or e-mailed pornographic material. The company is responsible for the actions of its employees; therefore, it is highly recommended that the company do the following:

1. Create a policy memo detailing what can and cannot be done on the Internet (including e-mail). Make sure all employees sign and return this memo. Use tools such as those on surfcontrol.com to monitor employee Net usage.
2. Determine whether any e-mail monitoring software is used and determine its effectiveness.

Section 3

Coding Fundamentals

There are really two parts to the Web development equation: the front end and the back end. The front end is the part we see. It's full of HTML and graphics. It's the back end, however, that requires the hot and heavy programming skills.

What you'll learn in this section:

1. Everything you'll ever need to know about ASP (active server pages).
2. How to add classes to active server pages.
3. How to use Perl and CGI.
4. How to access databases via CGI.
5. What is object-oriented Perl.
6. Everything you'll ever need to know to code using VoiceXML.
7. All about Struts and Java server pages.

How to Create, Manage, and Deliver Your Web Content

Karen Brogno

Content management is a mix of business practices and technical processes for creating and collecting information for your Web site, keeping it current, then delivering (i.e., real-time publishing) that content in Web-based applications. Content management automates many time-consuming steps in producing Web pages and brings control and order to Web-based information. This chapter outlines a structure of business decision making for content management against which Web developers can adapt and develop their own processes. The guidelines apply, to a greater or lesser extent, to both business-to-business (B2B) and business-to-consumer (B2C) sites.

The Value of Content Management

The purpose of content management is to define the key technical tasks and the process-oriented work that will ensure your company's Web site reliably gets the most accurate and timely information out to its employees (in an Intranet deployment), suppliers, contractors, or end-customers. Done well, content management offers several valuable propositions:

Leverages an organization's information assets. A central idea of content management is the reuse of content so that it can be applied to multiple Web sites and possibly even different output media, such as for print manuals or newsletters or form factors (e.g., PDAs and Web-enabled phones). This is accomplished by managing content in a presentation-independent format. That means separating style (i.e., how the Web page looks) from the content (i.e., what the Web page contains). An effective content management system should also be able to deal with any form of content from any source and provide a platform for importing and integrating information from existing business applications.

Streamlines the publishing of Web content and speeds content rollout. A key reason for implementing content management is to automate all or portions of the authoring, editing, tagging, approving, tracking, publishing, and archiving of content on a Web site. Technical processes for template creation and workflow management, for example, allow an organization to respond more quickly to change while ensuring that the integrity of the site design is maintained and the site content is updated consistently, following standards.

Improves collaboration within an organization. A large Web site is a multidisciplinary project that involves graphic designers and other creative types, product managers, Web developers, programmers, and many others with responsibility for placing content of all kinds. Advanced content management solutions supporting workflow around content can make it easier to coordinate the activities and communication performed by Web team members. Workflow wed to content management also raises the overall confidence in each contributor's ability to meet standards because it makes clear how and when and by whom content can be altered.

Identifies errors before they are posted on the "live" Web site. A content management system in and of itself can't prevent technical glitches that produce errors (such as when the United Airlines Web site listed ticket prices in error and visitors were able to book flights from the U.S. to Paris for less than $30). (1) However, a content management system ideally has safeguards built in for reviewing and approving content and can bring such errors to light before they go online.

Maintains and enhances customer relationships. Customers want products or services that are useful, reliable, provide convenience, and are responsive to their needs through customization. These are the same expectations customers will have of your Web site. Effective content management processes make for better customer retention. The more consistent, current, and accurate a Web site is, the more value it provides customers and the more interest they'll have in using the site. Putting incorrect product prices or financials online will cause customer dissatisfaction or even more serious consequences. Providing continually refreshed pages with updated information, responding to customer e-mails promptly, or providing objective, outside experts to give occasional feedback wins customers.

Reduces operational costs. A well-implemented content management process not only improves overall time-to-market and quality of Web content, it can also minimize the number of people the Web staff needs or eliminate labor costs associated with filing paper requests and updates and changes to content. Content management with automated workflow can also reduce costs associated with poorly coordinated efforts that can produce inconsistent or inaccurate information.

Content Management Procedures/Issues

At the most basic level, content management can be broken down into three steps, each of which is a multistep process in and of itself with a defined sequence of tasks. The key steps are:

1. Creating and acquiring content. The starting point of content management is the acquisition of content from multiple sources, in multiple formats.
2. Managing content. The heart of a content management system is a workflow system that directs what happens to content after it's collected, including the review, approval, updating, and archiving of content.
3. Delivering (i.e., publishing) content in Web-based applications. This final step makes content available to a Web site in a file that resides on the server (or multiple servers), where the content is then available for general consumption.

How simple or advanced the implementation of content management is will depend on the organization's goals for its site, its size, and its budget. A very simple process for content management would be an author editing an HTML page on a Web server. However, a medium-size Web site with 500 to 2,000 pages is too large to manage manually, since there can be dozens of contributors submitting page changes. Then, multiple copies of a page need to be tested, verified, reviewed, and approved before the content is ready to be deployed to a production server. For Web sites of this scale, content management software can be very useful in managing portions of the content life cycle (Figure 16-1) within a browser-based environment and usually in conjunction with home-grown procedures as well. A very large site that has hundreds of thousands of pages of constantly changing information, integrates transactional systems, and gets millions

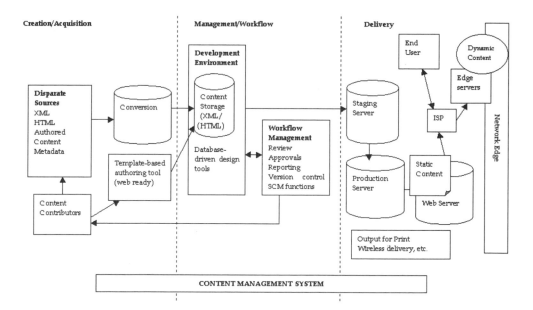

Figure 16-1. Life cycle of content.

of visitors a month may require the assistance of third-party integrators or outsourced providers for advanced forms of content management and delivery.

The following sections give recommended yet generic guidelines to instruct an organization on how to proceed, and what issues they need to consider, when putting in place a content management solution.

Creating and Acquiring Content

Because one of the previously mentioned objectives of content management is to manage content in a presentation-independent format, a good starting point is to know what the individual pieces of content are that ultimately make up Web pages. In the context of Web pages, content can be broken into two broad categories:

- Assets. Assets are pieces of information that the organization owns and that often are used to establish brand. Examples are your company's logos, trademarks, and patents. Legal and financial documents, purchase orders, corporate knowledge base, database records (how most product information is stored), and source code are also assets. These assets are often kept digitally as text files, graphics and images, and Portable Document Files (PDFs), but may also include audiotapes or videotape.
- Content. Content is everything that becomes part of the Web site, including assets the company owns as well as information that others own. Content comes from multiple sources and is created in multiple formats (see Figure 16-2). A content management system must have mechanisms for handling human-generated content (e.g., financial information in spreadsheets, brochure-ware, advertisements), programming code, and database information.

Authored Content

Much of the information on a Web site is human-generated. People from within and outside the organization will create and own certain information that's under their sphere of influence and accountability. These contributors provide business domain expertise that you need to call upon regularly or occasionally to keep Intranet and Web site information relevant and accurate. They include:

- Finance (e.g., expenses and revenue reports)
- Human resources (e.g., job postings, employee handbook information with corporate policies and procedures on timekeeping, benefit programs, travel policies)
- Marketing and sales (e.g., brochure-ware, competitive reports, forecasts)
- Product managers (e.g., product price lists, product specifications, white papers)
- Training (e.g., training materials, newsletters)
- Legal (e.g., copyright, regulatory information, legal disclaimers)

Content Types	Common Formats	Common Uses
Graphics	Bitmaps .JPEG .GIF .TIFF	Banner ads Product shots Company logos Design items (e.g., tabs, buttons)
Text	Word processor formats (e.g., MS Word, WordPerfect) Desktop publishing formats (e.g., QuarkXPress) ASCII Rich Text Format (RTF)	Product information Investors information Annual reports, brochures Press releases Search results E-mail
Multimedia	Animated GIFS QuickTime Shockwave RealAudio/RealVideo Windows Media Player	Animated tutorials Presentations Streaming media (used for press releases, education purposes, virtual seminars, analysts calls)
Databases	ORACLE Sybase SQL Server MS Access Database-driven XML	Dynamic and static content including: Product information Order information Search result pages Personalized information Help desk data Banner ad schedules Documentation Training materials
Downloads	RFT Acrobat PDF (Portable Document File) Microsoft Word ZIP .GIF and other graphics formats	Downloadable and/or online viewable files such as: Product specifications Annual reports
Applications and programs	CSV files Active Server Page (ASP) files Java Server Page (JSP) files Server and client-side scripts (e.g., CGI, Perl)	Page templates for: Order processing Credit card authorization Fulfillment processing Order reconciliation Customer service functions Event-driven customer e-mail services
Markup Languages	SGML HTML/Dynamic HTML XML	Structured information (tables, math) Static content Active content Dynamic content

Figure 16-2. Elements of Web content.

- Corporate communications (e.g., press releases, annual reports, branding elements)
- Graphics design (e.g., graphical text, illustrations, backgrounds, images, buttons, icons, tabs, banners, and other visual design elements)
- Outside contributors (e.g., advertisers' banner ads; user-supplied feedback on products or services; buyer and seller ratings)

A content management system defines how these contributors prepare their material and submit it. Options include the use of:

Standardized desktop applications. Many (if not most) of your contributors routinely work in office applications such as word processing and spreadsheet programs. The Microsoft Office suite that includes Microsoft Word, Excel, and Powerpoint is by far the most common program for creating documents using text and/or graphics. Content created in desktop publishing programs such as Quark XPress, Microsoft FrameMaker, and Adobe PageMaker will ultimately be destined for conversion into HTML or XML for Web site presentation, too. Contributors should be permitted to create their material in the program of their choice when:

1. The individual makes regular contributions. When people are regularly tapped to supply information it is usually because they are experts on a subject, but not necessarily expert in formatting or tagging. Allowing regular contributors to work in the program(s) they're most familiar is also an author-friendly policy. It allows the contributor to focus on content; it can also prevent errors from happening, as might be the case if the contributor were forced to use another authoring tool.
2. The contributor is creating content for both the Web and other information channels. For example, corporate may want to retain Quark files to produce printed company brochures or the annual report, even though the same content needs to work into the Web site workflow for posting on the company Intranet and Web site.

In the case where content exists in both print and online formats, policies for content control should be made clear to specify which format takes precedence. The policy could be as simple as stating that the online document is the primary authority because it is refreshed most frequently and a paper copy or other medium is secondary. If anomalies arise and a printed document is released before the online document, then the previous version of the online document is removed from the Intranet by the Webmaster.

Browser-based forms or templates. The easiest way to add new Web pages or update and maintain content in existing Web pages is to manage it right within a Web browser using a template or form. A Web developer will design the template or form with predefined or preprogrammed fields. The content contributor (e.g., a product manager) then adds information by typing in each field and sends the page to a Web server. A common gateway interface (CGI) or Perl script or some other custom application-server program may be required to automate the submission process. The system automatically knows how to serve that page because it acts on the information according to how it is preprogrammed. Templates are recommended when:

1. A contributor makes occasional or infrequent contributions. Using a template removes any worries about technical incompatibilities. Contributors who aren't standardized on the organization's preferred office suite application or who work on different platforms can still submit material.
2. There are many contributors, working from many locations. The browser allows

universal content entry. In a sense, browser-based authoring as a policy should allow more people to contribute. Contributors at any distributed location can update content as long as they have Web access on a desktop or laptop.

3. The reuse of design elements is desired. The prebuilt template can format the actual page design so that the organization's logo and other corporate branding elements are always displayed, as well as a navigation bar.

4. Consistency control is imperative. Because the template standard establishes the structure and design of the page, formatting errors can't be introduced.

5. Minimal approvals are required. Because the structure and design of the content is built in, templates would allow contributors to self-publish their content by submitting a final version to the corporate portal desktop for all employees to access. If contributors are submitting content from a different time zone, time synchronization can present the content at the right time through preset publishing dates or times. Most content management systems will still require users to obtain publishing rights for preapproved documents before they can publish to the live Web site without an administrator's assistance.

6. End-user or customer content is being collected. For example, if you create a Web version of a product catalog, you can set up one of your Web pages as an order form so that a customer can order your products using the Web.

HTML/XML editors. Editor applications are popular ways to create or integrate Web content. These are stand-alone, generally low-cost programs that place predefined tags around content as it is being written, so the contributor is in effect writing HTML or XML code at the same time he or she is writing text. Editors are available for different platforms (e.g., Windows, Mac, and Java). As authoring tools, these programs may be appropriate for:

1. Power users in the organization. Although a WYSIWG user interface may be implemented, this kind of tool requires that the user have at least some knowledge of coding and tagging, different code dialects, and different HTML extensions for Netscape Navigator and Microsoft Explorer.

2. Limited content management. HTML/XML editors can be used as general-purpose conversion utilities to tag existing content that's imported into the program, especially if they are simple documents or ones that are particularly well styled but would exclude more complicated file outputs, like from Quark XPress, that have special characters and tables. Some editors also have features that include limited support for workflow, site design, collaborative development, and Web site publishing (deployment).

Programming

In addition to authored content such as text and graphic formats, content management systems need to support code. A large-scale Web site is built with a lot of code. A large manufacturer such as Compaq could easily have 1 million pages of information on products on its Intranet for its sales force and contractors to access. That product list requires both extensive content and source code management to keep daily changes (more than 1,000 updates a day) under control.

In the context of Web-content-oriented materials, the programming code generally used is a markup language. A markup language encapsulates various content elements (e.g., photos, text, tables) in a single package. Within that package, each content element is enclosed in a content tag that describes what the content is, or a format tag that determines how the information is to be visually rendered or presented. Standard generalized markup language (SGML) is an International Standards Organization (ISO) format for maintaining large amounts of structured information; SGML is often used by publishers to generate content for multiple outputs, including print, CD-ROMs, and the Web. There are also application- or industry-specific markup languages such as MathML (used in scientific formulas and equations by scientific and technical authors), ChemicalML (used by chemists in the pharmaceutical industry for presenting molecular information), and NewsML (developed by Reuters and used for distributing news feeds to multiple editorial systems). At minimum, though, the coding schemes needed for Web content are hypertext markup language (HTML) and extensible markup language (XML).

HTML file sources. If a Web site is publishing mostly static information, then content can be standardized into HTML. HTML source content uses format tags. The keywords when thinking about HTML are content style (e.g., boldface, italics) and content positioning (e.g., placement of tables, images). If you were reading hypertext code alone, you wouldn't be able to tell whether the content is identified as a footer, footnote, or sidebar, for example. Content coded in HTML also produces "hard-coded" pages, which means that each time there's a new HTML version of the source content it becomes a separate source, rather than a variation of the original. For this reason, it can be difficult to modify and track large numbers of HTML pages to accommodate new or revised information.

XML file sources. XML file sources are becoming the standard for content management systems. In XML code, content is separate from content tagging, and content tagging is distinct from format tagging, so the content is entirely separate from presentation. XML is about describing content; style sheets handle issues of presentation (e.g., fonts, colors, and margins). For this reason, XML is considered an important technology for driving the transition to more open forms of electronic business where organizations can share and repurpose content more readily. In XML, anyone can interpret or understand the content's nature because the content is identified by a custom tag definition; that is, an organization can define its own set of markup elements, such as for a manufacturer's name, an employee name, or a price. Thus, in a business-to-business (B2B) market exchange, suppliers can provide content that can feed directly into its customers' content systems.

Unlike HTML, XML content can serve multiple purposes. It can be used for simple data representation and exchange, but it can also be used to produce content for different target audiences: for example, to publish Web pages, output for message-oriented computing (e.g., for browser-enabled cell phones or pagers), or hard copy.

XML Metadata. XML markup can also be used to store and link to metadata; XML generated from a database could have custom tags directly related to database metadata definitions. The most common definition of metadata is that it's "data about data." Each individual piece of content needs self-describing metadata to tell, at minimum, who the creator of the document is, when the document was released, the rights holders, and a unique identifier. The metatags would read: <Author>, <Date>, <Copyright>, <ID#>. This is an example of management metadata used for tracking purposes. Contextual information can also be embedded into the metadata. Adding context might mean including metadata on the purpose of the content; the frequency with which the content is used; the value of the content to the organization; when the content was last edited; the existence of any special agreements or arrangements on the content's use; etc. The more information that can be stored in metadata the better, because it can reduce the need to maintain separate records and make it easier to reuse the content. Metadata allows a Web site to understand and interpret what the content is, which makes it useful for:

- Management and archiving of content.
- Search and retrieval of Web site content.
- Preparing content for delivery to multiple devices.

Conversion Programming

Content conversion to a master format (e.g., HTML or XML) for Web publishing happens once the creative or authored content is passed on to the Web development or the IT staff. Conversion procedures may include any or all of the following:

- Development of a template set to convert text into uniformly formatted Web pages.
- Use of Save As function to save original word processing documents in HTML if a built-in or appropriate plug-in capability is available.
- Manual coding.
- Running a batch program using a conversion utility.
- Using the services of a third-party format conversion facility (i.e., outsourcing).

Key considerations in content conversion programming are:

Manual or batch conversion. Manual or batch conversion of authored documents will depend on how many documents there are and how large and complex they are. Creating a policy that requires that content be submitted in a consistent format (e.g., standardized on one word processing format with style sheet) will save time and effort in conversion. However, when materials are authored by different contributors at different locations at different points in time, there will be files that incorrectly apply style conventions, use a variety of manual formats, or lack markup altogether. These files will require some human intervention because any conversion utility will expect the source document to follow some style (i.e., have some logic) before it can be programmed with macros to automatically add code to the source file.

Third-party conversions. The conversion effort also depends on the size and skills of the current (and planned) technical team, so you must quantify the volume of content and the resources it would take to manage the conversion in-house. Unless you have ten or more full-time programmers working solely on a content management application, large-scale conversions can be difficult. For example, ten programmers converting 200 product manuals to XML, with ten chapters per manual and each programmer converting and testing one chapter a day, would become a 40-week effort. Hiring additional programmers can cut the time down to a few weeks. Another option is to outsource the work to a format conversion service that can convert structured documents created in common desktop authoring environments. Conversion facilities may be a good solution when there are very large numbers of source documents and when those source documents contain complicated tables and special characters that may deviate from the standard templates a commercial conversion utility may be able to handle. For example, because Quark XPress doesn't have a true table editor (only plug-ins that can build a table structure but not export it), converting Quark desktop publishing files to XML can be very time- and labor-intensive. A format conversion service may already have a suite of pre-built filters and processes that can analyze the text and tab structures and use specific Quark-style names. (2)

HTML to XML to HTML. XML-based content management systems may be most useful for companies without legacy content. As a practical matter, the amount of HTML that needs to be converted to XML can be enormous. The database-driven XML solution should have utilities for importing content, but it may also require coding or arduous manual effort. Tools that read or parse XML tags are available, but because browsers so easily read HTML, it may be necessary to translate XML back into HTML.

Database Content

The definition of Web site content must also be expanded to include transactional data. Transactional information stored in databases is routinely used for Web pages whenever a company's Web site is used to sell products or services. Transactions can be purchases or advanced search queries. During an e-commerce transaction, such as an online order, the Web site is drawing from database records for information such as product description and product specifications. The database is linked to a Web page template by inserting a database query at each place on the page where you want to call up content from the database. The pages are updated by running these database queries. When content is changed, the queries are rerun and updated images or text are automatically uploaded to replace the previous versions.

In the database-driven approach, the Web site is drawing not only on the content but also on the database procedure and middleware components that go and query the database and bring back the page. Middleware such as WebObjects, Active server page (ASP) technology, and Java server pages (JSP), among others, create the applications needed to enable an online order. For this reason a requirement for content management systems is that they be able to manage database processes and the interchange between creative content (i.e., text, images, page elements) and application content.

Database-driven content management is associated with:

Dynamic content. Database information is essential for publishing Web pages "on the fly" where the page content is modified automatically without changing the design of the Web site. An example is a page that's dynamically generated for a user to present information on products, orders, accounts, shipments, or promotions that 20 seconds later will actually change.

Personalized content. Because storing content in a database allows for efficient searches, it is possible to provide each customer with different search criteria (e.g., by product price, by product name, or by manufacturer), which personalizes the Web page for the end-user.

Batch publishing. Database-driven Web content management can do regular, scheduled exports of database content to a separate database used to run a Web site so that static content is updated.

CRM-enabled content management. A content management system may tie in with a customer relationship management system (CRM) in order to capture incoming customer correspondence (which typically arrives as e-mail and fax documents) and store it in a database. The inbound user-generated content is then available to customer service representatives the next time a customer calls. Outbound correspondence can also be generated through a template-based service request that automatically records the customer name, address, service request number, and the customer rep's name. This outbound correspondence can be queued for review and approval through the content management system's workflow system (described in the section on managing content) or sent through a batch print process. The correspondence is ultimately archived. Or service reps can reuse correspondence from reassigning one service request to another and updating the outbound document. (3)

Some content management solutions rely on relational databases from Oracle, IBM, Microsoft, and Sybase to store the bulk of content (saved as text within fields) and templates as well as metadata. Commercially available content management systems may also use a proprietary XML repository to maintain and manage the large quantities of content for reuse and repurposing.

Licensed Content

Organizations may also license content from third parties and publish that alongside their own content, rather than attempting to provide extensive content capabilities themselves. Organizations license content so that they can offer different kinds of content, keep the Web site fresh, and have visitors stay longer on their site. Organizations may license popular content (e.g., news, weather), interactive content (e.g., polls), or specialized content (e.g., industry information catalogs and advanced search technology) that is relevant to the highly targeted audience.

Policies for securing the right to use copyrighted content are fairly standard. They are:

Request permission to use the content. This means simply asking the copyright owner to grant permission. It is an informal method and may not be acceptable to your organization's legal department.

Obtain a nonexclusive license. Here you are asking for permission to use the content in a specific way and for a specified or limited time. Nonexclusive licenses do not have to be in writing.

Obtain an exclusive license. An exclusive license gives permission to use the content in a specified way but can be granted to only one licensee at a time.

Request a transfer of ownership (assignment of copyright). This is a request to purchase, often for lump sum, the copyright from another party. This assigned right transfer may need to be recorded in the Copyright Office.

Licensing arrangements can be outsourced through content aggregator services such as Screaming Media. Rather than licensing content directly from a content owner, a business organization contracts with the content aggregator. The aggregator does the work of providing content, from multiple sources, in a Web-ready format for a monthly service fee. Server-side software with custom content filtering is installed at the customer site, so the customer can in effect receive only content items that match its requirements. Organizations can also deliver their content to others participating in this kind of content services network (discussed later in this chapter under the heading "Syndicating Content").

Managing Content

Before content can be moved onto a local network and Web server, it must go through a series of content-related activities intended to ensure that the content is accurate and adheres to company standards (e.g., standards for common language and format to ensure any content coming from the company clarifies rather than confuses the company's position for customers and investors). The principle activities are:

- Approving the content.
- Updating the content.

- Performing version control.
- Performing quality assurance checks.
- Archiving or deleting content.

This part of content management requires a mix of project and workflow management and software configuration management (also known as source code management) techniques.

Approving Content

Policies for reviewing, approving, and updating content may vary from company to company or even within departments of the same company. Policies may be to:

1. Include a representative from each department or company division that is a source of content. The representative would be the main pipeline of information for a given group.
2. Tie Web content management to the larger Web development effort. For example, the marketing department may be in charge of Web projects and it may have an established process for collecting the information it needs for public relations initiatives and for passing that information quickly to the normal Web developers. Although content management is actually distinct from site development, the two tasks are becoming linked more and more; the thinking here is that if an organization already has a process for analyzing and assessing new Web projects, it can be brought to bear on the content management project, too.
3. Automating the review and approval process by implementing workflow management alongside a content management system. The workflow can be developed in-house through a process of scripting or by creating workflow templates with dynamic page-serving and database interfaces. If the organization is using a content management product, it may include a workflow system. This is the most accommodating method for large-scale Web sites where there could easily be dozens of individual types of workflow that result in the management of thousands of documents.

The review and approval of content requires procedures for:

1. Submission. At the outset the procedure for submission should be that only controlled content can be submitted. Controlled content is content that includes certain required information such as:

   - Unique ID
   - File name
   - Author name

- Title of the document
- Date on which the document was published/written
- Published (i.e., whether the document has already been put on the server)

Contributors also should have guidelines for how their content is to be transmitted. For example, the site administrator may specify uncompressed versus compressed files. To put content on the server contributors may be required to either upload the file themselves, via FTP, to an appropriate directory name or use a Web form built for their content.

2. Submission notification. A submission should automatically generate an e-mail notification. This step notifies the Web site administrator and next person in the content approval process that the material has been put on the server. For example, if an HR manager submits a job posting, the HR director would receive an automatic e-mail notification that the posting needs review/approval to be published. The e-mail notification could contain a link that the recipient clicks to access an editable version of the job posting.

3. Approval. Different content types may have different approval processes, but generally speaking, content approval protocols will fall into one of these categories:

- The original creator of the content is the sole approver.
- A group approves content. For example, a press release may be written by one copywriter in marketing but requires the approval of the marketing department as a group.
- Team-managed approval where two or more individuals or approving groups approve content. Example: A job posting goes to both human resources and finance for approvals, with the groups receiving the material at the same time so that they can review it simultaneously. The content isn't approved, however, until both groups approve it.
- Team-managed approval where two or more individuals or approving groups approve content, but the approval process is serial and the content is approved when the last in the series approves it. (4)

Approval procedures should also specify a time frame and fallback procedure in the event someone in the workflow can't perform his duties. For example, if approver A doesn't approve content within two days, the policy might be to either:

- Return to author for follow-up.
- Automatically pass the content to the next stage in the process (e.g., editing).
- Automatically pass the content to another approver, with a VP designated as the only person to give approval.

In some cases higher management may need approval at all times on certain types of content. Corporate may need to be notified every time the company logo is used in order to authorize that the logo is used appropriately each time it appears. Legal departments may wish to review all content to be sure libelous statements haven't slipped through the cracks.

4. Approval status notification/reporting. It is important to make sure each approver knows what happens to the content once it's moved to the next step. For example, the original author should be sent an e-mail notification when the text has been modified. A workflow system should be able to generate reports that provide status information to either control or track content. Reports are necessary to:

- Tell whether the content has been submitted, is being edited, has been returned to the author for rework, or has been accepted in its final form.
- Identify duplicate content or trigger action if content becomes stalled in the workflow process.
- Provide alerts when specific tasks have to be done. For example, a report could be generated if there is date-sensitive material that is about to expire. Or, in a workflow for an image, a report can be programmed if the image needs to be reformatted to reduce file size.

Reports are commonly delivered as e-mail alerts but can also be formatted in XML, HTML, or CSV format.

5. Access and usage control. The organization must have policies and access control lists that define who can write, create, and delete content. Authorized users can be contributors (i.e., content creators), content approvers, Web site administrators, or other Web project leaders. At minimum, a protected directory is used that only authorized users can access. Some content management systems allow additional authorization systems such as LDAP (lightweight directory access protocol) for secure directory access. Access control mechanisms that grant user permissions may include the following:

- Individuals can access data related to their own content only.
- Approvers have write access to make changes and approve the document.
- Approvers can be grouped according to roles (e.g., graphic artists, marketing writers) for accessing content related to their own resources and products.
- Individuals can be given authorized read-only or write access to confidential information, but the access must be logged.

Updating Existing Content

The process of updating Web content is a distributed one in which the various contributors throughout the organization—such as legal, marketing, human resources—handle the updating of their content. Distributing the responsibilities for content updates releases the Web development staff from the task of implementing content changes. The shared-responsibility model is dependent on:

- The availability of tools such as pre-built templates that make it easy for content contributors to update existing material.
- An approval process that is automated or at least isn't overly complicated or cumbersome. Remember, content updates aren't the same as a new development project and don't require the same steps for analysis and requirements definition.

Web content is updated weekly, daily, hourly, or minute by minute. Update frequency may be influenced by factors such as:

The type of content. Some content needs to be posted and replaced on a scheduled basis (e.g., weekly sales promotions). On a mature Web site, there will be content components that change infrequently. A datasheet and technical specification for a flat screen monitor will need to be updated far less frequently than the company's investors relations page. Ultimately all content will need to be updated, tested, and deployed during daily updates.

The chain reaction of changes. A single change can affect one or thousands of pages. How long it takes to identify and update all pages could influence how updates are scheduled.

Content sources. How many content contributors you have or where they are physically located shouldn't matter, yet these factors may be relevant in one sense. If a company has multiple content contributors overseas, the process for collecting and updating content may be affected by the availability of technical resources and tools to support multiple languages and time zones.

Performing Version Control

Versioning is a basic control mechanism. A version control system stores multiple versions of a source file and records the history of the file, such as the date it was created, who created it, who approves it, and who publishes it on the site. Any kind of content should be able to be saved to a version control system, including text documents, source code, and graphics. This step is important for two reasons:

- It provides a way for content contributors to refer back to an earlier version of material if an error occurs in a later version and needs correcting.
- It provides accountability for changes. A site administrator can look back and determine which developer made a change and on what date. This information may be necessary if ever a full site audit has to be performed for legal reasons.

Version control is a feature of most commercial content management systems, or it may be under the control of a separate source code management system. The version control system resides on a production server behind a site's firewall and may be on the same machine as the staging server.

From the perspective of the content contributors, version control means that the contributors can always access a copy of what their content looked like when they first contributed it and can then follow the content through its changes. From the perspective of site development teams, version control relates to source code management. Version control of source code is important for managing system builds and releases.

Procedures for version control include:

File-based check-in/checkout. Authorized users can check in or check out files or directories from the version control system. On checkout, a file can be locked so that no one else can access the same file while it's being updated. After the user updates the file or directory, the user undoes the lock by checking it back into the system. The site administrator sends e-mail notifications to other content contributors when files are checked back into the system. All Web contributors should be given their own directory hosted on the server for saving their original content contribution or works in progress. Some commercial content management systems set up the directory so that it contains a complete virtual copy of the entire Web site, which allows each contributor to stage and test changes in the context of the entire site without affecting other contributors' work.

Version history and rollback. If the organization is using a content management system for both Web publishing and print publishing, the system can track which version of a document or image has appeared in which output medium. The content management system can then maintain serial versions of content so that an earlier version can be accessed if necessary. A version control system also identifies source code versions and identifies what release developers are on and who is doing what with the Web site code they are working on. The system can do version-compares and rollback to a previous version based on a version number or label.

Security. The version control system grants contributors access to files based on their access privileges.

Archiving or Deleting Content

Although the flow of Web content may not seem to have a clear-cut end (it just keeps changing continuously), there will be a point when content must be retired either because it is too old to be accurate any longer or because it is unpopular. Three common policies for retiring content can be implemented:

- Content may be removed from a site entirely.
- Content may be removed from the site and archived for reference (e.g., informational purposes) or other purposes (e.g., to have an evidentiary record).
- Content may be selectively archived.

Archiving policies for Web content may be built on any existing policies and procedures for appraising schedules for how long the organization maintains other electronic records and offline archives. Guidelines for archiving Web content can be grouped as follows:

Content of temporary use by customers. Dynamically generated content has a limited life span and may be blocked after a preset time (e.g., when it is one day or two hours old), so the rest of the site still operates. Content that has lost its newsworthiness but is still otherwise relevant may be moved to another section of the site, then moved to a searchable archive.

Content needed for immediate or long-term reference. Any company newsletters or formal documents may automatically be identified for archiving. Image archiving policy may state that the highest-quality digital image be retained. Because an image digitized for use on the Web site will always be of an inferior quality, a master digital image may be kept in a separate image bank in a format such as encapsulated postscript (EPS), where it can be accessed and used to create a Web-ready image when needed.

Content necessary for legal purposes. For organizations that operate in certain industries such as financial services, utilities, or pharmaceuticals, procedures for deleting or archiving content need to be developed around government or regulatory policies, since there may legal requirements to retain content for a statutory period of up to seven years. It may be necessary to archive multiple versions of a site, reflecting certain points in time, and to archive content in all formats the content was originally delivered in or accessed by (e.g., print and CD-ROM as well as the Web).

Content with selective value. Identifying a content artifact that needs to be preserved can be accomplished by adding archiving meta-tag codes. This provides the capability to automatically identify and retrieve individual pages or individual elements that are so referenced while excluding directories, and additional files.

Delivering Content

Once content is approved, having completed its workflow, it is then ready to progress to the next phase of its life cycle—publishing. Publishing is when the content is copied to a "live" Web site where the general public can view it or, if deployed to an Intranet, a target audience can access it.

Whereas policies for content acquisition and its related workflow give employees and workgroups in the organization responsibility for creating and managing their own localized content (stored on development servers in the previous steps), the work of putting content onto production servers is handed off to the IT staff or a site development team. Commercial content management solutions as they exist today work within firewalls and have automatic deployment capabilities to handle the content's initial move off the local servers to a staging server application.

Application Staging

The staging server is a temporary holding area for the final versions of all files that will be distributed to a production server at the hosting facility. The staging area is designed to emulate the production site in every way possible, but because the staging server is behind the company's firewall, it is used for testing the site in a secure environment that cannot be accessed by the general public. Security can be enforced so that access is limited to only the site developers.

Staging procedures would include:

1. Loading the content onto the staging site. A file transfer utility and an FTP upload area separate from the staging area may be used for copying files into the staging server for testing. If the load is done under the control of a content management system with version control, then the system would detect where there are content changes based on where the approval workflow posts changes to each file (logged in a version history). Consequently, the process would know which file versions to update and would deploy those versions automatically, staging all the changes in unison rather than file by file.

2. Integration testing. The staging server is where content is assembled into a final page presentation and delivered through a Web browser. The content management systems coordinates changes comprised of files, database assets, application logic, and other information. New and existing application content and new creative (i.e., authored) content are brought together and the interactions between them and page elements are tested thoroughly in the staging area, where another approval process by site administrators happens. At the staging server you will also integrate advertising placements (banner ads) into the page presentation. Approval of locations for advertisements is usually done with templates. This testing of the staging site is to ensure changes are correct. The content management system should have automated procedures to undo changes to a staging file, if necessary, or to recover a file that's been deleted from staging. Further testing is then required to confirm any overwrite files.

3. QA testing. The following quality assurance (QA) and testing procedures may or may not be part of an off-the-shelf content management solution, but they are routinely done by the technical staff:

   - Code or unit testing (to verify coding of any individual programmer by another programmer)
   - Load testing (to determine how many simultaneous users can access the site, the number of transactions the site can process, average response times)
   - Compatibility testing (to test that the site can be accessed by different types of computers, operating systems, browser versions)
   - Usability testing (to check that links are working properly)

- Functional testing (to uncover problems with content and design)
- Regression testing (to resolve all items or "bugs" entered in the QA database; regression testing occurs every time a new release of the Web site is produced)

4. Scheduling the launch. After testing, launch requirements for content and applications are scheduled. This is an automated process in content management, so launching content may only involve changing the content's status from "working" or "live" in its management record. Then the content will be copied from staging to production from within the content management system. Content changes can be set to launch:

- Automatically when their workflow completes.
- At a scheduled time (e.g., a press release scheduled for automatic publishing at 8:00 A.M. on a specific day).
- On demand.

5. Deploying content to production server(s). After passing final staging tests, content is replicated to a public Web site by an automated process. Under the control of a content management system, the content may be bundled and moved as one from the staging area to the Web site by selecting a deployment option and indicating when and how the site update should occur (e.g., across a virtual private network using FTP). The ability to deliver the content to Web hosting facilities outside of the organization (i.e., outside of the firewall), and deploy content to multiple sites if the organization's environment involves more than one live site, may or may not be a feature of commercial content management platforms.

Issues in Advanced Content Publishing

At the publishing/deployment end of content management, organizations with highly complex Web sites typically work with Internet hosting and specialized content delivery service providers. They provide a layer of infrastructure for replicating and synchronizing content, site mirroring, load balancing, caching, securing digital content distribution, and performing other content management functions across a wide range of platforms. Key issues in advanced content delivery are:

- Speed (to reduce the time it takes to download Web pages)
- Performance reliability (to prevent outages during peak traffic)

Caching Services

Web caching was developed as a technology to speed up downloads around the global Internet and ensure the availability of Web pages. The basic idea is to bring content closer to the user requesting information, thereby reducing errors in data transmission. Caching technology may be a pure hardware solution from companies that have proprietary operating systems, or a software solution that runs on multiple platforms.

Many service providers use some kind of caching technology to reduce the number and size of round-trips back to databases or other servers so that the most heavily trafficked sites can serve pages quickly. Access to pages that are frequently updated by a Web site—dynamic and personalized pages such as those containing database-driven financial information—often cannot perform as fast as static Web pages. Caching service works provided there is access to the originating server. If a primary or origin server delivering dynamic content is down, the cache service will not deliver.

To get the same performance and fast downloads from dynamic or personalized Web pages that caching provides for static content (or flat files), a content management system may integrate cache management capabilities. In this model, the solution is to nest the small transactional component inside a cached formatting component. If a Web page is made up of six components and only one (e.g., a bank balance) is transactional, the system would only need to retrieve one piece of data from a back-end data source. Component-level caching can also be used to select and arrange the elements on personalized pages. (5)

Content Delivery Networks (CDNs)

While an organization may want to self-host its content, when its traffic volumes are very large and when the organization is using live streaming video and audio content or Webcasting large events, Web sites will usually require content delivery services. Although caching brings content closer to users, it doesn't address performance and reliability issues associated with delivery of rich content across the multiple networks that comprise the Internet.

CDN companies such as Akamai, Digital Island, Mirror Image Internet, and competitors maintain a network of their own servers at leading ISPs. They host replicas of an organization's content in cache servers (so-called edge servers) located within network edge points of presence (PoPs). This design allows the CDN to provide rich content, enhance Web site response times, and avoid delays and outages caused by peak demand and public network congestion.

If you are a customer of a CDN, the CDN would supply your organization with content management tools that the organization can use to render its content CDN-ready. A Web-based front end lets the organization see what content is being served and purge and update its content on the CDN edge servers as necessary. Usage histories and usage trends are provided to customers as part of the CDN service; these reports allow the organization to hone or adjust the content by, for example, moving more personalized or localized content to the edge of the CDN provider's network to better target users in a given geographical area.

Selling and Securing Digital Content

E-commerce is a major distribution method to access content from within organizations. Because of the drive to make more money from e-commerce, everything needs to be digital. As that occurs, any organization that publishes large amounts of content—textbooks, research reports, journals, magazines, or educational materials—wants to protect its digital property. The highest corporate officers are looking into content management solutions with digital rights management (DRM). The MP3 phenomenon is an example of how easy it is to get content with no rights management.

DRM bundles rights management technology and services together. The technology piece involves packaging up and securely encrypting a piece of digital content. The services piece involves transaction processing, information transaction processing to collect information on end-consumers, customer support, royalty management, and territory management (i.e., preventing the consumption of goods across geographic regions).

DRM is mentioned in this chapter because it should be on your organization's watch list. It is a developing technology that will probably impact content management solutions in the near future (by the time this book is published, there'll probably be broader adoption of DRM).

Syndicating Content

Syndication isn't a new concept, but it is increasingly used by organizations as another way to deploy their content assets. Some commercial content management systems offer business-user interfaces and support for building e-business syndication networks by offering deployment options across several formats (e.g., Web, print, wireless). Source content of any type (down to database rows or pieces of installable software) can be prepared for each deployment and sent to an affiliate or business partner.

Syndication allows organizations to reach new customers for their content. A successfully managed syndication program can generate additional revenues for an organization. Because the syndicator usually has no control over the affiliate's environment and gives up control over its information assets when they are transferred to another company, the key is to partner with the right syndicator who can target the audience you want and provide feedback.

Content Management Checklists

The following checklists are meant to help readers assess their content management needs. Use them as a starting point in deciding whether the solution is to develop a system in-house, have a customized system built, or use an off-the-shelf package.

Content Acquisition Checklist

1. Identify all the diverse types of content that your Web pages include, such as HTML files, graphic images, CAD or engineering drawings, sound clips, applets, and information from databases.

2. Identify information assets, or those pieces of content the organization owns. If content exists in both print and online formats, set policy for which format takes precedence. Usually the online document is the primary authority because it is refreshed most frequently, and a paper copy or other medium is secondary.

3. Assess how large your site is by the number of active pages (e.g., 400? 2,000? 1 million?). How many new active pages will be added to your site in the next month?

4. Know how many people or groups are contributing site content and where they are located. Determine whether there are language requirements for contributors in foreign offices.

5. Be author-friendly. For content contributors:

- Provide an easy-to-use authoring platform, including templates and tutorials.
- Make sure employees who originate business information can also contribute content to the Web site using tools of their choice (it will reduce their need for technical skills or assistance).

6. Provide contributors with guidelines for submitting controlled content that includes:

- Unique ID
- File name
- Author name
- Title of the document
- Date on which the document was published/written

7. Provide contributors with guidelines for how their content can be transmitted and received. Requiring electronic submission of documents will ease workflow. List the transmission methods contributors are allowed to use to submit content; the connectivity may determine what kind of format contributors must use:

- Private ISDN line
- DSL
- Cable modem services
- T1 lines
- HTTP
- FTP (it may be necessary to supply contributors with an FTP program)
- Dial-up connection

8. Provide contributors with a list of the technical formats that will be accepted electronically (e.g., compressed files, uncompressed files, word processing formats, graphics formats).

If you are using a commercial content management system to do authoring, know whether it:

- Can support content from users and repositories. You will want to import authored content that includes a variety of unstructured data (e.g., text, images, video, and sound) and structured data from different databases.
- Has a built-in authoring tool, supports third-party authoring tools, or requires a proprietary product.
- Comes preloaded with page templates that can be modified if required.
- Has appropriate interfaces to well-known development tools for producing static content (e.g., Microsoft FrontPage, Adobe PageMill, Notepad, etc.)
- Has appropriate interfaces to well-known dynamic Web page development tools (e.g., Macromedia Dreamweaver, ColdFusion, Net Objects Fusion, and Blue Sapphire).
- Can support industry-specific formats such as MathML or ChemicalML if necessary.

Content Conversion Checklist

1. Assess the volume of content you're collecting. Whether to manually or batch-convert content depends on how many documents or images there are. To assess if you can manage conversion in-house or need format conversion services, consider your existing content requirements:

- Word processor documents to formatted HTML or XML text
- Word processor tables to HTML/XML
- Documents to RTF or Microsoft Word downloadables
- Scanned documents to PDF files
- Document scans or faxes to TIFF
- Desktop publishing files to HTML/XML
- Presentation graphics (e.g., Powerpoint) to HTML
- Bitmapped graphics to GIF/JPEG (modification or compression of images or changing image formats is done to ensure that images load faster on a Web page)
- URLs to hyperlinks
- Spreadsheets to run-time files (if using Envoy for Corel WordPerfect Suite)

- Spreadsheets tables to HTML/XML
- Modification of database elements to include metadata

2. If managing the conversion using a batch utility, allow for post-software manual cleanup.

3. If using an XML-based commercial content management system, know whether the product has utilities for importing all your legacy content. If not, and coding or a manual effort is necessary, find out who does the integration work—you or the vendor.

4. If using XML, know whether your applications need an extra conversion to translate XML into HTML before use.

Content Workflow Checklist

1. How often are pages updated?

2. What is the current process for updating and approving content? Is a paper request used to request changes to a Web page? Is there a project tracking system? When a change is made, what is the procedure? For example, does it involve:

- Management notification?
- Sales and support staff notification?
- Legal notification?
- Customer notification?
- Other notifications?

3. When multiple contributors access the system, how is content control implemented? Does the existing system:

- Identify author or owner of documents?
- Identify who has write access to documents?
- Display date, time, file size, and current status of document?
- Give warnings to prevent deleting or overwriting another's work when work is being accessed simultaneously?
- Track the time spent on document?
- Enforce a naming convention internal to a workgroup?

The following is a preliminary list of the features to look for in a content management platform. This process of assessing off-the-shelf product capabilities may prompt you to reassess and better understand your current workflow and the impact a content management system will have on it.

A	Technical Issues (Hardware/Software)	Comments
1	What hardware platforms are supported?	
2	Which client operating system(s) does the product run under (e.g., the developer client may be Windows NT–based/the content contributor client may be browser-based)?	
3	Regarding Internet functionality, what languages are used in the product (e.g., Java, HTML, XML, JavaScript)?	
4	What native databases are supported? Does it use an XML repository, relational, or object-oriented database to store content?	
B	**Content Acquisition**	
1	What are the native authoring tools (e.g., is there forms-based authoring? Native Microsoft Word support?)?	
2	What content formats are supported?	
C	**Content Life Cycle**	
1	Can the product do full searches on content? On metadata?	
2	Does the product have a workflow system that can coordinate efforts among multiple users and groups?	
3	What other channels of communication integrate into the workflow (i.e., e-mail)?	
4	Are there reporting capabilities to produce graphical reports?	
5	Can the product do version control (i.e., maintain, archive, and retrieve multiple versions of document)? Can it keep an audit trail of changes?	
6	What methods of check-in/checkout are available (e.g., single files? Batch?)?	
D	**Dynamic Publishing & Personalization**	
1	Is language translation software bundled with the content management system? Is there a multilanguage browser interface? If not, is that a planned capability? (Relevant for global businesses.)	
2	Does the product repurpose content for multichanneled publishing or personalization (e.g., Web browser, wireless device, print)?	

E	Site Management	Comments
1	Is there capability to roll back to a previous version of site? If so, are rollbacks automatic or manually created?	
2	Is there a file-access security schema to be defined for either an individual user or a group? Is LDAP available for handling user access?	
3	Is there an advanced staging facility for publishing and quality control? Does the product integrate with ad servers and marketing campaign management tools?	
F	**Installation**	
1	Is wizard-like client installation and removal available?	
G	**Administration**	
1	Does the product include a graphical user interface as well as a command-line interface for administrators?	
2	Can the administrator manage multiple sites and servers from the administrative interface?	
3	How many users, and how much content, can the product support and still maintain good performance? (Compare that with your assessment of the number of contributors, approvers, workgroups you have using the systems and the number of active pages on your Web site.)	
4	How long is the lead time for software setup?	
5	Does the product rely on any proprietary code?	
H	**Nontechnical Considerations**	
1	What is the vendor company's financial history?	
2	What is the maturity of the product line (e.g., what percent of revenue is derived from content management)?	
3	What is the vendor's target market? (e.g., large media companies? Catalog producers? International Web site operators?)	
4	Is there pricing, licensing, and other helpful commercial information?	
5	Does the product support the preparation of content for syndication?	

Worksheet for Evaluating Off-the-Shelf Content Management Software Packages

References

1. Jane Costello, "United Site Quotes Super-Low Fares, Balks at Honoring the Ticket Prices," WSJ.com, 15 February, 2001.
2. Michael Gross, "Converting Quark to XML," Fresh Meadows, NY: Data Conversion Laboratory, 21 February 2001. Accessible at ww.dclab.com/QuarktoXML.html.
3. Rita Lochner and Karen Ross, "Adding Content to CRM," *DB2 Magazine* 6 (1): 12 (2001).
4. This framework is based on Andre McMillan, "Control Your Content," *e-Business Advisor,* 1 October, 2000, 42.
5. Bob Pierce, "Vignette Content Management Server," White Paper (Austin, TX: Vignette Corp.), 8 February 2001, 13.

Readings

1. Danielle Anthony and Bryan Formidoni, "Streamlining Content Management," *Unix Insider* Webmaster column (August 2000). Available at www.unixinsider.com/unixinsideronline.
2. "The Ins and Outs of Content Delivery Networks," White Paper (Los Gatos, CA: Stardust.com), December 2000.
3. Nancy McCluskey-Moore, "Untangling Web Content Management: Intranet, Extranet and Otherwise" (Vancouver, BC: NCompass Labs, Inc.). Available at www.ncompaslabs.com/Resources/Content+Management/White+Papers.htm.
4. Jim Reynolds and Arminder Kaur, "Content Management," Microsoft Enterprise Services White Paper, E-Commerce Technical Readiness (Redmond, WA: Microsoft Corp.), April 2000. Available at www.microsoft.com/technet/ecommerce.

KAREN BROGNO is an independent industry analyst covering the telecommunications and Internet industries. She is a contributing editor to U.S. e-Services Report (Fuji-Keizai USA). She has worked as an editor in professional book and consumer magazine publishing. Her editorial experience includes SGML for print and CD-ROM production, and SGML context-based tagging for a large data conversion project for a major bank. She is the former Webmaster for a community nonprofit animal welfare organization. She can be reached at KayBrogno@worldnet.att.net.

Active Server Pages Primer

Don Franke

Active server pages (ASP) is Microsoft's version of CGI (common gateway interface), which turns static Web pages into dynamic, database-driven content. ASP is free, installed with an option pack for Windows NT, or with Personal Web Server for Windows 95 and 98. ASP has become so popular that there are even UNIX and Linux versions available by such vendors as ChiliSoft! With Microsoft's growing dominance in the Web server marketplace, and the fact that it is ostensibly free (save the cost of downloading the 20MB option pack) there are now a large percentage of Web and e-commerce sites that run ASP, including Nasdaq, Barnes & Noble, and Dell. To better understand ASP let's take a step back and review the basics: HTML. (Please skip ahead to the section "Time to Code" if you are already familiar with HTML and CGI concepts.)

Think of an HTML page as blueprints for a house. The code describes what goes where, how things are formatted, what images to use, etc. What transforms this dry code into an engaging experience is the Web browser. When you go to a Web site, you are always requesting a specific Web page (i.e., index.html) The server reads in the code of the requested page and sends it to the client over the Internet as shown in Figure 17-1. The Web browser receives the code and translates it into tables, words, and pictures, resulting in the Web page.

HTML code is received by the browser just as it is delivered: left to right, top to bottom, just like you are reading this page. If you have never seen HTML code, just right-click on any Web page and select View Source. The first main tag you will see is <HTML>. This tells the Web browser that all the text the Web server is sending is hypertext markup language (HTML). At the end of the page will be </HTML>, which marks the end of the code. Between these two bookends are the stuff of the Web page. If you would like to learn more about HTML, there are many sites available offering beginner tutorials, as well as the definitive source: the World Wide Web Consortium at www.w3.org.

An HTML page is a collection of HTML tags and text, and it typically ends with the extension .htm or .html. When a client (the person using a Web browser) requests a page

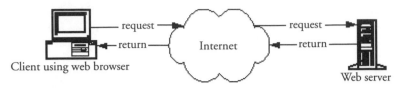

Figure 17-1. Client/server logic.

that ends in .htm or .html, this tells the Web server that the page in question is "just a basic Web page, don't do anything special." The Web server pulls the requested page into memory and delivers the text stream over the Internet to the client's Web browser, which the Web browser then translates into a visual page, pictures and all.

Sequence

1. User types URL in the URL field, or clicks a hyperlink to a specific page (e.g., http://www.newarttech.com).
2. Request is sent to the server at the specified address.
3. Web server locates default Web page (i.e., index.html).
4. Web server reads index.html text file into memory (if it isn't already in memory) and sends file text over Internet to requesting client machine.
5. Client Web browser receives text, reads it into memory, and displays translated Web page.

And this was how things began, all Web pages being static text files sent from a Web server to the Web browser (Figure 17-2). Any changes in content meant re-saving the page.

Then along came CGI. CGI gave life to these otherwise dead pages. Within the lines of HTML code could be a CGI script name; for example, `"<IMG SRC='images/counter.cgi?type=odometer'>."` This tells the server to run the CGI script using a CGI interpreter (Figure 17-3). The interpreter is a program on the server that needs to be set up on the Web server beforehand. When the CGI-capable Web server encounters this line, it loads this script (counter.cgi) into memory and the CGI interpreter runs the specified CGI script. The Web server continues reading the HTML file to the end, then delivers the result, including the counter-graphic, to the client browser. CGI, for the most part, ran only on UNIX/Linux Web servers, but Microsoft quickly entered the fray and introduced ASP. The scripting language of choice for ASP is VBScript. (Note: JScript could also be used, but I have yet to see an ASP page scripted in JScript.) Microsoft went with VBScript for the language for ASP, largely because of the immense popularity of Visual Basic. What makes Visual Basic so popular is that it's easy and powerful, requiring only a few lines of code to get results. Think of VBScript as Visual Basic Lite. The biggest difference between VBScript and Visual Basic is that you use Visual Ba-

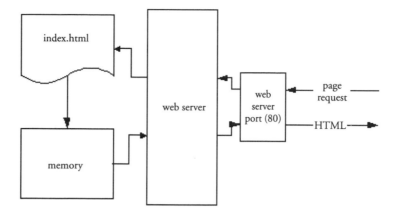

Figure 17-2. *Static Web server logic.*

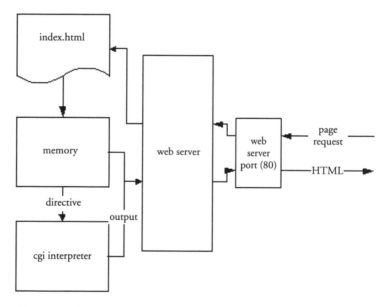

Figure 17-3. *Web server logic using CGI.*

sic to create "compiled" stand-alone applications or objects; VBScript is scripting only. If you have been exposed to Visual Basic, learning ASP will be that much easier.

Active server pages Web pages end with the extension .asp. When an .asp page is requested from an ASP-capable Web server (which will be assumed to be Windows NT 4.0 IIS for this chapter), the extension .asp tells the Web server, "be prepared to interpret any server-side scripting when reading in this page for delivery" (Figure 17-4). So, in addition to doing basic Web-server duties, there is now the additional responsibility

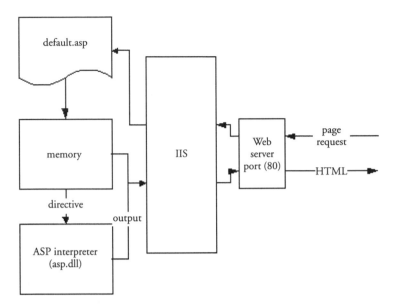

Figure 17-4. *IIS logic.*

of interpreting VBScript. This is the same scenario as running embedded CGI, just replace "CGI interpreter" with ASP interpreter (or asp.dll).

Notice that the Web page in question in Figure 17-4 is default.asp instead of index. html. Default.asp is what index.html is to non-IIS Web servers: the default or main page. IIS does support index.html also, and you can set IIS to make index.html your site's default page instead of default.asp. But the page must end in the extension .asp in order for the server to process the server-side VBScript. Otherwise, files ending with .htm or .html will be treated as basic HTML pages; any ASP code in these static pages will be unprocessed and displayed as text on the screen.

Time to Code

"How many programmers does it take to screw in a light bulb?"

"None. That's a hardware problem."

Now on to the fun stuff. ASP pages are coded using (at least) two languages combined: HTML and VBScript. The VBScript is intermingled with the HTML code. The following are three versions of everyone's favorite "Hello World." The first listing shows "Hello World" using just plain HTML:

```
<HTML>
<HEAD>
<TITLE>Hello World</TITLE>
```

```
</HEAD>
<BODY>
<CENTER>
<H1>Hello World</H1>
</BODY>
</HTML>
```

The following listing shows HTML with ASP "Hello World":

```
<HTML>
<HEAD>
<%
     ' dimension variables
     sTitle = "Hello World"
%>
<TITLE><%=sTitle%></TITLE>
</HEAD>
<BODY>
<CENTER>
<H1><%Response.write sTitle%></H1>
</BODY>
</HTML>
```

The next version is an all-ASP version:

```
<%
  response.write "<HTML>"
  response.write "<HEAD>"
  response.write "<TITLE>Hello World</TITLE>"
  response.write "</HEAD>"
  response.write "<BODY>"
  response.write "<CENTER>"
  response.write "<H1>Hello World</H1>"
  response.write "</BODY>"
  response.write "</HTML>"
%>
```

All three listings are very basic examples and all have the same results: "Hello World" in big letters centered on the screen. But for the Web server to the second and third listings, the Web server had to use its ASP-handling capabilities to interpret the VBScript. VBScript is presented between the <% . . . %> tags. When an ASP-capable server encounters <% as it reads in the page, the ASP interpreter processes all the following text until encountering the terminating %> tag. If you forget the closing tag you will most likely get an error. So, if the page is meant to be just a simple "Hello World," code it all in static HTML: this will be less work for the Web server to process. Lastly, run the third listing, then right-click on the Web page and select "View Source." You should see one long line of HTML code, not too pretty. To have each line of code presented as a separate line in the source, end each response.write line with "& vbCRLF" without quotes.

The Ten Squares Example

Here is another ASP example, called tensquares.asp:

```
<HTML>
<HEAD>
<TITLE>Ten Squares</TITLE>
</HEAD>
<BODY>
<CENTER>
<H1>Ten squares</H1>
<TABLE BORDER=1 WIDTH=400>
<TR>
<TD>   </TD>
<TD>   </TD>
<TD>   </TD>
<TD>   </TD>
<TD>   </TD>
<TD>   </TD>
</TR>
<TR>
<TD>   </TD>
<TD>   </TD>
<TD>   </TD>
<TD>   </TD>
<TD>   </TD>
<TD>   </TD>
</TR>
</TABLE>
</BODY>
</HTML>
```

What follows is a more maintainable, ASP version:

```
<HTML>
<HEAD>
<%'dimension variables
  Dim x
  Dim iTotalSquares
%>
<TITLE>Hello World</TITLE>
```

```
</HEAD>
<BODY>
<CENTER>
<H1>Ten Squares</H1>
<TABLE BORDER=1 WIDTH=400>
<TR>
<%iTotalSquares = 10
  For x = 1 to iTotalSquares
    If x = (iTotalSquares/2)+1 Then%>
    </TR>
    <TR>
  <%End If%>
  <TD>   </TD>
<%Next%>
</TR>
</TABLE>
</BODY>
</HTML>
```

While perhaps not too practical, the Ten Squares example shows two ways of presenting a grid of ten squares (see Figure 17-5). The ASP version has a For . . . Next loop (and one less line of code!). For each iteration in the loop a cell is drawn. If the iteration number (x)

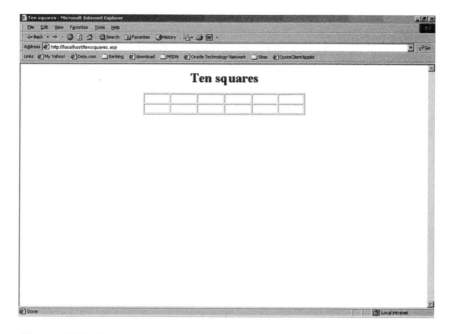

Figure 17-5. Tensquares.asp.

is greater than half the total number of squares, a new row is created. Now what if you wanted 12 squares? In the static HTML version you would have to code two more <TD></TD> pairs, as well as figure out where to put the <TR></TR> break to make the rows even on the top and bottom. For the ASP page, however, you just change the value of iTotalSquares to 12, and that's it; the logic in the For . . . Next loop takes care of the rest. This way, most of your work as a developer can go into coding the release version, rather than on forever maintaining the page.

The following listing is the ASP Ten Squares code, but now with the value of iTotal-Squares fed by parameter:

```
<HTML>
<HEAD>
<%'dimension variables
 Dim x
 Dim iTotalSquares

 'get/set variables
 iTotalSquares = Int(Request.QueryString("ts"))
 If iTotalSquares = 0 Then iTotalSquares = 4
%>
<TITLE>Hello World</TITLE>
</HEAD>
<BODY>
<CENTER>
<H1>Ten Squares</H1>
<TABLE BORDER=1 WIDTH=400>
<TR>
<%For x = 1 to iTotalSquares
  If x = (iTotalSquares/2)+1 Then%>
  </TR>
  <TR>
 <%End If%>
 <TD>   </TD>
<%Next%>
</TR>
</TABLE>

</BODY>
</HTML>
```

With the above example the number of squares presented on the page can be changed simply by changing the parameter you feed the page. To feed a page a parameter you follow the page name with a question mark, then parameters with their value: Pagename. asp?parameter=value.

Save the code as a page called tensquares.asp at the Web root of your Web server (i.e., c:\inetpub\wwwroot). Presently, when you want to call the page to see those ten squares, you type in the URL field of your Web browser http://localhost/tensquares.asp and the result is the page with the grid. Now, with the latest version, if you type http://localhost/tensquares.asp?ts=16 you will see a page with a grid of 16 squares, eight on top, eight on the bottom. If you don't provide a ts value, four squares will be drawn. The code examples up to now just offer a glimpse of the power VBScript makes available; for a more comprehensive reference visit http://msdn.microsoft.com/scripting and select VBScript. The key to success with active server pages is just plain playing around. I have learned the most by viewing other people's code and examples made available on the Web. Experiment with the Ten Squares example, make the squares different colors by using the <TD BGCOLOR="RED"> tag, put words in the cells, put the cell number in the cells by putting <%=x%> between the <TD></TD> tags. To creatively and effectively mix HTML and VBScript you need to get a feel for how they work together. And as you move on to JavaScript, you will see that mixing JavaScript and ASP can get really interesting, which is discussed later on.

Talking to the Database

Interfacing with a database is a very strong argument for using ASP. In just a handful of lines data can be retrieved and displayed on the page. A good starter database is one created in Microsoft Access (Access is an excellent learning tool for database design and SQL), and this section will offer examples that use an Access database. The example will be a simple Web-based address book. First, create a new Access database. This database will have one table called "person" with the structure shown in Figure 17-6. Set person_id as the primary key. Next, let's put some data in the database, as shown in Figure 17-7.

PERSON

Person_id	AUTONUMBER
First_name	TEXT (50)
Last_name	TEXT (50)
Phone_number	TEXT (50)

Figure 17-6. *Addresses database schema.*

Person_id	first_name	last_name	phone_number
1	Bill	Smith	713/ 555-1212
2	Ted	Johnson	914/ 555-1213
3	Susan	Williams	303/ 555-1214

Figure 17-7. *Person table data.*

Now that we have a database setup we need to make this database available for Web sites to connect to. For this example we will use ODBC, as this is the most common method. To create this data source, open the ODBC manager from Control Panels and do the followings steps:

1. Select the Microsoft Access Driver (*.mdb) and click "Finish" (see Figure 17-8).
2. Click the System tab and click "Add." For Data Source Name enter the name of the database (i.e., "addresses"). You can enter something like "Address Book" for the description (see Figure 17-9).
3. Click "Select . . ." and locate the .mdb file of the database you have created.
4. Click "OK" and you will then see your new data source listed (see Figure 17-10).

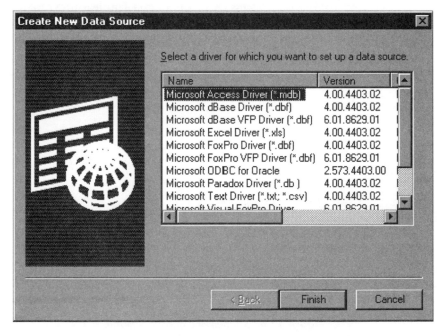

Figure 17-8. *Select Microsoft Access Driver (*.mdb) and click "Finish."*

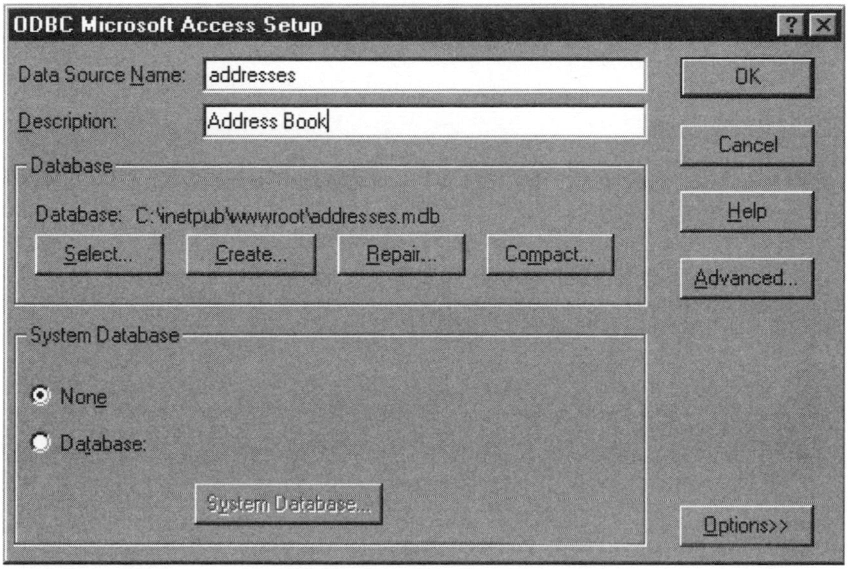

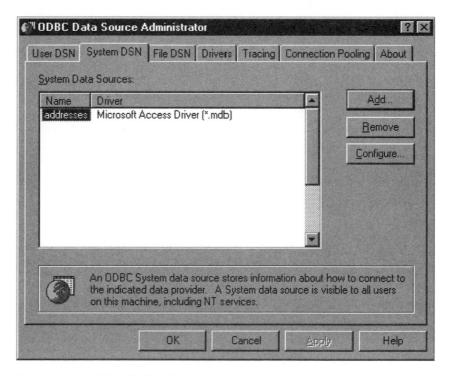

Figure 17-9. Enter Data Source Name, Description (optional),
and click "Select . . ." to select Access .mdb file.

Figure 17-10. Click "OK" and see data source "addresses" listed.

Figure 17-11. *Addresses.asp with form.*

Now let us create an ASP page to interface with this new data source. Below is the code for a page to be saved as addresses.asp (Figure 17-11):

```
<%'dimension variables
 Dim Conn
 Dim rsPeople
 Dim sSQL

 ' create db objects
 Set Conn = CreateObject("ADODB.Connection")
 Set rsPeople = CreateObject("ADODB.Recordset")

 ' open db connection
 Conn.Open "addresses"

 ' get list of people
 sSQL = "select person_id, first_name, last_name, phone_number
from person" & _
 " order by last_name asc"
   rsPeople.Open sSQL, Conn

%>
```

```
<HTML>
<HEAD>
<TITLE>Address Book</TITLE>
</HEAD>
<BODY BGCOLOR="#FFFFFF">
<CENTER>
<H1>Address Book</H1>
<BR>
<TABLE BORDER=1>
 <TR>
  <TH>Name</TH>
  <TH>Number</TH>
 </TR>
<%Do Until rsPeople.EOF%>
 <TR>
  <TD><%=rsPeople("last_name")%>,
<%=rsPeople("first_name")%></TD>
  <TD><%=rsPeople("phone_number")%></TD>
 </TR>
<% rsPeople.MoveNext
 Loop

  ' close and destroy db objects
 rsPeople.Close
 Set rsPeople = Nothing
 Conn.Close
 Set Conn = Nothing%>

</TABLE>

</BODY>
</HTML>
```

A quick dissection: The first part creates an ADO connection object that connects to the database, and an ADO record set object to hold information retrieved from the database. The next section is an HTML table. The rows of the table are drawn similar to the loop in the Ten Squares example, except in this case instead of using a For . . . Next loop a Do Until rsPeople.EOF loop is used. This loop will keep looping until the end of the record set is reached. Important: To iterate through the record set you must remember to include the MoveNext method (i.e., "rsPeople.MoveNext" in the loop). I have timed out many a server by forgetting this critical line. Without this line the loop continues ad infinitum because the end of the record-set is never reached without the MoveNext method.

The page is concluded with closing and destroying the database objects and </HTML> tag. Always stay in the habit of closing and destroying (i.e., Set Conn = Nothing) database objects as soon as possible. These database (ADO) objects can take up a lot of memory and should be managed aggressively to help ensure a responsive Web site.

Run addresses.asp and you should see a list of names and phone numbers. But what about adding entries? Sure, we could just use Access to open the database and type them in, but let's step into the Internet age and do it through the Web. Add a form to this page to allow you to enter data to be saved in the database. Add the following code beneath the </TABLE> tag:

```
<BR>
 <FORM NAME="frmMain" ACTION="saveentry.asp">
 First name: <INPUT TYPE="textbox" NAME="firstname" SIZE="20">
<BR>
 Last name: <INPUT TYPE="textbox" NAME="lastname" SIZE="20">
<BR>
 Phone number: <INPUT TYPE="textbox" NAME="phonenumber"
SIZE="15"> <BR><BR>
 <INPUT TYPE="submit" VALUE="Save entry">
 </FORM>
```

The action of this form is the name of the page to be redirected to when the form is submitted. When the form is submitted it will pass the names and values of the form controls (i.e., firstname, lastname, and phonenumber) to the action page (saveentry.asp). In other words, when values are entered into the form and Submit is clicked, the following line is fed to the URL field of your Web browser: http://localhost/saveentry.asp?firstname=John&lastname=Doe&phonenumber=408/555-1212.

But first the page saveentry.asp must be created. This page will never be seen by the user unless there is an error. It is intended to run on the server only, inserting the new entry information and redirecting the user back to addresses.asp. Below is the code for saveentry.asp:

```
<%On Error Resume Next

 ' dimension variables
 Dim Conn
 Dim sSQL
 Dim sFirstName, sLastName, sPhoneNumber

 ' get/set values
 sFirstName = Trim(Request.Querystring("firstname"))
 sLastName = Trim(Request.Querystring("lastname"))
 sPhoneNumber = Trim(Request.Querystring("phonenumber"))

 ' create db objects
 Set Conn = CreateObject("ADODB.Connection")
```

```
' open db connection
Conn.Open "addresses"

' insert entry
sSQL = "insert into person (first_name,last_name,phone_number)"
& _
  "values " & _
  "('" & sFirstName & "', '" & sLastName & "', '" & sPhoneNumber
& "')"

Err.Clear
Conn.Execute(sSQL)
If Err.Number <> 0 Then%>
 <HTML>
 <HEAD>
 <TITLE>ERROR</TITLE>
 </HEAD>
 <BODY>
 <CENTER>
 <H1>Error: Unable to save entry</H1>
 Error: <%=Err.description%><BR>
 Click 'back' to try again
 </BODY>
 </HTML>
<%End If

' close and destroy db objects
Conn.Close
Set Conn = Nothing

Response.redirect("addresses.asp")

%>
```

If the entry saves without error the user is immediately redirected to the address book page, displaying the new entry in the table. Note: By default Internet Explorer caches pages on your computer. While this can speed up the Web browsing experience, there is the chance you will not see changes made—you will be viewing a cached copy instead. This can get very frustrating, thinking your code change didn't take when all the while it's your browser that's the problem. In Internet Explorer go under Tools Internet Options; in the Temporary Internet Files frame click Settings; for "Check for newer versions of stored pages," select "Every Visit to the Page." This way, every time you request a page a fresh copy is always pulled from the server.

In saveentry.asp, if there is an error, ten lines of HTML code are written to the page to tell the user than an error has occurred. The On Error Resume Next line at the very top of the page enables ASP error handling. Otherwise, without error handling, user would receive cryptic server errors like "ADODB.Recordset error '800a0cc1' Item not found in this collection." What is a user going to do with that?

Now that we have a basic address book that entries can be added to, after using this a few times the need to edit and delete entries will be sorely missed. So let us add this functionality. First, change the loop that draws the list of addresses in addresses.asp to the following:

```
<%Do Until rsPeople.EOF%>
 <TR>
  <TD><A
HREF="editentry.asp?personid=<%=rsPeople("person_id")%>">
<%=rsPeople("last_name")%>, <%=rsPeople("first_name")%></A></TD>
  <TD><%=rsPeople("phone_number")%></TD>
 </TR>
<% rsPeople.MoveNext
 Loop
```

This will make each name a hyperlink, pointing to editentry.asp. The following is the code for a new page to be saved as editentry.asp:

```
<%'dimension variables
 Dim Conn
 Dim rsPerson
 Dim sSQL
 Dim iPersonID

 ' get/set values
 iPersonID = Int(Request.Querystring("personid"))

 ' create db objects
 Set Conn = CreateObject("ADODB.Connection")
 Set rsPerson = CreateObject("ADODB.Recordset")

 ' open db connection
 Conn.Open "addresses"

 ' get list of people
 sSQL = "select * from person where person_id = " & iPersonID
 rsPerson.Open sSQL, Conn
%>

<HTML>
<HEAD>
<TITLE>Edit Entry</TITLE>
<SCRIPT LANGUAGE="Javascript">
```

```
function confirmDelete(iPersonID) {
 if(confirm("Are you sure you want to delete this entry?"))
   document.location="saveentry.asp?personid=" + iPersonID +
"&mode=delete";
}

</SCRIPT>
</HEAD>
<BODY BGCOLOR="#FFFFFF">
<CENTER>
<H1>Edit Entry</H1>
<BR>
<FORM NAME="frmMain" ACTION="saveentry.asp">
<TABLE BORDER=1>
<TR>
 <TD><B>First Name</TD>
 <TD><INPUT TYPE="textbox" NAME="firstname"
VALUE="<%=rsPerson("first_name")%>"></TD>
</TR>
<TR>
 <TD><B>Last Name</TD>
 <TD><INPUT TYPE="textbox" NAME="lastname""
VALUE="<%=rsPerson("last_name")%>
"></TD>
</TR>
<TR>
 <TD><B>Phone Number</TD>
 <TD><INPUT TYPE="textbox" NAME="phonenumber"
VALUE="<%=rsPerson("phone_number")%>">></TD>
</TR>

<%
 ' close db objects
 rsPerson.Close
 Set rsPerson = Nothing
 Conn.Close
 Set Conn = Nothing%>

</TABLE>
<BR>
<BR>
<INPUT TYPE="submit" VALUE="Save Changes">
<INPUT TYPE="button" VALUE="Delete entry"
onClick="javascript:confirmDelete(<%=iPersonID%>)
">
</FORM>
</BODY>
</HTML>
```

As you probably notice, this page uses some JavaScript. Just as ASP gives power to the server when it renders and delivers Web pages, JavaScript adds power to the Web page on the client side. The JavaScript snippet in editentry.asp below is to confirm the user actually wants to delete the entry. The function confirmDelete takes one parameter, the person ID. If the user does click "OK" to the confirmation, the page is redirected to saveentry.asp, passing to this page the parameters person ID and mode. Now some changes need to be made to saveentry.asp to support both deleting and editing an entry. Right now, if you edit an entry and click "Save Changes" you will only add another entry. The following are new versions of saveentry.asp and editentry.asp:

```
'editentry.asp
<%'dimension variables
 Dim Conn
 Dim rsPerson
 Dim sSQL
 Dim iPersonID

 ' get/set values
 iPersonID = Int(Request.Querystring("personid"))

 ' create db objects
 Set Conn = CreateObject("ADODB.Connection")
 Set rsPerson = CreateObject("ADODB.Recordset")

 ' open db connection
 Conn.Open "addresses"

 ' get list of people
 sSQL = "select * from person where person_id = " & iPersonID
 rsPerson.Open sSQL, Conn
%>

<HTML>
<HEAD>
<TITLE>Edit Entry</TITLE>
<SCRIPT LANGUAGE="Javascript">
function confirmDelete(iPersonID) {
 if(confirm("Are you sure you want to delete this entry?")) {
  document.frmMain.mode.value="delete";
  document.frmMain.personid.value = iPersonID;
   document.location="saveentry.asp?personid=" + iPersonID +
"&mode=delete";
 }
}

function saveChanges(iPersonID) {
 document.frmMain.personid.value = iPersonID;
```

```
  document.frmMain.submit();
}
</SCRIPT>
</HEAD>
<BODY BGCOLOR="#FFFFFF">
<CENTER>
<H1>Edit Entry</H1>
<BR>
<FORM NAME="frmMain" ACTION="saveentry.asp"> <TABLE BORDER=1>
 <TR>
  <TD><B>First Name</TD>
  <TD><INPUT TYPE="textbox" NAME="firstname"
VALUE="<%=rsPerson("first_name")%>"></TD>
 </TR>
 <TR>
  <TD><B>Last Name</TD>
  <TD><INPUT TYPE="textbox" NAME="lastname"
VALUE="<%=rsPerson("last_name")%>"></TD>
 </TR>
 <TR>
  <TD><B>Phone Number</TD>
  <TD><INPUT TYPE="textbox" NAME="phonenumber"
VALUE="<%=rsPerson("phone_number")%>"></TD>
 </TR>

<%
 ' close db objects
 rsPerson.Close
 Set rsPerson = Nothing
 Conn.Close
 Set Conn = Nothing%>

</TABLE>
<BR>
<BR>
<INPUT TYPE="hidden" NAME="mode" VALUE="edit">
<INPUT TYPE="hidden" NAME="personid" VALUE="">
<INPUT TYPE="button" VALUE="Save Changes"
onClick="javascript:saveChanges(<%=iPersonID%>)">
<INPUT TYPE="button" VALUE="Delete entry"
onClick="javascript:confirmDelete(<%=iPersonID%>)">
</FORM>
</BODY>
</HTML>

'saveentry.asp
<%On Error Resume Next
 ' dimension variables
```

```
Dim Conn
Dim sSQL
Dim sFirstName, sLastName, sPhoneNumber
Dim sMode
Dim iPersonID

' get/set values
sFirstName = Trim(Request.Querystring("firstname"))
sLastName = Trim(Request.Querystring("lastname"))
sPhoneNumber = Trim(Request.Querystring("phonenumber"))
sMode = Trim(Request.Querystring("mode"))
iPersonID = Int(Request.Querystring("personid"))

' create db objects
Set Conn = CreateObject("ADODB.Connection")

' open db connection
Conn.Open "addresses"

Select Case sMode
  Case "delete"
    ' delete entry
    SSQL = "delete from person where person_id = " & iPersonID
  Case "edit"
    ' edit entry
    SSQL = "update person set" & _
      " first_name='" & sFirstName & "'" & _
      ", last_name='" & sLastName & "'" & _
      ", phone_number='" & sPhoneNumber & "'" & _
      " where person_id = " & iPersonID
  Case Else
    ' insert entry
    sSQL = "insert into person
(first_name,last_name,phone_number)" & _
    "values " & _
    "('" & sFirstName & "', '" & sLastName & "', '" &
sPhoneNumber & "')"
End Select

Err.Clear
Conn.Execute(sSQL)
If Err.Number <> 0 Then%>>
  <HTML>
  <HEAD>
  <TITLE>ERROR</TITLE>
  </HEAD>
  <BODY>
  <CENTER>
```

```
  <H1>Error: Unable to save entry</H1>
  Error: <%=Err.description%><BR>
  Click 'back' to try again
  </BODY>
  </HTML>
<%End If

  ' close and destroy db objects
  Conn.Close
  Set Conn = Nothing

  Response.redirect("addresses.asp")

%>
```

The new version of editentry.asp has some more JavaScript and a couple hidden form elements. The values of these hidden elements changed per the action (update or delete), their values changed by the JavaScript function at the top of the page. Netscape has a great JavaScript resource site at http://developer.netscape.com/tech/javascript/index.html.

The new version of saveentry.asp introduces the Select Case statement. Think of this as a better version of multiple if-then statements. This Select Case statement determines what SQL statement to execute; insert, update, or delete, based on the value of sMode. The Case Else is for when a value for sMode is not matched by any of the other Case statements. Therefore, if no mode is sent as a parameter to saveentry.asp, it defaults to insert, which then inserts the new entry into the database.

Conclusion

By reading this chapter you have now gained a Web-based address book and hopefully some knowledge about HTML, VBScript, SQL, and JavaScript. And you thought ASP was just one language! Again, I cannot stress enough the value of viewing the HTML code of other pages and experimenting with the code. This is what is so great about Web development, especially with ASP—it satisfies both sides of the brain!

References
1. WWW Consortium at http://www.w3.org.
2. Microsoft Scripting site at http://msdn.microsoft.com/scripting.
3. Netscape JavaScript development site at http://developer.netscape.com/tech/javascript/index.html.
4. http://www.15seconds.com.
5. http://www.4guysfromrolla.com.
6. http://www.aspkicker.com.

DON FRANKE is a programmer at a Fortune 500 technology company in Austin, Texas. He has written several technical articles on Web-related topics, and has worked for several high-tech companies in the Chicago area before uprooting his family for the warmer weather of the Southwest. He has two children, Ciana and Noah, and his wife, Lisa, without whose support such side projects as this could not be done. He can be reached at donfranke@yahoo.com.

How to Use ASP Classes

David Cline

The concept of objects in programming exists because objects simplify coding tasks. This is by no means the only reason, but for this discussion it will be our primary one.

Objects, or rather instances of them, um . . . what is an instance? Imagine an apple; that apple's image is a conceptual object, you can give it imagined properties: color, crispness, price, etc. But it doesn't exist, yet. But when you have purchased a Golden Delicious and are holding it in your hand—that we will consider an instance of our imagined apple object.

Our topic of examination in this chapter will be simplifying active server pages Web coding tasks by the use of classes (objects).

Classify Your Objects

To simplify, to ease one's Web creation and maintenance workload is a goal all Web developers strive for. To this goal we will explore the ASP Class concept:

```
Class cClassName
    Public vVariableName1
    Private vVariableName2
    Public Property Let Prop2(byval vValue)
      vVariableName2 = vValue
    End Property
    Public Property Get Prop2()
      Prop2 = vVariableName2
    End Property
    Public Sub SubOne([var1,var2, . . . ])
    End Sub
    Public Function FuncOne([var1,var2, . . . ])
      FuncOne = vValue
```

```
      End Function
      Private Sub Class_Initialize()
      End Sub
      Private Sub Class_Terminate()
      End Sub
   End Class
```

We will begin by designing with a bit of abstraction and objectifying (yes, it's in the dictionary!) using the ASP Class construct to encapsulate both functional code and functional concept in an easy-to-use and easy-to-understand package.

Now let's put our apple instance back in the fridge and use another object, one that performs work; how about your car? To start your car's engine you might do the following:

1. Insert key.
2. Turn key.
3. Listen to engine turning over.
4. Release key when engine starts.
5. Stop if engine cranks for more than ten seconds.
6. Repeat if engine not started.
7. Stop after ten tries (or when battery is dead).

Instead of these lengthy steps (okay, they're not that lengthy, but for my '67 Barracuda they would be) you could construct a car object and do this:

```
Set car = new cCar
car.start myKey
```

With our car object we've simplified the "lengthy" starting sequence substantially. By objectifying our vehicle into a generic car object and abstracting the starting process into a single object method or command, I'd have to say starting a car couldn't be much simpler.

Now our lengthy sequence didn't just disappear. No, we still have to "insert key" and "repeat if not started" but we've taken those steps and hidden them within our object. We've simplified a complex process by hiding the inherent complexity.

Months down the road, 'scuse the pun, when we need to start our car and because our Web developing lives are so detailed and demanding, we've managed to forget *how* to start our car. Instead of looking up the lengthy sequence in our car manual we just use our handy car object and its equally handy method "car.start(key)" and off we go, tooling down the highway.

Okay, stepping away from such poetic analogies (yeah right), allow me to cut right to how an ASP Class might be constructed and used. We will consider the words "class" and "object" as equivalent here.

```
<%
Class cPerson
    Public id
    Public firstName
    Public lastName
    Public birthDay
    Private mEmail
    Public Property Let email(vEmail)
      mEmail = vEmail
    End Property
    Public Property Get email()
      email = mEmail
    End Property
    Public Property Get fullName()
      fullName = firstName & " " & lastName
    End Property
End Class
%>
```

The class "cPerson" represents a person object. The "c" at the beginning is just my shorthand for saying "class." Our person object has six properties: id, firstName, lastName, birthDay, email and fullName. You'll notice that four of them are declared "Public":

1. Public id
2. Public firstName
3. Public lastName
4. Public birthDay

This means that we have placed them within our person class and given access to them to the public or to other code outside of this class. One property, mEmail, is declared "private":

```
Private mEmail
```

This signifies that only code within this person class can use or even see this property. We have, however, exposed mEmail through a formal property declaration; that is, Let email and Get email.

```
Public Property Let email(vEmail)
    mEmail = vEmail
```

```
End Property
Public Property Get email()
   email = mEmail
End Property
```

This formal property works the same way as declaring it "Public" but wrapping it all up in Lets and Gets allows us to perform additional manipulations of what the property does or what its value is. Which methodology should you choose? It's really up to you. Technically, properties should be declared formally using private variables to store their values. But that may entail numerous Lets and Gets, which end up adding little to no value. I opt for public variable declaration when no additional processing or validation is necessary; otherwise I prefer formal property declaration. Now notice the property fullName:

```
Public Property Get fullName()
   fullName = firstName & " " & lastName
End Property
```

This demonstrates that we can assemble existing class properties (and methods) into extended properties that simplify the use of our person class.

Now, to perform work inside our person class. Adding the below code to our cPerson class will allow us to retrieve the age in days for our person:

```
Public Function daysAlive()
   If Not isDate(birthDay) Then Exit Function
   daysAlive = datediff("d", birthDay, Date())
End Function
```

Demonstrating the use of this class we have the following:

```
<!--#include file="classes/cPerson.clas"-->
<%
   Dim person
   Set person = New cPerson
   person.firstName = "Billy Bob"
   person.lastName = "Thorton"
   person.birthDay = "4/15/49"
   Response.Write person.fullName & " has been alive for " & _
   person.daysAlive & " days."
   Set person = Nothing
%>
```

And behold, our person class has come to life. "Igor, it's alive!"

Now, maybe your definition of life is a bit more, shall we say, vivacious than what we've shown so far. Never fear. After we review the mechanics we'll get right back into building the perfect beast—and saving you time, as well.

ASP Class General Syntax

As we saw on the first page of this chapter:

```
<%
Class cClassName
    Public vVariableName1
    Private vVariableName2

Public Property Let Prop2(byval vValue)
    vVariableName2 = vValue
    End Property
    Public Property Get Prop2()
      Prop2 = vVariableName2
    End Property

Public Sub SubOne([var1,var2, . . . ])
    End Sub

Public Function FuncOne([var1,var2, . . . ])
      FuncOne = vValue
    End Function
Private Sub Class_Initialize()
End Sub

Private Sub Class_Terminate()
End Sub
End Class
%>
```

The structure is really quite simple. We have a class declaration:

```
Class cClassName
End Class
```

A few variable declarations:

```
Public vVariableName1
Private vVariableName2
```

A property (or two, the public "vVariableName1" is really a property, too):

```
Public Property Let Prop2(byval vValue)
   vVariableName2 = vValue
End Property
Public Property Get Prop2()
   Prop2 = vVariableName2
End Property
```

A subroutine and a function:

```
Public Sub SubOne([var1,var2, . . . ])
End Sub

Public Function FuncOne([var1,var2, . . . ])
   FuncOne = vValue
End Function
```

And two private events:

```
Private Sub Class_Initialize()
End Sub

Private Sub Class_Terminate()
End Sub
```

I've included every possible bit of functionality here just to show the complete picture of what a class may encompass. From a minimalist's perspective, the class declaration could be the only part of our class we need to include. But it wouldn't do much. At least a variable or two would be necessary for the class to actually provide any value in programming.

A class's variables (properties) are its personal property. They hold the primitives and objects that comprise the class's personality and parts. All variables of an ASP Class are variants (as well as all variables in general within VBScript). When I say primitives I mean numbers, strings (character data), and arrays all stored as variants. A class can contain other objects, also stored as variants, such as a person class having multiple address class objects contained within it or perhaps a file utility class having an instance of "Scripting.FileSystemObject" contained within.

For instance:

```
Class cPerson

   Public id
   Public name
   Private address1
   Private address2

   Private Sub Class_Initialize()
      Set address1 = New cAddress
      Set address2 = New cAddress
   End Sub
End Class

Class cAddress
   Public address
   Public city
   Public state
   Public zip
End Class

Class cFileUtility
   Private FSO
   Public Property Get Folder(Byval strFolderPath)
      Set Folder = FSO.GetFolder(strFolderPath)
   End Property
   Private Sub Class_Initialize()
      Set FSO = Server.CreateObject("Scripting.FileSystemObject")
   End Sub
End Class
```

Formally declared properties:

```
Public Property Let Prop1(byval vValue)
   vVariableName2 = vValue
End Property
Public Property Get Prop1()
   Prop1 = vVariableName2
End Property
```

As mentioned above, formally declared properties are the prescribed method of exposing a class's variables. Simply opening up your class's variables by "Public vVariable1" is not considered appropriate programming standards. Well, okay, but this simpler method requires about one-fifth of the typing and for most of my purposes doesn't leave me in too much of a compromising position. Formal properties come into play when either validation or post/pre-assignment processing is in order.

Say you had a property "phoneNumber" and you wanted to make sure you had at least ten digits in your property variable after being set by the owner of your class:

```
Private vPhone
Public Property Let phoneNumber(byval vPhoneNum)
    Dim rawNumber
    rawNumber = vPhoneNum
    rawNumber = replace(rawNumber,"-","")
    rawNumber = replace(rawNumber,"(","")
    rawNumber = replace(rawNumber,")","")
    rawNumber = replace(rawNumber,".","")

    If Len(rawNumber) < 10 Then _
       Err.Raise 29292, "", "Phone::Number::Incomplete Phone
       Number"
    If Not IsNumeric(rawNumber) Then _
       Err.Raise 29292, "", "Phone::Number::Non Numeric Phone
       Number"

    vPhone = rawNumber
  End Property

  Public Property Get phoneNumber()
    Number = vPhone
  End Property
```

Here we clean the incoming phone number, check it for length and numeric consistency, and store it. I've opted to raise an error if validation fails, but one would probably rather set an error string to indicate back to the user the phone number problem.

Subroutines and functions operate just like they might outside of a class structure. Subroutines execute code and do not return a result; functions (may) return a variant value. However, to execute a class-owned routine the name of the instance of the class must prefix the routine:

```
Class cClass
   Public Sub SubOne(var1)
     Response.Write var1 & "<br>"
   End Sub

   Public Function FuncOne(var1, var2)
     FuncOne = var1 & var2
   End Function
End Class

Dim myClass
Set myClass = new cClass
```

```
'-- run the subroutine--
myClass.SubOne "bingo"

'-- run the function--
Response.Write myClass.FuncOne("bingo", 12)

Set myClass = Nothing
```

Lastly in our discussion of ASP Class syntax—the two "events":

```
Private Sub Class_Initialize()
End Sub

Private Sub Class_Terminate()
End Sub
```

These are intended to provide a location for initialization code and cleanup code. These events get "fired" when, respectively, the New keyword is used to create an instance of a class

```
Dim myClass
Set myClass = New cClass
```

and when the object is destroyed, either through the use of the Nothing keyword

```
Set myClass = Nothing
```

or when the object goes out of scope. This could happen when the ASP engine releases the executing page code for the Response buffer contents return to the browser, or, if the object was declared within a subroutine or function, when the routine ends.

```
Sub TestObjectDestroy()
   Dim myClass
   Set myClass = New cClass
   MyClass.firstName = "David"
End Sub
```

The class instance myClass will be destroyed as the subroutine TestObjectDestroy complete execution.

A Few Technical Points

While we're on the internals of ASP Classes, you should be made aware of a couple of caveats. First, you'll want to avoid circular references. Example: Object A owns a reference to object B and object B owns a reference to object A. When both objects go out of scope or are destroyed by being set to Nothing, the memory each was occupying will not be released because there is one remaining reference to each object just hangin' about. As long as a reference to an object is left floating (ghosted), the memory cannot be reclaimed.

```
Class cExample
    Dim classHandle
End Class

Set A = New cExample
Set B = New cExample

Set A.classHandle = B
Set B.classHandle = A

Set A = Nothing
Set B = Nothing
```

The classHandle for each class instance was left holding the bag. And since we no longer have access to the A or B objects, we cannot retrieve the memory held by each; ergo, memory leak.

When the script engine is taken out of memory by shutting down either the IIS process or the COM+ host process, the lost memory would be reclaimed. But this may take a while (how often do you shut down a production Web server?). Better to be careful and be mindful of such circular, covetous code.

Caveat two: class persistence. One might be led to believe that once one creates and populates a class instance, say our above cPerson object, that that object might be storable (persisted) in the Application or Session ASP objects.

```
Dim person
Set person = New cPerson
Person.firstName = "Bob"
Set Session("myPerson") = person
```

Then, later, in a subsequent page,

```
Dim person
Set person = Session("myPerson")
Response.Write person.firstName
```

Sorry. No can do. As these classes are constructs created within the scripting engine; they vanish when the scripting engine goes out of scope. Currently there is no way to persist such a class (e.g., Java's serializable interface). There are ways, though, to persist the data held within the class to either a database, a cookie, or file system record-set—subsequently reconstituting the class on demand from the persisted data source.

VBScript or JScript

In this section we'll discuss the differences between using VBScript and JScript in writing our scripting classes.

Yes, classes can be written in JScript (JavaScript). In fact, objectifying data within JavaScript has been possible since early versions of JavaScript.

```
<script language=Jscript runat=server>

function cApple(variety, color, crispness, price, weight){
    this.variety = variety;
    this.color = color;
    this.crispness = crispness;
    this.price = price;
    this.weight = weight;
}
myApple = new cApple('Granny Smith','green',4,.45,.60)

</script>
```

Here we declare our apple object using a function as a class constructor (the code that actually causes the object to be created). Within the function the keyword "this" is used to reference the properties of the function (now a class).

To add more than just properties to a JavaScript class, we can even assign other functions to our original constructor function.

```
function fJuice(){
    if(this.crispness >= 3){
      return this.weight/5;
    }else{
      return this.weight/3;
    }
}
function cApple(. . . . .){
    this. . . ;
    this.juice = fJuice;
}
```

This is really just a tease to tempt you into learning on your own about JavaScript classes. As for a complete explanation of such code, I'd like to point you to some excellent references on JavaScript classes (found at the end of the chapter) where you can discover just how versatile they are. For consistency's sake I'll be sticking to VBScript classes.

Which language should you use to build your classes? It's really up to you. VBScript classes appear to be more formal and easier to write and understand. JScript classes have built-in circular reference traps and are capable of pseudo-inheritance as well as the prototype feature, which is sort of a method overloading (having routines of the same name accept alternate parameters as well as performing different functions). VBScript is VB-like in syntax, which sports millions of developers. JScript has a C-like syntax, which results in much shorter code than VBScript's. VBScript is English-like, with little convoluted coding styles. JScript supports inline conditions (var==2?'Monday','Tuesday'). JScript has both single-line and multiline comments. JScript fully supports optional arguments in functions. JScript fully supports try, catch, and throw, resulting in specific and concise error handling. Many people use JScript on the client side, and it's much easier to use the same language on the server side, as well.

We could go on for some time (maybe another minute, at least), but when it all boils down, your choice depends on, well, you.

Simple Examples

Hello World Class

```
'—- definition—-
Class cHello
   Public Sub sayHelloWorld (byval vPerson)
     Response.Write "Yo " & vPerson & ", Hello World."
   End Sub
End Class

'—- usage—-
Dim myHello
Set myHello = New cHello
myHello.sayHelloWorld "Bob"
Set myHello = Nothing
```

Code Timer Class (This is a JScript Class file—the reason we use JScript here is because it allows millisecond precision using the getTime() function.)

```
<script language="jScript" runat="server">
//~~~ CLASS DECLARATION ~~~~~~~~~~~~~
```

```
   function timer(){
   //—- internal variables
     var datStarted = null;
     var datStopped = null;

   //—- assign functions as methods
     this.start = fStart;
     this.stop = fStop;
     this.diffMils = fDiffMils;
     this.displayFormatted = fDisplayFormatted;
   }
//~~~~~~~~~~~~~~~~~~~~~~~~~~~
   function fStart(){
 var d = new Date();
 this.datStarted = d.getTime();
   }
//~~~~~~~~~~~~~~~~~~~~~~~~~~~
   function fStop(v){
 var d = new Date();
 this.datStopped = d.getTime();
   }
//~~~~~~~~~~~~~~~~~~~~~~~~~~~
   function fDiffMils(){
     return this.datStopped—this.datStarted;
   }
//~~~~~~~~~~~~~~~~~~~~~~~~~~~
   function fDisplayFormatted(){
   var intDiff = this.datStopped—this.datStarted;
 var diffSecs = 0;
 var diffMins = 0;

 diffSecs = Math.floor(intDiff/1000);
 intDiff = intDiff % 1000;

 diffMins = Math.floor(diffSecs/60);
 diffSecs = diffSecs % 60;

   var strOut = "Timer Result: "
       + ('00' + diffMins.toString()).right(2) + ":"
         + ('00' + diffSecs.toString()).right(2) + "."
         + (('00' +
Math.round(intDiff/10).toString()).right(2)).substr(0,2);
   response.write(strOut);
   }
//~~~ CONSTRUCTOR ~~~~~~~~~~~
   function cTimer(){
     return(new timer());
   }
```

```
//~~~~~~~~~~~~~~~~~~~~~~~~~~~~~
 function stringReverse () {
  var r = '';
  for (var i = this.length—1; i >= 0; i—){
  r += this.charAt(i);}
  return r;
 }
 String.prototype.reverse = stringReverse;

//~~~~~~~~~~~~~~~~~~~~~~~~~~~~~
 function stringRight(intChars) {
     return this.reverse().substr(0, intChars).reverse();
 }
 String.prototype.right = stringRight;

//  var strTest = "1234567890";
//  response.write("test:"+strTest.right(5));
</script>

<!—#INCLUDE file="Classes/cTimer.clas"—>
<%'—- usage—-
   Dim timer
   Set timer = cTimer()
   timer.start
   For i = 0 to 123456 'complex loop
      j = s/33 + .999
   Next
   timer.stop
   Response.Write timer.diffMils() & "<br>"
   timer.displayFormatted
%>
```

Let me make a few points about this class file. First, to instantiate a JScript class from VB, a special "constructor" function must be provided that creates a new object within JScript first and then passes this object (or its reference) back to the calling VBScript code:

```
//~~~ CONSTRUCTOR ~~~~~~~~~~~
   function cTimer(){
     return(new timer());
   }
```

Second, notice the VBScript code that calls this function:

```
Set timer = cTimer()
```

The fact that there is no "New" keyword in this code line is not a mistake. The "constructor" function already created a new class instance (object) and here we are only assigning it a local handle.

Two additional items of interest in this code are the

```
String.prototype.reverse = stringReverse;
```

and

```
String.prototype.right = stringRight;
```

These two lines extend the "String" object with additional functionality. This is an example of one of the benefits of JScript mentioned above. Used here, these two extensions provide "reverse" and "right" capabilities, which JScript does not inherently provide.

Event Logger Class

```
<%
Const    SUCCESS = 0
Const    ERROR = 1
Const    WARNING = 2
Const    INFORMATION = 4
Const    AUDIT_SUCCESS = 8
Const    AUDIT_FAILURE = 16

Class cEventLogger

    Public Sub Post(intType, strMessage)
      Set WshShell = Server.CreateObject("WScript.Shell")
      Set WshNetwork =
      Server.CreateObject("WScript.Network")

      WshShell.LogEvent intType, strMessage & _
        "Domain = " & WshNetwork.UserDomain & ": " & _
        "Computer Name = " & WshNetwork.ComputerName & ":
        " & _
        "User Name = " & WshNetwork.UserName
    End Sub
End Class
%>

<!--#INCLUDE file="Classes/cEventLogger.clas"-->
<%
```

```
'—- usage—-
Dim myEventLogger
Set myEventLogger = New cEventLogger
Dim myConnection
Set myConnection = Server.CreateObject("ADODB.Connection")
myConnection.Open "DSN=privateDB;USR=sa;PWD="
If err
   Then myEventLogger.Post ERROR, "Connection to privateDB
failed"
   Response.End
End If
%>
```

This class contains scripting components, namely the "Network" and "Shell" components, which are part of the Windows Scripting Host. These interfaces give access to some of the basic environment objects found in Windows. They are quite powerful (e.g., Wscript.Shell.Run()) and must be used with care and understanding. These same objects have been used by such viruses as "Melissa" and the "I Love You" virus. Here we use them for the much more benign use of logging an event into the Application Event Log.

Database Class

```
<!—metadata name="Microsoft ActiveX Data Objects 2.5 Library"
   type="TypeLib" uuid="{00000205-0000-0010-8000-
   00AA006D2EA4}"—>
<%
Class cDatabase
   private mConn
   private mDatabaseLocation
   public Debug
   private mError
   private mErrorDescription

   '~~~~~~~~~~~~~~~~~~~~~~~~~~~~~~~~~~~~~~~~~~~~
   Function getConnection()
   If Not Debug Then On Error Resume Next
    Dim strDataPath

   If Not IsObject(mconn) Then
       If mDatabaseLocation = "" Then
         errorRaise 911, "class::database::Database
         location not set"
         Exit Function
       End If
```

```
      set mconn = Server.CreateObject("ADODB.Connection")
        If Lcase(Left(mDatabaseLocation, 3)) = ".mdb"
        Then
         strDataPath = "DBQ=" &
          server.mappath(mDatabaseLocation)
          mconn.Open "DRIVER={Microsoft Access Driver
(*.mdb)};" & _
           strDataPath
        Else
        mconn.Open mDatabaseLocation
        End If

     If Err.Number <> 0 Then
         mError = Err.Number
         mErrorDescription = "An error occured
         connecting to the " & _
         "database: " & strDataPath & ":" &
         Err.Description
    End If
    End If

    Set getConnection = mconn
  End Function

'~~~~~~~~~~~~~~~~~~~~~~~~~~~~~~~~~~~~~~~~~~~
  Function getRecordset(sql)
    If Not Debug Then On Error Resume Next
   If Not IsObject(mconn) Then
      getConnection
    End If

   Dim tempRs
   Set tempRs = mconn.Execute(sql)
   If Err.Number <> 0 Then
      mError = Err.Number
   mErrorDescription = "An error occured executing this SQL:
   " & _
      sql & ":" & Err.Description
   End If
   Set getRecordset = tempRs
   Set tempRs = Nothing
  End Function

'~~~~~~~~~~~~~~~~~~~~~~~~~~~~~~~~~~~~~~~~~~~
  Function execute(sql)
    If Not Debug Then On Error Resume Next
   If Not IsObject(mconn) Then
      getConnection
    End If
```

```vb
        mconn.Execute sql

    If Err.Number <> 0 Then
        mError = Err.Number
    mErrorDescription = "An error occured executing this SQL:
     " & _
        sql & ":" & Err.Description
    End If
  End Function


'~~~~~~~~~~~~~~~~~~~~~~~~~~~~~~~~~~~~~~~~~~~
  Public Sub beginTrans()
   If Not IsObject(mconn) Then
        getConnection
    End If
   If Not IsObject(mConn) Then Exit Sub
    mConn.BeginTrans
  End Sub


'~~~~~~~~~~~~~~~~~~~~~~~~~~~~~~~~~~~~~~~~~~~
  Public Sub rollbackTrans()
    If Not IsObject(mConn) Then Exit Sub
    mConn.RollbackTrans
  End Sub


'~~~~~~~~~~~~~~~~~~~~~~~~~~~~~~~~~~~~~~~~~~~
  Public Sub commitTrans()
    If Not IsObject(mConn) Then Exit Sub
    mConn.CommitTrans
  End Sub
''~~~~~~~~~~~~~~~~~~~~~~~~~~~~~~~~~~~~~~~~~~
  Public Property Let databaseLocation(v)
    mDatabaseLocation = v
  End Property


'~~~~~~~~~~~~~~~~~~~~~~~~~~~~~~~~~~~~~~~~~~~
  Public Property Get databaseLocation()
    databaseLocation = mDatabaseLocation
  End Property


'~~~~~~~~~~~~~~~~~~~~~~~~~~~~~~~~~~~~~~~~~~~
  Sub printRecordset(rs)
   Dim fld, intCols
   If Not IsObject(rs) Then Exit Sub
   Response.write "<table border=1>"
    If rs.EOF Then
    Response.write "<tr><td>" & "Recoredset is
    empty" & _
```

```
                    "</td></tr>"
      Else
      Response.write "<tr>"
        For Each fld In rs.Fields
          Response.write "<th>" & "<font size=2
          face=""arial "">" & _
          fld.Name & " </th>"
        Next
          Response.write "</tr>"

        Do While Not rs.EOF
          Response.write "<tr>"
        For Each fld In rs.Fields
          Response.write "<td>" & "<font size=2
          face=""arial "">" &
          fld & " </td>"
        Next
          Response.write "</tr>"
            rs.MoveNext
        Loop
      End If
    Response.write "</table>"
    End Sub

'~~~~~~~~~~~~~~~~~~~~~~~~~~~~~~~~~~~~~~~~~~
    Public Property Get error()
      Error = mError
    End Property


'~~~~~~~~~~~~~~~~~~~~~~~~~~~~~~~~~~~~~~~~~~
    Public Sub errorRaise(errNum, errDesc)
      mError = errNum
      mErrorDescription = errDesc
    End Sub


'~~~~~~~~~~~~~~~~~~~~~~~~~~~~~~~~~~~~~~~~~~
    Public Sub errorClear()
      mError = 0
      mErrorDescription = ""
    End Sub


'~~~~~~~~~~~~~~~~~~~~~~~~~~~~~~~~~~~~~~~~~~
    Public Property Get ErrorDescription()
      ErrorDescription = mErrorDescription
    End Property


'~~~~~~~~~~~~~~~~~~~~~~~~~~~~~~~~~~~~~~~~~~
    Private Sub Class_Initialize()
```

```
    End Sub

'~~~~~~~~~~~~~~~~~~~~~~~~~~~~~~~~~~~~~~~~~~
    Private Sub Class_Terminate()
      Set mconn = Nothing
    End Sub
End Class
%>
```

Ah, yes, a favorite class of mine, the database class. What better way of easing code maintenance than by wrapping up often used and sometimes troublesome database calls. You will want to experiment with this class, as there are many ways to skin a database and the ways I've shown here may not necessarily be your own.

For starters I'll point out that when used, this class needs no more setup than to set the "databaseLocation" with an appropriate DSN string (either ODBC or OLEDB—I prefer file-based UDL files calling OLEDB) and fetching a record-set.

```
<!-#INCLUDE file="Classes/cDatabase.clas"->
<%
Const DATABASE_NAME_LOCATION = "../data/MyData.mdb"
Const DEBUG_MODE = True

dim myDatabase, rs
Set myDatabase = New cDatabase

myDatabase.debug = DEBUG_MODE
myDatabase.databaseLocation = DATABASE_NAME_LOCATION

Set rs = myDatabase.getRecordset("SELECT * FROM authors")
If Not rs.EOF Then
    Do While Not rs.EOF
      Response.Write rs("name") & "<br>"
      rs.MoveNext
    Loop
End If

If myDatabase.error Then Response.Write
myDatabase.errorDescription
Set myDatabase = Nothing
%>
```

Within the "getRecordset" function a check is made to make sure we have an open connection. If a connection is not found, then getConnection automatically creates one. This class is rudimentary and should be updated to use the more efficient "Command" object, but for simple use it is sufficient.

You'll notice that the ADODB.Connection's Transaction capability is also wrapped within this class. So if you really wanted, you could perform multiple "myDatabase. execute()"s within a connection-based transaction of your own creation. You would want to actually do this only if you were, perhaps, hitting multiple record sources or placing a CyberSource credit card order as well as updating an orders database. For database-only transactions the preferred method is to wrap database DML (data modification language) calls in stored procedures.

Cookie Class

```
<%
'~~~~~~~~~~~~~~~~~~~~~~~~~~~~~~~~~~~~~~~~~~~~~~~~~~
'-- dim a new Xession class and instance it--Const
A_SESSION_USES_COOKIE = 1
Const A_SESSION_INFO_COOKIE = "WebXession"
Const A_SESSION_COOKIE_SCOPE_DOMAIN = 0
Const A_MY_DOMAIN = ".mountainstream.com"

Public Xession
Set Xession = New cXession

'~~~ Class definition ~~~~~~~~~~~~~~~~~~~~~~~~~~~~
Class cXession

'-- NOTE the "Default" here----------
   Public Default Property Get Item(vntName)
     If A_SESSION_USES_COOKIE Then
        Item =
        Request.Cookies(A_SESSION_INFO_COOKIE)(vntName)
     Else
        Item = Session(vntName)
     End If
   End Property
'~~~~~~~~~~~~~~~~~~~~~~~~~~~~~~~~~~~~~~~~~~~~~~~~~~
   Public Property Let Item (vntName, vntValue)
     If IsNull(vntValue) Then Exit Property
     If IsEmpty(vntName) Then Exit Property
     If vntName = "" Then Exit Property
     If A_SESSION_USES_COOKIE Then
       If A_SESSION_COOKIE_SCOPE_DOMAIN Then
     Response.Cookies(A_SESSION_INFO_COOKIE).Domain =
     A_MY_DOMAIN
       End If
       Response.Cookies(A_SESSION_INFO_COOKIE)(vntNa
me)
       = vntValue
```

```
      Else
      Session(vntName)  = vntValue
      End If
   End Property
End Class
%>
```

Looking at this simple class one would not immediately appreciate its beauty. This class actually performs miracles. Well, not real, bona fide miracles, but, well, have a look at this:

```
<!-#INCLUDE file="Classes/cXession.clas"->
<%
Xession("firstName") = "Bob"
Xession("birthLocation") = "Kalamazoo"
Response.Write "Hello" & Xession("firstName") & " from " &
Xession("birthLocation") & "."
%>
```

And not only that, but since all data is saved in the cookie, on a subsequent ASP page we can, without resetting Bob's Xession level variables, do this:

```
<!-#INCLUDE file="Classes/cXession.clas"->
<%
Response.Write "Thanks " & Xession("firstName") & " for
visiting.<br>" Response.Write "Say HI to your friends in " &
Xession("birthLocation")
%>
```

The skinny on how this works is this: We use a "Default" keyword on the "Get" function on the "item" property of this class. This means that when a handle to the class is referenced without a specific property or method attached (e.g., Xession and not Xession.extraMethod), the default property of "item" is assumed. Also, cookies are domain- and directory-specific. With the inclusion of the below line:

```
Const A_MY_DOMAIN = "mountainstream.com"
```

All cookies written will be accessible by any host within the mountainstream.com domain, as well as any directory upstream in the directory tree; for example, "www.mountainstream.com/testing/source." We could have included a specific directory path on the cookie, but that would defeat our purposes. Also, you'll notice we do not have an "Expires" specified on the cookie. This means our cookie is Session-based and will not be saved to the Web guest's hard drive.

With this class, and pay close attention here, your server farm can now be stateless! That's right—turn off those ASP Sessions. Throw away Site Servers SQLServer–based state management. You can use this class anywhere you used the old Session. With two exceptions: one, keep the size of your total cookie to less than 3kb. Two, no variables beyond primitive can be stored here (arrays included). You can store numbers, strings, and dates—that's all. Of course, for good state management that should be enough, right?

Response Wrapper

```
<%
const CACHE_SIZE = 1000 'lines to buffer

Class cResponseWrapper
    dim aCache
    dim intNextSlot
    dim sv

    Public Sub write(s)
      aCache(intNextSlot) = s
      intNextSlot = intNextSlot + 1
    End Sub
'~~~~~~~~~~~~~~~~~~~~~~~~~~~~~~~~~~~~~~~~~~~
    Public Sub writenl(s)
      aCache(intNextSlot) = s & "<br>"
      intNextSlot = intNextSlot + 1
    End Sub
'~~~~~~~~~~~~~~~~~~~~~~~~~~~~~~~~~~~~~~~~~~~
    Public Property Get size()
      size = Len(Join(aCache,""))
    End Property
'~~~~~~~~~~~~~~~~~~~~~~~~~~~~~~~~~~~~~~~~~~~
    Public Sub flush()
      Response.write Join(aCache,"")
      aCache = array(intCache)
    End Sub

'~~~~~~~~~~~~~~~~~~~~~~~~~~~~~~~~~~~~~~~~~~~
    Public Function getSV()
      getSV = sv("ALL_HTTP")
    End Function

'~~~~~~~~~~~~~~~~~~~~~~~~~~~~~~~~~~~~~~~~~~~
    Private Sub Class_Initialize()
```

```
        redim aCache(CACHE_SIZE)
        Set sv = Request.ServerVariables()
    End Sub


'~~~~~~~~~~~~~~~~~~~~~~~~~~~~~~~~~~~~~~~~~~~~~~
    Private Sub Class_Terminate()
        Response.write "Class TermTest Terminate"
        Response.write Join(aCache,"")
        Set sv = Nothing
    End Sub


end class
%>
```

This class is mainly a toy. I included it here for one reason, to show that you can wrap other objects in ASP Classes within which you can modify how the "base" class handles properties and methods.

Here we wrap the intrinsic Response object and provide our own "buffered" output capability. With this you could: cache often used page parts, cache whole pages (both in application variables), dump the entire buffered response to disk in HTML files for static serving, and optimize string concantenation calls (VBScript string concantenation is one of the slowest around).

You'll see we loaded up a class property with the entire content of the ServerVariable "ALL_HTTP," which we could log to our cEventLogger if we wanted to trap absolutely all information about a request during an error condition.

Presentation Class

Optimizing our time (yes, we're still working on that) remains primary in our Web lives. Intelligent consolidation of code into like-minded modules is a great way to leverage our limited time. For instance, presentation HTML tends to be scattered all around our sites. A header done this way, a footer done that way, navigation links coded higgledy-piggledy mixed with images and tables all coded whichever way was popular at one time. Adding new pages into such a Web-stew makes for a maintenance nightmare.

Enter the "Display Class"

```
<%
Class cDisplay
'~~~~~
  Public Sub header(byval vPageTitle)
```

```
  out "<html><head>"
"<title>" & vPageTitle & "</title></head><body>"
  End Sub

'~~~~~
  Public Sub footer(byval vBackLink, byval vNextLink)
    out "<p class='footer'>This has been a production "
    out "of The Mountainstream Group © 2001</p>"
    out "<a href='/" & vBackLink & "'>&LT;&LT;&LT; back</a>"
    out "  |  "
    out "<a href='/" & vNextLink & "'>next &GT;&GT;&GT;</a><br>"
    out "</body>"
    out "</html>"
  End Sub

'~~~~~
  Public Sub nav(byval vThisPage)
    dim s
    s = s & "<br><a href='/'>Home</a><br>"
    s = s & "<a href='/company.asp'>Company</a><br>"
    s = s & "<a href='/products.asp'>Products</a><br>"
    s = s & "<a href='/cCare.asp'>CustomerCare</a><br>"
    s = s & "<a href='/career.asp'>Career</a><br>"
    s = s & "<a href='/login.asp'>Login</a><br>"
    out replace(s,"/" & vThisPage & ".asp","#")
  End Sub

'~~~~~
  Private Sub out(byval s)
    Response.write s
  End Sub
End Class
%>
```

Within our cDisplay class we have four subroutines: header, footer, nav, and out. The first three are self-evident; the third, "out," is merely a wrapper around the Response.Write call—for brevity's sake.

The use of cDisplay is as follows:

```
<--!#include file="classes/cDisplay.clas"-->
<%
Dim display
Set display = new cDisplay
display.header "test page"
display.nav "home"
Response.Write "Content for Test Page."
```

```
display.footer "last ", "next"
%>
```

Here we have sent a standard header, navigation, content, and footer to the browser with nine lines of code. So you can see that having a team of Web programmers adopt a common class system can ease some of your maintenance woes. Why didn't I merely put these into an include file? Well, I could have. But we're trying to maintain a pure class-based development environment and the use of "class.method" helps us remember where each method lives. When a large site starts to become unwieldy you may have tens of include files. Remembering where the routine "PrintClientWestCoastHeader" happens to be stored may be no easy feat. But with "header.PrintClientWestCoast" all of your developers will know exactly in which file to find this routine—in the header class.

You'll notice that the header and footer use different output methods than nav. In "nav" we concatenate onto a single string and then do a Replace on the assembled string to remove the link from the page we are on. This is the cleanest way to perform this conditional substitution. We could have had six If/Then/Else statements, but this method is the simplest. Note: String concatenation is one of the slowest processes in VBScript. Avoid it wherever possible. If you find you must perform stored string assembly, try using the method found in the cResponse class found in the source.zip file, which uses an array and the array's Join method to avoid continuously resizing the memory allocated for your building string.

OOD Design Considerations

Objects are all the rage. They have been for years. Now, ASP developers can share in the excitement. Purists will argue, of course, but our apple, our car, and our person are all "objects" in my book. No, we can't inherit. No, we can't implement or extend. No, we don't have polymorphism. But if you're looking to save some time and headaches and additionally want a simple way to standardize data access or file manipulation or HTML presentation—objects are a handy way out.

For our discussion object design becomes quite flat. What I mean is that when I say person I don't mean a class that extends the object class that extends the animal class that extends the primate class that implements the Webmaster class. No, when I say person I mean you, me, or a Web guest who has a name, age, occupation, address (a minor second-layer object), etc.

Done. That's it. No complicated hierarchy of business objects stacked to facilitate massive code reuse and object normalization across an entire enterprise.

We don't want to complicate our tasks too much by trying to build level upon level, but a bit of application division is a healthy and happy medium.

For instance, we have our presentation class, which handles general look and feel. This feels like a natural separation of function. We'll call this layer 1: it's not really a separate tier because we are performing the assembly all within the confines of the Web server application tier. This is just our first layer of application division.

Now we have our person class, which abstracts how we handle users in our Web site. We authenticate them (person.authenticate(username, password)), we load them, save them, and modify them. We'll call this layer 2. Again, a rather comfortable balancing of logical entities.

Finally we have our database class, handling all our calls to the actual third tier of our complete application. We'll finish and call this layer 3. This will house our mechanical workings, which will deal with our raw data.

So a rather crude layout might be:

Tier 1: User presentation (browser)
Tier 2: Application (Web server)
    Layer 1: Presentation
    Layer 2: Business object abstraction
    Layer 3: Database abstraction
Tier 3: Database

By dividing and conquering we have simplified our understanding of what our Web site is composed of—as well as identifying pieces that can be logically grouped and abstracted into containers or, if you will, objects.

References

1. www.themountainstream.com/brag/amacom/source.zip
2. www.webmonkeys.com/

DAVID CLINE (dave@themountainstream.com) is a dedicated Internet architect experienced in project management, design, construction, and maintenance of complex, multilanguage Web applications. He has successfully architected and constructed multiple document generation and publishing Web sites; effectively designed, coded, extended, and maintained Web sites for shipment tracking, sales management, and financial management; and published in multiple print and online technical journals.

Perl: How to Use the Most Widely Used Internet Programming Language Effectively

Peter Karlson and Benjamin Cole

This chapter covers the fundamentals of Perl as an Internet scripting language. Created originally in the late 1980s by former NASA system administrator Larry Wall, as a utilitarian scripting language for automating system administrator tasks, Perl (Practical Extraction and Report Language) has evolved into the most widely deployed language on the Internet today. This chapter will cover a brief introduction to Perl, how it fits into your Web site, what you need to get started, basic implementation examples, and an overview of more advanced topics.

What Is Perl Used for?

People have been known to do everything from simple system administration automation to full-blown electronic commerce initiatives with Perl. For this reason it is often referred to as the "Swiss-army chainsaw" by its creator and proponents. Since Perl is so flexible, it is easy to use it for many different levels of development, and is also famous for adapting to the style of programmers and not constricting them as much as other languages. The most popular uses of Perl usually involve the use of the common gateway interface (CGI) facility. CGI is a means to provide a standard interface from the browser to the back-end operations of the Web server. By allowing parameters to be passed from an HTML page to a server-side script, the developer can perform operations based on the user's input.

By far, the most popular use of Perl/CGI is simple information-gathering scripts that process data entered by an HTML form. No doubt you have experienced these forms while requesting information about a particular organization, when you have been asked to submit your name and address to receive something in return. Most likely this was a simple Perl script.

The second most popular use of Perl is to provide some level of interactivity to your

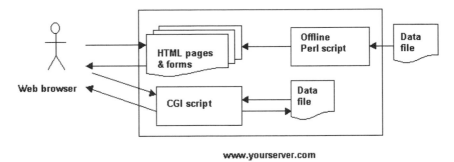

www.yourserver.com

Figure 19-1. Web site components.

Web site users (Figure 19-1). Interactivity in this case is defined by a two-way dialog between the server and the user. For example, it can be querying a data source such as an employee directory.

Dynamic content is a deep and dark quagmire that can be explored a million different ways. The scope of this chapter will cover dynamic content as it refers to anything that is displayed to a Web browser that is generated by a Perl script. For example, information that comes from a data source, such as stock information or system information, like date and time, are useful examples of simple dynamic content.

Perl can be used in a number of different ways on your Web site. As we have said above, the most popular way is to use Perl as the scripting language for CGI scripts. Another excellent use of Perl is to perform tasks that are too complex for normal shell scripts or batch files. For example, processing large text files offline on a nightly basis for online display via the web.

What Do I Need to Run Perl?

This chapter assumes that you are running your Web site on a Unix or Linux machine. Perl also runs reasonably well on Windows NT servers, but some of the functions are not supported or may act differently (read, your mileage may vary). For a vendor-supported version of Perl on NT you can go to www.activestate.com to download ActivePerl. You can also download the latest community-supported versions from www.perl.com.

Language Conventions

You will notice a few things about Perl immediately. The first is that it is a very simple programming language to read. It is crafty programmers that make it hard to read. Figure 19-2 represents the variation of the "Hello World" starter program with annotations.

Although many of Perl's language conventions resemble C, the variables have been

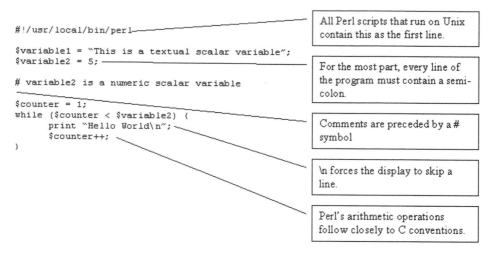

Figure 19-2. Perl "Hello World."

simplified to three basic types: scalars, arrays, and hashes. Scalar variables are numeric or textual information that may be manipulated by performing various operations such as concatenating one string onto another or adding two numbers together. Scalar variables can be identified by the preceding dollar sign. Since Perl is not a strongly typed language, it will automatically convert the data if you place a number where a string is expected and vice versa. This is usually seen as a fault to advanced software developers and a bonus to novices.

Offline Perl Script

Offline Perl scripts can be used to perform repetitive functions; used in conjunction with the Unix crontab utility, they can make a Webmaster's life much easier. The example below demonstrates the preprocessing of a data file that needs to be used by an online script. Say the data file needs to be reformatted and stripped of some content before being used by an online script. In order to save processing time, a Webmaster may decide to do some of the preprocessing in an offline script on a daily basis so that the CGI script does not need to waste time on the stripping and reformatting of the data every time a user wants to access the file.

```perl
#!/usr/local/bin/perl

# first set a scalar variable with each log file path

my $incoming_datafile = "/data/incoming_file.txt";
my $webready_datafile = "/www/data/data.txt";
```

```
# use the open function to open a file handle
# or call die to output an error message
# the open function takes 2 parameters
# first the filehandle name, second the variable containing #the
file path
# the file path is preceded by
# < for read only
# > for write only

open(DATA_1, "< $incoming_data") or die "can't open
$incoming_data: $!";
open(DATA_2, "> $outgoing_data") or die "can't open
$outgoing_data: $!";

# use a while loop and the diamond operator to read each
# line. The diamond operator returns a single line in a
# scalar context (undef if all the lines have been read).
# each time we go through the loop a new line of the log
# file is put into the variable "$_" which in turn can be
# written to the new log file.
# The diamond operator (<>) is used to iterate through a #chunk
of memory
while (<DATA_1>) {
   ($field1,$field2,$field3,$field4) = split("\t",$_);
# since the datafile contains tab delimited data the split
# function is used to split the line into 4 separate #variables
   print DATA_2 "$field1\t$field4";
# only two of the fields are needed so those are copied to
# the new file
}

}

# Clean up by closing the files
close(DATA_1)       or die "can't close $incoming_data: $!";
close(DATA_2)       or die "can't close $outgoing_data: $!";
```

You may notice some strange variables being used in this script, such as $_ and $!. These are called global special variables. The most commonly used special variable is $_, which contains the default input and pattern-searching string. In the preceding script we also used $!; this contains current value of the errno variable. The errno variable identifies the last system call error. You can use the errno variable in a string context to print out the corresponding system error string. It is always a good idea to use the "die" function when dealing with files. If "die" is not used it may take you some time to debug a problem in your script.

CGI

Common gateway interface (CGI) was created to solve a very simple problem; the Web was not just a set of static HTML files to be displayed. CGI allowed software developers to communicate with the Web browser in a standardized manner. CGI should be set up by your systems administrator or Webmaster and is probably already running on your Web server. Normally CGI scripts are installed in the cgi-bin directory. This can reside anywhere on your Web server; for sake of simplicity it is probably under your main content directory. It is also possible to set up your server to recognize anything that has a .cgi extension as a CGI script. Either way, all of your CGI scripts should have the extension .pl or .cgi, which are recognized by the Web server as special file extensions.

How Do I Use It?

Let's create a simple CGI script that displays the date and time and a simple message. If this were saved as a file called test.cgi in your cgi-bin directory, it would be accessible via a hyperlink such as http://www.yourserver.com/cgi-bin/test.cgi.

```
#!/usr/local/bin/perl—w
# the -w turns on warnings that may be output

# first use built in localtime function of Perl, this is a pre-
formatted
# set of time variables such as day, hour, minute etc.
my $timestamp = localtime();

$message = "Hello world, it's $timestamp";

# because this is going to a web browser print out
#Content-type
print "Content-type: text/html\n\n";
print "$message\n";
```

The example above does not take advantage of CGI's greatest strength, the ability to pass information to the script via parameters. Parameters are passed to CGI scripts in a standard name value pair format with the "&" symbol to separate each pair. For example, if we wanted to pass information to the script, such as the first name and the last name, the script would be called like this:

```
http://www.yourserver.com/cgi-
bin/test.cgi?firstname=John&lastname=Smith
```

The question mark denotes the separation of the script name and the beginning of the parameters.

Simple HTML Form to CGI

Normally you would not pass CGI variables by typing them into a URL window on your Web browser as given in the example above. This is where the concept of an HTML form comes into play. The HTML form is a set of HTML tags that are used to solicit information from the user, and once submitted to the script the parameters can be deconstructed into individual variables to be processed. In the example below, we create a simple HTML form, which lets the user interact with the Perl script. We will take our example from above and let the user enter his or her name; then, instead of printing out "Hello World," we will print out "Hello User."

First we need our HTML form.

```
<HTML>
<HEAD>
<TITLE>Example 3</TITLE>
</HEAD>
<BODY>
<FORM method="POST" action="/cgi-bin/example3.cgi">
Name: <INPUT type="text" name="name"></INPUT>
<INPUT type="submit" name="submit"></INPUT>
</FORM>
</BODY>
</HTML>
```

We need to create our Perl script that will process the form and print out a reply.

```
#!/usr/local/bin/perl
# Get the input

read(STDIN, $buffer, $ENV{'CONTENT_LENGTH'});

# Split the name-value pairs

# Load the FORM variables
foreach $pair (@pairs) {

# Put all the name value pairs into a hash table called #@pairs
    ($name, $value) = split(/=/, $pair);
    $value =~ tr/+/ /;
# This ensures that there are only "legal" characters in
# the values A through Z and 0 through 9
# any + in the value is replaced with a space
# decode any url encoded values with hex code
# decoding functions

$value =~ s/%([a-fA-F0-9][a-fA-F0-9])/pack("C",hex($1))/eg;
```

```perl
# Finally assign the value to a name in the hash table #called
FORM
$FORM{$name} = $value;
}

# first use built in localtime function of Perl
my $timestamp = localtime();

$message = "Hello $FORM{name}, it's $timestamp";

# because this is going to a web browser print out
# Content-type as text/html this will ensure that the web
# browser will recognize the output
print "Content-type: text/html\n\n";
print "$message\n";
```

This script introduced the concept of arrays and hashes. An array is a list of data such as "one, two, three." In Perl this is denoted by an "@" symbol. For example:

```perl
@number_list = ("one", "two", "three");
```

You can refer to the first element in the array as @number_list[0]. Note: The arrays always start with 0 and not 1.

A hash can be viewed as a two-dimensional array or a list of references to data. To convert our array example to a hash we could link the label to the value so that the label of "one" would have a value of 1. In Perl, this would be denoted like this:

```perl
%number_hash = ( "one"=>1, "two"=>2, "three"=>3 );
```

Perl Modules

Along with flexibility, the other great trait that ties the Perl community together is Perl's modularity. This allows other programmers to extend the functionality and share their code in a standardized manner. Modules are similar to a library or shared library in other languages. They are named with the .pm extension and are called with the "use" directive. There are literally hundreds of Perl modules that others have written and posted for your use on the popular Comprehensive Perl Archive Network, or CPAN, Web site (www.cpan.org). There is no sense in reinventing the wheel. Many modules come with your Perl install and are called "the standard Perl library."

The example above was the "old school" way to handle CGI input. Fortunately for the Perl community, a benevolent individual named Lincoln Stein created a standardized module to handle all the mundane tasks of dealing with CGI input and output called CGI.pm. This module is now part of the standard distribution of Perl and should be available on your Web server. The example below uses CGI.pm.

```perl
#!/usr/local/bin/perl

# the use statement pulls in the required module
# it also does some checking to make sure it exists
# if the module is not available the script will exit

use CGI qw/:standard/;

# notice we got rid of all that name value pair processing

# first use built in localtime function of Perl
my $timestamp = localtime();

# here is one way to use CGI.pm to get the name=value pair
my $name = param('name');
$message = "Hello $name, it's $timestamp";

# because this is going to a web browser print out
# Content-type via the
# header function that is available with CGI.pm

print header();
print "$message\n";
```

As you can see from the example above, the use of modules simplifies the script considerably. Fortunately, with a vast array of available Perl modules, dealing with a new programming task is very easy. In many cases, someone has already built a solution to your task. Unfortunately, these modules come with no warranty, and often the author of the module is very accessible. In fact, we have sent e-mails to some of the authors of Perl and gotten a response almost immediately. But in the off case that the documentation does not solve your problem or you cannot get in touch with the author, you will need to work it out yourself. That means that if you run into a problem, you will need to become familiar with some of the more complex features of Perl. You will want to do this anyway as you write more and more complex Perl scripts.

Advanced Perl

The examples mentioned were meant to give you a brief overview of the language, how it is structured and some of its uses. As we stated in the beginning of this chapter, Perl rises to meet the challenges of more advanced programming tasks.

Mod_Perl

One of the biggest drawbacks of using Perl in the CGI environment is that each time a Perl program runs, a new Perl process is started. These new processes are not a problem on a low-traffic Web site; however, for a larger site this will have a detrimental effect on other CGI processes and server performance in general. If this is the case, then it seems to rule out Perl as a solution for high-traffic sites. However, there is a solution available to lighten the load, and that is mod_Perl. Mod_Perl was written by Doug MacEachern and solves the process problem by embedding the Perl interpreter directly into the Web server. The bad news is that mod_Perl will only work with one Web server, Apache. The good news is that mod_Perl will only work with one Web server, Apache. The Apache Web server, like Perl, is a very successful piece of open-source software. Currently, the Apache Web server is the most used in the world. It also has the advantage of being free and often comes preinstalled with many Linux distributions.

This combination of Apache and Perl has many advantages. You will get the obvious CGI advantage, which is a tremendous boost in speed, but you will also gain an advantage on the Web server side. With mod_Perl you can now write server-side includes in Perl or put Perl code directly into the Apache configuration files.

Find out more about mod_Perl at the Apache website at www.apache.org or in the various Perl books mentioned later.

Databases

The next logical step after providing some user interaction would probably involve storing the data from these interactions in some type of database. When you talk about Perl and database interaction, you are talking about the set of Perl modules that comprise DBI/DBD. DBI is a database independent programming interface for Perl. The DBD, or database driver, does the work of implementing the DBI methods for each unique database. Therefore, there is a separate DBD module for each database. Some examples are DBD::MySQL and DBD::Oracle. The advantage of this is that you can write a program, which uses a MySQL database, and then migrate to an Oracle database with minimal work because you just need to swap in the Oracle DBD module without re-writing your application code.

Let's look at an example building upon our "Hello World" example once again. This time we will use the form as a login form that searches a database for a valid user, then displays the secure page.

```
#!/usr/local/bin/perl -w

# first we include the DBD module for the MySQL database
# we also include the CGI.pm module once again this time with
some more hooks
use DBD::mysql;
```

```perl
use CGI qw/:standard :html3 :netscape/;

# first we set some variables with the database name,
# database user and database password
my $thedb = "client_db";
my $dbuser = "db_user";
my $dbpwd = "dbpass";

# then as in the previous example we load the login name
# from the html form
my $name = param('name');

# now we will query the database for a match to the user
# name from the form. A standard sql query with the user
# name is stored in a variable

my $newquery = "SELECT * from user where userid=\'$name\'";

# here we call a subroutine to do the actual query the
# return goes into $datafound
$datafound =&query_db($thedb, $dbuser, $dbpwd, $newquery);
$numrows = $datafound->rows;

# next we just count the number of returned rows to make
# sure we got a match notice we use == and not eq this does
# a numeric comparison instead of a string comparison
if ($numrows == 0) {
   &system_error("User \"$name\" Not Found.<BR> Contact
   Technical Support");
   exit;
}

# since we know it should return just 1 row, put them in
# variables. Here we use one of the DBI methods to fetch a
# row as an array
my($fname, $lname, $email, $thezip, $city, $firsttime) =
$datafound>fetchrow_array;

# once we have data about the valid user we can check the
# fisrttime field band see if they have been here before
if ($firsttime eq "Y") {
   print header;
   print "Hello $name\n";
   my $value = "firsttime = \"N\"";
# now we must update the firsttime field so they get a
# different message next time
   update_db('user', $value);
} elsif ($firsttime eq "N") {
```

```perl
      print "Welcome back $name \n";
}
} #end else

} #end of main program

####————sub-routines follow————#####

# This sub will update data in "$table"
# required arguments (table name, columns, values)
# here is where the actual work is done
# the update_db sub-routine first makes a database
# connection
sub update_db {
 my($table, $values) = @_;
 $dbh = DBI-connect("DBI:mysql:$thedb",'$dbuser','$dbpwd')
    or die "Can not connect to $thedb: $dbh->errstr\n";
# just like the query we store the update query in a
# variable we use qq to quote the values within {}
    $statement = qq{UPDATE $table
          SET $values
            WHERE userid = '$theuser'
            };
# this is a DBI method, which prepares the statement
    $sth = $dbh->prepare($statement);
# if something goes wrong print out the error and an email
# address for tech support
  $sth->execute
  or
  display_error("Unable to execute $statement $dbh->err
  str. Please contact tech_support\@yourcompany.com");
  my $uid = $sth->{'insertid'};
  $sth->finish;
#   print "$statement\n";


}

sub query_db {
# This subroutine accesses the db and returns the 2D array
# of results Inputs are: DB name, username, password, SQL
# query to run the query sub-routine like the update sub-
# routine makes a connection to the db then fetches all the
# rows it can based on the query.

  my ($thedb, $user, $pwd, $newquery) = @_;
 $dbh = DBI->connect("DBI:mysql:$thedb",$dbuser,$dbpwd)
 or die "Can not connect to $thedb: $dbh->errstr\n";
 $qline = $dbh->prepare($newquery);
```

```
    $qline->execute or die "Unable to execute query on
    $thedb: $dbh->err,$dbh->errstr\n";
    $dbh->disconnect;
    return $qline;
}

# this sub prints out any error message passed to it.
sub system_error {
  local($ename) = @_;
  print header;
  print "<P>$ename</P>\n";
}
```

Object-Oriented Perl

Many would believe that if a language is not object oriented, then it is not a true programming language. Fortunately Perl code can be written either procedurally, as shown above, or in an object-oriented (OO) manner. The widest use of OO Perl is in the writing of modules. Almost all recent modules are written using OO Perl and some, like CGI.pm, are written so you can call methods in either a procedural style or OO style. This is yet another example of the power and flexibility of Perl.

References

1. Larry Wall, Tom Christiansen, and Jon Orwant, *Programming Perl*, 3rd Edition.
2. Tom Christiansen, et al., *Perl Cookbook*.
3. Randal L. Schwartz, et al., *Learning Perl*, (O'Reilly & Associates), July 2001.
4. Randal L. Schwartz, et al., *Learning Perl on Win32 Systems*.
5. Sriram Srinivasan, *Advanced Perl Programming*, (O'Reilly & Associates), August 1997.
6. Ellen Siever, et al., *Perl in a Nutshell*, (O'Reilly & Associates), December 1998.
7. www.perl.com.
8. www.cpan.org.
9. www.apache.org.
10. www.mysql.com.

PETER KARLSON has been involved with developing Internet technologies since 1991. As chief technology officer at Harrison & Troxell, Inc., he is responsible for researching, evangelizing, and espousing new technologies and processes to build durable Internet solutions for a wide array of clients.

BENJAMIN COLE is a senior software engineer at Harrison & Troxell, Inc. As a member of the R&D team he is responsible for creating the next generation of durable Internet solutions. He has spent the past few year's evangelizing the open source movement as well as the wider adoption of Perl, Apache, and Linux as a commercial delivery platform for e-business.

VoiceXML, How to Talk to the Internet

Srdjan Vujosevic and Robert Laberge

The Internet is in yet another expansion phase. First we had Web browsers, not so long ago we were introduced to the Internet via WAP-enabled cellular phones, and now we have VoiceXML, the latest addition to the Internet anywhere. This new portal is based on the XML tag–based subset called VoiceXML, which functions in cooperation with voice browser technology.

VoiceXML is a language for creating voice-user interfaces. It uses telephone-style speech recognition and DTMF (dual tone multi frequency) touchtone (keypad entry) for input, and previously recorded audio, text-to-speech synthesis, and dictionaries for output. This is not voiceover IP or long distance over the Internet as advertised by Internet providers. This is voice-enabling Internet Web sites and is based on the World Wide Web Consortium's (W3C) Voice Browser Working Group. W3C ensures that this new technology is portable and standardized so that any vendor or developer can take advantage of the open architecture.

VoiceXML can be used in two general methods. The first enables voice access to a Web site, and the second builds and enables nonproprietary IVR (interactive voice response) services.

When developing applications using VoiceXML, the Web's basic components and infrastructure remain the same. The main difference is that instead of using a Web browser such as Internet Explorer or Netscape, a voice browser is used. This voice browser is really a VoiceXML interpreter, which resides on a highly specialized server, with the user interface being a simple telephone.

This chapter will introduce VoiceXML technology in several steps: history, VoiceXML architecture, step-by-step dynamic example using database-driven content, and an overview of tools and platforms that can be used to quickly develop and deploy voice-enabled applications.

History

Changes in today's computer technologies, especially in the field of how we are using and accessing information available over the Internet, is changing at a greater speed than ever before. When President Bill Clinton went to office, there was only a handful of Internet Web sites. When George W. Bush took office eight years later, there were over 25 million Web sites—how times are changing. The next phase of expansion is voice-controlled Internet, starting with VoiceXML.

VoiceXML, or the "dialog markup language," as it's been referred to by the VoiceXML forum, has roots in XML, the extended markup language first presented in November of 1996.

Initial attempts to create a phone markup language started way back when with AT&T Bell Laboratories with a research project called "PhoneWeb." But efforts were set back with the AT&T split into AT&T and Lucent. Not much happened afterward until September 1998, when Motorola announced a new method to merge telephony (wire and wireless technologies) with the Internet via a new XML subset called VoxML. Motorola realized early on the importance of hands-free voice commands, and an integral part of their strategy was to focus on speech recognition as that input mechanism.

On March 2, 1999, AT&T, Lucent Technologies, and Motorola joined forces in the formation of a new voice extensible markup language forum called VXML forum. This was later renamed to the VoiceXML forum. On May 22, 2000, the VoiceXML Forum announced that the World Wide Web Consortium, regulators of Web standards, acknowledged the submission of version 1.0 of the VoiceXML specifications. And at the May 10–12 meetings in Paris, the W3C's Voice Browser Working Group agreed to adopt VoiceXML 1.0 as the basis for the development of a W3C dialog markup language, a big step in voice technology acceptance.

As of the beginning of 2001, along with the forum's founding members (AT&T, Lucent Technologies, Motorola, and later IBM), over 350 VoiceXML members have joined the group.

Architecture

As seen in Figure 20-1, there are many pieces to the VoiceXML architecture. In order to enable communication between the wire and wireless telephone devices (sections 1 and 2) and the Internet (everything above section 3), a specialized piece of hardware/software called the VoiceXML gateway is required.

The VoiceXML gateway is basically one or more computer servers residing on the same platform and running interpreters called voice browsers. These voice browsers understand and interpret VoiceXML dialogs (or commands). The VoiceXML gateway facilitates communication between the dialogs and the Internet by controlling resources such as Automatic Speech Recognition, message recording and play, Text to Speech,

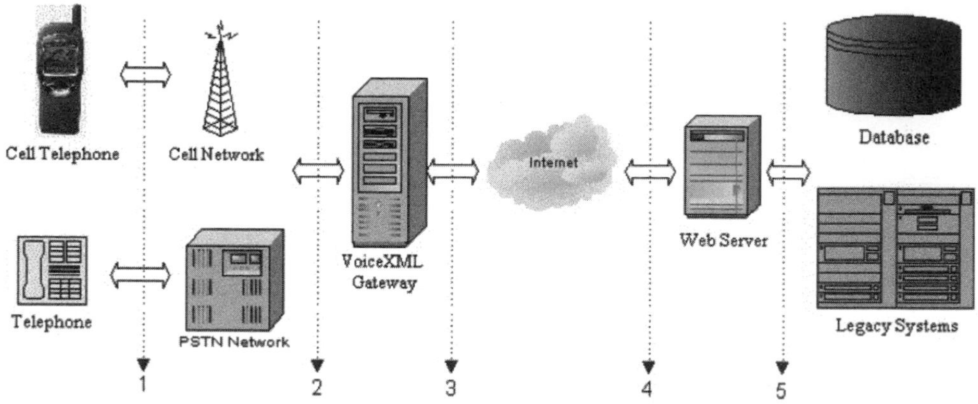

Figure 20-1. *The VoiceXML architecture.*

DTMF tone recognition, and the PSTN network connectivity. Apart from the VoiceXML interpreter (Motorola also includes the VoxML interpreter), each voice gateway includes Automatic Speech Recognition Engine (ASR), which supports multiple languages; in the case of Nuance, more than 15 languages are available. Also included are: Text-to-Speech Engine, system dictionaries, and an Internet interface (ranging from dial-up to high-speed links).

One of the most important parts of the VoiceXML gateway is the voice browser. In order to explain how this software differs from a traditional Web browser, let's concentrate for the moment on Figure 20-2.

In a PC environment (Figure 20-2, section A), a classic Web browser simply collects and presents data. Same idea for mobile browsers (Figure 20-2, section B) called microbrowsers, used on Web phones. It is important to note that in both cases, the browser resides on the client device (personal computer, WAP-enabled wireless device, or PDA) and the code begins its execution on the client side. Sections A and B of Figure 20-2 both represent client-side browsers.

It's a completely different story for voice browsers. Voice browsers reside within the VoiceXML gateway (Figure 20-2, section C) or are built into a PSTN (public switched telephone network). These browsers allow the users to place calls from any telephone and navigate through the VoiceXML application by selecting options on voice menus and executing simple voice input commands. Navigation can also be based on end-user voice input.

Voice browser program code resides on the Web server or on the VoiceXML gateway and is therefore a server-side browser similar to active server page code (ASP). VoiceXML developers would then maintain the code in the same fashion as they would regular HTML or ASP code.

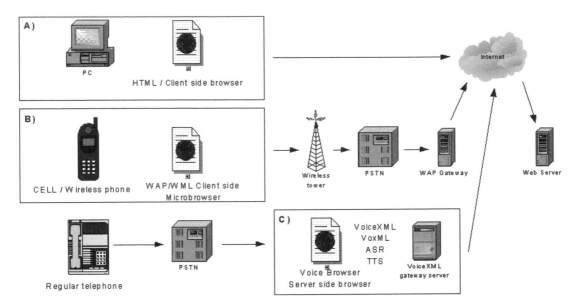

Figure 20-2. *How a voice browser differs from a traditional browser.*

In General

If you've had previous experience programming HTML, XML, or an XML subset, you shouldn't have any problem picking up the VoiceXML language. This chapter doesn't cover all VoiceXML tag details with all possible tag attributes but will explain the basic layout of a working application with basic tag introductions. For a detailed explanation of VoiceXML tags visit www.voicexml.org.

In a VoiceXML document (or program), the user is always in a conversational state called a dialog. Each dialog determines the flow to the next dialog, all depending on which selection is chosen or which command is given. In Web programming, execution is halted when a screen is displayed. The user then enters information and clicks OK (or whatever), selects a hyperlink, or chooses a form item. In VoiceXML, instead of a screen being presented, the system tells the user a selection to make or an informational statement. Execution is then paused until the user returns a voice command.

From the program's point of view, transitions to new dialogs are specified via URLs (relative or explicit). If no specific dialog is specified on the URL, the first dialog in the document is assumed. Execution is terminated when a dialog does not specify a successor, or if it has an element that explicitly exits the conversation. When programming, always guide the user by letting him or her know the next possible choices; if none exist, say so.

Step-by-Step

Rather than explaining the language, this chapter introduces the language via a working and functional application. As we go, we'll explain the basic usage of certain key tags; however, not all the attributes of the tags will be explained, as the goal here is to introduce the language and not every specific detail.

This chapter's example is based on the imaginary company called eDiapers that has one simple goal: "To provide the best quality and cheapest delivery of diapers to its customers."

Prerequisites to understand and test our dynamic database-driven VoiceXML application are Microsoft Access database, a Web server (Internet or Intranet based), a VoiceXML development tool (we used Motorola Mobile ADK 2.0), and a scripting language such as VBScript, JavaScript, or Perl. To generate the VoiceXML code, we used server-side VBScript.

Dialog Definition

The first step in creating a voice-enabled Web application is to define the conversation between the user and the system. This conversation is called the dialog. Designing a voice application is nothing more than defining the dialog flow for specific transactions. Think of this process as writing down the anticipated conversation between your salesperson and the client. Simply direct the conversation and only allow predefined responses to questions.

Here's the general anticipated conversation flow for the eDiaper voice application:

← Start of dialog →

System: Hello, and welcome to eDiaper, the cyber diaper store with the best e-diaper selections.

System: To purchase diapers, you must be a registered eDiaper member. To sign into the system please provide your customer number. Please say your customer number or say help for more information now.

User: 1-2-3-4-5.

System: Sorry, I didn't hear exactly six digits.

System: To purchase diapers, you must be a registered e Diaper member. To sign into the system please provide your customer number. Please say your customer number or say help for more information now.

User: 1-2-3-4-5-6.

System: Welcome back, Mary Twins.

System: Please select from the following list of available diaper types:

Say Plampers for Plampers 32 diaper per pack at the price of 6.5 dollars.

Say Muggies for Muggies 24 diaper per pack at the price of 6 dollars.

Say NoName for NoName 24 diaper per pack at the price of 5 dollars.

User: Muggies.

System: Please select the quantity in increments of one pack. Maximum quantity is 20 packs per order.

User: 21.

← Customer has requested more than 20 packs for this order →

System: Sorry, you have selected more than 20 packs for this order. Try again.

System: Please select the quantity in increments of one pack. Maximum quantity is 20 pack per order.

User: Ten.

← Customer has requested more than is currently available in stock →

System: Sorry, you have requested more diapers than we currently have available in stock, so we've given you all we have.

System: You have placed an order for eight packs of Muggies diapers for a total cost of 48 dollars.

System: Please say yes to commit this transaction or say no to cancel and start over.

← Quantity ordered is available in stock →

System: You have placed an order for eight packs of Muggies diapers for a total cost of 48 dollars.

System: Please say yes to commit this transaction or say no to cancel and start over.

User: Yes.

← Order delivered to address on file for registered customer →

System: Your order will be delivered to: Mary Twins living at 21 Kid Street.

System: Thank you for shopping at eDiaper.

← End of dialog →

Once you have a firm understanding of the anticipated dialog flow, it's highly recommended that you create a "state diagram." A state diagram (Figure 20-3) will help you

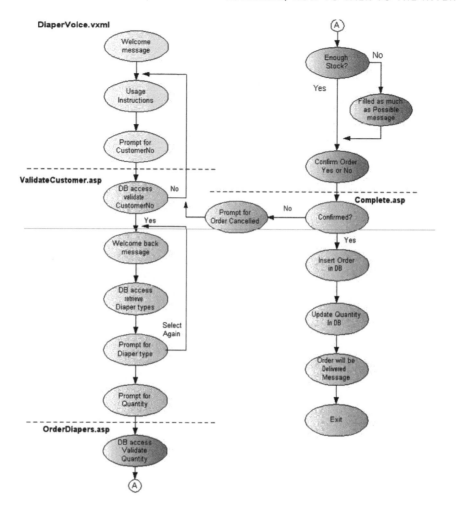

Figure 20-3. State diagram.

visualize the flow of information through your application, which is the key to a successful design. It will help you notice possible shortcomings in your conversation designs as well as possible logical improvements even before you start coding the programs. Not only will this diagram save you lots of reprogramming later on but it'll also be used as your system documentation once you're done.

As seen in the diagram, every general step of the application is highlighted. Developers can easily see the breaking points, the conversation flow, and overall logical flow. Rather than reading through the program code or the dialog definition, one can simply glance at the state diagram to quickly understand the individual programs and overall application.

Database Design

What kind of dynamic VoiceXML application would we have if we didn't connect to some sort of back-end database. In our application we're using a Microsoft Access database to hold all information pertaining to customers (Customers table), available stock (DiaperType table), and customer orders (Transactions table).

Refer to Figure 20-4 below for the basic table layouts and Figure 20-5 for the detailed table structures. Create a database called eDiaper.mdb and place it and its DSN file in your Web server's root directory. You could place the database in some other location on the server, but you'd also have to change the eDiaper.dsn file (Figure 20-6) location, too, as per coding in the programs—as you'll see later in this chapter.

In order to connect to a back-end database from the VBScript and ASP code, as we do in our programs, a connection string is required. There are many methods of defining a connection string. You can hard-code the string into the program logic, define a DSN file as we do here, or use the ODBC administrator (Start → Settings → Control Panel → ODBC Data Sources application, which will guide you through the creation process).

> Note: The "File DSN" entries default location is in "C:\Program Files\Common Files\ODBC\Data Sources." If you do not specify a fully qualified path to the file location (as we do in ValidateCustomer.asp, lines 4–11, which appears below) you'll have to place the eDiaper.dsn file in the default location, as noted above.

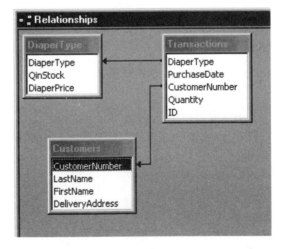

Figure 20-4. Table layouts.

Table: Customers

Column Name	Type	Size
CustomerNumber	Long Integer	4
LastName	Text	50
FirstName	Text	50
DeliveryAddress	Text	50

Table: DiaperType

Column Name	Type	Size
DiaperType	Text	50
QinStock	Long Integer	4
DiaperPrice	Currency	8

Table: Transactions

Column Name	Type	Size
DiaperType	Text	50
PurchaseDate	Date/Time	8
CustomerNumber	Long Integer	4
Quantity	Long Integer	4
ID	Long Integer	4

Figure 20-5. *Detailed table structures.*

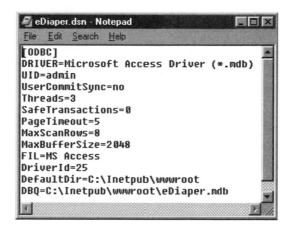

Figure 20-6. *The eDiaper.dsn file.*

At this point the dialog definitions are created, the state diagram is designed, and the database is in place and populated with some test data. Now we're all set to start coding our eDiaper application.

Let's Code

The first two programs in our application, DiaperVoice.vxml and ValidateCustomer.asp will be shown in this chapter. Again, our goal is not to ramble on but to introduce the programming aspects of VoiceXML. The first program is a pure static VoiceXML program, as denoted by its extension .vxml. The second program will demonstrate dynamic VoiceXML code and back-end database connectivity in an ASP program.

We highly suggest that the first program in your application always be a pure VoiceXML program ending with the .vxml extension. This is to ensure that crawlers and robots (programs that index Web pages automatically) will discover your application program and properly categorize it as a voice application in their indexed database search engine, for all the world to see.

Line numbers have been added to our programs for ease of reference. When executing the programs, line numbers will cause errors, so if you're copying the programs in this chapter, be sure to omit the line numbers.

The following VoiceXML program initiates the application with an introduction to the caller followed by a prompt for the user to say his or her customer number. This application assumes the user is preregistered with eDiaper.

DiaperVoice.vxml:

```
1.  <?xml version="1.0"?>
2.  <vxml version="1.0">
3.  <meta name="author" content="WaveDev"/>
4.  <meta name="maintainer" content="marketing@wavedev.com"/>
5.  <form>
6.   <block>
7.   Hello, and welcome to e Diaper, the cyber diaper store with
     the best e diaper selections.
8.   </block>
9.   <field name="login" type="digits">
10.  <prompt>
11.  To purchase diapers, you must be a registered e Diaper
     member. To sign into the system please provide your
     customer number.
12.  <break size="medium"/>
13.  Please say your customer number or say help for more
     information now.
14.  </prompt>
15.  <filled>
16.   <if cond="login.length != 6">
17.    <prompt>Sorry, I didn't hear exactly 6 digits.</prompt>
18.    <assign name="login" expr="undefined"/>
19.   <else/>
20.    <submit next="http://127.0.0.1/ValidateCustomer.asp"/>
21.   </if>
22.  </filled>
23.  <catch event="help">
24.  Please provide your six digit customer number.
25.  </catch>
```

```
26.   <catch event="nomatch noinput" count="3">
27.     <prompt>Sorry I did not understand what you said. !
      Goodbye.</prompt>
28.   <throw event="telephone.disconnect.hangup"/>
29.   </catch>
30. </field>
31. </form>
32. </vxml>
```

The first line in the above program defines the program as an XML document. Following this is the <vxml></vxml> tag pair (lines 2 and 32). These will encapsulate the remaining code to be VoiceXML tags. Lines 3 and 4 are simple meta-tags similar to HTML code. Next is the <form></form> tags (lines 5 and 31). These tags are key components of VoiceXML documents and contain the body of the program.

Lines 6–8 define a one-time executed block of code. Line 7 within this block is the initial application greeting to the end-users.

Line 9 defines an input field, which will be used to gather the customer number from the user. The field type attribute defines the login field as digits only.

Lines 10–14 define the first <prompt></prompt> tag pair. The programmable prompt tags prompt the user for input for, in this case, the login field. These tags are used quite often in VoiceXML programs.

Lines 15–22, the <filled></filled> tags, specify an action to perform when the login field is filled by the user input. In our case, if the login length is not exactly six digits long, the user will be prompted with an error message and the assign tag will reinitialize the login field to undefined, thus reinitiating the entire logic by sending control back to line 9. If, however, the login length is exactly six digits, control will be rerouted to another program via the submit command on line 20, which will also pass the login field variable.

Lines 23–29 are used for events (error, help, and no input from the user). In the first catch tag, if the user says "help" the message on line 24 is spoken by the system. If the user continues to say an invalid customer number more than three times, line 27 will relay a message to the user and finally disconnect the application by hanging up, line 28.

This is a very simple VoiceXML program with all the basics. For more information on VoiceXML tags and their attributes, visit the VoiceXML forum at www.voicexml.org.

Once valid input is accepted in the login field on line 20 control is passed to a second program called ValidateCustomer.asp, as seen in the state diagram flow. Here the input customer number is validated against our back-end database, and if it's valid, control will continue. Else the flow will return to the initiating program.

This second program has three forms for three distinct user interactions. The first welcomes the user back. The second asks the user to select the type of diaper he or she wishes to purchase. This process is followed by a database query looking at the DiaperType table and telling the user all the diapers eDiaper has available for sale. Of course, if there are no diapers for a specific diaper type, the program will not allow that particular diaper type to be told to the user. Finally, the third form prompts the user for the quantity of diapers desired.

ValidateCustomer.asp

```
1.  <%@ LANGUAGE="VBSCRIPT"%>
2.  <%
3.  '——Open connection to database
4.  DB = "eDiaper.mdb"
5.  Dir = Request.ServerVariables("SCRIPT_NAME")
6.  Dir = StrReverse(Dir)
7.  Dir = Mid(Dir, InStr(1, Dir, "/"))
8.  Dir = StrReverse(Dir)
9.  Path = Server.MapPath(Dir) & "\"
10. File = "eDiaper.dsn"
11. DSN = "filedsn=" & Path & file & ";DefaultDir=" & Path &
    ";DBQ=" & Path & DB & ";"
12. dim sql, Conn, RS
13. dim strLastName, strFirstName, strDeliveryAddress
14. Set Conn = Server.CreateObject("ADODB.Connection")
15. Set RS = Server.CreateObject("ADODB.RecordSet")
16. '——See if customer exists
17. sql = "Select LastName, FirstName, DeliveryAddress from
    Customers where CustomerNumber = " & request("login")
18. Conn.Open DSN
19. RS.Open sql, Conn, 1,1
20. if RS.EOF or RS.BOF then
21.   WrongCustomer = true
22. else
23.   WrongCustomer = false
24.   strLastName=RS("LastName")
25.   strFirstName=RS("FirstName")
26.   strDeliveryAddress=RS("DeliveryAddress")
27. end if
28. Conn.Close
29. set RS = nothing
30. set Conn = nothing
31. %>

32. <?xml version="1.0"?>
33. <vxml version="1.0">
34. <meta name="author" content="WaveDev"/>
35. <meta name="maintainer" content="marketing@wavedev.com"/>
36. <var name="SelectedType"/>
```

```
37. <form id="init">
38. <help> Please select valid diaper type.</help>
39. <noinput>I didn't hear anything, please try
    again.</noinput>
40. <error>Sorry I did not understand, please select from the
    following list of options:</error>
41. <%if WrongCustomer then%>
42. <block>
43. <prompt bargein="false">
44.  Customer <%response.write request("login")%> does not
     exists please try again.<break size="large"/>
45. </prompt>
46. <goto next="DiaperVoice.vxml"/>
47. </block>
48. <%else%>
49. <block>
50. <prompt bargein="false">
51.  Welcome back <%response.write strFirstName & " " &
     strLastName%><break size="large"/>
52. </prompt>
53. <goto next="#SelectDiaperType
54. </block>
55. <%end if%>
56. </form>

57. <form id="SelectDiaperType">
58. <%
59. Set Conn = Server.CreateObject("ADODB.Connection")
60. Set RS = Server.CreateObject("ADODB.RecordSet")
61. sql = "select DiaperType, DiaperPrice from DiaperType where
    QinStock > 0"
62. RS.Open sql, Conn, 1,1
63. %>
64. <field name="DiaperType">
65.  <prompt>Please select from the following list of available
     diaper types :<break size="large"/>
66.   <%RS.MoveFirst
67.   do while not RS.EOF%>
68.   Say <%response.write left(RS("DiaperType"),8)%> for
      <%response.write RS("DiaperType")%> at the price of
      <%response.write RS("DiaperPrice")%> dollars.
69.    <%RS.MoveNext
70.   l oop%>
71.  </prompt>
72.  <%RS.MoveFirst
73.  do while not RS.EOF%>
74.   <option value="<%response.write RS("DiaperType")%>">
      <%response.write left(RS("DiaperType"),8)%>
```

```
75.    </option>
76.      <%RS.MoveNext
77.    loop%>
78.    <filled>
79.      <assign name="SelectedType" expr="DiaperType"/>
80.      <goto next="#DiaperQuantity"/>
81.    </filled>
82.  </field>
83.  <%
84.  Conn.Close
85.  set RS = nothing
86.  set Conn = nothing
87.  %>
88.  </form>
89.  <form id="DiaperQuantity">
90.    <field name="DiaperQty" type="digits">
91.      <prompt> Please select the quantity in increments of one
         pack. Maximum quantity is 20 packs per order.<break
         size="large"/>
92.      </prompt>
93.      <filled>
94.        <if cond="DiaperQty > 20">
95.          <prompt>Sorry, you have selected more than 20 packs for
           this order, try again.</prompt>
96.          <assign name="DiaperQty" expr="undefined"/>
97.        <else/>
98.        <submit
         next="http://127.0.0.1/OrderDiapers.asp?CustomerNo=
         <%request("login")%>" namelist="DiaperQty SelectedType"/>
99.        </if>
100.   </filled>
101.   <catch event="help">
102.     Please choose the quantity of diapers for your order.
103.   </catch>
104.   <catch event="nomatch noinput" count="3">
105.     <prompt>Sorry I did not understand what you said. !
         Goodbye.</prompt>
106.     <throw event="telephone.disconnect.hangup"/>
107.   </catch>
108.   </field>
109.</form>
110.</vxml>
```

The first section of this second program is to connect to a back-end database and validate the customer number. Lines 1 through 31 do this simple task with a predefined Microsoft Access database. Notice the DSN file logic, lines 5–10. The logic here will determine exactly where on the Web server machine (wherever it's located in the world) to find the DSN file. We could have simply defined an ODBC connection to the database via the ODBC administration utility, but we prefer this method because we have more control over the dataset name.

The next minor but important section is the setting up of the VoiceXML header and meta-tags, lines 32–35. Line 36 defines a variable called SelectedType to be used in a later form.

The first form, called "init," lines 37–56, is used to reply to the customer number task. If the number is valid, the program will welcome back the member by name and proceed to the next form. If the number does not exist in the database, the user will be told a message and control will return to the invoking program.

The second form, called "SelectDiaperType," on lines 57–88, will prompt the user to select from the stated list of diaper types. A command will query the database to find all the diaper types available and in stock to relay back to the user. This is done via a while loop on lines 67–71. For each diaper type, the user will hear a prompt as follows:

Say diapertype *for* diapertype explanation *at the price of* diaperprice *dollars.*

The italic words would be replaced with the values returned from the database query, very simple and very effective.

Once this new input field, "DiaperType," is filled, lines 78–81 will assign the defined variable SelectedType from line 36 the value of this field. Then control will pass to the next form via a goto command on line 80.

The last form, "DiaperQuantity," on lines 89–110, will again prompt the user but this time for the quantity of diapers desired. The DiaperQty field is used and defined as digits on line 90. First the user is prompted with an instructional message to select a quantity. Once the input field is filled, if the quantity is less than 20, control is passed to another program via a <submit . . . > tag as done in the previous program. If the quantity is greater than 20, the user is told an error message, the field is reinitialized to nothing, and execution awaits another input from the user.

Lines 101–107 are used to catch special conditions or events. In our case, if the user says help, a brief instructional message is told and execution returns to a wait state. As with the first program, if three invalid attempts are performed, a final message is told and the application terminates by hanging up via the <throw> tag on line 106.

There are more programs in the eDiaper application as seen in the state diagram, but only the first two are required to explain VoiceXML programming basics. Hopefully this brief introduction has helped you understand the hows and whys of the VoiceXML language.

Development Tool

In order to develop VoiceXML applications, you'll require certain specific tools. Once you know the tags, putting the program together via an editor such as Notepad is a nice

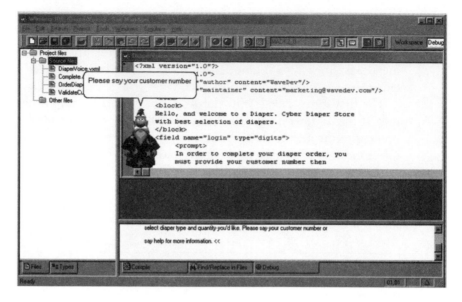

Figure 20-7. *Motorola ADK 2.0 tool.*

fast development method. But to test, debug, and run the application on the spot you'll require an ADK such as the free Motorola ADK 2.0. It's more or less an all-in-one integrated development environment for VoiceXML, VoxML (VoiceXML predecessor), as well as WML (wireless markup language used for creating WAP application).

This ADK is a nicely packaged tool that will run on Windows 98, Windows NT, or Windows 2000. Figure 20-7 shows a typical screen shot of the tool while it was being used to develop the eDiaper application.

It's important to utilize tools that will help you shorten the development and test life cycle of your VoiceXML applications. Motorola's ADK 2.0 is a great tool that can certainly help reduce development efforts, and since the little wizard on the screen actually talks, the entire development process is really quite fun.

Conclusion

In summation, VoiceXML:

- Is another portal to Internet applications.
- Is an XML subset used for quick development and deployment of voice applications that interact with the Web.
- Optimizes interactions in a client-server environment by allowing multiple dialogs per document.
- Allows the application developers to concentrate on application rather than developing low-level speech functionality.

- Is platform independent.
- Separates user interaction code (in VoiceXML) from service logic (CGI scripts, JavaScript, ASP).
- Provides portability, as VoiceXML is a common language for content providers, tool providers, and platform providers.

The eDiaper example presented is a completely functional application. We have developed and tested the application on our systems and it is 100 percent ready to go. Just recopy the code and use it in accordance with a VoiceXML gateway and you're off and running. Not all the programs in the application are supplied but the two that are will certainly give you a great introduction to VoiceXML.

References

1. http://studio.tellme.com.
2. http://www.motorola.com/MIMS/ISG/spin/mix/.
3. http://www.alphaworks.ibm.com/tech/voiceserversdk.
4. http://extranet.nuance.com/developer/.
5. http://www.generalmagic.com.
6. http://www.voicexmlcentral.com/.
7. http://www.xml.org/.
8. http://www.voicexml.org.
9. http://www.voicexml.org/voicexml1-0.dtd.
10. http://www.w3.org/TR/2000/NOTE-speechobjects-20001114.
11. http://www.alphaworks.ibm.com/tech/voicexml.
12. http://www.oasis-open.org/cover/sable.html.

SRDJAN VUJOSEVIC and ROBERT LABERGE are the creators of Wave-Dev.com, a firm specializing in "wireless enabling" of Internet sites and legacy systems via voice technology, WAP (HDML and WML), iMode, and MME. They're also the founders of WorldJobMart.com, the first Internet job site available on wireless handheld devices. They can be reached at authors@wavedev.com. For detailed information on WAP or VoiceXML, see their latest book, WAP Integration: professional developers guide *(John Wiley & Sons, 2001).*

The Struts Initiative:
Leveraging JavaServer Pages to
Meet the Demands of E-Business

Shaun Connolly

Many organizations understand the potential of technology provided by the Java 2 Platform, Enterprise Edition (J2EE). Developers are being asked to utilize J2EE technology like Java servlets and JavaServer Pages (JSPs) in their applications.

What many developers may not realize is that they can use this technology to separate application logic from presentation logic. By enabling content specialists to update and deploy content on their own, developers free themselves from these tasks so that they can focus on more application-level projects.

In the past year, an open source framework called Struts has emerged to further extend the capabilities of J2EE technology and help developers further separate business from presentation logic.

This chapter guides developers through the creation of a Struts-based application, then discusses some of the ways in which developers can utilize the Struts framework to meet other content presentation challenges.

Introduction

The Java 2 Platform, Enterprise Edition (J2EE) architecture is a great advance for developers. Its standardized framework defines and supports a multitiered programming model, freeing application developers to concentrate on solutions.

Developers can gain even more freedom for themselves by leveraging J2EE technology to separate application logic from business logic. In other words, developers can use J2EE technology to empower people with knowledge of specialized departmental content to easily update and deploy Web content on their own. With others able to focus on the look and feel, developers can really get down to the work at hand.

The J2EE specification outlines several technologies that help the developer create this separation—JavaServer Pages (JSPs), Enterprise JavaBeans (EJBs), and tag libraries (taglibs). Furthermore, in the past year a new initiative called Struts has exploded onto the development scene, promising to take the separation of business from application logic to an even higher level.

Struts

The Jakarta Project—sponsored by the Apache Software Foundation—is managing the open source initiative called Struts to create a framework for developing Web-based applications. Struts provides a well thought out design that allows developers to focus their attention on developing business logic and presenting it effectively, rather than peripheral functionality like program flow, validation, localization, and request dispatching. Struts accomplishes this by providing specific components in the form of Java classes and taglibs.

Struts is based on the Model-View-Controller design pattern (MVC), which emerged out of the SmallTalk programming language and works very well with JSP technology. MVC provides a clean separation of data, presentation, and application logic, and is illustrated in Figure 21-1.

The Model deals with the business data and logic that forms the basis of your application and is implemented using JavaBeans or EJBs. The View handles the visual presentation of the Model and is implemented using JSPs and tag libraries (taglibs). The Controller defines the way that a View responds to user input and is implemented as either a servlet or a JSP.

Using the powerful MVC paradigm, less technical people can work with the HTML and JSP tags that call the beans, while the Java developer creates the taglibs and beans that make up the business component stack.

This chapter will guide you through the creation of a complete Struts-based application, then discuss the ways in which the Struts framework can help a developer meet some of the challenges of separating business from application logic.

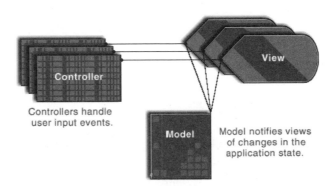

Figure 21-1. Model-View-Controller (MVC) architecture.

Developing a Logon Application Using Struts

Here is a simple logon application that prompts for a username and password and then lets the user know if the logon was successful or not. Remember, we're working from the MVC paradigm, so the View will be built first, followed by the Model, then the Controller, and finally the Application configuration file.

View

The View portion of this application consists of three JSP pages and a LogonForm Bean. The logon page prompts for the username and password, and the success and failure pages acknowledge successful/failed user login.

```
<%@ page language="java" %>
<%@ taglib uri="/WEB-INF/struts-form.tld" prefix="form" %>

<form:form action="logon.do">
Username: <form:text property="username" /><br />
Password: <form:password property="password" /><br />
<form:submit value="Logon" />
</form:form>
Listing 1: logon.jsp: demonstrates the use of the form tag

<%@ page language="java" %>
<html>
<head>
<title>Successful Logon</title>
</head>
<body>
You have successfully logged on.
</body>
</html>
Listing 2: success.jsp: displays our success message

<%@ page language="java" %>
<html>
<head>
<title>Logon Failure</title>
</head>
<body>
You have incorrectly logged on.
</body>
</html>
Listing 3: failure.jsp: displays our failure message
```

The LogonForm Bean extends the standard Struts ActionForm class and provides the support for the form tag's username and password properties that are accessed in logon.jsp.

```
package logon;
import org.apache.struts.action.ActionForm;

public class LogonForm extends ActionForm
{
  // A String variable representing our username form field
  protected String username;

  // A String variable representing our password form field
  protected String password;

  // A method to get the username form field. Will be used
  // by our LogonAction class to retrieve the username
  public String getUsername()
  {
   return username;
  }

  // A method to set the username form field. This method is
  // called on using introspection from the ActionServlet
  // controller
  public void setUsername(String username)
  {
   this.username = username;
  }

  // A method to set the password form field. This method is
  // called on using introspection from the ActionServlet
  // controller
  public void setPassword(String password)
  {
   this.password = password;
  }

  // A method to get the password form field. Will be used
  // in our LogonAction class to retrieve the username
  public String getPassword()
  {
   return password;
  }
}
```

Listing 4: LogonForm.java: extends the ActionForm class to add username and password support to the form tag used in logon.jsp

Model

The Model portion of this application consists of the action class that will handle the logon action. For the sake of simplicity, this class simply checks for the "test" username and password.

```java
package logon;
import javax.servlet.http.HttpServletRequest;
import javax.servlet.http.HttpServletResponse;
import org.apache.struts.action.*;

public class LogonAction extends Action
{
  // This is the method called on by ActionServlet when a
  // request is made for our logon action.
  // "mapping" is a class representation of our logon action
  // as defined in action.xml.
  // "form" is our form bean that we created for this action,
  // it should be an instance of "LogonForm".
  public ActionForward perform(ActionMapping mapping,
              ActionForm form,
              HttpServletRequest request,
              HttpServletResponse response)
  {
  // turn our form instance into our custom form bean
  LogonForm theForm = (LogonForm) form;

  // get the username and password from our form, they were
  // set using the struts form tags in logon.jsp
  String username = theForm.getUsername();
  String password = theForm.getPassword();

  // hardcode the username and password for simplicity
  if ((username.equals("test")) && (password.equals("test")))
  {
    // return an ActionForward that maps to the success page
    return mapping.findForward("success");
  }
  else
  {
    // return an ActionForward that maps to the failure page
    return mapping.findForward("failure");
  }
  }
}
```

Listing 5: LogonAction.java: handles the logon request

Controller

Struts implements the Controller in its ActionServlet class. The ActionServlet determines which action to take based on the requesting URI and its configuration file: struts-config. xml. The struts-config.xml file provides logical mappings that the ActionServlet will use to determine which Struts components to use and what the program flow is. This is done by providing a mapping for each requested uniform resource locator (URL) to an Action class and an ActionForm class.

Specifically, the Struts struts-config.xml file allows you to specify which Java classes will be used as the Action and ActionForm classes, so when a Web browser requests www.xyz.com/mystrutsapp/logon, for example, the desired classes and functionality get executed. The benefits of using an XML file for configuration are that a particular Action class can be leveraged for multiple requests and changes can be made to application behavior simply by modifying the struts-config.xml text file rather than the Java code.

```xml
<?xml version="1.0" encoding="ISO-8859-1" ?>
<!DOCTYPE struts-config PUBLIC
"-//Apache Software Foundation//DTD Struts Configuration
1.0//EN"
"http://jakarta.apache.org/struts/dtds/struts-config_1_0.dtd">

<struts-config>
  <form-beans>
   <form-bean name="logonForm" type="logon.LogonForm"/>
  </form-beans>
  <!--This tag defines the action mappings for the app.-->
  <action-mappings>
   <!-- ActionServlet uses the path to map to the action.-->
   <action path="/logon> type="logon.LogonAction"
            name="logonForm">
    <!-- The pages that ActionMapping may forward to.-->
    <forward name="success" path="/success.jsp" />
    <forward name="failure" path="/failure.jsp" />
   </action>
  </action-mappings>
</struts-config>
```
Listing 6: struts-config.xml: configures the ActionServlet

Application

Every Web application requires a web.xml file that contains important configuration and deployment settings. Most noteworthy are the <servlet-class> and <servlet-mapping> sections, which specify the Controller servlets and the mapping of which URL requests these Controllers will handle.

```xml
<?xml version="1.0" encoding="ISO-8859-1" ?>
<!DOCTYPE web-app PUBLIC
"-//Sun Microsystems, Inc.//DTD Web Application 2.2//EN"
```

```xml
"http://java.sun.com/j2ee/dtds/web-app_2_2.dtd">
<!—The servlet specification describes these sections.—>
<web-app>
  <servlet>
   <servlet-name>action</servlet-name>
   <!—This is the controller for our application.—>
   <servlet-class>
     org.apache.struts.action.ActionServlet
   </servlet-class>
   <init-param>
     <param-name>config</param-name>
      <param-value>/WEB-INF/struts-config.xml</param-value>
   </init-param>
   <init-param>
     <param-name>validate</param-name>
     <param-value>true</param-value>
   </init-param>
   <load-on-startup>1</load-on-startup>
  </servlet>

  <servlet-mapping>
   <!—Send requests with ".do" extension to ActionServlet.—>
   <servlet-name>action</servlet-name>
   <url-pattern>*.do</url-pattern>
  </servlet-mapping>

  <welcome-file-list>
   <welcome-file>logon.jsp</welcome-file>
  </welcome-file-list>

  <taglib>
   <!—Here, we define how to access the struts taglib.—>
   <taglib-uri>/WEB-INF/struts-form.tld</taglib-uri>
   <taglib-location>/WEB-INF/struts-form.tld</taglib-location>
  </taglib>
</web-app>
```
Listing 7: web.xml: configures the Logon application

Struts Request Processing

Now that we've put together a complete application, let's take a look at how it all fits together. Figure 21-2 illustrates how a request flows through the Struts framework.

1. The request calls the ActionServlet with a certain logical input form name.
2. This logical form name is then resolved according to mapping entries defined in struts-config.xml. Once the mapping is resolved, the ActionServlet will look in the

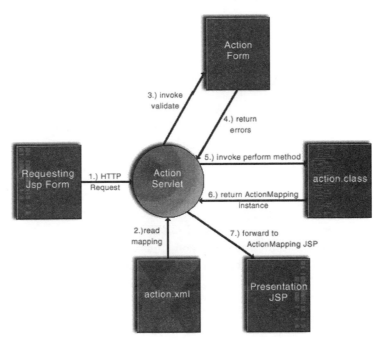

Figure 21-2. How a request flows through the Struts framework.

session for the ActionForm class associated with the request. If one does not exist, a new instance will be created and added to the session. The ActionForm attributes are then populated by calling the corresponding set methods. It's worth noting that the ActionForm bean's purpose is to represent the last input state of all entries on a particular form. This enables the framework to easily redisplay the last input screen (plus some error messages) prepopulated with what the user last entered.

3. Next, the ActionServlet calls the validate method on the ActionForm. The validate method returns either null (indicating success) or an array of errors (indicating an error condition).

4. If the ActionForm's validate method returns an array of errors, the ActionServlet populates the requesting input form and displays the errors to the user.

5. If the validate method returns null, the ActionServlet will instantiate an Action class (if one has not already been instantiated) as indicated by the mapping in struts-config.xml. The Action's perform method is then invoked by ActionServlet. The perform method is responsible for processing the request.

6. The perform method is required to return an ActionMapping instance. This instance indicates to the ActionServlet which JSP (if any) to forward the request off to for rendering of the presentation.

7. The presentation JSP is responsible for generating the appropriate response based on the results of executing the perform method.

Supporting Your Global Needs

We've put together a complete MVC application and have analyzed step-by-step how a request flows through the Struts framework. Now, if your company does any work outside the United States—if they have partners in Italy and a branch office in France, for example—the application needs to be localized so that it speaks many languages.

According to the MVC paradigm, the right way to handle localization is for the developer to create tools for the people focused on the look and feel to use. Struts provides the tools to change our logon application so that it not only supports our English friends, but also our *Français amis* and *Italiani amici*.

In order to localize our logon application, we need to create the associated resource bundles for English, French, and Italian, and rework the JSP pages to use the Struts message tag. Once this work is done, our application is ready to handle requests from English, French, and Italian users and greet them with prompts and messages that make sense to them.

Create Resource Bundles

To support multiple languages in your application using Struts, you must provide a resource bundle for each locale that you want to support, along with the appropriate extension.

```
logon.username=Username:
logon.password=Password:
logon.success=You have successfully logged on.
logon.failure=You have incorrectly logged on.
Listing 8: Logon.properties: the default (English) resource
bundle

logon.username=Nom:
logon.password=Mot de passe:
logon.success=Procédure de connexion réussie.
logon.failure=Procédure de connexion non réussie.
Listing 9: Logon_fr.properties: the French resource bundle

logon.username=Nome:
logon.password=Parola d'accesso:
logon.success=Inizio attivitá riuscito.
logon.failure=Inizio attivitá infruttuoso.
Listing 10: Logon_it.properties: the Italian resource bundle
```

Rework JSP Pages

Struts provides a message tag that handles obtaining the properly localized string. In order to successfully use the message tag, the application simply needs to store a Locale object within the user's session under the LOCALE_KEY of the Struts Action class. This Locale object is configured to match the user's language preference. If Struts finds no Locale object, then the default resource bundle will be used.

Let's take a look at the three reworked JSP pages to see how the message tag is used to replace the hard-coded text.

```
<%@ page language="java" %>
<%@ taglib uri="/WEB-INF/struts-bean.tld" prefix="struts" %>
<%@ taglib uri="/WEB-INF/struts-form.tld" prefix="form" %>

// Put a Locale object in the user's session describing
// the Locale that is specified by the browser's
// language preference (obtained via http header).
String lang = request.getHeader("Accept-Language");
session.putValue(org.apache.struts.action.Action.LOCALE_KEY, new
java.util.Locale(lang.substring(0, 2), "") );

<form:form action="logon.do">
<struts:message key="logon.username" />
<form:text property="username" /><br />
<struts:message key="logon.password" />
<form:password property="password" /><br />
<form:submit value="Logon" />
</form:form>
```
Listing 11: `logon.jsp`: reworked to store the Locale object and use the message tag

```
<%@ page language="java" %>
<%@ taglib uri="/WEB-INF/struts-bean.tld" prefix="struts" %>

<html>
<head>
<title>Successful Logon</title>
</head>
<body>
<struts:message key="logon.successful" />
</body>
</html>
```
Listing 12: `success.jsp`: reworked to use the message tag for success message

```
<%@ page language="java" %>
<%@ taglib uri="/WEB-INF/struts-bean.tld" prefix="struts" %>
```

```
<html>
<head>
<title>Logon Failure</title>
</head>
<body>
<struts:message key="logon.failure" />
</body>
</html>
```

Listing 13: `failure.jsp`: reworked to use the message tag for failure message

Conclusion

Throughout this chapter we have stressed the importance of separating business logic from its presentation. It is important to enable people to focus on their areas of expertise. By utilizing the Struts framework, we have demonstrated how to harness the efficiencies of the MVC design pattern and create applications that truly meet your global business needs.

In addition to your global business' language needs, global device needs—cell phones, pagers, and handheld PC's—also need to be addressed. Supporting applications with these kinds of "global" requirements will no doubt be added to the Struts framework in the near future. In the meantime, you can support these many devices by enhancing your Struts-based applications to utilize XML (extensible markup language) and XSLT (extensible stylesheet language for transformations) within your JSP views. You are strongly encouraged to browse the references below for more information on this topic, as well as all of the technologies covered in this chapter.

For those of you interested in participating in the Struts project, there are two mailing lists that you can subscribe to. You can subscribe to the Struts users' mailing list by sending e-mail to struts-user-subscribe@jakarta.apache.org, or you can send e-mail to struts-dev-subscribe@jakarta.apache.org to subscribe to the Struts developers' mailing list. The user mailing list is made up of users of the Struts framework, while the developer mailing list is made up of developers who are interested in furthering the Struts framework.

References

1. JavaServer Pages Technology page: http://java.sun.com/products/jsp/.
2. Java Servlet Technology page: http://java.sun.com/products/servlet/.
3. JavaServer Pages Tag Libraries: http://java.sun.com/products/jsp/taglibraries.html.
4. Jakarta Project Struts Framework: http://jakarta.apache.org/struts/.
5. Bluestone Labs Gallery Web site that contains Struts demo: http://gallery.bluestone.com.

6. Jakarta Project home page: http://jakarta.apache.org/.

7. XML Project home page: http://xml.apache.org/.

8. Apache Software Foundation home page: http://www.apache.org/.

9. World Wide Web Consortium (W3C) home page: http://www.w3.org/.

10. W3C XML Architecture domain page: http://www.w3.org/XML/.

11. W3C XSL Architecture domain page: http://www/w3.org/Style/XSL/.

SHAUN CONNOLLY has product management responsibility for Bluestone's Total-e-Server, which is the open-standards foundation for all Bluestone products. Mr. Connolly brings a strong technical presence to Bluestone's Corporate Program Management team, having spent 15 years in software development.

Before joining Bluestone, Mr. Connolly served as vice president of product design and development at Primavera Systems, a leading project management software company. Mr. Connolly held a variety of technical and management positions during his 12 years at Primavera. He helped guide Primavera's technical and product strategy by working with the executive management and such key customers and partners as Boeing, Bechtel, PECO, Vignette, Bentley Systems, and I2.

Mr. Connolly holds a BS in electrical engineering from Drexel University.

Section 4

Tips and Tricks

If you search the Web you'll find a plethora of freebie code written by Web development experts. In this section, I've invited some of these experts—who come in all shapes, sizes, ages, and nationalities—to share what I consider to be the most useful of scripts.

This section is intended as a sampling of what it is possible to do with tools such as JavaScript.

What you'll learn in this section:

1. How to code cookies.
2. How to build a Web site login using ASP, ADO, and SQL.
3. How to use JavaScript to write a shopping cart system.
4. How to build redirection into your Web site.
5. How to use JavaScript to create a rotating banner or image.
6. How to use JavaScript to mimic the Windows drop-down menu system on the Web.

Magic Cookies

Duncan Crombie

Cookies are one of the most useful and yet least understood tools available to a Web developer. They were originally conceived by Netscape and implemented in their Navigator 1.1 browser to provide a means for Web sites to store state variables between visits.

Cookies are described in RFC 2109 as an "HTTP State Management Mechanism." This essentially means that they enable variables to be stored in the browser and recalled by the site that set them even if the browser is shut down and the next visit is not for a number of days.

Without the ability to store state information, Web sites are unable, unless they force users to login at the start of each session, to provide any level of customization, as each visitor is forgotten as soon as they leave the site.

There are alternative means of identifying visitors, such as by their IP address. This, however, will only work where a browser has a static IP address. Dial-up users receive a dynamic IP address each time they connect, which makes this method of identification unreliable.

What Are Cookies?

A cookie is no more than a text string that a Web server or Web page can place into a file or directory on your computer for later reference. A real-life parallel would be the sticker that your local garage places inside your vehicle, indicating the date of your last service or oil change so that when you come back they have easy access to that information.

The implementation of cookies differs in one crucial way from the above example in that *only the server that placed the cookie on your computer is able to read it.* This means that information stored on your computer by one Web site, which could include your username or e-mail address, cannot be read by another server. The only exception to this is when different servers share the same domain and the cookie is set to be available across that domain (more about that later).

DOMAIN	AVAIL	PATH	SECURE	NAME	VALUE
www.chirp.com.au	FALSE	/	FALSE	name	Anonymous
www.ozemail.com.au	FALSE	/~dcrombie	FALSE	name	Anonymous
cnn.com	TRUE	/	FALSE	language	en

Figure 22-1. How cookies are stored.

You can easily view the cookies that have been stored on your computer as they are stored in plain text format. The location and format differ slightly for different browsers and platforms. On Windows you can search for a file named cookies.txt or a directory called cookies or Temporary Internet Files. If you are working on the Macintosh platform, look for a file called MagicCookie or cookies.txt in your Preferences folder.

Your cookies will be stored in either a single text file or in a directory structure with a separate file for each cookie (Figure 22-1). In either case the same information is stored and the format is roughly the same. The various pieces of information that make up a cookie will be described later.

What Can I Use Cookies for?

By skillful use of cookies on your site you can give your visitors the impression that they are being dealt with on a personal level. This can range from simple features, such as addressing them by name, up to personalization of the site graphics and content.

Remember that cookies will only give you information that visitors have entered on your site themselves—you can't detect their name, e-mail address, or any other piece of information from the browser using cookies!

The most common uses for cookies are:

• Storing personal information (e.g., name, e-mail, last visit) or user preferences associated with a site.
• Storing an ID that is used as a database reference. This minimizes the security risks in passing cookie information between the server and the browser, although for some sites, having access to the ID will enable you to access user information or to pose as another user on the site.
• Storing state variables, such as values entered or selected in forms, so that they are not lost as the browser moves to different pages. An example of this would be a site that remembers which section of a shopping catalog you searched last time and sets that as the default value when you return.

Another, more controversial application of cookies is where advertisers have banners from their own server appearing on a number of client sites. The banners themselves can set and receive cookies that identify users and allow the advertisers to follow them across all sites that carry their banners.

This is the practice that generated so much paranoia about cookies, and since then many browsers give you the option of automatically blocking cookies that are sourced from a different domain than the one you are visiting.

How Do I Set a Cookie?

The syntax for setting a cookie through an HTTP header is:

```
Set-Cookie: NAME=VALUE ; expires=DATE ;
path=PATH ; domain=DOMAIN_NAME ; secure
```

This header is passed from the Web server to the browser before the requested page is downloaded.

The meta-tag equivalent for setting a cookie is as follows:

```
<META http-equiv="Set-Cookie" content="NAME=VALUE; expires=DATE;
path=PATH; domain=DOMAIN; secure">
```

The header can also be generated by a server-side script such as PHP or using a CGI script, generally written in a language such as Perl or C.

PHP, for example, provides its own setcookie function:

```
setcookie (name, value, expire, path, domain, secure);
```

This function must be called before any page content is output, as it simply generates an HTTP header.

An alternative method for setting cookies is to use JavaScript, which sets the cookie instantly to the browser without requiring an HTTP header. The benefit of this is that it does not require any server-side support and so can be written into any Web page and can be set even after the page has loaded.

The syntax for setting a cookie in JavaScript is very similar to those above:

```
document.cookie = "NAME=VALUE; expires=DATE; path=PATH;
domain=DOMAIN; secure";
```

In either case, the only fields that you are required to supply are NAME and VALUE. The others will default, as shown in Figure 22-2.

These values determine when a cookie is going to be made visible to the Web server.

DATE	If you do not set an expiry date then the cookie will be set to expire as soon as the current browser session ends (i.e., by the user quitting the browser).
PATH	This will default to the path of the current directory.
DOMAIN	This will default to the domain of the current document.
SECURE	Default value is false.

Figure 22-2. Cookie fields.

Rules for Matching Cookies

The rules that determine when a browser should pass a cookie to the server are as follows:

Secure: If this value is set to TRUE, then the cookie is only passed if there is a secure channel. The URL in this instance will start with https:// instead of http://.

```
https:// . . .
```

Domain: If you do not specify the domain, then the AVAIL variable stored with the cookie with be FALSE and only servers that exactly match the domain stored will be able to see the cookie.

```
http://DOMAIN . . .
```

If you override the default value of DOMAIN you can make the cookie available across multiple sites. In this case AVAIL will be set to TRUE and all domains ending in the specified value can view the cookie.

```
http://* + DOMAIN . . .
```

There are limitations as to what can be set as the DOMAIN of a cookie. You can refer to the Netscape Specifications for details.

Path: If you are setting a cookie from a subdirectory of your domain and want it to be available from areas of the site outside that directory, then you can override the PATH variable. All addresses meeting the above criteria and starting with PATH will be able to view the cookie.

```
http://DOMAIN + PATH + *
```

Date: This variable determines when the cookie expires. The date is always set in GMT. To delete a cookie you need to set a cookie with the same PATH, DOMAIN, and SECURE values but with a past or negative DATE value.

How Do I Read a Cookie?

Every time you go to a new page or new domain, your browser checks to see if there are any cookies it should pass to the server along with the HTTP request. Any cookies that match the DOMAIN and the PATH of the current page should be made available to the server. Cookies that have expired or are set to be passed only over secure channels should not be sent.

Cookies that meet the above criteria are passed to the Web server using the format:

```
Cookie: NAME1=VALUE1 ; NAME2=VALUE2 . . .
```

Note that only the NAME=VALUE pairs are passed; no information about the expiry date or other attributes of the cookie are made available!

Cookie values can be read in a number of ways: using a server-side scripting language such as PHP; via a CGI script; or on the client side using JavaScript.

Because multiple cookies with the same NAME but different PATH and VALUE can be accessible on the same page, the more specific cookie (i.e., the cookie with the longest PATH value) will be sent first. For most methods of parsing cookies, the first cookie of a given NAME is used in preference to those that follow.

A CGI script can read the cookie values directly from the header. PHP creates a global associative array, $HTTP_COOKIE_VARS, storing all cookie values, and also creates a variable for each cookie.

In JavaScript you can access the variable document.cookie, which is a string of all the cookie values for the current page. To view the cookies available from any page you can type into the location bar of your browser the following command:

```
JavaScript: alert (document.cookie);
```

Parsing of this string is left up to the programmer. Some useful functions will be introduced later in this chapter.

How Secure Are Cookies?

The information stored in cookies is passed to the server in an HTTP header. This information is generally in plain text format, which means that anyone in between the Web server and the client can read the cookie information as it passes through. The exception would be if the page was being displayed over a secure channel (https).

If you want to pass sensitive information in a cookie, you can set the final parameter of the cookie, SECURE, to TRUE and the cookie will be passed *only* to the server where there is a secure channel. In any case, cookies stored on the visitor's computer are always in plain text format, so it is best not to store sensitive information or passwords in this way.

In addition to the above, some versions of Internet Explorer for Windows have a security hole that allows cookies to be read from any domain. Details of the problem and a work-around are available at www.peacefire.org/security/iecookies/.

Using Cookies in PHP and JavaScript

Setting and reading a cookie using PHP:

```php
<?PHP
  if ($submit) {
    $myName = $HTTP_POST_VARS["myName"];
    setcookie ("myName", $myName, time()+24*3600);
  } else {
    $myName = $HTTP_COOKIE_VARS["myName"];
  }
?>
<HTML>
<HEAD>
  <TITLE>Cookie Test Page</TITLE>
</HEAD>
<BODY bgcolor="#ffffff">

<H1>Cookie Test Page</H1>
<?PHP
  if ($myName) {
    echo ">Welcome back $myName</P>\n";
  }
?>
<FORM method="post" action="<?PHP echo $PHP_SELF; ?>">
Name: <INPUT type="text" name="myName" size="24">
<INPUT type="submit" name="submit" value="Set Cookie">
</FORM>

</BODY>
</HTML>
```

Setting and reading a cookie using JavaScript:

```html
<HTML>
<HEAD>
  <TITLE>Cookie Test Page</TITLE>
  <SCRIPT language="JavaScript">
  <!—Hide from older browsers

  var today = new Date();
  var expiry = new Date(today.getTime()+24*3600*1000);

// Simple setCookie function
  function setCookie(name, value) {
    if (value != null && value != "")
      document.cookie = name + "=" + escape(value) + ";
expires=" + expiry.toGMTString();
  }

  function getCookie(name) {
    var bites = document.cookie.split("; ");
    for (var i=0; i < bites.length; i++) {
      nextbite = bites[i].split("=");
      if (nextbite[0] == name)
        return unescape(nextbite[1]);
    }
    return null;
  }

  function getName() {
    var myName = prompt ("Enter your name:", "");
    setCookie ("myName", myName);
  }

  // Stop hiding—>
  </SCRIPT>
</HEAD>
<BODY bgcolor="#ffffff">

<H1>Cookie Test Page</H1>

<SCRIPT language="JavaScript">
<!—Hide from older browsers

  var myName = getCookie ("myName");
  if (myName != null) {
    document.write (">");
    document.write ("Welcome back " + myName);
    document.write ("</P>");
  }
```

```
// Stop hiding-->
</SCRIPT>

<FORM name="myForm">
<INPUT type="button" value="Set Cookie" onClick="getName();">
</FORM>

</BODY>
</HTML>
```

The two examples above do essentially the same thing. They each prompt users to enter their name, set that value as a cookie, and then display a personalized message when they reload or revisit the page. There are clear differences, however, between how this is implemented in PHP (server side) and JavaScript (client side).

When you work with a server-side language, nothing can be processed until you submit or reload the page. For the variable "myName" to be passed to the server it has to be entered into a form that is then submitted. This causes the same page to reload, but now the form value is available to the server as $HTTP_POST_VARS["myName"], which we use to set the cookie. The setcookie function has the effect of passing an HTTP header to the browser that sets the cookie.

Note that at this stage the server does not know about the cookie, the browser did not pass it as part of the HTTP request because this *preceded* the setcookie header. Only on subsequent visits to this page will the browser pass the cookie, which then becomes available to the server as $HTTP_COOKIE_VARS["myName"].

Using JavaScript on the client side, you can have the cookie *immediately* stored in the browser and *immediately* available in the document.cookie object without requiring an HTTP header to be passed from the server. There can be advantages in using JavaScript to set cookies, even when you have access to server-side scripting, because you avoid having to reload the page every time.

Finally, you will note that in both examples the cookie is set to expire after 24 hours. In PHP you specify the time value in seconds since epoch, whereas in JavaScript you need to specify it in milliseconds. In JavaScript you also have to convert this numeric value to a GMT string, whereas the PHP function setcookie does this transparently.

If you omit the expiry date, then both examples would still work, but the cookies would be lost as soon as you quit the browser. By setting an expiry date you allow the cookies to *persist* beyond the current session and be available at any time up until the expiry date.

Browser Limitations

The original cookie specifications from Netscape called for a limit to be placed on the number of cookies that a given site could set on your computer at one time. There is also a limit on the total number of cookies on your computer and the size of each cookie. The purpose of this is to prevent a malicious programmer from setting an infinite number of cookies and overloading your hard drive.

The suggested limits are as follows:

- Size limit per cookie: 4 kb (4,096 characters)
- Total number of cookies: 300
- Cookies per domain: 20

When either of the latter two limits are exceeded, the least recently used cookie is deleted, making way for the new one. If you try to store more than 4kb in a cookie, it will be truncated.

While sensible, these limitations will cause problems for programmers that are unaware of them or have not catered to them.

Common Mistakes

The following are the most common problems encountered when working with cookies.

Stale Cookies

A cookie is "stale" when it has passed its expiry date. Stale cookies are cleaned out of the cookie cache when you quit the browser.

This is a very common problem because it is not immediately obvious that it is a problem when you start writing cookies. Imagine that the algorithm used on your site is as follows:

```
Has the browser got a cookie?
IF NO: setcookie( . . . )
end
```

That looks simple enough. You only set the cookie if the browser hasn't already got one. Then, the next time the user visits, the cookie is already set, so you do nothing.

The problem with this is that no matter how far ahead you set the expiry date, it will get closer and closer until the cookie finally expires, even if that browser visits the site every day. Imagine if that cookie is used to store all of that user's preferences for a site. These values can be irretrievable because the cookie has become stale.

The amended algorithm is:

```
Has the browser got a cookie?
IF YES: setcookie( . . . ) with existing cookie values
        (moving forward the expiry date)
```

```
IF NO: setcookie( . . . )
end
```

This will ensure that a regular visitor to your site never has a stale cookie. A similar problem is encountered when people think that they can get around this problem by setting a cookie to expire in ten years and so don't bother updating it. These cookies could easily be swapped out of the cookie cache in the browser in favor of more recently updated cookies.

Cookie Spamming

The cause of this problem stems from the solution that is discussed above. The algorithm introduced as a solution to the stale cookie problem requires that setcookie() be called once for each cookie on each page of the site. This results in the browser being bombarded by multiple setcookie headers when it is necessary for the cookie to be updated only once.

This can be achieved by using a temporary cookie "updated" that is set to TRUE once the cookies have been updated. If another page is loaded during the same browser session, the presence of this cookie means that further setcookie() calls are not required.

```
if (getcookie ("updated") == true) end;
Has the browser got a cookie?
IF YES: setcookie( . . . ) with existing cookie values
        setcookie("updated", true);
IF NO: setcookie( . . . )
end
```

Note that the cookie "updated" should not be set with an expiry date unless that date is well short of the expiry date of the cookie that you are trying to preserve.

A very similar method is used when you want to count the number of times that a browser has visited your site. The only change is that instead of setting the cookie with the existing value, you initially set it to 1 and increase its value once for each visit.

PATH Problems

It is always tempting to just focus on the first three variables when setting a cookie: NAME, VALUE, and DATE. If you are running a site that has only a single directory of HMTL pages and runs under a single domain, then that really is all you need. If, on the other hand, you work with multiple directories, then you may also need to set the PATH variable to ensure that your cookies are visible where you think they are visible.

The solution is to set PATH=/ for all cookies in the site. If you are planning on having different cookies for different directories, then you should draw up a site map so that you have a clear idea of the scope of each cookie. See the section Rules for Matching Cookies as an aid.

Too Many Cookies

It is very tempting to use a new cookie for each variable that you want to store, particularly if you are setting up a shopping site and want to use cookies for the shopping cart. If you do this then you will very quickly run up against the 20-cookie limit. People using the site will start to see their initial selections disappear once they exceed the limit of 20 items.

The solution is to store all of your variables in a single cookie. Remember that each cookie has a 4kb limit. In theory you could store an entire Web page in that space. In order to store multiple values in a single cookie you have to provide your own code to "pack" and "unpack" the cookie contents.

As an example, you could set three values into one cookie using "!" as the major delimiter, separating the NAME/VALUE pairs, and ":" to separate NAME and VALUE for each pair.

Sample cookie:

```
poetry=rosesred!violets:blue!sugar:sweet
```

JavaScript Unpacking Example

This code introduces a more generic function, getValue(), that can be used to unpack cookies as well as values in our cookie array.

```
<SCRIPT language="JavaScript">
<!—Hide from older browsers

function getValue(str, name, delim1, delim2) {
  var bites = str.split(delim1);
  for (var i=0; i < bites.length; i++) {
    extbite = bites[i].split(delim2);
    if (nextbite[0] == name)
      return unescape(nextbite[1]);
  }
  return null;
}

var bikky = document.cookie;
var poetry = getValue (bikky, "poetry", "; ", "=");
```

```
var roses = getValue (poetry, "roses", "!", ":");
var violets = getValue (poetry, "violets", "!", ":");
var sugar = getValue (poetry, "sugar", "!", ":");

// Stop Hiding-->
</SCRIPT>
```

PHP Unpacking Example

The following code will extract all variables from the "poetry" cookie and create a new variable for each.

```
<?PHP
  $poetry = $HTTP_COOKIE_VARS["poetry"];
  $parray = explode ("!", $poetry);
  for ($i=0; $i < count ($parray); $i++) {
    list ($key, $val) = explode (":", $parray [$i]);
    $$key = $val;
  }
?>
```

As you can see from these examples and from those presented previously, most of the work involved in using cookies is in manipulating strings to store and extract values. Because that functionality is a basic part of any programming language, there is nothing to stop you writing your own code in another language such a Perl, C, or ASP.

References

THE ORIGINAL COOKIE SPECIFICATION AND THE OFFICIAL RFC
1. Netscape Specification: http://www.netscape.com/newsref/std/cookie_spec.html.
2. Request for Comments: 2109: http://www.cis.ohio-state.edu/htbin/rfc/rfc2109.html.

U.S. GOVERNMENT REPORT ON COOKIES
CIAC: Internet Cookies: http://ciac.llnl.gov/ciac/bulletins/i-034.shtml.

SAMPLE CODE
1. Duncan's Cookie Pages: http://www.ozemail.com.au/~dcrombie/cookie.html.
2. PHP: Manual: setcookie: http://www.php.net/manual/en/function.setcookie.php.
3. irt.org: JavaScript Cookie Articles: http://tech.irt.org/articles/script11.htm.
4. Cookie Central: http://www.cookiecentral.com/.

DUNCAN CROMBIE is managing director of Chirp Web Design, an Australian-based Web development company that specializes in customized database Web sites. Chirp has created sites for companies across Australia, the United States, and regions of Europe.

Before starting Chirp Web Design, Duncan completed degrees in engineering (systems) and economics at the Australian National University in Canberra. During this time, Duncan was exposed to the burgeoning WWW and quickly became proficient and started coding in HTML and JavaScript.

Duncan's home page provides code examples and tutorials that have been used and referenced around the world. His JavaScript cookie code has been particularly popular and is used on hundreds of sites including, at one time, the home.microsoft.com Web site.

This is Duncan's first published article, although visitors to his home page will find the framework of a JavaScript reference and tutorial that may eventually see the light of day.

Duncan Crombie Chirp Internet Pty Ltd ⟨dcrombie@chirp.com.au⟩ http://www.chirp. com.au

Secured Web Page Login with ASP

Corby Kissler

Web sites on the Internet are designed to provide information that is easily accessible from anywhere in the world. But what happens when you need to use the benefits of the Internet's mass availability, connectivity, and thin client architecture but have confidential information that is meant for a specific audience? Securing your Web site with a login page is a good way to make sure that the audience you want to give information to are the only ones capable of viewing it. One way to implement this is to use ASP, ADO, and SQL to design your login and security system.

Designing a Login page

The basic premise of designing a login and page security system using ASP, ADO, and SQL is to provide a way to secure pages in a Web site by checking permissions that have been assigned to the user accessing your site. Implementing this system can be broken down to the following steps:

- Infrastructure setup
- Database
- Application setup
- Scalability issues
- Login page
- Page security
- Administration

Infrastructure Setup—What You'll Need

In order to implement the code outlined in this chapter you will need the following items. We are assuming you have a server to install the software on:

- NT 4.0 SP 4 or above
- NT Option Pack—Internet Information Server (IIS) v4.0
- Relational Database Management System—Access/SQL Server/Oracle
- Administrative access to the server for configuration purposes

For the purposes of this chapter, we will assume that you have administrative privileges and are familiar with the proper setup of these items. You should also have at least a familiarity with HTML, ADO, SQL, ASP, VBSCRIPT, and JavaScript. Through the course of this development, we have relied on Microsoft's Visual Interdev v6.0 for our editing needs.

Database

For this application, we have chosen to persist information about our users, their login information, and specifics of their session in a database. While there are many ways to save this information, a database offers many unique benefits. A principle reason for using a relational database system is the ease with which data can be collected and then reported for management purposes.

Thus, we have created an Access database with two tables, UserInfo and Sessions. We recommend a more robust database system for production systems, but Access is sufficient for our purposes. As you may have already guessed, UserInfo contains information about the user, such as userid, username, password, as well as personalized information such as address, city, state, and zip. The Sessions table contains information about what the user did while at the site. Specifically, it stores login time, last visit time, and number of visits per session. The total session time may be derived from this data as well. The field names and data types for these tables are shown in Figure 23-1.

After creating this database, we now need a way to access it from our Web site. We chose to implement this database connectivity using ODBC and DSN's configured in the Windows ODBC control panel.

We chose the name "ASPLogin" for our DSN (data source name). We made this DSN a system DSN. A DSN is defined by Microsoft's MSDN Library as follows:

---

data source name (DSN)

An ODBC term for the collection of information used to connect your application to a particular ODBC database. The ODBC Driver Manager uses this information to create a connection to the database. A DSN can be stored in a file (a file DSN) or in the Windows Registry (a machine DSN). Compare with data connection.

Source: MSDN Libray—July 2000

Sessions Table	Datatype
UserID	Text (Key)
SessionID	Text (Key)
StartTime	Date/Time
LastVisit	Date/Time
Visits	Number
UserInfo Table	Datatype
UserID	AutoNumber (Key)
UserName	Text
Password	Text
FirstName	Text
LastName	Text
Address	Text
Address1	Text
City	Text
State	Text
Zip	Text

Figure 23-1. *The Sessions table.*

A system DSN is unique to the machine and does not differentiate between users. For a complete discussion of DSN choices and what makes sense in your scenario, please see the excellent resources at http://msdn.microsoft.com.

Application Setup

Every Internet application using IIS contains a file in the application root named global.asa. This file acts as a kind of initialization file. IIS looks here when the application starts, or when a user accesses the site, for session or application variables that can be used to define default values. An example of an application level default is where we want to limit the length of time a user can visit our protected site without taking some action. In our case, we have chosen 20 minutes as the maximum amount of time a user can remain idle. We set this value in the global.asa file by defining an application variable, SessExpiretime, and setting its value to 20. Figure 23-2 illustrates what a typical global.asa file looks like and also shows the initialization of our session expires parameter.

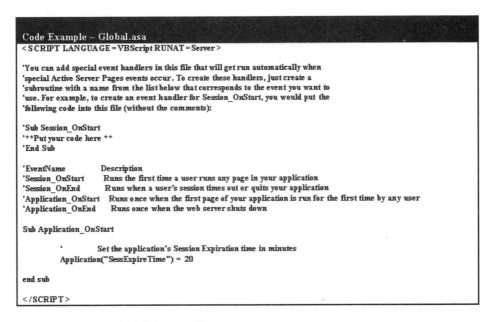

```
Code Example – Global.asa
< SCRIPT LANGUAGE = VBScript RUNAT = Server >

'You can add special event handlers in this file that will get run automatically when
'special Active Server Pages events occur. To create these handlers, just create a
'subroutine with a name from the list below that corresponds to the event you want to
'use. For example, to create an event handler for Session_OnStart, you would put the
'following code into this file (without the comments):

'Sub Session_OnStart
'**Put your code here **
'End Sub

'EventName               Description
'Session_OnStart         Runs the first time a user runs any page in your application
'Session_OnEnd           Runs when a user's session times out or quits your application
'Application_OnStart     Runs once when the first page of your application is run for the first time by any user
'Application_OnEnd       Runs once when the web server shuts down

Sub Application_OnStart

        '           Set the application's Session Expiration time in minutes
            Application("SessExpireTime") = 20

end sub

</SCRIPT>
```

Figure 23-2. A typical global.asa file.

Scalability Issues

A key concern for any Web application designer is scalability. The reason for this is that the very nature of the Web means that our application could be taking more hits than it was designed for in very short order. Therefore, we need to ensure that our application meets two criteria. First, that we can rely on the application to service the number of requests it was designed for, as well as a reasonable number above, and second, if we do encounter increased demand for the application, that the infrastructure and application can be modified easily to accept the increased demand.

In order to persist data about who is visiting our application, we need a way to track users as they navigate our site. One way to do this is to use cookies, a method that writes an index file on the user's computer. We then read the values stored in the cookie and present the correct information. This approach works, but there has been some negative press about cookies and the privacy implications of using them. This topic is outside the scope of this document, but deserves some attention.

Another way to track user persistence is to use the session object and session variables provided by IIS. While this is also a valid approach, we want to avoid using it. A little known fact about session variables is that they do not scale well. The main reason for this is that each session variable takes up a small amount of memory on the server. This does not become an issue until there are hundreds or thousands of users at the site using the application.

An easy and effective solution to these issues is to store the session information in the URL that is passed from page to page using the query string. The benefits of storing the session in the query string are outlined below:

1. Server memory resources are not used.
2. Client privacy issues are preserved.
3. Application scales to the capabilities of the hardware, not the software.
4. Conversion to a Web farm infrastructure is eased.

The syntax of this method is shown below:

```
http://www.myserver.com/validateuser.asp?SessionID=12345678
```

Our application implements this by generating a unique sessionid and storing this information in the database and passing the query string to the user. Figure 23-3 illustrates how we have generated the unique sessionid. We use a combination of serializing today's date, the userid, and segments of the current date.

To persist this information, we simply make sure that the first thing we do on any secure page is to read and validate the session information against the database. On all links to secure pages, we make sure to pass the session information in the query string as follows:

```
http://www.myserver.com/validateuser.asp?SessionID=12345678
```

This method is flexible enough to be used in a Web farm environment that validates the session information back to a centralized database, thus ensuring that our application scales well.

```
Code Example – Generate Session ID – Figure x-3
Function GetSessionID()

GetSessionID = clng(now()) & UID & CStr(Minute(Now()) & Hour(Now()) & Second(Now())& _
Month(Now()) & Year(Now()) & Day(Now()) )

End Function
```

Figure 23-3. Generate Sessionid.

Figure 23-4. *Sample login screen.*

Login Page

If we want users to log in to our secure site, we'll need a login page. I've included a sample screen shot of the login page (Figure 23-4) and a code snippet to illustrate the HTML. This is a basic login screen that you will see at many sites around the Web. The code sample listed below is worth noting. Let's take a look at it.

```
'LOGIN.ASP
<!—#INCLUDE FILE="LOGIN.INC"—>
<%

dim UID,Username, PWD, strSql
dim boolError
dim dbrecordset
dim strErrorMsg, strSessionID

'    Check to see if we have arrived here via the submit
'    button on this form
'    If yes, then we validate the username and password.
'    If the user exists, we assign a session variable,
'    update the session table
'    and redirect the user to the main secured page

strErrorMsg = Request.QueryString("ErrMsg")

if Request.Form.Count > 0 then
    set dbrecordset = server.CreateObject("ADODB.Recordset")
```

```
      Username = trim(Request.Form("UID"))
      PWD = trim(Request.Form("Password"))
      strsql = "SELECT * FROM UserInfo where username = '" &
UserName & "' and password = '" & PWD & "'"
      dbopen dbconnection
      set dbrecordset = dbconnection.execute(strsql)
      if not (dbrecordset.BOF and dbrecordset.EOF) THEN
            '     We have found the Username, Password in the
            '     database
            '     so we need to assign the session variable and
            '     update
            '     the session table, then redirect the user to
            '     the secured page
            UID = dbrecordset.fields(0).value
            dbrecordset.close
            strSessionID = GetSessionID
            strsql = "Insert into Sessions (userid, sessionid,
            starttime, lastvisit, visits) values (" & _
            "'" & UID & "','" & strSessionID & "','" & now() &
            "','" & now() & "', 1)"
            dbconnection.execute strsql
            Response.Redirect "mainpage.asp?Session=" &
            strSessionID
      else
            strErrorMsg = "User not found. Please check your
            username and password and try again!"
      end if
end if
%>


<HTML>
<HEAD>
<META NAME="GENERATOR" Content="Microsoft Visual Studio 6.0">
<TITLE></TITLE>
</HEAD>
<BODY>

<form action="Login.asp" method="post" name="login">
<P><center>
<TABLE border=1 cellPadding=1 cellSpacing=1 width="50%">
  <TR>
    <TD colspan=2>Welcome to the Acme employee site.
    Please enter your username and password below.
    <% if strErrorMsg <> "" then %>
    <font color = red> <%=strErrorMsg %></font>
    <% end if%>
    </TD>
  </TR>
```

```
  <TR>
    <TD>UserName:</TD>
    <TD><INPUT id=UID name=UID></TD>
    </TR>
    <TR>
    <TD>Password:</TD>
    <TD><INPUT type=password id=Password
    name=Password></TD>
    </TR></TABLE>
<P><INPUT id=button1 name=button1 type=submit
value=Login></P></center>
</form>
</BODY>
</HTML>
```

The first thing we do on this page is to include the file, "login.inc," which includes the functions we need. Then we assign the value of the error message from the query string, if any.

```
strErrorMsg = Request.QueryString("ErrMsg")
```

We then check the number of form fields that are being passed, if we find them, and read them into the appropriate variables.

```
if Request.Form.Count > 0 then
    set dbrecordset = server.CreateObject("ADODB.Recordset")
    Username = trim(Request.Form("UID"))
    PWD = trim(Request.Form("Password"))
```

The next step is to validate the username and password against the database. If successful, we write the session information to the sessions table and redirect the user to the main page of our secured area.

```
strsql = "SELECT * FROM UserInfo where username = '" & UserName
& "' and password = '" & PWD & "'"
    dbopen dbconnection
    set dbrecordset = dbconnection.execute(strsql)
    if not (dbrecordset.BOF and dbrecordset.EOF) THEN
            '    We have found the Username, Password in
            '    the database   so we need to assign the
            '    session variable and update
            '    the session table, then redirect the
```

```
'     user to the secured page
UID = dbrecordset.fields(0).value
dbrecordset.close
strSessionID = GetSessionID
strsql = "Insert into Sessions (userid,
sessionid, starttime, lastvisit, visits)
values (" & _
"'" & UID & "','" & strSessionID & "','" &
now() & "','" & now() & "', 1)"
dbconnection.execute strsql
Response.Redirect "mainpage.asp?Session=" &_
strSessionID
```

If not successful, we set an error message that will be displayed to the user on the login screen.

```
strErrorMsg = "User not found. Please check your username and
password and try again!"
```

The actual HTML form is worth noting as well. Basically, what we have done is to implement a standard HTML form using the POST method and submit the form to the same page for validation. We also include the error message, if any, to prompt the user for the response we want.

```
<form action="Login.asp" method="post" name="login">
<P><center>
<TABLE border=1 cellPadding=1 cellSpacing=1 width="50%">
  <TR>
    <TD colspan=2>Welcome to the Acme employee site.
      Please enter your username and password below.
      <% if strErrorMsg <> "" then %>
    <font color = red> <%=strErrorMsg %></font>
      <% end if%>
      </TD>
    </TR>
  <TR>
    <TD>UserName:</TD>
    <TD><INPUT id=UID name=UID></TD>
    </TR>
  <TR>
    <TD>Password:</TD>
        <TD><INPUT type=password id=Password
name=Password></TD>
    </TR></TABLE>
```

```
<P><INPUT id=button1 name=button1 type=submit
value=Login></P></center>

</form>
```

Page Security

Next, we need a way to make sure that the user visiting our page has a valid login. If we include the following two lines of code in each of the Web pages that we want to secure with our login system, we will ensure that our Web pages remain available to only those users who are in our database.

```
<!-#include file="login.inc"->
<%
VerifyUser = Validateuser(Request.QueryString("Session"))
%>
```

We include our validateuser function with the include file. The session information is taken from the query string and passed to the validateuser function from the include file. The result is stored in VerifyUser. This gives us an opportunity to analyze the functions in the "login.inc" file. The following figure contains the code from the include file:

```
<%
Function GetSessionID()
     GetSessionID = clng(now()) & UID & CStr(Minute(Now())
     & Hour(Now()) & Second(Now())& Month(Now()) &
     Year(Now()) & Day(Now()) )
End Function

Sub DBOpen(ByRef conn)
     Set conn = Server.CreateObject("ADODB.Connection")
     conn.open "DSN=ASPLogin"
End Sub

Function ValidateUser(ByVal usersession)
     DBOpen dbconnection
     strSql = "select * from Sessions where SessionID =
     '" & usersession & "'"
     Set dbrecordset = dbconnection.Execute(strsql)

     if not (dbrecordset.eof and dbrecordset.bof) then
         UID = dbrecordset.fields(0).value
```

```
              LastVisit = dbrecordset.fields(3).value
              dbrecordset.close

              'Check for Expired Session Variable
              if datediff("n",cdate(lastvisit), now()) >
                  Application("SessExpireTime") then
                  'Expired Session
                  response.redirect
                       "login.asp?ErrMsg=Session Expired"
              end if

              'Update the Session Information
              strSql =
              "UPDATE Sessions SET Sessions.LastVisit = Now(),
              Sessions.Visits = Sessions.Visits + 1 " & _
              " WHERE (((Sessions.UserID)='" & UID & "'))
              AND         Sessions.SessionID = '" &
                  usersession & "'"
                  dbConnection.Execute(strSql)
       else
                  response.redirect
                  "login.asp?ErrMsg=Access Denied. Please Login."
       end if

End Function

Function GetUserInfo(byVal UID)

              strSql = "select * from UserInfo where UserID = "
              & UID
              set dbrecordset = dbconnection.Execute(strSql)
              GetUserInfo = dbrecordset.getrows

End Function

%>
```

Let's analyze this code, specifically the ValidateUser function, which is where most of the real work of the application happens.

First, we open the data connection and compare the passed in session value with values in the database. This is accomplished in three lines of code.

```
DBOpen dbconnection
    strSql = "select * from Sessions where SessionID = '" &
    usersession & "'"
    Set dbrecordset = dbconnection.Execute(strsql)
```

We then check to make sure that we have a valid match and read the userid and the last time visited into local variables. If we don't find a match, we redirect the user to the login page with the appropriate error message.

```
if not (dbrecordset.eof and dbrecordset.bof) then
    UID = dbrecordset.fields(0).value
    LastVisit = dbrecordset.fields(3).value
    dbrecordset.close

    'Check for Expired Session Variable
    if datediff("n",cdate(lastvisit), now()) >
        Application("SessExpireTime") then
        'Expired Session
          response.redirect "login.asp?ErrMsg=Session
          Expired"
          end if
else
    response.redirect "login.asp?ErrMsg=Access Denied.
    Please Login."
end if
```

We also check to make sure that the user has not passed the session expiration time limit. If the user has passed the time limit, then we redirect them to the login page along with an error message.

Assuming that we have a valid login and the database has returned matching records, we then update the sessions table with the latest information.

```
'Update the Session Information
strSql = "UPDATE Sessions SET Sessions.LastVisit = Now(),
Sessions.Visits = Sessions.Visits + 1 " & _
  " WHERE (((Sessions.UserID)='" & UID & "')) AND
  Sessions.SessionID = '" & usersession & "'"

  dbConnection.Execute(strSql)
```

The update query listed above does a few things. First, it looks for the matching record in the database by userid and sessionid. Next, it sets the lastvisit field to the current date and time, giving the database the most current visited time. Finally, the query increments the hit counter (the field "visits") by one.

Using these simple premises, we have secured our Web site by requiring users to login with a valid username and password.

Personalization

One of the benefits of requiring users to log in to your Web site is that you know who they are once they get there. Depending on the type of information you store about your users, you can offer a Web site that is personalized to each specific user very easily. In this example, I have included a function that returns all the information stored about a particular user. This function takes one parameter, a userid, and returns an array containing the user information. You could use this information to greet users by name when they log in to your site, or to fill out their shipping information for them when they order a product from you. Here is the function:

```
Function GetUserInfo(byVal UID)

        strSql = "select * from UserInfo where UserID = "
        & UID
        set dbrecordset = dbconnection.Execute(strSql)
        GetUserInfo = dbrecordset.getrows
End Function
```

While we are looking up the sessionid and the user information, we have an opportunity to present information that has been customized especially to individual users. This type of personalization creates a friendly environment for your users.

Administration

The nice thing about using this method is that we are able to provide reports on what our users are doing while they are at the site. For instance, we can easily write a query against the database to give us the average time spent at the site. This would be valuable information to gauge the usefulness of the site. We could also easily modify the database table and update query to save the page that was being visited. From this information we could discern what section of the Web site was getting the most traffic, allowing us to analyze what users are using and what they are not. Using a database to store this information really gives us tremendous flexibility to do these things and, with a little imagination, much, much more.

References

Excellent sources of information regarding this topic can be found at:
1. http://msdn.microsoft.com.
2. http://www.cgvb.com.
3. http://www.asptoday.com.
4. http://www.wroxpress.com.

CORBY KISSLER has been involved in the Internet industry since 1994, when he planned and supported the launch of a successful ISP. After founding two successful Internet companies, Mr. Kissler is currently the president of the Marant Group, a national consulting firm, specializing in providing Internet solutions to the financial and health-care management industries, respectively. Corby has several Internet-based products to attest to his development skill. He has been programming Web sites and database applications to solve business problems for his entire career and is pleased to be able to contribute his experience to this publication.

JavaScript Shopping Cart

Richard Graeber

There are some hard realities in coding with JavaScript:

JavaScript size limitations: Because the current convention of the Internet limits the size of a JavaScript program to 200K, it is important to have efficient, low-fat code.

Error; line 22: When confronted with the venerable error message that points to a particular in the script, do this: With the HTML/JavaScript page loaded into a text editor, line 1 will be the uppermost line of text (code). Place cursor at bottommost line and hit the ^ (up arrow) the required line count. When you have hit the key the required number of times, the line with error will be the uppermost line.

JavaScript vs. Java: Some people confuse JavaScript with Java and vice versa. They may be named similarly and owned by the same company (Sun Microsystems), but they are fundamentally different. Java allows a Web developer to control the actions of a small window in the browser's main window. JavaScript, on the other hand, because of its integral nature to HTML, controls the entire browser window.

The JavaScript shopping cart must do the following:

1. Calculate running totals, including quantity discounts, as customer selects products.
2. Show running total in separate frame in same window.
3. Send selected choices as CGI function, evoking send-mail with auto-responder from server.
4. Encrypt the transaction through SSL.

Using the Order-Processing Function

Step 1. User views products and makes selection.
Step 2. User edits selection, chooses tax rate and shipping options.

Step 3. User enters shipping information; JScript validates form.
Step 4. User chooses Submit button as cash or credit card payment.

- If cash, list of selection, total amount, and shipping info is sent back to user with instructions to print out and mail with check.
- If credit card or i-check, SSL window opens for CC or i-Check info.

List of selection, total amount, shipping info, and financial info is sent to server. Send-mail with auto-responder sends receipt, e-mail confirmation, and sales order to appropriate recipients.

Basic Structure of the JavaScript Shopping Cart Script

Frameset, the Frames Window (JavaScriptCartX.htm)

This is the page that holds the pieces of the JSSCart, as shown in Figure 24-1. It is a frameset that is split horizontally. In the top half of the frameset appears the product catalog, sales order, shipping info form, and purchase receipt. On the bottom half is the running total with shipping options selection, state tax selection and Edit Cart, View Cart, Checkout buttons. This "totals" section is always in view.

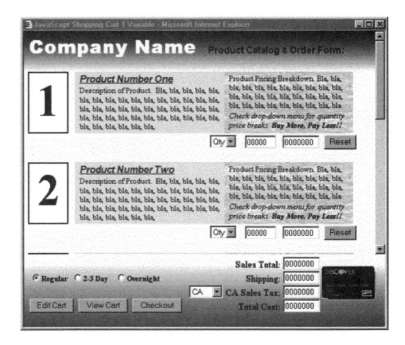

Figure 24-1. *The shopping cart windows.*

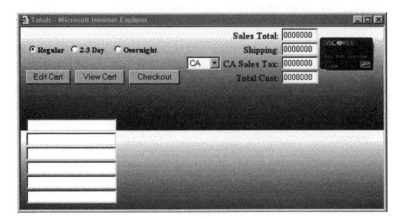

Figure 24-2. *The totals page.*

Totals, S&H, Tax (JavaScriptTotalsX.htm)

The totals page (Figure 24-2) is where the running total is displayed. Also provided are methods to select the tax option, shipping option, and navigation buttons for the shopping cart. The tax method is done with a drop-down menu, while the shipping method option is done with radio buttons. The navigation buttons consists of "Edit Cart," which is a back function that detects the current page and reacts appropriately. The "Show Cart" function displays the information in the shopping cart storage area. The "Checkout" button is linked to the shipping information page. The totals code is universal for all versions of JSSC and can be used basically unaltered. An exception is the cart text boxes, which will correspond with the quantity of products. Shipping charges and tax rates are calculated as a percentage of total. To change the tax rate and shipping rate, you'll have to change the following function:

```
function computeFinalTotal() {

state=document.forms[0].statE.options[document.forms[0]
.statE.selectedIndex].text
if(state == "CA" || state == "ca" || state == "Ca" ){
document.forms[0].tax.value =
parseFloat(document.forms[0].Sub.value) * .0825 //Tax Rate
document.forms[0].tax.value =
format(document.forms[0].tax.value, 2)
   } else {
document.forms[0].tax.value = 0
document.forms[0].tax.value =
format(document.forms[0].tax.value, 2)
}
```

```
if ( document.forms[0].Ship[0].checked ){
document.forms[0].Sub1.value = parseFloat(
document.forms[0].Sub.value) * .15 //Ship 1
document.forms[0].Sub1.value = format(
document.forms[0].Sub1.value, 2)
   } else if( document.forms[0].Ship[1].checked ) {
document.forms[0].Sub1.value = parseFloat(
document.forms[0].Sub.value) * .3 //Ship 2
document.forms[0].Sub1.value = format(
document.forms[0].Sub1.value, 2)
   } else if( document.forms[0].Ship[2].checked ) {
document.forms[0].Sub1.value = parseFloat(
document.forms[0].Sub.value) * .6 //Ship 3
document.forms[0].Sub1.value = format(
document.forms[0].Sub1.value, 2)
   }
```

One last thing to note about the totals page: It makes a decision about which page to display when the "View Cart" button is clicked. This is a navigation method that checks to see what page is open and acts accordingly. What follows is the code that does this:

```
var CurWin
function ViewCart()    {
            CurWin = parent.frames[0].document.title ==
("JavaScript Cart Catalog 1")
     if ( CurWin ) {
                     parent.viewCart3()
                } else {
                 parent.frames[0].history.back()  }  }
```

If the current window is the catalog page, then the function viewCart3 is triggered. If not, the window goes back one page.

Shopping Cart (The Holder)

Data produced by the user's selections must be stored and retrieved. This is done by placing the data in some kind of holder. This holder can be a text box or cookie file. The text box provides temporary storage of data, while the cookie method provides for more enduring records. The current JavaScript shopping cart utilizes the text box method for this data storage. The text boxes that store the purchase data are contained in the totals page.

Product Catalog (JavaScriptCatalogX.htm)

The product-catalog page (Figure 24-3) is set up to display a photo of the item with description and pricing (when the product photo is clicked, a brochure window opens). It

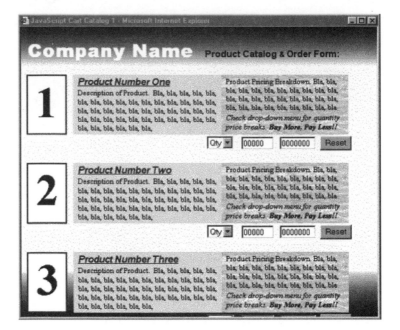

Figure 24-3. *The product-catalog page.*

also contains the JavaScript code that calculates the running totals as item and quantity is selected. These sums are passed to the totals page for calculation and display of subtotal and final grand total. The functions that reside in the totals page are triggered from the catalog page with the code below:

```
parent.frames[1].document.forms[0].Sub.value=computeSub()
    }
parent.frames[1].computeFinalTotal()
    }
```

The product-catalog page is an evolution of a calculating order form. By adapting it to the concept of framesets, greater versatility is achieved. It is here that product selection values are assigned. Below is the code for product-price-quantity assignment:

```
function product(name, One, Two, Three, Four, Five, Six, Seven,
Eight, Nine, Ten, Doz, Case ){
        this.name=name
        this.One=One
        this.Two=Two
        this.Three=Three
```

```
            this.Four=Four
            this.Five=Five
            this.Six=Six
            this.Seven=Seven
            this.Eight=Eight
            this.Nine=Nine
            this.Ten=Ten
            this.Doz=Doz
            this.Case=Case
       }
Product1 = new product("Product 1", "29.95", "29.35", "28.75",
"28.15", "27.55", "26.95", "26.35", "25.75", "25.15", "24.55",
"23.96", "17.97")
{}
Product2 = new product("Product 2", "11.95", "11.70", "11.45",
"11.25", "11.00", "10.75", "10.50", "10.25", "10.00", "9.80",
"9.56", "7.29")
{};
Product3 = new product("Product 3", "11.95", "11.70", "11.45",
"11.25", "11.00", "10.75", "10.50", "10.25", "10.00", "9.80",
"9.56", "7.29")
{};
Product4 = new product("Product 4", "9.95", "9.75", "9.55",
"9.35", "9.15", "8.95", "8.75", "8.55", "8.35", "8.15", "7.96",
"5.97")
{};
Product5 = new product("Product 5", "9.95", "9.75", "9.55",
"9.35", "9.15", "8.95", "8.75", "8.55", "8.35", "8.15", "7.96",
"5.97")
{};
Product6 = new product("Product 6", "6.95", "6.80", "6.70",
"6.55", "6.40", "6.25", "6.10", "6.00", "5.85", "5.70", "5.56",
"4.17")
{};
```

Below is the code that declares the variables that define the options presented to the customer during product selection. The cart is the product. The type is an arbitrary quality (that affects the price) such as size or color. And finally, there is the quantity.

```
var whatCart = ""
var whatType = ""
var whatQuan = ""
```

The variable values are assigned below. The values are produced from the selections that the customer makes while perusing the catalog order form:

```
function calculate(form){
 whatCart=(form.Cart.options[form.Cart.selectedIndex].value)
 whatType=(form.Type.options[form.Type.selectedIndex].value)
 whatQuan=(form.Quan.options[form.Quan.selectedIndex].value)
```

The cascade coded on the next page shows the general use of the variables assigned to a specific object. The cart is the product. The type is the size, in this case jumbo. And, finally, quan (quantity). The expanded code that is used for the JSSCart demos uses this basic structure. The only difference is that the quantity breakdown is more extensive. For less or more variables, this is where all the work occurs. In the example that follows, quantity options are 1 and 3 or more:

```
if (whatType == "Jumbo" )      {
if (whatCart =="Product1" )    {
if (whatQuan >= 3 )             {
  form.each.value=Product1.Three
    }     else
      form.each.value=Product1.One
}
 if (whatCart =="Product2")                    {
   if(whatQuan >= 3)                           {
     form.each.value=Product2.Three
   }        else
     form.each.value=Product2.One
   }
 if (whatCart =="Product3")            {
   if(whatQuan >= 3)                   {
     form.each.value=Product3.Three
   }        else
     form.each.value=Product3.One
   }
 if (whatCart =="Product4")         {
   if(whatQuan >= 3)          {
     form.each.value=Product4.Three
   }        else
     form.each.value=Product4.One
   }
 form.total.value=format(form.each.value * whatQuan, 2)
//Takes values, multiplies and makes 2 digit
 }
```

Shipping Information (JavaScriptCheckoutX.htm)

This page consists of text boxes and a text area for users to input their shipping information (Figure 23-4). This form uses a form validator triggered by the "Charge It" button.

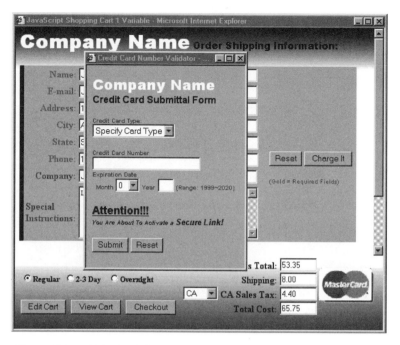

Figure 23-4. *Shipping information page.*

What's tricky about this form is that the shipping data, from the user, the shopping cart data, and the credit card information is submitted to the CGI from the ChargeIt.htm page.

General Payment Validator (JavaScriptChargeItX.htm)

This script validates not only the empty entries in the text boxes but also the parameters for credit card numbering schemes (Figure 24-5). This program pops up in its own window when the "Charge It" button is selected. Once the validator is satisfied, an onSubmit action is triggered, submitting all the data from the underlying form to a PERL forms-processor script, through the CGI.

CGI Form Processor (JSSCOrderProcessX.pl)

This PERL program processes the data sent to it by the JSSC. Not only does it send back a copy of the sales order to the shopping cart window and send the customer an e-mail confirmation that the order was received, but it also sends the store owner the purchase order. This PERL script is a basic send-mail with auto-responder, but has an addition. It uses regular expressions to remove unwanted HTML from the name-value pairs of the data string. Figures 24-6 and 24-7 shows this script in action:

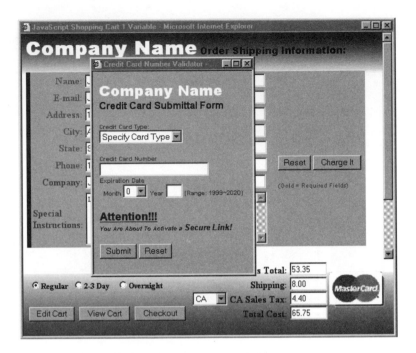

Figure 24-5. *Payment validator.*

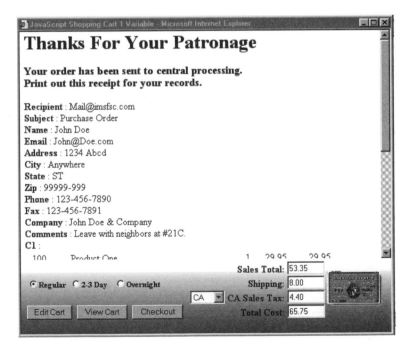

Figure 24-6. *Thanks for your patronage screen.*

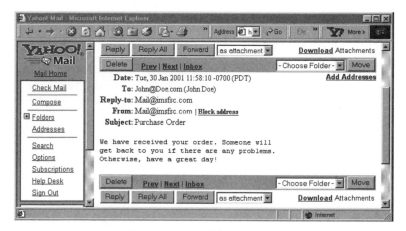

Figure 24-7. *The auto-responder.*

```
#!/usr/bin/perl
$mailprog = '/usr/sbin/sendmail';
$date = '/usr/bin/date'; chop ($date);

print "Content-type: text/html\n\n";
print "<html><head><title>Thank You E-
Mail</title></head>\n";
print "<body bgcolor=#ffffff><h1>Thanks For Your
        Patronage<br></h1>
        <h3>Your order has been sent to central
        processing.<br>
        Print out this receipt for your
        records.</h3>\n";
read(STDIN, $buffer, $ENV{'CONTENT_LENGTH'});
@pairs = split(/&/, $buffer);
foreach $pair (@pairs) {
  ($name, $value) = split(/=/, $pair);
$value =~ tr/+/ /;
$value =~ s/%([a-fA-F0-9][a-fA-F0-9])/pack("C",
hex($1))/eg;
$name =~ tr/+/ /;
$name =~ s/%([a-fA-F0-9][a-fA-F0-9])/pack("C",
hex($1))/eg;
$FORM{$name} = $value;
print "<strong>$name</strong> : $value<br>\n";
)
  open
(MAIL, "|$mailprog $FORM{'Recipient'}") || die "Can't open
mailprog!\n";
print MAIL "From: $FORM{'Email'} ($FORM{'Name'})\n";
```

```perl
print MAIL "Reply-To: $FORM{'Email'} ($FORM{'Name'})\n";
print MAIL "To: $FORM{'Recipient'}\n";
print MAIL "Subject: $FORM{'Subject'}\n\n";
print MAIL "Below is a purchase order.\n";
print MAIL
"It was submitted by $FORM{'Email'} ($FORM{'Name'} on
$date\n";
print MAIL
"----------------------------------------------------------
-----\n";
 foreach $pair (@pairs)
 {
 ($name, $value) = split(/=/, $pair);

#This section uses the regular expression to remove
unwanted form
#characters (un-webify).
    $value =~ tr/+/ /;
    $value =~ s/%([a-fA-F0-9][a-fA-F0-9])/pack("C",
    hex($1))/eg;
    $name =~ tr/+/ /;
    $name =~ s/%([a-fA-F0-9][a-fA-F0-9])/pack("C",
    hex($1))/eg;

#This section removes unwanted HTML from the shopping cart
string.
    $value =~ s/<\/td\>/ /g;
    $value =~ s/<td width="42" align="center">/ . . /g;
    $value =~ s/<td width="165" align="left">/ . . /g;
    $value =~ s/<td width="27" align="right">/ . . /g;
    $value =~ s/<td align="right" width="39">/ . . /g;
    $value =~ s/<td align="right" width="44">/ . . /g;
    $value =~ s/<\/tr\>/ /g;
    $value =~ s/<tr>/ /g;
    $value =~ s/<\/table\>/ /g;
    $value =~ s/<table border="0" width="540">/ /g;

$FORM{$name} = $value;
 print MAIL "$name: $value\n";
  }
 close (MAIL);
 open
 (MAIL, "|$mailprog $FORM{'Email'}") || die "Can't open
 $mailprog!\n";
 print MAIL "To: $FORM{'Email'} ($FORM{'Name'})\n";
 print MAIL "Reply-To: $FORM{'Recipient'}\n";
 print MAIL "From: $FORM{'Recipient'}\n";
 print MAIL "Subject: $FORM{'Subject'}\n\n";
```

```
print MAIL "We have received your order. Someone will\n";
print MAIL "get back to you if there are any problems.\n";
print MAIL "Otherwise, have a great day!";
close (MAIL); print "</body></html>";
```

It is important to note that this Perl script is the simplified version. As you saw, each of three separate sections are associated with corresponding screen shots. You can get really inventive with the outputs from the form-processing script. Add some HTML tables, font styles, or graphics to customize the output to your liking or creative bend. Maybe add an Order Number function to create a unique document number from the day and time.

Programming Interrelationships

This chapter describes the interacting elements of the JSSC. Because this program uses frames and pop-up windows, getting the right information to the right place at the right time is critical to the correct functioning of the JSSC. This section shows the connections between the different parts of the program. With a complete understanding of this area, you will be able to customize the JSSC to your heart's content.

JavaScriptCartX.htm

After a customer makes a product selection, upon clicking the "View Cart" button a JavaScript routine checks to see what page is open in the upper frame. If it is the check-out page, then the "back" command is issued. If the catalog page is open, then the "view-Cart3" function is activated and shopping cart data is displayed in the "Product Order Form Invoice" window (Figure 24-8). The HTML is created on the fly.

```
//The below function takes the user selections from the Catalog
page.
    function viewCart3(Product,Qty,Each,Total){
        for (i=0; i<6; i++) {
// i<6 because that is the number of products in the catalog.
    p =         frames[0].document
    Product = p.forms[i].Cart.text;
        // Type = additional form qualities can be inserted.
    Qty =
    p.forms[i].Quan.options[p.forms[i].Quan.selectedIndex].
    text;
    Each =   p.forms[i].each.value;
    Total =  p.forms[i].total.value;

    var Item = "10"+ i;
```

```
//The shopping cart string is stored in a data array in
accordance to
//the relationships below.
     viewCart3[i] = new Array(Item + Product + Qty + Each +
     Total)
//JSSCart1Var shown.

//Below is the HTML where the shopping cart data is inserted.
   if (Qty !== "Qty") {
//The following string must be a single line (shown in word-wrap
style
//for ease.)
     viewCart3[i] =
   ' <table border="0" width="540">
    <tr> <td width="42" align="center"> '+Item+' </td>
    <td width="165" align="left"> '+Product+' </td>
    <td width="27" align="right"> '+Qty+' </td>
    <td align="right" width="39"> '+Each+' </td>
    <td align="right" width="44"> '+Total+' </td>
    </tr> </table> ' ;
   }   else      { viewCart3[i] = (" ");        }       }
```

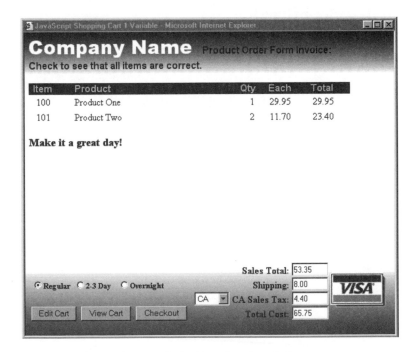

Figure 24-8. *The Product Order Form Invoice window.*

This JavaScript generates the HTML for the invoice page from the JavaScriptCartX.htm page using the Write command.

```
p.write (viewCart3[0])
  p.write (viewCart3[1])
  p.write (viewCart3[2])
  p.write (viewCart3[3])
  p.write (viewCart3[4])
  p.write (viewCart3[5])
  //p.write (viewCart3[6])  This is where to add additional
  products.
  //In the viewCart3 function, the counter is
  //set for 6 passes through the loop, because there are 6
  products
  //listed.

  p.write ("<br><h3> Make it a great day!</h3><br></BODY></HTML>
  ")
  //Put any message you want
  p.close()
  frames[1].document.forms[0].C1.value = viewCart3[0]
  //Text box from the Totals page.
  frames[1].document.forms[0].C2.value = viewCart3[1]
  //Add more for additional products.
  frames[1].document.forms[0].C3.value = viewCart3[2]
  frames[1].document.forms[0].C4.value = viewCart3[3]
  frames[1].document.forms[0].C5.value = viewCart3[4]
  frames[1].document.forms[0].C6.value = viewCart3[5]
        }
```

References
Actual download file name is http://www.1stcart.net/JSCartDownload2F.htm.

RICHARD GRAEBER is a lifetime resident of the Silicon Valley. He has worked in electromechanical engineering for 25 years, specializing in new product design and development, and has utilized IBM compatible computers since 1986. In 1998 he acquired HTML and TCP/IP skills and in 1999 discovered Java, JavaScript, and Perl. In 2000 he published

JavaScript Shopping Cart. "I was interested in pushing the JavaScript envelope. With Java, a Web programmer controls a small window in the browser's main window—while JavaScript, because of its integral nature to HTML, controls the entire browser window." He can be contacted at Richard@imsfsc.com.

## CHAPTER 25

Building Redirection into Your Site's Front End

Brian Reagan

In the early days of Web development a home page was little more than a logo and menu. Times have changed and Web sites are now dynamic structures. Today, the front end of a Web site may contain a login page, authentication logic, object and variable creation, as well as a home page. As for the home page, it serves more than aesthetic needs; it is the information center of the overall Web site, defining navigation and personalization. If designed properly, a home page can also be built to serve as a passage to more targeted information—launched from e-mail, other Web sites, or even from banner ads from within the site.

An Example

Consider the following use case: You are launching a new developers-only content area on your site and want to send e-mail to your users. The address of this new section is www.website.com/DevelopersOnly/. You'll probably generate a mailing list from your user profiles and send a simple note that drives interested users back to the Web site (as shown in Figure 25-1).

Easy enough, right? Yet what happens if your Web site is password-protected and each page checks to ensure that a user session is defined before allowing navigation? In this event, your users will probably be driven back to a login page, that will force them into the home page. Thanks to a hard-coded login page, you've lost the power of the e-mail's direct link.

Fortunately, the answer is straightforward: Build redirection into your site's front end, especially in password-protected sites. Rather than dumping users into a standard home page once they've been authenticated, you can redirect them directly to the specific path and/or page they desire.

The logic is described in the flowchart shown in Figure 25-2.

Figure 25-1. *E-mail with direct link.*

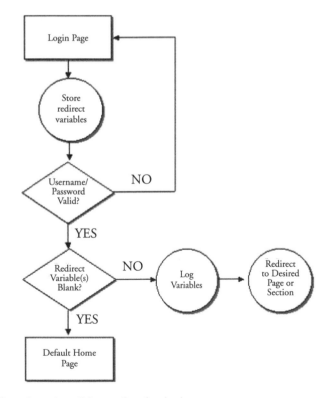

Figure 25-2. *Flowchart describing redirection logic.*

Example, Redux

To modify the previous e-mail message, use a predefined variable (named "strRedir" in this example) to store the path and send the users to the default page of the Web site: www.website.com/default.asp?strRedir=/developersonly.

Now, when a user hits the login page, the path to/developersonly/ is stored in a redirect variable. Once the user is authenticated, that variable is tested, logged, and the user's browser is sent to the path in question. Note the logging step in the flowchart. If you're taking the trouble to send mail to your users, you might as well log the success of the mailer. By introducing a simple step in the code, you'll create a log (either file or database table) that captures more meaningful data than simple HTTP logs.

Take a look at the sample code to do this.

```
<%
    Option Explicit
    Response.Buffer = True
    Dim strUser, strRedir
    strUser = session("strUser")
    strRedir = request.QueryString("strRedir")

    If strRedir <> "" then
        Call RedirLog(strRedir, strUser)
    Else
        strRedir = "default.asp"
    End if

    Response.redirect strRedir
%>
```

The first two lines of code are simply good practice when coding active server pages. Option Explicit will ensure that errors are flagged if the code runs across undeclared variables. As such, we need to dim all variables assigned in the script. The response.buffer set to true ensures that the page will not display until all server-side script is finished processing. This sends a single set of HTTP headers to the browser, providing a more efficient transmission between server and client. Buffering the response is also essential when sending a redirect back to the browser. An error will occur if a set of HTTP headers is encountered by a browser *before* reaching the redirect script.

The next snippet of code tests for the strRedir variable being passed on the URL. If it is present the RedirLog subroutine adds a row to a log file for page and user. (1) On the other hand, if the condition is false, the user is redirected to the standard home page. Note that this example assumes the username is being stored in a session variable named "strUser."

The RedirLog subroutine is as follows:

```
<%
    Sub RedirLog(strPath, strUser)
        StrLogText = strPath & "," & strUser & "," &
        CStr(Date)
        On error resume next

        Set objFSO =
        Server.CreateObject("Scripting.FileSystemObject")
        Set objLogFile =
        objFSO.OpenTextFile
            ("D:\logs\redirlog.txt",8, true)
        ObjLogFile.WriteLine(strLogText)
        ObjLogFile.close
    End Sub
%>
```

The first part of the subroutine creates a single text line of Path, User, and Date to be inserted into the file.

```
StrLogText = strPath & "," & strUser & "," & CStr(Date)
```

The output is displayed in Figure 25-3.

The next part of the subroutine instantiates the built-in FileSystemObject component, opens a text file, and appends the strLogText line. (2)

```
OpenTextFile("D:\logs\redirlog.txt",8, true)
```

Note the required path to the file—D:\logs\redirlog.txt. Even though this is server-side scripting, I would recommend placing this file somewhere on the file system that is inaccessible to the Web server, for security's sake. The second argument identifies the iomode for the OpenTextFile method—in this case 8 = ForAppending, as opposed to ForReading. The third argument is optional; when set to true, a new file will be created if it doesn't already exist.

```
ObjLogFile.WriteLine(strLogText)
ObjLogFile.close
```

Lastly, use the WriteLine method to ensure a line break after each entry. And, of course, it's necessary to close any files that you've opened during the course of the subroutine.

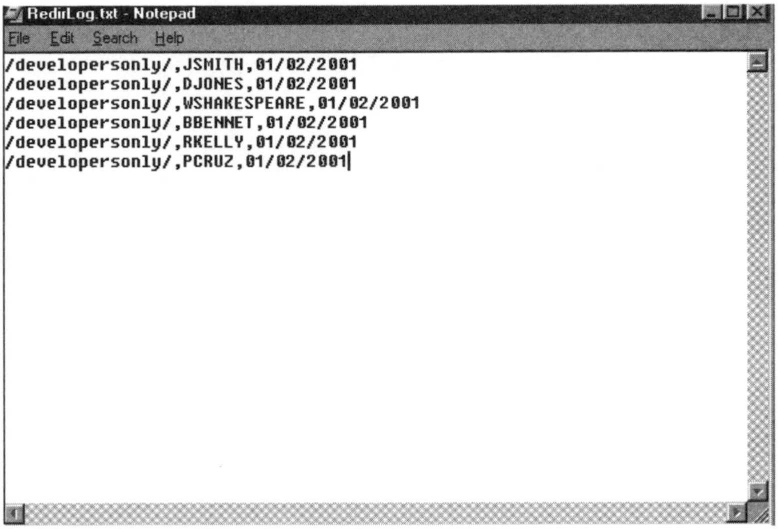
RedirLog.txt - Notepad
File Edit Search Help
/developersonly/,JSMITH,01/02/2001
/developersonly/,DJONES,01/02/2001
/developersonly/,WSHAKESPEARE,01/02/2001
/developersonly/,BBENNET,01/02/2001
/developersonly/,RKELLY,01/02/2001
/developersonly/,PCRUZ,01/02/2001

Figure 25-3. *Sample output of the RedirLog subroutine.*

Tracking More Data

The beauty of this approach is its flexibility. Today, the redirection path and user might be the most important items for reporting. However, you might add direct mail to your overall broadcast strategy. In which case, you might consider adding an additional attribute to the RedirLog subroutine to indicate the means by which the user found the site. For example, you could use a strType variable to distinguish between direct mail and e-mail.

For direct mail use:

```
StrRedir=/developersonly/&strType=mail0001
```

For e-mail broadcasts use:

```
StrRedir=/developersonly/&StrType = email0002
```

To do so, make the following changes to the RedirLog subroutine:

```
<%
     Sub RedirLog(strPath, strUser, strType)
          StrLogText = strPath & "," & strUser & "," &
```

```
        strType & "," & CStr(Date)
        On error resume next

        Set objFSO =
        Server.CreateObject("Scripting.FileSystemObject")
        Set objLogFile = objFSO.OpenTextFile
            ("D:\logs\redirlog.txt",8, true)
        ObjLogFile.WriteLine(strLogText)
        ObjLogFile.close
    End Sub
%>
```

Make sure to test for the strType variable in your default page. And in this case, if the strType variable is not defined it's filled with the word "unknown." Also, be sure to add the third argument to the RedirLog subroutine call.

```
<%
    Option Explicit
    Response.Buffer = True
    strUser = session("strUser")
    strRedir = request.QueryString("strRedir")
    strType = request.QueryString("strType")
    if strType = "" then
        strType = "unknown"
    end if

    If strRedir <> "" then
        Call RedirLog(strRedir, strUser, strType)
    Else
        StrRedir = "default.asp"
    End if

    Response.redirect strRedir
%>
```

A Refinement

Of course, the default.asp?strRedir=xyz&strType=abc is not the friendliest URL. And similarly, you might want to provide others the ability to link to major sections within your Web site without having to append their URLs each time you make a change. A refinement is shown below.

```
<%
    Option Explicit
    Response.Buffer = True
    Dim strQuery, strQueryRedir, strType, strPath, strRefer,
    strRedir, strUser
    StrQuery = request.QueryString
    StrQueryRedir = request.QueryString("strRedir")
    StrType = request.QueryString("strType")
    StrPath = request.ServerVariables("PATH_INFO")
    StrRedir = "default.asp"
    StrUser = session("strUser")

    If strQuery = "" then
        If strPath <> "" then
            StrRedir = strPath
            StrType = strRefer
        End If
    Else
        strRedir = strQueryRedir
    End
        Call RedirLog(strRedir, strUser, strType)
    Response.redirect strRedir
%>
```

A couple of additions here:

1. The default redirect is explicitly defined (strRedir = "default.asp").
2. Notice that the entire QueryString is now being stored in a variable called strQuery. In addition, we're also storing the ServerVariables("PATH_INFO") into another variable, strPath. This latter variable captures all information after the domain name. So, if the URL is www.website.com/developersonly/, the PATH_INFO would be "/developersonly/."
3. The next step is to test for the presence of a query string. If it's found, the redirect is assigned to the passed strRedir value. If it's not found, the next test is for PATH_INFO. If both are missing, the default redirect stays in place. If the PATH_INFO is not blank, the path info becomes the new redirect parameter.
4. The RedirLog subroutine call has been modified to include the strType parameter.

One additional line you might consider adding is:

```
StrRefer = request.ServerVariables("HTTP_REFERRER")
```

This will capture the referring URL—especially useful for banner ad placemets on remote sites. This could be built into the RedirLog subroutine as follows:

```
<%
    Sub RedirLog(strPath, strUser, strType, strRefer)
        StrLogText = strPath & "," & strUser & "," &
        strType & "," & strRefer & "," & CStr(Date)
        On error resume next

        Set objFSO =
        Server.CreateObject("Scripting.FileSystemObject")
        Set objLogFile = objFSO.OpenTextFile
            ("D:\logs\redirlog.txt",8, true)
        ObjLogFile.WriteLine(strLogText)
        ObjLogFile.close
    End Sub
%>
```

More Benefits

Once you've built these capabilities into your Web site's front end, you should consider using the same redirection technique for banner ads on your site. Again, it's a simple way to report on site traffic and also give you useful data on the effectiveness of banners (or any other image links on your site).

```
<A
HREF="/default.asp?strRedir=/developersarea/&strType=banner1"><I
MG SRC="images/banner1.gif"></A>
```

Conclusion

Once your Web site has moved beyond a simple set of static HTML pages, the level of complexity of reporting, coding, and site administration increases. By building a simple, scalable approach to redirection into your Web site's front end, you'll find that managing your e-mail campaigns, site promotion, and even internal banner ad placement is much easier. And, with the approach detailed above, you can continue to modify or enhance the logging capabilities as your site needs to evolve.

Notes

1. A database insert is recommended for high-volume sites, as the file I/O required in this function is expensive. This example is merely to demonstrate a simple logging technique.

2. The FileSystemObject is a special scripting object provided with active server pages in the Microsoft Scripting Runtime, found in the SCRRUN.DLL.

ACKNOWLEDGMENTS

The RedirLog subroutine was inspired by the WriteToLog function defined by the Wrox publication "Professional Active Server Pages 2.0," by Francis, Federov, Harrison, et al., 1998.

BRIAN REAGAN is an avid writer and a frequent contributor to technical journals and Web sites. For the past six years, he has managed large Web development groups within Fortune 100 companies. He's currently the director of e-business strategy for EMC Corporation.

## CHAPTER 26

Creating a Rotating Banner or Image

Mary Higgins

As you should already know, HTML is the language you use to create Web documents. Figure 26-1 shows a normal Web document incorporated with JavaScript. To create a rotating image or banner you will use JavaScript. Banners are a great way to advertise your business or products. The script for the banner is pretty simple.

For this project you will need a word processor, such as Notepad or Microsoft Word. If you do not have Microsoft Word, Notepad will be fine. I would not recommend using Wordpad; if you try to write JavaScript or HTML using Wordpad it can become a tangled mess. You will also need a couple banners, or images. The images can be any width or height. You can create your own banners or have a company make one for you. There are a lot of companies on the Internet that will let you create banners for free. Just look around and find one that meets your needs. You will need to have your banners or images in the same folder as your banner script.

Open Notepad by clicking on the Start button on your task bar (Windows 95 and higher), go to Programs, then to Accessories, click on Notepad. In Notepad you are going to want to type the JavaScript code that is written below. Remember that JavaScript is case sensitive. All examples in this chapter in JavaScript that are uppercase need to remain uppercase or the script will not work.

Please notice the semicolons at the end of each statement. The semicolons tell the browser that it has reached the end of the statement. The // tells the browser not to show any text following it. Using the // is a good way to leave notes for yourself, or to add comments.

The following listing includes line numbers for reference; be sure to type the script without the line numbers.

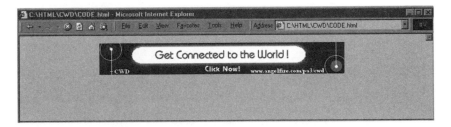

Figure 26-1. *A normal Web page.*

```
 1: <HTML>
 2: <HEAD>
 3: <SCRIPT LANGUAGE="JavaScript">

 4: var interval = 10; // delay between rotating images (in seconds)
 5: var random_display = 1; // 0 = no, 1 = yes
 6: interval *= 1000;
 7: var image_index = 0;
 8: image_list = new Array();
 9: image_list[image_index++] = new imageItem("img1.gif");
10: image_list[image_index++] = new imageItem("img2.gif");
11: image_list[image_index++] = new imageItem("img3.gif");
12: image_list[image_index++] = new imageItem("img4.gif");
13: image_list[image_index++] = new imageItem("img5.gif");
14: image_list[image_index++] = new imageItem("img6.gif");
15: var number_of_image = image_list.length;
16: function imageItem(image_location) {
17: this.image_item = new Image();
18: this.image_item.src = image_location;
19: }
20: function get_ImageItemLocation(imageObj) {
21: return(imageObj.image_item.src)
22: }
23: function generate(x, y) {
24: var range = y - x + 1;
25: return Math.floor(Math.random() * range) + x;
26: }
27: function getNextImage() {
28: if (random_display) {
29: image_index = generate(0, number_of_image-1);
30: }
31: else {
32: image_index = (image_index+1) % number_of_image;
33: }
34: var new_image = get_ImageItemLocation(image_list[image_index]);
35: return(new_image);
```

```
36: }
37: function rotateImage(place) {
38: var new_image = getNextImage();
39: document[place].src = new_image;
40: var recur_call = "rotateImage('"+place+"')";
41: setTimeout(recur_call, interval);
42: }
43: // End-->
44: </script>
45: </HEAD>
46: <BODY OnLoad="rotateImage('rImage')">
47: <center>
48: <img name="rImage" src="cwd1.gif">
49: </center>
50: </body>
51: </html>
```

The code is great, but what is the use in just copying it if you do not understand it? Let's take one line at a time to go over what it does and what you might need to change to customize it to your rotating banner or image.

The first two lines of code are normal HTML. The tag <html> will always come at the beginning of an HTML document, and you must close the <html> tag at the end. To do so just type </html>. Every HTML tag you open you must close, with the exception of the line break tag <br /> and a few others.

Please notice that most of this code goes *inside* the <head> tags. Only a few lines are in between the <body> tags.

The third is the beginning of the JavaScript. This tells the browser what type of code you will be using. There are many different types of code you could use for a rotating banner, such as ASP or C++. For now, though, we will be using JavaScript.

The fourth line tells the browser how many seconds you want each banner, or image, to be delayed. In this example the time is set to 10 seconds. To change the rate at which the image or banner is delayed, just increase or decrease the number. This will also increase how fast your banners rotate.

In line 5 the code var random_display = 1; specifies if you want the image to be randomly displayed or not. 1 tells the browser that you do want a random display, 0 says you do not want it to display the images in a random order.

In line 8, image_list = new Array(); tells the browser that you want to create a new array. Lines 9–14 show that you want to have six images be displayed and rotated. In between the quotations in this section of the code, new imageItem("img1.gif");, is where you would put the name of your image or banner. You may have as many images as you want. Once again, make sure that you have your images in the same folder as the banner script.

On line 15, var number_of_image = image_list.length; tells the browser that you want to create a new variable, (var). The variable is the number of images, number_of_image, and it equals the image list length, image_list.length, that was used in the above lines, 9–14. And to finish that line just add a semicolon.

Variables are named containers that can store data, like, for example, a number, an object, or a text string. There are some rules you need to follow when choosing a name for your variables.

A variable can include upper- and lowercase letters, any digits 0 through 9, and can include an underscore (_). Variables cannot include spaces or other punctuation. Also, variables are case sensitive, so if you have named a variable TargetNetwork_1, you would need to type it exactly like that each time.

Lines 16–19 explain the location of each image or banner. In line 20, the code function get_ImageItemLocation(imageObj) { tells the browser to get the image item location, and in line 21 to return it, return(imageObj.image_item.src).

Lines 23–26 generate the image, and if you put a 1 on line 5, var random_display = 1;, then it will be displayed randomly. Lines 27–30 tell the browser that after it has displayed one image, it should know to display another, function getNextImage() {.

Lines 32–42 return the image, get a new image, place it, rotate the images or banners, and set a time-out.

```
image_index = (image_index+1) % number_of_image;
}
var new_image = get_ImageItemLocation(image_list[image_index]);
return(new_image);
}
function rotateImage(place) {
var new_image = getNextImage();
document[place].src = new_image;
var recur_call = "rotateImage('"+place+"')";
setTimeout(recur_call, interval);
```

Line 43 is a comment, note the //. Line 44 is closing tag for the JavaScript, </script>. Line 45 closes the <head> tag, </head>.

In the <body> tag you need to place OnLoad="rotateImage('rImage')." It loads the image, rImage, which you named above. Then all you need to do is place <img name= "rImage" src="img1.gif"> in your normal HTML document, where you would like the banner or image to be at. Then make sure you close the <body> tag and <html> tag, lines 50 and 51, </body> </html>.

For this project you do not have to use banners, you can use any image. It is great for professional-looking sites. You could use the pictures to show off your artwork or products. Almost every site on the Web has some sort of advertising. Get your site noticed with professional-looking banners to show what you do or sell.

References
Current code can be downloaded from http://WebPros.at/onepoint.

MARY HIGGINS is a 17-year-old, home-schooled 11th grader from Berks County, Pennsylvania. She started writing code three years ago and since then has started her own business. She creates many sites for churches, nonprofit organizations, and small businesses. She enjoys computers, writing, painting, and horseback riding. You can visit her company Web site at http://QualityWork.at?OnePoint and e-mail her at OnePoint@mail.com.

Building a Drop-Down Menu

Peter Stevenson

The object of this chapter is to demonstrate step-by-step how to construct a drop-down menu that mimics the system used by Microsoft and other application writers.

We will go through the various stages of building each of the elements to demonstrate how the program works:

Stage 1: Simple menu with one element and five sub-elements.
Stage 2: Adding the controls for the menu.
Stages 3, 4: Using arrays to scale up the menu.
Stage 5: Using an MS Access database to drive the program.
Stage 6: Using the menu we have created to amend the database to self-update.

The source code for each of the stages can be found, copied, and pasted to your text editor at http://www15.brinkster.com/huddstgc/dropdown.

Stage 1: A Simple Drop-Down Menu (stage1.htm)

The code in this exercise can be created in a text editor and viewed in a browser that supports HTML 4.0.

The comments need not be included in your code.

```
<!DOCTYPE HTML PUBLIC "-//W3C//DTD HTML 4.0 Transitional//EN">

<html>
<head>
     <title>Stage 1</title>
<style>
```

```
<!—Setting up the style classes for each of the elements within
a style block. Notice that this block is placed in the head
section of the document. Each class starts with ".", is enclosed
in "{}" and an element is divided by ":" and separated by ";"—>

 .topline{position:absolute; top:0; left:0; width:60;
background-  color:silver; font-size:11; font-family: Tahoma;
height: 22px; }
 .mainpage{position:absolute; top:23; left:0; width:100%;
background-color:white; height:100%; border-top: 2px solid
silver; border-left: 2px solid silver;border-bottom: 2px solid
black; border-right: 2px solid black;}
 .dropdownstyle{position:absolute; width:150; background-
color:silver; border-top: 2px solid white; border-left: 2px
solid white;border-bottom: 2px solid black;border-right: 2px
solid black; }
.sub{font-size:11; font-family:Tahoma; height:22px; line-
height:1.3; }
.border{border-top: 1px solid silver; border-left: 1px solid
silver; border-bottom: 1px solid silver; border-right: 1px solid
silver; background-color:silver; color:black; width:60;}
</style>
</head>

<body bgcolor="silver">
<!—A Table to Contain the Menu Headings—>
<table align="left" width="300" border="0" cellpadding="1"
cellspacing="1" ID="topline" class="topline" >
<tr>
< align="left" class="border">   Element0</td>

</tr>
</table>
<!—A Division to Contain the Main Display—!>
<div id="mainpage" class="mainpage" >
<!—A Division to Contain the Dropdown Element—!>
<div class="dropdownstyle" style="left:0;top:0;">
<!—A Table to Contain the Sub-Headings—!>
<table width="100%" class="sub" border="0" cellpadding="3">
<tr><td>Sub1.1</td></tr>
<tr><td>Sub1.2</td></tr>
<tr><td>Sub1.3</td></tr>
<tr><td>Sub1.4</td></tr>
<tr><td>Sub1.5</td></tr>
</table>
</div>
</div>
</body>
</html>
```

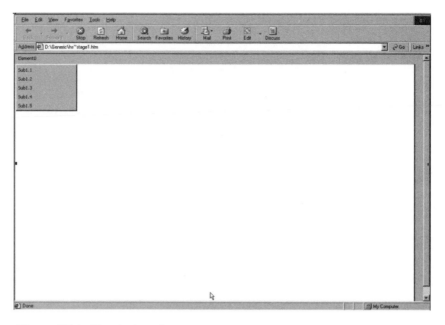

Figure 27-1. *Simple drop-down menu.*

This should produce the result shown in Figure 27-1.

Stage 2: Adding the Controls (stage2.htm)

We'd like to add the following features:

1. Hide the drop-down menu.
2. The mouse pointer hovers over the element name and a raised button appears.
3. The mouse leaves the element and the button disappears.
4. Click on the element name and the drop-down menu appears and the element becomes a depressed button.
5. The mouse pointer hovers over a sub-element and the background color and text color change.
6. Click on the display area and the screen reverts to its original appearance.

To do this the following code needs to be added:

```
.dropdownstyle{position:absolute; width:150; background-
color:silver; border-top: 2px solid white; border-left: 2px
solid white;border-bottom: 2px solid black;border-right: 2px
solid black; visibility:hidden;}
```

Add the following code to the table cell containing the element we wish to work on:

```
<td ID="EO" align="left" class="border"
onmouseover="toggle_element('EO','on')" >
  Element0</td>
```

Notice the double and single inverted commas. We now need to write the code that will perform this operation.

First create a script block in the head of the document. I have placed mine immediately under the style block, but it can go anywhere within the head.

```
<script language="javascript1.2" type="text/javascript">
</script>
```

This tells the browser what to expect in terms of the language and form of the information within the block.

We can now write the routine to display the button within the script block. Variables in JavaScript are case-sensitive, so take care when typing or you may get some surprising results.

```
function toggle_element(element,mode)
{
var TargetObj=document.all[element].style;
    if (mode=="on")
    {
            TargetObj.borderTop="1px solid white";
            TargetObj.borderLeft="1px solid white";
            TargetObj.borderBottom="1px solid DarkGray";
            TargetObj.borderRight="1px solid DarkGray";
    }
}
```

Perhaps this needs some clarification. The variables element and mode are passed to this function by the calling routine in the body that you have just written. We then create an object "TagetObj" that we point to the "all" and "style" collections of the browser. To learn more about these and many other collections and events that are too numerous to detail here and beyond the scope of this chapter, you need to obtain a copy of an appropriate scripting reference or your browser's API.

We now add the code to turn the button off to the "toggle_ element" function:

```
if (mode=="off")
    {
            TargetObj.borderTop="1px solid silver";
            TargetObj.borderLeft="1px solid silver";
            TargetObj.borderBottom="1px solid silver";
            TargetObj.borderRight="1px solid silver";
    }
```

Then add the control to the table cell:

```
<td ID="E0" align="left" class="border"
onmouseover="toggle_element('E0','on')"
onmouseout="toggle_element('E0','off')" >
  Element0</td>
```

Simple, isn't it?

Now comes the interesting bit: making the menu drop-down. We need to add one more control to the same table cell:

```
<td  ID="E0" align="left" class="border"
onmouseover="toggle_element('E0','on')"
onmouseout="toggle_element('E0','off')"
onclick="dropdown('drop0')">   Element0</td>
```

Then we identify the drop-down division we need to act on:

```
<div  id="drop0" class="dropdownstyle" style="left:0;top:0;">
```

Now we can add this code to the script block:

```
function dropdown(element)
{
     TargetObj=document.all[element].style;
     TargetObj.visibility="visible"
}
```

"Well, that's fine! It now appears but it doesn't drop down," you say. So we will now put that right.

Change the dropdownstyle class to:

```
.dropdownstyle{position:absolute;width:150;background-
color:silver;border-top: 2px solid white;border-left: 2px solid
white;border-bottom: 2px solid black;border-right: 2px solid
black; visibility:hidden; filter:revealTrans(Duration=1.0,
Transition=5);}
```

Change the drop-down function to:

```
function dropdown(element)
{
     var TargetObj=document.all[element];
      TargetObj.filters.item(0).Apply()
      TargetObj.style.visibility="visible";
      TargetObj.filters.item(0).Transition = 5
      TargetObj.filters(0).play(0.3)
}
```

You can vary the transition between 0 and 23-23 being a random transition and the "play(0.3)," which is the time taken to complete the display in seconds. Have a play and see which suits you best.

Now to highlighting the sub-elements in the drop-down box. Make the changes below to the cells in the drop-down table:

```
<tr><td id="Sub1.1" onmouseover="toggle_cell('Sub1.1','on')"
onmouseout="toggle_cell('Sub1.1','off')" >Sub1.1</td></tr>
<tr><td id="Sub1.2" onmouseover="toggle_cell('Sub1.2','on')"
onmouseout="toggle_cell('Sub1.2','off')">ub1.2</td></tr>
<tr><td id="Sub1.3" onmouseover="toggle_cell('Sub1.3','on')"
onmouseout="toggle_cell('Sub1.3','off')">Sub1.3</td></tr>
<tr><td id="Sub1.4" onmouseover="toggle_cell('Sub1.4','on')"
onmouseout="toggle_cell('Sub1.4','off')">Sub1.4</td></tr>
<tr><td id="Sub1.5" onmouseover="toggle_cell('Sub1.5','on')"
onmouseout="toggle_cell('Sub1.5','off')">Sub1.5</td></tr>
```

Then add the function below to the script block:

```
function toggle_cell(element,mode){
cell=document.all[element].style;
     if (mode=="on"){
     cell.backgroundColor="midnightblue";
```

```
          cell.color="white";
          }
          if (mode=="off"){
          cell.backgroundColor="silver";
          cell.color="black";
          }
    }
```

To complete this section of "Stage 2" all we need to do is to turn the drop-down off by clicking on the display division like this:

```
<div  id="mainpage" class="mainpage" onclick="closedrop()" >
```

Then add the function below to the script block:

```
function closedrop()
{
document.all["drop0"].style.visibility="hidden";
}
```

That's the easy bit; now let us consider how we can assign HotKeys to the project.

Assigning HotKeys (hotkeys.htm)

As an exercise and for the sake of completeness I have included this next section in the chapter. The source code can be obtained from http://www.brinkster.com/huddstgc/dropdown. I do not intend, at this moment in time, to apply this to the full program; but should you wish to apply it to yours, the method would be similar and with judicious use of flag variables would work for the full application.

Your browser uses the Alt and Control keys for its own operations, so we will apply HotKeys by using the Shift key.

To the script block add the following code:

```
function hotkey()
{
key=event.keyCode;

        if (event.shiftKey)
        {
                switch (key)
                {
```

```
                case 69 :
                 dropdown('drop0');
                break;
                case 33 :
                toggle_cell("Sub1.1","on");
                break;
                case 34 :
                toggle_cell("Sub1.2","on");
                break;
                case 163 :
                toggle_cell("Sub1.3","on");
                break;
                case 36 :
                toggle_cell("Sub1.4","on");
                break;
                case 37 :
                toggle_cell("Sub1.5","on");
                break;
                }
        }
}
```

To the body section add:

```
<script language="javascript1.2" type="text/javascript">
document.onkeypress=hotkey;
</script>
```

Amend the HTML as follows:

```
<td  ID="E0" align="left" class="border"
onmouseover="toggle_element('E0','on')"
onmouseout="toggle_element('E0','off')"
onclick="dropdown('drop0')">   <u>E</u>lement0</td>

<table width="100%" class="sub" border="0" cellpadding="3">
<tr><td id="Sub1.1" onmouseover="toggle_cell('Sub1.1','on')"
onmouseout="toggle_cell('Sub1.1','off')"
>Sub1.<u>1</u>    Shift 1</td></tr>
<tr><td id="Sub1.2" onmouseover="toggle_cell('Sub1.2','on')"
onmouseout="toggle_cell('Sub1.2','off')">Sub1.<u>2</u> &nbs
p;  Shift 2</td></tr>
<tr><td id="Sub1.3" onmouseover="toggle_cell('Sub1.3','on')"
onmouseout="toggle_cell('Sub1.3','off')">Sub1.<u>3</u> &nbs
p;  Shift 3</td></tr>
```

```
<tr><td id="Sub1.4" onmouseover="toggle_cell('Sub1.4','on')"
onmouseout="toggle_cell('Sub1.4','off')">Sub1.<u>4</u> &nbs
p;  Shift 4</td></tr>
<tr><td id="Sub1.5" onmouseover="toggle_cell('Sub1.5','on')"
onmouseout="toggle_cell('Sub1.5','off')">Sub1.<u>5</u> &nbs
p;  Shift 5</td></tr>

<script language="javascript1.2" type="text/javascript">
document.onkeypress=hotkey;
</script>
```

This is very basic and a lot more code is required to make it work properly, but I am sure you get the idea.

Stages 3, 4: Let's Scale It Up (stage3.htm)

We now have the basic HTML and JavaScript to produce a drop-down menu, and by copying, pasting, and renaming you could make as many elements and sub-elements as you wish. But that, although it would work very well, is as elegant as a brick hammer.

Let's say that we store the names of the elements and sub-elements in arrays within the program. Then, instead of going through the program every time you want to create a new drop-down menu or alter an existing one, instead of spending hours doing the deleting, copying, pasting, and then the debugging, all you need to do is alter the values of the variables stored in the arrays and start the computer going—and presto, a new drop-down menu. Now that would be elegant.

So How Do We Go About It?

Well, let's start with the sub-element table. First, put the relevant details into an array. We need the array to be a global variable, so we create it in the JavaScript block outside any function. Like this:

```
//create an array
sub_element1 = new Array();
qt='"';
//populate the array
sub_element0[0]="Sub1.0";
sub_element0[1]="Sub1.1";
sub_element0[2]="Sub1.2";
sub_element0[3]="Sub1.3";
sub_element0[4]="Sub1.4";
```

Replace the "mainpage" and "drop0" divisions and elements in the table with this piece of code:

```
<script language="javascript1.2" type="text/javascript">
document.write("<div id='mainpage' class='mainpage'
onclick='closedrop()' >")
document.write("<div id='drop0' class='dropdownstyle'
style='left:0;top:0;'>")
document.write("<table width='100%' class='sub' border='0'
cellpadding='3'>")

for (i=0; i<sub_element0.length; i++)
{
document.write("<tr><td id='"+sub_element0[i]+"'
onmouseover="+qt+"toggle_cell('"+sub_element0[i]+"','on')"+qt+"
onmouseout="+qt+"toggle_cell('"+sub_element0[i]+"','off')"+qt+"
>"+sub_element0[i]+"</td></tr>")
}

document.write("</table></div></div>");
</script>
```

Notice that all the double quotes (") in the original code have been changed to single quotes ('). If you get an error message, not changing these is probably the reason.

Now we know that we can write a table dynamically. So can we write a whole set of menus like that? The answer is of course, otherwise I wouldn't be writing this. Look at the code below:

```
<script language="javascript1.2" type="text/javascript">
document.write("<table align='left' border='0' cellpadding='1'
cellspacing='1' ID='topline' class='topline' ><tr>")
for (i=0; i<element.length; i++) //loop 1 iterations determined
by no of elements
{
document.write("<td ID='E"+i+"' align='left' class='border'
//this sets each menu title
onmouseover="+qt+"toggle_element('E"+i+"','on')"+qt+"
//and the controls, this needs
onmouseout="+qt+"toggle_element('E"+i+"','off')"+qt+"
//to be on one line
onclick="+qt+"dropdown('drop"+i+"')"+qt+">
  "+element[i]+"</td>");
}
document.write("</tr></table>");
document.write("<div id='mainpage' class='mainpage'
onclick='closedrop()' >");
```

```
for (i=0; i<element.length; i++) //loop 2 iterations determined
by no of elements

{
document.write("<div id='drop"+i+"' class='dropdownstyle'
style='left:"+55*i+";top:"+top+";'>");
document.write("<table width='100%' class='sub' border='0'
cellpadding='3'>");
      for (j=0; j<temp[i].length; j++)
      //loop 3 iterations determined by no of sub-elements
      {
      document.write("<tr><td id='Sub"+i+"."+j+"'
onmouseover="+qt+"toggle_cell('Sub"+i+"."+j+"','on')"+qt+"
onmouseout="+qt+"toggle_cell('Sub"+i+"."+j+"','off')"+qt+">"+
temp[i][j]+"</td></tr>");
      }
document.write("</table></div></div>")
}
</script>
```

You also need to add the array details and some global variables and alter the "close-drop()" function and the dropdown() function:

```
//****************************
//** Define GLOBAL VARIABLES **
//****************************
//Create an array for the Element names & populate
var element = new
Array("element0","element1","element2","element3","element4");
//Create an arrays for the Sub-Elements & populate
var sub_element0 = new
Array("Sub0.0","Sub0.1","Sub0.2","Sub0.3","Sub0.4");
var sub_element1 = new
Array("Sub1.0","Sub1.1","Sub1.2","Sub1.3","Sub1.4");
var sub_element2 = new
Array("Sub2.0","Sub2.1","Sub2.2","Sub2.3","Sub2.4");
var sub_element3 = new
Array("Sub3.0","Sub3.1","Sub3.2","Sub3.3","Sub3.4");
var sub_element4 = new
Array("Sub4.0","Sub4.1","Sub4.2","Sub4.3","Sub4.4");
//create a temporary array to hold pointers to the sub-element
arrays for display
// basically this is an array of arrays
var temp=new
Array(sub_element0,sub_element1,sub_element2,sub_element3,sub_el
ement4);
```

```
var qt='"'; //define the substitute for double Quotation marks
var top;

function closedrop()
{
     for (var i=0; i<element.length; i++) //close all dropdowns
     {
     document.all["drop"+i].style.visibility="hidden";
     }
}

function dropdown(element){
closedrop(); // close the last dropdown before opening another
by closing them all
 var TargetObj=document.all[element];
 TargetObj.filters.item(0).Apply()
 TargetObj.style.visibility="visible";
 TargetObj.filters.item(0).Transition = 5
 TargetObj.filters(0).play(0.3)
}
```

Now by simply altering the arrays you can alter the drop-down menus. We just need to tidy up the functions so that the application works like Internet Explorer. And this is the full listing of the program (stage4.htm):

```
<!DOCTYPE HTML PUBLIC "-//W3C//DTD HTML 4.0 Transitional//EN">
<html>
<head>
     <title>Stage 4</title>
<style>
.topline{position:absolute;top:0;left:0;width:60;background-
color:silver;font-size:11;font-family:Tahoma;height: 22px; }
.mainpage{position:absolute;top:23;left:0;width:100%;background-
color:white;height:100%;border-top: 2px solid silver;border-
left: 2px solid silver;border-bottom: 2px solid black;border-
right: 2px solid black;}
.dropdownstyle{position:absolute;width:150;background-
color:silver;border-top: 2px solid white;border-left: 2px solid
white;border-bottom: 2px solid black;border-right: 2px solid
black; visibility:hidden; filter:revealTrans(Duration=1.0,
Transition=5);}
.sub{font-size:11;font-family:Tahoma;height: 22px;line-
height:1.3; }
.border{border-top: 1px solid silver;border-left: 1px solid
silver;border-bottom: 1px solid silver;border-right: 1px solid
silver;background-color:silver; color:black; width:60; }
</style>
```

```
<script language="javascript1.2" type="text/javascript">
//****************************
//** Define GLOBAL VARIABLES **
//****************************
//Create an array for the Element names & populate
var element = new
Array("element0","element1","element2","element3","element4");
//Create an arrays for the Sub-Elements & populate
var sub_element0 = new
Array("Sub0.0","Sub0.1","Sub0.2","Sub0.3","Sub0.4");
var sub_element1 = new
Array("Sub1.0","Sub1.1","Sub1.2","Sub1.3","Sub1.4");
var sub_element2 = new
Array("Sub2.0","Sub2.1","Sub2.2","Sub2.3","Sub2.4");
var sub_element3 = new
Array("Sub3.0","Sub3.1","Sub3.2","Sub3.3","Sub3.4");
var sub_element4 = new
Array("Sub4.0","Sub4.1","Sub4.2","Sub4.3","Sub4.4");
//create a temporary array to hold pointers to the sub-elements
for display
var temp=new
Array(sub_element0,sub_element1,sub_element2,sub_element3,sub_
element4);
var qt='"'; //define the substitute for double Quotation marks
var top;
var clicked=false
var dropon=false

function toggle_element(element,mode,target)
{
var TargetObj=document.all[element].style;
    if (mode=="on")
    {
        if (clicked)
        {
        TargetObj.borderTop="1px solid white";
        TargetObj.borderLeft="1px solid white";
        TargetObj.borderBottom="1px solid DarkGray";
        TargetObj.borderRight="1px solid DarkGray";
        if (dropon){
        dropdown(target)
        }
        }else{
        TargetObj.borderTop="1px solid DarkGray";
        TargetObj.borderLeft="1px solid DarkGray";
        TargetObj.borderBottom="1px solid white";
        TargetObj.borderRight="1px solid white";
        }
    }
```

```
        if (mode=="off")
        {
                TargetObj.borderTop="1px solid silver";
                TargetObj.borderLeft="1px solid silver";
                TargetObj.borderBottom="1px solid silver";
                TargetObj.borderRight="1px solid silver";

        }
}

function dropdown(element){
closedrops()
 var TargetObj=document.all[element];
 TargetObj.filters.item(0).Apply()
 TargetObj.style.visibility="visible";
 TargetObj.filters.item(0).Transition = 5
 TargetObj.filters(0).play(0.2)
 dropon=true
}
function toggle_cell(element,mode){
cell=document.all[element].style;
if (mode=="on"){
      cell.backgroundColor="midnightblue";
      cell.color="white";


      }
      if (mode=="off"){
      cell.backgroundColor="silver";
      cell.color="black";
      }
}

function closedrops()
{
      for (var i=0; i<element.length; i++)
      {

      document.all["drop"+i].style.visibility="hidden";
      }
}

function closealldrops()
{
      for (var i=0; i<element.length; i++)
      {

      document.all["drop"+i].style.visibility="hidden";
      }
clicked=false
dropon=false
```

```
}
function setclick(){
clicked=true
}
</script>

</head>

<body bgcolor="silver" >
<script language="javascript1.2" type="text/javascript">
document.write("<table align='left' border='0' cellpadding='1'
cellspacing='1' ID='topline' class='topline' ><tr>")
for (i=0; i<element.length; i++)
{
document.write("<td ID='E"+i+"' align='left' class='border'
onmouseover="+qt+"toggle_element('E"+i+"','on','drop"+i+"')"+qt+
" onmouseout="+qt+"toggle_element('E"+i+"','off')"+qt+"
onclick="+qt+"setclick();dropdown('drop"+i+"')"+qt+">
  "+element[i]+"</td>");
}
document.write("</tr></table>");
document.write("<div id='mainpage' class='mainpage'
onclick='closealldrops()' >");
for (i=0; i<element.length; i++)
{
document.write("<div id='drop"+i+"' class='dropdownstyle'
style='left:"+55*i+";top:"+top+";'>");
document.write("<table width='100%' class='sub' border='0'
cellpadding='3'>");

        for (j=0; j<temp[i].length; j++)
        {
        document.write("<tr><td id='Sub"+i+"."+j+"'
onmouseover="+qt+"toggle_cell('Sub"+i+"."+j+"','on')"+qt+"
onmouseout="+qt+"toggle_cell('Sub"+i+"."+j+"','off')"+qt+">"+
temp[i][j]+"</td></tr>");
        }
document.write("</table></div></div>")
}
</script>
</body>
</html>
```

Stage 5: Using an MS Access Database to Drive the Program (stage5.asp)

I know what you are saying! We have spent a lot of time writing a fancy program, but what does it do? The answer at the moment is *nothing*, but we are just about to remedy that. We will also look into the question of "server-side" programming by means of ASP.

To get the full benefit of this section you will need access to a personal Web server such as PWS or IIS—or sign up with a server that supports ASP—and a database program. If you are using Windows 98 or above, then you already have a copy of PWS on your Windows 98 CD. It is another of Microsoft's best-kept secrets. You will find it in a file called "add-ons/pws." Just simply run the "setup.exe" and you are in business. There are other servers with ASP enabled, such as Chilli!ASP, and more will become available, I have no doubt.

The program below will generate the HTML to display the menu on your browser.

First of all we must set up the database. On your hard drive create a new folder called "dropdown," and within that three sub-folders named "common," "content," and "db." Next bring up your Access database and open a new file called, let's say, "dropinfo.mdb."

Open a table and name it "Control," and in Design View create two fields, "ID" and "Element." Set the Properties of ID to "auto number" and Element to "text," "length=50," "Required=NO," and "Allow zero length=YES."

Add ten more fields for each of ten sub-elements with properties of "text," "length=50," "Required=NO," and "Allow zero length=YES." Name the fields Sub0 through Sub9.

Repeat this procedure for another table named "Target," creating 12 fields named "ID," "dummy," and "target0," through "target9."

These will hold the URLs for the programs for your application. Now save the database to your "db" sub-folder on your hard drive.

You have just created a database for your program that will allow you to manipulate a drop-down menu with as many elements as you require with ten sub-elements. If you require more sub-elements, simply add more fields to your tables.

Locate the "adovbs.inc," which, if you have loaded PWS or IIS, will be found at C:\ Program Files\Common Files\system\ado. Copy this to your "common" folder.

Copy the "dropdown.htm" program as detailed above to the "content" file and rename it "dropdown.asp."

We now just need to create three more blank files: "global.asa" and "Default.asp," which we will store in the root directory "dropdown," and "sessionvars.inc," which is to be saved to the folder named "common."

This may seem complicated and a lot of work but it will save time and effort in the long run. Your "dropdown" directory should look like Figure 27-2.

Add this code to the "sessionvars.inc":

```
strProvider="DRIVER=Microsoft Access Driver (*.mdb); DBQ=" &
Server.MapPath(".") & "\db\dropinfo.mdb"
qt=Chr(34)
```

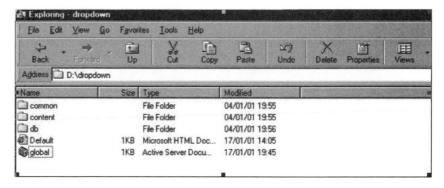

Figure 27-2. The "dropdown" directory.

> **strProvider:** This is the database connection string that tells the program where to find that database. We put it in an include file so that if the location of the database change, which it would if you were to upload the application to an external server, then only this file would need to be amended.

> **qt:** This is a constant representing a double quotation mark.

As the "sessionvars.inc" is included in each ASP page immediately after the <body> tag, any information contained in this file will be available to each routine in the application.

Now we are ready to start writing the code. I have provided a blank ASP file, called "blank.asp," on the Web site for you to use. Omit the last include line, as that is to show the code on the site. If you don't you will receive an error message, as you will not have a copy of this file in your application.

You can copy and paste this from the Web site.

Stage 6: (stage6.asp)

This is the code for the program.

```
<%@ Language="VBScript"%>
<%Response.buffer=true%>
<!--#include file="../common/adovbs.inc"-->
```

```
<html>
<head>
      <title>Stage 6</title>
<style>
.topline{position:absolute;top:0;left:0;width:60;background-
color:silver;font-size:11;font-family:Tahoma;height: 22px; }
.mainpage{position:absolute;top:23;left:0;width:100%;background-
color:white;height:100%;border-top: 2px solid silver;border-
left: 2px solid silver;border-bottom: 2px solid black;border-
right: 2px solid black;}
.dropdownstyle{position:absolute;width:150;background-
color:silver;border-top: 2px solid white;border-left: 2px solid
white;border-bottom: 2px solid black;border-right: 2px solid
black; visibility:hidden; filter:revealTrans(Duration=1.0,
Transition=5);}
.sub{font-size:11;font-family:Tahoma;height: 22px;line-
height:1.3; }
.border{ border-top: 1px solid silver;border-left: 1px solid
silver;border-bottom: 1px solid silver;border-right: 1px solid
silver;background-color:silver; color:black;}
</style>

<script language="javascript1.2" type="text/javascript">
//*****************************
//** Define GLOBAL VARIABLES **
//*****************************
var elements = new Array()
var top;
var clicked=false;
var dropon=false;

//**********************
//** Define FUNCTIONS **
//**********************
function setarray()
{
var index=document.earray.index.value //get the number of
elements from the index input
      for (var i=0;i<index;i++)
      {

      elements[i]=document.all["heading"+i].value;
      }
}

function toggle_element(element,mode,target)
{
var TargetObj=document.all[element].style;
```

```
      if (mode=="on")
      {
            if (clicked)
            {
            TargetObj.borderTop="1px solid DarkGray";
            TargetObj.borderLeft="1px solid DarkGray";
            TargetObj.borderBottom="1px solid white";
            TargetObj.borderRight="1px solid white";
                  if (dropon)
                  {
                  dropdown(target);
                  TargetObj.borderTop="1px solid DarkGray";
                  TargetObj.borderLeft="1px solid DarkGray";
                  TargetObj.borderBottom="1px solid white";
                  TargetObj.borderRight="1px solid white";
                  }
            }else{
            TargetObj.borderTop="1px solid white";
            TargetObj.borderLeft="1px solid white";
            TargetObj.borderBottom="1px solid DarkGray";
            TargetObj.borderRight="1px solid DarkGray";
            }
      }

      if (mode=="off")
      {
            if (!clicked)
            {
            TargetObj.borderTop="1px solid silver";
            TargetObj.borderLeft="1px solid silver";
            TargetObj.borderBottom="1px solid silver";
            TargetObj.borderRight="1px solid silver";
            }else{

            TargetObj.borderTop="1px solid DarkGray";
            TargetObj.borderLeft="1px solid DarkGray";
            TargetObj.borderBottom="1px solid white";
            TargetObj.borderRight="1px solid white";

            }
      }
}

function dropdown(element)
{
closedrops();
 var TargetObj=document.all[element];
 TargetObj.filters.item(0).Apply();
```

```
 TargetObj.style.visibility="visible";
 TargetObj.filters.item(0).Transition = 5;
 TargetObj.filters(0).play(0.3);
 dropon=true;

}

function toggle_cell(element,mode)
{
cell=document.all[element].style;
      if (mode=="on")
      {
      cell.backgroundColor="midnightblue";
      cell.color="white";
      }
      if (mode=="off")
      {
      cell.backgroundColor="silver";
      cell.color="black";
      }
}
function closedrops()
{
      for (var i=0; i<elements.length; i++)
      {

      document.all["drop"+i].style.visibility="hidden";
      var TurnoffObj=document.all["E"+i].style
      TurnoffObj.borderTop="1px solid silver";
      TurnoffObj.borderLeft="1px solid silver";
      TurnoffObj.borderBottom="1px solid silver";
      TurnoffObj.borderRight="1px solid silver";
      }
dropon=false
}

function closealldrops()
{
      for (var i=0; i<elements.length; i++)
      {

      document.all["drop"+i].style.visibility="hidden";
      var TurnoffObj=document.all["E"+i].style
      TurnoffObj.borderTop="1px solid silver";
      TurnoffObj.borderLeft="1px solid silver";
      TurnoffObj.borderBottom="1px solid silver";
      TurnoffObj.borderRight="1px solid silver";
      }
```

```
clicked=false;
dropon=false;
}

function setclick(element)
{
clicked=true;
var TargetObj=document.all[element].style;
TargetObj.borderTop="1px solid DarkGray";
TargetObj.borderLeft="1px solid DarkGray";
TargetObj.borderBottom="1px solid white";
TargetObj.borderRight="1px solid white";
}
</script>

</head>

<body bgcolor="silver" >
<!--#include file="../common/sessionvars.inc"-->
<%
     Set objConn=Server.CreateObject("ADODB.Connection")
     objConn.Open strProvider
     Set rst=Server.CreateObject("ADODB.Recordset")
     rst.open "Control" , objConn,
adOpenKeySet,adLockOptimistic, adCmdTable
     Dim i  ' counter for loop 1 & 2
     Dim j  ' counter for loop 3
     Dim epos(10)  'An array to set the location of the
elements & dropdown boxes to ensure that the positions coincide
(user alterable)

     Dim xpos
     xpos=0
     epos(0)=xpos
     xpos=xpos+35
     epos(1)=xpos
     xpos=xpos+55
     epos(2)=xpos
     xpos=xpos+55
     epos(3)=xpos
     xpos=xpos+55
     epos(4)=xpos
     Response.write"<form name='earray'><table align='left'
border='0' cellpadding='1' cellspacing='1' ID='topline'
class='topline' ><tr>"
     i=0 'reset counter
     while not rst.EOF
          if rst(1)<>"" then
```

```
            response.write"<td ID='E"&i&"' align='left'
class='border' style='position:absolute; left:"&epos(i)&";'
onmouseover="&qt&"toggle_element('E"&i&"','on','drop"&i&"')"&qt&
" onmouseout="&qt&"toggle_element('E"&i&"','off')"&qt&"
onclick="&qt&"setclick('E"&i&"');dropdown('drop"&i&"')"&qt&">&nb
sp; "&rst(1)&"</td>"
            'set up a form to pass the heading parameters to
Javascript
            response.write"<input name='heading"&i&"'
type='hidden' value="&rst(1)&">"
            i=i+1
            end if
      rst.MoveNext
      wend
      response.write"<input id='index' type='hidden'
value="&i&">"
      rst.close
response.write"</tr></table></form>"
response.write"<div id='mainpage' class='mainpage'
onclick='closealldrops()' >"
      rst.open "Control" , objConn,
adOpenKeySet,adLockOptimistic, adCmdTable
      Set objConn2=Server.CreateObject("ADODB.Connection")
      objConn2.Open strProvider
      Set rst2=Server.CreateObject("ADODB.Recordset")
      rst2.open "Target" , objConn,
adOpenKeySet,adLockOptimistic, adCmdTable

      i=0
      dim top
      dim strtarget
      top=0
      while not rst.EOF
      if rst(1)<>"" then

      response.write"<div id='drop"&i&"' class='dropdownstyle'
style='left:"&(epos(i)-3)&";top:"&top&";'>"
      response.write"<table width='100%' class='sub' border='0'
cellpadding='3'>"
      i=i+1
            for j=2 to rst.Fields.count-1 'loop 2
                  if rst(j)<>"" then 'if there is no Sub-element
then skip to the next

                  if rst2(j)<>"" then 'if the target is not
available then omit the onclick command

strtarget="onclick="&qt&"location.href='"&rst2(j)&
```

```
"'"&qt
                else
                strtarget=""
                end if

                response.write"<tr><td id='Sub"&i&.""&j&"'
onmouseover="&qt&"toggle_cell('Sub"&i&.""&j&"','on')"&qt&"
onmouseout="&qt&"toggle_cell('Sub"&i&.""&j&"','off')"&qt&"
"&strtarget&" >"&rst(j)&"</td></tr>"
                end if
        next
    end if
    response.write"</table></div>"
    rst.MoveNext
    rst2.MoveNext
    wend
    rst.close
    Set rst=Nothing 'tidy up the database connections
    objConn.close
    Set objConn=Nothing
    Set rst2=Nothing
    objConn2.close
    Set objConn2=Nothing
%>
<script language="javascript1.2" type="text/javascript">
//pass the array variables to the Javascript routines
setarray();
</script>
<!—remove the next line as it is not required for your
application.—>
<!—#include file="../common/footer.inc"—>
</div>
</body>
</html>
```

What does all that mean? Well, the JavaScript is almost the same, except that the arrays have been removed (as they are now redundant) and a new function "setarray()" has been added to take the "element" strings and place them in an array, which is when the page has been loaded.

The rest is the VbScript, which accesses the database to retrieve the information to be displayed. The method is identical to the JavaScript program, using three loops. If you are new to ASP programming and wish to take it further, then a good book to read is *ASP 2.0* (Wrox Press).

Go back to the database and populate the tables with information for the drop-down boxes (Figure 27-3 and Figure 27-4). Here are screen shots of what I did.

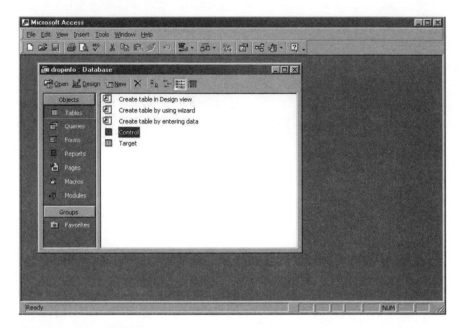

Figure 27-3. *Creating the tables.*

ID	Element	Sub0	Sub1	Sub2	Sub3	Sub4	Sub5	Sub6	Sub7	Sub8	Sub9
1	File	Alter Head	Alter Sub	Add Sub-Eleme	Delete Sub-Elei						
2	Element 2	Sub0	Sub1	Sub2	Sub3						
4	Element3	Sub0	Sub1	Sub2	Sub3						
5	Element4	Sub0	Sub1	Sub2	Sub3						
7	Element5	Sub0	Sub1	Sub2	Sub3						
(AutoNumber)											

Figure 27-4. *Naming the elements and sub-elements.*

Altering the Elements (alterhead.asp)

We can now write routines to modify the database dynamically. The first routine will alter the elements. I have called it "alterhead.asp," and the code is as follows:

```
<%@ Language="VBScript"%>
<%Response.buffer=true%>
<!-#include file=.."/common/adovbs.inc"->

<html>
<head>
     <title>Alter Headings</title>
</head>
```

```
<body>
<!-#include file=.."/common/sessionvars.inc"->
<%
if request.form("message")="alteredhead" then
Set objConn=Server.CreateObject("ADODB.Connection")
     objConn.Open strProvider
     Set rst=Server.CreateObject("ADODB.Recordset")
     strQuery="SELECT * FROM Control WHERE ID="&ID
     rst.open strQuery, objConn, adOpenKeySet,adLockOptimistic,
adCmdText
     rst(1)=request.form("alteration")
     rst.Update
     rst.close
     Set rst=Nothing 'tidy up the database connections
     objConn.close
     Set objConn=Nothing
end if
if request.QueryString("message")="alter" then
     ID=request.QueryString("ID")
     Session("ID")=ID
%>
<form name="newhead" action='alterhead.asp' method='post'>
<table align="center">
<tr><td>What is the new Heading <input
name="alteration"></td></tr>
<tr><td align="center"><input type="submit" value="Save New
Heading"></td></tr>
<input type="hidden" name="message" value="alteredhead">
</form>
<%

else
     Set objConn=Server.CreateObject("ADODB.Connection")
     objConn.Open strProvider
     Set rst=Server.CreateObject("ADODB.Recordset")
     rst.open "Control" , objConn,
adOpenKeySet,adLockOptimistic, adCmdTable
     response.write "The Current Headings are:-<br>"
     response.write "<table align='center' border='1'>"
     while not rst.EOF

     response.write "<tr><td><a
href='alterhead.asp?message=alter&ID="&rst(0)&"'>
Alter</a></td><td>"&rst(1)&"</td></tr>"
     rst.MoveNext
     wend
     response.write "</table>"
     rst.close
```

```
        Set rst=Nothing 'tidy up the database connections
        objConn.close
        Set objConn=Nothing
        end if
%>
<form id="return" action="stage6.asp" method="post">
<table align="center">
<tr><td><input type="submit" value="Return To Drodown Menu">
</table>
</form>
<!-remove the next line as it is not required for this
application.->
<!-#include file=.."/common/footer.inc"->
</body>
</html>
```

You will notice that this routine calls itself twice. The first time to make the alterations and the second to save the details back to the database.

To make this work correctly you need to add this code to the "global.asa" file:

```
<script language="vbscript" runat="server" >
Sub Application_OnStart

End Sub

Sub Session_OnStart
Session.Timeout=20 'Sets the length of time of the session
Session("ID")=""

End Sub
Sub Session_OnEnd

End Sub

Sub Application_OnEnd

End Sub
</script>
```

Add this code to the "sessionvars.inc," ID=Session("ID") (sessionvars.inc.htm). An HTML page is stateless—that is, it cannot retain any variables created in it. One of the advantages of using ASP is that the state of a variable can be maintained throughout the lifetime of a visit to the site, termed a session.

This is done by initializing the session variable in the "global.asa" file, which is accessed each time an ASP page is loaded, and referring to the variable in the "inc" file—which is what we have done above. The transfer of the variable then appears to be seamless and can be accessed without any further problems.

I have used two other methods of passing information: the query string and the form. The query string is passed as an addendum to the URL, as in the example below.

```
href='alterhead.asp?message=alter&ID=1'
```

This uses the Get method for transferring data. The disadvantage of this method is that the information passed is visible to the user.

The Form method passes the values of the input in pairs using the format name= value& for each input tag. The information is then translated by the server. An example of a form (altersub.asp) from the routine above is given below; this information is not seen by the user:

```
<form name="newhead" action='alterhead.asp' method='post'>
<input name="alteration">
<input type="submit" value="Save New Heading">
<input type="hidden" name="message" value="alteredhead">
</form>
```

Forms are also useful for storing data to be used by routine within the program and passing variables from one scripting language to another.

Altering the Sub-Elements

I have made this a combination routine that displays all the data contained in the database and enables the user to modify that data, which is then reflected in the other routines that use the database.

This is the source for the program:

```
<%@ Language="VBScript"%>
<%Response.buffer=true%>
<!—#include file=."./common/adovbs.inc"—>

<html>
<head>
    <title>Alter Sub-Headings</title>
</head>

<body>
<!—#include file=."./common/sessionvars.inc"—>
```

```
<%
    If request.form("message")="savesub" then
    Set objConn=Server.CreateObject("ADODB.Connection")
    objConn.Open strProvider
    Set rst=Server.CreateObject("ADODB.Recordset")
    strQuery="SELECT * FROM Control WHERE ID="&ID
    rst.open strQuery , objConn, adOpenKeySet,adLockOptimistic,
    adCmdText
    rst(Cint(item))=request.form("new_sub")
    rst.Update
    rst.close
    Set rst=Nothing 'tidy up the database connections
    objConn.close
    Set objConn=Nothing
    end if

    If request.form("message")="saveurl" then
    Set objConn=Server.CreateObject("ADODB.Connection")
    objConn.Open strProvider
    Set rst=Server.CreateObject("ADODB.Recordset")
    strQuery="SELECT * FROM Target WHERE ID="&ID
    rst.open strQuery , objConn, adOpenKeySet,adLockOptimistic,
    adCmdText
    rst(Cint(item))=request.form("new_url")
    rst.Update
    rst.close
    Set rst=Nothing 'tidy up the database connections
    objConn.close
    Set objConn=Nothing
    end if
    if request.QueryString("message")<>"" then
      ID=request.QueryString("ID")
      Session("ID")=ID
      item=request.QueryString("item")
      Session("item")=item
      subname=request.QueryString("subname")
      element=request.QueryString("element")

      if request.QueryString("message")="sub" then
      response.write"<center>You have Chosen to alter the Sub-
      Element called "&subname&"<br>In the Dropdown Menu with
      the Title of "&element&"<br>Enter the New Sub-Element Name
      in the box below. <br>"
          response.write"<form action='altersub.asp'
          method='post'>"
          response.write"<input type='text' name='new_sub'
          value='"&subname&"'><br><br>"
          response.write"<input type='submit' value='Save
```

```
              Alterations to Database'>"
              response.write"<input type='hidden'  name='message'
              value='savesub'>"
              response.write"</form></center>"
         end if

         if request.QueryString("message")="target" then
         response.write"<center>You have Chosen to alter the Target
         URL "&subname&"<br>In the Dropdown Menu with the Title of
         "&element&"<br>Enter the New URL in the box below.<br>"
                response.write"<form action='altersub.asp'
                method='post'>"

                response.write"<input type='text' name='new_url'
                value='"&subname&"'><br><br>"
                response.write"<input type='submit' value='Save
                Alterations to Database'>"
                 response.write"<input type='hidden'  name='message'
                 value='saveurl'>"
                 response.write"</form></center>"
                 end if
         else
         Set objConn=Server.CreateObject("ADODB.Connection")
         objConn.Open strProvider
         Set rst=Server.CreateObject("ADODB.Recordset")
         rst.open "Control" , objConn,
         adOpenKeySet,adLockOptimistic, adCmdTable
         Set objConn2=Server.CreateObject("ADODB.Connection")
         objConn2.Open strProvider
         Set rst2=Server.CreateObject("ADODB.Recordset")
         rst2.open "Target" , objConn,
         adOpenKeySet,adLockOptimistic, adCmdTable
         response.write "The Current Content of the Database is:-
<br>"
         response.write "<table align='center' border='1'
         cellpadding='5'>"
         response.write"<tr>"
         for i=1 to rst.Fields.count-1
         Response.write "<td>"&rst(i).Name&"</td>"
         next
         response.write"</tr>"
         while not rst.EOF
         response.write"<tr>"
         for i=1 to rst.Fields.count-1
         if rst(i)<>"" then
         response.write "<td><a
href='altersub.asp?ID="&rst(0)&"&item="&i&"&message=sub&
subname="&rst(i)&"&element="&rst(1)&"'>"&rst(i)&
```

```
"</a></td>"
        else
        response.write "<td><a
href='altersub.asp?ID="&rst(0)&"&item="&i&"&message=sub&
subname="&rst(i).Name&"&element="&rst(1)&"'>Empty</a></td>"
        end if
        next
        response.write"</tr><>"
        for i=1 to rst2.Fields.count-1
        if rst2(i)<>"" then
        response.write "<td><a
href='altersub.asp?ID="&rst2(0)&"&item="&i&"&message=target&
subname="&rst2(i)&"&element="&rst(1)&"'>"&rst2(i)&"</a></td>"
        else
        response.write "<td><a
href='altersub.asp?ID="&rst2(0)&"&item="&i&"&message=target&
subname="&rst2(i).Name&"&element="&rst(1)&"'>Empty</a></td>"

        end if
        next
        response.write"</tr>"
        rst.MoveNext
        rst2.MoveNext
        wend
        response.write"</table>"
        response.write"<br><br><center>Click on an Item to
Alter</center>"
        rst.close
        Set rst=Nothing 'tidy up the database connections
        objConn.close
        Set objConn=Nothing
        Set rst2=Nothing
        objConn2.close
        Set objConn2=Nothing
        end if
%>
<form id="return" action="stage6.asp" method="post">
<table align="center">
<tr><td><input type="submit" value="Return To Dropdown Menu">
</table>
</form>
</body>
</html>
```

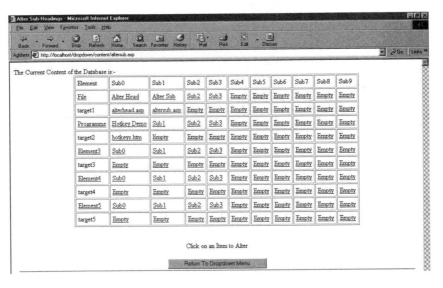

Figure 27-5.

Figure 27-5 is what you should get.

You are now in a position to use the menu in any of your applications. I am afraid that you will not be able to see this working on the Web site, as it is not practical to allow manipulation of the database. However, that should be no problem, as you should now have a working program yourself.

PETER STEVENSON is an amateur programmer who is completely self-taught. He lives in England and can be contacted via e-mail at pandc@bigger.com.

Section 5

Web to Database Connectivity

You can't create wonderful Web sites without having great content. While some content can be static (i.e., hard-coded directly into the Web site), most content comes from existing data sources such as files and databases.

Look at Amazon.com. Do you think that information on each book (price, publisher, author info, etc.) is hard-coded by some tireless Amazon programmer? Actually, most of Amazon's data come from databases that either they own or are owned by third-party sources such as publishers and credit card companies.

What you'll learn in this section:

1. Using an application service provider to host your database.
2. The concepts of database modeling.
3. How to use Oracle synonym tables in Web application integration.
4. How to produce a static HTML table.
5. How to deal with dynamic data using active server pages.
6. Dealing with dynamic data using Perl.

Web Database Publishing Using an Application Service Provider

Soo Kim

Since the onset of the Internet, businesses have experienced an energetic exchange of information. Speedy data exchange solutions have become the determining conditions for success in a shrinking global network. However, while Web databases have become a basic necessity, the financial and time costs, and the technical integration requirements, have prevented many entrepreneurs from benefiting from such existing technology. With such a market in mind, several companies have developed a Web database publishing facility to offer entrepreneurs the opportunity to create searchable and data-entry databases on the Web without any database programming experience. Three such companies are Bitlocker, Quickbase, and eCriteria. By easily uploading and downloading data in plain-text or XML, an entire enterprise could transfer its data securely to and through the Internet, escaping the financial costs and time burdens of creating customized Web software. This chapter details the exact method to publish a "shrink-wrap" Web database using the technology provided by a particular database service provider, and shows examples of how to utilize this emerging technology to expand your Web presence and to bring data-driven efficiency to your personal and work space.

Using the service of one database service provider (DSP), you can create three kinds of databases: (1) data entry, (2) searchable, or (3) both data entry and searchable. Although the concept of a database may seem foreign to many people, people all around the world use databases for their business and personal lives. For the purpose of this chapter, a database is simply a collection of data that is organized in rows and columns. You can imagine a database as looking like a table or a spreadsheet. However, there are differences between databases and spreadsheets that make databases significantly more useful and valuable.

1. You can allow people to add information into a database without being able to view all the other entries, or records, in the database. You can add an entry to a database by opening the database as a form, much like a registration form or a

poll, as commonly seen on the Web. When you type in information into a registration form, you cannot see the contents of the whole database. That is, you cannot view any of the entries that other people added when they used the registration form. Only the person maintaining the database can view, modify, download, or delete the collective data, in a private administrative area only accessible by a username and password. This sense of using a database through a form and allowing only the administrator to maintain the database makes a database a considerable upgrade from spreadsheets for a variety of business situations.

2. You can search through a database by performing queries, or asking questions to the database. That is, you can type in a value in a text box, or select a value from a pull-down list, to find any record with the value that you specified. As a huge advantage over having to pore through every cell in a spreadsheet to find a certain value, a database allows users to quickly search for a specific word or value.

This chapter provides detailed instructions on how to create (1) a data entry form, and (2) a data entry and searchable database. The first part will explain how to publish a 1040EZ tax form onto a Web site using eCriteria, one of a few emerging database service providers. The second part will explain how to create and use a sales database to keep track of personal or corporate sales efforts.

Part I: Web Form

Section 1: A Look at the End Result

Figure 28-1 represents the end result. This screen shot shows a database-enabled 1040EZ form, hosted by a database service provider. "Database-enabled" means that when someone completes the form, then clicks on the "Submit" button at the bottom of the form, the data immediately enters into a database. Only the database administrator (the member of eCriteria who created the database) has access to the data and can view, modify, search, or delete the collective data. This person can also download the data into his desktop or corporate application in a text format, by clicking on the button "Download data" in his eCriteria Workspace (Figure 28-3). If this form was not database-enabled, then the data would just be sent to a person in an e-mail, and someone would have to manually type the data into the desired application.

Section 2. How to Create a Database-Driven Web Form

Creating the 1040EZ Web form using eCriteria takes seven steps. (1)

Step 1: Go to the www.eCriteria.net. A home page resembling Figure 28-2 should appear. Click on the button to register and complete the registration process.

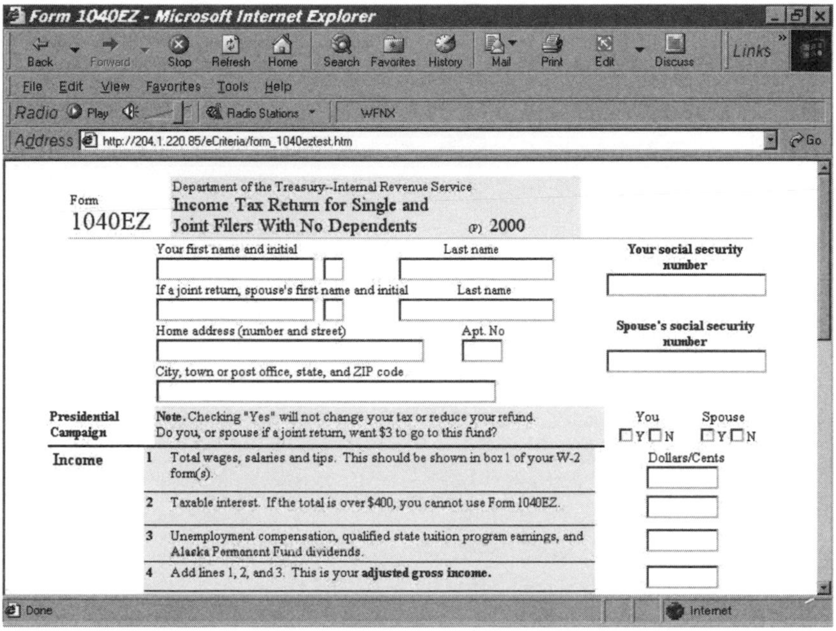

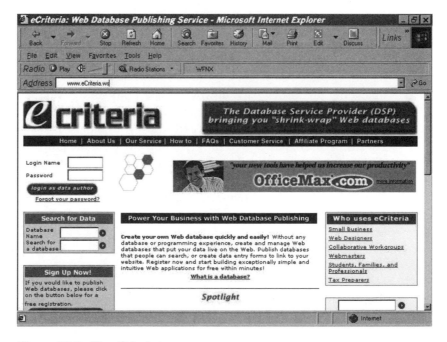

Figure 28-1. A database-enabled form.

Figure 28-2. The eCriteria home page.

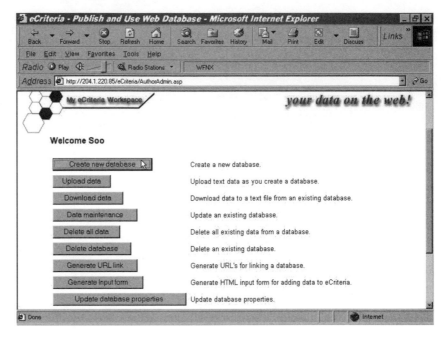

Figure 28-3. The eCriteria Workspace.

Step 2: You should arrive in your eCriteria Workspace, which is your private administrative area. Please refer to Figure 28-3. This is essentially where you will execute all actions regarding your Web databases. You can create a database on the fly, create a database by uploading preexisting data, download data from your eCriteria database to your local computer, maintain your database (search, add, delete, or edit data in a database), delete a database, generate the URL link to attach your database to a Web site, generate the HTML to customize a Web form, and update database properties. To start creating a Web form, you should click on the button "Create database." This will take you through a click-through process to create an empty database.

Step 3: Please type in the number of columns that your database will require. At this time, you may want to take a piece of paper and write down all the columns (also referred to as "fields" in database terminology) that your database needs. You should visualize your database as a table, with column headings at the top. Each column should represent each question in your form. There are 39 questions on this 1040EZ tax form, so you should type "39" on the screen shown in Figure 28-4. Then, click "Continue."

Step 4: You will then arrive at a page (Figure 28-5) to type the column names, the column types, and if required or desired, the column width and column label for the 39 columns.

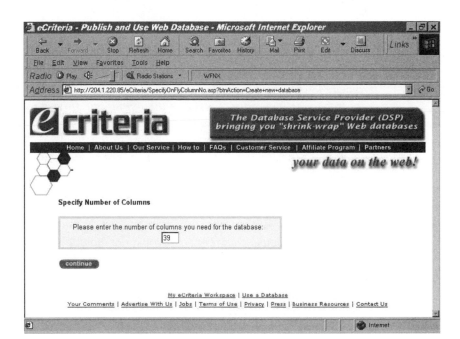

Figure 28-4. *Entering the number of columns you need.*

Column name: *This should be one word that describes the data that a person would input into this column (field); eCriteria does not allow special characters or spaces in the column name, so each column name should be composed of only letters and/or numbers.*

Column type: *This is the type of data that should be inputted for each column. The available types are: text, numeric with decimal (such as 2.34 or .09), numeric without decimal (such as 1, 2048, –50), money ($12.23), or date (2/3/2001). This is to define and restrict what kind of data is inputted for each question of the database, and is useful when you download your data into a spreadsheet or another calculator to perform data analysis.*

Column width: *This is the number of maximum characters that a column can store. For data of type text, you must specify how wide you would like the columns. The number you type in this box represents the number of characters (typically letters, numerals, and symbols) each data value could hold. You may want to allow a few more characters than what you think someone will need to input the data, to accommodate the largest value that a column might need in the future. This way, any data that you upload in the future will fit nicely into the columns you specify now. If the column is not of type text, then you do not need to specify the width of the column.*

Column label: *Because column names must not include spaces or special characters, eCriteria allows you to provide column labels, which will be viewable to the person using your Web form to input data into your Web form. This is optional; for example, if you had wanted to add spaces in your column names, you would type the newly revised column label in the spaces provided. If you designated the column name to be "LODate," you can make the column label "Last Order Date" (with spaces). "Last Order Date" is what other people would see on your Web form, and this is what you would see when you seek to view, edit, add, delete, or search data in your eCriteria Workspace. If you do not type a column label, the column name will remain the default.*

For the 1040EZ form, you should enter the following column names, types, widths, and labels, and then click "Continue." (See Figures 28-5a and 28-5b.)

Step 5: On this page, you are asked to define several properties of your database. Please refer to Figure 28-6.

1. You must create a unique name for your database. This name must not include any spaces.
2. You may classify your database as either a business or personal use, and select a category that best describes your database. If you specify your database to be public, anyone may use a keyword search (found on eCriteria's home page) to find a database with the properties that you gave it (such as the database name and category).
3. If you allow people to search your database, you may allow them to also download their results. If you do not want people to have this ability, please click "No."
4. You must specify your database to have the following characteristics: (1) add-only (a data-entry Web form), (2) search-only (a searchable database), or (3) both.

Column Name	Column Type	Column Width	Column Label
FirstName	Text	25	First Name
Initial	Text	1	Middle Initial
LastName	Text	25	Last Name
SSN	Text	10	
SpouseFirstName	Text	25	Spouse First Name
SpouseInitial	Text	1	Spouse Initial
SpouseLastName	Text	25	Spouse Last Name
SpouseSNN	Text	10	Spouse SSN
HomeAddress	Text	50	Home Address
AptNo	Text	10	Apt. No.
CityStateZip	Text	50	City, State, Zip
CampaignYou	Text	3	Wish to give $3 to Presidential fund?
CampaignSpouse	Text	3	Spouse: wish to give $3 to Presidential fund?
Wages	Money		
TaxableInterest	Money		Taxable Interest
Compensation	Money		
AGI	Money		
Claim	Text	3	
ClaimAmount	Money		Claim Amount
TaxableIncome	Money		Taxable Income
FederalIncomeTax	Money		Federal Income Tax
EIC	Money		
NontaxableEarned Type	Text	30	Nontaxable Earned Type
NontaxableEarned Amt	Money		Nontaxable Earned Amt
TotalPayments	Money		Total Payments
Tax	Money		
Refund	Money		
RoutingNumber	Text	10	Routing Number

Figure 28-5a. *A partial 1040EZ form database table.*

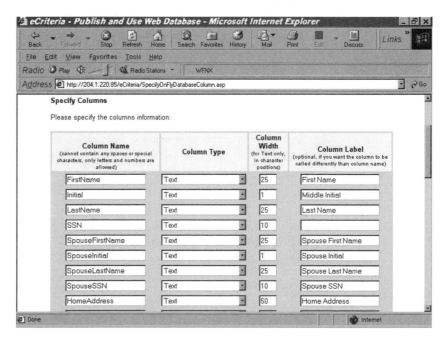

Figure 28-5b. *The same table as seen online.*

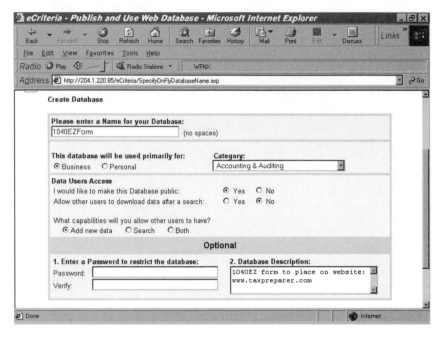

Figure 28-6. *Defining database properties.*

You should define this database as "add-only" because it will request sensitive personal and tax information, and should not be searchable by anyone other than you. If you are the only person allowed to search your database, you should define your database as "add-only" to keep your database secure and unsearchable by others.

> *Optional: If desired, you can limit accessibility to your database with a password. If you want to protect your database with a password, then those wanting to use your Web form will need a password to access your database. This password is different from the password you created when you registered for eCriteria.*

If you are placing this form on your Web site, creating a password for someone to complete your Web form may not be practical, because only those knowing the password will be able to fill out the form.

> *Optional: You may write a line to describe your database so that people who find it through eCriteria's keyword search can immediately understand how to use your database.*

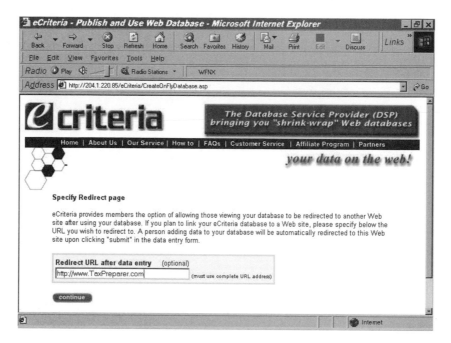

Figure 28-7. *The specify redirect page.*

Step 6: Because eCriteria allows you to link your Web database to your Web site, eCriteria provides a redirect feature (Figure 28-7). After a person uses your eCriteria Web database by accessing it from your site, when he clicks on the Submit button he will be immediately redirected from the eCriteria database to your Web site. This helps to make your Web site and Web databases intuitive and seamless for your users. The redirect URL should be the Web address of the page that a person should arrive at after using your database. For example, it could be a thank-you page, or a page with links to more databases.

Step 7: You can customize the look and feel of your data form by adding your own custom logo and eliminating eCriteria's banner advertisements (Figure 28-8). To place your logo is simple; you just click on "Browse" and select the appropriate drive and folder on your local computer or network to find the graphic you would like to appear at the top of your Web form.

You have now created a Web database (Figure 28-9)!

Section 3: The Result Without Further HTML Customization

You can see how your database would look to someone who accessed it from your Web site. Go to My eCriteria Workspace and click on "Generate URL Link" (Figure 28-10).

Select the database you want to view (Figure 28-11) and click "Continue."

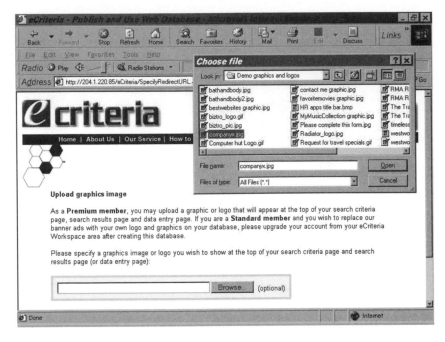

Figure 28-8. *Adding your own logo.*

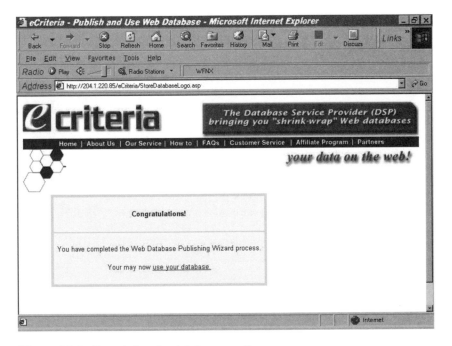

Figure 28-9. *Completing the database creation process.*

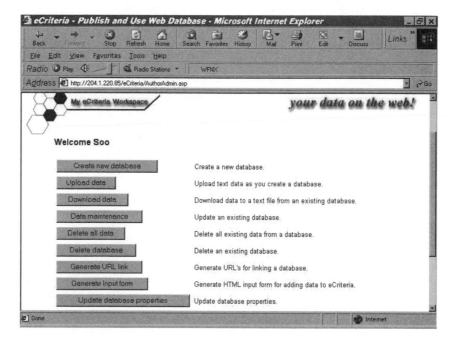

Figure 28-10. *Viewing the completed database.*

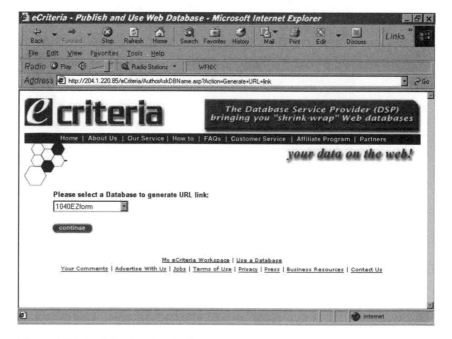

Figure 28-11. *Selecting the database.*

The following screen, as shown in Figure 28-12, should appear. This is the HTML tag you need to place on your Web site in order to link your Web form to your Web site. To see how your database would appear to someone who clicked on that link to your database, you should highlight the URL with your mouse and copy/paste the URL onto your browser.

Figure 28-13 shows how a user would see your Web form.

This Web form has incorporated the company logo, uploaded during the process of creating the database. However, if you want to customize the appearance of your Web form, similar to Figure 28-1, you must utilize another feature of eCriteria, accessible in your eCriteria Workspace.

Section 4: Customizing the HTML to Enhance the Web Form Appearance

In order to enhance the appearance of your Web form to make it look like Figure 28-1, you must use the HTML code accessed from the button "Generate input form." You should copy and paste the HTML provided, as shown in Figure 28-14.

You should copy/paste the HTML code into another file so that you can customize the appearance by adding different colors, fonts, and text. If you are not familiar with

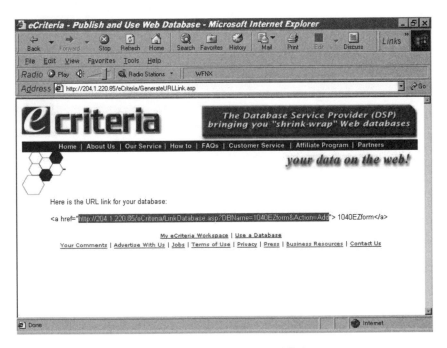

Figure 28-12. *The tag you need to enter into your HTML.*

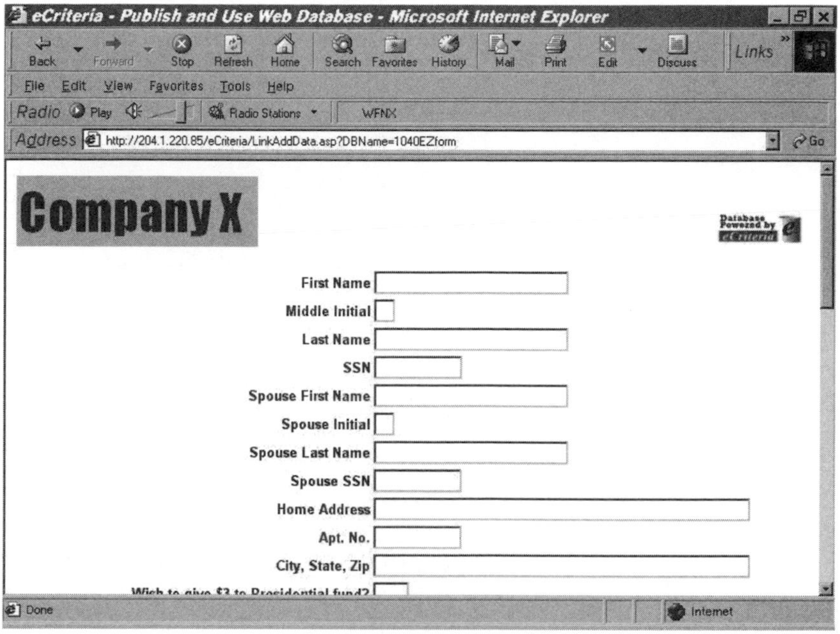

Figure 28-13. A user view of the database.

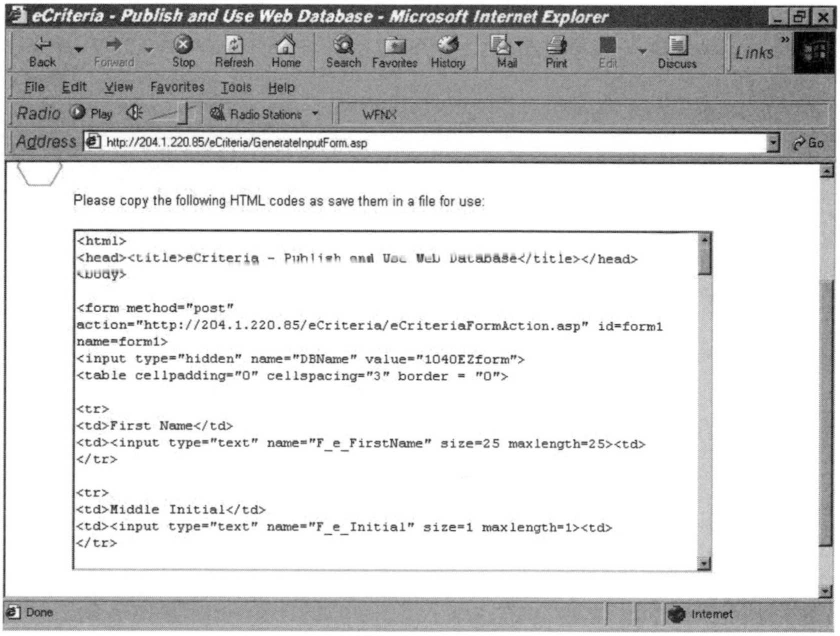

Figure 28-14. Generate input form.

HTML, you can use an HTML editor (such as FrontPage or Dreamweaver) to create a professional-looking Web form.

If you are creating this exact 1040EZ tax form, then you can make use of a premade HTML file to make your Web form look exactly like the one in Figure 28-1. Here is how:

1. Go to www.eCriteria.net.
2. Click on "Tax Preparers" within the section "Who uses eCriteria."
3. Click on the 1040 EZ form.
4. Right-click on the form, and select "View Source," as shown in Figure 28-15.
5. A HTML file should appear on your screen. Near the top of the file, there should be the following code:

```
<input type="hidden" name="DBName" value="Form_1040EZ">
```

You should delete "Form_1040EZ" and replace it with the name of the database you just created.
6. Save the file onto your Web site server.

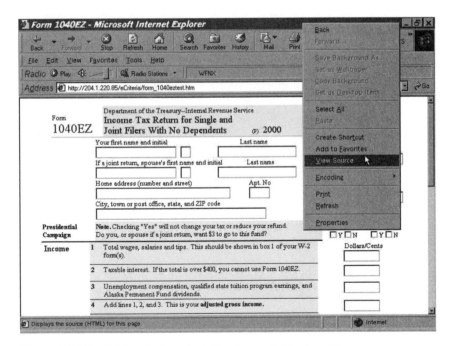

Figure 28-15. Making the form look like the one in Figure 28-1.

Part II: Searchable and Data-Entry Database

Section 1: The End Result

Part II explains how to create a sales database. For anyone conducting sales in a company, sales data can prove vital to a concentrated sales effort. Using a database service provider such as eCriteria, you can create a database to keep track of your company's sales efforts. The end result is twofold: (1) a form to enter the data, as demonstrated in Figure 28-16, and (2) a searchable database to search for specific data, as shown in Figure 28-17.

Section 2: How to Upload and Create a Database

Step 1: If you already have preexisting data in an Excel spreadsheet, you can upload the file as you create your database. (2) The spreadsheet should look like Figure 28-18.

The most important item to observe is the first row of data in the spreadsheet. The first line contains the column names, as described in Part I, Section 2, Step 4. As before, the column names must not include any spaces or special characters. Thus, in this example, the column name "NextAction" contains no spaces.

Step 2: Go to File/Save As. If your installation of Excel allows exporting to text with comma delimitations, you should see the item "CSV (Comma delimited)(*.csv)" in the list called "Save as type" (Figure 28-19). If not, you must go back to your Mi-

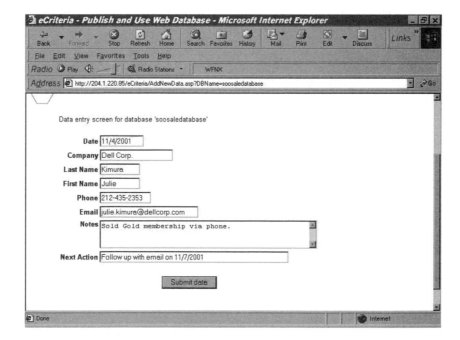

Figure 28-16. *A form used to enter the data.*

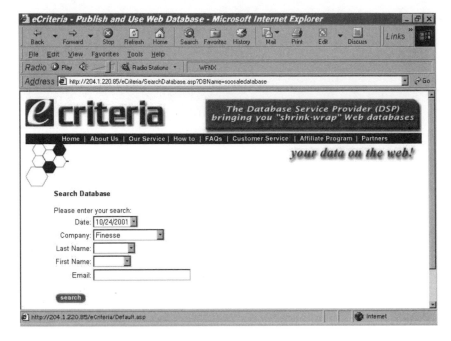

Figure 28-17. *A searchable database.*

	A	B	C	D	E	F	G	H
1	Date	Company	Last	First	Phone	Email	Notes	NextAction
2	10/30/01	Intershop	Ling	Linda	310-120-0124	Linda@intershop.com	Secured Letter of Inte	Thank you email
3	10/16/01	TechCoast	Bradford	Harry	310-876-7845	Harry@techcoast.net	Discussed the Add-or	Email info
4	11/4/01	Handel	Chang	Christina	562-894-7846	Christina@Handel.com	Intro-ed our service th	Expect reply within 1 w
5	10/25/01	Terren	Dulay	Elena	421-457-9753	Elena@Terren.com	Received an email rep	Email a fax notice
6	10/27/01	Eckhart A	Eckhart	Martin	548-876-8492	Martin@eckhart.com	Introduced our service	Email white paper
7	10/19/01	Wan Inc.	Fontana	Nancy	652-849-5453	Nancy@WanCorp.com	Applied for Partners-	Phone follow up
8	10/19/01	Microsoft	Gutierrez	Alice	310-897-3546	Alice@corp.microsoft.cor	Discussed partner fee	Phone in 3 days
9	10/19/01	Intel	Howards	Eileen	310-897-8954	Eileen@intel.com	Partner to add our ser	Phone follow up
10	9/18/01	Cisco	Igloo	Tina	310-894-8765	Tina@cisco.com	Showed our HR applic	Phone follow up
11	9/15/01	CenterBea	Jackson	Ben	562-864-5462	Ben@centerbeam.com	Gave me new contact	Email follow up
12	10/31/01	CentralExc	Kendall	Peter	213-513-8765	Peter@centralexchange.c	Replied eagerly to our	Phone follow up
13	9/12/01	TerraEarth	Lee	Matthew	213-897-8954	Matthew@terraearth.com	Sent partner app and	Phone follow up
14	10/13/01	SevenUp	Mitchells	Dan	213-854-8795	Dan@sevenupcorp.com	Discussed placement	Phone follow up
15	9/11/01	Pepsi	Nam	Eunme	213-897-5462	Eunme@pepsi.com	Left message	Phone in two days
16	9/11/01	MarchOne	Oh	Angie	310-897-8954	Angie@marchone.com	Wrote email concernir	Phone follow up
17	10/9/01	EvenNum	Patel	Grace	310-564-8765	Grace@evennum.corp.co	Third response to new	Email today
18	11/1/01	TreeHouse	Quiztol	Joy	213-567-8465	Joy@treehouse.com	Emailed White paper	Email follow up
19	11/2/01	Motley Fo	Reese	Janet	562-567-3416	Janet@mf.com	Meeting: positive feed	Phone follow up
20	11/2/01	Hyatt	Smith	Sandra	909-572-5612	Sandra@hyatt.com	Meeting: positive feed	Phone follow up
21	11/5/01	Regina As	Therana	Michael	945-897-8954	Michael@regina.com	Meeting: postponed ti	Meeting
22	11/5/01	Lindenberg	Uganda	Timothy	568-846-8942	Timothy@lind.com	Applied for Solutions/	Phone follow up
23	10/24/01	Finesse	Vasquez	Miguel	546-892-5612	Miguel@finesse.com	Discussed email news	Phone follow up
24	10/24/01	Herbal Ess	Waterford	Robert	546-597-5683	Robert@herbalessence.c	Thinks it would be gre	Phone follow up
25	10/31/01	TheraFlu	Xillo	Derek	213-454-5462	Derek@theraflu.com	Emailed me back, I c	Phone follow up
26	10/30/01	Advil	Yamada	Victor	126-979-7541	Victor@advil.com	Prelim discussion of	Phone follow up

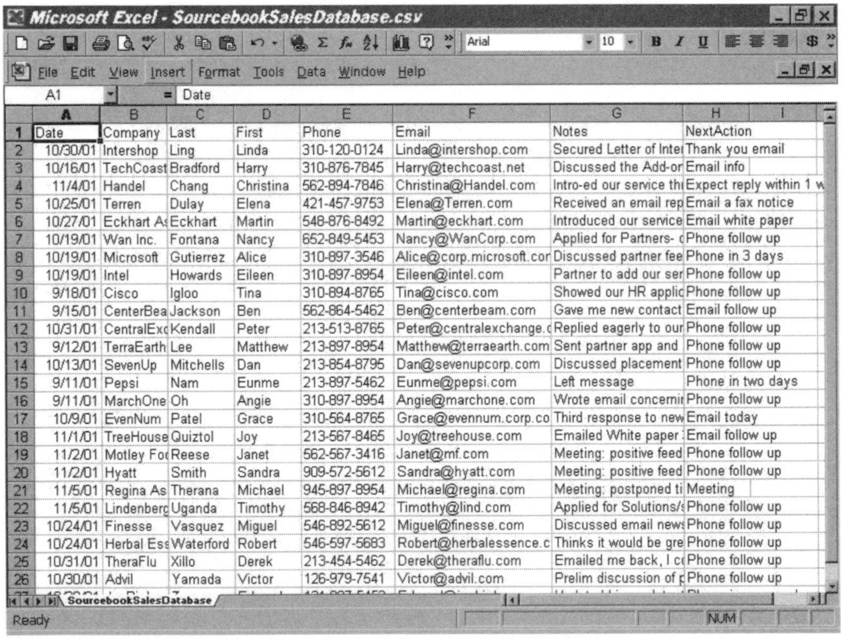

Figure 28-18. *Uploading an Excel spreadsheet.*

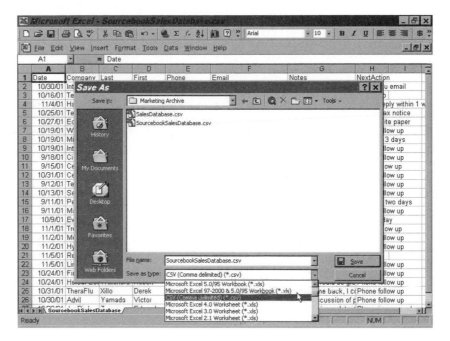

Figure 28-19. *Exporting as a CSV file.*

crosoft Office CD and rerun the Setup program to select this feature in Excel. Fortunately, Microsoft does automatically install text features in a "Typical" install. Save your file as a .csv file. You should remember what you name this file, for you will be uploading this file into eCriteria.

If the following message appears, please click "Yes" (Figure 28-20).

Step 3: Now, you must open up your Internet browser and go to www.eCriteria.net. Register or log in, and you will view the following screen. This is your eCriteria Workspace (Figure 28-21).

Click on the button "Upload data."

Step 4: On this page, you are asked to import the Excel file that you saved with a .csv extension. You can do this by browsing through your local computer and clicking on the file that you wish to import (Figure 28-22).

Step 5: On this page, you can specify the column types, widths, and labels, if appropriate (Figure 28-23). When you uploaded your Excel file to eCriteria, eCriteria automatically filled in the column names with the first row of data that you specified on your spreadsheet. Because you were restricted to make each cell in the first row of your spreadsheet only one word with no spaces or special characters, you can use this page to type column labels. Please see Part I, Section 2, Step 4 for more explanation regarding this page.

Step 6: Here, you must define a name for your database (Figure 28-24). This name must be unique and may not contain any spaces. You can specify your database as public under

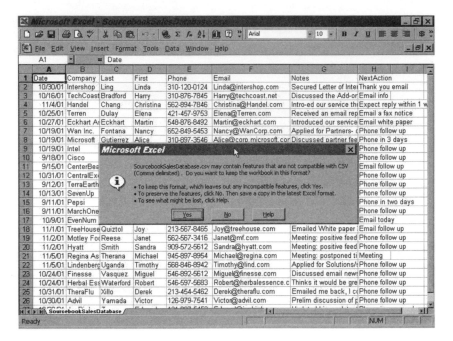

Figure 28-20. Exporting to CSV.

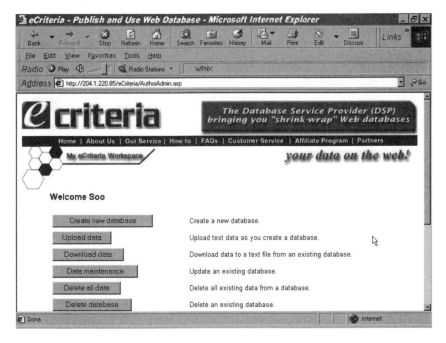

Figure 28-21. Uploading to eCriteria.

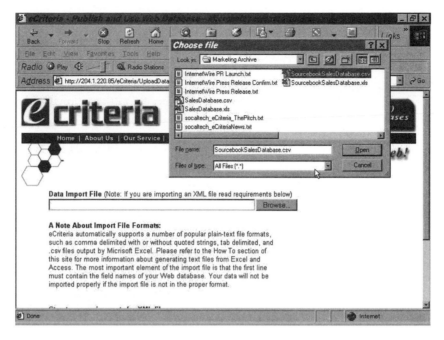

Figure 28-22. *Choosing the Excel file.*

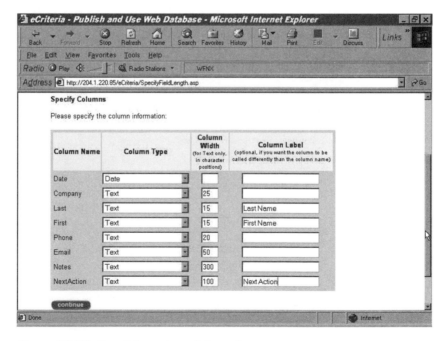

Figure 28-23. *Specifying column information.*

a business or personal category, so that anyone using eCriteria's keyword search for a database can find your database.

On this page, you also define how people can use your database. Allowing users to "add new data" means that they will be able to see your Web form and type the data through the form. "Search" means that users will be able to search through your database using the search criteria you will specify on the following page. "Both" means that users can both add new data and search the database.

Please refer to Part I, Section 2, Step 5 for more detailed explanations.

Step 7: eCriteria successfully imported all of the data records in your Excel spreadsheet. Click "Continue" (Figure 28-25).

Step 8: Since this sales database was specified as both data entry and searchable, this screen asks you to define which columns should be searchable. eCriteria currently offers two options:

1. If you click on a box in the column "Check if column will be used in searching," a person using your searchable database will be able to type in a value to search if the value exists in that particular column.
2. If you click on a box in the column "Check if column will be used as search pull-

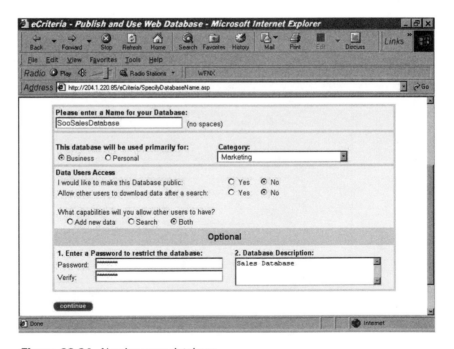

Figure 28-24. Naming your database.

down list," a person using your searchable database will be able to select a value from all the unique values in that particular column, shown in a pull-down list.

As Figure 28-26 shows, a user will be able to type an e-mail address to find a particular record in the database, or select a date, company, last name, or first name from a list to find a particular entry in the database.

Below this table, you can choose a column to use to sort the data. That is, search results will appear in the sort order you specify here.

Step 9: If you plan to link your database to a Web site, then you can specify a redirect page. Whenever someone has finished using your database on your Web site, he will be redirected to the Web page you specify here. Figure 28-27 shows that this database will be redirected to http://soosales.homestead.com/index.html.

Step 10: You can upload a company logo or a favorite graphic to customize the appearance of your database, as shown in Figure 28-28.

You're done (Figure 28–29)!

Section 3: A Look at the End Result

You can input up-to-the-minute sales data to your database in one of three ways:

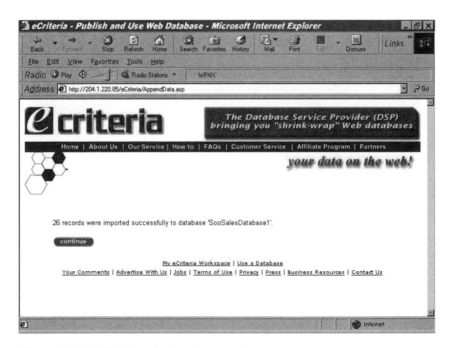

Figure 28-25. Finishing the database creation process.

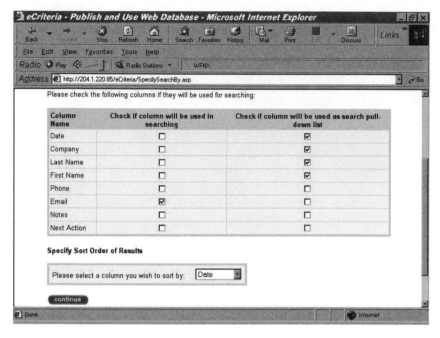

Figure 28-26. Choosing a column to sort the data.

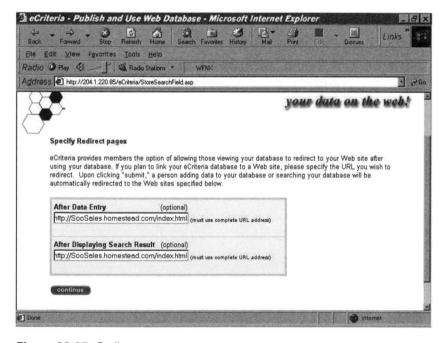

Figure 28-27. Redirect your page.

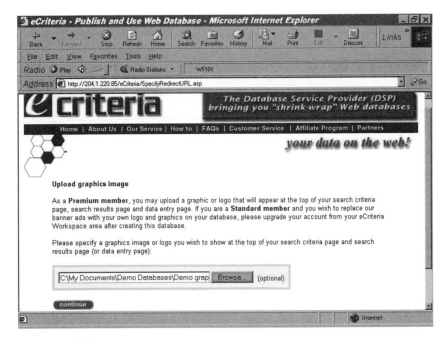

Figure 28-28. *Uploading the logo.*

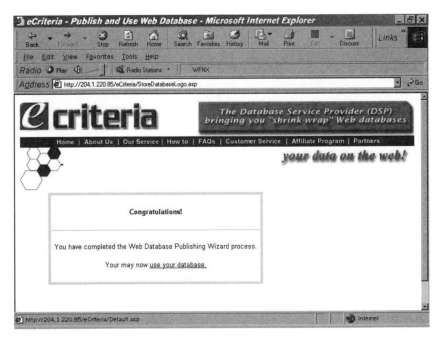

Figure 28-29. *The finished message.*

1. By accessing your database from your Web site.
2. By typing the name of your database into eCriteria to use it while at the eCriteria Web site.
3. By adding new data through your private administrative area.

Figure 28-30 shows how the database would appear if you accessed it directly from eCriteria's Web site. After you input the new information, you can click "Submit data" (Figure 28-31). To perform a search, you also have three options. You can:

1. Access your database via your Web site.
2. Access your database by using the "Use a database" link on the eCriteria Web site.
3. Access your database via your Data Maintenance area.

Figure 28-32 shows how to search your database using the eCriteria Web site. You can search by selecting a value in any of the pull-down lists or typing in the e-mail address.
   The search results will appear as shown in Figure 28-33.

Section 4: Maintaining Your Database
If you log into eCriteria and click on the button "Data Maintenance," you will see a

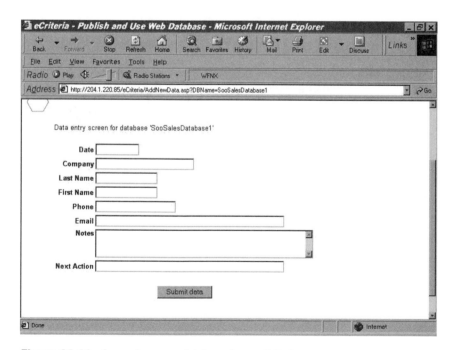

Figure 28-30. *Accessing your database from eCriteria.*

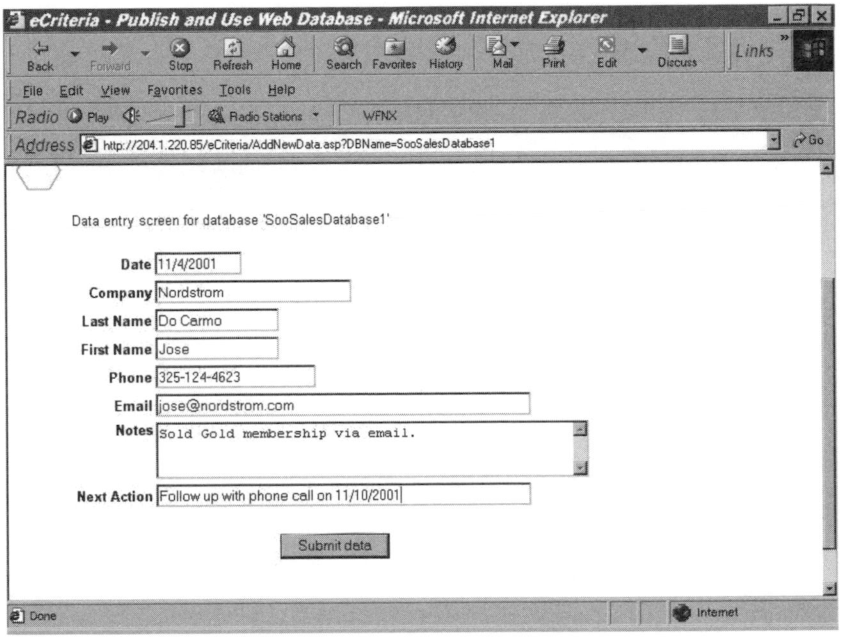

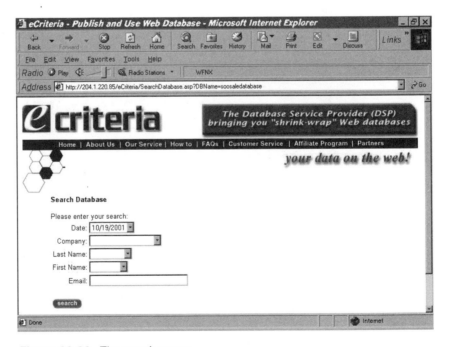

Figure 28-31. *Data entry screen.*

Figure 28-32. *The search screen.*

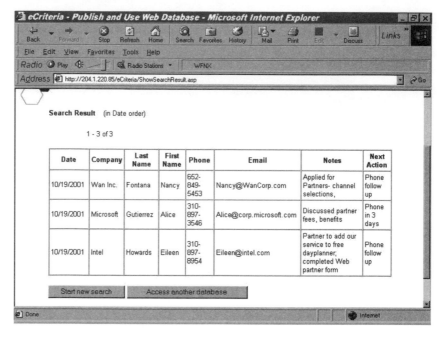

Figure 28-33. Search results.

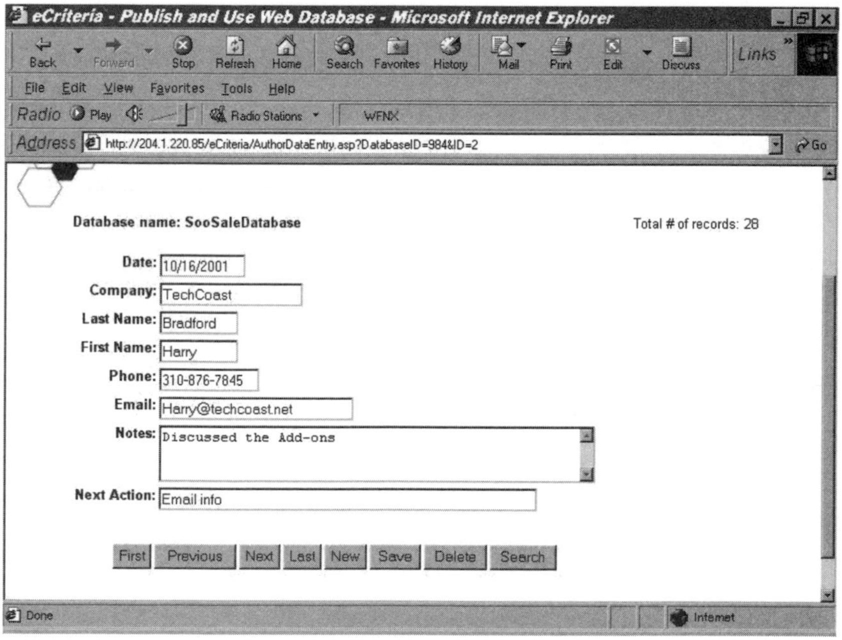

Figure 28-34. The data maintenance screen.

screen similar to Figure 28-34. In your Data Maintenance area, you can perform the following activities:

1. Add a new record.
2. Edit an existing record.
3. Delete an existing record.
4. Search for a particular record.

Notes

1. Because database service providers such as eCriteria are constantly evolving and adding more features, these instructions and screen shots may be slightly outdated and may not precisely reflect the current process needed for creating a Web database.
2. You can upload data from a variety of desktop applications, including Microsoft Excel, Access, Word, Outlook, Palm Pilot, and Notepad. Instructions on uploading from these applications appear on www.eCriteria.net.

SOO KIM is the business development manager at AMULET Development Corporation, a Los Angeles–based developer of database-enabled and e-commerce Web sites. At AMULET, Ms. Kim directs general business development for the company and its spin-off venture, eCriteria. Responsible for securing business partnerships, Ms. Kim handles corporate communications with a variety of Internet and Web-based firms. In this role, she documents eCriteria's technology and business development through a series of popular white papers. While managing eCriteria's beta test, Ms. Kim also directed the relaunch of eCriteria's data exchange portal-style architecture. She also acts as the coordinator of eCriteria's affiliate program. Prior to working at AMULET, Ms. Kim handled various computer network responsibilities for two years in the computer and technology department of the Office of Residential Life, UCLA. Ms. Kim received her B.A. degree in history from UCLA.

Data(Base) Modeling Design for the Web

Renzo Miletich

When it comes to Internet database development, knowing how to construct a data model—and subsequently the database to support future growth, constant changes, and added functionality—requires you to go through a five-step process, beginning with the gathering of requirements that will let you identify purpose, functions, and activities that end-users will need to perform once the system is up and running. It will also help you understand how the data flows through the different systems and/or people throughout the organization: You will perform a series of interviews of system's stakeholders and translate them into decomposition and data-flow diagrams for ease of understanding. After the first phase is completed, you begin the conceptual design by graphically representing those business, data, and information requirements through an entity relationship diagram that defines the people, places, and/or things that you want to gather information about, as well as the relationships among them.

The third phase of this process, referred to as the logical design, lets you achieve third normal form for all entities, by identifying and removing repeating group attributes to another entity and taking those attributes that are partly dependent on the primary key into their own table. The fourth phase, called the physical design, lets you map the entire data model to a specific platform. The final stage, called the physical implementation, will let you create all the database objects for the development as well as the maintenance of your database system.

Step 1: Gather Requirements

The goal at hand is to identify the purpose, functionality, events, and long-term expectations about the system. Therefore, initiate the process by creating a team of individuals with complementary skills that together will be able to perform a series of interviews of system's stakeholders to help you identify and understand the data required for processing, the natural data relationships, and the software platform for the database implementation—as well as the types of users that will be accessing the system. A copy of the strategic plans for the corporation, the departments, and the groups you are working with can tell you where they need to be in three, five and ten years so that you may design accordingly. Once those requirements have been identified, proceed to arrange them into a simple hierarchy chart like Figure 29-1, which will show you the breakdown of the system functions and activities.

Now, in order to understand the flow, and the processing of data performed as it moves through the system, you need to create a data-flow diagram like the one shown in Figure 29-2.

Here you are able to expose the external entities, represented by the rectangles, to which the system needs to interact. Even though they might be outside the scope of your development, it will help you plan the handoffs and/or presentation of this data as it moves through your system. It will also let you define the data stores of information, which will eventually become tables on your database.

Step 2: Conceptual Design

After the gathering and analysis of requirements have taken place and the scope of the system has been defined and understood by all the system stakeholders, proceed to the creation of an entity relationship diagram by identifying the major entities, or principal data objects, from which information is to be collected. They usually denote a person, place, thing, or event of informational interest. Group them in relation to one another, as shown in Figure 29-3, using one of the three ER notations (Chen's, Crow's Foot, or

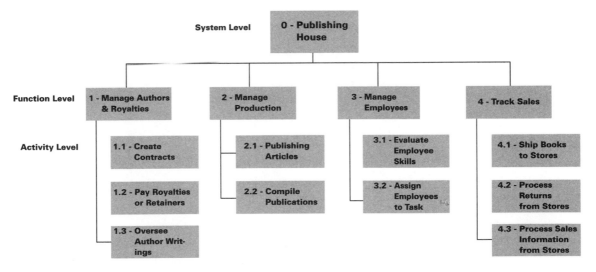

Figure 29-1. *Decomposition diagram.*

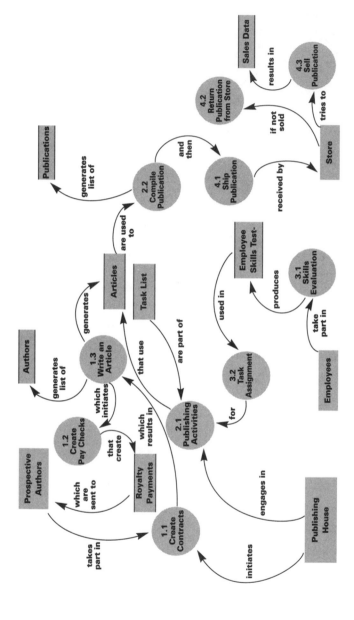

Figure 29-2. Top-level data-flow diagram.

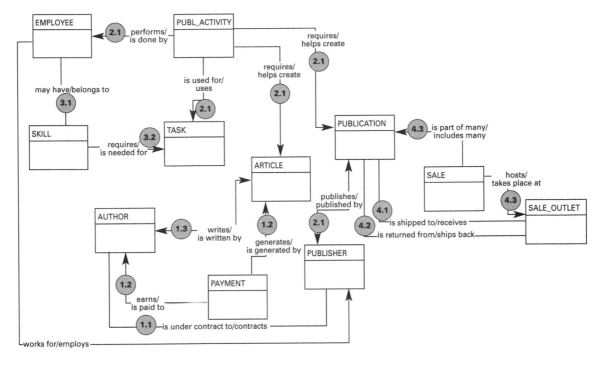

Figure 29-3. Using ER notation.

IDEF1X) and define the degree of the relationship among the entities, which helps you represent real-world associations among them. The most common meaning associated with the term relationship is indicated by the connectivity between entity occurrences: one-to-one, one-to-many, and many-to-many, with a role name at one end to clarify the relationship's purpose. The rationale is quite simple. If an "Employee" has many "Skills," use a one-to-many-degree relationship to relate them with one another.

Step 3: Logical Design

The third phase of the data modeling process is to forward-engineer the ERD created in the previous phase into a logical model, which will give you a closer representation of the evolving database. Start iterating your ERD by defining entity's properties or attributes, using descriptive characteristics that will provide more detail about them. There are two types of attributes: identifiers and descriptors. An identifier, or primary key, is used to uniquely determine an instance of an entity, which will ensure unique row-level access. A descriptor, or non-key attribute, is used to specify a non-unique characteristic of a particular entity instance.

Then, continue your iterations by applying data normalization techniques that consist of arranging data into logical groupings in such a way that each group describes a small part of the whole, minimizing the amount of data duplicated. Also, organize the data so that when you modify it, everything is in one place. Without data normalization, your database system will be inaccurate, slow, inefficient, and it might not produce the results that you expected.

A collaborative session with two or more data modelers and domain experts can help you better understand this situation. Remember that data modeling requires a great deal of thought and is best completed by trial and error. As you define more details about your model, you'll often find more than one way to satisfy the same condition or rule; each approach has its benefits and drawbacks, and only you can determine which model works best for your business. The ability to model your business "on paper" allows you to test out and debug ideas before implementing them, saving money, other resources, and much, much aggravation.

You can use a CASE tool with your favorite notation to facilitate this process. I use ER/Studio CASE tools from Embarcadero Technologies, and IDEF1X and Crow's Foot notations.

Step 4: Physical Design

Up to this point, everything has been vendor-neutral. During the physical design phase you must already know which platform (SQL, Access Oracle) you're going to use for the physical implementation of your database. But before you generate the scripts necessary for the implementation, you must first perform some final activities.

First, you need to validate your model by checking for entities without any attributes, primary keys or unassigned data types. Second, add flag and time-stamp columns to your tables to facilitate data processing. Finally, define a security plan for secure access to your database system by identifying groups or roles, mapping them to the different tables in your data model, and defining the type of access (select, insert, update, and/or delete).

Step 5: Physical Implementation

Now that you have successfully completed the design for your database, the next step will be to physically implement it for the development and maintenance to commence. Start this by creating your database on your selected target platform and defining its initial data and log sizes. Then proceed to the creation of all database objects (tables, indexes, primary keys) by using the Data Definition Language commands create, alter, and drop (see creating_database_objects script).

Add complementary data by either generating a script or using a data aggregation tool and finally running the security scripts (see security script).

RENZO MILETICH is a senior consultant who spends his days designing, developing, and deploying databases for multiple companies. He is also an experienced Web project manager who works with ASP, Visual Basic, and SQL Server.

Using Oracle Synonym Tables in Web Application Integration

Paul W. Brassil

Integrating legacy systems into a new Web site is one of the thorniest issues you will face as an Internet developer. As the promise of the Web evolves from a simple text and graphics distribution system to a true living and breathing software application, you will grapple with remote systems assimilation sooner or later. The possible solutions run the gamut from a low-tech batch feed transferring flat files via FTP to an expensive third-party, message-oriented middleware (MOM) product. Before you rush out to invest in a complex EAI architecture, check first if your Web site and the legacy system are both built on Oracle databases. If so, you might find that accessing remote data via Oracle synonym tables is an elegant alternative that is surprisingly easy to implement.

Overview of Synonym Architecture

Synonym tables are table pointers from a local Oracle database table to a remote Oracle database table. Applying SQL statements against the local instance of the pointer acts simultaneously on the remote table. By way of an example let's assume that a remote system has a table named USER that your Web application needs to read from and write to. You can create a USER synonym table in your local Oracle database that is named LOCAL_USER that could be manipulated locally but act remotely against the USER table. To look up the e-mail address of a user in the remote USER table, run a select statement against the LOCAL_USER table that actually acts on the remote USER table. This allows you much better control over the remote data than would be possible with a more complex middleware solution (as the database will control the flow of data between the systems).

Creating the Database Link

So how do you go about creating and using synonym tables? Well, first you need to create a link between your local database and the remote Oracle system. This requires the creation of a database link between the two systems. Database links essentially contain the following information:

1. The network protocol for communication (TCP/IP, SPX, etc.).
2. The host name and port number of the system.
3. The SID of the database with which you want to communicate.

It is necessary for SQL*Net (an Oracle product that allows two or more databases to communicate over a network) to be installed on both systems for database links to work. If you have a dedicated DBA on your team, you may want to leave the implementation details to him or her. The steps are:

1. Create an entry in the TNSNames.ora file that has the networking information needed by the database link. If you are using Oracle 8x, the easiest way to do this is with the Oracle Net8 Easy Config utility (Figure 30-1).
2. Use the following SQL syntax in SQL*Plus to create the link:

```
Create [public] database link REMOTE_CONNECT
Connect to username identified by password
Using 'connect string';
```

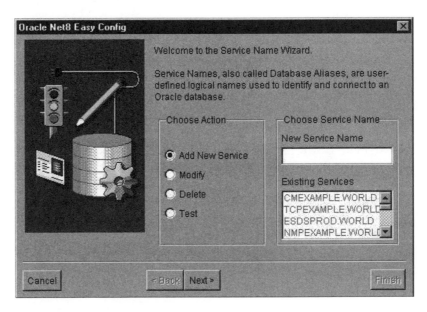

Figure 30-1. The Net8 Easy Config utility.

You might, for example, use the following query to create a database link to the remote database containing the USER table:

```
Create database link USER_DATABASE
Connect to jsmith identified by soccer
Using 'USERDB'
```

where:

- The username on the remote database is jsmith.
- The password for user jsmith is soccer.
- The TNSNAMES.ora entry for the remote system is USERDB.

The "public" argument, if used, will allow all users access to the database link. It is important to note that this is not always desirable, as it can compromise the security of the remote system. Talk with your DBA before using this argument. Either way, you now have a remote database connection that you can link one or more synonym tables to.

Creating the Synonym Table

Once the database link is in place, it is a simple matter to create the synonym table. The syntax is:

```
Create [public] synonym tablename
For remotetable@REMOTE_CONNECT
```

Again, the use of the public argument will give access to all users (and again, its use is something you should run by your DBA). Create the following synonym table for the remote USER table with this query:

```
Create public synonym LOCAL_USER
For USER@USER_DATABASEremotetablename@REMOTE_CONNECT
```

This will create a link in your database that you can use as if it were a local table. To test the linkage to the remote system, run the following SQL query:

```
Select count(*) from LOCAL_USER
```

and get back:

```
COUNT(*)
---------
6374
```

This indicates that there are 6,374 records in the remote USER table. At this point you should begin to see how powerful synonym tables can be.

Overview of Code Access

Because this is a guide on how to improve your Internet development skills and not a manual for database administrators, it is now time to see how synonym tables can be used in a Web application. It goes without saying that you need a way to imbed business objects in your code that will allow access to your database. This could be an ADO call in ASP or a Java object in JSP using JDBC. Once you have database connectivity, you are ready to go.

Walk-through of Example

Let's suppose that you are responsible for your company's Extranet, a site that allows downloads of your company's software products. Users register their software online (after first purchasing the software and receiving a registration key in the mail) and download updates and patches after the registration number has been validated. In this example, the registration data is actually maintained in a separate Oracle database (which we'll call the "Software Entitlement" database), but the company has decided that *your* Web site's database is the system of record for user accounts. That means that when you create or update a user account in your system, that same information needs to be updated in the Software Entitlement database. Likewise, when a user logs into your Web site to download software, you need to query the Software Entitlement database to verify that the user has been approved for distribution of the requested software. Synonym tables provide the perfect solution.

First create (following the aforementioned steps) a local synonym table to the USER table and a local synonym table to the SOFTWARE_DOWNLOAD table on the Software Entitlement database. On the local system call the tables LOCAL_USER and LOCAL_SOFTWARE_DOWNLOAD. Also, create a table called WEB_USER on the local database to store the local user information used for personalization. Assume the tables on the remote system are structured as shown in Figure 30-2.

The user creation flow will be:

1. Create the user in the local WEB_USER table. Figure 30-3 displays an example of how a user will enter data in the Web site.

USER

Column	USER_ID	FNAME	LNAME	ADDRESS	CITY	STATE	ZIP	EMAIL
Example	U12345	John	Smith	2 Oak St.	Medfield	MA	02052	js@abc.net

SOFTWARE_DOWNLOAD

Column	USER_ID	SOFTWARE_ID	SOFTWARE_NAME
Example	U12345	SW4567	Online TimeClock Version 1.2

Figure 30-2. *Possible structure of tables on remote system.*

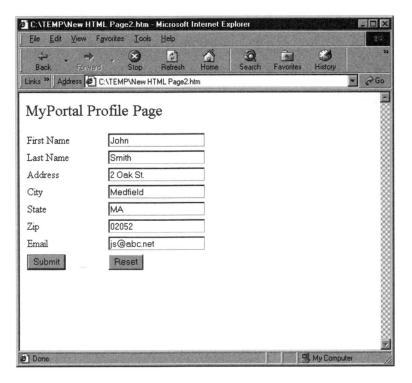

Figure 30-3. *Entering data into the database.*

2. Retrieve the unique USER_ID you've created in the WEB_USER table for the new row. Use the user's unique e-mail address to select the unique USER_ID.

3. Create an account in the remote USER table with the unique USER_ID and user data (via the LOCAL_USER synonym table).

Figure 30-4. *The software package lookup.*

4. The administrator of the Software Entitlement database will configure the software a user can download (when the user registers the software online).

To look up a software package that a user can download:

1. Get the USER_ID of the Web user from the WEB_USER table.
2. Look up the software package in the remote SOFTWARE_DOWNLOAD table that the user has access to (via the LOCAL_SOFTWARE_DOWNLOAD synonym table).
3. Display the software packages the user can download.

Figure 30-4 shows an example of this.
The following Java class illustrates each step:

```
class WebConnect{
        Connection GetDBConnect() //Method to connect to
Database
```

```
        throws SQLException, ClassNotFoundException
        {
                String connect = "jdbc:odbc:WEBDB";
                String user = "webuser";
                String password = "webpass";
                Class.forName("sun.jdbc.odbc.JdbcOdbcDriver");
                return (DriverManager.getConnection(connect,
                user, password));
        }
        void CreateNewUser(String fname, String lname, //Method
        to create a new user
                            String add, String city,      //in
                            local table and remote
                            String state, String zip,     //table
                            String email)
throws SQLException, ClassNotFoundException
{
                String uid = null;
                String table =  "WEB_USER";
                Connection lconnect = GetDBConnect();
                Statement lstate = lconnect.createStatement();
                lstate.execute(CreateInsert(table, uid, fname,
                lname, add, city, state, zip, email));
                ResultSet lresult = lstate.executeQuery("select
                USER_ID from WEB_USER where EMAIL = '" + email +
                "'" );
                lresult.next();
                uid = lresult.getString("USER_ID");
                table = "LOCAL_USER";
                lstate.execute(CreateInsert(table, uid, fname,
                lname, add, city, state, zip, email));
                lstate.close();
        }
        String CreateInsert(String table, String uid, String
        fname, String lname,            //Method
                            String add, String city, String state,
                            String zip,         //to
                            String email)    //create
        {                                         //insert
                String insert = "Insert into ";
                        insert+= table +" values ";
                        insert+= "(";
                        insert+= uid+ ",";
                        insert+= "'" +fname+ "',";
                        insert+= "'" +lname+ "',";
                        insert+= "'" +add+ "',";
                        insert+= "'" +city+ "',";
                        insert+= "'" +state+ "',";
```

```
                        insert+= "'" +zip+ "',";
                        insert+= "'" +email+"'";
                        insert+= ")";
                return insert;
        }
        String GetEntitlement(int uid) //method to get
        registered software
        throws SQLException, ClassNotFoundException
        {
                String software_ent;
                Connection lconnect = GetDBConnect();
                Statement lstate = lconnect.createStatement();
                ResultSet lresult = s.executeQuery("select
                SOFTWARE_NAME from LOCAL_SOFTWARE_DOWNLOAD where
                USER_ID =" + uid );
                lresult.next();
                software_ent =
lresult.getString("SOFTWARE_NAME");
                lstate.close();
                return software_ent;
        }
}
```

First, look at the CreateNewUserUser method. After connecting to the Web database via the GetDBConnect JDBC method, an insert statement writes the user information to the WEB_USER table. A trigger in the WEB_USER table generates the USER_ID.[1] Using the unique e-mail address of the user, the USER_ID is selected and, with the rest of the user profile data, written to the remote USER table via the LOCAL_USER synonym table:

---

[1]You can create a sequence trigger in the WEB_USER table that will generate a new, serial user ID every time a row is written to the WEB_USER table. This will save you from having to create a USER_ID and ensuring its uniqueness each time. The syntax to create the trigger is:

```
create sequence USERSEQUENCE;
create trigger USER_ID
before insert on pb_USER for each row
begin
 if ( :new.USER_ID is null ) then
   select USERSEQUENCE.nextval into :new.USER_ID from DUAL;
 end if;
end;
```

Next, the GetEntitlement method looks up a user's registered software in the remote SOFTWARE_DOWNLOAD table. The USER_ID is passed and, via the LOCAL_SOFTWARE_DOWNLOAD synonym table, a string containing the name of the software the user has access to is returned:

```
ResultSet lresult = s.executeQuery("select SOFTWARE_NAME from
LOCAL_SOFTWARE_DOWNLOAD where USER_ID =" + uid );
lresult.next();
software_ent = lresult.getString("SOFTWARE_NAME");
lstate.close();
return software_ent;
```

The class is unsophisticated and serves only as a simple example of the concepts discussed above. To make this more robust, you would want to wrap the WEB_USER and LOCAL_USER inserts in transactional logic so that inserts to both tables either commit completely or roll back. The importance of this example is an understanding of the location transparency offered by synonym tables and how simple they can be to implement.

Conclusion

Synonym tables are flexible and scalable tools that are a natural fit for application integration development. You can save a lot of development time when you adopt this approach, and will be spared the cost and potential administrative issues that come from more involved EAI implementations.

References

1. George Koch and Kevin Loney. *Oracle: The Complete Reference, Electronic Edition* (Berkeley, CA: Osborne McGraw-Hill, 1997).
2. Bruce Eckel. *Thinking In Java, 2nd Edition* (Upper Saddle River, NJ: Prentice-Hall, Inc., 2000).

PAUL W. BRASSIL is manager of e-business technology at EMC Corporation. He has a B.S. in business management and M.S. in computer information systems, Brassil has over ten years of software engineering and management experience, including positions as principal software engineer (C++/COM/Web), project lead, and software manager.

Database-Internet Connectivity

Greg Griffiths

This chapter provides an overview of how to get information stored in a database to be displayed on the Internet and how that information can be updated in the database via the Internet.

We will also give a brief overview of the technologies involved in Internet database connectivity and will illustrate with three simple practical examples, which are intended to provide a trivial example with plenty of scope for improvement by the user.

Three approaches will be discussed in this chapter. Firstly, publishing a static HTML table from a program such as Microsoft Access; then we shall look at an approach using active server pages (ASP) and one using the DBI module of Perl.

There are several ways to put database content on the Internet, and although we shall only be examining three in this chapter, the fundamentals explored here should provide a basis for similar work using other tool sets or languages.

It is assumed that the reader has a basic understanding of:

1. Databases.
2. The structured query language (SQL).
3. Programming/scripting languages. (1)
4. Web programming languages such as HTML and its variants.
5. The setup of associated software and hardware such as a Web server, ODBC, modem.

A listing of books and Web sites for all levels on all of these subjects is included at the end of this chapter. The basis of this section is from work that I did for my B.S. in computer science dissertation at the University of Wales, Aberystwyth (http://www.aber.ac.uk).

A Little Background

HTML

The creation of the language we refer to today as HTML is attributed to Tim Berners-Lee, who created it while working at CERN. Over the past decade, the Internet has exploded in terms of growth and HTML is the language that holds it all together. To ensure maximum accessibility to this media, it is important that we all speak the same language, HTML. However, there are some "extras" that some people or organizations have included in their systems, hence the need for and use of an independant HTML standard. HTML was revamped and relaunched as HTML 2.0 in late 1995—see RFC1866 for further info—by the Internet Engineering Task Force (IETF). Other slight modifications included HTML+ (1993) and HTML 3.0 (1995), which contained many new features, although neither were adopted as "offical" standards.

Following on from these and the increased use of the Web, the World Wide Web Consortium's HTML Working Group produced HTML 3.2 (January 1997).

I am sure that all of you have seen sites that contain the immortal phrase "best viewed in," which normally translates to "probably only usable in." This issue has promoted the cause of standards with HTML and adherence to them by the various groups involved. If this were not the case, the users experience would be significantly reduced, which could inflict mortal blows on the Web.

Thus, each new revision of the official HTML specification is backward-compatible as well as forward-looking, embracing the latest "custom" add-ons from various companies as well as accommodating new user requirements. HTML has also been developed to be platform- and device-independent.

ODBC

This is a method in which applications can interact with an SQL-compliant database in a DBMS-independent manner. Thus, a series of programs written using ODBC to work with an Oracle database will work just as well with an SQL server.

A committee of industry experts from the X/Open and SQL Access Group committees developed it.

Microsoft supports ODBC, which is probably the reason for its dominance as the main method for this purpose.

Before we begin, however, it is worth taking a few moments to examine what we are doing. Database hosting for a Web site is normally a reasonably expensive business, and if you are displaying data that changes on a regular basis—say, once a week for sports results, or quarterly for a department phone book—then perhaps providing full database-Internet connectivity is not the most appropriate solution.

A server-side script—such as a Perl or an ASP script—is called by a standard HTML link to the HTML file, such as:

```
<a href="\cgi-bin\asp\phonebook.asp">Phone Book</a>
```

Alternatively, it can be used to process input from an HTML form. In which case, it needs to be included as part of the FORM tag:

```
<form name="myform" action="\cgi-bin\asp\phonebook.asp"
method="post">
```

The script in the context of this chapter will need to perform the following actions:

1. Accept any values passed to it by the calling page or form.
2. Declare and instantiate any variables that it will use.
3. Make a database connection and run a query.
4. Process the results of the query.
5. Prepare and send a response to the user.

In some instances, you may need to run several queries and/or use database connections to achieve your required goal, but for this example we will only use a single connection and query. The response to the user may be a thank-you page if the user has submitted a form, or it may be a results page if the user is querying the database.

At this point, it is also worth defining some terminology that we shall use in this section; these definitions should give you some insight into the rest of the section.

Static publishing involves taking a snapshot of your data and then saving the result as a file and making that output file available via the Internet; it could simply be the result of a query or a report. This is considered to be the better approach if you have data that changes on a regular basis such as sports results or accounts.

Dynamic publishing is where any change to the database by any user is immediately updated to the copy that the server holds. In many cases, the database is directly attached to the server via one of the tools described herein. This results in more up-to-date information and is a better approach if you have data that frequently changes such as stock prices, or if you want your users to always have the latest information.

Although most of this section concerns the latter of these two approaches, you may—due to your ISP or cost, for example—have to use the first method to produce your output and then publish that on the Web instead of having live "dynamic" information.

Producing a Static HTML Table

If you are only going to be displaying reasonably static information, you only need to display the data to the user; then you may be able to use the functionality of your database

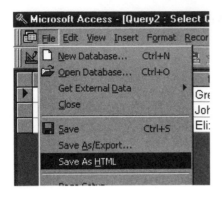

Figure 31-1. *Saving as HTML.*

to save the results of your query in a "Web-friendly" format. This will allow you to save your results as an HTML file and then either add this directly to your site or include it in an existing page.

This approach requires no extra support from your Internet Service Provider (ISP), as you are only using standard HTML files. One of the most common databases that provide this sort of functionality is Microsoft's Access, and we shall use this for our example.

To save the results as an HTML file you need to do the following:

1. Create your query as normal in Access and save it.
2. Open the File drop-down menu.
3. Select the Save As HTML option—as shown in Figure 31-1. This will then run the Publish to the Web wizard.
4. Press the Next button on the first screen.
5. On the next screen, click on the Queries tab and then select the checkbox next to the required query. Then press the Next button.
6. If you have a file that is a template for your site, select it here. Otherwise just press the Next button.
7. Select Static HTML on the next screen and then press the Next button.
8. Provide a directory to save the file to and ensure that the "No, I want to publish objects locally" option is selected. Then press the Next button.
9. On the next screen press the Finish button.

You can now take your snapshot of your data in the file the wizard created and alter it, as you need to get it to fit in with the rest of your Web site.

Alternatively, you could use your preferred HTML editor such as Microsoft FrontPage or Macromedia's Dreamweaver to create a simple table and then put the values into this table.

Dynamic Data

For some systems, the method outlined above may not be what you need. You may, for example, have stock prices to display or want a user to be able to see any changes they make have immediate effect and not wait for someone to update and then republish the snapshot, or you may need to pull data about an ongoing process into an inquiry form for a user or manager.

If this is the case, then the following data flow occurs between the user and the database via the Web server:

Client → Web Server → Application Server → Database

The client is a browser such as Microsoft's Internet Explorer or Netscape's Navigator or Opera Software's Opera. The Web server is the program that handles requests from the client; examples include IIS and Apache.

The application server is the program that handles the executable code that is called by the client via the Web server; in some cases this may be built into the Web server (for example, with ASP and IIS) or may be an additional program (for example, the Perl executable or Allaire's Cold Fusion toolset). This server connects to the specified database using the selected method (commonly ODBC or JDBC).

If you are using a Microsoft Windows machine as your Web server, it is likely that you or the administrator will be required to set up an Open DataBase Connectivity connection for the Web server to use to communicate with the database. A similar connection will need to be defined on any other platform, such as Linux, Unix, or Mac.

We shall firstly define an HTML Web page that can capture the information that we require for our program. In this example, our form will allow the user to enter a surname into the form and will then return a list of all matches on that surname. This example should be enough to allow you to build more complex queries so you can search for multiple criteria as well.

Here is our simple HTML form for this example.

```
<html>
<body>
<form name="phonebook" action="\cgi-bin\phonebook.asp"
method="post">
Surname : <input type="text" name="surname" size="20"><br>
<input type="submit">
</form>
</body>
</html>
```

We shall use the same HTML form that we defined in the previous section for this section as well.

Dynamic Data Using ASP

For our first example, we will look at interacting with a database using active server pages, commonly known as ASP. ASP was initially introduced in December 1996 as part of Microsoft's Internet Information Server 3 product. Being a Microsoft product, it has not been fully ported onto other platforms. Although companies such as ChilliASP! have made most of the core functionality available, it still remains generally a Windows-only approach. The most common platform for ASP is the Microsoft Webserver IIS, although others may support ASP. Check out the documentation for your specific Web server for further information.

Microsoft has recently released a new version of ASP, called ASP+, as part of their Net strategy. Although there are many similarities, there are also several differences. This tutorial will focus only on ASP, but the concepts explored here can easily be expanded using ASP+.

ASP is not a language, it is more of an approach to doing something, in the same way as word processing or sport. Generally, most ASP pages are written in VBScript—the Web scripting subset language of Microsoft's Visual Basic tool, although they could also be written in another language such as JavaScript, for example. Server-side scripts written in Java or JavaScript these days are referred to as Java server pages, although many of the concepts are shared with the ASP model.

Microsoft has produced a tool called InterDev to provide a tool for ASP that is similar to what their FrontPage product does for HTML. However, a text editor such as Word-Pad or Vi will suffice for most applications.

Our Example

The sample form that we are using will provide the input to our ASP page. The following ASP page has been heavily commented to show you what exactly we are doing as you progress through it.

```
<%
' declare our variables
Dim surname
Dim SQLString
' put the value the user entered into our variable SURNAME
surname=request.Form("surname")

' send back the first bit of our document to the user
response.write("<html><head><title>PhoneBook</title></head><body
>")

' build our SQL Statement and append the value of SURNAME to the
end
SQLString="SELECT firstname,lastname,ext FROM tbl_phonebook
WHERE lastname like '%" & surname & "%'"
' create our database connection
set dbConn = server.createobject("ADODB.connection")

' open the connection for to an Oracle Datbase using an
Microsoft ODBC driver for Oracle
```

```
' in the format "<DSN Name>","<Username>","<Password>"
dbConn.open "PhoneBook", "myphone", "telephone"

' run our query and put the results into the object RESULTS
set results=dbConn.execute(SQLString)

' move through all the results brouhgt back by the query
Do While Not results.EOF

    ' assign each value to variable
    forename=results("firstname")
    surname=results("lastname")
    extension=results("ext")

    ' send back that row in the format firstname lastname
    ' extension
    response.write(forename & "  " & surname &
    " " & ext &"<br>")
loop

'close the results object
results.close()
' close the datbase
dbConn.close()

' send the HMTL footer to complete the HTML document
response.write("</body></html>")
%>
```

In this example, we get the user input, send back the top part of our HTML page, create our query, open the connection and run the query, process the results, and then close both the results object and the database connection before sending some more HTML to complete the page returned to the user using the response.write command.

The reason for keeping the database and results connections open for as little as possible is firstly a performance issue—we only use the system resources to create the connections just before we need them and then close them afterward to give the system back the resources. Secondly, it promotes clean coding and maintainability—why open them well before you need to use them and then close them long after you have finished with them? Could you follow this program when it is ten or even a hundred times the size?

What is returned to the user via the Web server would be something like:

```
Greg Griffiths 2203
Craig Griffith 6231
Diane Griffiths 8889
Larry Harper-Griffiths 6668
```

Dynamic Data Using Perl

We shall continue to use the phone book example from the previous section and look at how we would implement it using Perl. Perl was created by Larry Wall in the 1980s as a language to improve system administration, but with the advent of the Internet it has found a niche as the main language for server-side scripting in the world. Resources abound for this language in all media formats—check out www.perl.com or do a search for it at an online bookseller such as Amazon.com.

This product is also open source, and embraces changes and enhancements made by the user group, so much so that a constantly growing repository for Perl modules has been created on the Internet—CPAN (www.cpan.com). The popularity of Perl as a language for this type of work means that support is never far away, from newsgroups discussions such as comp.lang.perl to hired Perl consultants. Hiring staff with Perl skills is also reasonably easy.

Perl runs on Unix and Windows—although there are some differences between the two versions due to the underlying operating system. While it is extremely common on Unix and Linux platforms—it is part of the standard install for most of them—it is slightly less known on Windows environments. The best install of Perl for Windows can be found on the ActiveState site (www.activestate.com) and this version comes with an installer and instructions to get you started.

Perl has several approaches to Internet—database connectivity, but we shall only examine one in detail, the DBI module. Other alternatives include Dave Roth's Win32::ODBC module, which is bundled with the ActiveState install but limited to Windows platforms, or the Text::CSV module, which acts as an interface to the Windows CSV file format. Others include Data::Dumper, AnyDBM_File, and Storable.

Our Example

As before, we shall use a heavily commented Perl script to show you what is going on:

```perl
#!/usr/bin/perl

# include the modules that we will use in this script, in our
case, just the DBI module
# and the strict module to promote good coding practice
use DBI
use Strict


# declare our variables
my $SQLStatement;    # our SQLString
my $firstname;       # }
my $lastname;        # } variables to store the results of our
query
```

```perl
my $ext;          # }
my $Surname            # the variable storing the user input
my $buffer;            # Input buffer
my %FORM;        # Array holding form data
my @pairs;             # Array holding form input
my $pair;        # Instance of @pairs
my $name;        # Variable name from form
my $value;             # Variable value from form


# Print content return type
print <<"EOF";
Content-type: text/html

EOF

# Get the input
read(STDIN, $buffer, $ENV{'CONTENT_LENGTH'});

# decode the submitted form

foreach $pair (@pairs)
{
    ($name, $value) = split(/=/, $pair);

    # Un-Webify plus signs and %-encoding
    $value =~ tr/+/ /;
    $value =~ s/%([a-fA-F0-9][a-fA-F0-9])/pack("C", hex($1))/eg;

    # Uncomment for debugging purposes
    # print "Setting $name to $value<P>";

    $FORM{$name} = $value;
}

# put the users input into the variable Surname
$Surname=$FORM{'surname'};

# send back the first part of our response, don't forget to
escape some characters by using
# a \ before them.
print "<html><head><title>PhoneBook<\/title><\/head>";

# build our SQL Statement
$SQLStatement="SELECT firstname,lastname,ext FROM tbl_phonebook
WHERE lastname like '%$Surname%'"

# Define the connection to the database in the format
# ("dbi:<Connection Type>:<DSN Name>","<Username>","<password>")
```

```perl
my $dbh = DBI->connect( "dbi:ODBC:PhoneBook", "myphone",
"telephone" )
    or die "Unable to connect: " . $DBI::errstr . "\n";

# Prepare the query and then execute it
my $query = $dbh->prepare($SqlStatement);
$query->execute
    or die "can't run SQL";

# Get the results and assign them to our variables
while (($firstname,$surname,$ext) = $query->fetchrow_array)
{
    print "$firstname $surname $ext <br>";
}

# Close everything down
$query->finish;
$dbh->disconnect;

# send the rest of the HTML page back
print "<\/body><\/html>"
```

Although this script is longer than the example in the previous section, they both achieve the same result. This second script can be used as is on either the Windows or Unix version of Perl. This platform independence is one of the weaknesses that ASP is slowly overcoming.

Where Now?

Now that you have seen—and hopefully understood—these examples, you will be looking to expand upon them and adjust them to your particular needs. Keeping with the phone book example, you may wish to add extra search criteria such as first name and department.

On the technical side, you are probably going to want to alter the HTML that is used here so that it fits in with the rest of your site. Also consider using some validation on both the client (browser) and server (script) side to ensure as far as you can that the users are entering data that will not either crash your code or cause other problems for you.

These sample scripts are simply used to provide you with a basic showcase of what the chosen approach can do; they lack many of the features that you would require for a production application, including data integrity checking and validation both on the client and server side. For client side validation, I recommend JavaScript. This is because it is the de facto standard scripting language on the client side and is included in all of the mainstream browsers, such as Internet Explorer, Netscape, and Opera. VBScript, the Microsoft scripting language, is supported out of the box only by Internet Explorer, and their version of JavaScript—JScript—has some differences with JavaScript that may cause problems on your page.

Your ISP or company may not provide support for ASP or Perl, so you may need to setup a Web server and the relevant files on your local computer. This also has the added bonus of not crashing or causing problems with their servers while you "try something out."

If your ISP does not support ASP, you should be able to find a company such as Brinkster (www.brinkster.com) who provide free ASP and ASP+ hosting with plenty of tutorials for free. On the Perl side, consider companies such as UKLinux (www.uklinux.net).

Possible Alternatives?

Although I have illustrated simple examples using both ASP and Perl to give you a flavor of what they can do, they are not by any means the only two ways of connecting a database to the Internet. Other tools that will do this include:

- Perl using Win32::ODBC rather than DBI
- Allaire Cold Fusion: http://www.allaire.com
- JDBC (Java): http://java.sun.com/products/jdbc/
- Jagg (Java): http://www.bulletproof.com/jagg/
- Netscape's LiveWire: http://webreview.com/wr/pub/97/07/25/webdev.htm
- Galileo: http://www.esemplare.com/galileo.html
- ODBiC: http://freeweb.digiweb.com/business/ODBiC/
- Other: http://www.webdeveloper.com/database/

Some of these tool sets can be used in a similar way to FrontPage or Dreamweaver in terms of their interface. Others, however, require some form of coding, which, depending on the product, could be a large investment of resources and money. A quick search using any search engine on some of the mentioned keywords in this section will bring up a plethora of approaches as well as many other supporting items such as reviews and tutorials.

Conclusion

I hope that this chapter has given you an overview of the concepts behind connecting a database to the Internet and provided you with some working examples. The books, Web sites, and other resources listed in the reference section should give you the information you need to develop your particular solution.

In addition to the approaches explored here, there are many others. You will need to consider your skill sets, resources, budget, time scale, and the operating systems and Web server software that are on the computers that house your Web server and database, among other factors.

References

ASP

Web Sites
1. http://www.aspin.com
2. http://www.asp-zone.com
3. http://www.chillisoft.net
4. http://www.4guysfromrolla.com
5. http://wdvl.com/Authoring/ASP/
6. http://www.zdnet.com/pcmag/pctech/content/16/22/it1622.001.html

Books
1. de Cali, James, et al. *Professional ASP Data Access.* Wrox Press, Inc, ISBN 1861003927.
2. Denault, Dan, et al. *ASP 3.0 Programmer's Reference.* Wrox Press, Inc, ISBN 1861003234.
3. Homer, Alex. *Alex Homer's Professional ASP Web Techniques.* Wrox Press, Inc, ISBN 1861003218.
4. Homer, Alex, et al. *Professional Active Server Pages 3.0.* Wrox Press, Inc, ISBN 1861002610.
5. Kaufman, John, et al. *Beginning ASP Databases.* Wrox Press Inc, ISBN 1861002726.
6. Mitchell, Scott. *Designing Active Server Pages.* O'Reilly & Associates, ISBN 0596000448.
7. *Sams Teach Yourself Web Development with ASP in 24 Hours.* Sams Publishing, ISBN 0672317907.
8. Weissinger, A. Keyton. *ASP in a Nutshell.* O'Reilly UK, ISBN 1565928431.

Mailing lists
1. http://p2p.wrox.com

Newsgroups
1. microsoft.public.inetserver.asp.db
2. microsoft.public.inetserver.asp.general

PERL

Web Sites
1. http://www.activestate.com
2. http://www.hermetica.com/technologia/DBI/
3. http://www.perl.com

Books
1. Christiansen, Tom, et al. *Perl Cookbook.* O'Reilly UK, ISBN 1565922433.
2. Descartes, Alligator, and Tim Bunce. *Programming the Perl DBI.* O'Reilly UK, ISBN 1565926994.

3. Gundavaram, Shishir, et al. *CGI Programming with Perl.* O'Reilly UK, ISBN 1565924193.
4. Lemay, Laura. *Teach Yourself Perl in 21 Days.* Sams Publishing, ISBN 0672313057.
5. Scwartz, Randal, et al. *Learning Perl.* O'Reilly UK, ISBN 1565922840.
6. Spainhour, Steven, et al. *Perl in a Nutshell.* O'Reilly UK, ISBN 1565922867.
7. Wall, Larry, et al. *Programming Perl.* O'Reilly UK, ISBN 0596000278.
More can be found reviewed at http://www.perl.com/reference/query.cgi?books.

Mailing Lists

1. http://www.perl.com/reference/query.cgi?lists

Newsgroups

1. comp.lang.perl
2. comp.lang.perl.misc
3. comp.lang.perl.moderated
4. comp.lang.perl.modules

OTHER RESOURCES OF INTEREST

Web Sites

1. http://developer.netscape.com/docs/manuals/javascript.html
2. http://hotwired.lycos.com/webmonkey/programming/javascript/
3. http://wdvl.com/Authoring/JavaScript/
4. http://www.cookiecentral.com
5. http://www.extropia.com/Scripts/
6. http://www.htmlgoodies.com
7. http://www.htmlhelp.com
8. http://www.javascript.com
9. http://www.javascriptsource.com
10. http://www.killersites.com
11. http://www.ncsa.uiuc.edu/General/Internet/WWW/HTMLPrimer.html
12. http://www.php.net
13. http://www.webdeveloper.com
14. http://www.w3.org/People/Raggett/tidy/
15. http://www.w3.org/TR/html401/
16. http://www.webreference.com
17. http://www.yahoo.com/Computers_and_Internet/Internet/World_Wide_Web/

Books

1. Blank, Jon, et al. *Beginning PHP Programming.* Wrox Press, Inc, ISBN 1861003730.
2. Castro, Elisabeth. *HMTL 4 for the World Wide Web.* Peachpit Press, ISBN 0201354934.
3. Flanagan, David. *Javascript: The Definitive Guide.* O'Reilly UK, ISBN 1565923928.
4. Goodman, Danny. *Dynamic HTML.* O'Reilly UK, ISBN 1565924940.

5. Moncur, Micheal. *Teach Yourself Javascript in 24 Hours.* Sams Publishing, ISBN 0672320258.
6. Musicano, Chuck, et al. *HTML & XHTML.* O'Reilly UK, ISBN 059600026X.
7. Oliver, Dick. *Teach Yourself HTML in 24 Hours.* Sams Publishing, ISBN 0672317249.
8. Scollo, Chris, et al. *Professional PHP Programming.* Wrox Press, Inc, ISBN 1861002963.
9. Wilton, Paul. *Beginning Javascript.* Wrox Press, Inc, ISBN 1861004060.

Newsgroups
1. alt.html
2. alt.html.dhtml
3. alt.html.editors.enhanced-html
4. alt.html.editors.webedit
5. alt.html.server-side
6. alt.html.webedit
7. alt.www.webmaster
8. comp.infosystems. www.authoring.html
9. comp.lang.javascript

Note

1. It is necessary to have an understanding of these languages to help the reader fully understand and possibly use some of the examples. For example, some knowledge of Java is needed to fully understand and implement the example code in the JDBC section. However, a basic understanding of the concepts of computer programming languages will aid understanding.

GREG GRIFFITHS is a recent graduate (1999) of the University of Wales, Aberystwyth, UK, with a B.Sc. (Hons) in computer science. His dissertation topic was database-Internet connectivity and involved creating a Web-based search engine that provided added functionality for administrators and users who had a site listed in the index.

Greg has been working with various Web technologies from Perl to ASP, HTML to JavaScript for the past few years. He is currently involved in several Web-related projects, including the development and maintainance of several Web sites, and is responsible for a Web-based Knowledge Management system used by a large U.S. corporate UK subsidiary. He is currently based in Hereford, UK with his new wife Elizabeth. He can be contacted at greg@greggriffiths.org or through his Web site at http://www.greggriffiths.org.

Section 6

Server and Performance Dynamics

When most folks get into the business of building Web sites, they see only the creative part of the Web development equation—the writing of content, the creation of graphics, etc. What they don't see—or even choose to ignore—is the grunt work of "serving" up that content to Web surfers.

This is the stuff of server administration, and if it's not done right your Web site literally won't see the light of day.

What you'll learn in this section:

1. How to perform Web site quality assurance.
2. About Web page creation best practices.
3. About page load time standards.
4. How to perform Web site maintenance.
5. How to handle applet to server communication.
6. How to use Open Source Rsync to handle redundancy and replication.
7. How to package existing Web applications into interactive Web services using WSML (Web services markup language).
8. Tricks for improving the performance of Java server-side applications.
9. Just how data is routed over the Internet.
10. What you need to know about e-commerce security: encryption, SSL, digital signatures.

Improving Web Site Performance

Tom Dahm

The goal of your e-commerce company should be the operation of a high quality Web site that quickly serves well-formed pages. This seems obvious, yet many e-commerce sites never establish practices to ensure the performance of their Web site. Site quality assurance should never be overlooked, as it has a direct impact on the ability of a Web site to generate revenue. There are too many choices on the Internet for customers to waste their time at bad sites.

Consider these sobering statistics about "bail out" (the extent to which online sales are at risk due to poor Web site quality).

- Slow performance costs e-commerce sites an estimated $362 million per month (Zona Research).
- 43 percent of Internet shoppers failed to complete a purchase in the last year (Boston Consulting Group).
- 46 percent of users have left a preferred Web site because of a site-related problem (Jupiter Communications).

Internet Week states that customer expectations of online sales experiences have been increasing steadily. As seasonal peak shopping times draw closer, online shoppers grow even more impatient with sites that don't deliver. It is clear that businesses striving to have successful Web sites must continue to elevate their quality in order to meet user expectations and encourage customer retention.

In the business-to-consumer (B2C) world, sales predictions for the 2000 holiday season topped $10 billion. Forrester Research, Jupiter Communications, and Gartner Group all estimated that online holiday sales for the year 2000 would total between $10 billion and $11.6 billion.

Tapping into the Internet's potential can be critical to the success of a small business. A well-designed and working Web site levels the playing field by giving small operations access to the same markets as large multinational corporations. Access Markets International (AMI) Partners have projected that online purchases from small businesses alone will register $118 billion for the year 2001. This amount will continue to grow as the Internet expands. Small businesses must be ready to take advantage of the opportunity while large businesses need to rise to the challenge as well.

Quality assurance problems and the resulting loss of revenue are not in any way limited to retail e-commerce sites. Business-to-business (B2B) e-commerce has even higher projected revenue in coming years than B2C. B2B sites are subject to the same pitfalls as B2C sites and can pose even greater financial risks than consumer site problems.

Learn from the Mistakes of Others

On the Web, your competitors are just one click away.

A Web site with poorly designed, slow, or broken pages will send visitors to your competitor's sites in droves. Customers expect a site to be attractive, fast-loading, and easy to use. If your site doesn't meet those specifications, most customers just won't bother with you.

Boo.com learned this the hard way. The British high-fashion site promised to be "a gateway to the world of cool" and a place where "you could use the Internet to fulfill your fantasies." Boo soon found that customers expected a working Web site and were not at all impressed with theirs.

"Boo was so convinced it was changing the world of e-commerce that it overlooked the truth that working technology matters more than fancy features," reported *The Standard* in May 2000. "In the end, Boo is a testament to the unglamorous idea that panache will only take you so far."

Panache doesn't get you anywhere if customers can't access your site. Full access to Boo's site required customers to have high-speed Internet access, Flash, and the most recent browser versions. Initially, the site didn't work at all on Apple computers—and it was slow, very slow.

"Inattention to customers is unwise, considering the stakes," report Ted Kemp and Scott Tilett of *Internet Week*. The winners will be those who "answer customers' questions and close the deal with minimal hassle. That means moving shoppers through checkout lines efficiently with smoother transaction processes and giving customers easier access to product information, assistance and details about when and how products will be shipped."

Boo's failure was a big one. Investors lost an estimated $125 million on the deal, and many potential investors turned away from future investments in such start-ups. Reassure investors and avoid costly mistakes on your e-commerce site by instituting an effective Web site quality assurance program.

Web Site Quality Assurance

Web site quality assurance involves two distinct tasks:

- Establish procedures for Web page creation.
- Establish procedures for ongoing site maintenance.

The first task involves the design and enforcement of organization-wide quality standards for each page on the Web site. Such universal coding standards help eliminate page errors and incompatible technologies on the site. The design standards maintain a consistent "look and feel" that enables visitors to be more successful at navigating through the site and encourages repeat visits.

In addition, even the best-designed sites require regular maintenance or their quality may degrade over time. Establishing clear procedures and timetables for regularly scheduled site maintenance means that this important task doesn't get overlooked during the frenetic pace of other design projects.

Successful e-commerce companies understand the importance of both these tasks and enforce the organizational discipline required to make them work.

Web Page Creation Best Practices

Companies often encounter problems when they begin defining their Web page creation standards because they're aiming at a moving target. The market is flooded with new design tools and browser versions, all promising tremendous benefits. Most Web developers are highly receptive to change and eager to work with the leading-edge tools such as Flash, Dynamic HTML, Java, and Cascading Style Sheets.

However, on the Internet, the leading edge often becomes the "bleeding edge" because most Internet users are somewhat resistant to change. A surprising number of visitors to your site are using older Web browsers that won't understand the latest technologies. As a result, your Web site won't display correctly and your pages will be out of alignment.

Leading e-commerce sites such as Amazon and eBay make little or no use of the latest technologies. In fact, both of these sites have a distinctly trailing-edge flavor. As they are two of the most successful e-commerce sites on the Internet, businesses of all sizes would be wise to learn from their success.

Browser Compatibility Standards

The first step in a robust Web site quality assurance program is therefore to establish company-wide browser compatibility standards. This decision is important and will drive the rest of your Web site design process. Expect that these standards will need to be changed over time as new technologies are introduced and Internet users upgrade their systems.

Most businesspeople reflexively instruct developers to "make my site compatible with 100 percent of Web browsers." While that's a worthy goal, 100 percent compatibility is all but impossible to achieve. There will always be one customer using an ancient version of Netscape Navigator. In practice, compatibility goals of about 98 percent are about the best you can achieve, and some Web sites are willing to accept even lower rates of compatibility.

Browser plug-ins cause many compatibility problems, so use them carefully. A plug-in is a piece of software installed to perform a task that the browser is unable to do by itself, such as playing a song or movie. Macromedia's Flash is an exciting multimedia technology that requires such a plug-in to view. The latest versions of Netscape and Microsoft browsers come with this plug-in already installed. Yet approximately 10 percent of Internet users are still using older browsers that don't include it.

Although the plug-ins are easy to download and install, don't expect visitors to be so committed to your site that they will take the time to do it. If your Web site compatibility goal is to appeal to 90 percent of your audience, then Flash is definitely a technology you can comfortably include on your pages. However, if your goal is 95 percent compatibility, then you'll want to avoid using it for a while yet.

So how do you know? If you already have an established Web site, that task is easy. Your Web server's log files contain detailed information on what browsers are being used to access your Web site. All major commercial log file analysis software, like Web Trends and Market Wave, can analyze this data and help define what technologies are compatible. If you're launching a new site, then do what brick-and-mortar businesses do on a regular basis: Know your customers and tailor your catalogs and advertising to appeal to them.

In addition, some Web tools and reference sites will tell you what technologies are compatible with each browser version. NetMechanic HTML Toolbox includes a browser compatibility checker that tests your Web pages for problems. Many excellent reference sites, such as Web Review and ZDNet's Web Developer channel, include detailed HTML references that help you make compatibility decisions.

Web Page Testing

All developers in your organization must be familiar with your design guidelines and build pages that conform to the standard. Make it easy for them to validate their designs with a testing lab. Developers can test pages in the lab and immediately see how design techniques display across browsers and operating systems.

At a minimum, your lab should contain the following equipment (as shown in Figure 32-1):

If you don't yet have the space or financial resources to maintain such a lab, you should still check your site on as many browsers and operating systems as possible. Netscape maintains an archive of older browser versions that you can download to your computer. WebTV offers a free download of a simulated WebTV browser that you can use to test your site.

Another option is to use automated validation tools to check for HTML errors and specific tags that may not be compatible across browsers. This is not as reliable as compatibility testing in a lab and can't guarantee compatibility, since the tools can only ap-

Figure 32-1. Test lab components.

proximate how your pages will display across browsers and operating systems. However, automated page validation tools can be very accurate and will provide you with the knowledge you need to correct potential problems.

Many companies offer automated tools at a reasonable price:

- HTML Toolbox: NetMechanic's site maintenance product scans your page for HTML coding errors, repairs them, and alerts you to techniques that aren't compatible with all browsers.
- W3C Validator: The World Wide Web Consortium (W3C) offers an online HTML validator.
- HTML Editors: Many Web page editors (such as HomeSite and Dreamweaver) offer embedded validators. You can use them to check your code while you're designing the page.

Thorough Web page testing is critical. It is the only way to find errors on your page before your customers do!

Page Load Time Standards

Decisions about technologies directly impact another vital aspect of your Web site: page load time. The importance of a fast-loading Web site cannot be overstated. If your pages don't load quickly, you'll lose money. Period.

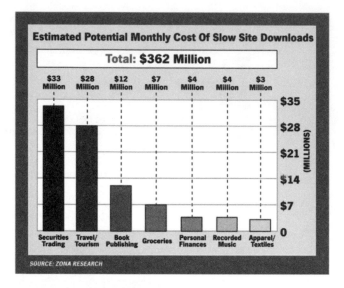

Figure 32-2. *Estimated potential monthly cost of slow site*

As previously stated, Zona Research reports that as much as $362.2 million in e-commerce sales in the United States may have been lost per month in 1999 due to un-acceptable download speeds (shown in Figure 32-2). In addition, of the 43 percent of Internet shoppers who failed to complete a purchase in the last year, half said they abandoned a site due to slow page downloads. (Another 45 percent ditched Web sites because of confusing content or poor navigability.)

Many factors affect your site's load-time performance. The reliability of your network and your Web server hardware can slow sites considerably. However, poor design decisions are the main reason for slow Web pages.

The three primary factors that can cause you problems are:

- Large graphic images
- Lengthy dynamic HTML scripts
- Badly designed HTML code

Use your Web page creation standards to address these problems during the design phase and avoid costly problems later on. Figure 32-3 shows the variation in download times caused by different modem speeds. Set a goal for the maximum-allowable page download times across different modem speeds.

If you plan to target consumers surfing the Internet from home, then your pages should load within ten seconds over a 56kb modem. If your site is designed for businesspeople accessing the Web over an office network, then you have considerably more freedom. Again, know your customers and base decisions on what works best for them.

A number of tools can help you estimate the load time of your Web pages. HTML

Load Time by Modem Speed	
Modem Speed	**Download Time**
14.4k	55.79 seconds
28.8k	29.90 seconds
56k	17.18 seconds
ISDN(128k)	9.83 seconds
T1 (1.44MB)	4.52 seconds

Figure 32-3. *Load time by modem speed.*

editors such as Dreamweaver now include load time estimators. Online Web site tools such as NetMechanic's HTML Toolbox and WebPartner's InstaCheck include similar features.

See Figure 32-4 for a checklist of activities critical to assuring the quality of Web page creation.

Ongoing Site Maintenance Best Practices

While every change you make to your pages needs to be tested thoroughly, you also need to schedule ongoing testing and site maintenance to eliminate sporadic and recurring problems like broken links and malfunctioning servers.

Link Checking

A study by Cyveillance shows the rapid and accelerating growth of the Internet. They report that if growth continues at its current trend, the now 2.5 billion pages on the Internet will become 4 billion pages by February 2001. Of the estimated 350 million links that currently exist on the Internet, 10.43 percent are broken at any given time. Links can break for two reasons:

- External sites you've linked to move or delete pages.
- Links to pages inside your own site break when you make changes and don't thoroughly test their effects.

Link checking on a small site is relatively easy, but it can be a time-consuming nightmare on sites with hundreds of pages. Automated link-checking tools save you time; they test each link in your site and alert you to problems.

Server Monitoring

Server monitoring is the most important ongoing quality assurance process. Simply put, if your Web site isn't up, customers can't buy anything.

Figure 32-4. *QA checklist: Web page creation.*

According to NetMechanic's research, at any given moment on the Internet, 2 percent of Web sites are down due to problems with their server. Cahners In-Stat-Group totaled the cost of an outage at two time-sensitive commerce sites. They calculated that a 22-hour outage at an auction site could cost $2.8 million and that an eight-hour outage during the trading day at a brokerage site could cost $5.2 million.

Some Web site downtime is inevitable. Web servers are complex devices that will fail eventually. If your Web site uses a Linux server, you can expect a mean time between failures of about a month. If your site uses a Windows NT server, your mean time between failures will be considerably less than that. A study by the Standish Group, as shown in Figure 32-5, shows that downtime for mission-critical applications did not improve from 1998 to 1999.

The goal of Web server monitoring is to quickly identify problems with your site, then alert your technical staff via pager or cell phone so they can immediately fix the problem.

A number of online services exist to monitor your Web site for you. Typically, these services will access a Web page every 15 minutes, 24 hours a day, seven days a week. Low-end monitoring services, such as RedAlert and NetMechanic's Server Check, will access a page in your site and verify that its content was served correctly. High-end services, such as Mercury Interactive's ActiveWatch and WebPartner's Secret Shopper, offer full

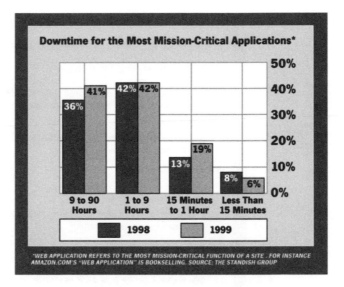

Figure 32-5. Downtime for most mission-critical

transaction monitoring. These services simulate a shopper moving through the checkout line to verify that your shopping cart software is working.

Server Scalability

According to analyst Geri Spieler of the Gartner Group, a lot of the stores don't understand what happens when a gazillion people hit their Web site. They may not have a problem in early August, but the same well-run system doesn't work so well in early December.

If you expect your e-commerce site to be successful, then you should expect to handle thousands of customers visiting your site every hour. A site that attracts one million visitors per month will average 33,000 visitors per day!

Despite that, Web sites consistently underestimate the strains that a surge of traffic can place on their servers. ABC first debuted its Interactive TV during the 1999 Fiesta Bowl, inviting TV viewers to play armchair quarterback through the ABC Web site. Within 15 minutes of kickoff, the site was crushed by traffic and unable to respond to visitors.

In an even more dramatic example, when the *Encyclopedia Britannica* made itself freely available over the Internet, the resulting traffic kept the site offline for over a month.

If you expect your company to succeed online, you should be prepared to handle the consequences of that success. Prior to launch, therefore, you'll need to run a number of scalability tests on your site. Software packages such as Rational Software's Performance

Figure 32-6. QA checklist for on-going site maintenance.

Suite and Mercury Interactive's Astra LoadTest will simulate thousands of visitors accessing your site simultaneously. These packages can help you identify performance bottlenecks and solve them before they cost you customers.

See Figure 32-6 for a checklist of activities critical to assuring the quality of ongoing site maintenance.

Create Customer Loyalty

Once a visitor to your site decides to become a customer, you've won half the battle. However, a sizable percentage of customers who have a negative shopping experience on your site will not return. According to Jupiter Communications, of the 46 percent of users who have left a preferred Web site because of a site-related problem, 20 percent never returned to the site and 80 percent returned only after visiting a competitor's site.

Create customer loyalty to your site by not giving customers a reason to leave the site. If your site is fast and error free, you'll see a benefit to your bottom line.

Invest Company Resources in Your Site

Eliminating or neglecting quality assurance standards is like running a brick-and-mortar business without a sales force or a retail operation without a cashier. In e-business your Web site is your primary—sometimes your only—customer interface. It is your market-

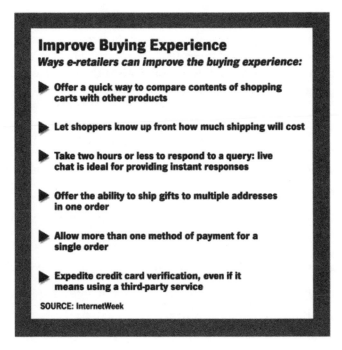

Figure 32-7. *Improving buying experience.*

ing brochure, your direct-mail literature, your sales force, cashier, and customer service representative all in one.

Traditional businesses that are successful take great care in selecting their staff for these key positions. They also invest significant resources in assuring the quality of the services their employees deliver. This same care and investment of resources is necessary in e-business: If they're executed properly, the payoff will be great! If not, the penalties and revenue loss can drive you out of business.

In addition, *Internet Week* recommends a variety of ways that e-businesses can improve the online buying experience for their customers (shown in Figure 32-7). Since a customer's first shopping experience can make or break future purchases, dedicating time and resources to taking care of current customers can have a big payoff.

Increasing Revenue

The Internet market is growing larger every year: 66.9 percent of Americans use the Internet and, according to the Roper-Starch poll by AOL, 51.7 percent purchase products online. This same poll also shows that the number of online shoppers has doubled in the past two years. If your Web site doesn't work or shoppers don't trust it, you'll lose customers, revenue, and investors.

The primary reason any business invests in a Web site is to increase revenue potential. Yet, businesses often neglect many of the details necessary to maintain high quality and efficient operation of their Web site. Establishing a quality assurance program with best practices and company-wide standards is the surest way to successfully obtain that increased revenue.

TOM DAHM is a founder of NetMechanic, Inc., and currently serves as the company's COO. NetMechanic is the leading independent provider of online Web site maintenance, monitoring, and promotion tools and has tuned over 32 million Web pages. Mr. Dahm is active in the Internet industry and is one of the organizers of Huntsville's Internet Circle, a peer advisory group of Internet start-up companies. He has been published on Web Developer's Journal *and has been interviewed by and quoted in* Internet Week, Information Week, *and* Building Online Business.

With a technical background in software development and systems engineering, Mr. Dahm holds a B.S. degree in electrical engineering from the University of Alabama in Huntsville and has over 15 years of experience in the defense industry. He is a native of Huntsville, Alabama.

NetMechanic, Inc. is a member of the Web Host Guild, founded in 1998, with the goal of setting Internet industry standards related to Web site hosting service, support, and speed. NetMechanic is also a member of the Alabama Information Technology Association (AITA), an organization founded in September of 1999 that is comprised of more than 1,500 Alabama IT companies employing 20,000 people. AITA advocates, educates, and promotes Alabama organizations engaged in providing IT products and services.

Applet to Server Communication

Andy Katz

Many Web application books have discussed the topic of serving dynamic "real-time" content to the browser. One option is to provide the user with a "refresh" button that allows them to explicitly update the content. The problem with this type of communication is that it requires the client to "ask" for the latest content from the server. Another option is to use the HTML meta-tag to refresh the content on the user's browser. Unfortunately, this has the undesirable side effect of adding each request to the browser's history cache, thus altering the results of the browser's "Back" button. In this chapter I will discuss an alternate means of providing dynamic content using Java applet to server communication.

The Assignment

For the purpose of our discussion, let's pretend you've been assigned the task of providing real-time stock quotes to your end-users. We'll assume your target audience is using a Java-enabled browser such as Internet Explorer or Netscape Navigator to peruse your Web site. After some thought and due diligence, you've decided that the best way to provide the dynamic stock data is via an applet. Now that you've chosen how to present the data, you must determine how to most efficiently extract the data from your server. Let's take a look at some of our options.

JDBC Connectivity

If the financial information you are trying to retrieve is persisted in a relational database, you could connect directly using a vendor-specific JDBC driver. The problem with this solution is threefold.

The first issue has to do with database security. In order to establish a database connection the applet will need to provide a valid username and password to the database engine. This means the applet must be privy to that username and password (each could be hard-coded within the applet class or passed in via the applet PARAM tag).

The second issue relates to the browser's own Java security manager. In a vanilla application (not using trusted applets), the applet can only establish network connections to the machine from which it was downloaded. In other words, if your corporate database server resides on a separate machine from your Web server(s), the applet would be restricted from establishing a connection to your database server.

Lastly, another consideration must be evaluated when trying to connect directly to a database server. It has to do with the client's corporate firewall policy. Many corporate firewalls restrict the transmission of data to ports 80 (typical unsecure port, e.g., http://yourwebsite.com) and 443 (typical secure port, e.g., https://yourwebsite.com). Since most database engines listen for requests on ports other than 80 and 443, the client may be stifled when the applet attempts to make the database connection.

RMI

Using RMI (remote method invocation) would allow us to communicate with remote Java objects, but then we have to deal with the RMI registry, and we still have the Web browser compatibility issue(s) to address.

HTTP Access

Another option is to make use of some of the Java networking classes to speak directly to the Web server. This option would alleviate the security restrictions posed in the aforementioned JDBC connectivity solution and simplify our overall design by decoupling the applet from the actual data source.

Our Design Approach

What do we need to consider in our design? We know the applet will be communicating directly with a Java servlet–enabled Web server via HTTP. Since we have the luxury of using a Web server that supports the Java servlet API, we have a few different options regarding the way we pass data back to the applet.

One approach is to send back raw text. This would fulfill our requirement to provide real-time stock data to the end-user, but with a price. If the HTTP response contains textual data, the applet must know how to parse out that data. This creates a binding relationship between the program creating the text and the program parsing the text. If one day the requirements change and we need to display more information to the end-user, we must re-code our parser. This could potentially introduce new bugs into our application.

A better approach is to send over a Java object. Since Java objects are much more user-friendly than raw textual strings (e.g., providing the client with a set of publicly accessible

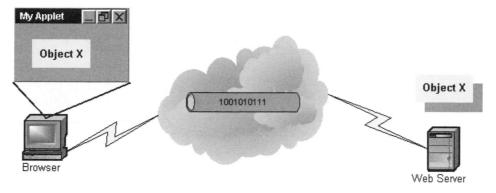

Figure 33-1. *A Web server creating a Java object.*

methods), we can use this to our advantage. Now the question is, how do we get a live Java object that resides on our Web server across the Internet and into our applet? Let's take a look at Figure 33-1.

Figure 33-1 depicts a Web server creating a Java object, serializing the object, and sending it back in the form of an HTTP response to the requesting applet. Once the applet receives the HTTP response, it must then resurrect those bytes back into their original form, that of a Java object. This might sound a bit complicated, but as you'll see, it's really quite simple!

A good design would encapsulate the applet from the actual communication details. This allows us to alter the way we transmit information from the applet to the server and vice versa. Our design will use three classes to hide the implementation details from the applet. Let's take a look at our communication classes:

- NetworkConfiguration: This container class holds all the necessary data to connect to the Web server and build the actual HTTP request.
- NetworkCommunicator: This class implements the runnable interface and submits HTTP requests on behalf of the client on a timed basis.
- NetworkRequestExecutor: This class knows how to build the HTTP query string, connect to a Web server, and deserialize the bytes held within the HTTP response.

The applet would create a NetworkConfiguration object and place relevant Web server and query string information into it. Take a look at some example applet code below:

```
NetworkConfiguration networkConfiguration = new
NetworkConfiguration();
networkConfiguration.setURL("http://myserver.com/servlet/MyServl
et");
networkConfiguration.setDelay(10000);
```

```
String stocks = "ORCL,SUNW,IBM,MSFT";
StringTokenizer st = new StringTokenizer(stocks,",");

while (st.hasMoreTokens()) {
   String sym = st.nextToken();
   networkConfiguration.addQueryKeyValue("COMPANYID",sym);
}
```

As you can see, the applet maps the server properties such as the URL and how often to submit a request onto the NetworkConfiguration object. Afterward, the applet parses a set of stock symbols and adds them via the addQueryKeyValue(String s1, String s2) method. The "COMPANYID" string represents a "key" that will be used in the construction of the HTTP request. For example, http://myserver.com/servlet/MyServlet? COMPANYID=ORCL,SUNW . . .

Next, the applet would get access to a NetworkCommunicator object and pass the previously created NetworkConfiguration into the NetworkCommunicator. See the code snippet below:

```
NetworkCommunicator networkCommunicator =
NetworkCommunicator.getInstance();
networkCommunicator.addNetworkConfiguration("StockQuote",network
Configuration);

The "StockQuote" string is there to designate a particular
NetworkConfiguration object. This is because you can have
multiple NetworkConfiguration objects within the
NetworkCommunicator. Once the NetworkCommunicator is assigned
one or more NetworkConfiguration objects, it will begin to
submit requests on behalf of the client using the
NetworkRequestExecutor. The client can then ask the
NetworkCommunicator for the dynamic data retrieved from the
server.

String key = "StockQuote";
networkConfiguration =
networkCommunicator.getNetworkConfiguration(key);

Hashtable resultsHash = null;
if (networkConfiguration!=null) {
   resultsHash = networkConfiguration.getResultsHash();
}
```

Now let's take a look at the NetworkRequestExecutor. As stated earlier, its purpose is to create the HTTP request, submit it to the Web server, and parse out the response. Well, we know that the Web server response is going to contain a serialized Java object; hence it will have to deserialize the object using the java.io package. Below is the code used to resurrect the Java object:

```
// sb is a StringBuffer containing the bytes read from the HTTP
response
String response = new String(sb).getBytes();
ByteArrayInputStream bais = new ByteArrayInputStream(response);
ObjectInputStream ois = new ObjectInputStream(bais);
Hashtable tempHash = (Hashtable)ois.readObject();
.
```

And voilá, we have a Java object, in our case a java.util.Hashtable! Lastly the Network-RequestExecutor swaps the newly created Hashtable for the older Hashtable in the NetworkConfiguration object via the following code:

```
if (tempHash!=null)
    synchronized (networkConfiguration.getResultsHash())
        networkConfiguration.setResultsHash(tempHash);
```

Design Considerations

Now that we've successfully built and tested our application, we should think about how we could improve it, allowing for more flexibility when incorporating future enhancements. One restriction we've placed upon our design is the need for a Java-enabled Web server due to the serialization of the Java object. This might be a very important issue if your corporate Web site is written in C/C++ or Perl. One way to get around this issue is with the use of XML. Instead of passing a serialized object back to the applet, the server could return XML. The applet could use an XML parser to extract the pertinent data and construct its own internal Java object. This would allow our applet to communicate freely with *any* Web server capable of generating XML.

The Source Code

Source code can be found online at this book's Web site at CHAPT33.doc <www.newartech.com>.

ANDY KATZ brings nearly seven years of software development experience to Tacpoint Technologies. Prior to joining Tacpoint, Mr. Katz was a technology consultant with Sage IT Partners, where he was responsible for designing and implementing e-commerce solutions across a broad array of vertical markets including manufacturing, sales, and finance.

Before joining Save, Mr. Katz was a senior consultant with Andersen Consulting LLP, specializing in the telecommunications industry. Mr. Katz led development efforts for several telephony billing applications, where he oversaw requirements definition, object design, data model design, and testing strategies.

Prior to this position, Mr. Katz was an associate with Arthur Andersen & Company, SC, where he participated in the development and production support of an internal worldwide accounting application. His client list includes Pacific Bele Telesis, Motorola, Netscape Communications, Charles Schwab, Wyle Electronics, and Pacific Gas & Electric Energy Services.

He holds a B.S. in mathematics and economics from Illinois State University.

Redundancy and Replication with Rsync: Replicated Content Across Redundant Servers

Peter Karlson

This chapter explores the topic of replication, specifically with regard to an open source tool called Rsync. By introducing replication, we open the door to redundancy as well as higher availability of Web services.

Redundancy and Replication Basics

This chapter presupposes that you are interested in creating higher availability of Web services for your users. The first step to higher availability is to have redundant Web servers, so that if one fails the other one can take over. Redundancy requires that your content be replicated between the servers. As your need for higher availability increases, so does the investigation and eradication of the number of single points of failure. You must systematically follow the flow of requests from the Internet from your ISP into your network and to the Web server. At each junction examine the implications of that piece of equipment failing and what steps you need to take to reduce or eliminate that threat. In order to explain the composition of a high available solution we will look at a typical architectural view of a higher available Web solution.

Key Components

A high-level architectural view outlines only the key components to a higher availability Web solution.

Web Servers

The Web servers must be set up and receiving Web traffic. Typically the servers are identical machines if you are doing load balancing. In fail-over scenarios one machine may be only a backup machine, so it may not be as high performance as the primary server.

Another consideration is the placement of the Web servers. The Web servers need not be in the same data center. Geographically dispersing the Web servers decreases the chance that you will have an outage due to a location-specific issue such as a network or power failure.

Load Balancers/Traffic Director

There are many different types of load balancers and traffic directors. These devices range from simple "HTTP sprayers" that literally take the incoming HTTP requests and redirect them to a set of Web servers to sophisticated algorithms that take into consideration server availability and load before sending traffic to the Web servers.

DNS

Some of the more sophisticated load-balancing solutions are configured to replace the domain name service (DNS) entries for your Web servers with the IP address of the load balancer. Therefore all traffic hits the load balancer and is redirected to an appropriately available server.

Higher Availability

In order to have a true high-availability configuration you would need to at least double every single point of failure. This means multiple Internet connections, which in turn involves a much more complicated routing scheme such as border gateway protocol (BGP), not to mention the additional hardware to support the routing. A high-availability solution would also entail redundant load balancers, switches, and firewalls.

What to Replicate

When deciding what to replicate, you need to think of all the things that change periodically that are crucial for the operation of your Web server. This would include things like content, configuration information, and data. Content is the first thing that comes to mind when it comes to replication. If your content is constantly updated on an hourly or daily basis, you probably would like to replicate that content automatically.

Configuration files are the not so obvious "content" that should also be replicated. If a configuration changes on one server, the changes should be automatically replicated to ensure similar server behavior. Data can be tricky to replicate and corporations have spent millions of dollars on database vendor solutions to replicate data from one server to another. The subject of database replication is nontrivial and far too complicated to tackle in this chapter, but I can give you some pointers on how to back up data from one server to another in case of a catastrophic failure where you need to switch to a backup server.

Rsync

What is Rsync?

Rsync is an open source tool written by Andrew Tridgell and Paul Mackerras that allows users to replicate files from one Unix server to another. Unfortunately there is not a fully functioning version of Rsync for the Windows platform. The authors give some pointers on how to compile a version that will run on Windows, but this will only work for the Rsync client and not for the server. One of the major points about Rsync is that it only copies the bytes that have changed in a file; therefore it is very efficient and fast. Rsync is freely available under the GNU Public License from http://rsync.samba.org.

What Else Is There?

Many people use plain old FTP to transfer files from one server to another. Unfortunately FTP is continually under scrutiny for being insecure, not to mention that if you have a number of large files that need to be transferred, you will need to transfer the entire file every time there is a change to the file. The other alternative is rcp. Again, the security implications of rcp are often questioned, since it falls under the dreaded "r-commands" that are generally among the first things to be shut off by savvy systems administrators. Rcp also has some other issues with symbolic links and permission problems. For those users that are running their Web services on the Windows NT platform, there are a number of commercial packages, such as SureSync from Software Pursuits, that contain similar functionality to Rsync.

How Is It Used?

Rsync is used in a number of different configurations. Generally there is one primary server that transfers files to one or more secondary servers. In some cases the primary server will be a staging server that content is prepared and tested on; the content is then replicated to the live servers after a quality assurance inspection is made. Some Webmasters prefer the content to be moved in two steps, first from the staging to the live server and then another move to replicate the content from the primary live servers to the secondary live servers. In some cases the staging server resides on the same physical Web server as the primary live server, so the content can be copied from one directory to another. In this case the synchronization is done from the primary live servers to the secondary servers.

How Do I Get It?

Download the gzipped/tarred binary files from http://rsync.samba.org. Generally there are two to three files contained in the bundle, the main pages and the Rsync binary built for your particular operating system.

Example 1

```
myhost% mkdir rsync
myhost% cd rsync
myhost% gunzip rsync-2_3_1_Solaris26_sparc_tar.gz
myhost% tar xvf rsync-2_3_1_Solaris26_sparc_tar
```

How Do I Install It?

The beauty of Rsync is that you do not need to "install it" in the traditional Unix software sense because it is a single binary that can act both as the server daemon and a client. For example, after you have completed the unpacking of the bundle (Example 1), you move the Rsync file into the directory where it will live. The most common location is /usr/local/bin, but you will probably need root access to copy the file to this location.

How Do I Configure It?

The two critical configurations are the server and the client. The Rsync server is a simple daemon that runs on TCP port 873. It requires the use of a configuration file in order to know what to allow the server to do. Generally the rsyncd.conf file resides in the /etc directory but can be placed anywhere on your system by specifying the —config parameter. Example 2 below shows how to start up the Rsync server daemon with the —daemon option as well as an alternative configuration file location.

Example 2

```
myhost% ./rsync rsyncd—daemon—config /tmp/rsyncd.conf
```

The configuration file contains information about who is allowed to transfer files, where the files will be placed on the server, and logging. Rsync refers to groupings of content as modules. Example 3 shows a sample configuration file. The module is "www"; you see that the content user (cu) is allowed to transfer from the staging host into the /www directory.

Example 3

```
# Sample rsyncd.conf file
#
log file = /tmp/rsync.log
[www]
        path = /www
        hosts allow = staging.mycompany.com
        uid = cu
        gid = content
        read only = false
#
```

There are a number of different parameters that can be configured when using Rsync as a client. I will highlight the most useful features; for the complete parameter list you should refer to the Rsync Web site or type rsync —help to get the complete list of options.

Example 4 illustrates a simple client configuration to transfer all of the /www content that has changed to the secondary server. The archive option is a combination of a number of useful options, —recursive used to recursively transfer a directory structure, —links, which preserves all symbolic links, —perms, which ensures that the file and directory permissions are preserved, and —owner and —group, which preserve the ownership and group access rights of the files transferred.

The —verbose and —stats options give you back valuable information about the files transferred, such as how many files, how fast, and how many bytes were transferred. The —compress option uses a compression algorithm on the content before sending it to the other server. If you have a very fast connection between the servers, you will be better off not doing compression, since this will add CPU load on both machines. On the other hand, if you are transferring on a slower speed line, the transfer will take less time when using the compress option.

Example 4

```
rsync—archive—verbose—compress—stats /www/*
cu@secondary.mycompany.com::www
```

Secure Installations

If you require more security, there are a number of ways Rsync can be made more secure. The first is to change the transport for Rsync to ssh. This is accomplished by setting the remote shell parameter (-e or —rsh) on the client to ssh. This assumes that you have ssh installed on the target server. Example 5 shows the client example with the new remote shell option.

Example 5

```
rsync—e ssh—archive—verbose—compress—stats /www/*
cu@secondary.mycompany.com::www
```

How to Replicate

I have already given you some examples of how to replicate content using Rsync above; now I will tie it together using specific examples for content, configuration, and data-replication scenarios.

Content Replication

Generally when you set up your Web server, you try to keep your content in one place to avoid confusion and mistakes when transferring files. In most cases Webmasters will point their document root to something useful such as /www. Under the /www directory you can have your /images and other site-specific directories. The best way of implementing content replication is to do it on a wholesale complete directory basis to ensure all files are identical on all servers, as shown in the above examples.

However, if you have more than one person working on content or images, you may want to do a selective transfer of just the file(s) that you want to transfer. This is relatively straightforward to do with a simple shell script. You can use your favorite scripting means—Perl, Bourne shell, Korn shell, or C shell. Example 6 is illustrated using C shell.

Example 6

```
#! /bin/csh -f
#
################################################################
####
set the_content=$1
set current_directory='pwd'

rsync—archive—verbose—compress—stats
$current_directory/$the_content cu@secondary.mycompany.com:www
```

Configuration Replication

Configuration files come in many different shapes and sizes. Fortunately many of the configuration files necessary to run Web services are similar enough that we can make some general assumptions. The first is that the configuration files are plain text files; therefore you can manipulate the files with sed/awk to modify them before replicating them to another server. The second assumption is that your servers are set up identically from a file location perspective.

Depending on the type of configuration file, you may have to do some pre- or post-processing in order for the configuration to take effect. [In the example below, which shows the manipulation of a Web server configuration file, such as a httpd.conf, to change the IP address of the server from the primary server to the secondary server, the file may need to be run through a sed script to replace one IP address with another in order for it to be used on another server; see Example 7.]

Example 7

```
myhost% cat httpd.conf | sed 's|
192.233.86.10|192.168.1.10|g' > /tmp/configs/httpd.conf
myhost% rsync—archive—verbose—compress—stats
/tmp/configs/httpd.conf
Webmaster@secondary.mycompany.com:wsconfig
```

Example 7 assumes that you have set up a content module called wsconfig that points to the configuration directory for the Web server; normally this would be /usr/local/apache/conf. The post-processing step may involve restarting the Web server in order for the changes to take effect.

Data Replication

As stated above, data replication is a nontrivial exercise and should not be taken lightly. For the sake of brevity Example 8 assumes that you are backing up a MySQL database from the primary server to a secondary server for fail-over purposes.

Example 8

```
myhost% rsync—archive—verbose—compress—stats
/usr/local/mysql/data/customer.frm
dba@secondary.mycompany.com:data
```

Example 8 assumes that you have set up another content module called data and have a user called dba with the appropriate permissions to copy files in to the data directory.

Replication Initiation Schemes

There are a number of ways to initiate an Rsync session; the two most popular are via cron and triggered by some time of event. The Unix crontab utility is one of the singularly powerful mechanisms available to users. It enables you to schedule events to occur anytime and as often as you like. This is critical for automating repetitive tasks such as replicating content from one server to another. For example, you can automate your content replication on an hourly basis by adding the following line to your crontab.

Example 9

```
0 * * * * (/usr/local/bin/rsync—archive—verbose—compress—stats
/www/* cu@secondary.mycompany.com::www > /tmp/hourly_rsync.log)
2>/dev/null
```

There are two things to note about Example 9. The first is that Rsync should have a fully qualified path; in this case I am assuming that it is installed in /usr/local/bin. The second is that this example assumes that you would like to capture the output of Rsync to a temporary log file that is overwritten every hour.

We have been indirectly discussing event-based replication throughout this chapter. This involves adding an Rsync operation to another event such as the example above to replicate a specific piece of content; this is a simple example of event-based replication.

PETER KARLSON has been involved with developing Internet technologies since 1991. As chief technology officer at Harrison & Troxell, Inc., he is responsible for researching, evangelizing, and espousing new technologies and processes to build durable Internet solutions for a wide array of clients.

Syndication: Understanding How to Package Existing Web Applications into Interactive Web Services

Eilon Reshef

Syndication has become a central business model in the Internet world. Application syndication technology allows companies to share Web-based applications between sites. This chapter provides an overview of the process of packaging existing Web applications into interactive Web services using WSML (Web services markup language) and Web-Collage Syndicator. It then shows how interactive Web services can be integrated into other sites. The chapter provides an example that illustrates how an insurance company can integrate its car insurance application into agent sites and into online car buying sites.

Overview

Syndication Background

The concept of syndication made its way into the Internet world from the media industry. Production studios syndicate TV programs to broadcast networks and local stations. Writers syndicate articles to various publications. Essentially, reuse of the same assets in multiple contexts is a fundamental economic model for generating revenue.

It was not easy for the Internet world to accept the idea of syndication. Early entrants believed that every company—from manufacturers to financial services—would attract customers directly to its own Web site, disintermediating all channels. However, as Internet business models evolved, it was soon realized that to succeed, companies must "be everywhere"—make their content, their services, and transactions accessible in as many Web sites as possible.

This chapter focuses on application syndication, a technology that allows companies to share interactive Web applications from their existing sites with business partners. Unlike other forms of syndication, syndication of applications allows businesses to distribute complete branded business processes across their distribution chain.

Application syndication has been successful in facilitating various types of business scenarios:

In the case of online distribution, companies can offer their e-commerce products and services not only on their own Web site, but also on multiple partner Web sites that act as their online distribution channels. The need to create such channels for various types of industries has been amply advocated in the industry literature. (1, 4, 5) For example, in the insurance industry, insurance companies can offer insurance policy applications on Web sites where buyers purchase insurable products, such as real estate or cars.

In the case of channel empowerment, companies can share applications that support sales with their channel partners. (6) For example, a computer manufacturer can share an application that configures laptops with its resellers, so that a user visiting a reseller's Web site would be able to configure a laptop directly on that site.

Application syndication technology is also used in other contexts where applications must be shared between Web sites. In many cases, syndication can share applications internally within an organization, through a corporate Intranet.

Interactive Web Services

In the context of application syndication, an interactive Web service is a syndicatable Web application, that is, a multistep application—including the user experience—that can be reused in the context of another site. Much like some types of component architectures in the object-oriented world, an interactive Web service encapsulates business logic (such as providing an insurance quote) with the user interface that enables it. Essentially, any self-contained section of a Web site can be thought of as an interactive Web service.

The concept of interactive Web services creates the need for some new terminology. A provider is a company or organization with Web applications that are packaged as interactive Web services for syndication. A host is an organization that embeds interactive Web services into its Web site. A host site prepares container pages that embed the Web service.

Syndication enables end-users to reach a host site that contains functionality from the provider site. The user interacts with an application that integrates functionality from both. The application is integrated in such a way that each page is dynamically composed from HTML content served by both the host and provider sites. Depending on the syndication software used, pages can be merged at the server level or at the browser level.

WebCollage Syndicator

The process of packaging a Web application into an interactive Web service depends on the syndication solution you choose. To illustrate the application syndication process, we use a high-end syndication server—Syndicator—provided by WebCollage. (10) WebCollage Syndicator uses an XML-based standard called WSML (Web services markup language) to define interactive Web services. This standard—or a similar one—should be available in your syndication solution of choice.

With the architecture we follow in this chapter, pages are assembled at the browser level. Essentially, pages are produced in such a way that the browser issues two HTTP requests for each page—one to the host site and one to the provider site. The standard browser merges the two pages and returns a single page to the user. With client-based integration, session handling, cookies, and security are fully carried out by the browser and are transparent to the application.

An Example: Syndicating Automobile Insurance Application

To provide a clearer picture of the way syndication operates, the following example takes you through the steps of creating an interactive Web service and syndicating it to business partners.

As the head developer of a Web site of an insurance company we will call BigInsurance (www.biginsurance.com), you need to share your automobile insurance application with two partners.

The first partner is a traditional agent, BestAgent (www.bestinsuranceagent.com). BestAgent has just launched an independent Web site and should be able to sell your insurance policies online—as it does in the real world.

Another partner recently signed up by your marketing department is an online car sales site, BuyACarOnline (www.buyacaronline.com). By syndicating your automobile insurance application to that site, your company can reduce customer acquisition costs by reaching customers at the moment they complete the purchase of a new car.

The following discussion shows the steps required to package your automobile insurance application as an interactive Web service and share it with your partners. For simplicity, we will assume that the application has four different pages, the first two illustrated in Figure 35-1 later:

1. The "teaser" (http://www.biginsurance.com/index.html)—a part of the static home page of BigInsurance—requests the state in which the customer lives.
2. The data entry page (http://www.BigInsurance.com/carapplication.jsp) processes the entered state and requests all the customer's additional information.
3. The quote page (http://www.BigInsurance.com/quote.jsp) processes the full customer and car information and produces a quote, which the user can accept or reject.
4. The confirmation page (http://www.BigInsurance.com/confirm.jsp) processes the user's acceptance by creating a policy and showing its details.

In the real world, application providers will have different requirements for the content they present. The insurance agent, BestAgent, prefers to use the car insurance application with BigInsurance's brand (present at the top right part of the page). In contrast, BuyACarOnline should use the application in a private-label mode, without the BigInsurance brand. In the sequel, we go over the steps of packaging the insurance application

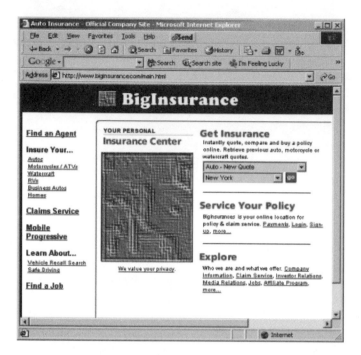

Figure 35-1. *Sample insurance application.*

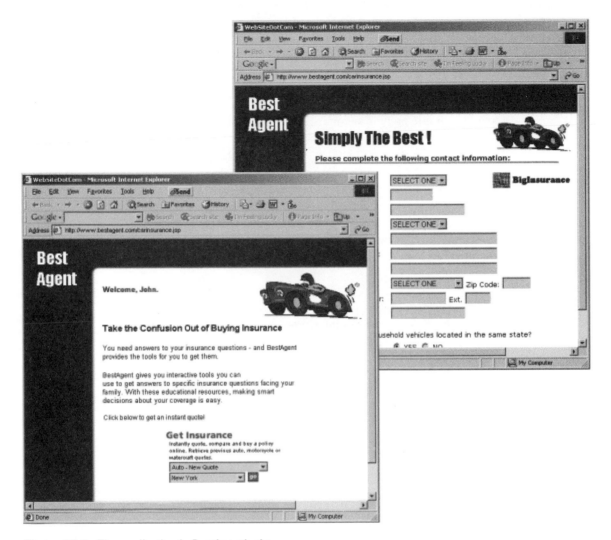

Figure 35-2. The application in BestAgent's site.

as a Web service and syndicating it to the two partners. Figure 35-2 shows how the application would appear in Bestinsurance agent's site.

The remainder of this chapter illustrates how to create a basic Web service, how the Web service can be integrated into your partners' sites, and how application integration can be added. Then, it provides an overview of how application syndication technology works. Finally, it lists several criteria to help you evaluate a syndication solution.

Building an Interactive Web Service

An interactive Web service has two aspects: the application-to-user part (user interface) and the application-to-application part (functional integration). To define a Web service, you can choose to define one or both of the two aspects. In this example, you first define the user interface part of the interactive Web service and integrate it into a host site. Then, you add a simple programmatic interface that exchanges data with the host site.

Your first step in building an interactive service is to create a Web service file. You can do it with your software of choice. With WebCollage Syndicator, a Web service file is an XML file that conforms to the WSML schema. Syndicator provides a GUI interface to create new services.

Defining the User Interface

To define the user experience in the interactive Web service, you should carry out these steps:

1. Identify which pages are part of the Web service.
2. Identify which sections in the pages are part of the Web service.
3. Identify which HTML attributes can be customized by host sites.

The first step is required; the other steps are optional. The rest of this section elaborates on these three steps.

Identifying the Pages

At the first step, you should go to each of the pages that are part of the application. In this case, these are the four HTML and JSP pages listed in "An Example: Syndicating Automobile Insurance Application." WSML allows you to declare the pages that belong to the interactive Web service. WSML provides the following syntax:

```
<link rel="wsml:component" href=" /carinsurance">
<!—some code here—>
```

The URL above is the Web service's relative URL.

Selecting Page Sections

In most cases, you will want to syndicate only sections of pages and not complete pages. After you select the pages to syndicate, define which sections of those pages you want to syndicate. With WSML, you can define sections that are always syndicated by adding a wsml:section attribute to any HTML element. All the HTML code within this element is considered part of the Web service. In the BigInsurance application, the car insurance teaser content appears in an HTML table, so you can mark it up as follows:

```
<table wsml:section="*">
  <!—some code here—>
</table>
```

Any section marked with this attribute will appear in the host sites.

You can also define some sections to be included at your discretion. This will allow you to decide later—on a host-by-host basis—whether a section is to appear in a particular host site. In our example, the syndicated Web service provided to BestAgent—the reseller—includes the BigInsurance brand in the upper right part of the page, whereas BuyACarOnline hosts the Web service without the brand. With WSML, you can define optional sections by adding a section name (in this case, "brand") as part of the wsml:section attribute:

```
<table wsml:section="brand">
  <!—some code here—>
</table>
```

Identifying Look and Feel Customization Options

In many cases, you may need to allow host sites to customize the application's look and feel to fit their container pages. WSML provides elements called "properties" that allow customization of any HTML attribute for individual hosts. Add a wsml:property attribute to any HTML tag that can be customized. The example below shows how you can mark up a table's background color, which is white by default, to customize it for different host sites.

```
<table bgcolor="white" >wsml:property="bgcolor:main-color">
  <!—some code here—>
</table>
```

The code above associates the background color with a property called "main-color." The section, Customizing the Look and Feel, shows how you can customize "main-color" for each host site.

Integrating Interactive Web Services

Once you define an interactive Web service, a host can integrate the Web service into its site. This section discusses what the host should do to embed an interactive Web service.

Embedding an Interactive Web Service

When you define a Web service with Webcollage Syndicator, embedding the service in a host site is relatively straightforward. Below we illustrate how your agent—BestAgent—can embed the car insurance application into its site. To do so, BestAgent defines a container HTML page, typically a generic BestAgent Web page. In our example, the page is placed at http://www.bestagent.com/carinsurance.jsp. In that page, BestAgent inserts an "import" line in the page location where the service is to appear. This import line is a line of external JavaScript that pulls in the Web service, as illustrated below:

```
<script
src="http://syndicator.www.biginsurance.com/bigagent/car"></scri
pt>
```

When a customer reaches BestAgent's Web page, the interactive Web service is integrated into the page in real time (see Figure 35-2). As the user navigates within the car insurance application, the user remains in BigAgent's site, receiving the next steps of the insurance application still at BigAgent's site. For more details on how the syndication technology facilitates this process, see "How Interactive Web Services Work."

You can repeat the same procedure with other host sites. For example, BuyACar-Online would also prepare a container page, give it a URL (for example, http://www.buyacaronline.com/getinsurance.jsp), and add a similar HTML line.

```
<script
src="http://syndicator.www.biginsurance.com/buyacaronline/car"><
/script>
```

Note that a different import line is used for each host site, with a different URL. That line uniquely identifies the host site and the Web service.

Selecting Sections

As you may recall, "Selecting Page Sections" defined the "brand" part of the car insurance service as an optional section. This means that this section can be selectively syndicated to some host sites, such as BestAgent, but not to others, such as BuyACarOnline.

Your syndication software should allow you to customize the syndication for each host site with a GUI interface, but you can also implement this by providing each host site with a slightly different import line.

For example, where BigAgent will receive a "standard" import line, BuyACarOnline will receive an import line that excludes the brand by passing a corresponding URL parameter:

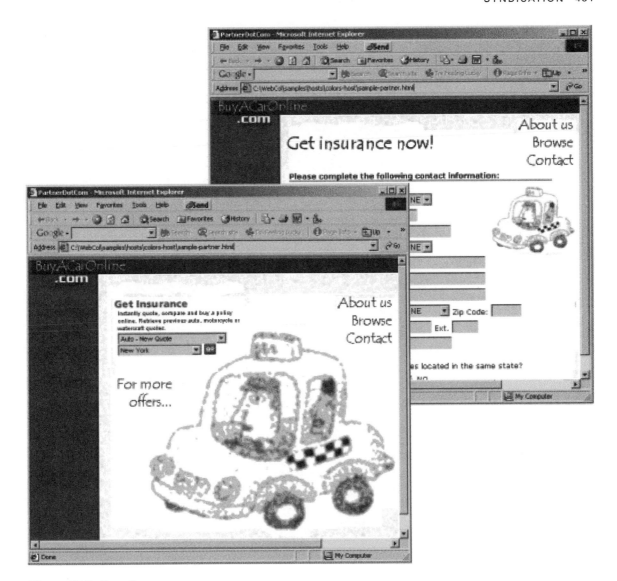

Figure 35-3. Branding.

```
<script
src="http://syndicator.www.biginsurance.com/buyacaronline/car?
brand=no"></script>
```

Consequently, the application on BuyACarOnline will not contain the BigInsurance brand, so it can place its own brand (see Figure 35-3).

Customizing the Look and Feel

Similarly, you may need to customize the properties you defined in your Web service for each host site. Your syndication software should allow you to customize the Web service. This can be done in many ways. WebCollage Syndicator provides a GUI interface for this purpose, and also allows you to customize the service using the import line. So Buy-ACarOnline can change the background color—even dynamically—using the import line (see Figure 35-3).

```
<script
src="http://syndicator.www.biginsurance.com/buyacaroline/car?mai
n-color=yellow"></script>
```

Controlling the Context

Consider your auto insurance application from the host's standpoint. The application consists of multiple pages, each with a different content and size. The host site may want to place each such page in a different container page, either for aesthetic reasons or to provide additional content at different steps of the Web service. The syndication software should allow the host site to choose the container pages. WebCollage Syndicator provides an interface for each host site, allowing it to associate different container pages with different pages in your application.

Defining Application Integration

After integrating the Web service into the host pages, it is time to integrate the two applications. To define application integration scenarios, you can define parameters and messages. Parameters allow you to transfer data back and forth between your interactive Web service and the host application. Messages generalize this by allowing you to transfer complex data structures securely. This section only covers parameters. For more information on messages, see reference 10.

Using input parameters

A Web service can allow parameters to customize its behavior. For example, you can define an input parameter called "state." If a host site knows the state in which the customer lives, it can pass that parameter to your application, allowing the user to skip a redundant step—providing a better user experience.

To pass values, a host site would embed them in the import line that integrates the Web service, for example:

```
<script
src="http://syndicator.www.biginsurance.com/bigagent/car?state=N
Y"></script>
```

The host site can generate the container page dynamically to provide the information. Your application would receive the parameter values as URL parameters.

Using Output Parameters

In many cases, your application needs to pass data to the host site. For example, whenever a user completes the application for an automotive insurance policy, you need to pass the policy number to your agent. An easy way to do it is to pass the policy number via an output parameter. You can use WSML to do this by placing a parameter in the header part of the confirmation page:

```
<wsml:output-parameter parameter="policy-id" value="2281991A"/>
```

Because your application is generating the confirmation page (the confirm.jsp page) dynamically, you can easily add the policy number to the page. As part of the syndication process, the value is passed to the host site as a URL parameter. So the next request to the host site would be to the URL:

```
http://www.bestagent.com/carinsurances.jsp?policy-id=2281991A
```

BestAgent's application can interpret the additional policy-id parameter and store it in its database.

To pass data in a more secure and robust manner, you can use the messages mechanism, which is not covered in this chapter.

How Interactive Web Services Work

As discussed in the section, Interactive Web Services, integration of interactive Web services can be performed at the browser level, which is how WebCollage Syndicator operates. This works as follows: A user accesses a host site (e.g., www.bestagent.com) and receives a page from that site. The page contains the import line, which instructs the browser to fetch some HTML code from the provider site (BigInsurance). The syndication software receives the HTTP request and clips the relevant section from its page at the live BigInsurance Web site. The browser integrates the section into the container page. This process is somewhat similar to the way banner ads work. However, application syndication also modifies all the links in the syndicated page to ensure that when the user interacts with the application, the user remains at the host site.

Evaluating Syndication Solutions

In the early days of Web development—before the availability of third-party solutions—companies tried to implement application syndication in-house. Companies attempted to customize their Web sites to appear like every one of their business partners' sites—essentially simulating real syndication. Soon, these companies discovered that this method is not scalable, because of the growing number of both applications and partners.

Today, using a syndication solution developed by a third-party vendor is increasingly common. When you evaluate a syndication solution, you should carefully examine the ways it will address your business needs. Some of the criteria you should consider are:

- Flexibility in application packaging. You should be able to easily syndicate multiple applications (that is, create separate Web services from your Web site) and customize them for multiple hosts.
- Integration into partner sites. Users must feel they have never left the partner Web site. For example, the page URL should be the partner URL (such as www.bestagent.com), and partners should be able to provide dynamic, personalized content as they would on other sections of the Web sites.
- Application integration. You should be able to exchange parameters and data with partner applications to support features like integrated shopping carts, single sign on, and others.
- Business tools across sites. You should be sure that there are reporting mechanisms that allow both providers and hosts to analyze click-stream information. Also consider cross-personalization and cross-selling opportunities.
- Maintenance. You should consider how much work is required to integrate each partner. Ideally, adding a new partner should be as easy as clicking on a button in a GUI interface. Typically, the more "self-service" capabilities a solution has, the less maintenance work you will have to do.
- Technology. You should ensure that the software you select maintains security, supports fail-over scenarios, and scales to the required performance.

The syndication technology you use—whether developed in-house or purchased from a third party—directly affects the success of the business partnerships you build.

Conclusion

In the early days of the Internet, companies believed that the Internet would completely change the way they do business. It was argued that companies would be able to interact directly with their customers, effectively eliminating the need for their existing channels.

Now it is clearer than ever that this has not happened. On the Web, companies must still use distribution channels—whether traditional channels or new online channels—to reach out to customers. In fact, according to the Patricia Seybold Group, "the service you offer as a utility to marketing partners will enhance your brand and broaden your reach. Remember, on the Web you can be everywhere at once!" (7)

Application syndication and Web services are becoming the de facto standard for encapsulating business logic and sharing it with business partners. Successful implementation of these technologies is key to keeping in step with the Internet's evolution.

References:

1. Online Insurance Distribution Beyond Web Sites," *Gartner Research Note,* October 2000.
2. Web Services: Starting Simple, Growing Over Time," *Gartner Research Note,* October 2000.
3. Syndication: The Emerging Model for Business in the Internet Era, *Harvard Business Review,* May–June 2000.
4. "Retailers Must Court Suppliers to Prompt Collaboration Online," *Jupiter Concept Report,* October 2000.
5. "General-Purpose Information Exchanges Can't Stand Alone," *Jupiter Concept Report,* April 2000.
6. "Manufacturers' Aisles: Managing Customers' Brand Experience." Patricia Seybold Group, December 1999.
7. "Preparing for the E-Services Revolution," Patricia Seybold Group, April 1999.
8. "Syndicating End-to-End Services," Patricia Seybold Group, June 2000.
9. "The Web Goes into Syndication," *Release 1.0,* July 1999.
10. "WebCollage Syndicator," http://www.webcollage.com/syndicator.

EILON RESHEF is WebCollage's vice president of products and one of the company's founders. He has held strategic technology and development positions with Gizmoz.com, Magic Software Enterprises, and other companies. Eilon also spent several years in the Israeli defense forces, where he developed a variety of software applications. He holds a bachelor's degree in computer science from the Technion, Israel Institute of Technology and a master's degree in computer science from the Weizmann Institute of Science in Israel. During his academic career, Eilon published several articles on software development and combinatorial problems.

Finding the Right Host and Publishing Your Application

John Christopher Kipple

Finding the right host for publishing your application, whether you are considering collocated, dedicated, or shared hosting, the process is no trivial matter—from determining what fire suppression system the data center uses, to ensuring the programming language of your application is supported by the provider's hardware and software architecture, to what skills the support staff possess. You have your application built, or perhaps you have just begun the planning process for its development. Be sure to prioritize a crucial tier in an application development project: choosing the right provider to host it and developing a requirements document. Distinct and essential criteria for finding the right fit between the application developer and hosting provider are suggested within a three-tier process. Suggestions are offered for fundamental questions to ask providers; configuration settings (within tier 2 and 3 considerations) to speed application operations and real-world examples are provided to exemplify the importance of this process, and to assist you in creating a comprehensive requirements document.

Procedures

International Data Corporation (IDC) estimated that application-hosting spending would rise to $633 million by the end of 2000 and will reach $7.8 billion by 2004. Others like Ovum have gone further by saying that such spending will hit $136 billion by 2006. (1) Assuming this to be the outlook for the application hosting market, we can expect even more providers to join in this somewhat frenzied battle for clients. Thus, the process of seeking and finding the right provider for your application hosting needs, as a developer, will grow increasingly more complex and problematic.

Jeanne Schaaf, an analyst with Forrester Research, reinforces these assumptions by stating recently in a *Web Hosting Magazine* article entitled "Data Center Craze," "We see high-level solutions required by customers and more and more managed solutions." (2)

Due to this complexity that is demanded by application developers as well as their applications' end-users, and due to the tremendous shortage of IT specialists, you may find yourself searching for a hosting provider for the application you developed for a client company.

According to the Information Technology Association of America (ITAA), "of the nearly 1.6 million IT positions opening in the next year, more than half will go unfilled." (1) Therefore, companies are less likely to attempt to host applications internally, considering the lack of technically skilled labor available and the high price of internal staffing. Thus, this chapter's discussion enjoins that context and assumes you are either strongly considering outsourcing your hosting needs or have already made that determination in the affirmative. Victor Inglese of DaimlerChrysler Capital was paraphrased as saying in a recent article regarding his company's outsourcing of SAP application servers, "Because there are so many new ASPs on the market, business users cannot ask too many questions or gather enough information." (9)

Essential considerations and questions regarding a hosting provider's capabilities and offers are separated into three tiers, namely:

Tier 1 begins with discovering your application project's minimum hosting requirements (e.g., from operation systems to service-level agreements to bandwidth needs to e-commerce to needs for shared versus colocated environments to security needs).

Tier 2 considerations involve comparing your minimum requirements to standard capabilities and offers by hosting providers (e.g., programming support for your specific application, hidden costs, SLAs, privacy policies, bandwidth conversions, restrictions on client uploads in shared configurations, third-party programs supported).

Tier 3 represents specific details that should be discerned by inquiring further into the true capabilities of your short-listed potential hosting providers (e.g., what partnerships/ accolades/alliances has the provider developed/earned; experience, training, and certifications of support staff; site-per-server ratios for shared environments; hardware/software/ networks; load-balancing capabilities; more security issues).

Please note that in various examples, the Microsoft Windows2000 IIS 5.0 Web server is used to demonstrate certain proclivities of a hosting environment both shared and dedicated, and this platform was chosen due to the author's familiarity with the OS and the ease of graphic illustration it affords. Using the following questions and qualifications (tiers), you can begin building a requirements document that will allow you to more fully communicate to a provider your expectations and needs for your outsourced hosting.

Determine Your Minimum Requirements for Hosting Your Application

You must first decide if you desire a shared or dedicated/colocated hosting environment for your application's Web site (shared hosting means multiple Web sites on the same machine that is owned by the host; dedicated or colocated hosting means that you lease or buy a server already located or placed, respectively, in a host's data center):

Tier 2: This determination hinges quite simply on three main factors:

1. How much traffic you anticipate for your Web site.
2. How much space you need for your site's files.
3. How much customization/control of the server you need.

Tier 3: If you are planning to have a lot of traffic (e.g., you are advertising your Web site URL on national TV, or you have been contracted to create a medium to large company's Web presence) and/or you plan to have movie files or multiple, large streaming audio files or downloads, there will definitely be diminishing returns both on price and value in a shared hosting configuration as the price increases to match the need for high traffic and/or valuable server hard-drive space that your site consumes.

On the value side, many hosts are extremely hesitant to allow customers to load custom components to a shared server (e.g., dll's). Thus, even if you are able to talk the provider into allowing you to load your own custom dll, do you really want your own site on such a system that may contain hundreds of custom, perhaps untested and unstable components? It would be a better option and would afford more control, stability, and flexibility if you had such needs mentioned in tier 2, to "pay now or pay later," and order a colocated or dedicated server. In a dedicated or colocated server you can control all functions of the server much like is done with a desktop PC using PCAnywhere, VNC, TridiaVNC, or similar remote control products (please see Figure 36-1 for a screen shot of a remotely managed dedicated server). (6) As you can see in Figure 36-1, you can hardly tell the difference between viewing the remote desktop and viewing a local computer's desktop.

In a shared hosting environment, you not only save money on hardware or leases for same, you also are not responsible for purchasing licenses for the OS and other loaded servers, even though you are able to make use of it. However, there are some things you should keep in mind: Drives are added at times to servers, they fail at other times, and the more portable your code the more resistant your application is to problems due to these environmental changes that result in absolute path changes (e.g., use the server.mappath command in VBscript and use relative references wherever possible in any other coding languages).

The number of providers offering shared hosting is increasing while the price for shared hosting is decreasing. This trend will undoubtedly continue. Hosting providers offer many standard benefits and options—some will be mentioned in more detail later in the chapter—that are not usually provided in colocated or dedicated hosting (e.g., client interfaces, Perl modules, proprietary tools like AspEmail, ASPmail, and sendmail). Thus, make sure you know the costs associated with these add-on products if you desire them in your dedicated or colocated service, as they are most likely only "free" on shared service offerings.

Figure 36-1. A remote desktop.

In What Operating System (e.g., Microsoft Windows NT, Redhat Unix, Solaris) Does Your Application Operate Best?

Tier 2: Rule of thumb, host your application on the same OS platform that it was developed in (e.g., if your application was developed in a Windows NT box, host it on a Windows NT or Windows2000 server). You might run into file permission issues not evident in testing and debugging phases of your development cycle if you publish an application, for example, built and tested in a Windows98 or Windows Me environment (which cannot and does not use the NT file system) to a server that does use NTFS partitions.

The same problem can arise when an application is built and tested using Windows NT or Windows2000 without NTFS partitions, or in publishing from a Unix-based environment to an NT-based environment.

Tier 3: Does the provider offer a way to change or manipulate your files permissions (e.g., using Telnet, a controller interface of some kind)? Please see the screen shots for an example of a controller interface, beginning in Figure 36-2, that allows for the manipulation of file permissions on Web sites on shared servers by clients simply connecting via a browser on the Web.

You can see in Figure 36-2 that we have selected the file that we would like to set permissions on but need to set the application's focus to it by clicking the "Select File" button. Then, in Figure 36-3 you will notice that the file has been focused upon and now

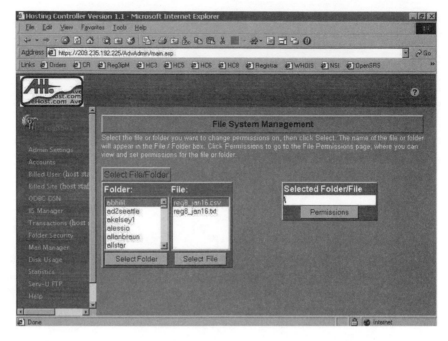

Figure 36-2. *Controller interface.*

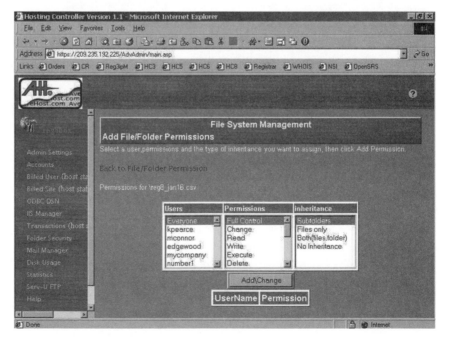

Figure 36-3. *Setting permissions.*

you are ready to set permissions for the file by selecting the users who you want to change the permissions assignment for. Then you can select the permissions assignment for that user in the middle selection list, and you can also select the inheritance in the far right selection box.

Once you hit the "Add/Change" button, the ACLs of the Windows2000 NTFS are manipulated with no interaction from the Web-hosting provider. This type of control can be essential to applications, especially when they need to interact with databases. For example, on Windows NT and 2000 IIS 5.0 Web server environments, any database below the root of the virtual Web server instance (i.e., available and publishable to the public Internet) should be inheriting standard permission setting for that location, which happens to be "READ" access and translates in NTFS ACLs to read and execute permissions but nothing else.

Thus, with such permissions, an Access database put in any directory below root will not allow update queries to be run against the database, as that would require "Write" permissions. Solution: Use an interface, similar in function to the one depicted in Figures 36-2 and 36-3, and change the permissions on either the database itself or, even better, on the folder it resides in (i.e., give the folder "CHANGE" or "READ/WRITE" permissions) so that any additional databases added to the folder won't require you changing their permissions, as they would be inheriting them from the folder. However, it must be mentioned that there is a justifiable security concern with placing a database below root especially when its permissions are even more open than other files below root.

From a security perspective, the best location for placement of a database in a virtual Web site is above root, which is at least one level higher in the folder hierarchy of the server's file system than the public Internet reach. Thus, folders "above root" can have permissions such that files in them already have more open permissions like that which would allow update queries on MS Access databases to fire.

What Programming Language Does Your Application Need to Run?

Tier 2: Does the hosting provider support that language; also, does it support it on both its shared and dedicated/colocated servers? For example, the host may state that it supports Perl, PHP, JRun (servlets, JSP pages), ColdFusion, Active Server Page, and Microsoft FrontPage. But they haven't told you anything about the versions supported of each of those languages, many times you won't find that information on their own Web site and it is not always apparent in host provider-listing Web sites.

Moreover, in host-provider-list Web sites, the owning organization in most cases has only check boxes next to various supported features and this leaves the provider with the limited ability to select or not select features offered. The best action to take is to e-mail and/or call the provider to discern this crucial information before you make use of the provider's convenient online signup script or before you sign and fax their contract back to them.

Tier 3: Ask the provider what programming expertise their staff possesses; are they knowledgeable enough in the programming language of your application to give you programming support if you were to need it? If not, and you were stuck on a question, it may be a more expensive proposition to find outside help from the aspect of searching and hiring time alone. Also, what types of affiliations if any does the hosting provider have with the vendors that support the programming language of your application?

For example, look for a provider being a Registered Web Presence Provider (WPP) if they claim to support; (4) or, if they claim to support Allaire Corporation's JRun, are they an Allaire Alliance Partner? Such a partnership shows the host's commitment to providing a higher level of expertise and customer service than typical providers of such products.

Also, keep in mind the advice presented in the tier 1 item previously mentioned (i.e., what operating system to choose); TopHosts.com stated it best when they advise customers on how best to choose what OS platform to host their Web site, "Your choice of [OS] platform will define the utility and type of software that you can use, the kind of applications that your site can run, what kind of server can host your site, the amount of control you have over your site and how efficiently your site will work as it grows in scale." (5)

What Networks and Hardware Does the Host Support/Provide?

Tier 2: One day while transferring files via FTP to an older server of my company's, I noticed the throughput of bandwidth was about 39 KB and thought that was okay but could be a lot better. Because the same files had to be copied to our new servers also, I was proceeding with that and noticed that the throughput with the same files, the same connection, from the same computer, to this new Dual Pentium server plugged into the same type of connection to the same WAN network was 286 KB. Now this was not scientific experimentation, but it was an observation that was noted.

After the new company servers were online for a few weeks, the customer comments started pouring in. They entailed remarks like, "Wow, did you guys add another T-3 or OC-xxx to your network, your servers fly!" Little did they know that the increased throughput had nothing to do with our network backbone's bandwidth, as it had not changed, but everything to do with our latest and fastest hardware. Thus, while you are looking at a provider's extensive fiber and backbone connections to the Internet, make sure you don't forget to inquire what hardware they are using in their boxes.

Tier 3: Most hosting providers and their data center providers (network operation centers, or NOCs; please see Figure 36-4 for a example of a NOC) appreciate the need for bandwidth and scale it to not exceed 50 percent utilization. Thus, my recommendation is to focus more on the hardware in the NOC, and to look for SCSI- and RAID-controlled hard drives in a host's servers, which are now able to bring information transfer speeds incredibly high within the server. IDE-connected hard drives, even with the latest mother-

Figure 36-4. *Network operation center.*

boards and chips, are not usually able to attain such transfer speeds. Also, the flexibility SCSI controller cards afforded by allowing multiple devices to be "daisy-chained together" allows for easier and better hot-swapping of hard drives in servers when drives fail.

RAID, which is the acronym for redundant array of independent disks, essentially means that more than one disk drive is used to form a container that allows for increased reliability and fault tolerance. And, depending on the RAID configuration, it usually provides increased performance. For example, with RAID 1 or RAID 5 configurations, you can have a hard drive fail but the data is not lost from the failed drive because it is saved on the other drive(s), and, in fact, you might not notice the failure at all if the system was set up properly.

Also look for dual CPUs, especially in shared servers' very busy boxes bombarded with requests to: send Web pages, run processes/services, parse code, accept and send FTP transfers, send and receive e-mail, log most activities, and communicate with other internally networked computers like domain controllers and namservers. Thus a server having an extra or multiple CPUs will enable it to divide its load and share some of those crucial tasks and allow for a speedier reaction, processing requests in a prioritized first-come-first-served fashion, to transfer requests for files, for instance, much faster.

What Is the Optimum Network Topology?

Tier 2: Network topologies of the host's data center or NOC are important but as long as there is redundant upstream provider connections (e.g., Sprint, MCI, UUnet) and the provider does *not* run beyond 50 percent utilization, and your route to servers in that data center from your main connection point appears stable and comparatively fast, the bandwidth you are purchasing is most likely adequate and reliable.

Tier 3: "Cold Potato" routing might be your next level of concern if your application is sensitive to things like network routes, packet latency, and so on to operate appropriately. "Cold Potato" routing can be illustrated this way: A person on the AT&T dial-up network requests that Web pages be sent from yahoo.com to his browser on his computer to view the site; if yahoo.com's network is engaging in "cold potato" routing, it will send the packets of data containing the yahoo.com Web page via its own network as far as possible, then route them onto the AT&T dial-up network and to the customer's computer. "Hot potato" routing would exist, using the same example, if the packets containing the yahoo.com Web page were routed back onto the AT&T dial-up network at the first opportunity, thus bypassing travel along yahoo.com's network (or their data center provider's network). "Hot potato" routing is what most networks' routers try to initiate. However, if your application is highly sensitive to things like latency (high ping or packet return times; e.g., video streaming), then cold potato routing should become an essential criteria in your requirements document.

The E-Mail Question (Spam, Policies and Procedures):

Tier 2: Decide if you want to keep e-mail in-house or to outsource it. One example of the complexity of outsourcing a large corporate environment's e-mail system is exemplified by United Airlines (UA) e-mail outsourcing to USA.NET. UA announced their Web e-mail outsourcing with USA.NET over 14 months ago and it has yet to be implemented, according to Carolyn Duffy's *NetWorld* article: "Delays plague record Web-based mail rollout." (7) Companies and individuals can either use the host's e-mail server or have their e-mail records (called MX records) forwarded elsewhere without affecting the packets that are used to request their Web sites (A records).

Tier 3: What type of spam blocks does the provider use? The provider's protection systems against e-mail spam, at a minimum, should consist of a requirement that all outbound traffic (SMTP) from its mail servers be from a local host. This will attempt to ensure that whoever is using the provider's SMTP servers to send e-mail will most likely be a current customer of the host and therefore is not likely to spam due to the practically universal anti-spam prohibitions of ISPs, ASPs, and the like. This will limit the amount of traffic on the e-mail server that you will be sharing (if your configuration was not dedicated or colocated) and it will also help prevent a large amount of junk e-mail deluging your inbox. The latter could be quite disconcerting if you had to wade through 100 junk e-mails daily just to find e-mail with meaning or significance.

Security, That Is the Question

Tier 2: Firewalls are common among companies that outsource their hosting and e-mail services, but this practice does not come without its own set of considerations. Without going beyond the scope of this chapter in a lengthy description of firewalls, suffice it to say that firewalls essentially function by blocking certain ports available to networks protected behind them. Now this can present quite critical issues with applications that call on ports that are blocked by the firewall. (8)

For example, Allaire's JRun 3.0 uses by default port 8000 for its Admin Interface. If a firewall were installed on the route to that server's NIC that blocked access to port 8000, one would be prohibited to access that port on that server without either accessing it locally on the machine itself or releasing the port from within the configuration of the firewall. Thus, before large sums of money are spent purchasing or renting a firewall for placement with your hosted application, make sure that there will be utility in doing so. Oftentimes, firewalls are required to be configured so "open" (most ports are able to transfer packets without restrictions) for applications to operate properly that they end up serving little purpose save draining your pocketbook.

You will also need a secure sockets layer (SSL) server certificate if you are planning to engage in e-commerce that captures sensitive data (e.g., credit cards) from customers. Most hosting providers allow you to use their own certificate on your site, which *does* allow your site visitors secure, encrypted communication. However, not having your own certificate can have other unintended consequences. For example, if you use the provider's SSL certificate (cert), your visitors must be warned of the fact that the certificate name does not match the domain name of the site being visited. That communication is intended to protect the visitor from someone hijacking another site's certificate and trying to pass it off as the same site.

However, visitors who might be already a little hesitant to put their credit card into an online form may be even less likely to do so if they see a message like that which appears in Figure 36-5 (notice the triangle with the exclamation point in the middle). How do you avoid that dialog box and message appearing? You can easily and relatively inexpensively obtain your site's own SSL certificate via your hosting provider or directly with a certificate authority (Thawte, Inc., or Verisign, Inc.).

Tier 3: Try to align with a hosting provider that fully understands security issues; you can look for clues of this on their Web site. Look to see how much discussion there is about security and you'll start to get a picture of how much attention they give it. This is not just important from the perspective of the host being to protect the server and network that your site resides upon, but also due to the fact that permissions, as discussed in the second tier 1 consideration, you should find a provider whose support staff is extremely well versed in permission settings and how they impact applications, with or without your access to or the availability of a client controller interface like tht depicted in Figure 36-2.

If you are not able to get your application to fire, even after adjusting permissions with a client interface, you will definitely want to reach someone on the end of a phone line that has a pretty good idea of what to do next.

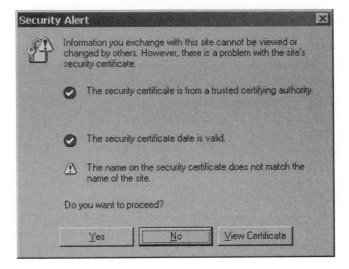

Figure 36-5. *Dialog box message that appears when using a provider's certificate to provide your site SSL.*

Privacy Policies and Service Level Agreements

Tier 2: Check the host's privacy policy to be sure that it clearly defines what the provider will or won't do with your personal information. This can become embarrassing if you are reselling the services provided by the Web host and your clients start to get e-mails listing promotions on their Web hosting, for example.

Tier 3: There has been a lot of talk and concern over the FBI's use of an e-mail–sniffing "black box" called Carnivore in data centers wherein it has received a court order granting access to install the unit. Find out what the provider's policy is surrounding this controversial practice and decide if they give you enough peace of mind that your privacy will be protected.

Referral/Reseller Programs; After All, You Have Clients Also

Tier 2: If you are interested in reselling the provider's services, make sure there is a solid reseller program in place that you can use to produce some ROI on the hosting service in addition to your development and/or application service offerings. Some hosts offer 50 percent discounts or greater on accounts you refer. Most will offer at least 10 percent referral commissions for accounts you send them. If you are seeking this kind of arrangement, then look for hosts that allow you flexibility in their billing system and/or in custom branding the client controller interface with your logo, for instance, so that your own customers are less likely to decide to skip the middleman.

Tier 3: If large company clients are involved, it would probably be best that you disclose your relationship to the hosting provider, since sooner or later they will have needs and/or questions/problems that perhaps surpass your ability to fully support them. It would be less embarrassing for you and might even help you close a deal if you tell them they are paying you to help them find the best service and not just trying to play middleman, which will raise costs. If you take this "objective procurer" stance, it could work well in your consulting paradigm.

Narrow Your Search and/or Short-Term Hosting Requirements?

Tier 2: Some portals can provide venues for acquiring quotes for hosting and other services. These ASPs (e.g., E-lance, respond.com, or Imandi) are uniquely designed to provide custom leads that are specific to the services hosting providers offer. Other sites provide comprehensive lists of hosts and what they offer (e.g., TopHosts.com, Microsoft FrontPage2000 Registered WPP List, CNET Web Services).

Tier 3: Perhaps you have a short-term project to test an application's function, for example, on the Web, but it is ultimately destined for a large Intranet at a company. In this case, you want to look for a host that has little to no penalties for cancellation and short contract lifes. Read the fine print and make sure you are aware of the amount of notice that must be given before you stop paying for the service. Not unlike power companies, the lights on your Web site can go out fairly quickly for overdue invoices.

Conclusion

You have been presented with the fundamental considerations in tier 1 questions and criteria; those were elaborated upon in the tier 2 and tier 3 levels. Thus, you have a focus for your search and a map for building a requirements document. Don't take "I am not sure" answers from hosting providers; there are enough providers in the market to avoid such time eaters. Again, the bottom line: Find a hosting provider that makes an investment in you and/or your company (especially if you are looking at a long-term project), or that will help you be successful in your hosting endeavor whether you are a short-term or long-term client. Seek courtesy, honesty, and integrity, because you and/or your business deserve nothing less.

References

1. "Custom Consulting Analysis, Application Hosting: A Customer Primer," Summit Strategies, Inc., July 2000, 3–14.
2. M. Smetannikov. "Data Center Craze," *Web Hosting Magazine,* 1 (3): 27, 2000.
3. For more information about ASP.NET, you may go to http://msdn.microsoft.com/voices/asp12282000.asp or go to http://www.asp.net.

4. To locate a Registered Web Presence Provider for Microsoft FrontPage2000 or to learn more about the program, you may go to http://www.microsoftwpp.com/wppsearch.
5. For more information, please visit: http://www.TopHosts.com.
6. You can find more information on Symantec's PCAnywhere by going to http://www.symantec.com; for more information on the free VNC (Virtual Network Computing), please follow this URL: http://www.uk.research.att.com/vnc/.
7. C. Duffy, "Delays Plague Record Web-based Mail Rollout. *NetWorld,* 18 (4): 1, 76, (22 January 2001).
8. Standard ports would be, for example, port 25 (SMTP), port 110 (POP3), port 80 (http://), port 443 (https:// or secure sockets layer [SSL]), port 21 and 22 (FTP).
9. D. Pappalardo, "Sharing wisdom on ASPs," *NetWorld,* 17 (48): 1, 96 (27 November 2000).
* Microsoft, Windows, and FrontPage are registered trademarks of Microsoft Corporation. All other trademarks mentioned are held by their respective claimants.

CHRIS KIPPLE is currently CEO and CTO at Avehost.com (a start-up, fast-growing international Internet hosting, application, and access-service provider) and of RegSearch(sm) International (a regulatory information publisher). AveHost.com's clients range from small businesses to Verizon Wireless and a district of the U.S. Coast Guard. Previously, Mr. Kipple worked at Pfizer as a regulatory safety associate where he, in addition to his main job functions, enhanced the worldwide safety department's Intranet Web site. He has a B.S. from the University of Houston—University Park and is completing an M.B.A. in technology management at the University of Phoenix. Mr. Kipple has recently been appointed to serve on the Republican Business Committee (RBC), which is part of the National Republican Congressional Committee to serve the interests of small business. He currently resides in New Jersey.

Java Performance Improvement Process

Stephen Kowalczyk and Madison Cloutier

Java Technology has emerged as the platform of choice for e-business systems because of its dynamic flexibility and development productivity. According to leading industry analysts, 70 percent of e-business systems will use Java by 2004. Despite its popularity, a major challenge with Java is execution performance.

Performance can be dealt with at three different levels—executive, management, and technical. At the executive level it is important to allocate the necessary resources and ensure appropriate processes are in place to ensure stable and scalable systems. Managers must oversee the activities of designing, development, testing, deploying, and management of systems. At the technical level it is important to follow best known practices, selecting appropriate software and hardware to successfully implement the required business system.

Many developers new to Java development lack knowledge about the performance implications of their design and coding practices. Java introduces many new language features and has different performance characteristics than older-generation programming languages—these differences require a new approach to guarantee high performance. In the fast-paced Internet world, organizations may compromise performance in the rush to be first to market with leading-edge functionality, believing that performance can be dealt with later. This is an unfortunate assumption, because performance is like quality—it must be addressed and designed in from the beginning.

This chapter provides useful information for all three levels of decision makers by exploring the key issues that affect the performance of server-side Java applications. It is not necessary to have a background in Java programming to understand all the content of this chapter. The first section covers basic performance concepts, the second provides guidelines for executives wanting to implement a Java performance management plan for their organization, the third provides a methodology managers can use to improve the performance of e-business systems, the fourth provides an overview of Java deployment platform technologies and the fifth reviews "best-known" Java coding practices.

Performance Basics

Before we discuss how to improve the performance of a Java server-side application, we need to review exactly what we mean by performance. This is not a simple task, since every application and developer has a different definition.

For the purpose of this chapter we will use the following five aspects to define performance:

1. Computational performance: Which programming algorithm performs best?
2. RAM footprint: How much memory does the application require to run effectively?
3. Startup time: How long does the application take to reach a useable state?
4. Scalability: How does the application perform under heavy user load?
5. Perceived performance: How does a user perceive the performance of the application?

All of these aspects must be considered for server-side applications, with a varying degree of importance for every application. For example, most server-side applications are launched a single time to run for relatively long periods, reducing the importance of startup time. Computational performance is important for applications that apply business logic to transactions. End-users primarily care about their perception of performance.

Which ones should you focus on? The business requirements for the application will determine the importance of each performance aspect, and any company that does not understand how their application performs in each of the five areas will undoubtedly suffer from performance complaints at some point.

What Affects Performance?

When you look at improving the performance of a Java application, there are four primary areas to consider: design, Java deployment platform, implementation, and hardware/operating system platform.

Design

A good design is absolutely necessary to deliver good performance. This is true for any application developed in any language, not just Java. If the application is well designed, it can take advantage of more resources such as memory and multiple CPUs. Covering the details of a good OO design is beyond the scope of this chapter, but there are numerous other books on the subject.

It is important to realize that technologies such as JSP, servlets, and EJB impose certain design constraints on the application. Understanding the performance impact of using each technology and applying them appropriately is equally important.

Java Deployment Platform

A key factor affecting Java performance is the choice of deployment platform. Originally, Java was a completely interpreted language, which contributed to poor performance. Innovations in Java deployment technology now offer many more options for organizations today, including just-in-time (JIT) compilers, mixed-mode interpretation, dynamic adaptive compilers, ahead-of-time compilers, and mixed-mode deployment technology. To ensure peak performance, it is important to choose the appropriate deployment platform for your Java-based applications.

Since the choice of deployment environments and tuning parameters is usually one of the easiest things to change in a Java application, it should be one of the first things examined after understanding the bottlenecks in a system and ensuring there is a good design.

Implementation

This is the area most developers jump to when looking at performance problems—the code. This makes sense, but it is important to ensure that any code changes are targeted at the portions of the code that are actually bottlenecks to performance. Be sure that performance bottlenecks are understood before making code changes. Bottlenecks can be identified by using profiling and performance analysis tools.

Hardware and OS

The most common misconception about improving the performance of a Java application is that a faster CPU and more memory are the only solution. Depending on the application bottlenecks, a change to the operating system, the disk subsystem, or the application design may prove most effective. Before adding new hardware to the system, be sure you have benchmarked and analyzed the application to determine the bottlenecks, and apply new hardware only as appropriate.

Implementing a Java Performance Management Plan

Java performance management is a systematic approach to designing, coding, measuring, assessing, optimizing, monitoring, and selecting appropriate tools and third-party software to ensure high levels of performance for Java-based e-business systems.

Appropriate planning allows organizations to utilize Java's benefits without sacrificing performance—or the company's bottom line. Failure to address Java performance issues can result in lost business opportunities and higher operating costs. The following are steps that you can take to initiate a Java performance management action plan for your organization.

Step 1: Educate software developers on best-known Java coding practices so that they understand the performance implications of their development choices. Java introduces new concepts such as object allocation, garbage collection, heap size management, data structures, and thread synchronization. The new features must be understood and applied properly.

Step 2: Ensure that an appropriate design and architecture are in place to meet system performance objectives, and that critical performance management points are identified. As a general rule, focus on a good design first and performance tune later. Deployment technology cannot overcome a bad design. When in doubt, engage Java design experts to assist.

Step 3: If planning to use third-party Java software in the system, thoroughly assess the software to ensure it meets performance objectives. Once third-party software has been selected and incorporated into a system it is difficult to change, so you do not want it to be the source of performance problems.

Step 4: Develop a testing plan that reflects anticipated real-world use. Tools are available for simulating usage of Internet-based systems and for monitoring Java system behavior. These tools provide valuable information needed for Java performance management.

Step 5: Implement a regular performance check plan. Assess performance early and often to ensure that applications behave as expected. It is important to develop performance matrix and base lines early during development for comparisons as new code is added to the system. Early benchmarking of third-party software, Java deployment technologies, and hardware/operating system platforms allow earlier decisions regarding production configuration and therefore more opportunities for performance tuning.

Step 6: Optimize the system for the chosen configuration. It is best to perform optimizations one at a time and reassess to verify achievement of desired results. Hardware, operating systems, Java deployment platform, and application combinations can vary considerably, so optimizing for the targeted deployment environment and application stack is critical.

Step 7: Instrument applications for ongoing monitoring and capacity planning. This will provide early warning of potential performance problems before they can seriously impact business.

Process for Improving Performance

The process of performance tuning is identifying bottlenecks in the application and then making choices to remove or minimize them.

All applications have bottlenecks—places where the application slows down, either waiting for something to happen before it can proceed or processing commands extraneous to the task at hand. Eliminating the bottlenecks in the application is the goal of performance tuning. However, you can never remove all the bottlenecks in an application, but the bottlenecks that can't be eliminated can be minimized.

Understanding the possible bottlenecks is the first step toward performance improve-

Bottleneck	The application is...
File and Network I/O	... waiting to read or write to the network or disk.
CPU	... waiting for the CPU to become available.
Memory	... busy allocating/de-allocating memory or swapping.
Exceptions	... busy processing exceptions.
Synchronization	... waiting for a shared resource to become available.
Database	... waiting for a response or processing the results from a database query.

Figure 37-1. *List of common bottlenecks.*

ment. Figure 37-1 is a list of common bottlenecks in Java applications and what each generally means.

Following is a performance improvement process that has been successfully used by professional Java performance consultants to identify and resolve performance bottlenecks.

Step 1: Define your performance requirements. Like all requirements, performance requirements should be specific and measurable. Ideally, they are already part of the requirements for the application and look something like:

- The application shall support 5,000 simultaneous users with five-second think time, with an average response time of less than ten seconds for the transfer transaction.

Be sure the performance requirements are specific and do not conflict with other requirements. If project requirements define deployment on a single processor server, don't expect it to support 1 million simultaneous users. Also, the performance requirements should generally be targeted at the system or component level of the application. This is primarily done to avoid wasting valuable time in trying to micro-tune a portion of the application that is not in the critical performance path. Lastly, be sure that performance goals mesh with the business goals of the application.

Step 2: Determine your current performance. Once performance requirements are identified, you should determine how the application currently performs in relation to the target. If the application meets all the criteria of your performance goal, then you are finished—release the application and get to work on the next release.

In the more normal case, you will now have a baseline to use for comparison as you further tune the application performance.

What performance measurements you take will depend on the application and the transactions you are testing, but the suggested minimum is response time and transactions per unit of time. It is also useful to record the CPU and memory utilization on the server during the tests for use in predicting the scalability of the application.

Be sure that you drive the system with a realistic load and mixture of transactions to simulate the expected workload. Use load-testing tools to drive the application and gather the required measurements. This will allow you to easily reproduce the load tests after tuning.

Beware of using only micro-benchmarks, which measure only small portions of code. This can lead you to miss the overall performance picture of the application and you can waste time trying to tune portions of the application that are not impacting overall system performance.

Step 3: Identify the bottlenecks. Once a baseline benchmark for the application is completed, you want to identify performance bottlenecks in the application. Using a profiler or analysis tool allows you to determine where the time is spent in the application stack. This will pinpoint places to make changes in the application to improve performance. These tools can also identify other potential problems such as excessive exception handling and garbage collection.

In general, an application spends 80 percent of its time executing 20 percent of the code. It is necessary to identify and isolate that 20 percent.

When profiling, be sure to drive the application for a sufficient time with a load that represents real use. This will provide a more accurate picture of system bottlenecks. If the test run is too short, the startup processing of the application will overshadow the actual execution profile, causing you to target areas that will not impact the run-time performance of the application.

If profiling reveals no obvious optimization target and performance is still not sufficient, look at the application design or deployment platform.

Step 4: Determine what can be done. Once a problem area in the application is identified, you need to decide what can be done to improve the performance. Remember that there are four areas in which you can make changes—the design, the code, the Java deployment platform, and the hardware/OS environment. Be sure to weigh all options for improving performance against the cost to make the changes.

Step 5: Implement a single change and benchmark. You want to be sure to implement changes one at a time and verify that the change actually improved performance. If you make multiple changes at once, it will be difficult to determine which helped and which didn't. Also, be sure to verify that the performance improvement didn't introduce any bugs into the application.

Continue this step until the bottlenecks identified in Step 4 are resolved.

Step 6: Return to Step 3. Performance tuning is an incremental process. Plan to continue measuring and profiling the application until performance requirements are met or it is no longer cost-effective to make improvements.

Java Deployment Environment

When planning to deploy a Java server application, there are important choices to make regarding deployment environment. This section examines the various choices for deploying a Java server application.

Hardware / Operating System

One decision to be made is what hardware/operating system platform to use. Factors to keep in mind when making the decision include:

- Performance of the OS in terms of disk and network I/O
- Maintainability of the OS
- Availability of OS administration knowledge
- Availability of any third-party tools or products
- Price/performance of the underlying hardware

Choosing the right hardware/OS for your application is out of the scope of this chapter, but realize that the choice, like other choices that need to be made in performance tuning, may end up being a compromise between performance and other total cost-of-ownership factors.

Java Deployment Platform

When deploying a Java application, the Java source code files are first compiled into a platform-independent, intermediate format known as "byte-code." This byte-code is then executed by a Java deployment platform using one of two fundamental technical approaches: one based on interpreter technology and the other based on "ahead-of-time" (AOT) native compilation (Figure 37-2).

Interpreter-Based Technology

The first-generation Java deployment platforms included virtual machines (JVM) that interpreted Java byte-code by reading the platform-independent byte-code and acting upon it. While this allowed the platform independence that originally made Java popular, it delivered very poor performance.

The second-generation Java deployment platforms incorporated the first performance enhancement such as just-in-time compilers (JITs). A JIT converts the language-independent byte-code to native machine code just before execution. This provided some performance improvement, but larger, more demanding Java applications continue to exhibit poor performance because code optimization is done very rapidly on small sections of the byte-code.

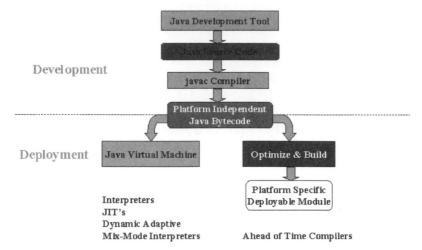

Figure 37-2. *Compiling a Java application.*

Another performance enhancement was the "dynamic adaptive compiler" or "mixed mode interpreter," which converts selected portions of the byte-code into optimized native code, based on execution patterns. Using the 80/20 rule, the idea is to begin with everything interpreted, monitoring the application for frequently executed or long-running code. These "hot spots" are then converted to optimized native code and patched back into the running application. In theory, the longer the application runs, the more optimized it should become.

Historically, interpreter-based technology, regardless of performance enhancements implemented, has never matched the performance and scalability of platform-specific, natively compiled code. This is because every CPU cycle that is spent trying to optimize and compile interpreted code on the fly takes cycles away from the business functionality of the application.

Ahead-of-Time Native Compilation-Based Technology

During the second generation of Java deployment platforms, AOT Java compilers were introduced to convert byte-code into binary native executables prior to the deployment and execution of the application.

The first AOT compilers worked on a class-by-class basis and relied on a standard JVM run-time. This class-by-class compilation improved performance some, but was limited in the optimizations that could be done and suffered from the reliance on the standard JVM.

The next AOT compilers included their own run-time as part of their native executables and did application-wide analysis to enable better optimization. This provided much better performance, but there were still drawbacks, the most notable being the lack of support for dynamic loading of Java byte-code.

The third generation of Java deployment platforms is represented by AOT compilers that have resolved the issue of dynamic loading with new features like built-in byte-code interpretation and the ability to dynamically include pre-compiled code during program execution. This ability to mix interpreted and pre-compiled code gives users the best of both worlds.

Which Technology Should We Use?

A common complaint of early AOT compilers was that they traded the platform independence and dynamic nature of Java for the performance of a native executable. This was true, but for server applications the loss of platform independence is not usually an issue, since companies generally do not regularly change their server platforms. The loss of the dynamic aspects of Java could indeed be a problem, but the latest generation of AOT compilation technologies now support this capability (Figure 37-3).

Native compilation has other advantages, such as security and reduced deployment complexities of Java applications—security, because it is no longer necessary to deploy Java byte-code, which can be easily de-compiled and reverse-engineered, even with obfuscation; and ease of deployment, because self-contained, native executables are easier to deploy and maintain than numerous files of Java byte-code.

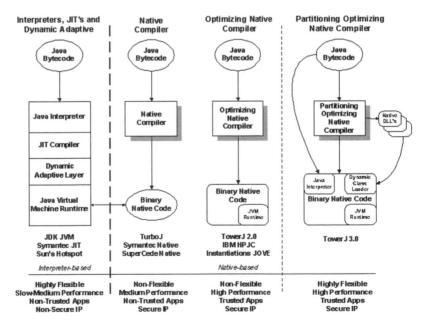

Figure 37-3. *Compilation technologies overview.*

The fact that AOT compilers are used before the application runs suggests they will continue to outperform interpreter-based technology. This is primarily because increasingly complex optimizations can be accomplished without negatively impacting the run-time performance. In addition, some AOT compilers expose an intermediate code layer and can utilize hardware-specific compilers, allowing engineers to apply advanced performance tuning like vectorization, software pipelining, and profile-guided optimization.

Both technologies have improved over the years and offer different performance characteristics. To determine which is best for your application, follow the performance improvement process outlined in the section "Process for Improving Performance."

Best-Known Java Coding Practices

What should be done with the "slow" portion of code? There are really two solutions—improve the performance of the code by changing the code, or call the slow section of code less often by improving the design. The best solution is to improve the design, since not calling code will always be faster than calling optimized code. Which solution you end up choosing will depend on how well optimized the code is currently—if changing the code doesn't create enough performance, there is no other choice but to change the design.

Performance optimization will oftentimes lead to a more specialized solution than originally desired, sacrificing flexibility, maintainability, or reuse. Weigh the benefits and cost of each optimization before making changes.

When looking at code changes for performance improvement, some of the following tips may help. The list does not contain every possible performance improvement but covers common, best-known practices. For more detailed code examples, refer to other books focused on Java performance improvement.

Object Creation and Resizing

One of the most common problems in Java programs is the over-creation of objects. This is not necessarily due to a design problem—the Java language includes rich libraries that abstract out the complexities of common computing tasks. However, very few programmers take the time to understand how a certain Java library actually implements the given functionality. A simple line of Java code may create more objects than one would expect. In the case where these objects are immediately unreferenced, you take a performance hit twice—once to create the object and then again to garbage-collect it. An interesting metric to look at in the application is the number of objects created per transaction or unit time. A very large number will usually indicate a performance problem due to excessive creation/destruction of objects.

Some tips for minimizing the number of objects used in the code follows.

Use static class variables. In cases where you have a variable in a class that never changes value for all of its instances, be sure to make it a static class variable so that only one instance of the variable is created for all instances of the class.

Instead of:

```
public class foo{
    SomeObject so = new SomeObject();
}
use
public class foo{
    static SomeObject so = new SomeObject();
}
```

Avoid excessive modification of immutable objects. Being an immutable object means that once the object is created it cannot be changed—a new object has to be created rather than just changing the already existing one. The most famous immutable object in Java is the String class. So if you say:

```
String foo = "Hello";
foo = "there";
foo = "Eveyone";
```

You actually have created three String objects, two of which are now available for garbage collection. It gets even worse as you start concatenating Strings together—the compiler creates other temporary objects in order to accomplish the concatenation. In the case of the String class, if you are going to continue to append strings to it, you are better off using the StringBuffer class instead.

Create objects with a reasonable size. If an object that has a dynamic internal buffer reaches the size limit on its buffer, it will have to create a new buffer and copy over the contents of the current one. Two examples are Vector and StringBuffer. These types of classes often have constructors that let you set the initial size of the internal buffer. In the case of StringBuffer, the default size is 16 characters. If you are expecting to append more than 16 characters to your StringBuffer, then you can spare yourself the performance hit of the auto-expansion of the internal buffer by setting it to a better value initially.

Avoid creating objects that are consistently created and thrown back. If you have objects that are constantly being created and then thrown away, you should try creating an object pool. The overhead of managing the pool should be less expensive than the excessive creation and garbage collection of the objects.

Only initialize objects in the scope they are used. Java allows you to declare and initialize objects anywhere in the code. This means that you can save the overhead of creating objects that are only used in a certain scope in the code. For instance, instead of saying:

```
SomeObject so = new SomeObject();
if (x == 1) then {
    Foo = so.getXX();
}
```

use

```
if (x == 1) then {
SomeObject so = new SomeObject();
    Foo = so.getXX();
}
```

This way, you only create the SomeObject when it is really necessary.

Don't initialize objects twice. Sometimes you will see code like:

```
public class foo {
    private SomeObject so = new SomeObject();

    public foo() {
        so = new SomeObject();
}
```

In this case, you are actually initializing the "so" variable twice, once as you specified in the constructor code, and once because the compiler inserts another so = new SomeObject() into the constructor for you. Just initialize the variable once by leaving it out of the constructor or not initializing it in the class variable definition.

Exceptions

The Java language includes functionality to handle exceptions, using a try/catch block. This functionality makes it easy to develop exception-handling code, but the overuse of try/catch blocks can have an impact on application performance. Some tips for using exceptions in the code follows.

Avoid using try/catch blocks for application logic. Depending on the JVM, simply setting up for exceptions even if they are not thrown will impact performance. Often an if block or while/for loop will provide the same logic. Exceptions should be used only in exceptional cases—if you are expecting it to happen with some regularity, look at rewriting the code.

Reuse the exception. If you find that you absolutely need to use an exception in a performance-critical path, try to reuse an existing exception object. Most of the time spent throwing an exception is in creating the exception object.

Threading

Almost every server application developed uses threads—they are key to fully utilizing the resources available to an application. Having many threads executing will allow the application to continue processing something if another thread gets blocked waiting for disk or network I/O.

However, poorly designed or implemented threading can be a big performance problem. Some tips for using threads in the code follows.

Watch out for over-synchronization. Be careful to not over-synchronize the code—synchronized methods are drastically slower than unsynchronized ones. Too much synchronization leads to a single threaded behavior with the overhead of synchronization—not a good combination. Remember that many Java classes, such as Vector, are already synchronized—there may be an unsynchronized alternative if you don't need the synchronization (ArrayList in the case of a Vector).

Synchronize methods, not code blocks. A synchronized method performs slightly better than a synchronized code block, so when you need to synchronize code, try to synchronize a whole method instead of just a code block.

Use multiple locks per object to maximize concurrency. By default, every object has a single lock object. This means that if two threads want to execute two different synchronized methods on a single object, they end up locking each other out, even if the two methods in question do not share any resources. To avoid this, you can create multiple locks per object:

```
class foo{
  private static int var1;
  private static Object lock1 = new Object();
  private static int var2;
  private static Object lock2 = new Object();

  public static void increment1() {
     synchronized (lock1) {
       var1++;
     }
  }
```

```
public static void increment2() {
    synchronized (lock2) {
        var2++;
    }
}
}
```

I/O

I/O covers many areas, but the most commonly used I/O relates to reading and writing from either disk, network, or database. The Java language includes a rich set of classes to handle disk and network I/O, with and without buffering. When it comes to database I/O, you will have some sort of JDBC driver to contend with. As with other provided classes, these classes can also introduce performance bottlenecks. Some suggestions for I/O coding practices follow.

Use buffered I/O. Buffered I/O is typically faster than non-buffered, so use it wherever possible. Be sure to set the buffer size appropriately—too small or large of a buffer will impact performance. Also, when using buffered I/O, only use flush() when absolutely necessary—if you must flush frequently, then non-buffered I/O might be better.

Output streams and Unicode Strings. When using output streams and Unicode Strings, there is a large amount of overhead in the various Writer classes, since they have to perform a Unicode character to byte conversion. If possible, perform this character to byte conversion outside of the critical performance path and use an OutputStream instead of a Writer class.

Use transient when using serialization. Whenever you have to serial an object, you want to minimize the amount of objects that need to be serialized (and then unserialized at some point). Any attributes that can be computed or otherwise re-created should be labeled as transient so that they are not serialized each time. This can be a big performance boost, especially if you are sending serialized objects across the network.

Cache. When data or objects are accessed often but rarely changed, you might want to create a cache to speed up access to them. This might include things like database result sets, full HTML response pages, etc.

Use the fastest JDBC driver available. JDBC drivers usually fall into two categories—Type 2, which is a Java wrapper around a native driver, and Type 4, which is an all Java driver. Which you should use will depend heavily on the application and Java deployment environment. Since the code changes needed to support a different driver are generally minimal, be sure to test all the available drivers for best performance.

Native Code

It is believed that writing native code will always outperform Java code. This is partially true, depending on the Java deployment environment under comparison and whether you take the overhead of calling the native code into account. In general, you want to use native code only when the overhead of calling the native code via JNI is eclipsed by the speed of the native code implementation.

Additional Tips

The following are additional tips for Java programming that didn't fall into the previous areas.

Use method variables. When possible, use a local method variable rather than an instance or class variable, since access to them is faster. If you refer or change it often enough in the method, making a local copy and updating it at the end may also be a performance win.

Avoid method call overhead. Most everyone is taught to write "get and set" methods for every class variable and to always use them. For use within the class itself, this is not always the best idea—setting a class variable directly using this.xx = foo instead of this.setXX(foo) is almost two times faster. If you don't need to use the set method for synchronization reasons, use the variable directly.

Avoid creating objects or re-calling a method with unchanged variables in loops. Creating objects or re-calling the same method with the same arguments in a loop is a waste of compute cycles. Place those kinds of calls prior to the loop.

Use static, final, and private. Compilers can only inline methods that are declared final, static, or private, so to take advantage of this optimization, be sure to use the keywords when possible.

Use System.arraycopy() for large arrays. If you need to copy and arrays of size 4 or larger, use System.arraycopy(). This is much faster than doing it manually.

Time stamping and logging. There are two common performance problems when it comes to server applications, both related to the time stamping of log entries. First, a lot of programmers use a call like new Date() to get the current time. On a busy server, this means they compute the date many times a second but really only care about second granularity. In this case, it would make sense to create a class that computes the date only every second. See Dov Bulka's book *Java Performance and Scalability* for an example of a "lazy" date class. Second, if there is no reason to have the actual date logged in a readable format like "Fri Dec 29 2000 17:58:12 EST 2000," just log the results of System.currentTimeMillis(). You can then post-process the log for a readable time.

Conclusion

Improving Java application performance is much like any other performance-tuning exercise, but with a few additional considerations. By defining performance goals that support business objectives, following a systematic approach, utilizing best-known practices, and choosing the right deployment environment, you can ensure that your Java-based systems help your company's top line without negatively impacting the bottom line.

STEPHEN KOWALCZYK is a senior consultant with Tower Technology Corporation's Professional Services Group. MADISON CLOUTIER is the vice president of technical marketing for Tower Technology. Tower is a leading provider of performance-oriented solutions for Java-based systems.

A Primer on Routing Algorithms

Gary S. Rogers

Before we discuss the *basics* of how data is routed over a network such as the Internet, it is important to see how routing fits into the larger picture of telecommunications. More advanced topics such as routing over autonomous systems and border routers are not covered in this chapter.

A Reference Model

During the time the Internet was taking shape in the early 1980s, an international body of experts from the International Standards Organization were also building something, namely a model of protocol standards called the Open Systems Interconnect (OSI) Reference Model. The predecessor to this model was the TCP/IP Model. The primary difference between the two is that the application layer (layer 7) of this model is roughly equivalent to layers 5 through 7 of the OSI Model. (3) Both models route packets at layer 3.

By using the word "open," the committee specified a set of standards for the exchange of information among systems that are "open" to one another due to their mutual use of the appropriate standards. What is a standard? A standard is a prescribed set of rules, conditions, or requirements. (4)

The OSI Reference Model, quite shrewdly, incorporated existing standards such as IEEE 802.3, or Ethernet. Basically, the OSI Model provides a conceptual and functional blueprint, and is *not* a set of implementation rules. The model employs the concept of layering. What essentially occurred was that a determination was made as to the *totality* of communications-related activities that had to be performed by the communications hardware and software on a host.

Next, this functionality or set of activities was broken up into seven vertical layers, essentially grouping the similar functions. As an example, all functions or activities having to do with message routing were placed in the OSI Reference Model's layer 3, or network layer.

Okay, so ISO established a model. But, how exactly does it work? First, the application programs interface to the communications stack via whatever method the operating system employs. Then, the appropriate layer 7 program is called, performs its processing, and attaches a header to the data and then calls the layer 6 program. This program performs its function, attaches its header, and then calls the layer 5 program and so on until the data, with all associated headers, is transmitted over the communications media to the destination computer. It should be made clear that each layer is attaching a header and incorporating into that header whatever information is necessary for its peer process on the destination computer. As an example, the layer 3 program adds its own source Internet address as well as the destination address. Also, the ISO committee established seven layers, but not all are used.

As mentioned, the primary layer involved in routing data over the Internet is OSI layer 3, the network layer. The network layer has one purpose, namely, controlling the activities of the subnet. Obviously, this requires that the network layer must determine how packets are routed from source to destination. Currently, IP (the Internet Protocol) is the most popular protocol used for routing. (2) And, IP is the primary routing protocol for the Internet. (6) Novell's anser to IP is Internetwork Packet Exchange (IPX). Like IP, IPX is a connectionless protocol. (5)

This can be a difficult endeavor in that routing can be either static or dynamic. Routing can be input by network administrators into routing tables (static) or a wide range of dynamic routing can take place based upon highly elaborate routing algorithms involving not only shortest path but traffic load, error rates, and even administrative aspects such as cost.

An Example of Layering and the OSI Reference Model

Let's assume that a user is using a chat application like AOL's Instant Messenger, or a similar product such as MSN Instant Messenger or ICQ Corporation's ICQ product.

The user types the message "Hi Susie!" The application layer passes the data ("Hi Susie!") from the user's application to the layer 6 presentation layer. At the presentation layer the data is translated and encrypted. Once this is accomplished, the presentation layer passes this data (and the header the presentation layer attaches to the data) to the session layer, where the dialogue is set for full-duplex communication (since chats function in this fashion). Next, the session layer calls the transport layer, where it packages the data as segments. The recipient's name is resolved to its corresponding IP address. The transport layer also adds check sums for the necessary error checking, because, as discussed, the transport layer is responsible for end-to-end reliability.

The transport layer then calls the layer 3 network layer. Remember, this layer is responsible for message routing.

The network layer packages the data as datagrams or packets (fragments or "chunks" of the message). If, after an analysis of the IP address, the destination is on a network that is not local, then the IP address for the next intervening device is added as the next destination. This is crucial in that this layer is concerned with the next hop that is necessary to route the datagram on its way to the final destination. Once this has been accomplished, then the data link layer process is called. The data link layer packages the datagram into frames. Then, the physical address of the device is resolved.

Typically, on a LAN, for example, this is the MAC address assigned by the manufacturer. This is the address belonging to the intervening device, which will forward the data on to its destination. In most cases, for LANS, the specific access type for the network is Ethernet. Token ring is the other most used access type.

The data link layer passes the data to the physical layer, where it is packaged as bits (0's and "1"s) and transmitted by the network adapter (usually a network interface card) across the transmission media. This transmission media may be copper-based or fiber-optic strands. The fact that a transmission is taking place is the relevant fact; how it is accomplished is up to the network adapter. For example, on a fiber optic network, the network adapter will use flashes of light instead of sending electrical impulses along a copper line.

At the other end of the physical media, the physical layer of the intervening device receives the bits off the network media. The process that was described before is repeated, except in the opposite direction. In this case, the data link layer takes the data and packages it as frames and the destination device's physical address is resolved to its corresponding IP address. Then, the data link layer calls the network layer, which then packages the data as datagrams. After the analysis is performed to determine the IP address of the destination device, the location of this device on the network is ascertained, usually by accessing routing tables. Once this has been accomplished, we go back down the layers once again and the data link layer is then called. As usual, the data link layer packages the data into frames and the IP address is resolved to the MAC address.

The data is then sent to the physical layer, where it is packaged as bits and transmitted across the network as before.

This process continues (layers 1-2-3, then 3-2-1) until the final destination is reached. At that point, the network layer on that computer passes the data to its transport layer, where it is reordered, reassembled into segments, and error checking is performed via the check sums that were incorporated earlier.

The transport layer calls the session layer, which acknowledges that the data has been received.

The presentation layer is called next, where the data is translated and unencrypted (in the TCP/IP Model, layers 5 through 7 are all-in-one). Finally, the application layer is called, who calls the "chat" application, in this case AOL's Instant Messenger, and the message "Hi Susie!" appears. This sequence hopefully provides an excellent viewpoint of the amount and complexity of the communications software needed just in order to send a simple message such as "Hi Susie!"

What Is a Routing Algorithm?

The routing algorithm decides which output line of a router an incoming packet or datagram should be transmitted out on. The process can be a complex one.

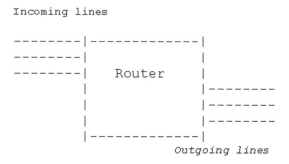

Figure 38-1. *Switching fabric.*

Routers have incoming and outgoing lines. The decision-making process internal to a router decides which outgoing line a packet travels in order to get to its destination (or another router in between). This is typically referred to as the switching fabric and can be seen in Figure 38-1.

Classifications of Routing Algorithms

Routing algorithms can be generally be grouped into two broad categories:

1. Nonadaptive algorithms
2. Adaptive algorithms

Nonadaptive algorithms are established by the network administrator. They then route packets based upon the rules of the routing algorithm.

Nonadaptive algorithms are loaded (i.e., "burned") into microprocessor chips that are then inserted onto the motherboards of routers, or they are downloaded onto them once they are initially booted.

This nonadaptive routing approach is called static routing. The key is that the routers then route data based upon these loaded algorithms. If network conditions or topology change, they simply follow the instructions comprising the algorithms. This makes them somewhat less efficient than their successors, adaptive algorithms. Adaptive, or static, routing algorithms are administered manually by the network administrator. (1)

Adaptive algorithms change their decisions on how to route data (i.e., packets or datagrams) as network conditions change. For example, if a line is upgraded from a 56 KB line to a T-1, then the adaptive algorithm takes this into account when it decides which line to output for the next packet.

There are several routing algorithms that have been developed and employed on the Internet. These routing algorithms have been developed and deployed basically in an evolutionary process.

Shortest Path Routing

The first routing algorithm developed was shortest path routing. It is a static algorithm and perhaps the easiest to understand, as well. What occurs is that basically the shortest path algorithm just locates the shortest path between two routers and transmits the packet on that line.

So, what do we mean by "shortest"? It can be either the number of hops or geographic distance in kilometers.

Shortest Path Routing: Geographic Distance

Using shortest path routing, a packet would go from Router A to Router B, not Router C, as shown in Figure 38-2.

Using shortest path routing:number of hops, the packet will traverse this path from Router A to Router G, as shown in Figure 38-3.

Shortest path routers also can use other attributes as metrics, such as queuing time or transmission delay.

Flooding Routing Algorithm

Flooding (Figure 38-4) is another static algorithm. With flooding, every single incoming packet is sent out on every outgoing line. The only exception to this is the line on which the packet came in on. For example, in the following graphic, if the packet came in from LA, it would be sent out to SEA, SD, and KC.

A major disadvantage of flooding is that it produces a massive network load, since there are so many packets present on a network.

Theoretically, an almost infinite number of packets could be generated as every router sends the packet out on every outgoing line. A way to minimize this effect is to place a hop counter in the header of each packet and then decrement it at each hop. The packet would eventually be "shedded" or dropped when the counter reaches zero. A big question would be how high to make the hop count. The typical answer is to

```
Router A -----> Router B
          \
           \--------> Router C
```

Figure 38-2. *Routing example.*

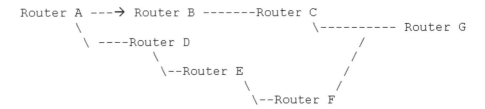

Figure 38-3. *Routing example.*

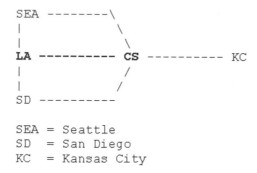

Figure 38-4. *Flooding routing algorithm.*

set the hop counter at the size of the full network minus one. As an example, if you have a network of 30 routers, then the hop count would be set to 29 (since the originating router is not counted).

Another method is to simply keep track of which packets have been flooded so that you will not send them out another time. Of course, this requires the router to establish yet another table, in order to keep track of this activity. This may tend to degrade performance.

A variation of flooding is selective flooding. Selective flooding employs the same primary logic, except it is direction oriented. For example, if you only wanted to flood in one direction, then selective flooding would be your answer.

Why ever employ such an algorithm that obviously overloads a network? Well, there are several instances. First, routers let all other routers know of new network nodes by flooding the network, typically at times of less traffic such as evening and/or weekend hours. Second, if you absolutely must assure (as much as humanly possible) that a message, via packets, gets through, then flooding is the answer. Granted, the message, via packets, may get through multiple times, but at least it gets through. As an example, what if you were the North American Air Defense Command and you needed to tell all military bases in the United States that a nuclear weapon was coming their way; this would be the way to do it.

Distance Vector Routing

Distance vector routing is a dynamic routing algorithm and is used in most networks today, including the Internet.

In distance vector routing, the routers maintain a routing table that contains one entry for every router in the network. This entry contains two distinct sections:

1. The preferred outgoing line to use to reach each network destination.
2. A "questimate" on the distance in kilometers or the time to that destination.

The metric used in conjunction with this table information may be number of hops or queue length or even delay. The way it works is that each distance vector router exchanges this information with its neighbors and updates its routing table accordingly. In this way, the router can get a more accurate picture of the network. How often does this "updating" occur? Well, that is where the experience of the network administrator plays a part. The routing tables are originally established by the network administrator and the timing of the updating process should be "tweaked" by the network administrator in the most efficient manner possible, such that the routers always have an accurate "picture" of the network while also not performing the update so often that the network is unduly burdened by this updating process.

Link State Routing

Link state routing is the most prevalent routing algorithm utilized today. It is a dynamic routing algorithm in that it can change its decisions on which outgoing line to send data when changes in the network occur.

Link state routers follow a process where they learn who their neighboring routers are (i.e., IP addresses), perform measurements on the delay or cost to each of these neighboring routers, and then tell this to all other routers in the network. Obviously, this provides a detailed perspective of the network.

When a router is initially booted, it first learns who its neighbors are by sending a special "Howdy" packet out on each of its outgoing lines. This Howdy (actually HELLO) packet is supposed to be returned by all neighbors. Thus, each router knows the unique address of each of its neighbors.

The router also computes the delay to its neighbors. This is performed by the router sending a special ECHO packet to all its neighbors. All neighbors are required to reply "send it back." The router then measures the round-trip time and an estimate of the delay can be computed. This is similar to sonar and the pinging process employed by that technology. You can also compute the load factor by measuring the time from when it gets queued in its outgoing line versus when it is actually sent out on the line.

Once this process has been completed, the router builds a packet containing this data. This packet typically looks as shown in Figure 38-5.

After a router has all the link state packets from every router on the network, then it proceeds to construct its "picture" of the network. This is obviously a much more accurate picture of the network than any of the other routing algorithms, but it does have its price. These packets are larger in size than those employed by distance vector routers. These induced a larger throughout delay and overhead on the network. Plus,

```
------------------------------------------------------------------------
| Originator's IP address | Seq no. | age of packet | List of Neighbors and delay    |
------------------------------------------------------------------------
```

Figure 38-5. *The packet.*

the time a router needs to construct them, process them, and construct its associated routing tables using this data can be significant. Is it worth it? Well, this answer is somewhat complex. If you have a rapidly changing network as in an organization that is adding new offices frequently and/or upgrading its lines periodically, then this is worth the price (in overhead) in that you can receive an accurate picture of the network in short-order time.

Conclusion

There are several routing algorithms employed today. Routing algorithms began with static routing performed by simple shortest path routing and now have evolved to the point where they dynamically change, where they send data based upon changing network conditions.

References

1. V. Amato, *Cisco Systems Networking Academy: First Year Companion Guide,* 1999.
2. S. Feit, *Wide Area High Speed Networks* (New York: MacMillian), 1999.
3. B. Forouzan, *Data Communications and Networking* (Boston: McGraw-Hill), 2001.
4. "NSPA79," National Standards Policy Advisory Committee, A National Policy on Standards for the United States, 1979.
5. E. Tittel and D. Johnson, *A Guide to Networking Essentials* (Boston: Course Technology), 1998.
6. J. Walrand, *Communication Networks: A First Course* (Boston: McGraw-Hill), 1998.

GARY S. ROGERS has almost 25 years' experience designing, developing, and implementing complex networking and system software in a wide variety of computer system environments. He has been involved in all phases of the system development life cycle from initial needs analysis to design development, software development, and testing through conversion and deployment of system to customer sites. He also has twelve years experience teaching a wide range of computer courses.

Currently, Dr. Rogers is an assistant professor at Macon State College, the fastest-growing institution of the 34-institution University of Georgia system. Dr. Rogers received his Ph.D. from Walden University, M.A. from Webster University, and his B.A. from the University of Florida.

Internet and E-Commerce Security

Kevin Lundy

In this chapter, we are going to have a brief history lesson as an introduction to cryptography. It is important to understand how and why cryptography works.

Early Algorithms

One of the earliest known utilizations of encryption was by Julius Caesar. Caesar used a simple mono-alphabetic substitution. Mono-substitution simply replaces one letter with another. Imagine simply shifting the alphabet one character at a time such that a=b, b=c, etc. So "Caesar" would be represented as "Dbftbs." In particular, Caesar used an offset of three (a=d, b=e, etc.)

This simple algorithm is easy to decipher. Techniques used to decipher mono-alphabetic encryption include the frequency distribution of letters. That distribution can then be used with short words, repeating letters, common initials, and final letters to break the code.

One method to overcome this frequency weakness is to use a poly-alphabetic substitution. This works by having multiple substitution tables. For example, for the odd letters, let's use a character shift of one, and for the even letters, let's use Caesar's shift of three.

Now, using the above tables, let's encrypt the phrase:

CAESARS ALLY

Would be encrypted as

ddfvbut dmoz

First, notice that the "CA" is encrypted as "dd." Then notice the repeating "LL" is encrypted as "mo." The poly-alphabetic substitution flattens the frequency distribution curve of the alphabet. Simultaneously, it removes repeating letters as an aid to deciphering the code.

It is important to note that in order to keep our examples simple, we are using a simple shift of the alphabet as our algorithm. In practical use, the substitution would be calculated by an equation using modular arithmetic. Modular arithmetic is used to ensure that the results remain in a predetermined range. For a one-to-one substitution using the English alphabet, this would be mod 26. Caesar's shift of three would then be written as:

$$(a) = (A) + 3 \bmod 26$$

These algorithms can now form the basis for encryption. The results of the algorithm give us a symmetric key. Symmetric implies that the key can be used to encrypt or decrypt the data. However, if the key is compromised, so is your encryption.

One-Way Functions

A one-way function is a function that is simple to compute, but the inverse computation is more difficult to compute. Consider for example the equation $y=x^3$. Given a value for x, it is relatively easy to calculate y. This can be done with paper and pencil. However, the inverse calculation, $x=\sqrt[3]{y}$, is significantly more difficult to calculate, especially manually.

Now consider $y=x^2$. This is another simple function. The inverse function, $x=\sqrt[2]{y}$, yields two results, a positive and negative.

One-way functions are particularly useful for authentication. This allows for storing passwords in an encrypted format. If the password file is compromised, the actual passwords are not inferred to an intruder. When users attempt to log in, they type their password, and the system applies the one-way function and compares the results to the stored encrypted password.

Public-Key Cryptography

This is a huge gray area among both developers and administrators. We know it works, but not how. Too many books go into the mathematical details and still keep us scratching our heads. Public-key encryption is often referred to as PKI. The simplistic description is that all encrypt/decrypt processes require two keys, a public key and a private key (asymmetric). If the private key encrypts a data stream, then only the public key can decrypt the data. Conversely, if the public key encrypts a data stream, then only the private key can decrypt the data.

It is important to remember that the private key is just that—it should never be available to anyone else.

How is this useful? Assume that I give you my public key. I now send you a data stream that I have encrypted using my private key. If you can decrypt this stream using the public key, you are then assured that I originated that data. You have just authenticated me! Now consider the inverse. You want to send me financial information (your credit card number). You encrypt that information with my public key. You can send that information confident that nobody can decrypt the data except the holder of the private key. If your encrypted information were intercepted, and the bad guy were to attempt to use the public key, the results would be ineligible.

There is another extremely useful benefit of public-key encryption. There needs to be only one pair of keys, for an unlimited number of users (assuming one-to-many or many-to-one). In traditional encryption, there needs to be an encryption key for every pair of systems communicating. Think of our e-commerce Web site. Using traditional encryption, the server would need to generate and track encryption keys for every customer. You can see that for a popular site this would quickly become unwieldy. Using public-key encryption, we only need one pair of keys.

Generating the Keys

The key (pardon the pun) to public/private keys is an algorithm that provides for two results (keys) that are mutual inverses. This algorithm was first proposed in 1978 as the RSA algorithm. The letters are the initials of the three inventors: Rivest, Shamir, and Adelman.

The mathematics of the RSA algorithm are beyond the scope of this book. Further information on RSA may be found at www.rsasecurity.com.

Generally speaking, keys are generated by taking two *large* prime numbers and multiplying them together to get an even larger number. By large, we mean numbers on the magnitude of 15 digits.

Now, just to reiterate, in symmetric encryption we take our clear text, use a single key and our encryption algorithm, and create our encrypted text. To decrypt, we use that same key and algorithm to decrypt. In asymmetric encryption, we use our private key and our algorithm to encrypt the data. The receiver then uses our public key to decrypt the text.

Locking and Unlocking Encrypted Data

Let's take a look at a simplistic data flow using public/private encryption. Let's assume two computers wish to have an encrypted dialogue—a server and a client.

1. Server obtains client's public key (from a key server or from the client).
2. Server uses client's public key and server's private key to generate a large key.

3. Server uses this large key and the algorithm to generate cypher text.
4. Client obtains server's public key (from a key server or from the server).
5. Client uses server's public key and client's private key to generate a large key.
6. Cypher text is descrypted.
7. The export issue.

In January 2000, the U.S. government significantly reduced the export regulations on cryptography products. Export of products is now allowed, except to the following countries: Cuba, Iran, Iraq, Libya, North Korea, Serbia, Sudan, Syria, and Taliban-controlled areas of Afghanistan. Regardless of U.S. export laws, encryption products have been available from non-U.S. vendors for a number of years. Further information on U.S. export laws may be found at www.bxa.doc.gov/.

Secure Sockets

What Is SSL?

SSL stands for secure sockets layer, originally developed by Netscape. SSL is a protocol that resides between the IP protocol stack and higher-level protocols (such as HTTP). Another important feature of SSL is that it is session based.

A session-based encryption aids us in that we can use symmetric keys for speed.

Rather than examine the mechanics of how SSL works, let's take a look at what SSL does for us:

1. Via the server's public key and a server certificate, authenticates to the client that the server is who it claims to be.
2. Optionally, with client certificates, can authenticate the client to the server (think of home banking).
3. Negotiate a common encryption algorithm and strength.
4. Generate and exchange an encryption key via public/private key encryption.
5. Initiate symmetric encryption for the remainder of the session.

As you can see, SSL solves many problems for an e-commerce Web site. In step 1, we have authenticated to the client that we are who we say we are. In step 2, we have optionally authenticated the client. Step 3 uses either 512- or 1024-bit encryption to protect our server keys while we negotiate a session key. Steps 3–5 have encrypted our data transfer, providing both security and integrity. Steps 3–5 have enabled us to utilize symmetric encryption for speed. Finally, since SSL is session based, it also enables us to use smaller keys, again resulting in higher performance.

If you are interested in the details of SSL, http://developer.netscape.com has some excellent white papers.

Encryption Levels

There are two primary levels of key sizes in use today on public e-commerce Web sites, 40-bit and 128-bit. At this point, we are discussing the key size for our symmetric encryption session. This is an important distinction. When trying to determine the level for your application, you must perform a risk analysis. Some factors to consider are:

1. Who your customers are
2. Where they are located
3. What you are protecting
4. How long it needs to be protected

40-Bit versus 128-Bit

Generally speaking, the key size is the determining factor in an algorithm's strength, although the actual algorithm plays a part as well; 128-bit encryption is approximately 3×10^{26} times stronger than 40-bit encryption. Prior to the relaxation of U.S. export laws, if you wanted to have an e-commerce site with customers outside the United States, you were relegated to 40-bit encryption. This was true even if your server were also located outside the United States, since the predominant browser vendors (Netscape and MS) are located in the United States. This prevented browsers capable of 128-bit security from being exported.

With your Web site, you have three options for encryption:

1. Require 128-bit encryption.
2. Suggest 128-bit, but settle for 40-bit if the client doesn't support 128-bit.
3. Require only 40-bit.

If your Web site has an international clientele, you may want to consider allowing 40-bit encryption for a short time period, until your clients have had sufficient time to install the newly available 128-bit software.

Implementing SSL on a Web Server

So, if SSL is so great, what do we need to do to use it? First we need a Web server that supports SSL; fortunately most current Web software does. Next we need a server certificate from an acceptable certificate authority (CA). You can be your own CA or you can use a public CA. Keep in mind, however, that the CA must also be acceptable to the client. Some public CA's include:

- Verisign, Inc., http://www.verisign.com
- Entrust.net, Limited, http://www.entrust.net
- Digital Signature Trust Comp., http://www.digsigtrust.com

Let's step through the process of setting up SSL for our Web site on IIS.

Step 1: Create a certificate request. To do this, we need to get to Key manager. We do this by starting the MMC, editing the properties for the Web site, choosing the security tab, and then pressing the key manager button, and follow the wizard (Figure 39-1).
Step 2: Submit the request to your chosen CA (including payment).
Step 3: Once you receive the certificate, install it via Key Manager.

This step highlights one limitation of SSL. You *must* bind the certificate to a single IP address and port. If you are hosting multiple Web sites on your server with a single IP address, you can have only one certificate. SSL does *not* work with host headers. Why doesn't SSL work with host headers? Because the http get request is in the data portion of our IP packet, which is encrypted, so IIS wouldn't know which site (and it's private key) to use.

Once we have a certificate, it's a simple matter to use the MMC to highlight a directory and enable encryption. Highlight the directory to be secured, right-click, choose properties, directory security, and click on Edit under Secure Communication. Put a check mark in the secure channel box, as shown in Figure 39-2.

The Dos and Don'ts of SSL

There are a couple of rules of thumb for SSL. These may seem obvious, but they are worth stating, as they are easily overlooked.

Figure 39-1. *Creating a new key.*

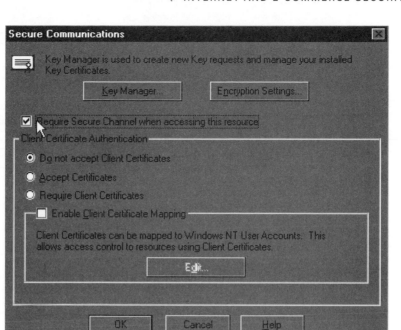

Figure 39-2. *The secure channel dialog.*

1. Don't encrypt everything. You don't want to encrypt everything on your Web site, only the sensitive information. Remember each session encryption key takes memory, and each encrypted page consumes CPU cycles. You may have a powerful server, but the client side has to decrypt your data as well, and the client may not be as powerful.

2. Don't use an encryption strength stronger than necessary. Why use a key that would take five years and millions of dollars of equipment to crack, when the session may last five minutes?

Know the data you are trying to protect, and know your customers and what is acceptable to them!

Digital Certificates Signatures

What Is a Digital Certificate?

A digital certificate is basically an electronic ID. This ID is associated with a public key. The combination of the certificate and public key allows for proof of a person, server, or company's identification. The standard for certificates is known as X-509.

Similar to obtaining a personal ID, such as a driver's license or social security card,

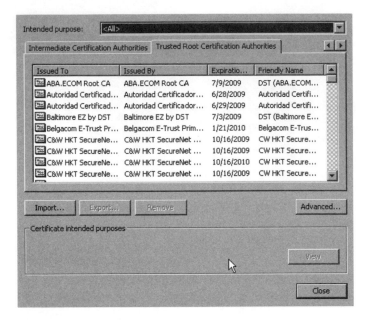

Figure 39-3. *Trusted root certificate authorities.*

you obtain a digital certificate from an authorized agency. In this case, this is a certificate agency (CA). For an Intranet or private site, you can run your own CA software. For a public site, you need to use a public CA entity. The various CAs have various requirements for identifying that you are who you say you are.

The CA issues a certificate that blinks a public key to the name on the certificate identifies (in our case a server). Certificates issued by a public CA help prevent the use of fake public keys for impersonation. This provides the client the confidence to know that when they send their credit card information to our site, only our server will be able to decrypt it. Certificates work via transitive trust. In other words, the client trusts the CA to truly identify the server. So once the client verifies the certificate, the client trusts the server (if the CA trusts the server, I trust the server). The transitive trust can be several levels from an eventual root CA. You can see the CAs that your browser currently trusts. Do this in IE5 by going to tools/internet options/content/certificates/trusted root certificate authorities. You should see a screen similar to Figure 39-3:

Establishing server authentication via a digital signature is a five-step process:

1. The server presents its certificate to the client.
2. Client checks the certificate's valid dates.
3. Client checks the name of the issuing CA to see if it trusts that CA.
4. Client validates the CA's public key to the certificate's digital signature.

5. Client compares the domain name in the certificate to the domain name of the server.

Once the server is authenticated, the two systems proceed with SSL as explained earlier.

What Is a Digital Signature?

A digital signature is used in much the same way as a handwritten signature. Digital signatures use the same technology as public/private encryption. Signatures are often used with e-mail, as they ensure the origin of an e-mail message.

Simply stated, an e-mail message is sent in clear text. The text is encrypted with the originator's private key and is sent along with the clear text. The recipient takes the clear text and encrypts it with the sender's public key. The recipient then compares the two encrypted texts, also known as the hash. If the hashes match, the signature is authenticated. It is impossible for the sender to deny sending the message at a later time. If an imposter were to send a signed message, the hashes would not match.

Securing the Client

Client certificates are another way to add security to your site. A client certificate works in much the same way as a server certificate. A client certificate is a method of authenticating a user to a server.

Obviously, you wouldn't want to use certificates for a general merchandise e-commerce site. So when would you want to use client certificates? Think about online banking as an example. The bank could provide the customer with a client certificate as an added layer of protection. Another example might be a business-to-business supplier. On the client side, only the purchasing agent is allowed to place orders. In that case, a client certificate could be installed on the purchasing agent's computer.

One significant difference between client and server certificates is the source for the certificate. In a server certificate, there is generally one certificate from a single CA (such as Verisign). With a client certificate, you may have several certificates installed from multiple CAs. For example, you might have a certificate issued by your online bank, and another certificate issued from your online brokerage. You can see any personal certificates you already have installed; in IE5 go to tools/internet options/content/certificates/personal.

Summary

In this chapter, we have introduced the concepts of encryption. We saw that encryption has been used since the days of Julius Caesar.

We have introduced a lot of basic information about encryption keys, digital signatures, digital certificates, and public key infrastructure that are important when writing applications that take advantage of the features of these technologies. We touched upon secure sockets layer and the advantages and limitations of that technology. Later in this book, we will be exploring these tools in more detail and will use them in our sample site.

KEVIN LUNDY attended the Florida Institute of Technology (now known simply as Florida Tech), where he earned a bachelor's degree in oceanography. After graduation, he began working as an offshore geophysical engineer out of New Orleans. Lundy earned an M.S. degree in computer systems management. He is now the director of IT for a prominent surviving dot.com.

Section 7

Web Development Power Tool Tutorials

Web development has become complex. As a result simple web design tools such as Microsoft's FrontPage are usually insufficient. Instead, we need a suite of tools that will create a complete and robust system for deployment on the web.

What you'll learn in this section:

1. How to use OracleMobile Online Studio.
2. How to connect SAP to the Web.
3. How to use a diagrammatic tool called 001 to generate complete Web sites.
4. How to use Oracle's PowerBuilder to generate Web sites.
5. The differences between Custom Tag Libraries and Javabeans.

mySAP : Connecting SAP to the Web

Mohamed H. Judi

mySAP is more than just an e-business solution; it is SAP's answer to integrating your enterprise's value chain from end to end. Therefore, by developing mySAP components, SAP is treating e-business as an integrated part of the whole business and demanding new IT architecture.

The new architecture in demand is a component-based, open, frictionless, and scalable environment. It uses the Internet as its main communication platform. The main four components of mySAP are Workplace, Marketplace, Business Scenarios, and Application Hosting.

Figure 40-1 shows that with a single sign-on to mySAP Workplace, you can have access to internal and external systems in your enterprise just from your Internet browser. In the coming sections, I will explain how to build a role-based and personalized employee portal, which demonstrates Figure 40-1 in practice.

SAP Middleware Technologies

Before we start building an employee portal, it is imperative to understand how SAP connects mySAP and non-SAP systems to the Internet. SAP uses three different ways to serve SAP applications over the Internet.

Internet Transaction Server

Internet Transaction Server (ITS) is the standard interface between all mySAP components and the Web. With the delivered IACs (Internet Application Components), standard business transactions from the R/3 world can be directly transferred to the Internet on a simple browser interface.

Since R/3 is using a proprietary communication protocol different from HTTP used between the Web browser and Web server, ITS is needed to translates HTML into RFC

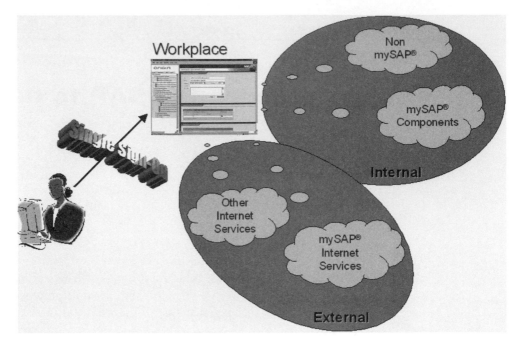

Figure 40-1. *Sign-in to mySAP.*

calls and vice versa. ITS is a relatively simple piece of software, which does principally the following actions repeatedly:

- Send an HTML form to the browser.
- Receive the filled form.
- Extract the form data from the form.
- Call the appropriate transaction in R/3.
- Catch the transaction result screen.
- Transform the result into an HTML page.
- Send the HTML page to the browser.

Technically, ITS is a Web server application that interfaces via HTTP with a Web browser, and via other protocols with the back-end component system. Server-side scripting is a powerful feature of Web servers. You can find such a server application behind most CGI scripts.

ITS is not a true programming language, such as Java or Perl. It barely reproduces SAP transaction into HTML code. This is a characteristic and major flaw of the ITS. In order to bring individual logic into the Web communication, you would have to write transactions in ABAP, thus putting all intelligence into R/3. However, SAP also provides an outside/in approach to connect mySAP components to the Web. This loosely couples

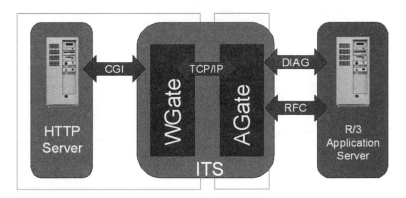

Figure 40-2. *ITS architecture.*

Web technology with SAP applications. In this case, most of the communication is attained in a stateless fashion. The logic is handled outside SAP, and a session is only opened with SAP application when objects are sent, or received, from the back-end application.

ITS consists of two main parts, AGate and WGate. The AGate is the part that integrates with the back-end component, and WGate is the part that integrates with the Web site. Both parts communicate via TCP/IP. It is required that you run AGate on an NT/2000 server. You can run WGate on any NT/2000 or Unix server. Figure 40-2 illustrates the ITS architecture.

Business Connector

The SAP Business Connector (BC) allows you to extend and enhance your SAP system using open and nonproprietary technology. The SAP Business Connector allows for bidirectional communication to and from the SAP server. With the Business Connector, you can:

Execute SAP Remote Function Calls (RFCs) from the SAP BC server. You can access all SAP functionality that is available via RFCs from SAP Business Connector server. It is possible to easily create XML-based SAP BC services that execute RFCs. Usually, you will create SAP BC services for SAP Business Application Programming Interfaces (BAPIs), which are formalized RFCs with well-defined input and output specifications. I will explain BAPIs in this document as the third method of integrating SAP systems. To execute an RFC on the SAP server, applications within your organization call up the SAP BC services. In the same way, your business partners can make requests over the Internet to call up a service that executes an RFC.

Execute SAP BC services from SAP systems. You can create remote function calls (RFCs) that call up SAP BC services residing on the SAP Business Connector server. Creating

SAP RFCs from SAP BC services allows the SAP users to access the information that is available to the SAP Business Connector server.

Route SAP business documents (IDocs) based on criteria you specify. SAP Business Connector server provides rich routing capabilities for IDocs. IDocs are EDI-equivalent data containers of SAP. You can configure the SAP Business Connector server to send an IDoc to another SAP system, the mySAP portal, non-SAP system, or to a remote URL in an XML format.

You can install and configure the SAP Business Connector in a very short time. By reusing existing infrastructure and expertise, the cost of deployment is low. Using the SAP Business Connector, you do not need software integration on your partners' side; you can directly link to XML and HTML Web sites over the Internet. The SAP Business Connector allows you to increase efficiency across the supply chain and customer loyalty by tightly integrating your business infrastructure with that of any partner.

The SAP Business Connector incorporates a fully developed RFC server and client. These provide real-time bidirectional communication to and from the SAP system. From SAP perspective, calling the SAP Business Connector is no different from calling any other RFC server. SAP converts its proprietary RFC format to XML or HTML, so you do not need SAP software on the other side.

The SAP Business Connector supports both synchronous (RFC) as well as asynchronous (tRFC) calls from SAP systems transparently. Therefore, BC supports BAPIs and ALE (SAP's EDI-equivalent protocol) scenarios.

SAP can convert IDocs to a structured document with direct access to each single field. This allows you to modify an IDoc's contents easily. For example, you can customize incoming IDocs based on local data format, if this is required. You also may simply access existing BAPIs in SAP systems from a browser or client application, or send XML documents to the SAP system. As you can see, developing applications with the SAP Business Connector requires no knowledge of SAP data structures, significantly reducing deployment time and cost.

Direct BAPI Calls

Business Application Programming Interfaces (BAPIs) are business functions in the SAP system written in its primary programming language, ABAP. As mentioned in the previous section, BAPIs are formalized RFCs (Remote Function Calls).

SAP has introduced object-oriented technology into the R/3 system by making R/3 processes and data available in the form of the SAP business object types.

A Business Object Type:

- Is a software representation of the real-world object.
- Encapsulates business logic.

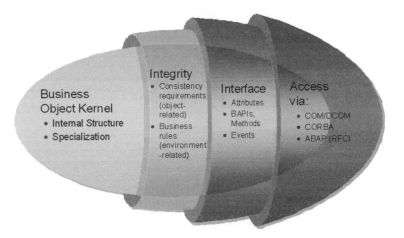

Figure 40-3. *A Business Object Type.*

- Allows access through only defined interfaces (BAPIs).
- Hides internal details, thus implementation can change, while the outside remains the same.
- Is stored and managed in SAP's Business Object Repository (BOR).

Figure 40-3 illustrates graphically the different layers in a Business Object Type. The diagram shows the different structural layers of the Business Object Type: The Kernel, Integrity, Interface, and Access.

An example of a Business Object Type would be a Customer. Figure 40-4 shows a Customer object with all associated methods and import-export parameters.

The GetDetail1 (Figure 40-5) method enables you to call up detailed information on a customer.

In Figure 40-6, a green light (i.e., those that don't say STOP) indicates that the method is released and can be used.

If you click on the green light beside the Create Online method, the system takes you to the Function Builder transaction, where you can display or make any changes. The following is the ABAP source code behind this method:

```
FUNCTION bapi_customer_create.
 DATA: verbuchter_kunde LIKE kna1-kunnr,
       msgv1 LIKE sy-msgv1.

 SET PARAMETER ID 'DEBITOR_VERBUCHT' FIELD ' '.
 CALL TRANSACTION 'XD01'.

 GET PARAMETER ID 'DEBITOR_VERBUCHT' FIELD verbuchter_kunde.
```

```
IF verbuchter_kunde is initial.
 CALL FUNCTION 'BALW_BAPIRETURN_GET1'
   EXPORTING
      type = 'I'
      cl   = 'F2'
      number    = 246
IMPORTING
   bapireturn = return.
ELSE.
 GET PARAMETER ID 'KUN' FIELD customer.
 customerno = customer.
 MOVE verbuchter_kunde TO msgv1.
 CALL FUNCTION 'BALW_BAPIRETURN_GET1'
 EXPORTING
  type   = 'I'
  cl     = 'F2'
  number    = 247
  par1   = msgv1
 IMPORTING
   bapireturn = return.
 ENDIF.
ENDFUNCTION.
```

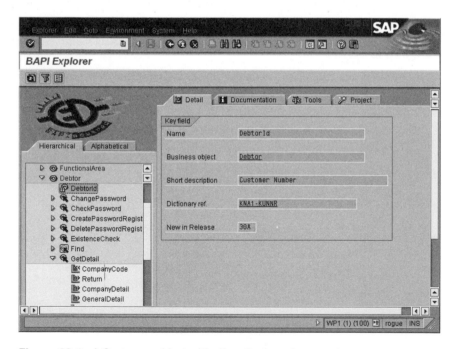

Figure 40-4. *A Customer object with all methods and parameters.*

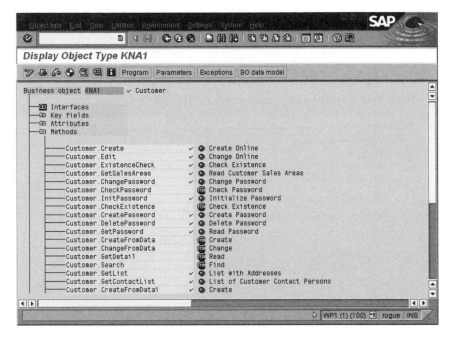

Figure 40-6. *Releasing a method.*

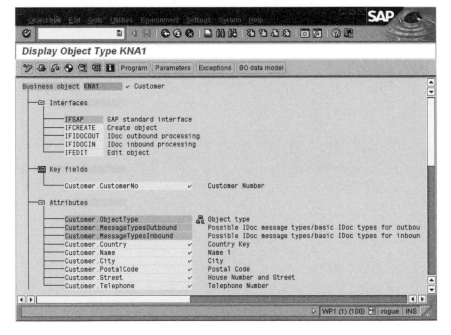

Figure 40-5. *Calling up detailed information on a customer.*

mySAP Workplace

mySAP Workplace is an enterprise portal providing users with fast, easy access to all the internal and external applications, business content, and services they require to perform their work tasks. It has a personalized, role-based interface that you can configure and customize according to personal user preferences. Features such as Roles, MiniApps, LaunchPad, and Drag and Relate transform the desktop into the ultimate productivity-enhancing engine.

Figure 40-7 shows mySAP Workplace architecture. Similar to other components within the mySAP landscape, Workplace needs middleware to connect to the Internet. ITS Middleware consists of two DLL instances, AGate (Application Gate) and the WGate (Web Gate). It is possible to install the ITS on the same box with its component, or, for scalability purposes, you can install each instance on a separate machine. However, for accessibility reasons, SAP does not recommend that you install Workplace with other components.

mySAP Workplace includes a number of predefined user roles to accommodate the individual user's preferences, corporate role, and level of authority. The mySAP Workplace Release 2.11 contains over 200 cross-component and cross-application templates for composite roles including single roles, which you can use or adapt according to your requirements. In addition to cross-industry templates, there are also industry-specific templates for composite roles and single roles. You can use these templates to help you organize your roles on the mySAP Workplace server more quickly.

Technically, the difference between single and composite roles is as follows:

A composite role template defines the LaunchPad in the mySAP Workplace and contains all the activities, functions, information, and services from different systems that a

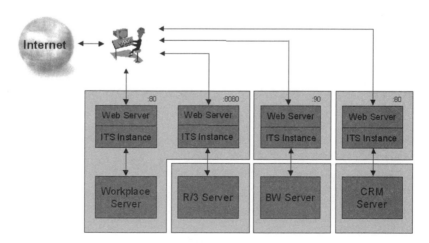

Figure 40-7. The mySAP Workplace architecture.

user with a certain role requires to accomplish his or her daily tasks. You can also assign more than one role to a user.

The following release-dependent information is contained in the composite roles:

- mySAP transactions
- URLs
- Documentation

The composite role templates are only on the mySAP Workplace Server.

A single role consists of a group of activities, functions, and services from just one target system (e.g., R/3). A single role contains the following release-dependent information:

- Transactions from one mySAP component
- Web addresses (URLs)
- MiniApps
- Documentation
- Authorizations for the included transactions
- Attributes for subsequent filtering or tailoring to your company-internal requirements. The role is tailored according to the following criteria: connected component system, country, industry, and application component.
- Component variable or logical system name (target system)

The single-role templates are available both in the respective component systems and on the mySAP Workplace server. As of release 4.6C, if you make any changes to single roles in the mySAP Workplace, the system will automatically update those roles in the respective component system via ALE. It is also still possible to get roles information from the component system in Workplace using RFC.

Generally, each composite role supplied to you in the Workplace Release 2.11 consists of several single-role templates. These single role templates contain access to all the activities and functions that are contained in the composite role. Note that each single role provides activities, functions, information, or services from just one component system.

Depending on your landscape, you need to copy the appropriate templates and modify them according to your special requirements. For example, a SAP pre-configured composite role could contain single roles targeting systems not in your landscape, such as Customer Relationship Management (CRM) or Business Information Warehouse (BW), and therefore you need to remove those roles from your composite role. Figure 40-8 shows an example of a composite role and its constituent single roles.

As you can see from Figure 40-8, each role has a target system assigned to it. For example, the R3100 variable is defined as the logical system WP1CLNT100 (SAP R/3 4.6C) in ALE. In case this target system changed, you only change the logical system assigned to the variable R3100, and that will ensure all roles assigned to this variable are properly assigned to the right logical system.

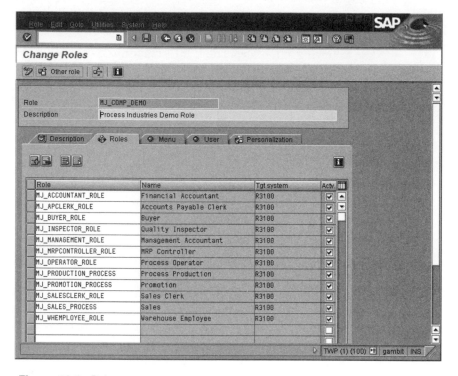

Figure 40-8. *Roles.*

Defining a Single Role

Before you can assign a role to a user, you have to define the role in transaction code PFCG first. As of Basis release 4.6C, you can define your roles in the mySAP Workplace server and distribute them to all target systems. The following example assumes that you have already fully configured Workplace and R/3 clients. In our case, we will work with mySAP Workplace 2.10 and SAP R/3 4.6C.

Starting from the Workplace server, go to transaction code PFCG. There are different ways to start this transaction. The easiest way is by clicking on the button "Create role" in the SAP Easy Access toolbar (Figure 40-9).

As shown Figure 40-10, enter a name for your role, then click on the "Create role" button.

After you click on "Create role," you need to give your role a brief description (Figure 40-11) and save before you can proceed to the other tabs. Next, you need to design a menu for your role.

Figure 40-9. *The Easy Access toolbar.*

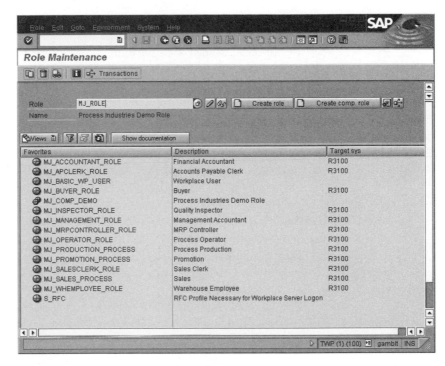

Figure 40-10. *Entering a name and then creating a role.*

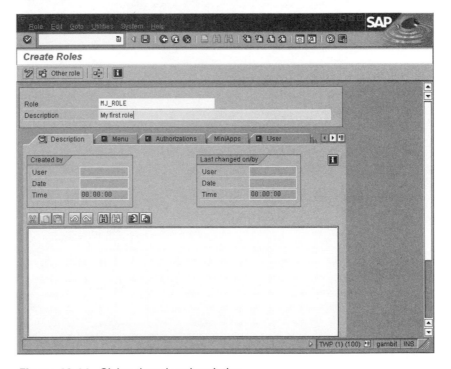

Figure 40-11. *Giving the role a description.*

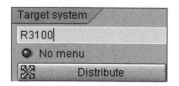

Figure 40-12. *Entering a Logical System code.*

In order to start building a menu for your role, go to the Menu tab to construct the menu structure for this role. Before you start inserting menu nodes, enter the target system that you will be calling R/3 transactions from. In this field, enter a logical system code or its variable (Figure 40-12).

To start building your menu, you can insert SAP transactions, reports from various sources, Web resources, and local files. If you have a list of transaction codes, reports, or other node that you would like to include in the menu, the top three buttons—Transaction, Report, and Other—will allow you to enter specific codes. However, if you do not know specific codes, it is also possible to insert transactions from the SAP standard menu, other roles, or area menus, or even to import a flat ASCII file (Figure 40-13).

In case you decided to insert transactions from menus, a pop-up dialog box will ask you to specify from which system you want to call these menus: local or remote target (Figure 40-14).

When you select the desired system, the menu from that system will show up. As you can see from Figure 40-15, it is a matter of selecting what you want to include in your

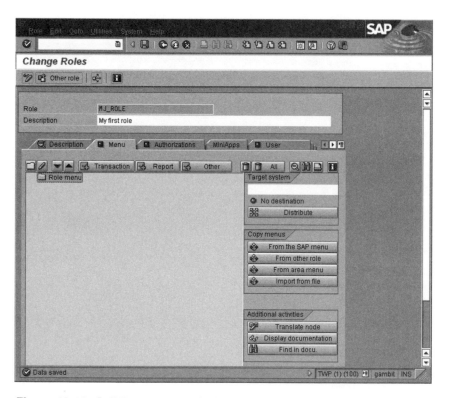

Figure 40-13. *Building your menu by inserting resources.*

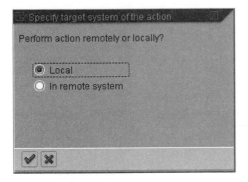

Figure 40-14. *Choosing the local or remote target.*

role menu. Select what you think should be in the role, and transfer all selected menu branches to your role. After you finish building your menu, save; you will be asked whether you want to distribute the role to the target system.

As soon as you add nodes to your role, the tab light indicator will turn green, indicating that you have menu structure now defined (Figure 40-16). This does not mean the user can execute any of the transactions you included in the role. You still need to give the user authorizations to run these transactions in the component system. Since your role has R/3 as the target system (component), we will have to generate authorizations in that system.

Before I take you to the component system to generate role profiles, let us add a MiniApp to the role (Figure 40-17). As you will see later, MiniApps are the "push" part of the Workplace portal. Through these small windows, you can push information to users as they sign on to their Workplace.

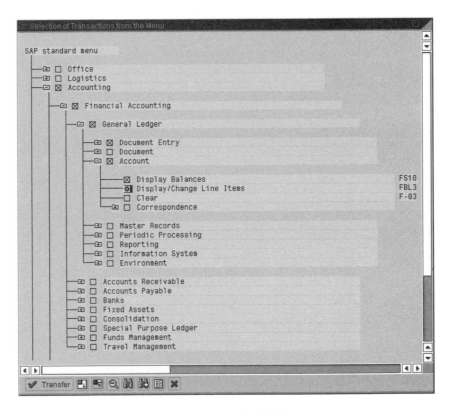

Figure 40-15. *Selecting what you want to include in your system.*

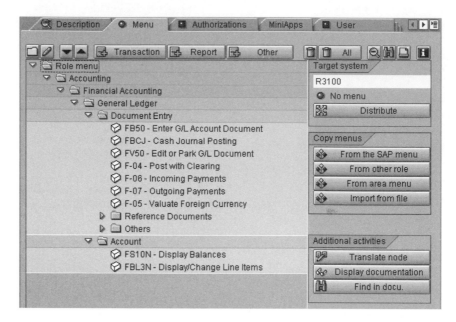

Figure 40-16. *The menu tab, shown here in gray, turns green, indicating that menu structure has been defined.*

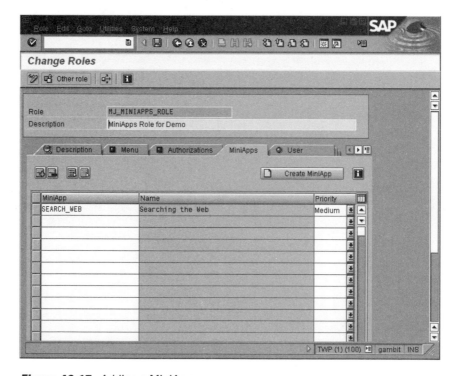

Figure 40-17. *Adding a MiniApp.*

For example, information pushed to users in the MiniApp can be performance indicators, news, and important messages from their Inbox.

As of Basis release 4.6C, you should centrally manage MiniApps from within the Workplace server in the Web Application Builder. If you have MiniApps included in your roles using the old procedure in prior Basis releases, it is still possible to maintain those MiniApps by accessing the old transaction from the Goto menu.

Figure 40-18 shows the Web Application Builder, where you maintain MiniApps and other Web applications under the new procedure.

The next step before we move to the component (target) system is assigning users to this role. As you can see in Figure 40-19, all users assigned to the role are listed under the User tab. When you add users to this list and save, the system will synchronize what you enter here with data in the user master record (transaction code, SU01).

By now, you are ready to generate an authorizations profile for this role in the component system. If you did all your ALE configurations properly, when you saved the role, the target system indicator light will turn green, indicating that the distribution of your role definition has been completed successfully.

In the mySAP Core (R/3 4.6C) component, you must generate authorization profiles for all the roles that you created in Workplace. You can simply do this in the transaction PFCG, Authorizations tab (Figure 40-20).

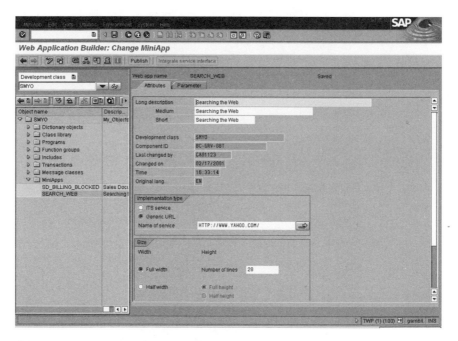

Figure 40-18. Maintaining MiniApps.

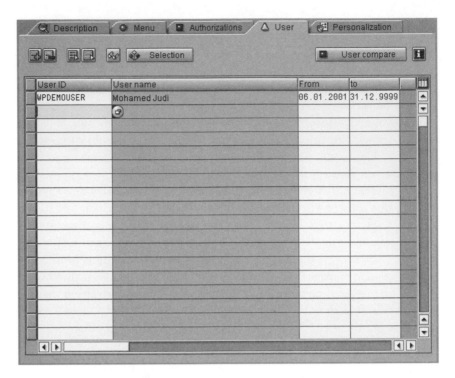

Figure 40-19. *Assigning users.*

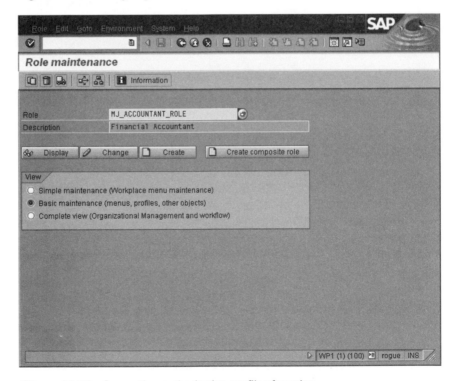

Figure 40-20. *Generating authorization profiles for roles.*

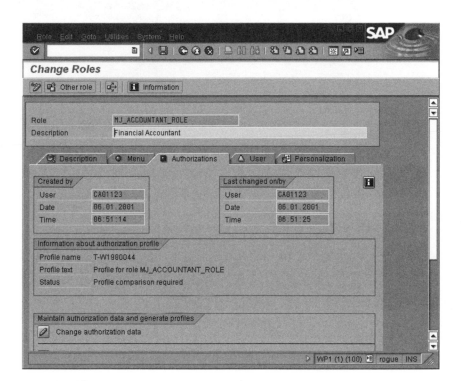

Figure 40-21. *Giving users authorization to run transactions.*

In the following steps, we are going to give users assigned to MJ_ACCOUN-TANT_ROLE authorization to run all transactions that you included in the menu structure (Figure 40-21).

If you click on the "Change authorization data" button at the bottom of the Authorizations tab, you will end up in the Profile Generator transaction, shown in Figure 40-22.

For some of you who worked with authorizations in SAP, the new Profile Generator is intuitively designed to facilitate what used to be a very painful experience. SAP uses indicator lights and other legends to explain the status of each authorization object. There are green, yellow, and red lights indicating whether profile can be generated.

After entering all missing values, all lights are green, and therefore technically generating the profile is now possible (Figure 40-23). This of course doesn't mean the user got the right authorizations in terms of business requirements.

After you generate the profile for your role, the Authorizations tab indicator light will be green, which means all users assigned to this role are now able to access every transaction you included in their menu structure (Figure 40-24).

Now you are ready to test your setup. In order to ensure a single sign-on to all systems without having to log on to each component system every time you launch a transaction,

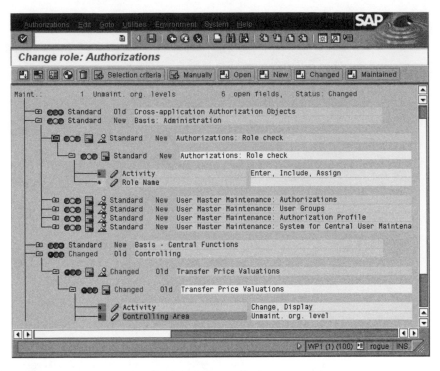

Figure 40-22. *The Profile Generator transaction.*

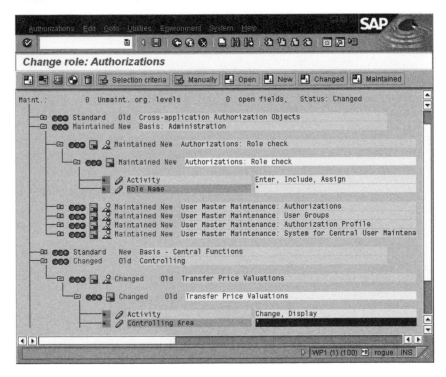

Figure 40-23. *Generation possible status.*

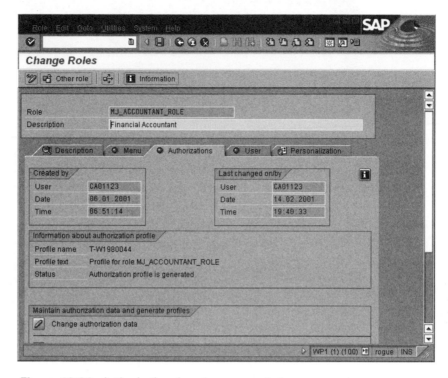

Figure 40-24. Authorizations have been generated.

the same username and password must exist in all components, using Cookies. This is an easy and free way of deploying Single Sign-On (SSO) in Workplace. The other more secured methods require digital certificates, which is not free.

Figure 40-25 shows the logon screen called by entering a URL in your browser window. After a successful sign-on, the PortalBuilder constructs your Workplace for you. As you can see from the following screen, the left-hand side of the Workplace is your LaunchPad, where you can "pull" information from the different target systems built in the menu structure. You can also drag and drop transactions from the role menu to your Favorites folder, or enter new Web addresses. The right-hand side of the Workplace represents the "push" portion of the portal, where MiniApps are shown. In the same area, transactions called from the LaunchPad are displayed, as you can see in Figure 40-26.

In our example, the MiniApp used is just a URL for the Yahoo Web site. In real-life situations, Web sites are not good examples of MiniApps. Due to their stateless nature, outside-in applications are very good candidates for MiniApp implementation. Examples of what could be a good MiniApp application are:

- Alerts
- Critical reports
- Corporate news

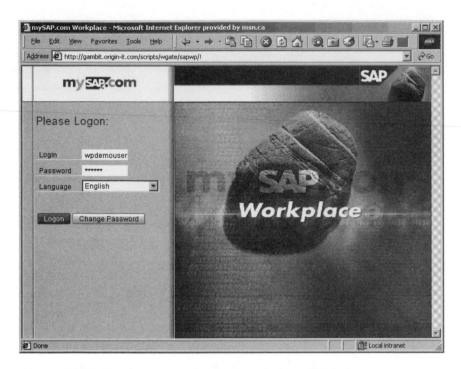

Figure 40-25. *The logon screen is called by entering a URL in the browser window.*

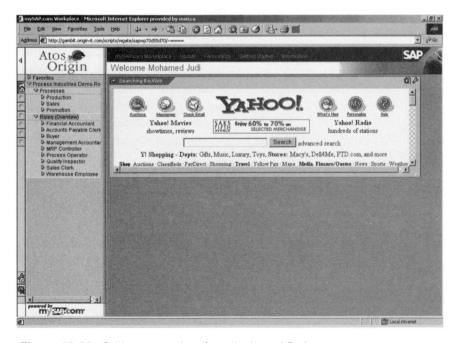

Figure 40-26. *Calling transactions from the LaunchPad.*

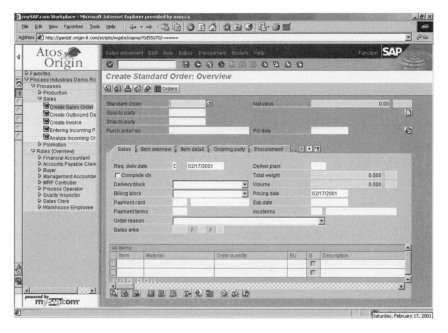

Figure 40-27. *Example of a good MiniApp.*

- Performance indicators
- Important e-mails and faxes
- Open orders (Figure 40-27)

A thorough discussion of the mySAP Workplace is certainly beyond the scope of this chapter; however, you should now have a high level understanding of what Workplace can offer your organization and how mySAP is currently structured. The landscape is constantly changing, but one thing is becoming a fact: SAP is moving away from the "one black box" model to the component and Web-based architecture.

> *Note: All trademarks, trade names, and logos contained within this document are used in an editorial context only and are the property of their respective owners.*

MOHAMED H. JUDI is a consultant in enterprise solutions at Atos Origin, Inc., a global end-to-end, front-to-back office business solutions enabler. At Atos Origin, Mr. Judi is one of 27,000 internationally experienced professionals partnering with Atos Origin's clients to transform them into e-communities. Throughout his career life, Mr. Judi helps organizations realize their information technology goals. In his role, he is assisting organizations in various industries to implement end-to-end enterprise solutions and customize solutions with speed and efficiency. Mr. Judi is a certified SAP and BaaN consultant with more than 12 years' experience in implementing ERP systems and more than two years of e-business experience. He has a unique mix of business, functional, and technical skills that best position him to understand his clients' business requirements and implement the wisest solution for them. Prior to working at Atos Origin, Mr. Judi handled various consulting responsibilities internationally for tier-one and tier-two organizations. Mr. Judi received his postgraduate certificate in business administration from Sheffield Hallam University, UK, and his B.Sc. degree in Operations Research from the University of Riyadh, Saudi Arabia.

Using OracleMobile Online Studio

Kai Li

OracleMobile Online Studio is an online environment for you to build, test, and deploy your mobile applications for the OracleMobile hosted platform. It provides an incredibly short time-to-market solution for wireless enablement of your web content allowing your content to be accessed by all mobile devices including phones, PDAs, pagers, and through multiple interfaces including voice. Content such as e-business applications can be enabled in days or even hours depending on the complexity of the content. The value proposition for you, the developer, is that you can focus on your business logic which is your core competency, and let OracleMobile focus on the device complexity, our core competency. To aid your development, this guide provides detailed information on how you can use OracleMobile Online Studio.

Online Studio's build, test, and deploy model is new and unique to software development. It presents a hosted approach to developing dynamic content. You do not need to download any software or tools to start using Online Studio. All you need to do is access the OracleMobile Online Studio website, register, and login. Once authenticated, you will have access to reusable modules, examples, documentation, runtime information, and other useful resources. Deploying your mobile application is seamless. With a few mouse clicks, you can deploy your application to OracleMobile's consumer website (http://www.oraclemobile.com) or your company's wireless website hosted by Oracle-Mobile (see the Deploying Your Application section for more information).

Advantages of Using OracleMobile Online Studio

Following are some of the many reasons you should use Online Studio as part of your mobile development effort:

- Support for any device and any network without any special programming or setup required. Online Studio is hosted and ready to go. OracleMobile's business is to support any device on any network or protocol.

- Allows mobile applications to seamlessly leverage pre-built services packaged as OracleMobile modules such as Driving Directions and Location modules.
- Enables a company's customers to instantly access mobile services from http://www.oraclemobile.com, a scalable and secure wireless website with 7×24 guaranteed service. Deployment of applications from Online Studio to this website is seamless and immediate with just a few mouse clicks. If you have a wireless website hosted by OracleMobile, deployment to that website is just as easy.
- Lets you market your new hosted mobile applications as modules for use by other developers.
- No cost to you. Testing and deployment are free of charge.

Building Your Application

The first step in building your mobile application is developing it using your own tools and platform. Your development infrastructure is transparent to Online Studio. This allows you to leverage the investment in your current infrastructure. Online Studio is also transparent to the mechanism used to generate the presentation logic of your mobile application. Examples of these mechanisms are CGI, JavaServer Pages, and Active Server Pages. For Online Studio to work, the presentation logic of your application must return content compliant with our MobileXML DTD (Table 41-1) MobileXML consists of a set of device-neutral XML tags specifically designed for small screen devices and voice.

Generating MobileXML

After trying some of the examples and understanding how MobileXML is rendered on devices, you can develop dynamic content on your own web server and provide the Online Studio with a link to that content through your web server. You simply need to set up a HTTP URL to link to your application's entry point which contains code that generates MobileXML. This XML will be transformed by Online Studio to the individual device content formats understood by each unique device, for example, WML for WAP-compliant devices.

To generate MobileXML, you can use any of the traditional means of generating dynamic HTML such as JavaServer Pages, CGI, or Active Server Pages. Hence, instead of generating HTML, the code or script generates MobileXML. The following code snippets illustrate how.

Using JavaServer Pages

JavaServer Pages (JSP) is the presentation layer for Java-centric web applications. In standard web applications where HTML browsers are the client, JSPs generate HTML to

SimpleContainer

The super element which is the parent of all the other elements in the MobileXML DTD.

Sample code:
```
<SimpleContainer>
 <SimpleText>
  <SimpleTextItem>Hello There!</SimpleTextItem>
  <SimpleTextItem>Hello Again!</SimpleTextItem>
 </SimpleText>
</SimpleContainer>
```

Action

This element defines a navigation point a user can use. This tag expects voice input of specified type, and if recognized, navigates to the destination specified by target attribute. The following are the attributes and values explained according to their usage.

Usage 1:
```
<Action type="nospeech | nomatch | badnext | anyerror"
    target=destination
    reprompt="Y | N"
    ordinal=integer
    label=label
    task="GO">text</Action>
```

where type values are:
nospeech—If there is no response in 3 to 4 seconds, target is invoked.
nomatch—If user's voice input is not recognized, target is invoked.
badnext—If illegal markup is returned after target is invoked.
anyerror—On any error condition, target is invoked.

This usage scenario allows error handling to be tuned based on the valid values for type. If *text* is not recognized, the appropriate error handling occurs based on value for type.

Usage 2:
```
<Action type="SOFT1"
    voicelabel=text | voicetitle=text
    target=destination
    task="GO"
    label=label></Action>
```

If the value of type is SOFT1, either *text* in voicelabel or voicetitle is expected. Note that label or title can also be used, but will be superceded by voicelabel or voicetitle respectively.

Usage 3:
```
<Action type="HELP"
    target=destination
```

```
      task="GO"
      label=label>help text</Action>
```

Input grammar "help" is expected and *help text* is output to user using text-to-speech.

Usage 4:

```
<Action type="PREV"
      target=destination
      task="GO"
      label=label></Action>
```

Input grammar "cancel" is expected and target is invoked.

Usage 5:

```
<Action type="ACCEPT"
      target=destination
      task="GO"
      label=label></Action>
```

If type is ACCEPT, this is an implicit link. There is no pause or prompt after current card has completed before target is invoked.

Sample code:

```
<SimpleContainer>
 <SimpleText>
  <Action label="Main" type="SOFT1" task="GO" target="">
  </Action>
  <SimpleTextItem>Hello World!</SimpleTextItem>
 </SimpleText>
</SimpleContainer>
```

SimpleText   This element contains one or more blocks of plain text (abstracted by SimpleTextItem).

Sample code:

```
<SimpleContainer>
 <SimpleText>
  <SimpleTextItem>Hello There!</SimpleTextItem>
  <SimpleTextItem>Hello Again!</SimpleTextItem>
 </SimpleText>
</SimpleContainer>
```

SimpleTextItem   This element contains one block of plain text, typically a single paragraph. By default, text-to-speech synthesis is used to represent the text enclosed in these tags. An attribute can be specified to override the default. This attribute has the syntax:

```
audiosrc="http://www.domain.com/filename.wav"
```

The WAV file specified should be in 8-bit mulaw.

Sample code:
```
<SimpleContainer>
 <SimpleText>
  <SimpleTextItem>Hello There!</SimpleTextItem>
  <SimpleTextItem>Hello Again!</SimpleTextItem>
  <SimpleTextItem>Hello<SimpleBreak/>a third
  time!</SimpleTextItem>
 </SimpleText>
</SimpleContainer>
```

SimpleMenu

This element represents a single menu with selectable links which are defined by the children SimpleMenuItem elements.

Sample code:
```
<SimpleContainer>
  <SimpleMenu title="Select one of the following foods:">
   <SimpleMenuItem target="?food=meat">Meat</SimpleMenuItem>
   <SimpleMenuItem target="?food=veg">Vegetables
   </SimpleMenuItem>
   <SimpleMenuItem target="?food=fruits">Fruits
   </SimpleMenuItem>
   <SimpleMenuItem target="?food=seafood">Seafood
   </SimpleMenuItem>
  </SimpleMenu>
</SimpleContainer>
```

SimpleMenuItem

This element represents a single, selectable option in a menu defined by SimpleMenu. <SimpleMenuItem> translates to voice as "Your options are . . . .". For example:
```
<SimpleContainer>

 <SimpleMenu title="Select one of the following colors:">
  <SimpleMenuItem target="?color=red">red</SimpleMenuItem>
  <SimpleMenuItem target="?color=blue">blue</SimpleMenuItem>
  <SimpleMenuItem
  target="?color=green">green</SimpleMenuItem>

 </SimpleMenu>

</SimpleContainer>
```

The above will be vocalized in text-to-speech as:

"Select one of the following colors. Your options are red, blue, green."

Additional parameters:

voiceitem
```
<SimpleMenuItem voiceitem="color red"
        target="?color=red">red</SimpleMenuItem>
```

The voiceitem attribute supercedes the text between the tags. In this case, "color red" will be synthesized to speech rather than "red."

voicekey

```
<SimpleMenuItem voiceitem="color red"
        voicekey="r"
        target="?color=red">red</SimpleMenuItem>
```

The voicekey attribute is used as input grammar instead of the voiceitem attribute. The above will be synthesized to voice as:

"Select one of the following colors. Your options are color red, blue, green. For color red, say r."

Sample code:

```
<SimpleContainer>
 <SimpleMenu title="Select one of the following foods:">
  <SimpleMenuItem target="?food=meat">Meat</SimpleMenuItem>
  <SimpleMenuItem
  target="?food=veg">Vegetables</SimpleMenuItem>
  <SimpleMenuItem
  target="?food=fruits">Fruits</SimpleMenuItem>
  <SimpleMenuItem
  target="?food=seafood">Seafood</SimpleMenuItem>
 </SimpleMenu>
</SimpleContainer>
```

SimpleForm   This element is used for displaying one or more input fields. The fields are presented using the SimpleFormItem and SimpleFormSelect elements.

Sample code:

```
<SimpleContainer>
 <SimpleForm target="processForm.jsp">
  <Action label="Cancel" type="ACCEPT" task="GO"
    target="cancel.jsp"></Action>
  <Action label="Main" type="ACCEPT" task="GO"
    target="../main.jsp"></Action>
  <SimpleFormItem name="zip"> Enter zip
code:</SimpleFormItem>
  <SimpleFormSelect name="genre" title="Category:">
   <SimpleFormOption value="Art">Art</SimpleFormOption>
   <SimpleFormOption
   value="Comedy">Comedy</SimpleFormOption>
   <SimpleFormOption
   value="Action">Action</SimpleFormOption>
   <SimpleFormOption value="Drama">Drama</SimpleFormOption>
   <SimpleFormOption
   value="Family">Family</SimpleFormOption>
   <SimpleFormOption
   value="Horror">Horror</SimpleFormOption>
```

```
    <SimpleFormOption value="Sci-Fi">Sci-
    Fi</SimpleFormOption>
    <SimpleFormOption value="Documentary">Documentary
    </SimpleFormOption>
   </SimpleFormSelect>
  </SimpleForm>
</SimpleContainer>
```

SimpleFormItem

For obtaining input from a user. This element opens a new card/screen, presents a prompt, and waits for input from the user. The content of this element, which is in parsable character format, specifies default values for the form item.

Sample code:
```
<SimpleContainer>
 <SimpleForm name="Starting"
            target="../processScripts/processStart.jsp">
  <Action label="OK" type="ACCEPT" task="GO"></Action>
  <SimpleFormItem name="addrInput">
            Driving Directions!
            Starting Street (OK if unknown)
  </SimpleFormItem>
  <SimpleFormItem name="zipInput">
            Starting Zip-Code or City State
            (e.g. 91305 or San Carlos CA)
  </SimpleFormItem>
 </SimpleForm>
</SimpleContainer>
```

SimpleFormSelect

This element opens a new card/screen and presents a number of selectable options to users.

Sample code:
```
<SimpleContainer>
 <SimpleForm target="processForm.jsp">
  <Action label="Cancel" type="ACCEPT" task="GO"
    target="cancel.jsp"></Action>
  <Action label="Main" type="ACCEPT" task="GO"
    target="../main.jsp"></Action>
  <SimpleFormItem name="zip"> Enter zip code:
  </SimpleFormItem>
  <SimpleFormSelect name="genre" title="Category:">
   <SimpleFormOption value="Art">Art
   </SimpleFormOption>
   <SimpleFormOption value="Comedy">Comedy
   </SimpleFormOption>
   <SimpleFormOption
   value="Action">Action</SimpleFormOption>
   <SimpleFormOption value="Drama">Drama</SimpleFormOption>
```

```
    <SimpleFormOption
    value="Family">Family</SimpleFormOption>
    <SimpleFormOption
    value="Horror">Horror</SimpleFormOption>
    <SimpleFormOption value="Sci-Fi">Sci-
    Fi</SimpleFormOption>
    <SimpleFormOption value="Documentary">Documentary
    </SimpleFormOption>
   </SimpleFormSelect>
  </SimpleForm></SimpleContainer>
```

SimpleFormOption　　This element is an item in a selectable menu. The content of this element, which is in parsable character format, specifies default values for the form item.

Sample code:
```
SimpleContainer>
 <SimpleForm target="processForm.jsp">
  <Action label="Cancel" type="ACCEPT" task="GO"
    target="cancel.jsp"></Action>
  <Action label="Main" type="ACCEPT" task="GO"
    target="../main.jsp"></Action>
  <SimpleFormItem name="zip"> Enter zip code:
  </SimpleFormItem>
  <SimpleFormSelect name="genre" title="Category:">
   <SimpleFormOption value="Art">Art
   </SimpleFormOption>
   <SimpleFormOption value="Comedy">Comedy
   </SimpleFormOption>
   <SimpleFormOption
   value="Action">Action</SimpleFormOption>
   <SimpleFormOption value="Drama">Drama</SimpleFormOption>
   <SimpleFormOption
   value="Family">Family</SimpleFormOption>
   <SimpleFormOption
   value="Horror">Horror</SimpleFormOption>
   <SimpleFormOption value="Sci-Fi">Sci-
   Fi</SimpleFormOption>
   <SimpleFormOption value="Documentary">Documentary
   </SimpleFormOption>
  </SimpleFormSelect>
 </SimpleForm></SimpleContainer>
```

SimpleImage　　Displays a WBMP or BMP image.

Sample code:
```
<SimpleContainer>
 <SimpleMenu title="Welcome to XYZ wireless news.
        What do you want to do:">
  <SimpleImage src="images/logo"/> <!—This will be rendered
                    above the SimpleMenu title.—>
```

```
<SimpleMenuItem target="?choice=lnews">Latest
News</SimpleMenuItem>
<SimpleMenuItem target="?choice=company">Company
Search</SimpleMenuItem>
<SimpleMenuItem
target="?choice=login">Login</SimpleMenuItem>
</SimpleMenu>
</SimpleContainer>
```

em   This element specifies text to be displayed in emphasized font. On different devices, this could be italic. This element is an OracleMobile hosting extension.

Sample code:
```
<SimpleContainer>
 <SimpleText>
  <SimpleTextItem><em>Welcome!</em></SimpleTextItem>
 </SimpleText>
</SimpleContainer>
```

strong   This element specifies text to be displayed in strong font. On different devices, this could be bold. This element is an OracleMobile hosting extension.

Sample code:
```
<SimpleContainer>
 <SimpleText>
  <SimpleTextItem><strong>Welcome!</strong></SimpleTextItem>
 </SimpleText>
</SimpleContainer>
```

SimpleBreak   Enables line breaks in a text string within SimpleTextItem.

Sample code:
```
<SimpleContainer>
 <SimpleText>
  <SimpleTextItem>Welcome<SimpleBreak/>to
  <SimpleBreak/>OracleMobile</SimpleTextItem>
 </SimpleText>
</SimpleContainer>
```

Table 41-1: *The MobileXML DTD defines the abstract device markup language used in the Online Studio application framework. The goal of the definitions is to be a superset of the markup languages for a variety of devices. Elements in the DTD represent elements of an abstract user interface which translate to device-specific formats. The following is a list of tag elements in the MobileXML DTD. Click on each element to see more details, and also, view the tag element tree. MobileXML is derived from the DTD of Portal-to-Go 1.0.2 with hosting extensions added. Note that the tag names are case-sensitive as below. Please note that the most current set of tags can be found online at http://studio.oraclemobile.com/omp/site/Documentation/tags/index.htm.*

these browsers. For mobile applications hosted by Online Studio, the JSPs output MobileXML instead of HTML. Consider the example below:

```
<?xml version="1.0" encoding="UTF-8"?>

<SimpleContainer>
    <%@ page language="java"
                import="java.util.*,
                        java.text.*
                "%>
<%
   Date date = new Date();
   String time = DateFormat.getTimeInstance().format(date);
%>

    <SimpleText>
       <SimpleTextItem>Current Time:
           <%=time%></SimpleTextItem>
    </SimpleText>
</SimpleContainer>
```

Note that this is very similar to generating HTML which implies that the learning curve for developing with Online Studio is very small.

Using CGI

Similar to JSPs, CGI can also be used to develop dynamic mobile applications simply by generating MobileXML instead of HTML. A simple example:

```
#!/usr/local/bin/Perl5
print "<SimpleContainer>";
print "<SimpleText>";
print "<SimpleTextItem>Hello There</SimpleTextitem>";
print "</SimpleText>";
print "</SimpleContainer>";
```

Linking to Modules

Modules allow you to link pre-built applications to your own thereby adding functionality beyond the scope of your own applications without having to develop them. The modules are provided to enable reuse of mobile services. For example, if you are developing an address book application, you can link the addresses in the book with our Driving Directions module. A user of your service can then select an address and obtain driving directions to it from an originating address. This can be achieved without you having to write another application to generate driving directions. You only need to specify the module's namespace reference in the "target" attribute of your service's XML tags and provide call back information to the module in the form of attributes.

Consider the following example which prompts a user for the starting address:

```
<!—Note: This example is not tested yet as the driving
     directions module is still in development.—>

<SimpleContainer>
    <SimpleForm target="omp://oraclemobile/directions/"
         callbackurl="" callbackparam="">
    <SimpleFormItem name="numStreet">
      Enter the number and street where you are starting:
    </SimpleFormItem>
    <SimpleFormItem name="city">
      Enter the city of your starting address:
    </SimpleFormItem>
    <SimpleFormItem name="state">
      Enter the state of your starting address:
    </SimpleFormItem>
    <SimpleFormItem name="zip">
      Enter the zip of your starting address:
    </SimpleFormItem>
    <Action type="ACCEPT" task="GO"
                  target="%value user.home.url%">
    </SimpleForm>
</SimpleContainer>
```

The syntax of the attributes required to use any module is:

```
target =
"omp://oraclemobile/moduleName&param1=value1&param2=value2"

callbackpath = "your_service's_path"

callbackparam = "paramName1=value&paramName2=value"
```

where:

moduleName is the name of the module shown in the modules list;

param1, value1, param2, value2 are parameters required by the module;

callbackpath is the path to the next service after module has completed execution (null if execution goes back to the same service which called the module);

callbackparam allows you to send state information to the next service specified by callbackpath after the module has completed execution. You can restore your application to the state it was in before it invoked the module or initialize it to another state. For a list of available modules and their parameter information, see http://studio. oraclemobile.com/omp/site/Documentation/modules/mobilemodules.htm.

Using Namespace References

A namespace system has been implemented to allow easy access to Mobile Modules. This namepsace is accessible using a URL-like syntax: omp://oraclemobile/*mobile_module_name*/. For example, the Location module can be accessed using omp://oraclemobile/location/.

A mobile application can invoke a Mobile Module by specifying this syntax in the "target" attribute of the appropriate MobileXML tag. For example, to invoke the Location module from <SimpleMenu>:

```
<SimpleMenu title="Address Finder">
  <SimpleMenuItem target="omp://oraclemobile/location">
  Look up address
  </SimpleMenuItem>
</SimpleMenu>
```

Using the callbackpath attribute, you can specify the next application or module execution should be transferred to after the invoked module has completed. Figure 41-1 depicts how this can be done.

Writing Scripts

In Online Studio, you can embed scripts in the MobileXML content of your application. Currently, the scripts allow your application to obtain a user's ID, name, and the

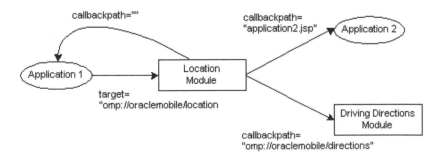

Figure 41-1. Invoking a Mobile module.

location of the user's home in the Online Studio namepsace. The functionality of the scripts will be expanded in the future. The script syntax is:

```
%value user.var_name%
```

where *var_name* is one of the following: id, name, or menu.home

---

Example:

```
<SimpleContainer>
  <SimpleText>
    <SimpleTextItem>
            Hello %value user.name%.
      </SimpleTextItem>
    <SimpleTextItem>
            This is your user ID %value user.id%.
      </SimpleTextItem>
      <SimpleTextItem>
            Your home is %value user.menu.home%.
        </SimpleTextItem>
  </SimpleText>
</SimpleContainer>
```

Adding Your Application to Online Studio

Once you have written application code to generate MobileXML and defined an HTTP URL to your web server, you can add an application in Online Studio to link to that XML content. Follow the instructions below:

1. Click My Studio on the navigation bar.
   Login if you haven't already.
2. Click Create New Application.
3. Edit the application details as follows:

Name—The name of your new application.
Remote URL—The HTTP URL to your content accessible on the internet (outside corporate firewalls).
Description—A description of your new application. This will appear in the modules list as the description of your application if you decide to make it a module.

Keywords—Searchable keywords used by the search engine in the www.oracle-mobile.com wireless website to find your application.

Comments—Information you can enter for yourself - will not be displayed to your users. You can bring up a history of comments for this application later.

4. Click Create Application. Your application is now registered in Online Studio.

Testing Your Application

Once you have specified the URL to your application in Online Studio, you can start running and testing it with actual mobile devices or simulators (see http://studio.oracle-mobile.com/omp/site/Support/resources.htm, simulator downloads).

To run your new application:

1. Click on My Studio in the left navigation bar.
2. Under My Applications, click on Edit link of your application.
   Take note of the last text box called Work Log. Use this box to view debug information when you run your application.
3. Invoke your application as follows:

   A. Using a small screen mobile device:
      1. Use your device's browser to go to http://studio.oraclemobile.com.
      2. Login with the same username/password as you did for the Online Studio website.
      3. Navigate to Applications.
      4. Select your new application.
      5. At the same time as you interact with your application, view the runtime messages in the debug log text box. If an error occurs, you can use the messages in this box for debugging. This box also shows the MobileXML generated by your application. You can see if there are any errors in the XML.
   B. Using a simulator:
      1. You can also use a simulator (phone, PDA, or voice in the near future) to test the application. With a phone or PDA simulator, go to the URL http://studio.oraclemobile.com. (Check out *Other Resources* to download simulators.)

Note that you can also run and test the supplied examples. Some of them can also be modifed (the static ones). By modifying the examples, you can prototype and test static services on Online Studio. This provides a way for you to quickly view the rendering of MobileXML on multiple devices and on voice when it becomes available.

Deploying Your Application

Once testing is complete, you can begin the deployment phase. Online Studio is an integrated component of the OracleMobile Hosting Platform and thus allows you to deploy an application to an OracleMobile-hosted website seamlessly (including www. oraclemobile.com).

The deployment process involves joining a domain other than the "default" domain. You are automatically a member of the "default" domain when you sign up, but you need to belong to a user-created domain in order to deploy. Domains other than the "default" domain are user-created. Domains in Online Studio are used to group applications together so that users who are members of the same domain can see the same applications. For the current version of Online Studio, this feature is not fully implemented. Domains can still be created and users can join them but users cannot yet see the common applications of each domain. However, when deploying an application, you still need to join a user-created domain for namespace uniqueness reasons. Others will be able to join your domain in the future if you supply them with your domain's password.

After you have joined a domain, the deployment process requires you to cut and paste a QuickLink Button from the Online Studio to your website. This button allows you to enable your users to invoke the actual deployment of your application to their specific user accounts in a OracleMobile-hosted website. When a user sees the button in your website and clicks on it, the HTTP URL for your mobile application is deployed to the associated OracleMobile-hosted website (the user is prompted for his/her username and password to the OracleMobile-hosted website when the button is clicked). When the user logs in to this website with a mobile device, he/she can see and invoke your application from the list of QuickLinks. (QuickLinks are services displayed at the top level of a user's menu of services. This allows the QuickLink services to be accessed without the need to navigate into the menu structure.)

The steps to perform deployment are:

1. Click the Deploy link next to your application's name.
2. Enter the information in the form fields. These are similar to those when you added your application.
3. Select either deployment to OracleMobile's consumer website or a website hosted by OracleMobile.
4. Follow the instructions on the screen to complete the deployment.

Sample Applications

```
1. Hello World

<SimpleContainer>
   <SimpleText>
```

```
    <SimpleTextItem>Hello World</SimpleTextItem>
   </SimpleText>
   <SimpleText>
    <SimpleTextItem>Hello Again</SimpleTextItem>
   </SimpleText>
</SimpleContainer>
```

On a WAP-compliant phone, the output looks like Figure 41-2.

```
2. Menu Example

<SimpleContainer>
  <SimpleMenu>
  <!—The JSP files targetted below generate dynamic content and
      return this content as MobileXML.—>
    <SimpleMenuItem
      Target="http://www.content.com/servicex/catalog.jsp">
      browse
    </SimpleMenuItem>

    <SimpleMenuItem
      Target="http://www.content.com/servicex/search.jsp">
      search
    </SimpleMenuItem>

    <SimpleMenuItem
      Target="http://www.content.com/servicex/cart.jsp">
      shopping cart
    </SimpleMenuItem>

  </SimpleMenu>
</SimpleContainer>
```

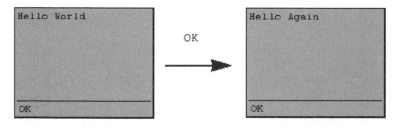

Figure 41-2. Hello World.

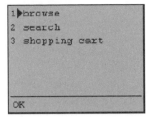

Figure 41-3. *The Menu Example.*

On a WAP-compliant phone, the output looks like Figure 41-3.

```
3. Form Example.

<SimpleContainer>
  <SimpleForm name="Starting" target="StartLocation.jsp">
  <Action label="OK" type="ACCEPT" task="GO"  target="">
  </Action>

    <SimpleFormItem name="addrInput">
     Driving Directions! Starting Street (OK if unknown)
    </SimpleFormItem>

    <SimpleFormItem name="zipInput">
    Starting Zip-Code or City State
    (e.g. 91305 or San Carlos CA)
    </SimpleFormItem>

  </SimpleForm>
</SimpleContainer>
```

On a WAP-compliant phone, the output looks like Figure 41-4.

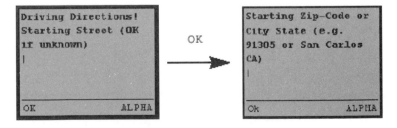

Figure 41-4. *The Form Example.*

KAI LI is a Senior Product Manager at OracleMobile. She can be reached at kai.li@ oracle.com.

Developing Web Applications with 001

Margaret H. Hamilton and William R. Hackler

In this chapter we show how software applications for the Web are developed with the 001 Tool Suite; also referred to as 001:Digital Gold, or simply 001, and pronounced "double-oh-one." (1–4) 001 was created to automate the mathematically based paradigm, Development Before the Fact (DBTF). (2–4) Along with its automation, DBTF has been used in research and "trail blazer" organizations; and is now being adopted for commercial use. (5–10)

In addition to its roots in real-world system design and software development, DBTF has roots in other worlds including systems theory, formal methods, formal linguistics, and object technology. Although it is new, it would be natural to make assumptions about what is possible and impossible based on its superficial resemblance to other technologies such as object technology. It helps, however, to suspend any and all preconceived notions when first introduced to DBTF, because DBTF is a world unto itself—a completely new way to think about systems and software.

Preventative Paradigm

What makes DBTF different is that it is a preventative paradigm instead of a curative one. Problems associated with traditional methods of design and development are prevented "before the fact" just by the way a system is defined. That is, DBTF concentrates on preventing problems of development from even happening; rather than letting them happen "after the fact" and fixing them after they've surfaced at the most inopportune and expensive point in time.

From the very beginning, a DBTF system inherently integrates all its own objects (and all aspects, relationships, and viewpoints of these objects) and the combinations of functionality using these objects; maximizes its own reliability and flexibility to change (including reconfiguration in real time, change of target requirements, and change of static and dynamic architectures and processes); capitalizes on its own parallelism; supports its own run-time performance analysis; and maximizes the potential for its own resource allocation, reuse, and automation.

Formal but Friendly Language

A formal systems language based on DBTF's foundations, 001AXES, is used to define a DBTF system. With this language, a system has properties that come along "for the ride" that in essence control its own destiny; because of these properties, many things heretofore not believed possible with traditional methods are now possible with DBTF (Table 42-1). DBTF's automation, 001, is used to ensure that these properties are captured throughout a system's design and development.

It is assumed a designer or developer would have received adequate training in 001 (in both its language and its environment) before using it. Although this chapter introduces 001's capabilities for developing Web applications, it is not our intent to provide a tutorial on 001AXES or 001.

Full Life-Cycle Environment

Although a total system engineering and software development environment, 001 can be used to coexist and interface with other tools. It can be used to prototype a system or develop a software system fully. 001 breaks the development life cycle into a sequence of stages, including: requirements and design modeling by formal specification and analysis; automatic code generation based on consistent and logically complete models; test and execution; and simulation.

001's motivation is to facilitate the "doing things right in the first place" development style, avoiding the "fixing wrong things up" traditional approach. To automate the theory, 001 is developed with the following considerations: error prevention from the early stage of system definition, life cycle control of the system under development, and inherent reuse of highly reliable systems.

001 provides traceability from requirements to design, implementation (for example, the code it generates has names corresponding to the original requirements), and testing; the system under development is manageable and maintainable. Systems being managed (e.g., a system of requirements and the system of specifications that implements those requirements) are objects from the viewpoint of 001. With 001, objects in one phase—say, requirements—are traceable to objects in the next phase of development, the specification phase. This feature is helpful for large, complex software systems, for which maintenance in traditional environments is even more time- and effort-consuming than development.

001AXES lies in the heart of 001. Although formal, this language is practical and friendly. It can be used to define any kind of system the human mind can envision and develop any software application that has the potential to be implemented. Based on a theory that extends traditional mathematics of systems with a unique concept of real-

Traditional (After the Fact)	001 (Before the Fact)
Interface errors (over 75% of all errors) ~Most found after implementation ~Some found manually ~Some found by dynamic runs analysis ~Some never found	*No interface errors* ~All found before implementation ~All found by automatic and static analysis ~Always found

Ambiguous requirements
~Informal or semi-formal language
~Different phases, languages and tools
~Different language for other systems than
   for software
	Unambiguous requirements
	~formal, but friendly language
	~All phases, same language and tools
	~Same language for software,
	   hardware and any other system

Automation supports manual process
~Mostly manual documentation,
   programming, test generation,
   traceability, etc.
	Automation does real work
	~Automatic documentation, programming,
	   test generation, traceability, etc.
	~100% code automatically generated
	   for any kind of software

No guarantee of function integrity after *implementation*	*Guarantee of function integrity after* *implementation*
Systems not traceable or evolvable ~Locked in products, architectures, etc. ~Painful transition from legacy ~Maintenance performed at code level	*Systems traceable and evolvable* ~Open architecture ~Smooth transition from legacy ~Maintenance performed at spec level
Reuse not inherent ~Reuse is adhoc ~Customization and reuse are mutually exclusive	*Inherent reuse* ~Every object a candidate for reuse ~Customization increases reuse pool

Mismatched objects, phases, products,
architectures and environment
~System not integrated with software
~Function oriented <u>or</u> object oriented
~GUI not integrated with application
~Simulation not integrated with software
   code
	Integrated & seamless objects, phases, products,
	architectures and environment
	~System integrated with software
	~System oriented objects: integration of
	   function, timing, <u>and</u> object oriented
	~GUI integrated with application
	~Simulation integrated with software code

Product x not defined and developed *with itself*	*001 defined with and generated by itself* ~#1 in all evaluations
Dollars wasted, error prone systems ~Not cost effective ~Difficult to meet schedules ~Less of what you need and more of what you don't need	*Better, faster, cheaper systems* ~10 to 1, 20 to 1, 50 to 1...dollars saved ~Minimum time to complete ~No more, no less of what you need

Table 42-1. *A Comparison*

time distributed control, 001AXES has embodied within it a natural representation of structured relationships of objects and their interactions as events.

System-Oriented Objects

All 001AXES models are defined and developed as system-oriented objects (SOOs). A SOO is understood the same way without ambiguity by all other objects within its environment—including all users, models, and automated tools. Each SOO is made up of other SOOs. Every aspect of a SOO is integrated, not the least of which is the integration of its object-oriented parts with its function-oriented and its timing-oriented parts. The philosophy that supports the theory that to integrate all the objects in a system you need to be able to integrate all aspects of each object in the system is strongly adhered to.

A SOO lends itself inherently to diverse forms of development, including that which is component based. Instead of systems being object-oriented, objects are systems-oriented. The means for capturing inherent and recursive reuse is provided by the formal definition mechanisms within 001 AXES. Not only does it have properties in its definitions to support the designer in finding, creating, and using commonality from the very beginning of a system's life cycle; commonality is ensured simply by using this language. This means the modeler does not have to work at making something become object-oriented. Rather he models the objects and their relationships, and the functions and their relationships; and the language inherently integrates these aspects as well as takes care of making those things that should become objects become objects.

Every SOO is a candidate to be a reusable—and is inherently integratable—within the same system, within other systems, and within all of these systems as they evolve. This is because every object is a system and every system is an object.

001AXES provides the necessary information in its definitions for an automated environment to know whether a system should be allocated to distributed, asynchronous, or synchronous processors; or whether two processors or ten processors should be selected. With traditional methods, it is up to the developer to incorporate such detail into his application. For any change in the architecture, it is necessary for the developer to then redesign and redevelop his applications that are impacted by that change. With DBTF, this is not necessary, since this process is inherent and automated.

A Client Record System Example

Throughout this chapter a simple client record system for the Web is used to illustrate the use of 001 in design and development. To access this Web service, a client logs in and then fills out some registration information. After registering, the client can add a new customer record, remove an existing customer record, list the set of existing customer records, or exit a login session.

Although the example life cycle process model in this chapter illustrates a means to perform DBTF processes of design and development, DBTF users are not tied to any particular process model for development when building an application (e.g., eXtreme Programming, spiral development, or waterfall development) other than that which is implied by the 001AXES language.

With DBTF the same language semantics is used throughout a life cycle to define all aspects of a system, including its requirements, system design, and software design models; enterprise, hardware, and software models; functional-, timing- (e.g., scheduling), and object-oriented parts of each model. Model examples provided here are defined and designed with 001AXES—and simulated (to understand a system's real-time distributed behavior), developed (to show a generated software implementation), tested, and maintained with 001.

Once 001AXES is used to capture the essence of DBTF in defining a system, complete software implementations (100 percent of the code) are automatically generated by 001 in a developer's language of choice (such as Java, C, or C++). The software code examples shown in this chapter have been automatically generated in Java or C (from their 001AXES requirements and specification models) using 001. Although the current commercial versions of 001 are hosted on UNIX and Linux, other environments can be cross-targeted with 001 from the host to the target architecture (for example, Web applications developed using 001 on Linux but generated by 001 to reside under NT).

Because it is based on DBTF, 001 is able to automatically generate all of (and any kind of) software system from a set of 001AXES-defined requirements, specifications, or design—for any configured architecture. This is in fact how the 001 Tool Suite itself was developed. That is, it is defined with itself and it automatically (re)generates itself as an ongoing evolving system on many diverse architectures.

Since all the components within 001 are inherently integrated as part of the same DBTF system (Figure 42-1 contains a simplified 001AXES object type definition of the tool suite's architecture), no additional time and effort is needed for integrating diverse products for developing different parts of a system, phases of the system, or for integrating the modules or views (e.g., use cases, data flow, timing, state transition, and object types) of a module created with or resulting from these disparate products. If one component is used for, say, definition and another for analysis and still another for generating code, there will not be interface mismatches between these components of the tool suite. Similarly, there are no interface mismatches between the components of the applications developed with the tool suite—and, no interface mismatches between each component's states of development.

Vertically, there are two model spaces in 001:

Definition space: the static specification of the system under development. Every model is defined in terms of Function Maps (FMaps[1]) to capture time characteristics and Type Maps (TMaps[2]) to capture space characteristics, which guide a designer in thinking through his concepts at all levels of system design (Figure 42-2). TMaps are used for defining types of objects and the relationships between those objects; FMaps are used for defining things done with the objects in the TMap (i.e., for defining functions and state

---

[1]FMaps are function graphs showing the potential functional interactions between objects in terms of their object states.
[2]TMaps are type graphs showing the potential relationships that can exist between types of objects.

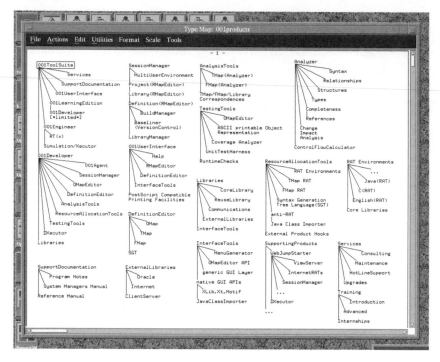

Figure 42-1. *The 001 Tool Suite architecture defined with 001.*

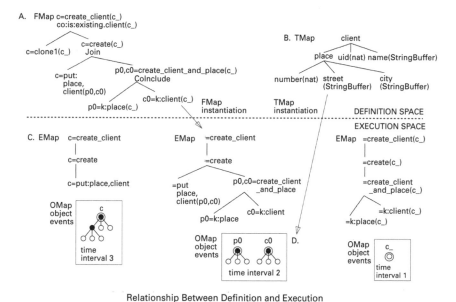

Relationship Between Definition and Execution

Figure 42-2. *Definition/execution space of 001AXES defined systems.*

transitions, including timing, ordering, and priorities). FMaps and TMaps are inherently integrated. In 001, FMaps exist either as FMap operations or as FMap Structures (user-configurable FMaps); TMaps exist simply as TMaps or TMap structures (user-configurable TMaps, called parameterized types).

Execution space: the realization of the definition space, reflecting the run-time performance of the system. This space is realized in terms of Execution Maps (EMaps, instantiations of FMaps) and Object Maps (OMaps, instantiations of TMaps, see Figure 42-2).

All 001AXES maps (sometimes referred to as control maps) are defined in terms of formal structures of control (control of input access, output access, input values, output values, error detection, invocation, timing, and priorities). Features such as polymorphism, encapsulation, inheritance, and persistence formally reside both on the function side as well as the object side of a system, where the functional side is defined in terms of the object side and vice versa, providing the ability to automatically trace within and between levels and layers of a system.

The TMap provides universal primitive operations of type—"Any"— for controlling objects and their object states, which are inherited by all types of objects. These universal primitive operations provide a means to create, destroy, copy, reference, move, access a value, detect and recover from errors, and access the type of an object. They provide an easy way to think about and manipulate different types of objects. With the universal primitive operations, building systems can be accomplished in a uniform manner.

Sometimes one would like to treat all objects in an identical way to make life easier. In addition to the universal operations and other reusables that can be used with all objects, there are the data types, TMap and OMap. With these types, one can take further advantage of the FMap and TMap environment when there is a need to use a more generic form of reuse when it comes to working with objects. For example, when an object needs to find out about itself, it is able to query the TMap from whence it came by using data type TMap. One may wish to do some of the same kinds of things to different types of objects, such as printing things about those objects or loading and storing them. Data type OMap is used for doing these kinds of things with and to objects.

Components within 001

One set of components within the tool suite, 001Developer, is used by a developer or designer to work with the definition space of a system; another set, 001Engineer, is used by the system designer to understand a system's execution space. Although this chapter focuses more on 001Developer's functions, we discuss 001Engineer's functions in order to understand how everything works together as one integrated system (see the section Systems Engineering).

001AXES can be thought of as operating in two distinct modes within the 001 environment:

Executable specification: 001AXES can serve as an executable specification language. In this mode, a 001AXES definition can serve as input to 001's simulator component (the Xecutor configured for simulation) for dynamic analysis during the design phase; or it can be layered onto 001's DXecutor (when the Xecutor is configured as a stand-alone distributed object manager) for distributed system development.

Automatic code generation: a 001 AXES definition serves as input to the code generator for purposes of prototyping or production software development. This feature facilitates the automatic programming of language-independent, platform-independent software development.

001Engineer contains components for systems design (system engineering, process modeling, enterprise modeling). It consists primarily of the requirements traceability component, $RT(x)$, for analyzing and tracing requirements, and a simulator component (Xecutor in simulation mode) that simulates a 001AXES model.

001Developer contains components used by both system designers and software developers. It consists primarily of graphical editing capabilities for defining models (Definition Editors), an analyzer component that checks models for consistency and logical completeness, a generator component (RAT) that automatically generates executable code or documentation from 001AXES models, the OMap Editor for viewing and testing objects, and a set of reusable building blocks.

In addition to other reusables supplied by 001Developer, the designer starts with a tool kit or foundation of primitive types and a set of existing types in the form of universal and core types. The designer also has the option of defining and building his own types as well as other types of reusables with 001.

In addition to the components within the 001 Tool Suite, other 001 developed components are available to support 001 users. An example of such a component is a product called WebJumpStarter, a "middleware" reusable for jump-starting 001-developed Web-based applications. The example in this chapter uses 001 along with the WebJump-Starter in its development process.

Architecture of the WebJumpStarter

A key objective of WebJumpStarter (WJS) is to raise the development level of Web-based systems. To bring this about, WJS capitalizes on unique properties of 001. WJS is an environment for developing reliable distributed object systems, layered onto 001's Distributed Xecutor (DXecutor). The developer of these distributed objects works on a layer above the traditional layer of development for distributed objects such as those provided by technologies Common Object Request Broker Architecture (CORBA), Distributed Component Object Model (DCOM), Java Remote Method Invocation (RMI), and Enterprise JavaBeans (EJB). The major reason for this is 001AXES has embedded within it characteristics that lend themselves to the automation of real-time and distributed systems. In 001 technology terms, any one of these lower-level distributed architecture technologies could be used as an implementation environment for the DXecutor.

The DXecutor is a distributed object manager used in conjunction with the 001 Tool Suite. It is a run-time environment that knows about the real-time and distributed semantics of a 001AXES specification. What this means to a developer is that he can use 001AXES to define the real-time functional process from the application perspective. The variables as inputs and outputs to the functions of the application correspond to real-time events in the actual system. In 001AXES, the developer no longer has to define event management, streaming of information, management of communications, and data transfer between clients and servers of the distributed object management system (DOMS) with data types in their application; it is intrinsic in the grammar of 001AXES.

Whereas in a traditional DOMS, the developer works with implementation artifacts of the DOMS, in the WJS the DOMS is under the hood, and the developer does not directly work with its implementation artifacts. This allows an application developer to concentrate on the application (e.g., the business rules) without the interference of implementation artifacts. The developer uses 001AXES to define the functionality of the application (*what* is to be done) and the rest is automated.

The other aspects of a 001 system specification used to accomplish this automation are the allocation architectures and the resource architectures. At a high level, the allocation architecture defines *who* does *what* and the resource architecture defines *who* is capable of *what*, again in terms of FMaps and TMaps. For each functional architecture there is one of a possible set of resource architectures. For each resource architecture, the allocation architecture maps each function of the functional architecture (the *what*) to functions in its resource architecture capable of performing it (the *who*). WJS and 001 determine how best to implement this correspondence (e.g., statically at compile time using an RAT or dynamically at runtime using the DXecutor).

In addition to using 001AXES with the 001 Tool Suite to define an application's functional architecture for WJS, 001 provides support for accessing traditional architectures (e.g., Java 2 Platform, Enterprise Edition, J2EE platform), standard Web application facilities and tools, and application service resources deployed as distributed agents (e.g., 001 agents for session management, dynamic page content services, and trading services). With WJS, many traditional technologies are no longer needed by a Web developer.

The DXecutor can be used to manage any type of distributed object system (e.g., enterprise or workflow management). It manages parallel threads of execution, inherent in any 001AXES specification. This entails activating primitive functions when objects arrive, starting new event-activated threads, activating and interrupting based on functional priorities, coordination of communication with other DXecutors, and automatic marshaling (or serialization) of object shipments to consumer functions resident in other DXecutors. With the DXecutor (which is at a higher layer of abstraction), designers and developers no longer have to program the event interactions of components as they would with Enterprise JavaBeans (EJB). The equivalent of what is accomplished by a human programmer using EJB's session and entity beans (e.g., object state management, remote and shared data access, object persistence) is automatic. The specification of business logic in a 001AXES functional specification is completely transparent, while an EJB specification still has embedded remnants of the class mechanisms used to manage distributed objects.

WJS's view server supports the integration of dynamic Web page content (i.e., OMap data) embedded within HTML pages. This allows a developer to define dynamic content based upon 001AXES OMap queries that are then embedded directly into an HTML page description being passed to the user's Web browser.

Extensible Markup Language (XML) technologies such as XHTML and XSLT all play a part in WJS. To a large extent, these are again under the hood. For example, XML Document Type Definitions (DTDs) can be automatically generated from a TMap with the appropriate RAT configuration; and an XML document can be generated from an OMap. In 001, data type OMap corresponds to the XML Document Object Model (DOM).

An OMap represents the information for a system that is to be remembered; and it is storable to disk as a persistent object. Other data stores (e.g., Oracle) have been used to store OMaps. An interface that automatically maps an OMap to ODBC or JDBC for the Enterprise Information Tier (EIS) is supported through the use of primitive type extensions mapped to appropriate class APIs. As an alternative to EIS interfaces, OMaps are persistently stored on disk in their native format. OMaps can be edited by the OMap Editor component of 001 and then converted to and from XML format as needed.

Current RAT configurations used for generating code implementations with the WJS are C (or C++) and Java. The main reason for a Java RAT is for its platform independence and its large set of supporting object class libraries. The main reason for C (or C++) on the Web is for its run-time efficiency. Using 001AXES specifications (which are transparent to any particular implementation language) allows a developer to choose the most appropriate solution to his implementation (e.g., Java for its large portable set of class libraries or C++ for efficiency).

Developing Web applications in the WJS is managed much the same as it is in the 001 Tool Suite. The main difference is in the types of objects being managed. In addition to the management of FMaps and TMaps, other Web-related artifacts such as HTML Web page specifications are managed from the Road Map (RMap). This allows a developer to see related Web development artifacts and their relationships.

The Genericity of the Process

There is commonality in every development process or discipline. Sometimes a manager designs. Sometimes he manages. Sometimes he verifies or analyzes. Sometimes a designer manages. Other times he designs. Or implements. Each such viewpoint is relative to a common view.

The most successful requirements definition process takes place in an environment where the user, designer, developer, and test engineer work out the requirements together, early in the game. This type of working relationship accelerates the understanding of the user's requirements by all parties involved. It uncovers misunderstandings between and among all parties, and it uncovers "user-intent" errors before development begins. In addition, there is often knowledge on the part of the designer, developer, or test engineer that the user does not have; having it, the user would often define the requirements differently. For example, the mere change of a specified accuracy could save "millions" during the development process and yet not affect the success of the application; this could mean less expensive equipment or fewer people needed to work on the project. Such understanding can be accelerated if all parties have a common means of formal communication.

The 001AXES language provides this kind of vehicle for understanding, for all disciplines involved. For each phase of development, whether it be process modeling, requirements, design, or testing, the process is, for all practical purposes, generic. If a designer begins by defining requirements, he can define them with 001AXES; if he begins at the specification or design phase, he defines his designs with 001AXES; or if his responsibility is testing, he can define his test cases with 001AXES. The generic development process described below can be applied to any and all of these phases, as well as others.

Management within the Tool Suite

001 has several manager components. Each manager is used to manage a portion of the life-cycle development of a system and artifacts about that system introduced by the developer (e.g., development issues and decisions made about a definition under development). Each manager manages an RMap of objects to be managed and may manage other managers (Figure 42-3).

In 001's life cycle management system in which definitions are managed, an RMap provides an index or table of contents to the user's system of definitions; it also supports the managers in the management of these definitions, including definitions for FMaps, TMaps, FMap and TMap defined structures, OMaps, primitive data types, objects brought in from other environments, and other RMaps. Managers use the RMap to coordinate multiuser access to the definitions of the system being developed. Each RMap in a system is an OMap of the objects in the system used to develop that system within each particular manager's domain.

The RMap editor is used to define an RMap as a relational hierarchy, the combination of the control system as a hierarchy and relations (as network, non-control–like connections) forming a web of communication or some other abstract form of dependency between two or more nodes in the RMap. These relations allow the manager to maintain cross-phase dependencies between the definition systems within each development phase of a system. For example, the relation of a requirement (as part of a system of requirements) to its dependent implementation FMaps or TMaps (as part of the target

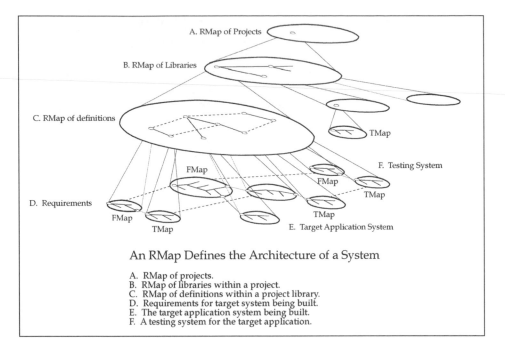

An RMap Defines the Architecture of a System

A. RMap of projects.
B. RMap of libraries within a project.
C. RMap of definitions within a project library.
D. Requirements for target system being built.
E. The target application system being built.
F. A testing system for the target application.

Figure 42-3. An RMap defines the architecture of a system.

system[3] under development) and testing FMaps and TMaps (as part of the testing system) can be visualized on the same RMap. Ultimately, these cross-phase system relations provide for the full traceability of requirements to generation artifacts (e.g., code) and back again.

001's managers include the Session Manager for managing all sessions, the Project Manager for managing all projects, the Library Manager for managing libraries within one project, the Definition Manager for managing definitions within a library, and the RT(x) manager for capturing information about objects in each of the above managers.

The Session Manager is the initial manager responsible for entry into 001 and authorizing administrative or normal Project Manager access (Figure 42-4). To start 001's Session Manager the user types oo1 and enters his name and password. If the user is authorized, the Session Manager starts a Project Manager for the user. To enter into the Project Manager's administrative interface, the user enters "oo1super" for the name field and the supervisor's password.

The Project Manager manages all projects and users (Figure 42-5). It lets the user create, enter, and delete projects; and it maintains a list of file system mount points on which projects may reside, watching them for adequate space. For each project, the Project

---

[3]"Target system" here means the application being developed for the end-user.

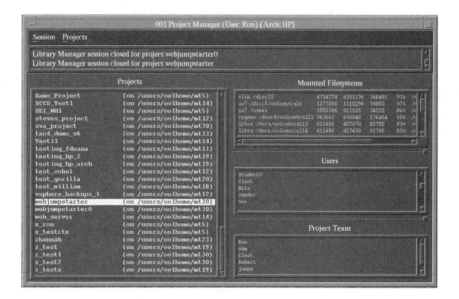

Figure 42-4. *Session Manager for managing 001 session.*

Figure 42-5. *Project Manager for managing projects.*

Manager also maintains a list of users who may access the project; and it enforces these access privileges.

The Library Manager manages a single project, where each object it manages is a library. (See Figure 42-6; note that this figure shows an example of a 001 printout as opposed to a screen shot.) The Library Manager allows the user to create, enter, and delete libraries within that project. Libraries may also be linked together into sub-trees; this enables one library to use the definitions in another library. Library utilities work on the currently selected library to provide error recovery, environment configuration, searching, and other useful support.

The Definition Manager manages a library, where each object it manages is a definition

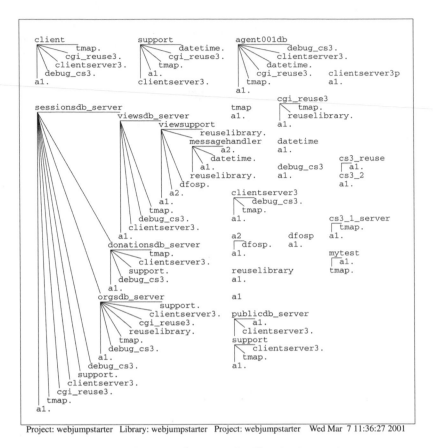

Figure 42-6. Library Manager for managing libraries in a project.

or another library (Figure 42-7). The Definition Manager allows a user to manage the life cycle of a definition. In addition to creating, editing, importing (definitions from other libraries), and deleting definitions, the Definition Manager provides the following for a selected definition (the other managers perform these functions implicitly):

Definition: A user can describe an application in terms of the 001AXES graphical language. The Definition Editor is provided for constructing map definitions as well as performing life cycle functions on the definition being edited. Examples of other utilities provided to support definitions are structure derivation, printing, searching, layout, scaling, and color coding of definition nodes.

Analysis: A user can verify the correctness of a definition in terms of itself and in terms of its integration with other related definitions. A status is associated with each step or phase of a definition along its life cycle path. Analysis may result in the status of a defini-

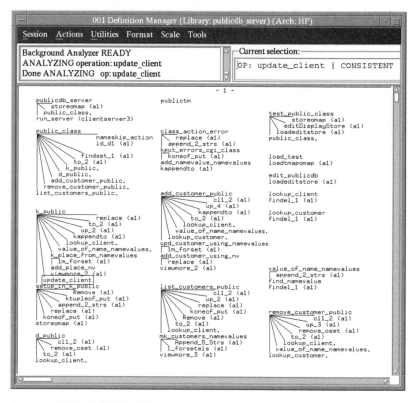

Figure 42-7. *Definition Manager for managing definitions in a library.*

tion changing, showing a transition to the new phase as the definition progresses though its life cycle development process.

Resource allocation: A user may define SGT configurations of the RAT that the Definition Manager applies when RATting. Each RAT configuration translates the definition being RATted to some export format, which could be generated code, English documents, or management information (artifacts about the definition such as who wrote the definition).

Execution: The user may run and test executable systems from the Definition Manager. The manager invokes a debugger for the user. During execution, the user can use standard debugger features native to the machine operating environment, the OMap editor, or print out an ASCII object representation to understand and experiment with the implementation being executed.

General support: A user has a general-purpose set of interactive functions (for example, searching, navigating, viewing, hiding of RMap details through filtering and coloring, and scaling the view of the RMap). In addition, sub-trees or the entire library of definitions

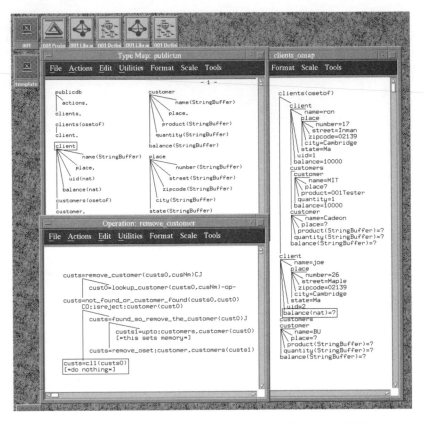

Figure 42-8. *Definition Editor for definining TMaps, OMaps, and FMaps.*

may be rebuilt using the Rebuild option (i.e., their life cycle phases of edit, analyze, and RAT are reinvoked), resulting in the regeneration of the system.

The Definition Editor of the Definition Manager is used to define TMaps, OMaps, FMaps, and SGTs in graphical tree form (Figure 42-8 shows individual Definition Editors managing a TMap, OMap, and an FMap, respectively). In addition to editing facilities used to construct graphical definitions, the Definition Editor can be used to manage the life-cycle process of the definition being edited.

The RT(x) Manager is used to enter the user's requirements and life-cycle artifacts into 001's environment, providing for user life-cycle management, requirements traceability, and metrics gathering (Figure 42-9). The user interface for RT(x) is a configuration of the OMap Editor using its programming API. This information about an object being managed and the relations between it and other managed objects (e.g., between a requirement, its target system implementation, and testing system) is captured in a persistent OMap database based upon a TMap that describes a default complex of development artifacts and relations.

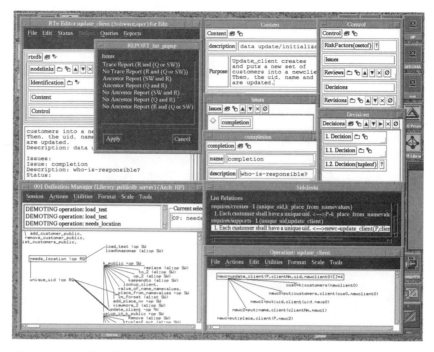

Figure 42-9. The RT(x) Manager provides for life-cycle management and traceability.

The Generic Life-Cycle Process

The development of a DBTF system follows a general pattern (see Figure 42-10) of definition (to state what the system is to do and be), analysis (to verify consistency and logical completeness), implementation (resource allocation), and execution (to validate performance). 001's Actions menu provides the functions for these development process disciplines from within a 001 manager (Figure 42-11).

Definition phase. The first part of the generic process is the modeling or definition phase, keeping in mind that all development phases include some form of definition. This is the time when the system designer organizes his system in terms of TMaps, OMaps, and FMaps (and structures of TMaps, OMaps, and FMaps), using a Road Map (RMap) as a management and organization tool. He also models the user interface for his application. Part of this process is finding maps in earlier developed libraries that can be reused.

Using editing facilities of the tool suite, models (for example, requirements, design, test cases, use cases) are defined in FMaps, TMaps, and predefined objects as persistent OMaps. During this process, the user defines what the system is to do in terms of the objects that exist. In order to define a map in 001, the user selects the option Create from the Actions menu from within one of 001's managers (Figure 42-11).

System Engineering Seamlessly Integrated with Software Development

System Engineering:

- Define FMaps and TMaps for system architecture
- Analyze
- Simulate real-time behavior

Software Development:

- Define FMaps and TMaps for application
- Analyze
- Generate production ready code
- Execute on target machine

Design Changes and Maintenance:

- Revise FMaps and TMaps
- Repeat engineering and/or development process

Management:

- Organize projects into working libraries
- Manage and trace requirements
- Generate product and process metrics
- Generate specification, design and test documentation

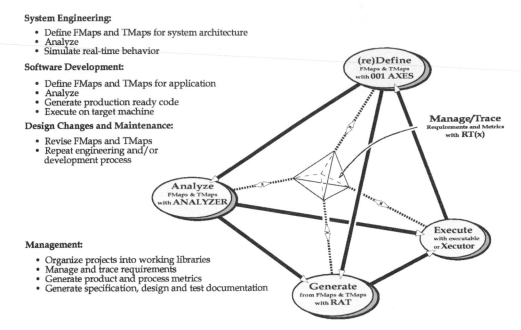

Figure 42-10. *The Generic Life Cycle Process.*

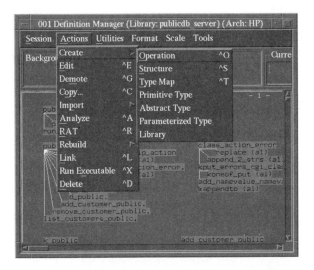

Figure 42-11. *Actions menu for selection of life-cycle functions.*

Typical DBTF Design Process

Typically, a designer or team of designers will begin to design a DBTF system by sketching a TMap (using the Definition Editor) of the application. This is where the designers decide on the types of objects, and the relationships between those objects, they will have in their system (see TMap in Figure 42-8).

Often an RMap will be sketched in parallel (using the RMap Editor) with the TMap and used to organize all system objects (including TMaps, OMaps, FMaps, and other RMaps). At each node of an RMap there is a pointer (visually a line) to other maps including FMaps, TMaps, and other RMaps. As we've been told by several SOO designers: "FMaps almost fall into place once a TMap has been agreed upon by the design team." This is a result of the natural partitioning of functionality (or groups of functionality) provided to the designers by the TMap system (Figure 42-7 contains an RMap and Figure 42-8 contains a TMap, OMap, and an FMap). Typically many managers and editors will be open at the same time during the development of a system (Figure 42-12).

The structure of a TMap by its very nature defines several universal mechanisms that support its life cycle. For example, a TMap has an inherent way to be instantiated, to be populated using a GUI, and to be stored persistently. The TMap provides the structural criteria from which to evaluate the functional partitioning of the system—for example,

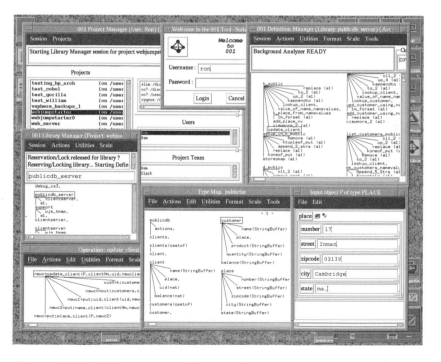

Figure 42-12. *001 managers working together.*

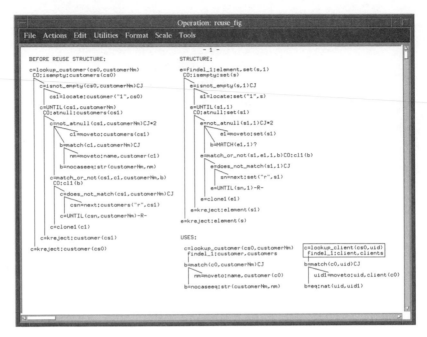

Figure 42-13. *User-defined reusable FMap structure.*

the shape of the structural partitioning of the FMaps is balanced against the structural organization of the shape of the objects as defined by the TMap.

In planning FMaps and TMaps, the more object types can be grouped into common TMap type patterns, the simpler the FMap definitions of the unique functional structure of the system will be. This is because common patterns in the TMap lend themselves to the construction of common functional reusables as generic FMaps (universal FMap operations having polymorphism or FMap structures encapsulating a functional environment in which a nodal family, operates[4]). Part of this process of abstraction (e.g., finding common TMap patterns and making generic FMaps from more concrete FMaps (Figure 42-13) is to determine if more abstract mechanisms can be formed and derived from existing mechanisms, either from earlier libraries or from newly defined FMaps and TMaps. Another part is to continue to look for commonalities within the new mechanisms and to remove redundant ones (by making and then referring to a common reusable definition). This process continues until all functions of the FMaps and all types

[4]A nodal family in 001AXES comprises a parent and some number of children being controlled by the parent. The structure used to group the parent and children together forms a background environment in which the children work together to perform the parent's function.

of the TMaps have been decomposed to the most primitive levels (primitive functions and primitive types, respectively)—primitive, that is, with respect to the particular layer of abstraction in question.

User interface. The GUI environment (as well as its interface to the Internet) is tightly integrated with the definition (and development) of any 001 application. GUI (support for Motif or AWT) is provided while preserving traceability, interface integrity, and control seamlessly between the GUI part of the application and the other parts of the application. Its automatic data-driven interface generator supports rapid program evolution. Layers of loosely to tightly coupled GUI integration are provided. At the lowest level of integration, a set of primitive data types is provided to access the power of Xlib, Xt, and the Motif windowing system. Each of these layers is defined with primitive operators and types that match the API for that layer. At this layer, all the raw power of the windowing system may be accessed (in Java, this could be AWT or Swing).

An intermediate layer above these base-level APIs (called GUI and GUIELEMENT) is provided that encapsulates most of the repetitive operational aspects of Widget management and construction of X widgets. Since this layer was defined as SOOs, the OMap Editor can be used to specify and view information about the window hierarchy. In addition, the GUI objects may be persistently stored as OMaps to be used during the initialization, modification, or analysis stages of GUI development. The GUI technology used to implement this layer is hidden. An application built on this layer is independent of its implementation (e.g., an implementation in Java using AWT).

The highest layer is tightly integrated with the TMap system. It is at this layer that the OMap Editor is always available to an application to populate and manipulate objects based on the TMap. The object editor has standard default presentations as well as a set of primitive operators that allow a user to use its presentation features to develop interactive GUIs that are tightly coupled to the TMap (e.g., automatic generation of a system of menus from a TMap description).

Other screen description technologies (e.g., WYSIWYG GUI builders) may also be used in conjunction with a translator of their export capabilities to a DBTF GUI specification (for example, a translator was developed to go from Motif UIL as an output of ICS's Builder Xcessory product to an OMap screen description usable by the OMap editor for its GUI).

In addition to the above GUI layers, users can define their own primitive type interfaces to user-chosen APIs, providing the end-user with freedom and flexibility of choice. Throughout all of these choices the APIs are integrated with the use of FMaps and TMaps.

The OMap Editor can be used throughout a system's development in major ways: as a general object viewer/editor, and as a full end-user interface. The OMap Editor chooses appropriate default visualizations for each data item to be displayed. For a specific OMap, it manages the visualization of specific data values for the user and the modification of the OMap by the user.

Several things drove the creation of the OMap Editor: Many applications center around the display and modification of data; the visualization of data structures may be generated and managed automatically by understanding the semantics of data description; automation is made useful by a wide array of configuration avenues, for both the developer and end-user; and the system may be configured in many ways. A set of reasonable defaults is always provided that allows rapid prototyping and gives the developer a concrete starting point.

The TMap is the repository for information about the structure of data and implies the operations that may be performed on it. The visualization of data created from the TMap consists of interface elements that display the values in the OMap and interface elements that trigger primitive functions on those values. For example, an ordered set might be depicted as a list, with buttons for insert and extract; a Boolean might be visualized as a toggle switch.

For each primitive and parameterized type, there is a group of modes of visualization from which to choose. For example, a number can be visualized as a text item with the number in it or a dial that can be turned to the desired value. In addition, advanced users can add new primitive and parameterized types. The OMap Editor produces forms-entry screens, much like conventional database screen painters, but supports the full semantic capabilities of a TMap. It will generate nested screens for arbitrary depth type hierarchies and has full support for 001AXES parameterized types including OSetOf, OrderedSetOf, TreeOf, OneOf and TupleOf. (2) The developer has control over the data that may be viewed or modified by the user. Data in the OMap may be reorganized, specified as view-only, or completely hidden from the user (Figure 42-14).

Using data type OMapEditor (the API to the OMap Editor functions), the developer has complete control over visualization and data modification from within the application. Here, the developer can add functions to capture run-time data events (like trigger functions), perform constraint checking, data analysis, and specialized graphics manipulations. Besides data specification, the developer has access to many graphical configuration options. Some of these may be carefully controlled while others may be left for users to change. A common capability allows end-users to save the locations and sizes of their windows between sessions.

Type OMapEditor provides an operational base upon which WJS's view server is constructed. The view server mixes form (presentation) and content (e.g., OMap object values). This consists of (X)HTML with embedded 001 query statements (to define the content). The embedded query statements select the content using control statements (e.g., to select a set of elements to be gathered) and object selection paths (OSP) to identify some location in an OMap, the tree of objects instantiated from a TMap. The OSP is a unique path down the tree (based on the node names of the TMap) to some descendent child object node. An OSP is like an XPath expression. These query statements in essence target the information content to be retrieved from the OMap content database. The view server generates dynamic HTML based on these embedded OMap query

Figure 42-14. *OMap Editor in a Windows presentation mode.*

statements and associated OSPs to be used for query and report presentation by a browser (Figure 42-15).

Analysis phase: The second part of the generic process is referred to as the analysis phase (often overlapping in time with the definition phase; the overlap is due to the interactive aspects of this phase), beginning when 001AXES definitions are provided as input to the Analyzer. This includes *static* analysis for preventative properties and *dynamic* analysis for user-intent properties. Since 001AXES is used to define inherently modular components, a small fraction of a system can be taken fully through analysis, long before the rest of the system is even conceptualized. When the Analyzer detects ambiguity (Figure 42-16), it provides precise information to the user as to the nature of the inconsistency or lack of logical completeness (consistency and logical completeness are prerequisites for integration between models). This phase is deliberately similar to having a DBTF expert look over your shoulder as you develop a system. In order to analyze in 001, the user selects the option Analyze from the Actions menu from within the Definition Manager.

Figure 42-15. *A WJS template for creating an HTML page.*

The Analyzer is involved in many life-cycle tasks, insuring completeness of functions and object types, and making sure definitions are defined until they stop at primitives. It insures consistency and traceability by making sure interfaces are correct. The Analyzer is also involved in overall integration by checking across independently developed modules and definitions of library modules. Many tasks of management are incorporated into this analysis process.

In the first part of analysis, models are submitted to the Dataflow Structure Calculator to provide, automatically, the structures with a static analysis of the local data flow for a given model. The Analyzer can then be used to ensure that each model or set of models was defined properly and follows the rules of 001AXES. For example the Analyzer uses static analysis to make sure the rules of the three primitive control structures (2) are followed; it also makes sure the rules inherited by abstract user-defined structures from more primitive structures are followed. This ensures no data conflicts,, timing conflicts or priority conflicts and no redundancies, ambiguities, or logically incomplete definitions. Other types of analysis are performed using 001Engineer's Xecutor, discussed further below.

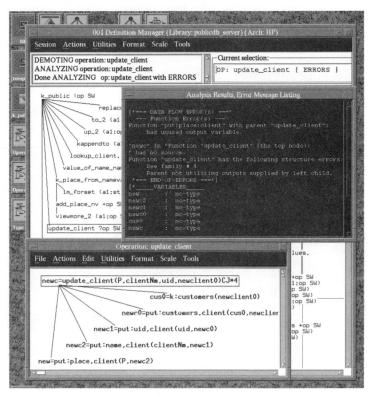

Figure 42-16. *The Analyzer discovers errors in a definition.*

Implementation phase (resource allocation): A software implementation consistent with the model is generated—for a selected target environment in the language and architecture of choice. Once a specification is determined to be consistent and logically complete by the Analyzer, it is handed over to the generator component: the Resource Allocation Tool (RAT) if it is intended to be transformed into a software system, or the Xecutor for simulation studies. If it is determined to be incorrect in either type of analysis, the user returns to the definition phase and changes his specification using 001AXES. In order to generate code in 001, the user selects the option RAT from the Actions menu from within the Definition Manager.

The RAT automatically generates complete, fully integrated, fully production-ready code for any kind of application, whether it be Web-based GUI, database, communications, real-time, distributed, client server, multiuser, or mathematical algorithms. The Java code, C code, and English have been automatically generated by the RAT from the same FMaps and TMaps (Figure 42-17). Instead of automatically supporting the user to do the work manually, as most traditional tools would do, the tool suite does the "real work" and generates a complete software solution. Even if a more traditional tool were

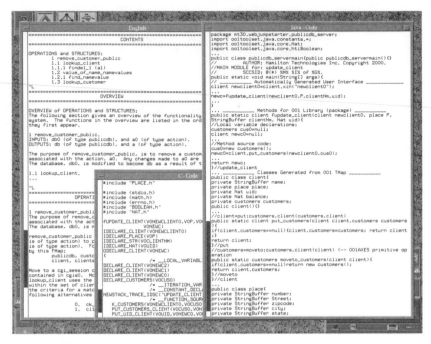

Figure 42-17. *Automatically generated Java, C, and English, each from the same FMaps and TMaps.*

to automatically do some of the real work, it would need to be finished or integrated with other code, manually. There is *no manual work* to be done to finish the coding task with the RAT.

RAT-generated code inherits all the SOO qualities from its 001AXES definitions, including interface correctness and traceability, from and to the requirements and design, from whence it came, and within the code layer itself.

The type part of the RAT generates object type templates for a particular application domain from one or more TMaps. The code generated by the functional part of the RAT, from one or more FMaps, is automatically connected to the code generated from the TMaps and code for the primitive types in the core library, as well as—if desired—extensions to code libraries developed from other environments (e.g., J2EE).

The generator can provide output information that can be used as input by other tools or for testing (such as generating code instrumented to determine path coverage of the decision alternatives taken during the execution of a system). This feature can also be used as another means of rapid prototyping for systems design studies. User-tailored documents can also be configured to be automatically generated by the RAT—with selectable portions of a system definition, implementation, and description—and projections such as parallel patterns, decision trees, and priority maps.

Having a completely open architecture, the RAT is illustrative of component-based development. Because 001's environment is open, it allows for interfacing to existing or future legacy code. Several options exist for such an interface. Interfaces or wrappers can be placed around existing or legacy code to create primitives for the generation environment to automatically code to; systems can be defined to have universal FMaps (having polymorphism) that result in code directly embedded as inline code; legacy code can call and send input to code generated by the RAT at execution time; and the generator can be configured to generate language-specific statements (such as "+") or statements that interface to the legacy code. In addition, shell scripts within the tool suite environment are open to end-user modification (e.g., modification of link and compile scripts).

The Java RAT Environment

RATting has two major aspects: mapping 001AXES TMaps and mapping 001AXES FMaps to the target language to be generated. The RAT supports openness by allowing a user to tailor the target language syntax being generated and extend 001AXES types by layering them onto corresponding target language types (called 001AXES-layered primitive types). Tailoring of the RAT is accomplished using a graphical Syntax Generation Tree (SGT) language specifically designed for easy specification of syntax transformations of a 001AXES specification. As an example, the Java mapping of 001AXES types makes the following correspondences:

- A 001AXES primitive type corresponds to a Java primitive type or to any Java class available in any of the wide range of packages supported by Java vendors.
- A 001AXES abstract type (with a different meaning than in Java or C++) corresponds to a Java top-level, nested, or inner class, depending on the TMap type context.
- A 001AXES structured type (traditionally called a parameterized type that may be polymorphic) corresponds to a Java extendable class that provides inheritable polymorphic methods for the 001AXES abstract type that is the head of the TMap type nodal family.

In order to layer a 001AXES primitive type onto a Java class, the user maps each of the primitive operations of the type to its corresponding implementation as a Java instance or class method. Because there is a fairly close correspondence between a 001AXES type and a Java class, much of the 001AXES type specification can be anti-RATted from Java (i.e., the process of reverse engineering or abstracting code into a system specification) using an import facility built upon the Java foundation and reflection class packages. This import facility allows a 001 user access to Java classes.

Since a Java class code specification that has been raised to a 001AXES code-independent type specification will be incomplete according to the formal requirements of 001AXES, information must be provided to complete the process. One example of the incompleteness of a Java class specification becomes apparent in the identification of a method's input and output objects. This stems from the problem that a method may have many arguments, some of which may be input objects and some of which may be output objects. While many output objects can be determined by the form of the method, some outputs can only be determined by reading the documentation of the method. For an automated anti-RATting tool, the user must identify some of the method output objects. As an example, consider the following correspondences:

```
Type: StringBuffer.
Primitive Operations:
StringBuffer=k:StringBuffer(Any); [* object creation *]
StringBuffer-1m=setCharAt:StringBuffer(StringBuffer-1,int,char)
CharArray-1m=getChars:StringBuffer(StringBuffer-
1,int,int,CharArray-1,int)
. . .
public class java.lang.StringBuffer extends java.lang.Object{
//constructors
public StringBuffer();
//instance methods
public synchronized void setCharAt(int index, char ch);
public synchronized void getChars(int srcBegin, int srcEnd,
char[] dst, int dstBegin);
. . .
```

In this example, the 001AXES primitive operation, k:StringBuffer, corresponds to the Java constructor, StringBuffer();. The differences in syntax are minimal and given a basic Java constructor of this form, it is easy to construct the 001AXES primitive operation associated with it. They differ in how they are used in an application. In 001AXES, a primitive operation is used as a function, for example:

```
buf=k:StringBuffer(x); [* where x is of type any *]
```

In Java, the corresponding constructor is used as:

```
buf=new StringBuffer();
```

This mapping is automated by the anti-RAT import facility. Whenever code is generated from an FMap, the SGT form "<@outputname-1>=new StringBuffer();" is applied by the RAT. When "<@outputname-1>" is replaced with the primitive function's first output, buf, the proper Java code is produced.

Most of the second primitive operation, "setCharAt:StringBuffer," can be inferred from the instance method setCharAt. The "this" reference maps to the "StringBuffer-1" part of the primitive operation's type mapping. The setCharAt instance method arguments are mapped to the other two input types, for example:

```
int index, char ch   ==>    int, char
```

The missing piece of information is the "m" (the semantic component of "StringBuffer-1m") that specifies the object has been modified. To determine this "m" component, a user must read the documentation associated with the setCharAt method.

The "m" specifier in 001AXES is really a symbolic shorthand for a commonly used axiom or constraint on a primitive operation of a type. Since the Java language does not support axiom or constraint specifications, it is not surprising that this part of the 001AXES specification has to be added in by the user manually.

```
CharArray-1m=getChars:StringBuffer(StringBuffer-
1,int,int,CharArray-1,int)
public synchronized void getChars(int srcBegin, int srcEnd,
char[] dst, int dstBegin);
```

The last mapping example shows that an automation cannot always determine the output type. For example, in the Java specification of getChars, the "void" statement states that nothing is returned from the method. However, there is one output object type from a functional perspective. The implicit "this" could be used as a pass-through reference-only object, but this is always the case for instance methods. In this case, the instance method does not modify the instance object, so it is not necessary as an output to the primitive operation. But, a 001AXES primitive operation must have at least one output. The documentation of the method provides us with a natural functional output; it is the "char[] dst" argument. This argument, as a reference object, is modified by getChars, so from a functional perspective, when an input state is modified, it must be returned as a new output object state. This mapping, for example:

```
char[] dst    ==>'s CharArray-1m = . . . ( . . . CharArray-1
. . . ),
```

must be identified by the user who gathers this information from the documentation and provides it as input to the anti-RATting process.

Translation of an FMap into the target language is a mapping between the grammar of 001AXES and that of the target language. This takes into consideration the capabilities (i.e., semantics) of the target language as well as its syntax. When mapping to a traditional sequential code language such as Java, many aspects of 001AXES's real-time rich language semantics are ignored (e.g., priority, interrupt, or event-driven characteristics).

In 001AXES, these real-time characteristics are built into the language (i.e., as part of its grammar) as opposed to providing them as add-on data-type capabilities (i.e., as a lexical element) as they are traditionally done (e.g., threads). In 001AXES, threads are not needed as an additional type, since 001AXES is event-driven and inherently defines multi-threaded control for all specifications, without the user having to be aware of it. When generating to Java, since Java is inherently sequential, the Java-generated code mapping uses a traditional approach subset (e.g., utilizing the Thread, ThreadGroup classes) rather than the 001AXES native threaded event-driven semantics.

The RAT-generated target language syntax for FMaps falls into two groups: control syntax for making decisions and loops; and call syntax for invoking operators and calling methods. In the current Java mapping, for example, all methods are defined in a generic way, so that only inputs are passed as arguments, and all outputs are returned via the return statement. When there are many outputs produced by a 001AXES function, a constructor is generated to return all the output objects as an object whose return class name is generated from the sequence of types of the outputs of the 001AXES function. If only one output is returned from the 001AXES function, then a new return class is not generated, since Java naturally supports this case.

Assume a 001AXES function producing several outputs, for example:

```
db,a=add_customer_public(db0,a0)-op-
```

This results in the following return class being generated:

```
public class OO{
public Object o1;
public Object o2;
public OO(Object i1,Object i2){
i1=o1;i2=o2;}
}
```

Inside the method implementation of add_customer_public an OO object is returned as:

```
public static OO fadd_customer_public(db0,a0){
. . .
return new OO(db,a);
```

And finally, the following code is generated for the add_customer_public method use:

```
OO out14=fadd_customer_public(db0,a0);
db=(publicdb)out14.o1;
a0=(action)out14.o2;
```

Following is the portion of the Java SGT responsible for the FMap generation of the use of the generated return class (Figure 42-18).

As mentioned earlier, the generator component is accessible to a user to tailor it for his own brand of generated code, documentation, or projections on an as-needed basis. For example, different RAT configurations can be used to generate different styles of code (e.g., embedded code, IDL, XML DTDs).

The RAT open architecture extension of 001AXES base types can be used to interface to an architecture of choice (e.g., Java J2EE) by making a set of 001AXES primitive types for each of the service technology APIs of interest. It can be configured to interface to a system at all levels, from high levels (such as a JDBC API or JavaSpaces) to low levels such as operating system calls (e.g., POSIX or the Java Virtual Machine instruction set). In so doing, the user maps a 001AXES primitive operation of a primitive type to some code implementation interface (e.g., a Java instance or class method). There is no limit to this type of extension other than that of the current software industry capabilities. This type of extension allows one to access database, graphics, client/server, legacy code,

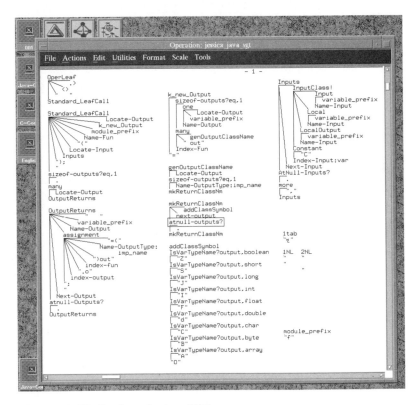

Figure 42-18. Portion of a Java SGT.

operating system, communications systems, Internet-based systems, and machine environments of choice.

Previous extensions have included databases (such as Oracle, SQL Server, or Versant), operating systems (including UNIX, Linux, and NT), user interfaces (including Motif and HTML), communication protocols (including TCP/IP and CGI), Web packages (such as FrontPage), and legacy code of choice; there is no need to lose time and resources to port to a new environment. Examples of interfaces currently available are UNIX including Linux, Motif, NT, and TCP/IP.

As can be seen from above, a choice of code generation from the perspective of language can be made using a single solution specification (also user configurable).

For a software system, the generator performs automatic generation of code or documentation (Java, C, English, or some other kind of code for which the generator has been configured) to allocate the definitions found in the 001AXES specification. Languages configured for the RAT have included APL, Lisp, Pascal, FORTRAN, ADA, COBOL, C, C++, Java, and English.

During this phase, code (or documentation, testing information, etc.) is automatically generated (or regenerated) for any part or type of a model in a system (and for any part of the system that has been changed). Obsolete code is automatically replaced or removed and new code is integrated into the current base of managed code without intervention by the developer (except in the case when a developer is extending the RAT's environment by interfacing to preexisting service technologies).

Once the generator is configured for a new environment, a system can be automatically regenerated to reside on that environment. Thus the RAT becomes an agent of reuse as well as an agent of reverse engineering (from a more modern perspective) across its target code implementations. For future modernization projects, rather than invest all the time and money required for significant training and reverse engineering, one could opt instead to use—and continue to use—a single definition languageand automatically generate the latest implementation environment. For example, developments using the tool suite have taken place on UNIX (Linux) and then were automatically cross-targeted for applications residing on architectures such as NT, IBM Mainframe, and the AS 4000.

If the selected environment has already been configured, the RAT selects that environment directly; otherwise, the RAT is first configured for a new language and architecture. The set of 001AXES definitions from which code is generated to one architecture (e.g., C) can be used to regenerate code to another architecture (e.g., Java). This means, for example, that developers (who are anxious to start development and want to use a new language but do not have its compiler and support tools or its configuration yet available) can define their system in 001AXES, generate to an existing language (e.g., C), and develop part or all of their system in this mode; they can then regenerate to the new language (e.g., Java or C#) using the same 001AXES definitions when the new compiler and support tools become available.

Each new configuration of the RAT becomes a reusable architecture component for layering a DBTF application onto a new architecture. In a relative sense the earlier version can be looked upon as legacy code to the new one. The implications are that already developed systems are never obsolete just because a new language or architecture appeared on the scene.

Once a system has been generated by the RAT, it is ready to be compiled, linked, and executed. The generated code can be compiled, linked, and executed on the machine where the tool suite environment resides, or it can be sent over to other machines for subsequent compilation, linking, and execution. The Link Actions menu option performs both compilation for all code being referenced and then links an executable file according to the Build Manager's settings. The link and execution tasks are selected and performed within the 001 environment. To link, the user selects the option Link from the Actions menu from within the Definition Manager.

Execution phase: The last part of the generic life cycle is the execution phase. To execute an FMap operation, the user selects the option Run Executable from the Actions menu from within the Definition Manager. This consists of performance testing (during which user intent errors are located) or final system operation (Figure 42-19). If the real system is software, it is ready to be tested dynamically for user intent errors or be to be placed into operation. During performance testing, each time a user intent error is found, previous life-cycle phases are repeated (altering the 001 AXES specification and redeveloping the application with 001) until the intended behavior is embodied in the system.

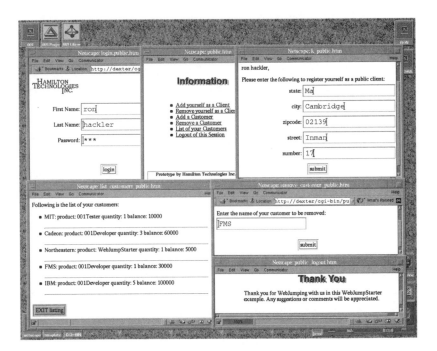

Figure 42-19. *Running the client record system.*

If the real system is hardware, enterpriseware, or peopleware, the generated system serves as one form of simulation (001Engineer's Xecutor component serves as the other form of simulation at the definition level) upon which the real system can be based.

Before-the-Fact Testing

A typical way to test within a traditional development environment is to build a system, then test it—that is, after-the-fact testing. The issues and problems of after-the-fact testing are well known by experienced managers, test engineers, and developers. In contrast, testing within the DBTF paradigm, by its very nature, is an integral part of each of the generic phases: definition, analysis, implementation, and execution.

Use of the "no more, no less" philosophy of DBTF removes the need for the majority of testing that would have been necessary with traditional techniques. This is largely because of reuse inherited with the use of 001AXES and that which has become automated within the 001 Tool Suite— and because all objects in a DBTF system are under control and traceable—again, obviating the need for another set of tests that are needed in a more traditional setting. Following are more specific reasons why this is the case:

Correct use of 001AXES eliminates (or prevents) the majority of errors, including all interface errors (which account for over 75 percent of all errors) at definition time (i.e., before implementation). Should the language be used incorrectly, 001AXES provides the necessary information to the Analyzer to find all the interface errors. Testing (dynamically, that is) for errors that fall into the category of interface errors is no longer necessary. Testing for other types of errors is minimized: There is less chance for some of them to exist (through implicit use in the formal systems language and the tool suite) and there is a high degree of inherent reuse in the language (thus avoiding errors that would have occurred if unnecessary systems had been developed).

All mechanisms of 001AXES contribute to these kinds of preventative testing. For example, TMap properties ensure the proper use of objects in an FMap. A TMap has a corresponding set of control properties for controlling spatial relationships between objects. One cannot, for example, put a leg on a table where a leg already exists; conversely, one cannot remove a leg from the table (or a Place in a Customer record) where there is no leg; a reference to the state of an object cannot be modified if there are other references to that state in the future (since a 001AXES variable refers to an object state, not the object directly); reject values exist in all types, allowing the FMap user to recover from failures if they are encountered.

Integration testing is minimized, since all objects within a system are by their nature integrated, another example of inherent reuse. Thus, integration testing as we have known it in a traditional environment is no longer needed. Since all code is automatically generated from FMaps and TMaps, no errors are made in going from design to code (i.e., there is no longer a manual process of coding). Again, fewer errors to test for. Other components such as 001Engineer's requirements traceability component automate processes of going from requirements to design to tests to use cases to other requirements and back again. The need for traditional testing, which helps make sure the implementation satisfies the design and the design satisfies the requirements, is minimized.

To support testing further, the developer is notified of the impact on his system of any changes; those areas that are affected (for example, all FMaps that are affected by a change to a TMap) are demoted.

Since the generator can be configured to generate to one of a possible set of architectures, no errors will be made because of a manual process of conversion, since conversions will be performed by the generator automatically. Again, fewer errors to test for.

Sometimes testing and analysis are indistinguishable processes. Such is the case when the Analyzer performs inspection by checking for consistency and completeness of the models. Semantic errors, interface errors, and data flow errors are found by such static checking. A classic example of DBTF properties in 001AXES is that which inherently forms the basis for the movement of some dynamic testing into the realm of static testing. Testing in 001 for relative timing of events, thread activation, and priority interrupt scheduling is a case in point, since these timing aspects of a system have been moved from traditionally residing as a type (i.e., an open class lexical element in a language) to residing in the grammar (i.e., in the closed class part of a language) in 001AXES. For example, all functions in a 001AXES specification are uniquely ordered. With an Include structure (the primitive control structure in 001AXES for independent functions), if a lower priority child is executed and its higher priority sibling receives enough input to execute, then the lower priority child gives up its resource. Thus, thread scheduling is inherent in any 001-developed application.

Dynamic Testing: For those tests that remain (far fewer test cases than would be needed in a traditional environment), testing itself can be viewed as a system of systems in terms of FMaps and TMaps: the environment of the target system as a system, the structures of testing scenarios including use cases as a system, and each instantiation of a scenario (a set of test cases) as a system.

Simulation and execution are examples of dynamic testing. Test cases, which can be defined by FMaps and TMaps, can be executed to test against requirements in simulated environments as well as the target system. Simulation can also be used for environment modeling or testing the target application. Specific constraints on the dynamic behavior of the system, such as sequence and data dependencies (which can also be defined by FMaps and TMaps) can be checked at run time.

Debugging can be performed at the code level with the use of the native debugger of the chosen architecture. 001 automatically generates a unit test harness code wrapper around a function to be executed. This incorporates data-entry prompts for primitive objects and the OMap Editor as a data-entry facility for populating complex objects. The code generated by 001 has variable and function names that closely match their corresponding names in the design specification of FMaps and TMaps, setting the stage for life-cycle traceability. The debugger is used to set breakpoints and examine values of simple object variables. The object editor (with its windowing interface as described earlier) is used to examine complex OMap objects (from within the debugger) and to modify their values or load other OMap objects having test values. Testing is also supported by ASCII output generation showing the object decomposition in terms of its structure and leaf node values of OMap objects from the debugger. The OMap Editor is used to perform testing by allowing a user to view and modify an OMap object from within the debugging environment. This lets a user determine the contents of any complex OMap object and to make changes to perform experiments while debugging the system. The following commands are used from within a typical debugger to invoke the OMap Editor and to print an ASCII representation of the object to file:

```
print debug_OMap(CLIENT1)
print ascii_OMap(CLIENT1.self,"./client.ascii")
```

The RAT automatically generates test code (that inherits rules from whence it came) that finds an additional set of errors dynamically. For finding user intent errors, at run time, dynamic testing is supported by invoking the object editor on objects from within the debugger of the native operating system. This allows one to perform "what if" experiments by changing an object on the fly and to load and store persistent objects. Run-time constraint tests (these are really universal axioms that must hold for objects to be well formed) are automatically generated to validate the universal constraints that "two objects cannot be in the same place at the same time" and the fact that "you can't get something from nothing." For example, it would not allow an engine to be put into a truck (or, as mentioned earlier, a leg onto a table or a Place into a Customer record) that already had one, nor allow an engine to be removed from a truck with no engine. A unit test harness for testing each object and its relationships is also automatically generated by the RAT.

An automatic user interface is provided with the OMap editor for populating and manipulating complex objects, including storage and retrieval for persistent objects. This provides the ability to test the target system at any input-output interface with predefined object test data sets.

Some kinds of testing that remain (e.g., code coverage analysis) are usually performed in later phases of the life cycle. The need for code coverage testing is minimized, since the use of 001AXES for defining the system ensures no interface errors. This means there will be no logic in danger of not being used properly due to interface problems in the models, since if the model contained an interface error, it would be caught by the Analyzer before the code was automatically generated from that model. This eliminates the need for wire-tracing-oriented tests that analyze code produced with traditional environments. Since all code is automatically generated from FMaps and TMaps, the chance for a human to miss either creating the code for part of a model or interfacing incorrectly to the other code in the system is eliminated.

For the test coverage analysis that remains, test coverage analysis can be performed by selecting a configuration of the generator component to generate coverage analysis FMap (and TMap) implementations for a particular subsystem to be tested. The topmost FMap of the subsystem has an associated set of test cases in which each test case represents the inputs (either primitive object values or OMaps) to run one scenario (i.e., a performance pass) of the system. After defining the test cases, the subsystem is executed. The generated code logs each decision alternative taken in each FMap with a reference to the current test case for all the test cases defined. When the test cases finish running, the output objects for each test case are stored (for possible pre- or post-condition analysis) and an analysis is automatically performed to determine the coverage within the system provided by test cases. This coverage analysis results in a listing of the percentage of coverage (the number of paths taken over the number of potential paths), and a listing by test case of the FMap decision alternatives taken. With this approach, regression testing is performed simply by rerunning the set of test cases for a particular subsystem.

Special analysis functions can be developed in terms of FMaps and TMaps as part of the test system to analyze the results (e.g., to analyze the post-conditions as output OMap objects and in terms of the pre-conditions as input OMap objects to see whether or not a particular function under test behaves as expected). The analysis FMap examining the pre- and post-conditions of a system under test can use test cases from the coverage database; or, the analysis FMap can be a stand-alone special-purpose test with its own inputs separate from those of the coverage database test cases.

Using DBTF and 001, the process of developing a software system to test software is the same as the process of developing any software system. (8) A solution for how to develop one solves the other. This includes the same generic phases, language, tools, and testing techniques (i.e., testing the application system is the same generic process as testing the system that tests the application system). The set of tests developed itself as a DBTF system can become a set of reusable tests for other systems as well. The same can be said about the applications it will be used to test.

FMaps and TMaps are used to model the testing system. Test cases are stored as OMap files providing pre- and post-conditions for the testing of FMaps in the target system. Just as with the application being tested, code is automatically generated from the FMaps and TMaps in the testing system. The tests are then ready to run. The results are captured as OMap files. Special analysis functions can be developed in terms of FMaps and TMaps as part of the test system to analyze the results (e.g., to analyze the output OMap objects and the input OMap objects to see whether or not a particular function behaves as expected for a particular test). The analysis FMap examining the pre- and post-conditions of a system under test can use test cases from the coverage database; or, the analysis FMap can be a stand-alone special-purpose test with its own inputs separate from those of the coverage database test cases.

Automatic documentation: The documentation environment of a 001-developed system is tightly integrated with the definition of the system. To document a system the user first selects the option Library Settings of the Utilities menu from within the Library

Manager for a selected library. This brings up the Environment Manager, which is used to set the characteristics for the selected library. The user toggles the documentation templates to be generated under the title "Documentation Resource Allocation Tools" from within the Environment Manager. When a user analyzes a 001AXES definition from within the Definition Manager for the selected library, documentation is automatically generated by the RAT, wrapping in the user's own comments should it be desirable to do so. That same 001AXES definition can itself become part of that same generated document (Figure 42-17). Documentation from the various model viewpoints of a system can be collected and integrated into the documentation of the system. This means, for example, that a resulting document could also include descriptions of the requirements, the testing, developer's issues, and developer's decisions made about the design of a system.

Configuration management: The Baseliner facility provides version control and baselining for all RMaps, FMaps, TMaps, and user-defined reusables, including user-defined FMap and TMap structures. To set up version control on a library, the user selects the option Set Version from the Utilities menu from within the Definition Manager. The Build Manager provides configuration control and manages all entities used in the construction of an executable. This includes source files, header files, and context information about the steps taken to produce the executable. This facility also provides options for controlling the optimization level, debugging information, and profiling information of the compiled code. To set build characteristics, the user selects the option Link Options from the Utilities menu from within the Definition Manager.

Maintenance: With traditional tools, after shell or partial code has been automatically generated, programmers add or change code manually. As they write more code, it becomes more difficult to regenerate the shell or partial code from changes in the requirements, because their code would be destroyed or made obsolete. The maintenance process becomes even more manual as the software evolves with 001.

The maintenance phase is simply redesign and redevelopment (iterations of development phases). DBTF systems are defined to handle changes both during development and operation.

Because all objects in a 001AXES system are under control and all objects are traceable, there is more flexibility and less unpredictability than with traditional systems.

Again, with 001, the developer *doesn't ever need to change the code*. SOOs are defined to handle changes both during development and operation, providing for more flexibility yet less unpredictability than with traditional systems. Application changes are made to the specification—*not to the code* (whether it be for simulation or for software). Changes to the architecture of the application are made to the configuration (either the SGT or layered primitive types) of the generator environment (which generates one of a possible set of implementations from the model)—*not to the code*. Once a change has been made to either the specification or the architecture configuration, only that part of the system that has been changed is regenerated and integrated with the rest of the application (again, automatically). The system is then automatically generated, compiled, linked, and executed *without manual intervention.*

Though each of these portions of the generic life cycle are conceptually distinct, in practice they tend to overlap considerably. The enhancement of productivity provided by automated analysis and automatic generation encourages rapid-prototyping style development (or eXtreme Programming). Often, a skeletal representation of the target system is defined first, to be subsequently fleshed out with greater functionality. The user is allowed to see the results of his ideas clearly as soon as they are consistent and logically complete (i.e., the 001AXES specification does not have any missing pieces, from a logical point of view).

System Engineering

In the previous sections, we concentrated on software development. The next section describes system designer/system engineering-related tasks within a 001 environment. Although the developer's tasks and the system designer's tasks often overlap, an application's life cycle would typically begin with the system design first, and the system design would need to be completed before all the developer's tasks are completed.

Requirements Capturing

A typical system design process begins with capturing requirements that are often in the form of a customer-supplied English document. If requirements are defined with English or a traditional requirements language (instead of with 001AXES), the requirements can then be modeled in 001AXES before proceeding to the design specification stage (where the system design is defined in 001AXES). To support the modeler in this endeavor, the automatic import facility of 001 reads the user's requirements document and builds an RMap of FMaps (including a beginning sketch of FMaps and TMaps), matching the requirements, to get a head start on the development of the FMaps and TMaps for the requirements.

The requirements component, RT(x), automatically parses the requirements document for key expressions (for example, "cash management system") and keywords (for example, "shall"). An RMap is then automatically generated that essentially is an outline of the sections in the requirements document, along with information the user chose for the purpose of establishing traceability and gathering metrics throughout the life cycle. Each node in the RMap corresponds to an FMap and its automatically generated functions, which continue to outline the paragraphs of a section of the requirements document. A sentence may contain one or more requirements. An FMap leaf node function under a parent function associated with a paragraph is associated with a requirement. Each requirement is uniquely identified and is numbered with a requirements identifier used to make correspondences to the target system, which will be defined by the user during the design process. As part of the design process, reusables can be used to fulfill some of the requirements associated with the nodes on the RMap. For others, some FMaps and TMaps may already have been defined for this system. Others are yet to be defined.

The modeler decides how much detail to provide in terms of FMaps and TMaps for the requirements. It becomes a trade-off for the requirements engineer. If it is important to have quality requirements that save on confusion and time later (both of which contribute to saving money), more detail will be provided in the FMaps and TMaps during the requirements phase.

Requirements traceability: A requirement in a definition (e.g., the currently selected requirement in an FMap or a TMap) can be graphically connected (via RMap intra- or intersystem model relationship connectors) by the system designer to other definition nodes (e.g., another set of requirements, a set of tests, a set of use cases, or a target system model) for the purpose of tracing that requirement to the other models. When an FMap is analyzed and it is determined that it needs other definitions (e.g., another FMap operation or structure), the RMap is automatically redrawn to reflect this dependency. Any preliminary dependencies that the user has manually drawn in are removed if they violate the consistency of the internal FMap dependencies as determined by the Analyzer. A traceability matrix can be automatically generated for any combination of RMap model relationships to provide traceability information. An RMap is printed as an encapsulated postscript file and able to be used within a user's generated documents. This supports a user in documenting system traceability.

With the RT(x) concept, a system design can be seamlessly integrated to software. RT(x) provides users with more control over their own requirements process. It allows users to enter requirements into the system and trace between those requirements and corresponding FMaps and TMaps (and corresponding generated code) throughout system specification, detailed design, implementation, testing, and final documentation. A user can define any relationship between objects and describe the complex dependencies between these objects. This allows the user to query on, for example, the relationships between a set of requirements and its supporting specifications, test cases, and implementations. The requirements editor allows the user to specify, query, and report on a database of information about a model (and its relationships) as well as about its development (and its relationships).

Requirements analysis: A requirements definition can have additional information about it and its relationships. Every node on the RMap has the ability to have information about it, its development, and relationships (within and between life-cycle phases) associated with it provided by the user. This information, together with its formal definition, is used for gathering metrics about the system and its development, providing a mechanism to trace from requirements to code and back again, ensuring that the implemented system meets the requirements. This information could include who is responsible for the object in question (e.g., who created this requirement or which target system function implements this requirement); constraints; TBDs; other requirements from the user; issues; and information about the contents of the model itself. The RAT can use this information to generate metrics and reports on the progress or state of the development of the current target system and its relation to the original requirements.

Detailed Design Document Generation

Documentation (e.g., detailed design documents) can be automatically generated (when analysis is completed or when needed) from the same SOO specifications that code is generated from. The documentation for the model is therefore always consistent with its generated code. Integration of documents and code is maintained by the Baseliner facility.

Documents can be generated using document templates or document artifacts corresponding to life-cycle phases. This documentation (partial or complete) can then be imported into document-publishing software for processing and/or direct incorporation into the final document.

System Analysis and Design

Simulation: If it is desirable to simulate the requirements, the FMaps and TMaps need to be defined to the level of primitives (functions for FMaps and types for TMaps) at their leaf nodes. The higher the level of the primitives, the higher the level of the requirements that can be simulated; the lower the level of the primitives, the more finely grained will be the simulated requirements. In 001, primitive types need not have an associated implementation for simulation. A user only has to define the primitive type (e.g., its name and its set of primitive operations). Implementation trade-offs are studied by identifying potential implementations for a primitive operation. FMaps and TMaps can be executed directly by the run-time executive component, the Xecutor (Figure 42-20).

The Xecutor can be configured to perform real-time distributed system simulation and analysis and/or it can be configured to be a stand-alone real-time distributed object executive (DXecutor). The functionality of the Xecutor can be extended by dynamic loading of external modules. The Xecutor component understands the real-time characteristics inherent in the grammar of a 001AXES definition (e.g., all functions to be executed have a unique priority). To perform simulation, the system is defined in terms of what it does (the functional architecture), how it can be done (the resource architecture), and who does what when (the allocation architecture).

To understand the system, the user defines time and other engineering characteristics of the system so that it can be analyzed. For example, to determine the viability of particular scheduling constraints on the system the user defines constraint (e.g., an interval within which a function must complete once started) and timing characteristics of the primitive functions (e.g., a fixed time or an algorithmically computed time using a random

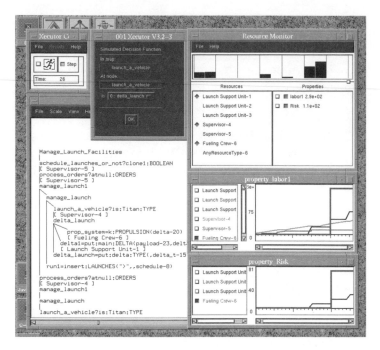

Figure 42-20. *Xecutor Running a real-time simulation experiment.*

number seed to provide for variances). Another feature is a behavior calculator that allows a user to roll up information (characteristics of the system associated with a primitive function such as cost and risk) to its parent function, which collects a sum of each child's value for each type of characteristic. This roll-up process continues until a parent with a monitor is reached to capture and log its subsystem characteristics.

In order to perform system analysis, the system designer goes through an iterative process of defining simulation experiments. System characteristics and system definitions continue to be revised until the system satisfies the engineering constraints of the system requirements. Along the way the system's requirements might need to be changed to further constrain or relax system needs due to unforeseen events (such as the availability of certain hardware not being completed on time). At this point the system is ready for full detailed design and full-scale development using a process of recursive refinement. This refinement process continues as more aspects of the target system are added throughout its development process (e.g., with its implementation, deployment, maintenance, and evolution). If the system being simulated has been designed to be a production software system, the same FMaps and TMaps used for the simulation can be used to automatically generate the production code. The Xecutor can be used to analyze processes such as those in a business environment (enterprise model), manufacturing environment (process model), or a software environment (e.g., searching for parallelism in an algorithm).

Mapping Changes to Code

Changes to the requirements can be made to the original requirements or to the requirements in FMaps and TMaps. If a user makes incremental changes to the English requirements document and then reimports it by generating a new RMap of FMaps for those requirements, the requirements component will allow for requirements document changes and then reimport those requirements with a minimum of disturbance to the established RMap of FMap requirements models and their associated links to other models (e.g., testing systems or the target system under development). If a user makes changes to the requirements at the level of FMaps and TMaps, they are in the form where the analyzer is able to automatically determine that the requirements are consistent, logically complete, and traceable.

Any relationship connections between models are automatically maintained. For example, if a requirement FMap has a dependency relation to a supporting target system (software) model and the requirement FMap is deleted, then the dependency relation is removed. Test models can be evolved as needed and regression tests performed as needed. The new design information is extracted and placed into the document based on the document configuration of the RAT. A change in a 001AXES specification is followed by an automatic regeneration of the code that has been impacted with the change using the generator in order to guarantee that the code matches the specification (again, as we discussed earlier, maintenance is always performed at the FMap and TMap level).

The user than instructs the generator to automatically regenerate the code. Only that part of the system that has changed will be regenerated. Once again the system is automatically compiled, linked, and executed.

Summary

DBTF's preventative philosophy, to solve a problem as early as possible, means finding that problem statically (before implementing it) is better than finding it dynamically at testing time. Preventing it by the way that system is defined is even better—better, faster, cheaper. Better yet is not having to define the system (and build and test) it at all. This is the philosophy adhered to in designing systems and developing software with 001.

Toward this end, we have described how 001 can be used to automate the development process within each phase and between phases, beginning when the user first inputs his thoughts and ending when testing his ideas. It has been shown that with this approach, the same language and the same tools can be used throughout all phases, levels, and layers of design and development. There are no other languages or tools to learn.

Systems developed with 001 (SOOs) are all candidates for reuse, because they are defined with 001AXES (and 001AXES is based on DBTF). All SOOs can be used in multiple or evolving projects, because they do not have "lock-in" characteristics. Each DBTF development phase is independent of a later phase. An application can be automatically generated for various alternative implementations without changing its original definition. A set of requirements allows for alternative specifications; a set of specifications allows for alternative implementations (for example, one project with code generated from a 001AXES definition to interface with a relational database environment and another generated from the same 001AXES definition to interface with an object-oriented database; one project with a client/server architecture and another with a mainframe architecture; or one project with C or embedded C, another with Java and another with C#).

Real-world experience sets the stage for the DBTF technology, the DBTF technology embodies the theory, the language supports its representation, and the 001 Tool Suite supports its application and use. Each is evolutionary (in fact, recursively so), with experience feeding the theory and the theory feeding 001AXES, which in turn feeds the 001 Tool Suite. All are used in concert to design systems and build software—for gaining built-in quality, built-in productivity, and built-in control.

References

1. 001 Tool Suite, Hamilton Technologies, Inc., Version 3.3.1, 1986–2001.
2. M. Hamilton, "Inside Development Before the Fact," *Electronic Design,* 4 April 1994, ES.
3. M. Hamilton, "Development Before the Fact in Action," *Electronic Design,* 13 June 1994, ES.
4. M. Hamilton and W. R. Hackler, *Object Thinking: Development Before the Fact,* In Press.
5. M. Ouyang and M. W. Golay, "An Integrated Formal Approach for Developing High Quality Software of Safety-Critical Systems," Report No. MIT-ANP-TR-035, Cambridge: Massachusetts Institute of Technology, September 1995.
6. U.S. Department of Defense, Strategic Defense Initiative, *Software Engineering Tools Experiment—Final Report,* Vol. 1, Experiment Summary, Table 1, 9. Washington, D. C., October 1992.
7. Krut, Jr., "Integrating 001 Tool Support in the Feature-Oriented Domain Analysis Methodology" (CMU/SEI-93-TR-11, ESC-TR-93-188), Pittsburgh: Software Engineering Institute, Carnegie Mellon University, 1993.
8. M. Hamilton and W. R. Hackler, "Towards Cost Effective and Timely End-to-End Testing," HTI. Prepared for Army Research Laboratory, Contract No. DAKF11-99-P-1236, 17 July 2000.
9. J. Keyes, *Internet Management,* ch. 30–33, on 001-developed systems for the Internet, Auerbach, 2000.
10. Keyes, J. and M. Hamilton, "Defining e . . . com for e-Profits," *Handbook of E-Business,* ch. F5, RIA, 2000.

MARGARET HAMILTON (mhh@htius.com) is the founder and CEO of Hamilton Technologies, Inc. (HTI), based in Cambridge, Massachusetts, (17 Inman Street, Cam-

bridge, MA 02139, 617-492-0058). A pioneer in the systems engineering and software development industry, her mission has been to bring to market a completely integrated and robust tool suite based on the unique systems theory paradigm she created called Development Before the Fact (DBTF). In bringing her product to market, her company leveraged the power of reusability and the reliability of seamless integration to provide a set of tools that sharply decrease errors while simultaneously increasing productivity. The result is an ultra-reliable system at a fraction of the cost of conventional systems. Hamilton's goal was to embed this formal and completely systems-oriented object (SOO) framework into a highly efficient, high-performance, completely graphical, portable workbench of smart tools that the planner, systems engineer, and software developer could use throughout the entire system design and software development life cycle. Today this ideal has been surpassed with the 001 Tool Suite.

Earlier in her career, as the leader of the software engineering division at MIT's Charles Stark Draper Laboratory, Hamilton was the director of the Apollo on-board flight software project and created Higher Order Software (HOS), a formal systems design theory.

Hamilton then founded and was CEO of Higher Order Software, where she was responsible for the development of the first comprehensive life-cycle development tool in the industry. This tool, called USE.IT, was based on her formal design theory, HOS.

Hamilton received the Augusta Ada Lovelace Award from the Association for Women in Computing in 1986.

WILLIAM R. HACKLER (ron@htius.com) is director of development at Hamilton Technologies, Inc. (HTI), based in Cambridge, Massachusetts. As part of his responsibilities, he is the lead engineer for the development of both current and future versions of the 001 Tool Suite, using 001 to define and generate itself. In addition, Hackler has been responsible for many areas of the DBTF technology.

Hackler has been responsible for many other 001-designed and -developed systems, including the development of a simulator for the University of California Los Alamos National Laboratory; a missile tracking simulation for a large aerospace company (HTI was nominated for SBA Subcontractor of the Year as a result of this effort); several asynchronous real-time distributed applications for SDI; a factory model for an aerospace manufacturing plant; and several Internet-related applications, including an accident record system for state highway departments, a trading system for financial systems, and a matchmaking system.

Prior to HTI, Hackler was director of advanced concepts at Higher Order Software, Inc., where he spent many years defining and developing technologies based on research using the foundations of the HOS methodology. Here he was responsible for many applications applying this methodology and its automation, USE.IT (many components of which he was responsible for designing and developing). These applications included the development of systems in the areas of battle management and aerospace manufacturing.

Prior to this he studied composition with composer Mertin Brown in the Charles Ives lineage of music and applied music theory to the objects of mathematics.

Note

001, 001 Tool Suite, 001:Digital Gold, Digital Gold, DBTF, Development Before the Fact, FunctionMap, FMap, TypeMap, TMap, ObjectMap, OMap, RoadMap, RMap, ExecutionMap, EMap, RAT, SOO, System Oriented Object, 001AXES, Xecutor, DXecutor, 001Engineer, 001Developer, 001LearningEdition, WebJumpStarter, Agent001Db are all trademarks of Hamilton Technologies, Inc.

Custom Tag Library versus JavaBeans

Jason Weiss

Java technology provides developers with JavaServer Pages (JSP) and servlets as a superior alternative to traditional CGI programs. The architecture of JSPs provides support for a logical and physical separation between the HTML page designers and the component developers, who specialize in implementing advanced business logic. Another advantage of a JSP is its ability to implement a custom tag library. These custom tags allow page designers to abstract themselves from a complex set of logic; include this tag and it will have this effect on the Web page.

Although examples can be located detailing how to build a custom tag library, developers are rarely educated on how to make a proper design decision on which to use, a custom tag library or a JavaBean.

It should be noted that this paper assumes that the reader has some knowledge of using JSPs to implement a Java 2 Platform Enterprise Edition (J2EE) Web Application.

JavaBean or Custom Tag Library?

There is no standard HTML or JSP tag that is capable of executing different logic based on different inputs fed into the page. In order to create a *reactive* page, Java code becomes a necessity. Both custom tag libraries and JavaBeans can be utilized to separate presentation from complex business logic, providing the ability to run different logic branches. It is at this point that it becomes imperative for a developer to understand the idiosyncrasies, strengths, and weaknesses of each of these options in order to make educated design decisions. We will take a brief look at both options, and provide a set of heuristics in table form that outline the capabilities and features of each. Use this table as a reference to help you decide which approach to use in your design, JavaBeans or a custom tag library.

JavaBeans

JavaBeans technology has been around for a while. Full coverage of JavaBeans is well beyond our scope here, but if you are interested in learning more about JavaBeans, there are numerous books on the subject, as well as documentation from Sun at http://java.sun.com/beans/docs/.

JavaBeans are a useful option for encapsulating logic and removing Java code from the middle of a JSP page. JavaBeans have been available for use inside of a JSP since the 1.0 JSP specification. JSPs are equipped with three dedicated tags that specialize in working with JavaBeans:

```
<jsp:useBean>
<jsp:getProperty>
<jsp:setProperty>
```

There are a number of attributes for each of these tags, which again are beyond our scope and will not be covered here. Suffice to say, each of these are empty tags (an empty tag has no text appearing between the opening and closing tags, and can be simplified to a single tag with a "/>" terminal) and cannot manipulate the contents of the JSP page in any way. To get a value out of the bean, the page designer declares his intention to use a bean first, for example:

```
<jsp:useBean id="myBean" class="com.some.company.MyBean"/>
```

The id attribute is the name that the page designer will use to reference the bean. The class attribute is the class that should be associated with the id provided. A JavaBean may store a color code and expose the value of that color code through a set of methods, for example:

- String getColorCode()
- void setColorCode (String color)

The bean is said to have exposed a property named colorCode. Read-only properties can be established by not defining a mutator method.

Once a bean is created through the <jsp:useBean> tag, page designers can access the bean properties elsewhere on the page. To work with the properties of a bean, the page designer uses either the <jsp:getProperty/> or <jsp:setProperty/> tag. For example, this tag would output the value of the color code to the JSP page:

```
<jsp:getProperty name="myBean" property="colorCode"/>
```

JavaBeans force developers to respect the notion of encapsulation. The methods used to manipulate the properties on the beans could do anything behind the scenes, including accessing a database and implementing complex validation rules. In fact, reading and writing properties from a JavaBean could fire off different actions. It is because of encapsulation that these JavaBeans can be thought of as "black-box" programming. Page designers can use these black boxes throughout the site without an iota of understanding of the complexities behind the values that mystically appear.

Here is a complete example of using a JavaBean inside of a JSP page:

```
<%@ page import="com.some.company.*"
    language="java"
    buffer="8kb"
    autoFlush="true"
    isThreadSafe="true"
    info="Copyright(C) 2001, Sybase, Inc."
    isErrorPage="false" %>

<jsp:useBean id="myBean" class="com.some.company.MyBean"/>
<HTML>
<HEAD>
<TITLE>Some Page</TITLE>
</HEAD>
<BODY>
    Here is something from the bean:
    <jsp:getProperty name="myBean" property="colorCode"/>
</BODY>
</HTML>
```

To reiterate a major point, the logic behind the method used to represent the colorCode property could be quite complex. For example, it might connect to a remote database or invoke a method running on an application server halfway around the world in order to find out the value of the property. Regardless of the approach, the page designer only needs to know the name of the property he's interested in using, not the details on how to obtain the value.

Although it is possible to invoke bean methods directly after declaring the bean using a <jsp:useBean> tag, the JSP 1.1 specification explicitly refers to the use of <jsp:getProperty> and <jsp:setProperty>. In other words, the specification is unclear about whether invoking methods directly is an acceptable practice or not. The safest course of action is to stick with these two tags and avoid calling methods on the bean directly.

JavaBeans are great for handling business logic. The aforementioned JavaBean tags have the built-in ability to work hand-in-hand with data obtained through a Web form. When setting a property on a JavaBean, page designers only need to remember to set the property attribute on the tag to the same name used inside of the form. The JSP will automatically assume that the value it should provide needs to come from the form that it is processing. In situations where the form name must be different from the property name on the bean, a combination of the property and param attributes can be set, thereby establishing a link between the two.

Bean tags also understand the notion of scope. Recall that scope provides an indication of where the bean is recognized. By specifying the optional scope attribute on the <jsp:useBean/> tag, the bean will only be instantiated if a matching id is not already present at the indicated scope level: page, application, session, or request. Although we won't go into the details between the different scopes here, this feature is unique to a JavaBean.

Finally, it is worth mentioning that our discussion on JavaBeans does not relate to Enterprise JavaBeans (EJBs), which are part of J2EE. There are proposals to introduce another standard JSP tag that provides similar capabilities, allowing a JSP to establish a reference to an EJB on a remote server, but as of this writing there is no standard. Also noteworthy is the fact that each of these tags is case sensitive, and attributes must be enclosed in either single or double quotes.

Custom Tag Libraries

The JavaServer Pages 1.1 specification provides a mechanism for defining new actions into a JSP page. A custom tag library is comprised of one or more Java classes (called tag handlers) and an XML tag library description file (tag library, for short). The tag library dictates the new tag names and valid attributes for those tags.

Tag handler classes, together with a tag library, determine how the tags, their attributes, and their bodies will be interpreted and processed at request time from inside a JSP page. Collectively, they provide an architecture that is arguably more apt than a JavaBean at encapsulating a complex operation from the page designer. Unfortunately, that power comes with a cost; it takes more effort to build and implement a custom tag library than a simple JavaBean.

Here is an example of a JSP page using a small custom tag library:

```
<%@ page import="com.some.company.*"
    language="java"
    buffer="8kb"
    autoFlush="true"
    isThreadSafe="true"
    info="Copyright(C) 2001, Sybase, Inc."
    isErrorPage="false" %>

<jsp:useBean id="myBean" class="com.some.company.MyBean"/>

<HTML>
<BODY>
```

Here is something from the bean:

```
<jsp:getProperty name="myBean" property="colorCode"/>
<%@ taglib uri="WEB-INF/tlds/tablib.tld" prefix="example"%>
```

Here is the output from a custom tag:

```
<example:myCustomTag someColor="#FFFF00"/>
</BODY>
</HTML>
```

At page request time, the Java classes associated with this custom tag are invoked, and the generated content is streamed back to the client in place of this tag. The classes that implement that tag library are distributed with the Web application either in the web-inf/lib directory, contained in a single .JAR, or in the web-inf/classes directory, as individual classes. The taglib page directive provides directions on where the tag library exists. This tag library defines the implementation details of the tag, in XML format. The following tag library was referenced inside of the JSP page by the taglib page directive (<%@ taglib . . . >), and it established the prefix of example for all the tags inside the library:

```
<?xml version="1.0" encoding="ISO-8859-1" ?>
<!DOCTYPE taglib PUBLIC
"-//Sun Microsystems, Inc.//DTD JSP Tag Library
  1.1//EN"
"http://java.sun.com/j2ee/dtds/web-jsptaglibrary_1_1.dtd">

<!--This is my tab library descriptor-->
<taglib>
  <tlibversion>1.0</tlibversion>
  <jspversion>1.1</jspversion>
  <info>
    Custom Tag Example
  </info>

 <!--Tags-->
 <tag>
<name>myCustomTag</name>
<tagclass>com.some.company.ExampleTag</tagclass>
<bodycontent>EMPTY</bodycontent>
<info>Just a small sample tag</info>
      <attribute>
            <name>someColor</name>
            <required>false</required>
```

```
        </attribute>
    </tag>
</taglib>
```

You can see that the library exposes a tag called myCustomTag with a single, optional attribute, someColor. The tag library also indicates that the body content (<bodycontent>) is empty and should be ignored.

Tag libraries typically (when built correctly) provide the page designer with a more meaningful, self-descriptive definition of what the tag is doing, possibly demonstrating a self-documenting characteristic. Instead of being restricted to a tag that begins <jsg:getProperty/>, the page can use a tag like <employee:PreferredColor/>, making the HTML more legible down the road for maintenance purposes.

Similar to a JavaBean, page designers can inform a custom tag of a value by setting attributes on the tag. However, tag libraries also have the unique ability of allowing the tag developer to directly expose variables to the JSP page. For example, a tag library could populate a variable called employee, permitting the page designer to reference the variable elsewhere on the page inside of a scriptlet or expression, like this:

```
<%= employee.getPreferredColor() %>
```

How Do I Access the Request Object?

Both JavaBeans and tag libraries can access the various methods and thereby the data associated with the request object. Tag library attributes can declaratively indicate that an attribute can be specified as an expression:

```
<rtnexpresssion>true</rtnexpression>
```

This means that the following syntax is valid for a custom tag:

```
<example:myTag
    myAttribute="<%= request.getContentLength() %>">
```

Similarly, if a JavaBean needs access to the same type of content, use the <jsp:setProperty> tag:

```
<jsp:setProperty
    name="myBean"
```

```
property="someProperty"
value="<%= request.getContentLenght() %>"/>
```

Comparison Chart

Figure 43-1 provides a one-stop reference to help developers choose which approach is right for their problem, JavaBeans or custom tag libraries.

	JavaBean	Custom Tag Library
Deployment Location	Accessible through the CLASSPATH on the server hosting the Web Application. Typically deployed as a .JAR file into the web-inf/lib directory.	Either as stand-alone classes deployed into web-inf/classes, or as a .JAR file inside of web-inf/lib.
Mappings	No concept of mapping the physical JavaBean JAR into a .WAR deployment descriptor.	The .WAR deployment descriptor can provide a logical mapping between the tag library descriptor URI and the physical tag library descriptor location. For example, the JSPs can reference /TagLibrary and the deployment descriptor will associate this with /web-inf/tlds/taglib.tld.
Tag Flow	Rigid; must use 1 of 3 well-defined tags to access the bean, each of which use the jsp prefix	Fluid; tag library author determines the names of the tags, the page designer determines the prefix
Variable Access	Page designers can only get/set values through the use of the standard bean tags: <jsp:getProeprty/> <jsp:setProperty/>	Page designers assign values through tag attributes, and tag developers can optionally expose custom variables for use elsewhere on the JSP page.
Scope	Can be defined at the page, application, session, or request level.	Page scope only; tag can only be used on a JSP page that references the tag library through the taglib page directive.
Manipulation of JSP Content	No	Yes
Ability to encapsulate complex business logic from the page designer	Yes	Yes
Ability to access the request object	Yes	Yes. Must remember to add the <rtnexpression> tag for each attribute that needs this capability.
Ability to provide a logical name for a complex business operation	No	Yes, the name of the tag is developer defined, and the name of the prefix is page designer defined.
Ease of development	Relatively Simple	More Complex
Version Introduced	JSP 1.0	JSP 1.1 (Sybase® EAServer 3.6.1 fully implements JSP 1.1)

Figure 43-1. *JavaBeans or custom tag libraries reference chart.*

Notes

Sybase and Power J are registered trademarks of Sybase, Inc., or its subsidiaries. All other company and product names mentioned might be trademarks of the companies with which they are associated.

Java and all Java-based marks are trademarks or registered trademarks of Sun Microsystems, Inc., in the United States and other countries.

JASON WEISS is a principal architect working with the Internet applications division of Sybase. His focus is on Internet development with EAServer. Jason coauthored *Taming Jaguar* and routinely lectures on Sybase technology solutions. When not writing code, he enjoys hiking, skiing, and scuba diving. He can be reached at weissj@sybase.com.

## CHAPTER 44

PowerBuilder 8 Web Development

Jason Weiss

PowerBuilder 8 represents a major milestone for developers seeking a true 4GL Web development environment. This version of PowerBuilder builds on the development environment's proven capabilities with the integration of a robust and full-featured HTML authoring environment, complemented with an array of wizards that assist in building a new Web site from scratch or simply performing some routine maintenance on an existing site. Tightly coupled with PowerBuilder is PowerDynamo, a dynamic page server that integrates seamlessly with any ISAPI, NSAPI, or CGI-enabled Web server.

Typically, robust, scalable, highly available Web applications are not developed by Power-Builder and PowerDynamo alone. Enterprise application development must leverage a robust application server, such as Sybase EAServer (EAS), a Java 2 Platform Enterprise Edition (J2EE) certified application server. In our example application, we will be leveraging PowerBuilder and EAServer (which includes both Jaguar CTS and PowerDynamo). It is worth noting here that evaluation versions of this software can be obtained from www.sybase.com. We will also be using web DataWindow technology. The web DataWindow allows developers to leverage the feature-rich DataWindow painter to create WYSIWYG Web pages full of data from a database.

Our sample Web application will be a small employee phone book application based on the sample database that ships with PowerBuilder. We will discuss the steps necessary to create this small Web site and provide some useful insight into the decisions behind many of the steps involved.

Creating a Workspace

The PowerBuilder 8 integrated development environment (IDE) uses a workspace/target metaphor. A workspace is comprised of many targets, and each target is an application, or possibly a subset of a much larger application represented by the workspace. The first thing we need to do is create a new workspace for our sample application. After starting

Figure 44-1.
Create a new
workspace.

PowerBuilder, you may see a Welcome splash screen, which provides a direct link for creating a new workspace. In the event you've launched PowerBuilder previously and disabled this splash screen, go to the File menu and select the New . . . Menu option. Click on the Workspace tab page, as displayed in Figure 44-1, select Workspace, and click the OK button. In our sample, we will create a new folder on the C drive called Sample (c:\sample\) and create a workspace named Phonebook inside of that directory (c:\sample\phonebook.pbw).

Creating the Web Target

A workspace all by itself is, for all intents and purposes, worthless until there are targets associated with it. In this next step, we will create our Web target. PowerBuilder provides two distinct types of Web targets. Briefly, the following types of Web targets are available:

- A Dynamo Web site target is a database-based Web site (the Web pages will be stored inside of a database).
- A Web site target is a file-based Web site (the Web pages will be stored as files inside of a root directory).

For our example, we will build a Dynamo Web site (database-based). The database will be an Adaptive Server Anywhere database (included with PowerBuilder). By locating the Web site inside of the database, the Web site can piggyback on the inherent features of the database, including the ability to replicate the Web site. The associated wizard will create our Web target, as well as the necessary deployment configuration for that target.

Inside of PowerBuilder, right-click on the workspace name (Phonebook) and select New from the pop-up menu. A tabbed dialog similar to the one in Figure 44-22 will display that automatically has the Target tab page selected. Locate the Dynamo Web site wizard in the second line and click the OK button. Clicking the OK button will launch a wizard that will help us create a database that will contain our Web site, as well as provide screens with which to tweak the deployment configuration. The exact number of screens in the wizard may vary depending upon your selections as you move through, but there are roughly a dozen pages to this wizard.

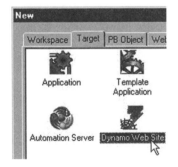

Figure 44-2. Create a
Dynamo Web site target.

Step 1: Review the informational screen. Click the Next button after you have reviewed the information and you are ready to proceed.

Step 2: Specify the Web target's name. After the first informational screen, we are prompted to provide several file names and locations. Recall that we created a new workspace inside of the c:\sample\ directory. We are going to continue developing inside that directory. Change the name of the Web target (the first field on the wizard page) to c:\sample\

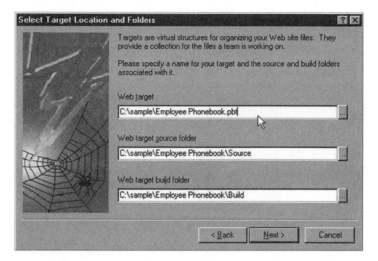

Figure 44-3. *Specify the Employee Phonebook target location.*

Employee Phonebook.pbt and tab off of the field. The other two fields will be updated to reflect the target's name. Your dialogue should look similar to Figure 44-3. Click the Next button to continue.

Step 3: Create the URL Prefix Mapping. Every Web application is associated with a URL prefix mapping. This permits a single server (www.somecompany.com) to host multiple applications. In our example, we will use /hr as the mapping into the Employee Phonebook application. Depending upon how you've configured your Web server, URLs may be case sensitive. In our example, we will use lowercase for the URL mapping, as displayed in Figure 44-4. Click the Next button to continue.

Step 4: Create an ODBC data source. Since we are creating a database-based Web site, we need to create an ODBC data source that will map to our new database. To clarify, the wizard will actually create the database for us when we are finished—the database doesn't have to previously exist (although that certainly is an option). For our sample application, we will create a new ODBC data source named phonebook. Click the Next button to continue.

Step 5: Specify a database file. In the previous step, we identified what the logical ODBC data source name would be. In this step, we need to specify the physical file name and location. In this case, we are going to leave the default name and location:

c:\sample\Employee Phonebook\Dynamo\phonebook.db

Click the Next button to continue.

Step 6: Provide the database login information. The default user ID of "dba" and password of "sql" is sufficient for our small sample. A production site should never accept

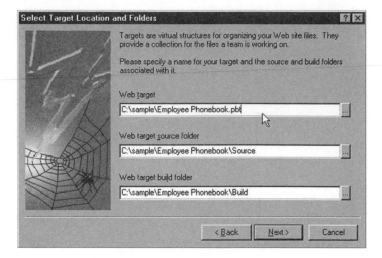

Figure 44-3. *Specify the Employee Phonebook target location.*

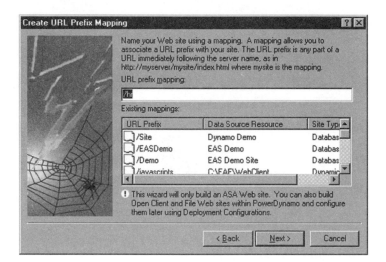

Figure 44-4. *Creating the URL mapping for the application.*

the default user ID and passwords, as it could lead to a security breach. Click the Next button to continue.

Step 7: Optionally include help files and a sample application. Leave the checkbox unchecked—we do not need to include the help files or the sample application inside the database that is about to be created. Click the Next button to continue.

Step 8: Provide a deployment configuration name. Again, this is a logical name and we are going to accept the default. Click the Next button to continue.

Step 9: Specify the Web server location. We will be using the personal Web server that is included with PowerBuilder for developing our sample application. Because this Web server will be started shortly on our development machine, we want to specify localhost for the HTTP server name. Leave the default port of 80, as displayed in Figure 44-5. Click the Next button to continue.

Step 10: Choose an object model. The Web sites developed with PowerBuilder can optionally utilize an object model. If you write server scripts using the default Web target object model, you can deploy the same content to several different servers. Leave the radio button selected next to the "I am using the default object model" option, as displayed in Figure 44-6, and click Next to continue.

Step 11: Specify deployment options. As you work on and modify the various pages inside the Web site, you may encounter the situation where a file may not deploy because of a file lock (i.e., the file is in use). This step allows you to choose an approach to handle these situations. We will again leave the default selection of "Deploy All or Nothing" and click the Next button to continue.

Step 12: Choose a local copy folder. This folder is used for making a local copy of the Web pages when a deploy executes. Again, we will accept the default directory. When we eventually deploy our Web pages, copies of the files will be made in this directory. Click the Next button to continue.

After walking through our wizard, we are presented with a summary screen containing all of the choices made along the way. If everything looks all right, click on the Finish button to begin building your Web site. On the 800 MHz laptop used to build this example, it took approximately 30 seconds for the wizard to create a new database, define an ODBC mapping, establish the URL mapping, and install the system files necessary to support the Web site. Times will vary based on your configuration.

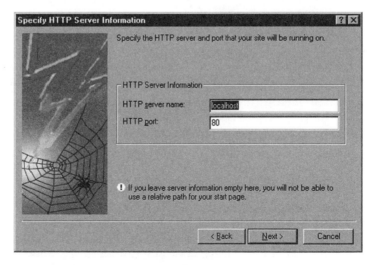

Figure 44-5. Pointing PowerBuilder to your Web server.

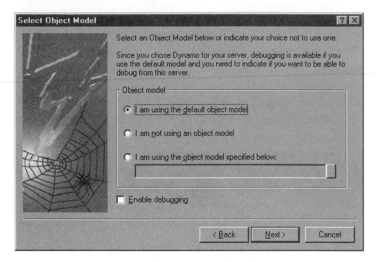

Figure 44-6. *Selecting an object model for the Web site.*

At this point, PowerBuilder has created our new Employee Phonebook Web target. You may need to expand the workspace tree view to see the new target. Presently, there aren't any Web files defined—just the shell to hold your Web site. Creating your Web pages is the next step!

Leveraging DataWindows

The PowerBuilder DataWindow has been a mainstay in client-server development since it was first introduced over ten years ago. PowerBuilder provides smooth integration of the DataWindow into a Web page. The DataWindow is very powerful technology, and in fact is patented by Sybase. There have been complete books written about DataWindow technology. Unfortunately, at this point we must make the assumption that you are comfortable with the concept of a DataWindow, although we will walk you through step-by-step to create the phone book's DataWindow.

To display data from the sample database (this is a different database than the one created as a result of the wizard above—this database contains business data), we need to build a DataWindow that retrieves the names and phone numbers of our employees. We will want to store these DataWindows inside of their own library. For simplicity, we will create another target for our workspace.

Right-click on the workspace and choose New. This target needs to be an application. Specify an application name of hr in the Application Name field and hit the tab key. The Library and Target fields should be automatically filled in, using the workspace's root directory c:\sample\. Click the Finish button to continue.

Next, we need to connect to the database that we will be pulling our list of employees from. The EAS Demo is a sample database that is installed with PowerBuilder 8 out of the box. Access the Database Profiles dialog, expand the ODBC database interface, highlight the EAS Demo database, and click on the Connect button.

> NOTE: If you receive any type of error message while trying to establish your database connection, you must resolve your connection problems before continuing.

Next, we need to create our DataWindow. Right-click on the hr target and choose New. Notice this time the New dialog defaults to the PB Object tab. We need to work with a different tab, the DataWindow tab. After selecting the DataWindow tab, choose the Tabular presentation style and click the OK button. Choose Quick Select and click on the Next button to continue. In the next step, a list of tables available from the EAS Demo database is displayed. Single-click on the employee table and click on the emp_fname, emp_lname, and phone columns, in that order. Click on the OK button to continue. For illustrative purposes only, select teal for the background color and click the Next button to continue. A summary screen of your choices is displayed—click on the Finish button after you have reviewed your selections. Again, for illustrative purposes only, click on the emp_lname column and click on the B toolbar button (bold). This will make the last-name column display in bold. Additionally, go to the Rows menu and choose the Sort menu item. Drag the emp_lname column over to the Columns box (using drag and drop). This will sort the list of employees by last name in ascending order. Click the OK button to close the sort dialog box.

DataWindows are represented using DHTML at run-time, and our purpose is to demonstrate how the visual development environment can be leveraged when designing your Web pages. Save the DataWindow as d_emp_phonebook and close the DataWindow painter.

Starting EAServer

The DataWindow that we just created will eventually be used inside our application server, Jaguar CTS. Before we continue, we need to start up Jaguar. From the Windows Start button, select Program Files, Sybase, Jaguar CTS, and finally Jaguar Server (jdk1.2). This will start up Jaguar CTS, which we will need in the upcoming steps. Feel free to minimize Jaguar's window to get it out of your way after you see "Accepting connections" on the console window.

If you are running PowerBuilder on a Windows 9x operating system, you will not be able to start Jaguar or, unfortunately, continue until you have located a box on your network that is running Jaguar. Jaguar works with a wide array of operating systems, including Windows NT, Windows 2000, Solaris, HP-UX, and AIX. To clarify, clients can access Jaguar from Windows 9x, but they cannot run Jaguar directly.

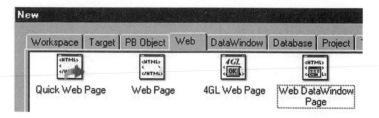

Figure 44-7. *Create a new Web DataWindow page.*

Create Web Pages

Now that we have established a Web target and our phone book DataWindow, we are ready to begin adding pages to the site. To begin, right-click on the Employee Phonebook target and choose New. This time, when the New dialog appears the Web tab page will be selected by default. Select the Web DataWindow Page from the list, as displayed in Figure 44-7, and click the OK button. Once again, PowerBuilder will present a wizard that will collect the necessary information and generate the corresponding code for us. We will be walking through seven distinct steps in this wizard.

Step 1: Review the informational screen. Click the Next button after you have reviewed the information and you are ready to proceed.

Step 2: Specify the new HTML file. Since we are building an employee phone book, let's give our new Web page a suitable name—Phonebook. Tabbing off of the field will automatically populate the file name for us:

c:\sample\Employee Phonebook\Source\Phonebook.htm

Click the Next button to continue.

Step 3: Choosing an EAServer profile. The Web DataWindow technology leverages components installed out of the box inside of EAServer. In order to access and execute a Web DataWindow Web page, we need to associate it with a server. Since we are running EAServer locally on our machine, highlight the localhost server and click Next to continue. If by chance you don't see localhost as an option, as displayed in Fgiure 44-8, cancel the wizard and create an EAServer profile (accessible from the Tools menu) with the following details:

```
Profile Name:    localhost
Server Name:     localhost
Port:            9000
Login Name:      jagadmin
Password: <no password, unless you've created one!!>
```

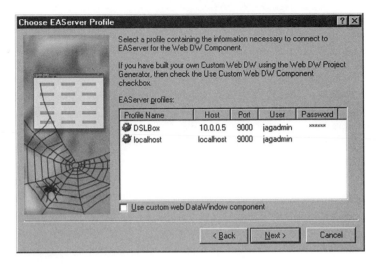

Figure 44-8. *Choosing an EAServer for deployment.*

Step 4: Specify the source of the DataWindow. In this step, we need to tell the wizard where our DataWindow will be coming from. In our case, we previously established a PowerBuilder library that contains the definition. Leave the default selection Power-Builder library or report file and click Next to continue.

Step 5: Specify the library. After indicating that our DataWindow definition would be coming from a PowerBuilder library, we need to point the wizard to the physical path, c:\sample\hr.pbl. Be sure to check the "Generate absolute path in script" checkbox for our example.

Step 6: Choose the DataWindow object. The wizard will open up the library specified and prompt you to pick one of the DataWindows to use on this Web page. Since we only created a single DataWindow, the choice is pretty limited! Highlight the d_emp_phone-book DataWindow and click the Next button to continue.

Step 7: Specify the database connection. Select the EAS Demo connection from the list of available connections. This is the same database profile that we used when we painted the DataWindow earlier.

After walking through our wizard, we are presented with a summary screen containing all of the choices made along the way. If everything looks all right, click on the Finish button to begin building your Web page. Shortly, the page will appear inside of PowerBuilder. Notice that the characteristics of the DataWindow are present inside of the page—the background color should be teal, there are three columns, etc. Be sure to remember to save the page before closing the window!

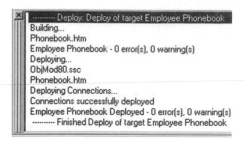

Figure 44-9. *Deployment log.*

Deployment

Congratulations! We are done developing the employee phone book. The only thing left to do is to deploy our Web site. Right-click on the Employee Phonebook Web target and choose Deploy. There won't be anything to configure—we answered those questions when we walked through the Web target wizard. The output window at the bottom of the IDE provides feedback about the progress of the deploy, as displayed in Figure 44-9. Yours should look similar to Figure 44-1.

Accessing the Web Site

Before we just fire up our browser, let's go through a final checklist of what needs to be running in order to access our employee phone book.

1. Ensure that Jaguar Server (JDK 1.2) has been started.
2. Start up the Personal Web Server (it can be found under the PowerDynamo program group). If you had previously started the Web server, you must stop and start it again in order for it to find the new URL mappings we created earlier.
3. Open up your favorite browser and access http://localhost/hr/Phone book.htm. You should see your new employee phone book, similar to the one displayed in Figure 44-10.

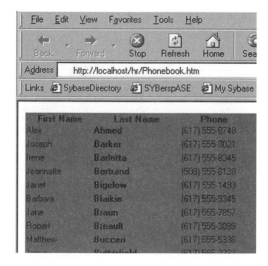

Figure 44-10. *Viewing your phone book in the browser.*

Troubleshooting

Hopefully, your phone book worked on the first try. However, anyone who has developed software before realizes that bugs can surface at any time! When developing this sample application, there was one "gotcha" encountered. Did your browser display something similar to this:

```
ERROR: SetDwObject('C:samplehr.pbl','d_emp_phonebook') failed =
-1
ERROR: DataWindow definition not set.
```

Notice the "\" marks are suspiciously missing from the path. Open up the Phonebook.htm file inside of PowerBuilder and access the Source tab page at the bottom of the painter's window. Navigate the code and replace each occurrence of c:\sample\hr.pbl with c:\\sample\\hr.pbl. For some reason, your "\" marks were being removed when the page was processed. Save the page, re-deploy, and try to access your phone book again—this time you should see your listings!

At the time of writing PowerBuilder 8 was still in beta. The name of the database profile was not finalized. Throughout the text, the database profile was referenced as EAS Demo. In reality, the name of the database may be something like EAS Demo V5 DB. Be sure to take this into account.

EAServer uses database connection caches to access the database. For our small example here, ensure that EAServer has a connection cache configured with a name that is identical to the profile inside of PowerBuilder.

Conclusion

PowerBuilder 8 provides a robust platform for development-interactive, database-driven Web sites. In our sample phone book, recall that we didn't have to manually write a single line of code! Our example here only scratches the surface of what PowerBuilder is capable of producing. I encourage you to experiment with the other features of Power-Builder 8 for developing complex, robust, and scalable enterprise-level Web sites.

Notes

Sybase, Adaptive Server, DataWindow, PowerDynamo, Jaguar CTS, and PowerBuilder are registered trademarks of Sybase, Inc., or its subsidiaries. All other company and product names mentioned might be trademarks of the companies with which they are associated.

Java and all Java-based marks are trademarks or registered trademarks of Sun Micro-systems, Inc., in the United States and other countries.

JASON WEISS is a principal architect working with the Internet applications division of Sybase. His focus is on Internet development with EAServer. Jason coauthored *Taming Jaguar* and routinely lectures on Sybase technology solutions. When not writing code, he enjoys hiking, skiing, and scuba diving. He can be reached at weissj@sybase.com.

Appendixes

HTML Quick Reference

This quick reference covers the following most frequently used HTML tags:

<!—comment—>

<A>

<ADDRESS>

<APPLET>

<AREA>

<B>

<BASE . . . >

<BASEFONT SIZE= . . . >

<BDO>

<BGSOUND>

<BIG>

<BLINK>

<BLOCKQUOTE>

<BODY>

<BUTTON>

<CAPTION>

<CENTER>

<CITE>

<CODE>

<COL>

<COLGROUP>

<DD>

<DEL>

<DIR>

<DIV>

<DL>

<DT>

<EM>

<EMBED>

<FIELDSET>

<FONT SIZE= . . . >

<FORM>

<FRAME>

<FRAMESET>

<H1>

<H2>

<H3>

<H4>

<H5>

<H6>

<H ALIGN= >

<HEAD>

<HP>

<HR>

<HTML>

<I>

<IMG>

<INPUT>

<ISINDEX>

<KBD>
<LABEL>
<LAYER>
<LEGEND>
<LI>
<LINK>
<LISTING>
<MAP>
<MARQUEE>
<MENU>
<META>
<MULTICOL>
<NEXTID>
<NOBR>
<NOEMBED>
<NOFRAME>
<NOLAYER>
<NOSCRIPT>
<OBJECT>
<OL>
<OPTGROUP>
<OPTION>
<P>
<P ALIGN=>
<PARAM>
<PLAINTEXT>
<PRE>
<Q>

<S>
<SAMP>
<SCRIPT>
<SELECT>
<SMALL>
<SOUND>
<SPACER>
<SPAN>
<STRIKE>
<STRONG>
<STYLE>
<SUB>
<SUP>
<TABLE>
<TBODY>
<TD>
<TEXTAREA>
<TFOOT>
<TH>
<THEAD>
<TITLE>
<TR>
<TT>
<U>
<UL>
<VAR>
<WBR>
<XMP>

Tags by type:

Miscellaneous
<!—comment—>
<APPLET>
<CODE>
<!DOCTYPE>
<MARQUEE>
<META>
<NOSCRIPT>
<OBJECT>

<PARAM>
<SCRIPT>

Sound
<BDO>
<BGSOUND>
<EMBED>
<NOEMBED>
<SOUND>

Frames
<FRAME>
<FRAMESET>
<IFRAME>
<NOFRAME>

Links and Images
<ADDRESS>
<A HREF>
<AREA>
<ILAYER>
<IMG>
<LAYER>
<LINK>
<MAP>
<NEXTID>
<NOLAYER>

Tables
<CAPTION>
<COL>
<COLGROUP>
<TABLE>
<TBODY>
<TD>
<TFOOT>
<TH>
<THEAD>
<TR>

General
<BASE>
<BASEFONT>
<BODY>
<HEAD>
<HTML>
<TITLE>

Alignment
<BLOCKQUOTE>
<CENTER>

Forms
<BUTTON>
<FIELDSET>
<FORM>
<INPUT>
<ISINDEX>
<KEYGEN>
<LABEL>
<LEGEND>
<OPTGROUP>
<OPTION>
<SELECT>
<TEXTAREA>

Lists
<DD>
<DFN>
<DIR>
<DL>
<DT>
<LI>
<MENU>
<OL>
<UL>

Dividers

<DIV>
<HR>
<MULITCOL>
<NOBR>
<SPACER>
<SPAN>
<WBR>

Format
<BIG>
<BLINK>
<B>
<CITE>
<DEL>

\<EM\>	\<SAMP\>
\<FONT\>	\<SMALL\>
\<Hx\>	\<STRIKE\>
\<INS\>	\<STRONG\>
\<I\>	\<STYLE\>
\<KBD\>	\<SUB\>
\<LISTING\>	\<SUP\>
\<P\>	\<TT\>
\<PLAINTEXT\>	\<U\>
\<PRE\>	\<VAR\>
\<Q\>	\<XMP\>
\<S\>	

\<!—comment—\>

To include comments in an HTML document that will be ignored by the HTML user agent, surround them with \<!—and—\>. After the comment delimiter, all text up to the next occurrence of—\> is ignored. Hence comments cannot be nested. White space is allowed between the closing—and \>, but not between the opening \<! and—.

Example:

```
<!—Id: The text between these two tags are comments—>
```

\<A . . . \> . . . \</A\>

The Anchor element is a marked text that is the start and/or destination of a hypertext link. Anchor elements are defined by the A element. The A element accepts several attributes, but either the NAME or HREF attribute is required.

Attributes:

HREF—If the HREF attribute is present, the text between the opening and closing anchor elements becomes hypertext. If this hypertext is selected by readers, they are moved to another document, or to a different location in the current document, whose network address is defined by the value of the HREF attribute.

Example :

```
<A HREF="http://www.microsoft.com">Microsoft's</A>Web site
```

With the HREF attribute, the form HREF="#identifier" can refer to another anchor in the same document.

Example:

```
The <A HREF="document.html#glossary">glossary</A> defines terms
used in the document.
```

In this example, selecting "glossary" takes the reader to another anchor (i.e., <A NAME= "glossary">Glossary</A>) in the same document (document.html). The NAME attribute is described below. If the anchor is in another document, the HREF attribute may be relative to the document's address or the specified base address.

METHODS—The METHODS attributes of anchors and links provide information about the functions that the user may perform on an object. These are more accurately given by the HTTP protocol when it is used, but it may, for similar reasons as for the TITLE attribute, be useful to include the information in advance in the link. The HTML user agent may chose a different rendering as a function of the methods allowed; for example, something that is searchable may get a different icon. The value of the METHODS attribute is a comma-separated list of HTTP methods supported by the object for public use.

NAME—If present, the NAME attribute allows the anchor to be the target of a link. The value of the NAME attribute is an identifier for the anchor. Identifiers are arbitrary strings but must be unique within the HTML document.

Example:

```
<A NAME=coffee>Coffee</A> is an example of . . .
An example of this is <A HREF=#coffee>coffee</A>.
```

Another document can then make a reference explicitly to this anchor by putting the identifier after the address, separated by the hash (#) sign:

```
<A NAME=drinks.html#coffee>
```

REL—The REL attribute gives the relationship(s) described by the hypertext link from the anchor to the target. The value is a comma-separated list of relationship values. Values and their semantics will be registered by the HTML registration authority. The default relationship if none other is given is void. The REL attribute is only used when the HREF attribute is present.

REV—The REV attribute is the same as the REL attribute, but the semantics of the link type are in the reverse direction. A link from A to B with REL="X" expresses the same relationship as a link from B to A with REV="X." An anchor may have both REL and REV attributes.

TITLE—The TITLE attribute is informational only. If present, the TITLE attribute should provide the title of the document whose address is given by the HREF attribute. The TITLE attribute is useful for at least two reasons. The HTML user agent may display the title of the document prior to retrieving it, for example, as a margin note or on a small box while the mouse is over the anchor, or while the document is being loaded. Another reason is that documents that are not marked-up text, such as graphics, plain text, and Gopher menus, do not have titles. The TITLE attribute can be used to provide a title to such documents. When using the TITLE attribute, the title should be valid and unique for the destination document.

URN—If present, the URN attribute specifies a uniform resource name (URN) for a target document. The format of URNs is under discussion (1994) by various working groups of the Internet Engineering Task Force.

<ADDRESS> . . . </ADDRESS>

The ADDRESS element specifies such information as address, signature, and authorship, often at the top or bottom of a document. Typically, an Address is rendered in an italic typeface and may be indented. The ADDRESS element implies a paragraph break before and after.

Example:

```
<ADDRESS>
Jessica Keyes<BR>
New Art Inc. New York NY <BR>
Tel (800) 276-1118
</ADDRESS>
```

<APPLET> . . . </APPLET>

The APPLET element is the mechanism to embed and invoke a Java application within an HTML document.

Attributes:

ALIGN—Specifies the alignment of text following the APPLET reference relative to the applet on screen. LEFT and RIGHT specify floating horizontal alignment of the applet in the browser window, and subsequent text will wrap around the applet. The other options specify vertical alignment of text relative to the applet on the same line.

ALT—Indicates text to be displayed for text-only browsers or browsers that do not understand the APPLET element.

ARCHIVE—This attribute can improve applet download time by reducing the number of HTTP connections required to fetch applet code.

CODE—This attribute indicates a URL pointing to the applet's code/class.

CODEBASE—This attribute indicates the base URL of the applet if the CODE attribute is relative. If the CODEBASE URL is relative, it is in relation to the current document URL or the BASE HREF element, if present.

HEIGHT—This attribute explicitly specifies the height of the applet in pixels. It can be used to speed up display of the document being downloaded so it can pre-render the document with an applet placeholder while the applet downloads.

HSPACE—This attribute specifies the horizontal spacing (left and right padding) around the applet in pixels.

MAYSCRIPT—This is a stand-alone attribute that permits the applet to access JavaScript functionality and data on a page. Attempts to access JavaScript when this attribute is not present results in a Java exception.

NAME—This provides a way for the applet to identify the applet to other applets in the current HTML page.

OBJECT—This attribute gives the name of the resource that contains a "serialized" representation of an applet. The applet will be deserialized by the browser. The init() method will not be invoked; but its start() method will. Attributes valid when the original object was serialized are not restored. Any attributes passed to this applet instance will be available to the applet.

VSPACE—This attribute specifies the vertical spacing (top and bottom padding) around the applet in pixels.

WIDTH—This attribute explicitly specifies the width of the applet in pixels. It can be used to speed up display of the document being downloaded so it can pre-render the document with an applet placeholder while the applet downloads.

Example:

```
<applet CODEBASE="http://www.xxx.com/java/"
CODE="javaexample.class" WIDTH=200 HEIGHT=300>
<param NAME=text1 VALUE="Example Text 1">
<param NAME=imagecaption VALUE="Image Caption">
<param NAME=bounceimage VALUE="bounce1.gif">
<img SRC="non_java_image.gif" WIDTH=200 HEIGHT=300 BORDER=0
ALT="You are missing the full Java Experience.">
</applet>
```

<AREA>

A part of the <MAP> tag. With this tag you specify the areas that are hyperlinked in an image and where they go.

Attributes:

HREF—Stands for "hyperlink reference." References the page or the action that the hyperlinked area is to do or go to.
NOHREF—Specifies the area is not to be hyperlinked anywhere.

Example:

```
<MAP NAME="mapbuttons">
<AREA SHAPE="rect" COORDS="10,10,49,49" HREF="about.htm">
<AREA SHAPE="rect" COORDS="20,20,49,49" HREF="services.htm">
<AREA SHAPE="rect" COORDS="30,30,49,49" HREF="index.htm">
</MAP>
<IMG SRC="image.gif" ALIGN=LEFT WIDTH=25 HEIGHT=25 ALT="Map of
Buttonsr" USEMAP="#mapbuttons>
```

SHAPE—Determines the shape of the hyperlinked area; can be rectangle (rect), polygon (poly), circles (circle), and default (default).
COORDS—Sets the coordinates of the area. For a rectangle and they are given as "left, top, right, bottom" and a cirle is defined as a center point and then a radius.

<B> . . . </B>

The Bold element specifies that the text should be rendered in boldface, where available. Otherwise, alternative mapping is allowed.

For example, the instructions: <B>must be read</B> before continuing would be rendered as follows: The instructions *must be read* before continuing.

<BASE . . . >

The BASE element allows the URL of the document itself to be recorded in situations in which the document may be read out of context. URLs within the document may be in a "partial" form relative to this base address. Where the base address is not specified, the HTML user agent uses the URL it used to access the document to resolve any relative URLs. The BASE element has one attribute, HREF, which identifies the URL.

Netscape addition—<BASEFONT SIZE . . . > This changes the size of the BASE-

FONT that all relative <FONT SIZE . . . > changes are based on. It defaults to 3, and has a valid range of 1–7. For example, <BASEFONT SIZE=5>

<BDO>

The bidirectional override is needed where absolute control over character sequence order is required (such as mixed-language directionality words) and use of the common attribute DIR on other elements fails to produce proper bidirectional rendering. It is also useful in dealing with short pieces of text in which the directionality cannot be clearly resolved from the surrounding context.

Attributes:

DIR—On block-level elements, the DIR attribute indicates the base directionality of the text in the block. If omitted it is inherited from the parent element. The default directionality of the overall HTML document is left-to-right. On inline elements, it makes the element start a new directional embedding level. If omitted, the inline element does not start a new embedding level.
LANGUAGE—Specifies a string indicating the language/character set used in in the BDO container.

```
Example:

Does this look <bdo DIR="rtl">Backwards</bdo> to you?

Result:

Does this look sdraw kcaB to you?
```

<BGSOUND> (Microsoft Extension)

This tag is a Microsoft extension that lets you play background sounds or soundtracks while the reader is looking at your page. Attributes include:
BALANCE—Determines how sound output will be balanced in right/left stereo output situation. A value of −10,000 is left-only balance, and a value of 10,000 represents right-only balance. A value of 0 represents balanced output between the two stereo output devices.
DELAY—Specifies the number of seconds to delay before playing the indicated sound file.
LOOP=n or LOOP=INFINITE—Specifies how many times a sound file will be played. If LOOP=INFINITE or LOOP=−1, the sound file will keep playing indefinitely.

Example:

```
<BGSOUND SRC=music.wav LOOP=5>
```

SRC=URL—Specifies the Internet address of the sound file to play.

<BIG> . . . </BIG>

This element applies a larger size font formatting to text (in relation to the default font size). BIG and its companion element SMALL answer the needs of having alternate character level elements for controlling font size while also not being specific in *how* to display the contents.

Attributes:

None.

Example:

```
<big>text</big>
```

<BLINK> (Netscape Addition)

Surrounding any text with this element will cause the selected text to blink on the viewing page. This can serve to add extra emphasis to selected text.

Example:

```
<BLINK>This text would blink on the page</BLINK>
```

<BLOCKQUOTE> . . . </BLOCKQUOTE>

The BLOCKQUOTE element is used to contain text quoted from another source. A typical rendering might be a slight extra left and right indent, and/or italic font. The BLOCKQUOTE element causes a paragraph break and typically provides space above and below the quote.

Single-font rendition may reflect the quotation style of Internet mail by putting a vertical line of graphic characters, such as the greater-than symbol (>), in the left margin.

Example:

```
JFK once said
<BLOCKQUOTE>
<P>ask not what your country can do for you . . . </BLOCKQUOTE>
but I am not sure.
```

<BODY> . . . </BODY>

The body of an HTML document contains all the text and images that make up the page, together with all the HTML elements that provide the control/formatting of the page.

Example:

```
<BODY>
The document included here
</BODY>
```

The <BODY> element has been enhanced in recent Netscape versions. It is now possible to control the document background.

Attributes:

BACKGROUND—The purpose of this attribute is to specify a URL pointing to an image that is to be used as a background for the document. In Netscape, this background image is used to tile the full background of the document-viewing area. Thus specifying:

```
<BODY BACKGROUND="URL or path/filename.gif">
Document here
</BODY>
```

---

would cause whatever text, images, etc. that appeared in that document to be placed on a background consisting of the graphics file (filename.gif) being tiled to cover the viewing area, much like bitmaps are used for Windows wallpaper.

BGCOLOR—This attribute changes the color of the background without having to specify a separate image that requires another network access to load. The format that Netscape 1.1 understands is:

```
<BODY BGCOLOR="#rrggbb">
Document here
</BODY>
```

Where "#rrggbb" is a hexadecimal red-green-blue triplet used to specify the background color. Clearly, once the background colors/patterns have been changed, it will be necessary to also be able to control the foreground to establish the proper contrasts. The following attributes are also recognized as part of the BODY element by Netscape 1.1. **LINK, VLINK, and ALINK attributes**—These attributes let you control the coloring of link text. VLINK stands for visited link, and ALINK stands for active link. The default coloring of these is: LINK=blue, VLINK=purple, and ALINK=red. Again, the format for these attributes is the same as that for BGCOLOR and TEXT.

```
<BODY LINK="#rrggbb" VLINK="#rrggbb" ALINK="#rrggbb">
Document here
</BODY>
```

TEXT—This attribute is used to control the color of all the normal text in the document. This basically consists of all text that is not specially colored to indicate a link. The format of TEXT is the same as that of BGCOLOR.

```
<BODY TEXT="#rrggbb">
Document here
</BODY>
```

Coloring Considerations—Since these color controls are all attributes of the BODY element, they can only be set once for the entire document. Document color cannot be changed partially through a document.

Setting a background image requires the fetching of an image file from a second HTTP connection; it will slow down the perceived speed of document loading. None of the document can be displayed until the image is loaded and decoded. Needless to say, keep background images small.

If the Auto Load Images option is turned off, background images will not be loaded. If the background image is not loaded for any reason, and a BGCOLOR was not also specified, then any of the foreground controlling attributes (LINK, VLINK, and ALINK) will be ignored. The idea behind this is that if the requested background image is unavailable, or not loaded, setting requested text colors on top of the default gray background may make the document unreadable.

<BUTTON>

The BUTTON element allows for the creation of richer form control widgets than the standard plain text used for BUTTON, RESET, and SUBMIT fields available via the INPUT element. The use of the BUTTON element allows HTML formatting to be encapsulated within these control widgets. The BUTTON element can contain most any non-interactive element such as character and block-level formatting.

Attributes:

ACCESSKEY—This is a method of giving access/focus to an active HTML element using a keyboard character. This is a common GUI paradigm also known as a "keyboard shortcut" or "keyboard accelerator." A single character is used as the value of this attribute. In addition, a platform-dependent key is usually used in combination with the ACCESSKEY character to access the functionality of the active field.

DISABLED—This is a stand-alone attribute that indicates the element is initially nonfunctional.

NAME—Associates a symbolic name to the field when submitted to a form-processing script.

ONBLUR—A blur Event Handler executes script code when a hyperlink loses focus.

ONFOCUS—A focus Event Handler executes script code when a hyperlink receives focus by tabbing with the keyboard or clicking with the mouse.

TABINDEX—"Tabbing" is a method of giving access/focus to an active HTML element using a standard keyboard sequence. All the active elements in a document can be cycled through using this sequence (e.g., Windows TAB key). The order of the active elements in this cycle is usually the order they occur in the document, but the TABINDEX attribute allows a different order to be established. The use of this attribute should create the following tabbing order cycle if the browser supports the attribute:

1. active elements using the TABINDEX attribute with positive integers are navigated first. Low values are navigated first.
2. active elements not specifying any TABINDEX attribute, and those elements carrying a DISABLED attribute or using negative TABINDEX values do not participate in the tabbing cycle.

TYPE—This attribute specifies the purpose that the button will fulfill: that of the traditional submit, reset, or multipurpose button.

VALUE—This attribute represents the symbolic result of the button when activated.

```
Example:

<button TYPE=submit NAME=helpbutton TABINDEX=1>
<img SRC="image.gif" ALIGN=middle> Get the
<strong>HELP</strong> that you need here . . .
</button>
```


The Line Break element specifies that a new line must be started at the given point. A new line indents the same as that of line-wrapped text.

The <BR> element has been Netscape-enhanced. With the addition of floating images, it was necessary to expand the <BR> element. Normal <BR> still just inserts a line break. A CLEAR attribute has been added to <BR>.

Attributes:

CLEAR=left—Will break the line and move vertically down until you have a clear left margin (no floating images).
CLEAR=right—Does the same for the right margin.
CLEAR=all—Moves down until both margins are clear of images.

<CAPTION . . . > . . . </CAPTION>

This represents the caption for a table. <CAPTION> elements should appear inside the <TABLE> but not inside table rows or cells. The caption accepts an alignment attribute that defaults to ALIGN=top but can be explicitly set to ALIGN=bottom. Like table cells, any document body HTML can appear in a caption. Captions are always horizontally centered with respect to the table, and they may have their lines broken to fit within the width of the table.

<CENTER> (Netscape Extension)

All lines of text between the begin and end of the CENTER element are centered between the current left and right margins.

<CITE> . . . </CITE>

The Citation element specifies a citation, typically rendered as italics. For example, this sentence, containing a <CITE>citation reference</CITE> would look like:

This sentence, containing a *citation reference* would look like:

\<CODE\> . . . \</CODE\>

The CODE element indicates an example of code, typically rendered as monospaced. Do not confuse with the Preformatted Text element.

\<COL\>

COL is used to define the generic properties of a table column rather than using the traditional row structure (TR, THEAD, TBODY, and TFOOT). COL is used within a COLGROUP grouping structure to define properties of a single column within the group (attributes specified in the COL element override those found in the parent COLGROUP structure). It can also be used at the same table structure nesting level as COLGROUP to define properties for single rows (those not participating in a column grouping).

Attributes:

ALIGN—This controls the horizontal alignment of text within the current column.
CHAR—This attribute specifies a character in the cell content to be used to align the data in each cell of the current column (the first occurrence should be used). The default value for this attribute is the decimal point character for the current specified language.
CHAROFF—This attribute specifies the spacing offset to the first occurrence of the alignment character (specified by the CHAR attribute) on each line of cells in the current column. The direction of the offset is determined by the current text direction (set with the DIR attribute or the BDO element).
REPEAT—This attribute specifies how many columns the current column definition applies to. This is a shorthand for providing column attributes to multiple columns at once.
SPAN—This attribute specifies how many columns the current column specification applies to (default value is 1). The number of total columns in a table should equal the number of cells specified later in the table structure, but it is possible to specify a SPAN value of 0, which indicates that the current COL element spans all remaining columns. Using the SPAN element does not actually *define* a column grouping, it is rather a method used to more easily specify shared column attributes.
VALIGN—This attribute specifies the vertical alignment of cell contents relative to the cell boundaries for all cells in the current column.
WIDTH—Specifies the overall width of the specified column.

Example:

```
<table BORDER="2" ALIGN="left" CELLPADDING="5"
BORDERCOLOR="#ff0000" COLS="4" FRAME="vsides" RULES="cols"
WIDTH="75%">
```

```
<colgroup>
<col ALIGN="right">
</colgroup>
<colgroup>
<col ALIGN="center">
<col ALIGN="center">
<col ALIGN="center">
</colgroup>
<caption ALIGN="top">Here's the caption</caption>
<thead>
<tr>
<th>One</th>
<th>Two</th>
<th>
<table>
```

<COLGROUP>

This element acts as a container for a group of columns (which are specified with COL elements), and allows the author to specify default properties for these columns. This element comes before any of the standard row grouping hierarchies (TR, THEAD, TBODY, and TFOOT) and only serves to more completely describe organizational characteristics of the row grouping data that follow (no cell data is contained in COLGROUPs).

If no COLGROUP elements are present, all columns in the table are assumed to be part of a single column group. Each COLGROUP grouping can contain zero or more COL elements.

Attributes:

ALIGN—This controls the horizontal alignment of text within the column group.
CHAR—This attribute specifies a character in the cell content to be used to align the data in each cell of the column group (the first occurrence should be used). The default value for this attribute is the decimal point character for the current specified language.
CHAROFF—This attribute specifies the spacing offset to the first occurrence of the alignment character (specified by the CHAR attribute) on each line of cells in the current column group. The direction of the offset is determined by the current text direction (set with the DIR attribute or the BDO element).
REPEAT—This attribute specifies how many columns the current column definition applies to. This is shorthand for providing column attributes to multiple columns at once.
SPAN—This attribute specifies a default for how many columns are in the current group. It provides a convenient way of grouping columns without the need to supply COL el-

ements. This attribute should be ignored if the current COLGROUP contains one or more COL tags.

VALIGN—This attribute specifies the vertical alignment of cell contents relative to the cell boundaries for all cells in the column group.

WIDTH—Specifies the overall width of the column grouping.

<DL> . . . </DL>
<DT> . . . </DT>
<DD> . . . </DD>

A definition list is a list of terms and corresponding definitions. Definition lists are typically formatted with the term flush-left and the definition, formatted paragraph-style, indented after the term.

```
Example:

<DL>
<DT>Term<DD>This is the definition of the first term.
<DT>Term<DD>This is the definition of the second term.
</DL>
```

If the <DT> term does not fit in the <DT> column (one-third of the display area), it may be extended across the page with the <DD> section moved to the next line, or it may be wrapped onto successive lines of the left-hand column.

Single occurrences of a <DT> element without a subsequent <DD> element are allowed, and have the same significance as if the <DD> element had been present with no text. The opening list element must be <DL> and must be immediately followed by the first term (<DT>).

The definition list type can take the COMPACT attribute, which suggests that a compact rendering be used, because the list items are small and/or the entire list is large.

Unless you provide the COMPACT attribute, the HTML user agent may leave white space between successive <DT>, <DD> pairs. The COMPACT attribute may also reduce the width of the left-hand (<DT>) column.

If using the COMPACT attribute, the opening list element must be <DL COMPACT>, which must be immediately followed by the first <DT> element:

```
<DL COMPACT>
<DT>Term<DD>This is the first definition in compact format.
<DT>Term<DD>This is the second definition in compact format.
</DL>
```

<DEL> . . . </DEL>

The DEL element is one of two elements used (the other being INS) to allow revision control in HTML documents. The DEL element is nestable and can be used in conjunction with the INS element to indicate content and/or markup that has been deleted after the document's initial creation—it is not really eliminated from the document, though. A date stamp is used to mark when the change was made and no destructive changes are ever made to the document. This is useful in areas such as the legal profession, where historical change information is important. HTML documents containing revision annotations will contain all content and markup ever applied to the document. Browsers that can interpret the DEL and INS elements could possibly display the "current" state of the document or display all content with a common visual cues for inserted or deleted text. More advanced revision systems could allow for chronological snapshots of a document at any point in its history.

Attributes:

CITE—Indicates the URL citing the reason for the change in the document.
DATETIME—Indicates the date and time when the contents were deleted.

Example:

```
<del>deleted text</del>
```

<DIR> . . . </DIR>

A Directory List element is used to present a list of items containing up to 20 characters each. Items in a directory list may be arranged in columns, typically 24 characters wide. If the HTML user agent can optimize the column width as a function of the widths of individual elements, so much the better.

A directory list must begin with the <DIR> element, which is immediately followed by a <LI> (List Item) element:

Example:

```
<DIR>
<LI>A-H<LI>I-M
<LI>M-R<LI>S-Z
</DIR>
```

\<DIV> . . . \</DIV>

The DIV (Division Marker) element is a generic, catch-all block formatting element with an implied line break before and after. Within the realm of style sheets, this element is nestable to allow hierarchies of sections, subsections, or chapters to be defined. This nesting ability also allows for powerful style sheet mechanisms to be applied.

The recent addition of the many linking attributes to DIV and SPAN appear to be an attempt to expand the generic block and inline capabilities of these two elements.

Attributes:

ALIGN—This indicates the horizontal alignment of the Division block text in the browser window. These values can be overridden by style sheets values.

CHARSET—This attribute indicates the character encoding of the destination resource of the HREF attribute.

HREF—This attribute indicates the URL to be loaded when the linked content is activated.

HREFLANG—This attribute specifies the base language of the resource indicated in the HREF attribute.

MEDIA—This attribute is a keyword representing the intended rendering destination for the style sheet properties applied to this element. Multiple destinations are given, delimited by commas.

REL—The REL attribute is meant to give the relationship(s) described between the current document and the document specified by the HREF attribute.

REV—The REL attribute is basically meant to be the same as the REL attribute, but the semantics of the relationship are in the reverse direction. A link from A to B with REL="X" expresses the same relationship as a link from B to A with REV="X". Both the REL and REV attributes may be used in the same element.

TARGET—This attribute specifies the named frame for the contents specified by the HREF attribute to load to when activated.

TYPE—This attribute specifies the MIME type of the resource indicated in the HREF attribute.

Example:

```
<div ALIGN="right" CLASS="greensection" STYLE="color:
lime">text</div>
```

\<EM> . . . \</EM>

The Emphasis element indicates typographic emphasis, typically rendered as italics.

> *Example:*
>
> ```
> The <EM>Emphasis</EM> element typically renders as Italics.
> would render:
> The Emphasis element typically renders as Italics.
> ```

<EMBED> (Netscape Extension)

This tag is only recognized by the Windows version of Netscape Navigator, versions 1.1 and above.

The EMBED element allows you to put documents directly into an HTML page. The syntax is:

```
<EMBED SRC="images/embed.bmp">
```

The EMBED element will allow you to embed documents of any type. Your user only needs to have an application that can view the data installed correctly on their machine.

If a width and height are specified, the embedded object is scaled to fit the available space. For example, this is the same bitmap as above, scaled:

```
<EMBED SRC="images/embed.bmp" WIDTH=250 HEIGHT=50>
```

Embedded objects can be activated by double-clicking them in the Netscape window. The application that supports use of the embedded object will be launched, with the object present.

> NOTE: Using the EMBED element, you should be sure that the user will have a suitable application available that is OLE compliant. Otherwise, the HTML document will not be displayed as hoped. Essentially this element produces the same results as embedding objects in Word for Windows—the object is displayed and can be edited in a suitable application by double-clicking on the object.

<FIELDSET> . . . </FIELDSET>

The nestable FIELDSET element is used to group related form fields together. The grouping of form fields allows for a more intuitive visual user interface while also giving speech-based navigation methods better cues of how to render a page.

The suggested rendering for the FIELDSET element is left of the browser, but will usually take the form of a box around the contents of the FIELDSET. If the optional LEGEND element is present directly after the opening FIELDSET tag, its contents are transposed on top of the region of the FIELDSET bounding box specified in the ALIGN attribute of the LEGEND element.

Attributes:

ALIGN—Specifies the alignment of the contents of the FIELDSET.

Example:

```
<fieldset>
<legend ACCESSKEY=G TABINDEX=1>Gender</legend>
<label ACCESSKEY=M>
<input TYPE=RADIO NAME=Gender VALUE=Male>Male</label>
<br>
<label ACCESSKEY=F>
<input TYPE=RADIO NAME=Gender VALUE=Female>Female</label>
</fieldset>
```

<FONT SIZE . . . > (Netscape Extension)

Netscape 1.0 and above supports different-sized fonts within HTML documents. This should be distinguished from Headings. The new element is <FONT SIZE=value>. Valid values range from 1 to 7. The default FONT size is 3. The value given to size can optionally have a "+" or "−" character in front of it to specify that it is relative that the document baseFONT. The default baseFONT is 3 and can be changed with the <BASEFONT SIZE . . . > element.

<FORM> . . . </FORM>

The FORM element is used to delimit a data input form. There can be several forms in a single document, but the FORM element can't be nested.

Attributes:

ACTION—The ACTION attribute is a URL specifying the location to which the contents of the form are submitted to elicit a response. If the ACTION attribute is missing, the URL of the document itself is assumed. The way data is submitted varies with the access protocol of the URL, and with the values of the METHOD and ENCTYPE attributes.

ENCTYPE—Specifies the format of the submitted data in case the protocol does not impose a format itself.

The Level 2 specification defines and requires support for the HTTP access protocol only.

When the ACTION attribute is set to an HTTP URL, the METHOD attribute must be set to an HTTP method as defined by the HTTP method specification in the IETF draft HTTP standard. The default METHOD is GET, although for many applications, the POST method may be preferred. With the post method, the ENCTYPE attribute is a MIME type specifying the format of the posted data; by default, it is application/x-www-form-urlencoded.

Under any protocol, the submitted contents of the form logically consist of name-value pairs. The names are usually equal to the NAME attributes of the various interactive elements in the form.

METHOD —Selects variations in the protocol.

> NOTE: The names are not guaranteed to be unique keys, nor are the names of form elements required to be distinct. The values encode the user's input to the corresponding interactive elements. Elements capable of displaying a textual or numerical value will return a name-value pair even when they receive no explicit user input.

<FRAME> . . . </FRAME>

The FRAME element defines a single frame in a frameset.

Attributes:

MARGINHEIGHT—Defines the margin height within a frame in pixels.
MARGINWIDTH—Defines the margin width within a frame in pixels.
NAME—Assigns a name to the frame to be used as a target of hyperlinks.
NORESIZE—Says that the user cannot change the size of the frame. There is no value assisted with the tag.

Example:

```
<FRAMESET COLS="50%, 50%">
<FRAMESET ROWS="50%,50%">
<FRAME SRC="cell.html" SCROLLING="yes">
<FRAME SRC="cell.html" NORESIZE>
</FRAMESET>
```

```
<FRAMESET ROWS="33%,33%33%">
<FRAMESRC="cell.html">
<FRAMESRC="cell.html">
<FRAMESRC="cell.html">
</FRAMESET>
</FRAMESET>

<NOFRAMES>
This page is designed for a frames-capable browser. Please see
our <A HREF="noframes.html">noframes version</A>.
</NOFRAMES>
```

SCROLLING—Defines whether the frame should have a scrollbar, and defaults to the value "auto."

SRC—The URL of the document to be displayed in this frame.

<FRAMESET> . . . </FRAMESET>

The FRAMESET element is used instead of the BODY element. It is used in an HTML document whose sole purpose is to define the layout of the frames that will make up the page.

Attributes:

COLS—Follows same format as rows, only tells the screen sections horizontally.

Example:

```
<FRAMESET COLS="50%, 50%">
<FRAMESET ROWS="50%,50%">
<FRAME SRC="cell.html" SCROLLING="yes">
<FRAME SRC="cell.html" NORESIZE>
</FRAMESET>
<FRAMESET ROWS="33%,33%33%">
<FRAMESRC="cell.html">
<FRAMESRC="cell.html">
<FRAMESRC="cell.html">
</FRAMESET>
</FRAMESET>

<NOFRAMES>
This page is designed for a frames-capable browser. Please see
our <A HREF="noframes.html">noframes version</A>.
</NOFRAMES>
```

ROWS—Tells how much of the screen each row is allotted in pixels, percentage numbers, or '*', meaning *take up the remaining space.*

\<H1> . . . \</H1>

HTML defines six levels of heading. A Heading element implies all the font changes, paragraph breaks before and after, and white space necessary to render the heading.

The highest level of headings is \<H1>. It is a bold, very large font, centered. One or two blank lines above and below.

\<H2> . . . \</H2>

Bold, large font, flush-left. One or two blank lines above and below.

\<H3> . . . \</H3>

Italic, large font, slightly indented from the left margin. One or two blank lines above and below.

\<H4> . . . \</H4>

Bold, normal font, indented more than H3. One blank line above and below.

\<H5> . . . \</H5>

Italic, normal font, indented as H4. One blank line above.

\<H6> . . . \</H6>

Bold, indented same as normal text, more than H5. One blank line above.

\<H ALIGN= >

ALIGN=left|center|right attributes have been added to the \<H1> to \<H6> elements.

```
Example:

<H1 ALIGN=center>Hello, this is a heading</H1>
would align a heading of style 1 in the center of the page.
```

<HEAD> . . . </HEAD>

The head of an HTML document is an unordered collection of information about the document. It requires the TITLE element between <HEAD> and </HEAD> elements, thus:

```
Example:

<HEAD>
<TITLE> Introduction to HTML </TITLE>
</HEAD>
```

The HEAD and /HEAD elements do not directly affect the look of the document when rendered. The following elements are related to the head element. While not directly affecting the look of the document when rendered, they do provide (if used) important information to the HTML user agent.

Attributes:

BASE—Allows base address of HTML document to be specified.
ISINDEX—Allows keyword searching of the document.
LINK—Indicates realationships between documents.
META—Specifies document information useable by server/clients.
NEXTID—Creates unique document identifiers.
TITLE—Specifies the title of the document.

<HR>

A Horizontal Rule element is a divider between sections of text such as a full width horizontal rule or equivalent graphic.

> NOTE: The HR element has been Netscape-enhanced. The <HR> element specifies that a horizontal rule of some sort (the default being a shaded engraved line) be drawn across the page. To this element Netscape has added four new attributes that allow the document author to describe how the horizontal rule should look.

Attributes:

<HR SIZE=number>—The SIZE attribute let the author give an indication of how thick they wish the horizontal rule to be.

<HR WIDTH=number|percent>—The default horizontal rule is always as wide as the page. With the WIDTH attribute, the author can specify an exact width in pixels, or a relative width measured in percent of document width.

<HR ALIGN=left|right|center>—Now that horizontal rules do not have to be the width of the page, it is necessary to allow the author to specify whether they should be pushed up against the left margin, the right margin, or centered in the page.

<HR NOSHADE>—Finally, for those times when a solid bar is required, the NOSHADE attribute lets the author specify that the horizontal rule should not be shaded at all.

<HTML> . . . </HTML>

This element identifies the document as containing HTML elements. It should immediately follow the prologue document identifier and serves to surround all of the remaining text, including all other elements. That is, the document should be constructed thus:

Example:

```
<HTML>
Here is all the rest of the document, including any elements.
</HTML>
```

The HTML element is not visible upon HTML user agent rendering and can contain only the HEAD and BODY elements.

<I> . . . </I>

The Italic element specifies that the text should be rendered in italic font where available. Otherwise, alternative mapping is allowed.

Example:

```
Anything between the <I>I elements</I> should be italics.
```

would render as :

```
Anything between the I elements should be italics.
```

<IMG . . . >

The Image element is used to incorporate inline graphics (typically icons or small graphics) into an HTML document. This element cannot be used for embedding other HTML text.

HTML user agents that cannot render inline images ignore the Image element unless it contains the ALT attribute. Note that some HTML user agents can render linked graphics but not inline graphics. If a graphic is essential, you may want to create a link to it rather than to put it inline. If the graphic is not essential, then the Image element is appropriate.

Attributes:

ALIGN—The ALIGN attribute accepts the values TOP or MIDDLE or BOTTOM, which specifies if the following line of text is aligned with the top, middle, or bottom of the graphic.

ALT—Optional text as an alternative to the graphic for rendering in non-graphical environments. Alternate text should be provided whenever the graphic is not rendered. Alternate text is mandatory for Level 0 documents.

Example:

```
<IMG SRC="triangle.gif" ALT="Warning:"> Be sure to read these
instructions.
```

ISMAP—The ISMAP (is map) attribute identifies an image as an image map. Image maps are graphics in which certain regions are mapped to URLs. By clicking on different regions, different resources can be accessed from the same graphic.

Example:

```
<A HREF="http://machine/htbin/imagemap/sample">
<IMG SRC="sample.gif" ISMAP>
</A>
```

NOTE: To be able to employ image maps in HTML documents, the HTTP server that will be controlling document access must have the correct cgi-bin software installed to control image map behavior.

SRC—The value of the SRC attribute is the URL of the document to be embedded; only images can be embedded, not HTML text. Its syntax is the same as that of the HREF attribute of the <A> element. SRC is mandatory. Image elements are allowed within anchors.

> *Example:*
>
> ```
> <IMG SRC ="triangle.gif">Be sure to read these instructions.
> ```

> *NOTE: The <IMG> element has received possibly the largest Netscape enhancement. The <IMG . . . > attribute is probably the most extended element.*

<IMG ALIGN= left|right|top|texttop|middle|absmiddle|baseline|bottom|absbottom>

The additions to your ALIGN options need a lot of explanation. First, the values "left" and "right." Images with those alignments are an entirely new floating image type.

ALIGN=left image will float the image down and over to the left margin (into the next available space there), and subsequent text will wrap around the right-hand side of that image.

ALIGN=right will align the image with the right margin, and the text wraps around the left.

ALIGN=top aligns itself with the top of the tallest item in the line.

ALIGN=texttop aligns itself with the top of the tallest text in the line (this is usually but not always the same as ALIGN=top).

ALIGN=middle aligns the baseline of the current line with the middle of the image.

ALIGN=absmiddle aligns the middle of the current line with the middle of the image.

ALIGN=baseline aligns the bottom of the image with the baseline of the current line.

ALIGN=bottom aligns the bottom of the image with the baseline of the current line.

ALIGN=absbottom aligns the bottom of the image with the bottom of the current line.

<IMG WIDTH=value HEIGHT=value>—The WIDTH and HEIGHT attributes were added to <IMG . . . > mainly to speed up display of the document. If the author specifies these, the viewer of the document will not have to wait for the image to be loaded over the network and its size calculated.

<IMG BORDER=value>—This lets the document author control the thickness of the border around an image displayed.

Warning: Setting BORDER=0 on images that are also part of anchors may confuse your users, as they are used to a colored border indicating an image is an anchor.

<IMG VSPACE=value HSPACE=value>—For the floating images it is likely that the author does not want them pressing up against the text wrapped around the image. VSPACE controls the vertical space above and below the image, while HSPACE controls the horizontal space to the left and right of the image.

LOWSRC—Using the LOWSRC attribute, it is possible to use two images in the same space.

Example:

```
<IMG SRC="highres.gif" LOWSRC="lowres.jpg">
```

Browsers that do not recognize the LOWSRC attribute cleanly ignore it and simply load the image called "highres.gif."

This means that you can have a very low-resolution version of an image loaded initially; if the user stays on the page after the initial layout phase, a higher-resolution (and presumably bigger) version of the same image can "fade in" and replace it.

Both GIF (both normal and interlaced) and JPEG images can be freely interchanged using this method. You can also specify width and/or height values in the IMG element, and both the high-res and low-res versions of the image will be appropriately scaled to match.

If the images are of different sizes and a fixed height and width are not specified in the IMG element, the second image (the image specified by the SRC attribute) will be scaled to the dimensions of the first (LOWSRC) image.

<INPUT>

The INPUT element represents a field whose contents may be edited by the user.

Attributes:

ALIGN—Vertical alignment of the image. For use only with TYPE=IMAGE in HTML Level 2. The possible values are exactly the same as for the ALIGN attribute of the image element.

CHECKED—Indicates that a checkbox or radio button is selected. Unselected checkboxes and radio buttons do not return name-value pairs when the form is submitted.

MAXLENGTH—Indicates the maximum number of characters that can be entered into a text field. This can be greater than specified by the SIZE attribute, in which case the field will scroll appropriately. The default number of characters is unlimited.

NAME—Symbolic name used when transferring the form's contents. The NAME attribute is required for most input types and is normally used to provide a unique identifier for a field, or for a logically related group of fields.

SIZE—Specifies the size or precision of the field according to its type. For example, to specify a field with a visible width of 24 characters:

```
INPUT TYPE=text SIZE="24"
```

SRC—A URL specifying an image. For use only with TYPE=IMAGE in HTML Level 2.

TYPE—Defines the type of data the field accepts. Defaults to free text. Several types of fields can be defined with the TYPE attribute:

- CHECKBOX: Used for simple Boolean attributes, or for attributes that can take multiple values at the same time. The latter is represented by a number of checkbox fields, each of which has the same name. Each selected checkbox generates a separate name-value pair in the submitted data, even if this results in duplicate names. The default value for checkboxes is "on."
- HIDDEN: No field is presented to the user, but the content of the field is sent with the submitted form. This value may be used to transmit state information about client-server interaction.
- IMAGE: An image field upon which you can click with a pointing device, causing the form to be immediately submitted. The coordinates of the selected point are measured in pixel units from the upper-left corner of the image, and are returned (along with the other contents of the form) in two name-value pairs. The x-coordinate is submitted under the name of the field with .x appended, and the y-coordinate is submitted under the name of the field with .y appended. Any VALUE attribute is ignored. The image itself is specified by the SRC attribute, exactly as for the Image element.

> NOTE: In a future version of the HTML specification, the IMAGE functionality may be folded into an enhanced SUBMIT field.

- PASSWORD—The same as the TEXT attribute, except that text is not displayed as it is entered.
- RADIO—Used for attributes that accept a single value from a set of alternatives. Each radio button field in the group should be given the same name. Only the selected radio button in the group generates a name-value pair in the submitted data. Radio buttons require an explicit VALUE attribute.
- RESET—A button that when pressed resets the form's fields to their specified initial values. The label to be displayed on the button may be specified just as for the SUBMIT button.
- SUBMIT—A button that when pressed submits the form. You can use the VALUE attribute to provide a non-editable label to be displayed on the button. The default label is application-specific. If a SUBMIT button is pressed in order to submit the form, and that button has a NAME attribute specified, then that button contributes a name-value pair to the submitted data. Otherwise, a SUBMIT button makes no contribution to the submitted data.
- TEXT—Used for single line text entry fields. Use in conjunction with the SIZE and MAXLENGTH attributes. Use the TEXTAREA element for text fields that can accept multiple lines.
- VALUE—The initial displayed value of the field, if it displays a textual or numerical value; or the value to be returned when the field is selected, if it displays a Boolean value. This attribute is required for radio buttons.

<ISINDEX . . . >

The ISINDEX element tells the HTML user agent that the document is an index document. As well as reading it, the reader may use a keyword search. The document can be queried with a keyword search by adding a question mark to the end of the document address, followed by a list of keywords separated by plus signs.

> NOTE: The ISINDEX element is usually generated automatically by a server. If added manually to an HTML document, the HTML user agent assumes that the server can handle a search on the document. To use the ISINDEX element, the server must have a search engine that supports this element.

<KBD> . . . </KBD>

The Keyboard element indicates text typed by a user, typically rendered as monospaced. It might commonly be used in an instruction manual.

<LABEL> . . . </LABEL>

The non-nestable LABEL element accomplishes two tasks: association of a description with a form field control and increasing the size of the active user interface region for selecting the form control. Description attachment is of greatest use to speech-based browsers, while the benefits of an increased user interface region are felt most by users of browsers that accommodate a pointing device (such as a mouse or pen). Activating a LABEL with a pointing device passes input focus on to its associated form field control.

Labels are attached either explicitly or implicitly. Explicit attachment is accomplished through the use of a form field ID as the value of the FOR attribute. This method allows attachment of a label to a field elsewhere in the document and has the advantage of allowing multiple labels to be attached to a single form field.

Form fields are attached implicitly to a label when they are in the contents of the label element. In this case, the label must only contain one form field within the LABEL contents.

Attributes:

ACCESSKEY—This is a method of giving access/focus to an active HTML element using a keyboard character. This is a common GUI paradigm also known as a "keyboard shortcut" or "keyboard accelerator." A single character is used as the value of this attribute. In addition, a platform-dependent key is usually used in combination with the ACCESSKEY character to access the functionality of the active field.

FOR—This attribute identifies which form field the label is attached to. If this attribute is not used, the label is associated with its contents.

ONBLUR—A blur Event Handler executes script code when a hyperlink loses focus.

ONFOCUS—A focus Event Handler executes script code when a hyperlink receives focus by tabbing with the keyboard or clicking with the mouse.

Example:

```
<fieldset>
<legend ACCESSKEY=G TABINDEX=1>Gender</legend>
<label ACCESSKEY=M>
<input TYPE=RADIO NAME=Gender VALUE=Male>Male
</label> <br>
<label ACCESSKEY=F>
```

```
<input TYPE=RADIO NAME=Gender VALUE=Female>Female
</label>
</fieldset>
```

\<LAYER> . . . \</LAYER>

This is a new element created by Netscape that allows an author to define precisely positioned two-dimensional layout consisting of overlapping layers of transparent or solid content on a Web page. All the content between the opening and closing LAYER tags can be treated as a single item of content that can be moved and altered in various ways.

Layers can have a stacking order that allows a virtual third z-dimension to be defined. Using this, layers can appear on top of other layers. Layers can also be transparent or solid; if transparent, the content of underlying layers shows through it. As if that weren't enough, background colors or tiled images can also be specified for a layer. (Setting these attributes for a layer will negate its transparency property and layers below it will be obscured.)

Layers can be nested and moved in a dynamic fashion via scripting. This type of layer-defining explicit positioning is also known as an "out-of-flow" or "positioned" layer. An alternate method of defining a layer is through the use of the ILAYER element, which allows the definition of layers whose position follows the flow of the page (like an image)—this is known as an "inflow layer."

Note: This element is curious in that it mirrors the functionality of the capabilities now offered through the positioning property extensions for Cascading Style Sheets. The LAYER and ILAYER elements are essentially HTML-based solutions to the same functionality that these CSS extensions provide. It is interesting to note that support for CSS positioning and the LAYER/ILAYER elements appeared in Netscape at the same time. However, CSS positioning has been created with the official sanctioning of the W3C, while it is unlikely that LAYER/ILAYER will ever gain such support.

Attributes:

ABOVE—This attribute specifies the name of the layer that will occur directly above the current layer in the layer stacking order (z-order). It overrides the default behavior of placing new layers on top of all existing layers. Only one of the Z-INDEX, ABOVE, or BELOW attributes can be used for a given layer. References to layers not yet defined result in default layer creation behavior—that is, the new layer will be placed on top of all existing layers.

BACKGROUND—This specifies a background image to be tiled on a layer. Default behavior for a layer is to be transparent.

BELOW—This attribute specifies the name of the layer that will occur directly below the current layer in the layer stacking order (z-order). It overrides the default behavior of placing new layers on top of all existing layers. Only one of the Z-INDEX, ABOVE, or BELOW attributes can be used for a given layer. References to layers not yet defined result in default layer creation behavior—that is, the new layer will be placed on top of all existing layers.

BGCOLOR—This specifies the background color of the layer. Default behavior for a layer is to be transparent.

CLIP—This parameter specifies the clipping rectangle (viewable area) of the layer, which can be less than the width and height of the content of the layer. If the CLIP attribute is omitted, the clipping rectangle of a layer is the same size as the HTML content of the layer. A layer will expand to contain all of its content by default.

HEIGHT—This parameter specifies the height of the layer's content and serves as a reference dimension for child layers.

LEFT—This specifies the coordinate position of the left side boundary position of the current layer in relation to a parent layer if present. If no parent layer exists, the value is relative to the main document window.

NAME—This attribute specifies the name of the layer in order to identify or reference it from other layers or scripting languages. Layers are unnamed by default.

ONBLUR—A blur Event Handler executes Script code when a layer loses keyboard focus.

ONFOCUS—A focus Event Handler executes Script code when a layer receives input focus by tabbing with the keyboard or clicking with the mouse.

ONLOAD—This attribute executes Script code with the completion of loading of the layer.

ONMOUSEOVER—A mouseOver Event Handler executes Script code once each time the mouse pointer moves over a layer from outside the layer.

ONMOUSEOUT—A mouseOut Event Handler executes Script code once each time the mouse pointer exits from the bounds of a layer from inside the layer.

PAGEX—This specifies the absolute horizontal (X) coordinate position of the left boundary position of the current layer in relation to the document window (this differs slightly in definition from the LEFT attribute).

PAGEY—This specifies the absolute vertical (Y) coordinate position of the top boundary position of the current layer in relation to the document window (this differs slightly in definition from the TOP attribute).

SRC—This attribute specifies the URL of an HTML "sub-document" to be inserted into the layer. The effect is similar to the IFRAME tag implemented by Internet Explorer.

TOP—This specifies the coordinate position of the top boundary position of the current layer in relation to a parent layer if present. If no parent layer exists, the value is relative to the main document window.

VISIBILITY—This attribute specifies whether the layer is visible or not. A layer will have the same visibility as its parent layer by default. Even if the visibility of a layer is set to SHOW, a layer can only be seen if there are no other visible, solid layers stacked on top of it. For top-level layers that are not nested inside other layers, a value of INHERIT has the same effect as SHOW, since the body document is always visible.

WIDTH—This parameter specifies the width of the layer's content. Specifically, it controls the right margin of the layer for wrapping purposes. Some elements may not be "wrappable" (like images) and extend beyond the width specified. Layer contents wrap at the right boundary of the enclosing block by default.

Z-INDEX—This attribute allows a layer's stacking order (z-order) to be specified in terms of an integer. Layers with higher-numbered Z-INDEX values are stacked above those with lower ones. Positive Z-INDEX values cause the layer to be stacked above its parent while negative values will cause the layer to be stacked below its parent. This attribute overrides the default behavior of placing new layers on top of all existing layers. Only one of the Z-INDEX, ABOVE, or BELOW attributes can be used for any given layer.

Example:

```
<layer NAME="two" LEFT=40 TOP=40 Z-INDEX=2>
<font SIZE=7 COLOR="#0000ff">Two</font>
</layer>
<layer NAME="one" LEFT=25 TOP=25 Z-INDEX=1>
<font SIZE=7 COLOR="#ffff00">One</font>
</layer>
<layer NAME="three" LEFT=55 TOP=55 Z-INDEX=3>
<font SIZE=7 COLOR="#ff0000">Three</font>
</layer>
```

<LI>

The Directory List element is used to present a list of items containing up to 20 characters each. Items in a directory list may be arranged in columns, typically 24 characters wide. If the HTML user agent can optimize the column width as function of the widths of individual elements, so much the better.

A directory list must begin with the <DIR> element, which is immediately followed by an LI (list item) element:

Example:

```
<DIR>
<LI>A-H<LI>I-M
<LI>M-R<LI>S-Z
</DIR>
```

<LEGEND>

The LEGEND element assigns a caption to a FIELDSET grouping of form elements. Using a LEGEND is most useful when pages are rendered using non-visual formats. The ALIGN attribute of this element will allow horizontal and vertical alignment of LEGEND content with respect to the FIELDSET in visual browsers.

Note: Use of the LEGEND element is optional within a FIELDSET, and if used must immediately follow the opening FIELDSET tag. If the LEGEND element uses the ACCESSKEY attribute, the form control within the parent FIELDSET with the lowest tabbing order receives the focus.

Attributes:

ACCESSKEY—This is a method of giving access/focus to an active HTML element using a keyboard character. This is a common GUI paradigm also known as a "keyboard shortcut" or "keyboard accelerator" A single character is used as the value of this attribute. In addition, a platform-dependent key is usually used in combination with the ACCESSKEY character to access the functionality of the active field.

ALIGN—Indicates the source URL of the quotation. No rendering directions are given for this attribute.

Example:

```
<fieldset>
<legend ACCESSKEY=G TABINDEX=1>Gender</legend>
<label ACCESSKEY=M>
<input TYPE=RADIO NAME=Gender VALUE=Male>Male</label> <br>
<label ACCESSKEY=F>
<input TYPE=RADIO NAME=Gender VALUE=Female>Female</label>
</fieldset>
```

<LINK . . . >

The LINK element indicates a relationship between the document and some other object. A document may have any number of Link elements.

The LINK element is empty (does not have a closing element), but takes the same attributes as the Anchor element. Typical uses are to indicate authorship, related indexes and glossaries, older or more recent versions, etc. Links can indicate a static tree structure in which the document was authored by pointing to a parent and next and previous document, for example.

Servers may also allow links to be added by those who do not have the right to alter the body of a document.

<MAP>

Allows certain areas of an image to be hyperlinked. Image map coordinates are usually created using a program such as mapedit (www.mapedit.com)

Attributes:

NAME—Names the image map to be referenced later.
USEMAP—Specifies what coding to refer to.

Example:

```
<MAP NAME="buttonmap">
<AREA SHAPE="rect" COORDS="10,10,49,49" HREF="about.html">
<AREA SHAPE="rect" COORDS="10,10,49,49" HREF="services.html">
<AREA SHAPE="rect" COORDS="10,10,49,49" HREF="home.html">
</MAP>

<IMG SRC="image.gif" ALIGN=LEFT WIDTH=25 HEIGHT=25 ALT="Our
Button Map" USEMAP="#buttonmap>
```

<MARQUEE> (Microsoft Extension)

The MARQUEE tag lets you create a scrolling text area. This is a useful space for advertising or other information. There are a number of attributes that let you control the use of Marquees:

ALIGN—Specifies the location of text around the marquee. Can be either TOP, MIDDLE, or BOTTOM.
BEHAVIOR—Determines how the text will move within the marquee. Use SCROLL and the text will move in from one side and disappear off the other. If you use SLIDE the text will move in from one side, then stop when it touches the other. Using ALTERNATE, the text will bounce back and forth within the marquee.
BGCOLOR—Specifies the background color for the marquee. Instead of using the hexadecimal RGB triplet (e.g., #FFFFFF), you can use a Color Name.
DIRECTION—The direction that the text should scroll toward. It can be either LEFT or RIGHT.
HEIGHT—The height of the Marquee, or as a percentage of screen height.

HSPACE—The distance between the left and right margins of the marquee and the surrounding text (in pixels).

LOOP=n; OP=INFINITE—Specifies how many times text will scroll across the marquee. If LOOP=INFINITE or LOOP=−1, the text will repeat indefinitely.

SCROLLAMOUNT—Specifies the number of pixels between each successive draw of the marquee text.

SCROLLDELAY—Specifies the number of milliseconds between each successive draw of the marquee text.

VSPACE—The distance between the top and bottom margins of the marquee and the surrounding text (in pixels).

<MENU> . . . </MENU>

A menu list is a list of items with typically one line per item. The menu list style is more compact than the style of an unordered list. A menu list must begin with a MENU element, which is immediately followed by an LI (list item) element.

```
Example:

<MENU>
<LI>First item in the list.
<LI>Second item in the list.
<LI>Third item in the list.
</MENU>
```

<META . . . >

The META element is used within the HEAD element to embed document meta-information not defined by other HTML elements. Such information can be extracted by servers/clients for use in identifying, indexing, and cataloging specialized document meta-information.

Although it is generally preferable to use named elements that have well-defined semantics for each type of meta-information, such as title, this element is provided for situations where strict SGML parsing is necessary and the local DTD is not extensible.

In addition, HTTP servers can read the content of the document head to generate response headers corresponding to any elements defining a value for the attribute HTTP-EQUIV. This provides document authors a mechanism (not necessarily the preferred one) for identifying information that should be included in the respomse headers for an HTTP request.

Attributes:

HTTP-EQUIV—This attribute binds the element to an HTTP response header. If the semantics of the HTTP response header named by this attribute is known, then the contents can be processed based on a well-defined syntactic mapping whether or not the DTD includes anything about it. HTTP header names are not case sensitive. If not present, the NAME attribute should be used to identify this meta-information and it should not be used within an HTTP response header.

NAME—Meta-information name. If the name attribute is not present, then NAME can be assumed equal to the value HTTP-EQUIV.

CONTENT—The meta-information content to be associated with the given name and/ or HTTP response header.

<MULTICOL> . . . </MULTICOL>

MULTICOL specifies that all contained text will be displayed in multi-column format. All columns will have the same width and data should be spread evenly across each of the columns to achieve roughly equal column heights.

Attributes:

COLS—This attribute indicates the number of columns the contained data will be split into. The browser should try to evenly distribute the content across each of the columns in order to achieve roughly the same column height.

GUTTER—This attribute controls the amount of pixel space between columns.

WIDTH—This optional attribute is supposed to control the width of an individual column. All columns are always the same width, so the overall width of a multi-column layout should be (as specified by Netscape):

```
(cols * width) + ((cols - 1) * gutter)
```

Through direct experimentation, this attribute seems to control the *total* width of the column apparatus, not the width of each individual column. The multi-column apparatus will remain left-justified if a width results in an amount less than the overall browser window size. If no WIDTH is specified, the default width is 100 percent (full screen width).

```
Example:

<multicol COLS=3 WIDTH=80% GUTTER=20>
This is multi-column layout text that should be distributed
evenly
across 3 columns </multicol>
```

<NEXTID . . . >

The NEXTID element is a parameter read by and generated by text editing software to create unique identifiers. This element takes a single attribute, which is the next document alphanumeric identifier to be allocated of the form z123 :

```
Example:

<NEXTID N=Z127>
```

When modifying a document, existing anchor identifiers should not be reused, as these identifiers may be referenced by other documents. Human writers of HTML usually use mnemonic alphabetic identifiers. HTML user agents may ignore the NEXTID element. Support for the NEXTID element does not impact HTML user agents in any way.

<NOBR> (Netscape Extension)

The NOBR element stands for NO Break. This means all the text between the start and end of the NOBR elements cannot have line breaks inserted. While NOBR is essential for those character sequences that don't want to be broken, please be careful; long text strings inside of NOBR elements can look rather odd. Especially if during viewing the user adjusts the page size by altering the window size.

<NOEMBED> . . . </NOEMBED>

This is used in conjunction with the EMBED element to indicate content/HTML markup that will only appear if the browser does not support the EMBED syntax. Browsers that DO support the EMBED element will ignore the contents of the NO-EMBED element.

Example:

```
<embed SRC-"http://www.xxx.com/embedded.object" HEIGHT="50"
WIDTH="75">
<noembed>
<b>Please</b> try this
<a HREF="http://www.xxx.com/embedded.object">media clip</a>
</noembed>
</embed>
```

<NOFRAMES> . . . </NOFRAMES>

Provides information or alternate page layout for non-frames-capable browsers.

Example:

```
<NOFRAMES>
This page is designed for a frames-capable browser. Please see
our
<A HREF=" noframes.html">
noframes version
</A>.
</NOFRAMES>
```

<NOLAYER> . . . </NOLAYER>

This element is used in conjunction with the LAYER and ILAYER elements to indicate content/HTML markup that will only appear if the browser does not support the LAYER/ILAYER syntax. Browsers that do support the layering syntax will ignore the contents of the NOLAYER element.

Example:

```
<layer NAME="two" LEFT=40 TOP=40 Z-INDEX=2
SRC="http://www.example.com/document.html">
Positioned content</layer>
<nolayer><b>Please</b> try this page for
browsers that can not handle Netscape 's LAYER syntax.
```

```
<a HREF="http://www.example.com/alternate.html">Simple Text
Page</a>
</nolayer>
```

<NOSCRIPT> . . . </NOSCRIPT>

This element is used in conjunction with the SCRIPT element to indicate content/ HTML markup that will only appear if the browser does not support the SCRIPT syntax. Browsers that *do* support the SCRIPT element will ignore the contents of the NOSCRIPT element.

```
Example:

<script LANGUAGE="JavaScript">
<!—document.write("Hello World.")—>
</script>
<noscript>
<b>Please</b> try this page for browsers that can not handle
scripting.
<a HREF="http://www.xxx.com/alternate.html">Simple Text
Page</a>
</noscript>
```

<OBJECT> . . . </OBJECT>

The OBJECT element replaces and absorbs the many methods in use to include multimedia and embedded content in HTML documents. This element can replace all of the functionality in the existing APPLET, EMBED, BGSOUND, SOUND, and IMG elements. In order to achieve this, the element has many attributes that require some explanation.

When using OBJECT in place of the APPLET element, the PARAM element is used exactly as it would be with the APPLET element.

Attributes:

ALIGN—This attribute specifies the alignment of text following the OBJECT reference relative to the object on screen. LEFT and RIGHT specify floating horizontal alignment of the object in the browser window, and subsequent content will wrap around the object. The other options specify vertical alignment of text relative to the object on the same line.

BORDER—This controls the thickness of the border around the object (in pixels).

CLASSID—This attribute is a URL indicating the implementation for the OBJECT. In some systems this is a class identifier.

CODEBASE—This attribute allows the author to specify the URL of the OBJECT's implementation, which some URL schemes require in addition to the CLASSID URL.

CODETYPE—This attribute specifies the MIME type of the code referenced by the CLASSID attribute in advance of actually retrieving it. Browsers may use this value to skip over unsupported MIME types without needing to make network access.

DATA—This attribute indicates a URL pointing to the OBJECT's data, such as a GIF file for an image. If the CLASSID attribute is absent, the media (MIME) type of the data is used to determine a default value for the CLASSID attribute. The implementation is then loaded as if the CLASSID attribute had been explicitly specified.

DECLARE—This is a stand-alone attribute that indicates an object that is not created or instantiated until needed by something that references it (i.e., late binding). Each such "binding" typically results in a separate copy of the object (this is class-dependent). So in such cases, DECLARE is treated as a declaration for making an instance of an object. See the DECLARE explanation in the OBJECT specification for more details.

EXPORT—This is a stand-alone attribute that allows an image map defined within this element's content to be exported to an enclosing OBJECT element. This is only useful when inner and outer OBJECT elements both are images and have the same size.

HEIGHT—This attribute explicitly specifies the height of the object in pixels. It can be used to speed up display of the document being downloaded so it can pre-render the document with object placeholders while the object downloads.

HSPACE—This attribute specifies the horizontal spacing around objects in pixels (left and right padding).

NAME—This provides a way for the object to participate in a FORM submission process. If the NAME attribute is specified and the DECLARE attribute is absent, then the browser should use the data obtained from the OBJECT (the method used to obtain the data from the object is specific to each object) paired with the NAME in the FORM submission process.

SHAPES—This attribute indicates that the OBJECT contains hyperlinks associated with shaped regions of the visible area of the OBJECT. When this attribute is used, the contents of the OBJECT element will be hyperlinks with new hybrid client-side image mapping attributes. These are used to create a backward compatible system for map navigation. Please see the attributes of the Hyperlink (A HREF) element for implementation details of this attribute.

STANDBY—This allows you to specify a short text string for the browser to display while it loads the OBJECTs implementation and data. The character data can include character entities.

TABINDEX—"Tabbing" is a method of giving access/focus to an active HTML element using a standard keyboard sequence. All the active elements in a document can be cycled through using this sequence (e.g., Windows TAB key). The order of the active elements in this cycle is usually the order they occur in the document, but the TABINDEX attribute allows a different order to be established. The use of this attribute should create the following tabbing order cycle if the browser supports the attribute:

1. active elements using the TABINDEX attribute with positive integers are navigated first. Low values are navigated first.
2. active elements not specifying any TABINDEX attribute.

Those elements carrying a DISABLED attribute or using negative TABINDEX values do not participate in the tabbing cycle.

TYPE—This attribute specifies the MIME type of the data referenced in the DATA attribute in advance of retrieving it. In the absence of the CLASSID attribute, it allows the browser to retrieve the code implementing the OBJECT concurrently with the data and to skip over unsupported MIME types without having to make network accesses.

USEMAP—This attribute specifies the URL (usually internal to the document) of the client-side image map specification to be used if the browser has that capability. If the argument to USEMAP begins with a "#" it is assumed to be in the current document. Client-side coordinate mapping is done by the browser, so is inherently faster in processing the coordinates than the old ISMAP process for the IMG element. This attribute is usually only used for static image OBJECTs.

VSPACE—This attribute specifies the vertical spacing around objects in pixels (top and bottom padding).

WIDTH—This attribute explicitly specifies the width of the object in pixels. It can be used to speed up display of the document being downloaded so it can pre-render the document with object placeholders while the object downloads.

```
Example:

<object CODETYPE="application/java-vm"
CODEBASE="http://www.xxx.com/applet.class"
CLASSID="java:program.start" HEIGHT="100" WIDTH="100">
<param NAME="options" VALUE="xqz">
If you can read this you are too close.<br>
AND your browser does not support Java.
</object>
```

<OL> . . . </OL>

The Ordered List element is used to present a numbered list of items, sorted by sequence or order of importance.

An ordered list must begin with the OL element, which is immediately followed by an LI (list item) element.

Example:

```
<OL>
<LI>Click the Web button to open the Open the URL window.
<LI>Enter the URL number in the text field of the Open URL
window. The Web document you specified is displayed.
<LI>Click highlighted text to move from one link to another.
</OL>
```

The Ordered List element can take the COMPACT attribute, which suggests that a compact rendering be used.

NOTE: The OL element has been Netscape-enhanced. The average ordered list counts 1, 2, 3, etc. Netscape authors have added the TYPE attribute to this element to allow authors to specify whether the list items should be marked with:

(TYPE=A) - capital letters. e.g. A, B, C . . .
(TYPE=a) - small letters. e.g. a, b, c . . .
(TYPE=I) - large roman numerals. e.g. I, II, III . . .
(TYPE=i) - small roman numerals. e.g. i, ii, iii . . .
(TYPE=1) - or the default numbers. e.g. 1, 2, 3 . . .

For lists that wish to start at values other than 1 the new attribute START is available. START is always specified in the default numbers, and will be converted based on TYPE before display. Thus START=5 would display either an E, e, V, v, or 5 based on the TYPE attribute.

<OPTGROUP> . . . </OPTGROUP>

The OPTGROUP element allows authors to group selection list choices into a hierarchy. This is particularly helpful to nonvisual user agents when large numbers of options are available to choose from. Possible rendering of this element could be a collapsible hierarchy list of OPTION element content or some presentation conveying the hierarchy relationship of the OPTION contents. Browsers not supporting this element will "see" only a traditional flat list of OPTION elements. The LABEL attribute for this element is used to provide shorter labels for the nodes of the hierarchical menus.

Attributes:

DISABLED—This is a stand-alone attribute that indicates the element is initially nonfunctional.

LABEL—This specifies a shorter alternate label for use in identifying the subgroup of options.

Example:

```
<select NAME="Familytree">
<option LABEL="Bill" VALUE="bill">Bill Smith
<option LABEL="Mary" VALUE="mary">Mary Smith
<optgroup LABEL="Joe">
<option VALUE="michael">Michael Smith
<option VALUE="susan">Susan Smith
<option VALUE="howard">Howard Smith
</optgroup>
</select>
```

<OPTION>

The OPTION element can only occur within a SELECT element. It represents one choice.

Attributes:

SELECTED—Indicates that this option is initially selected.
VALUE—When present indicates the value to be returned if this option is chosen. The returned value defaults to the contents of the OPTION element.

The contents of the OPTION element are presented to the user to represent the option. It is used as a returned value if the VALUE attribute is not present.

<P> . . . </P>

The Paragraph element indicates a paragraph. The exact indentation and leading of a paragraph are not defined and may be a function of other elements, style sheets, etc.

Typically, paragraphs are surrounded by a vertical space of one line or half a line. This is typically not the case within the ADDRESS element and is never the case within the Preformatted Text element. With some HTML user agents, the first line in a paragraph is indented.

Example:

```
<H1>This Heading Precedes the Paragraph</H1>
<P>This is the text of the first paragraph.
```

```
<P>This is the text of the second paragraph. Although you do
not need to start paragraphs on new lines, maintaining this
convention facilitates document maintenance.
<P>This is the text of a third paragraph.
```

<P ALIGN>

Provides the ability to align paragraphs. Basically, ALIGN=left|center|right attributes have been added to the <P> element.

> *Example:*
>
> ```
> <P ALIGN=LEFT>  . . . </P>—All text within the paragraph will
> be aligned to the left side of the page layout. This setting is
> equal to the default <P> element.
>
> <P ALIGN=CENTER>  . . . </P>—All text within the paragraph will
> be aligned to the center of the page.
>
> <P ALIGN=RIGHT>  . . . </P>—All text will be aligned to the
> right side of the page.
> ```

<PARAM> . . . </PARAM>

The PARAM element is used to pass values to an embedded OBJECT (usually an embedded program) or to an embedded Java APPLET. In both situations PARAM serves the same purpose and has almost the same implementation (mostly because the official OBJECT with PARAM usage was meant to absorb the APPLET with PARAM functionality.)

Attributes:

NAME—This attribute identifies a symbolic name for the current parameter. It is coupled to a VALUE attribute to complete the parameter assignment.
TYPE—This identifies the MIME type of the resource indicated by the VALUE attribute ONLY when the VALUETYPE attribute has a value of REF.
VALUE—This identifies a value for the current parameter. It is coupled to a NAME attribute to complete the parameter assignment.
VALUETYPE—This identifies the type of the value attribute.

> *Example:*
> ```
> Applet usage:
> <applet CODEBASE="http://www.xxx.com/java/"
> ```

```
CODE="javaexample.class" WIDTH=200 HEIGHT=300>
<param NAME=text1 VALUE="Example Text 1">
<param NAME=imagecaption VALUE="Image Caption">
<param NAME=bounceimage VALUE="bounce1.gif">
<img SRC="non_java_image.gif" WIDTH=200 HEIGHT=300 BORDER=0
ALT="You are missing the full Java Experience.">
</applet>

Object usage:
<object CODETYPE="application/java-vm"
CODEBASE="http://www.xxx.com/applet.class"
CLASSID="java:program.start"
HEIGHT="100" WIDTH="100">
<param NAME="options" VALUE="xqz">
If you can read this you are too close.<br>
AND your browser does not supportJava.</object>
```

<PRE> . . . </PRE>

The Preformatted Text element presents blocks of text in fixed-width font, and so is suitable for text that has been formatted on screen.

The PRE element may be used with the optional WIDTH attribute, which is a Level 1 feature. The WIDTH attribute specifies the maximum number of characters for a line and allows the HTML user agent to select a suitable font and indentation. If the WIDTH attribute is not present, a width of 80 characters is assumed. Where the WIDTH attribute is supported, widths of 40, 80, and 132 characters should be presented optimally, with other widths being rounded up.

Rules of use:

1. Line breaks within the text are rendered as a move to the beginning of the next line.
2. The P element should not be used. If found, it should be rendered as a move to the beginning of the next line.
3. Anchor elements and character highlighting elements may be used.
4. Elements that define paragraph formatting (headings, ADDRESS, etc.) must not be used.
5. The horizontal tab character (encoded in US-ASCII and ISO-8859-1 as decimal 9) must be interpreted as the smallest positive nonzero number of spaces that will leave the number of characters so far on the line as a multiple of 8. Its use is not recommended, however.

<S> . . . </S>
See <STRIKE>

\<SAMP\> . . . \</SAMP\>

The Sample element indicates a sequence of literal characters; typically rendered as monospaced.

\<SCRIPT\> . . . \</SCRIPT\>

The SCRIPT element is the method used by browsers to recognize scripting languages in an HTML document. Scripting allows Web pages to change dynamically in response to events such as screen exit and entry, or user mouse-clicks. The most popular browser scripting languages currently are JavaScript and VBScript. While discussing the full scope of scripting in HTML pages is not the intent of these documents, discussion of how scripting affects HTML authoring is *definitely* relevant. Many other sites have covered the details with far greater skill and detail than I could ever manage. Please see the Related Links section for pointers to good resources on the subject.

Scripts can exist either embedded within a document or may be located elsewhere. If the script code is contained within a Web page, it will be embedded within an HTML comment between the script container tags. (Nesting within a comment is important in order to make the script invisible to browsers that do not support the feature.) Statements are evaluated when the document is loaded. If a script attempts to reference document objects defined by HTML elements occurring later in the document, the attempt will fail. Because of this, it is generally safest to place a SCRIPT statement at the top of a document in the HEAD element.

NOTE: Scripts can also be invoked using the A element combined with Script code in place of the destination URL. This allows a script (either inline or located in a SCRIPT element) to be executed when the user clicks on a hyperlink.

Attributes:

CHARSET—This indicates the character encoding of the script contents.
DEFER—This stand-alone attribute is used to advise the browser that the script is not going to generate any rendered document content and thus the user agent can continue parsing and rendering.
LANGUAGE—This attribute indicates the scripting language the script is written in. It is required if the SRC attribute is not specified, optional otherwise.
ONBLUR—A blur Event Handler executes Script code when a form field or layer loses focus.
ONCHANGE—A change Event Handler executes Script code when a form field loses focus and its value has been modified. This Event Handler is used to validate data after it is modified by a user.

ONCLICK—A click Event Handler executes Script code when an object is clicked.

ONFOCUS—A focus Event Handler executes script code when a form field or layer receives input focus by tabbing with the keyboard or clicking with the mouse. Important: Selecting within a form field results in a onSelect event, not a onFocus event.

ONLOAD—This attribute executes Script code with the completion of loading of a window or layer, or when all frames within a Frameset have finished loading. In a Frame document scenario, an onLoad event in the BODY element of a sub-frame will occur before an onLoad event within the parent FRAMESET element.

ONMOUSEOVER—A mouseOver Event Handler executes Script code once each time the mouse pointer enters the bounds of an object from outside the object.

ONMOUSEOUT—A mouseOut Event Handler executes Script code once each time the mouse pointer exits the bounds of an object from inside the object.

ONSELECT—A select Event Handler executes Script code when a user selects some of the text within a form field.

ONSUBMIT—A submit Event Handler executes Script code when a user submits a form. It can also be used to prevent a form from being submitted; to do so, put a return statement that returns false in the Event Handler. Any other returned value lets the form submit. If you omit the return statement, the form is submitted.

ONUNLOAD—An unload Event Handler executes Script code when the user exits a document. In a Frame document scenario, an onUnload event in the BODY element of a sub-frame will occur before an onUnload event within the parent FRAMESET element.

Example:

```
<html>
<head>

<script LANGUAGE="JavaScript">
<!—hide script from old browsers
function getname(str) {
alert("Hi, "+ str+"!");
}
// end hiding contents—>
</script>

</head>
<body>

Please enter your name:
<form>
<input TYPE="text" NAME="name" onBlur="getname(this.value)"
VALUE="">
</form>
</body>
</html>
```

SRC—This attribute specifies an external source for the script code.

TYPE—This attribute specifies the MIME type of the scripting code.

<SELECT . . . > . . . </SELECT>

The Select element allows the user to choose one of a set of alternatives described by textual labels. Every alternative is represented by the Option element.

Attributes:

MULTIPLE—The MULTIPLE attribute is needed when users are allowed to make several selections, e.g., <SELECT MULTIPLE>.

NAME—Specifies the name that will be submitted as a name-value pair.

SIZE—Specifies the number of visible items. If this is greater than one, then the resulting form control will be a list.

   The SELECT element is typically rendered as a pull-down or pop-up list.

```
Example:

<SELECT NAME="flavor">
<OPTION>Vanilla
<OPTION>Strawberry
<OPTION>Rum and Raisin
<OPTION>Peach and Orange
</SELECT>
```

If no option is initially marked as selected, then the first item listed is selected.

<SMALL> . . . </SMALL>

See <BIG>. Opposite of.

<SOUND> . . . </SOUND>

Use of the SOUND element specifies an audio file to be played in the background while viewing a document.

Attributes:

DELAY—Specifies the number of seconds to delay before playing the indicated sound file.

LOOP—Allows the author to specify the number of times the sound will play.

SRC—Specifies the URL of the audio file.

```
<sound SRC="http://www.xxx.com/xxx.wav" DELAY="5">
```

<SPACER>

The SPACER element attempts to give the author more control over white space in HTML documents. The author can control horizontal-only spacing, vertical-only spacing, or block spacing (vertical and horizontal) as well.

Attributes:

ALIGN—This attribute only applies when the TYPE is Block. It controls alignment of the surrounding text relative to the spacing block.
HEIGHT—This attribute only applies when the TYPE is Block. It controls the pixel height of the Block (Rectangle) SPACER element.
SIZE—This attribute only applies when the SPACER has a TYPE of Horizontal or Vertical. It controls the pixel width or height of the SPACER element.
TYPE—The values for TYPE allow different types of control over white-space spacing.
WIDTH—This attribute only applies when the TYPE is Block. It controls the pixel width of the Block (Rectangle) SPACER element.

```
Example:

<spacer TYPE="block" ALIGN="left" WIDTH=100 HEIGHT=100>
text
<br CLEAR="left">
```

<SPAN> . . . </SPAN>

The SPAN element is used in situations where the author wishes to apply a style using Cascading Style Sheets to a content area (text, etc.) that does not have a structured or established HTML rendering convention. It is an in-place Character Formatting level element that does *not* have an implied line break before and after the enclosed content. For more information on style sheets, please see Appendix B.

The recent addition of the many linking attributes to DIV and SPAN appear to be an attempt to expand the generic block and inline capabilities of these two elements.

Attributes:

CHARSET—This attribute indicates the character encoding of the destination resource of the HREF attribute.

HREF—This attribute indicates the URL to be loaded when the linked content is activated.

HREFLANG—This attribute specifies the base language of the resource indicated in the HREF attribute.

MEDIA—This attribute is a keyword representing the intended rendering destination for the style sheet properties applied to this element. Multiple destinations are given delimited by commas.

REL—The REL attribute is meant to give the relationship(s) described between the current document and the document specified by the HREF attribute.

REV—The REL attribute is basically meant to be the same as the REL attribute, but the semantics of the relationship are in the reverse direction. A link from A to B with REL="X" expresses the same relationship as a link from B to A with REV="X." Both the REL and REV attributes may be used in the same element.

TARGET—This attribute specifies the named frame for the contents specified by the HREF attribute to load to when activated.

TYPE—This attribute specifies the MIME type of the resource indicated in the HREF attribute.

Example:

```
<span CLASS="sectiona" STYLE="color:blue ">text within a span
tag</span>
```

<STRIKE>. . . . </STRIKE>

These are physical style elements that indicate a sequence of characters that has a horizontal line striking through the middle. The HTML 2 specification had STRIKE as a proposed element that did not reach the final specification, but HTML 3 revised the syntax to S. The HTML 3.2 recommendation reverted to the earlier syntax, and HTML 4.0 now includes *both* usages. Many browsers support one or the other, or even both.

Example:

```
<strike>text</strike>
<s>text</s>
```

\<STRONG> . . . \</STRONG>

The STRONG element indicates strong typographic emphasis, typically rendered in bold.

\<STYLE> . . . \</STYLE>

The STYLE element is one of the three methods used to include style information in an HTML document. The STYLE element is used in the document HEAD section to indicate style information for the entire document. If a LINK element exists (used to specify a style sheet external to the document) in conjunction with the STYLE element, the rules indicated in the STYLE section should be used instead of the LINK styles (i.e., it is independent of the style sheet cascading mechanism.) For more information on Cascading Style Sheets, please see Appendix B.

NOTE: Because this HEAD element requires a start and end tag, older browsers may end up displaying the style content it contains. In order to prevent this, it is strongly *recommended to embed this style information within the HTML Comment structure (<!——>).*

Attributes:

DISABLED—This is a stand-alone attribute that indicates the style reference is initially nonfunctional.
MEDIA—This attribute is a keyword representing the intended rendering destination for the style sheet definitions. Multiple destinations are given delimited by commas.
TITLE—This attribute is for use when other style sheet methods are specified. It allows the browser to build a menu of alternative style sheets (such as if one or more external style sheets are specified through use of the LINK element.) It may also be used to identify the style sheet in order to allow the user to have control over turning it on or off.
TYPE—This attribute indicates the Internet media type (MIME) of the STYLE element content. This MIME type applies to style rules applied within the STYLE element area as well as to all inline styles in the current document specified by the STYLE attribute used in HTML elements.

Example:

```
<html>
<head>
<title>Style Sheet Example</title>
<style TYPE="text/css">
```

```
<!—h1 { font-weight: bold; font-size: 12pt; line-height: 14pt;
font-family:helvetica;
    font-style: normal}
—>
</style>
</head>
<body>
This is plain text
<h1>This is Heading 1 affected by a style sheet</h1>
This is plain text
</body>
</html>
```

_{. . .}

This physical style element makes contained text subscripted in relation to surrounding content (vertically lowered text).

Example:

```
<sub>text</sub>
```

^{. . .}

This physical style element makes contained text superscripted in relation to surrounding content (vertically raised text).

Example:

```
<sup>text</sup>
```

<TABLE> . . . </TABLE>

This is the main wrapper for all the other table elements, and other table elements will be ignored if they aren't wrapped inside of a TABLE . . . /TABLE element. By default tables have no borders; borders will be added if the BORDER attribute is specified. At the time of writing, the TABLE element has an implied line break both before and after it. This is expected to change, allowing as much control over placement of tables as is currently available for the placement of images, aligning them to various positions in a line of text, as well as shifting them to the left or right margins and wrapping text around them.

Attributes:

BORDER—This attribute appears in the TABLE element. If present, borders are drawn around all table cells. If absent, there are no borders, but by default space is left for borders, so the same table with and without the BORDER attribute will have the same width.

By allowing the BORDER attribute to take a value, the document author gains two things. First he gains the ability to emphasize some tables with respect to others; a table with a border of four containing a sub-table with a border of one looks much nicer than if they both share the same default border width. Second, by explicitly setting border to zero, he regains that space originally reserved for borders between cells, allowing particularly compact tables.

CELLSPACING—This is a new attribute for the TABLE element. By default Netscape uses a cell spacing of two. For those fussy about the look of their tables, this gives them a little more control. Like it sounds, cell spacing is the amount of space inserted between individual cells in a table.

CELLPADDING=—This is a new attribute for the TABLE element. By default Netscape uses a cell padding of one. Cell padding is the amount of space between the border of the cell and the contents of the cell. Setting a cell padding of zero on a table with borders might look bad because the edges of the text could touch the cell borders. CELLSPACING=0 and CELLPADDING=1 gives the most compact table possible.

WIDTH—When this attribute appears in the TABLE element it is used to describe the desired width of this table, either as an absolute width in pixels or as a percentage of document width. Ordinarily complex heuristics are applied to tables and their cells to attempt to present a pleasing-looking table. Setting the WIDTH attribute overrides those heuristics and instead effort is put into fitting the table into the desired width as specified. In some cases it might be impossible to fit all the table cells at the specified width, in which case Netscape will try and get as close as possible.

When this attribute appears on either the TH or TD element it is used to describe the desired width of the cell, either as an absolute width in pixels or as a percentage of table width. Ordinarily complex heuristics are applied to table cells to attempt to present a pleasing-looking table. Setting the <WIDTH> attribute overrides those heuristics for that cell and instead effort is put into fitting the cell into the desired width as specified. In some cases it might be impossible to fit all the table cells at the specified widths, in which case Netscape will try and get as close as possible.

<TBODY> . . . </TBODY>

This element is part of the Complex Table Model, which allows a finer level of control than the Simple Table Model while maintaining backward compatibility with the simpler model. The TBODY element is part of a trio of table grouping elements that organize a series of Table Rows (TR) into Header (THEAD), Body (TBODY), and Footer (TFOOT) sections.

The THEAD and TFOOT section markers are optional, but one or more TBODY sections are always required. If present, each THEAD, TBODY, and TFOOT element must contain one or more TR tag groupings. To allow for backward compatibility with the older Simple Table Model, if no TBODY structures exist in a table, the entire set of row groupings (TR) are assumed to be a single TBODY.

The TBODY section is used to distinguish rows in the main body of the table from the rows used to define the header and footer of the table. Multiple TBODY sections are used when divisions or rules are needed between groups of table rows. The TBODY section(s) are placed after any THEAD or TFOOT sections in the HTML markup to allow browsers to render the header and footer before receiving all of the Table Body (TBODY) data (in case a table must be broken up.)

Attributes:

ALIGN—This controls the horizontal alignment of text within each of the table cells in the specified grouping.

BGCOLOR—This attribute sets the background color to be used for the current table section (TBODY).

CHAR—This attribute specifies a character in the cell content to be used to align the data in the current cell. The default value for this attribute is the decimal point character for the current specified language. No handling instructions are given for scenarios with multiple occurrences of the same alignment character on a single line.

CHAROFF—This attribute specifies the spacing offset to the first occurrence of the alignment character (specified by the CHAR attribute) on each line of the cells within the current cell grouping. The direction of the offset is determined by the current text direction (set with the DIR attribute or the BDO element). In left-to-right scenarios (default), offset is from the left margin. In right-to-left scenarios, offset is from the right margin.

VALIGN—This controls the vertical alignment of text within each of the table cells in the specified grouping.

Example:

```
<table
BORDER="2" ALIGN="left" CELLPADDING="5" BORDERCOLOR="#ff0000"
COLS="4" FRAME="vsides" RULES="rows" WIDTH="75%">
<caption ALIGN="top">Sample table</caption>
<thead>
<tr>
```

```
    <th>Player</th>
    <th>Score</th>
    <th>Team 1</th>
    <th>Team 2</th>
  </tr>
  </thead>

  <tfoot>
  <tr>
    <th COLSPAN=4>NOTE: This is only a small sample</th>
  </tr>
  </tfoot>
  <tbody>

  <tr>
    <td>Pete</td>
    <td>5</td>
    <td>2</td>
    <td>5</td>
  </tr>

  <tr>
    <td>Mike</td>
    <td>2</td>
    <td>7</td>
    <td>6/td>
  </tr>

  <tr>
    <td>Jean</td>
    <td>1</td>
    <td>2</td>
  <td>20<br>
  </td>

  </tr>
  </tbody>
  </table>
```

<TD . . . > . . . </TD>

This stands for table data and specifies a standard table data cell. Table data cells must only appear within table rows. Each row need not have the same number of cells specified, as short rows will be padded with blank cells on the right. A cell can contain any of the HTML elements normally present in the body of an HTML document. The default alignment of table data is ALIGN=left and VALIGN=middle. These alignments are overridden by any alignments specified in the containing <TR> element, and those alignments in turn are overridden by any ALIGN or VALIGN attributes explicitly specified on this cell. By default, lines inside of table cells can be broken up to fit within the overall cell width. Specifying the NOWRAP attribute for a TD prevents line-breaking for that cell.

<TD . . . > . . . </TD> can also contain NOWRAP, COLSPAN, and ROWSPAN attributes.

<TEXTAREA> . . . </TEXTAREA>

The TEXTAREA element lets users enter more than one line of text.

Example:

```
<TEXTAREA NAME="address" ROWS=64 COLS=6>
New Art Technologies, Inc.
The Big Apple
</TEXTAREA>
```

The text up to the end element (</TEXTAREA>) is used to initialize the field's value. This end element is always required even if the field is initially blank. When submitting a form, lines in a TEXTAREA should be terminated using CR/LF.

In a typical rendering, the ROWS and COLS attributes determine the visible dimension of the field in characters. The field is rendered in a fixed-width font. HTML user agents should allow text to extend beyond these limits by scrolling as needed.

NOTE: In the initial design for forms, multiline text fields were supported by the Input element with TYPE=TEXT. Unfortunately, this causes problems for fields with long text values. SGML's default (Reference Quantity Set) limits the length of attribute literals to only 240 characters. The HTML 2.0 SGML declaration increases the limit to 1,024 characters.

<TFOOT> . . . </TFOOT>

See <TBODY>.

<TH . . . > . . . </TH>

This stands for table header. Header cells are identical to data cells in all respects, with the exception that header cells are in a bold FONT and have a default ALIGN=center.

<TH . . . > . . . </TH> can also contain VALIGN, NOWRAP, COLSPAN, and ROW-SPAN attributes.

<THEAD> . . . </THEAD>
See <TBODY>.

<TITLE> . . . </TITLE>
Every HTML document must have a TITLE element. The title should identify the contents of the document and in a global context, and may be used in history lists and as a label for the windows displaying the document. Unlike headings, titles are not typically rendered in the text of a document itself. The TITLE element must occur within the head of the document and may not contain anchors, paragraph elements, or highlighting. Only one title is allowed in a document.

The length of a title is not limited, however; long titles may be truncated in some applications. To minimize the possibility, titles should be fewer than 64 characters. Also keep in mind that a short title such as "Introduction" may be meaningless out of context. An example of a meaningful title might be "Introduction to HTML Elements."

This is the only element that is required within the HEAD element. The other elements described are optional and can be implemented when appropriate.

```
Example:

<HEAD>
<TITLE> Introduction to HTML </TITLE>
</HEAD>
```

<TR > . . . </TR>
This stands for table row. The number of rows in a table is exactly specified by how many TR elements are contained within it, irregardless of cells that may attempt to use the ROWSPAN attribute to span into nonspecified rows. TR can have both the ALIGN and VALIGN attributes, which if specified become the default alignments for all cells in this row.

<TT> . . . </TT>
The Teletype element specifies that the text should be rendered in fixed-width typewriter font.

\<UL\> . . . \</UL\>

The Unordered List element is used to present a list of items that is typically separated by white space and/or marked by bullets. An unordered list must begin with the UL element, which is immediately followed by an LI (list item) element:

```
Example:

<UL>
<LI>First list item
<LI>Second list item
<LI>Third list item
</UL>
```

The Unordered List element can take the COMPACT attribute, which suggests that a compact rendering be used.

```
NOTE: The UL element has been Netscape-enhanced. The basic bulleted list has
a default progression of bullet types that changes as you move through indented
levels—from a solid disc to a circle to a square. Netscape authors have added a
TYPE attribute to the UL element so that no matter what the indent level, the bul-
let type can be specified thus :

TYPE=disc
TYPE=circle
TYPE=square
```

\<VAR\> . . . \</VAR\>

The Variable element indicates a variable name, typically rendered as italic.

```
Example:

When coding, <VAR>LeftIndent()</VAR> must be a variable
```

<WBR>

The WBR element stands for Word BReak. This is for the very rare case when a NOBR section requires an exact break. Also, it can be used anytime the Netscape Navigator can be helped by telling it where a word is allowed to be broken. The WBR element does not force a line break (BR does that); it simply lets the Netscape Navigator know where a line break is allowed to be inserted if needed.

Cascading Style Sheet Reference

DHTML (Dynamic HTML) is composed of three components: style sheets, content positioning, and downloadable fonts. Used together, these three components give you greater control over the appearance, layout, and behavior of your Web pages.

Please note that in order to make effective use of CSS (Cascading Style Sheets) and DHTML (Dynamic HTML), the browser must be at least Netscape or Internet Explorer version 4.0 or greater.

This appendix provides a short reference to the art and science of using Netscape's implementation of the CSS component of DHTML.

Quick Example

Let's take a look at a simple HTML page using Style Sheets.

```
<html>
<STYLE TYPE="text/css">
P {
textAlign:center; margin-left:20%; margin-right:20%;}
H1 {
text-decoration:underline; color: green;}
H2 {
text-transform:uppercase; color: red;
border-width:4pt; border-style:outset;
background-color:yellow; padding: 4pt;
border-color:red;}
BLOCKQUOTE {
color:blue; font-style:italic;
line-height:1.5; text-indent:10%;}
</STYLE>
<h1>This is header 1</h1>
```

```
<br><h2>This is header 2</h1>
<br>This is some text
</html>
```

Now let's see how the code looks in a browser (Figure A-1):

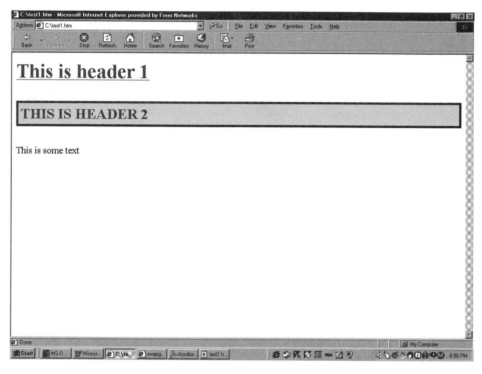

Figure A-1. *Simple style sheet example.*

CSS Tags

This appendix covers the following style sheet tags:

Comments in Style Sheets

CSS Resources

New HTML Tags
- <STYLE>
- <LINK>
- <SPAN>

New Attributes for Existing HTML Tags
- STYLE
- CLASS
- ID

New JavaScript Object Properties
- Tags
- Classes
- Ids

Font Properties
- Font size
- Font style
- Font family
- Font weight

Text Properties
- Line height
- Text decoration
- Text transform
- Text alignment
- Text indent

Block-Level Formatting Properties
- Margins
- Padding
- Border widths
- Border style
- Border color
- Width
- Alignment
- Clear

Color and Background Properties
- Color
- Background image
- Background color

Classification Properties
- Display
- List style type
- White space

Units
- Length units
- Color units

Comments in Style Sheets

Comments in style sheets are similar to those in the C programming language. For example:

```
B {color:blue;} /* bold text will be blue */
tags.B.color = "blue"; /* bold text will be blue */
```

JavaScript style sheet syntax also supports comments in the C++ style, for example:

```
tags.B.color = "blue"; // bold text will be blue
```

CSS Resources

1. http://jigsaw.w3.org/css-validator/. W3C CSS validation service.
2. http://222.zvon.org/xxl/CSS2Reference/Output/index.html. Complete CSS2 reference.
3. http://www.zvon.org/xxl/css1Reference/Output/index.html. Complete CSS1 reference.
4. http://www.w3.org/MarkUp/Guide/Style.html. A brief CSS tutorial including a table of browser safe colors.
5. http://www.w3.org/People/Raggett/tidy/. HTML Tidy, a utility to clean up markup errors.
6. http://www.hwg.org/resources/faqs/cssFAQ.html. CSS FAQ from the HTML Writers Guild.
7. http://wdvl.internet.com/Authoring/Style/Sheets/. Web Developer's Virtual Library on Cascading Style Sheets.
8. http://dmoz.org/Computers/Programming/Internet/CSS. Open directory links to CSS sources.
9. http://www.w3.org/TR/REC-CSS2/css2.pdf. CSS2 Specification W3C Recommendation.

New HTML Tags

This section lists the HTML tags that are useful for working with styles.

<STYLE>

The <STYLE> and </STYLE> tags indicate a style sheet. Inside <STYLE> and </STYLE> you can specify styles for elements, define classes and IDs, and generally establish styles for use within the document.

To specify that the style sheet uses JavaScript syntax, set the TYPE attribute to "text/javascript". To specify that the style sheet uses CSS syntax, set the TYPE attribute to "text/css". The default value for TYPE is "text/CSS".

For example:

```
<STYLE TYPE="text/css">
BODY {margin-right: 20%; margin-left:20%;}
PRE {color:green;}
all.CLASS1 {float:right; font-weight: bold;}
</STYLE>
```

<LINK>

Use the <LINK> element to link to an external style sheet for use in a document. For example:

```
CSS Syntax
<HTML>
<HEAD>
<TITLE>A Good Title</TITLE>
<LINK REL=STYLESHEET TYPE="text/css"
HREF="http://style.com/mystyles1.htm">
</HEAD>

JavaScript Syntax
<HTML>
<HEAD>
<TITLE>A Good Title</TITLE>
<LINK REL=STYLESHEET TYPE="text/javascript"
HREF="http://style.com/mystyles1.htm">
</HEAD>
```

<SPAN>

Use the inline <SPAN> and </SPAN> elements to indicate the beginning and end of a piece of text to which a style is to be applied.

The following example applies an individual style to a piece of text.

```
<P>Here is some normal paragraph text. It looks OK, but would
be much better if it was<SPAN style="color:blue; font-
weight:bold; font-style:italic"> in bright, bold, italic blue.
</SPAN>The blue text stands out much more.</P>
```

You can use the <SPAN> element to achieve effects such as a large initial letter, for example:

```
<STYLE TYPE="text/css">
init-letter.all {font-size:400%; font-weight:bold;}
</STYLE>
<P><SPAN class="init-letter">T</SPAN>his is . . . </P>
```

New Attributes for Existing HTML Tags

This section lists the new attributes for existing HTML tags that are useful for working with styles. These attributes can be used with any HTML tag to specify the style for that tag.

STYLE

The STYLE attribute determines the style of a specific element. For example:

```
CSS Syntax
<H3 STYLE="line-height:24pt; font-weight:bold; color:cyan;">
Cyan Heading</H3>

JavaScript Syntax
<H3 STYLE="lineHeight='24pt'; fontWeight='bold'; color='cyan'">
Cyan Heading</H3>
```

CLASS

The CLASSES JavaScript property allows you to define classes of styles in a style sheet. The CLASS attribute specifies a style class to apply to an element.

Although CSS syntax and JavaScript syntax use slightly different syntax to define classes of styles, the use of the CLASS attribute is the same in both syntaxes. For example:

CSS SyntaxExample
```
<STYLE TYPE="text/css">
H3.class1 {font-style:italic; color:red;}
</STYLE>
```

JavaScript Syntax Example
```
<STYLE TYPE="text/javascript">
classes.class1.H3.fontStyle="italic";
classes.class1.H3.color="red";
</STYLE>
```

Style Sheet Use
```
<H3 CLASS="class1">This H3 is in red italic letters.</H3>
```

Class names are case-sensitive. Each HTML element can use only one style class.

To specify that a class can apply to all elements, use the element selector "all" when you set the properties for the class. For example, the code sample below specifies that the class LEMON can be applied to any element, and all elements that use the style class LEMON are yellow.

CSS Syntax
```
<STYLE TYPE="text/css">
all.LEMON {color:yellow;}
</STYLE>
```

JavaScript Syntax
```
<STYLE TYPE="text/javascript">
classes.LEMON.all.color="yellow";
</STYLE>
```

Style Sheet Use
```
<H1 class="LEMON">A Nice Yellow Heading</P>
<P CLASS="LEMON">What a nice shade of yellow this paragraph
is.</P>
```

ID

When defining style sheets, you can create individual named styles.

An element can use a style class and also use a named style. This allows you to use named styles to express individual stylistic exceptions to a style class. To define an individual names style in CSS syntax, you use the # sign to indicate a name for an individual style, while In JavaScript syntax, you use the ID selector.

In both CSS syntax and JavaScript syntax, you use the ID attribute in an HTML element to specify the style for that element. ID names are case-sensitive.

ID styles are particularly useful for working with layers of precisely positioned HTML content. The following code shows an example of the use of individual named styles. In this example, the STYLE1 class defines a style with several characteristics. The named style A1 specifies that the color is blue. This style can be used to specify that a paragraph has all the style characteristics of STYLE1, except that its color is blue instead of red.

CSS Syntax
```
<STYLE TYPE="text/css">
P.STYLE1 {
color:red; font-size:24pt; line-height:26pt;
font-style:italic; font-weight:bold;
}
#A1 {color: blue;}
</STYLE>
```

JavaScript Syntax
```
<STYLE TYPE="text/javascript">
with (classes.STYLE1.P) {
color="red";
fontSize="24pt";
lineHeight="26pt";
fontStyle="italic";
fontWeight="bold";
}
ids.A1.color= "blue";
</STYLE>
```

Style Sheet Use
```
<P CLASS="STYLE1">Big red text</P>
<P CLASS="STYLE1" ID="A1">Big blue text</P>
```

New JavaScript Object Properties

This section discusses the new JavaScript object properties that are useful for defining style sheets using JavaScript syntax.

Tags

When using JavaScript syntax within the <STYLE> element, you can set styles by using the tags property of the JavaScript object document.

The following example uses JavaScript syntax to specify that all paragraphs appear in red:

```
<STYLE TYPE="text/javascript">
tags.P.color = red;
</STYLE>
```

In CSS syntax, this would be:

```
<STYLE TYPE="text/css">
P {color:red;}
</STYLE>
```

The tags property always applies to the document object for the current document, so you can omit document from the expression document.tags. For example, the following two statements both say the same thing:

```
document.tags.P.color = "red";
tags.P.color = "red";
```

To set default styles for all elements in a document, you can set the desired style on the <BODY> element, since all other elements inherit from <BODY>.

For example, to set a universal right margin for the document:

```
tags.body.marginRight="20pt"; /*JavaScript syntax */
BODY {margin-right:20pt;} /* CSS syntax */
```

Classes
See the CLASS section for a discussion of the classes JavaScript property.

Ids
See the ID section for a discussion of the ids JavaScript property.

Font Properties

Using styles, you can specify font size, font family, font style, and font weight for any element.

Font Size

CSS syntax name: font-size
JavaScript syntax name: fontSize

Possible values: absolute-size, relative-size, length, percentage
Initial value: medium
Applies to: all elements
Inherited: yes
Percentage values: relative to parent element's font size

- absolute-size
  An absolute-size is a keyword such as:
  xx-small
  x-small
  small
  medium
  large
  x-large
- relative-size
  A relative-size keyword is interpreted relative to the font size of the parent element. Note that relative values only equate to actual values when the element whose font size is a relative value has a parent element that has a font size. (A relative size has to have something to be relative to.)

  Possible values are:
  larger
  smaller

  For example, if the parent element has a font size of medium, a value of larger will make the font size of the current element be large.
- length
  A length is a number followed by a unit of measurement, such as 24pt.
- percentage
  A percentage keyword sets the font size to a percentage of the parent element's font size.

CSS Syntax
```
P {font-size:12pt;}
EM {font-size:120%};
BLOCKQUOTE {font-size:medium;}
B {font-size:larger;}
```

JavaScript Syntax
```
tags.P.fontSize = "12pt";
tags.EM.fontSize = 120%;
tags.BLOCKQUOTE.fontSize = "medium";
tags.B.fontSize="larger";
```

Font Family

CSS syntax name: font-family
JavaScript syntax name: fontFamily
Possible values: fontFamily
Initial value: the default font, which comes from user preferences
Applies to: all elements
Inherited: yes
Percentage values: NA

- fontFamily
  The fontFamily indicates the font family to use, such as Helvetica or Arial. If a list of font names is given, the browser tries each named font in turn until it finds one that exists on the user's system. If none of the specified font families are available on the user's system, the default font is used instead.

  If you link a font definition file to your Web page, the font definition file will be downloaded with the page, thus guaranteeing that all the fonts in the definition file are available on the user's system while the user is viewing that page.

  There is a set of generic family names that are guaranteed to indicate a font on every system, but that exact font is system-dependent. The five generic font families are:

- serif
- sans-serif
- cursive
- monospace
- fantasy

CSS Syntax Example
```
<STYLE TYPE="text/css">
H1 {fontFamily:Helvetica, Arial, sans-serif;}
</STYLE>
```

```
JavaScript Syntax Example
<STYLE TYPE="text/javascript">
tags.H1.fontFamily="Helvetica, Arial, sans-serif";
</STYLE>
```

Font Weight

CSS syntax name: font-weight
JavaScript syntax name: fontWeight
The font weight indicates the weight of the font. For example:

The possible values are normal, bold, bolder, and lighter. You can also specify weight as a numerical value from 100 to 900, where 100 is the lightest and 900 is the heaviest.
Possible values: normal, bold, bolder, lighter, 100–900
Initial value: normal
Applies to: all elements
Inherited: yes
Percentage values: N/A

```
CSS Syntax Example
<STYLE>
BLOCKQUOTE {font-weight: bold;}
</STYLE>

JavaScript Syntax Example
<STYLE>
tags.BLOCKQUOTE.fontWeight="bold";
</STYLE>
```

Font Style

CSS syntax name: font-style
JavaScript syntax name: fontStyle
Possible values: normal, italic
Initial value: normal
Applies to: all elements
Inherited: yes
Percentage values: N/A

This property determines the style of the font.
The following example specifies that emphasized text within <H1> elements appears in italic.

```
CSS Syntax Example
<STYLE>
H1 EM {font-style: italic;}
</STYLE>

JavaScript Syntax Example
<STYLE>
contextual(tags.H1, tags.EM).fontStyle = "italic";
</STYLE>
```

Text Properties

The use of style sheets allows you to set text properties such as line height and text decoration.

Line Height

CSS syntax name: line-height
JavaScript syntax name: lineHeight
Possible values number, length, percentage, normal
Initial value: normal for the font
Applies to: block-level elements
Inherited: yes
Percentage values: refers to the font size of the element itself

This property sets the distance between the baselines of two adjacent lines. It applies only to block-level elements.

- number:
  If you specify a numerical value without a unit of measurement, the line height is the font size of the current element multiplied by the numerical value. This differs from a percentage value in the way it inherits: when a numerical value is specified, child elements inherit the factor itself, not the resultant value (as is the case with percentage and other units).

  For example:
  fontSize:10pt;
  line-height:1.2; /* line height is now 120%, ie 12pt */
  font-size:20pt; /* line height is now 24 pt, */
- length:
  An expression of line height as a measurement, for example:
  line-height:0.4in;

line-height:18pt;
* percentage
Percentage of the element's font size, for example:
line-height:150%;
Negative values are not allowed.

Text Decoration

CSS syntax name: text-decoration
JavaScript syntax name: textDecoration
Possible values: none, underline, line-through, blink
Initial value: none
Applies to: all elements
Inherited: no, but see clarification below
Percentage values: N/A

This property describes decorations that are added to the text of an element. If the element has no text (for example, the <IMG> element in HTML) or is an empty element (for example, "<EM></EM>"), this property has no effect.

This property is not inherited, but children elements will match their parent. For example, if an element is underlined, the line should span the child elements. The color of the underlining will remain the same even if child elements have different color values.

For example:

```
BLOCKQUOTE {text-decoration: underline;}
```

The text decoration options do not include color options, since the color of text is derived from the color property value.

Text Transform

CSS syntax name: text-transform
JavaScript syntax name: textTransform
Possible values: capitalize, uppercase, lowercase, none
Initial value: none
Applies to: all elements
Inherited: yes
Percentage values: N/A

This property indicates text case.

Capitalize: Display the first character of each word in uppercase.
Uppercase: Display all letters of the element in uppercase.
Lowercase: Display all letters of the element in lowercase.
None: Neutralizes inherited value.

For example:

CSS Syntax Example
```
<STYLE TYPE="text/css">
H1 {text-transform:capitalize;}
H1.CAPH1 {text-transform: uppercase;}
</STYLE>
```

JavaScript Syntax Example
```
<STYLE>
tags.H1.textTransform = "capitalize";
classes.CAPH1.H1.textTransform = "uppercase";
</STYLE>
```

Style Sheet Use
```
<H1>This is a regular level-one heading</H1>
<H1 CLASS=CAPH1>important heading</H1>
```

Text Alignment

CSS syntax name: text-align
JavaScript syntax name: textAlign
Possible values: left, right, center, justify
Initial value: left
Applies to: block-level elements
Inherited: yes
Percentage values: N/A

This property describes how text is aligned within the element.

Example:

```
tags.P.textAlign = "center"
```

CSS Syntax Example
```
<STYLE TYPE="text/css">
all.RIGHTHEAD {text-align:right; color:blue;}
```

```
P.LEFTP {text-align:left; color:red;}
</STYLE>
```

JavaScript Syntax
```
<STYLE TYPE="text/javascript">
classes.RIGHTHEAD.all.textAlign="right";
classes.LEFTP.P.textAlign="left";
classes.RIGHTHEAD.all.color="blue";
classes.JUSTP.P.color="red";
</STYLE>
```

Style Sheet Use
```
<H3>A Normal Heading</H3>
<H3 CLASS=RIGHTHEAD>A Right-Aligned Heading</H3>
<P>This is a normal paragraph. This is what paragraphs usually
look like, when they are left to their own devices, and you do
not use style sheets to control their text alignment.</P>
<P CLASS = LEFTP>This paragraph is left-justified, which means
it has a ragged right edge. Whenever paragraphs contain
excessively, perhaps unnecessarily, long words, the raggedness
of the justification becomes more manifestly apparent than in
the case where all the words in the sentence are short.</P>
```

Text Indent

CSS syntax name: text-indent
JavaScript syntax name: textIndent
Possible values: length, percentage
Initial value: 0
Applies to: block-level elements
Inherited: yes
Percentage values: refer to parent element's width

The property specifies indentation that appears before the first formatted line. The text-indent value may be negative. An indent is not inserted in the middle of an element that was broken by another element (such as <BR> in HTML).

- length
  Length of the indent as a numerical value with units, for example:
  P {text-indent:3em;}
- percentage
  Length of the indent as a percentage of the parent element's width, for example:
  P {text-indent:25%;}

CSS Syntax Example
```
<STYLE TYPE="text/css">
P.INDENTED {text-indent:25%;}
</STYLE>
```

JavaScript Syntax Example
```
<STYLE TYPE="text/css">
classes.INDENTED.P.textIndent="25%";
</STYLE>
```

Style Sheet Use
```
<P CLASS=INDENTED>
The first line is indented 25 percent of the width of the
parent element, which in this case happens to be the BODY tag,
since this element is not embedded in anything else.</P>
<BLOCKQUOTE>
<P CLASS=INDENTED>
This time the first line is indented 25 percent from the
blockquote that surrounds this element. A blockquote
automatically indents its contents.</P>
</BLOCKQUOTE>
Block-Level Formatting Properties
Style sheets treat each block-level element as if it is
surrounded by a box.
Block-level elements start on a new line, for example, <H1> and
<P> are block-level elements, but <EM> is not. Each box can
have padding, border, and margins.You can set values for top,
bottom, left and right paddings, border widths, and margins.
```

Block-Level Formatting Properties

Style sheets treat each block-level element as if it is surrounded by a box. Block-level elements start on a new line; for example, <H1> and <P> are block-level element, but <EM> is not.

Each box can have padding, border, and margins. You can set values for top, bottom, left and right paddings, border widths, and margins.

Margins

CSS syntax names: margin-left, margin-right, margin-top, margin-bottom

JavaScript syntax names: marginLeft, marginRight, marginTop, marginBottom, and margins()

Possible values: length, percentage, auto
Initial value: 0

Applies to: all elements
Inherited: no
Percentage values: refer to parent element's width

These properties set the margin of an element. The margins express the minimal distance between the borders of two adjacent elements.

You can set each margin individually by specifying values for margin-left/ marginLeft, margin- right/marginRight, margin-top/marginTop, and margin-bottom/marginBottom.

In CSS syntax you can set all margins to the same value at one time by setting the margin property (note that the property name is singular). In JavaScript syntax you can use the margins() method to set the margins for all four sides at once. (Note that the function name is plural.)

The arguments to the margin property and margins() method are top, right, bottom, and left margins, respectively. For example:

```
CSS Syntax
/* top=10pt, right=20pt, bottom=30pt, left=40pt */
P {margin:10pt 20pt 30pt 40pt;}
/* set all P margins to 40 pt */
P {margin:40pt;}

JavaScript Syntax
/* top=10pt, right=20pt, bottom=30pt, left=40pt */
tags.BODY.margins("10pt", "20pt", "30pt", "40pt");
/* set all P margins to 40 pt */
tags.P.margins("40pt");
```

Adjoining margins of adjacent elements are added together, unless one of the elements has no content, in which case its margins are ignored. For example, if an <H1> element with a bottom margin of 40 points is followed by a <P> element with a top margin of 30 points, then the separation between the two elements is 70 points. However, if the <H1> element has content, but the <P> element is empty, then the margin between them is 40 points.

When margin properties are applied to replaced elements (such as an <IMG> tag), they express the minimal distance from the replaced element to any of the content of the parent element.

The use of negative margins is not recommended because it may have unpredictable results.

Padding

CSS syntax names: padding-top, padding-right, padding-bottom, padding-left, paddings
JavaScript syntax names: paddingTop, paddingRight, paddingBottom, paddingLeft, and paddings()

Possible values: length, percentage
Initial value: 0
Applies to: all elements
Inherited: no
Percentage values: refer to parent element's width

These properties describe how much space to insert between the border of an element and the content (such as text or image). You can set the padding on each side individually by specifying values for padding-top/paddingTop, padding-right/paddingRight, padding-left/paddingLeft, and padding-bottom/paddingBottom.

In CSS syntax you can use the padding property (note that it is padding singular) to set the padding for all four sides at once. In JavaScript syntax you can use the paddings() method to set the margins for all four sides at once.

The arguments to the padding property (CSS syntax) and the paddings() method (JavaScript syntax) are the top, right, bottom, and left padding values respectively.

```
CSS Syntax
/* top=10pt, right=20pt, bottom=30pt, left=40pt */
P {padding:10pt 20pt 30pt 40pt;}
/* set the padding on all sides of P to 40 pt */
P {padding:40pt;}

JavaScript Syntax
/* top=10pt, right=20pt, bottom=30pt, left=40pt */
tags.P.paddings("10pt", "20pt", "30pt", "40pt")
/* set the padding on all sides of P to 40 pt */
tags.P.paddings("40pt");
```

Padding values cannot be negative.

To specify the color or image that appears in the padding area, you can set the background color or background image of the element.

Border Widths
CSS syntax names: border-top-width, border-bottom-width, border-left-width, border-right-width, border-width
JavaScript syntax names: borderTopWidth, borderBottomWidth, borderLeftWidth, borderRightWidth, and borderWidths()
Possible values: length
Initial value: none
Applies to: all elements
Inherited: no
Percentage values: N/A

These properties set the width of a border around an element. You can set the width of the top border by specifying a value for border-top-width/borderTopWidth. You can set the width of the right border by specifying a value for border-right-width/border-RightWidth. You can set the width of the bottom border by specifying a value for border-bottom-width/borderBottomWidth. You can set the width of the left border by specifying a value for border-left-width/ borderLeft-Width.

In CSS syntax, you can set all four borders at once by setting the border-width property. In JavaScript syntax you can set all four borders at once by using the borderWidths() function.

The arguments to the border-width property (CSS syntax) and the border-Widths() function (JavaScript syntax) are the top, right, bottom, and left border widths, respectively.

```
/* top=1pt, right=2pt, bottom=3pt, left=4pt */
P {border-width:1pt 2pt 3pt 4pt;} /* CSS */
tags.P.borderWidths("1pt", "2pt", "3pt", "4pt"); /* JavaScript
syntax */
/* set the border width to 2 pt on all sides */
P {border-width:40pt;} /* CSS */
tags.P.borderWidths("40pt"); /* JavaScript syntax */
```

Border Style

CSS syntax name: border-style
JavaScript syntax name: borderStyle
Possible values: none, solid, double, inset, outset,
groove, ridge
Initial value: none
Applies to: all elements
Inherited: no
Percentage values: N/A

This property sets the style of a border around a block-level element. For the border to be visible, however, you must also specify the border width.

Border Color

CSS name: border-color
JavaScript syntax name: borderColor
Possible values: none, colorvalue
Initial value: none
Applies to: all elements

Inherited: no
Percentage values: N/A

This property sets the color of the border. The color can either be a named color or a six-digit hexadecimal value indicating a color or an rgb color value.

For example:

```
CSS Syntax
P {border-color:blue;}
BLOCKQUOTE {border-color:#0000FF;}
H1 {border-color:rgb(0%, 0%, 100%);}

JavaScript Syntax
tags.P.borderColor="blue";
tags.BLOCKQUOTE.borderColor="#0000FF";
tags.H1.borderColor="rgb(0%, 0%, 100%);
```

Width
CSS syntax name: width
JavaScript syntax name: width
Possible values: length, percentage, auto
Initial value: auto
Applies to: block-level and replaced elements
Inherited: no
Percentage values: refer to parent element's width

This property determines the width of an element.

Note that if you set the left and right margins, and also the width of a property, the margin settings take precedence over the width setting. For example, if the left margin setting is 25%, the right margin setting is 10%, and the width setting is 100%, the width setting is ignored. (The width will end up being 65% total.)

```
CSS Syntax Example
all.NARROW {width:50%;}
all.INDENTEDNARROW {margin-left:20%; width:60%;}

JavaScript Syntax Example
classes.NARROW.all.width = "50%";
classes.INDENTEDNARROW.all.width = "60%";
classes.INDENTEDNARROW.all.marginLeft = "20%";
```

Alignment

CSS syntax name: float
JavaScript syntax name: align
Possible values: left, right, none
Initial values: none
Applies to: all elements
Inherited: no
Percentage values: N/A
The term float is a reserved

The float property (CSS syntax) and align property (JavaScript syntax) determine the alignment of an element within its parent. (Note that the text-align/textAlign property determines the alignment of the content of text elements.)

The term float is a reserved word in JavaScript, which is why the JavaScript syntax uses the name align instead of float for this property.

Using the float/align property, you can make an element float to the left or the right and indicate how other content wraps around it.

If no value is specified, the default value is none. If the value is none, the element is displayed where it appears in the text.

If the value is left or right, the element is displayed on the left or the right (after taking margin properties into account). Other content appears on the right or left side of the floating element. If the value is left or right, the element is treated as a block-level element.

Using the float/align property, you can declare elements to be outside the normal flow of elements. For example, if the float/align property of an element is left, the normal flow wraps around on the right side.

If you set an element's float/align property set, do not also specify margins for it. If you do, the wrapping effect will not work properly. However, if you want a floating element to have a left or right margin, you can put it inside another element, such as a <DIV> block, that has the desired margins.

CSS Syntax Example

```
<STYLE TYPE="text/css">
H4 {
width:70%;
border-style:outset;
border-width:2pt;
border-color:green;
background-color:rgb(70%, 90%, 80%);
padding:5%;
font-weight:bold;
}
H4.TEXTRIGHT {text-align:right; margin-right:30%;}
```

```
H4.TEXTRIGHT_FLOATLEFT {text-align:right; float:left;}
H4.FLOATRIGHT {float:right;}
H4.FIXED_RIGHT_MARGIN {float:right; margin-right:30%;}
</STYLE>
```

JavaScript Syntax Example
```
<STYLE TYPE="text/javascript">
with (tags.H4) {
width="70%";
borderStyle="outset";
borderWidth="2pt";
borderColor="green";
backgroundColor = "rgb(70%, 90%, 80%)";
paddings("5%");
fontWeight="bold";
}
classes.TEXTRIGHT.H4.textAlign="right";
classes.TEXTRIGHT.H4.marginRight="30%;"
classes.TEXTRIGHT_FLOATLEFT.H4.textAlign="right";
classes.TEXTRIGHT_FLOATLEFT.H4.align="left";}
classes.FLOATRIGHT.H4.align="right";
classes.FIXED_RIGHT_MARGIN.H4.align="right";
classes.FIXED_RIGHT_MARGIN.H4.marginRight="30%";
</STYLE>
```

Style Sheet Use
```
<BODY>
<H4>Level-Four Heading</H4>
<P>I am a plain paragraph, positioned below a non-floating
level-four heading.
</P>
<H4 CLASS=TEXTRIGHT>H4 - My Text On Right, No Float</H4>
<P>I am also a plain paragraph, positioned below a non-floating
level-four heading. It just happens that the heading above me
has its text alignment set to right.
</P>
<H4 CLASS = FLOATRIGHT>H4 - Float = Right</H4>
<P>I am a regular paragraph. There's not much more you can say
about me. I am positioned after a level-four heading that is
floating to the right, so I come out positioned to the left of
it.</P>
<BR CLEAR>
<H4 CLASS=TEXTRIGHT_FLOATLEFT>H4 - My Text on Right, Float =
Left </H4>
<P>I'm also just a plain old paragraph going wherever the flow
takes me.
</P>
<BR CLEAR>
<H4 CLASS=FIXED_RIGHT_MARGIN>H4 - Float = Right, Fixed Right
Margin</H4>
```

```
<P>Hello? Hello!! I am wrapping round an H4 that is floating to
the right and has a fixed right margin. When I try to satisfy
all these requirements, you see what happens! For best results,
do not set the left and/or right margin when you set the float
(CSS syntax) or align (JavaScript syntax) property. Use an
enclosing element with margins instead.
</P>
<BR CLEAR>
<DIV STYLE="margin-left:30%;">
<H4 CLASS = FLOATRIGHT>H4 - Float = Right</H4>
<P>Notice how the heading next to me seems to have a right
margin.
That's because we are both inside a DIV block that has a right
margin.</P>
<BR CLEAR>
</DIV>
</BODY>
```

Clear

CSS syntax name: clear
JavaScript syntax name: clear
Possible values: none, left, right, both
Initial value: none
Applies to: all elements
Inherited: no
Percentage values: N/A

This property specifies whether an element allows floating elements on its sides. More specifically, the value of this property lists the sides where floating elements are not accepted. With clear set to left, an element will be moved below any floating element on the left side. With clear set to none, floating elements are allowed on all sides.

```
Example:

P {clear:left;}
tags.H1.clear = "left";
```

Color and Background Properties

Just as you can set color and background properties for a document as a whole, you can set them for block-level elements, too. These properties are applied to the "box" that contains the element.

Color

CSS syntax name: color
JavaScript syntax name: color
Possible values: color
Initial value: black
Applies to: all elements
Inherited: yes
Percentage values: N/A

This property describes the text color of an element, that is, the "foreground" color.

CSS Syntax Example
```
<STYLE TYPE="text/css">
EM {color:red;}
B {color:rgb(255, 0, 0);}
I {color:rgb(100%, 0%, 0%);}
CODE {color:#FF0000;}
</STYLE>
```

JavaScript Syntax Example
```
<STYLE TYPE="text/javascript">
tags.EM.color="red";
tags.B.color="rgb(255, 0, 0)";
tags.I.color="rgb(100%, 0%, 0%)";
tags.CODE.color="#FF0000";
</STYLE>
```

Background Image

CSS syntax name: background-image
JavaScript syntax name: backgroundImage
Possible values: url
Initial value: empty
Applies to: all elements
Inherited: no
Percentage values: N/A

This property specifies the background image of an element.

Partial URLs are interpreted relative to the source of the style sheet, not relative to the document.

CSS Syntax Example

```
<STYLE TYPE="text/css">
H1.SPECIAL {
background-image:url(images/glass2.gif);
padding:20pt;
color:yellow;
}
H2.SPECIAL {
padding:20pt;
background-color:#FFFF33;
border-style:solid;
border-width:1pt;
border-color:black;
}
P.SPECIAL B {background-image:url(images/tile1a.gif); }
P.SPECIAL I {background-color:cyan;}
</STYLE>
```

JavaScript Syntax Example

```
<STYLE TYPE="text/javascript">
classes.SPECIAL.H1.backgroundImage = "images/glass2.gif";
classes.SPECIAL.H1.paddings("20pt");
classes.SPECIAL.H1.color="yellow";
classes.SPECIAL.H2.paddings("20pt");
classes.SPECIAL.H2.backgroundColor="FFFF33";
classes.SPECIAL.H2.borderStyle="solid";
classes.SPECIAL.H2.borderWidth="1pt";
classes.SPECIAL.H2.borderColor="black";
contextual(classes.SPECIAL.P, tags.B).backgroundImage=
"images/tile1a.gif";
contextual(classes.SPECIAL.P, tags.I).backgroundColor="cyan";
</STYLE>
```

Style Sheet Use

```
<H1 CLASS=SPECIAL>Heading One with Image Background</H1>
<P CLASS=SPECIAL>
Hello. Notice how the portion of this paragraph that has an
<B>image background</B> is promoted to being a block- level
element on its own line.</P>
<H2 CLASS=SPECIAL>Heading Two with Solid Color Background</H2>
<P CLASS=SPECIAL>Hello, here is some <I>very interesting</I>
information. Notice that each <I>colored portion</I> of this
paragraph just continues right along in its normal place.
</P>
```

Background Color

CSS syntax name: background color
JavaScript syntax name: backgroundColor
Possible Values: color
Initial value: empty
Applies to: all elements
Inherited: no
Percentage values: N/A

This property specifies a solid background color for an element. See the previous section, Background Image, for a working example.

Classification Properties

These properties classify elements into categories more than they set specific visual parameters.

Display

CSS syntax name: display
JavaScript syntax name: display
Possible values: block, inline, list-item, none
Initial value: according to HTML
Applies to: all elements
Inherited: no
Percentage values: N/A

This property indicates whether an element is inline (for example, <EM> in HTML), block-level element (for example, <H1> in HTML), or a block-level list item (for example, <LI> in HTML). For HTML documents, the initial value is taken from the HTML specification.

A value of none turns off the display of the element, including children elements and the surrounding box. (Thus, if the value is set to none, the element is not displayed.)

Note that block-level elements do not seem to respond to having their display property set to inline.

CSS Syntax Example
```
EM.LISTEM {display:list-item;}
```

JavaScript Syntax Example
```
classes.LISTEM.EM.display="list-item";
```

List Style Type

CSS syntax name: list-style-type
JavaScript syntax name: listStyleType
Possible values: disc, circle, square, decimal, lower-roman,
upper-roman, lower-alpha, upper-alpha, none
Initial value: disc
Applies to: elements with display property value of list-item
Inherited: yes
Percentage values: N/A

This property describes how list items (that is, elements with a display value of list-item) are formatted.

This property can be set on any element, and its children will inherit the value. However, the list style is only displayed on elements that have a display value of list-item. In HTML this is typically the case for the <LI> element.

CSS Syntax Example

```
<STYLE TYPE="text/css">
UL.BLUELIST {color:blue;}
UL.BLUELIST LI {color:aqua;list-style-type:square;}
OL.REDLIST {color:red;}
OL.REDLIST LI {color:magenta; list-style-type:upper-roman;}
</STYLE>
```

JavaScript Syntax Example

```
<STYLE TYPE="text/javascript">
classes.BLUELIST.UL.color="blue";
contextual(classes.BLUELIST.UL, tags.LI).color="aqua";
contextual(classes.BLUELIST.UL,
tags.LI).listStyleType="square";
classes.REDLIST.OL.color="red";
contextual(classes.REDLIST.OL, tags.LI).color="magenta";
contextual(classes.REDLIST.OL, tags.LI).listStyleType="upper-
roman";
</STYLE>
```

Style Sheet Use

```
<UL CLASS=BLUELIST> <!—LI elements inherit from UL—>
<LI>Consulting
<LI>Development
<LI>Technology integration
</UL>
<OL CLASS=REDLIST> <!—LI elements inherit from OL—>
<LI>Start the program.
```

```
<LI>Enter your user name and password.
<LI>From the File menu, choose the Magic command.
</OL>
```

White Space

CSS syntax name: white-space
JavaScript syntax name: whiteSpace
Possible values: normal, pre
Initial value: according to HTML
Applies to: block-level elements
Inherited: yes
Percentage values: N/A

This property declares how white space inside the element should be handled. The choices are:

- normal (white space is collapsed)
- pre (behaves like the <PRE> element in HTML)

For example:

```
P.KEEPSPACES {white-space:pre;} /* CSS syntax */
classes.KEEPSPACES.P.whiteSpace = "pre"; /* JavaScript syntax
*/
```

Units

This section discusses units of measurement.

Length Units

The format of a length value is an optional sign character (+ or −, with + being the default) immediately followed by a number followed by a unit of measurement. For example, 12pt, 2em, 3mm.

There are three types of length units: relative, pixel, and absolute. Relative units specify a length relative to another length property. Style sheets that use relative units will scale more easily from one medium to another (for example, from a computer display to a laser printer). Percentage units and keyword values (such as x-large) offer similar advantages.

Child elements inherit the computed value, not the relative value, for example:

```
BODY {font-size:12pt; text-indent:3em;}
H1 {font-size:15pt;}
```

In the example above, the text indent value of H1 elements will be 36pt, not 45pt. The following relative units are supported:

- em—the height of the element's font, typically the width or height of the capital letter M
- ex—half the height of the element's font, which is typically the height of the letter x
- px—pixels, relative to rendering surface

The following absolute units are supported:

- pt—points
- pc—picas
- px—pixels
- in—inches
- mm—millimeters
- cm—centimeters

Color Units

A color value is a either a color name or a numerical RGB specification. The suggested list of color names is: aqua, black, blue, fuchsia, gray, green, lime, maroon, navy, olive, purple, red, silver, teal, white, and yellow.

```
tags.BODY.color = "black";
tags.backgroundColor = "white";
tags.H1.color = "maroon";
tags.H2.color = "olive";
```

You can specify an RGB color by a six-digit hexadecimal number, where the first two digits indicate the red value, the second two digits indicate the green value, and the last two digits indicate the blue value. For example:

```
BODY {color: #FF0000}; /* red */
BODY {background-color:#333333";} /* gray */
```

You can also specify an RGB color by using the rgb() function, which takes three arguments, for the red, green, and blue values. Each color value can either be an integer from 0 to 255 inclusive, or a percentage, as in this example:

```
P {color: rgb(200, 20, 240);) /* bright purple */
BLOCKQUOTE {background-color: rgb(100%, 100%, 20%); /* bright
yellow */
```

References:

1. http://developer.netscape.com/docs/manuals/dynhtml.html. Code presented in the introduction of this appendix was obtained from this source. This appendix is an edited version of the Netscape DHTML manual and from the sources listed in the resources section of that chapter.

Internet Development Resources

What follows is a list of interesting companies and their products. This appendix will get you started in the search for the perfect Web development tool.

Analysis Tools

Company: AccessWatch Inc.
Address: PO Box 60
Shady Side, MD 20764
Phone: (410) 955-0985
Web site: http://www.accesswatch.com
E-mail: sales@accesswatch.com
Product: AccessWatch

Company: Hi Software Inc.
Address: 6 Chennell Drive
Suite 280
Concord, NH 03301
Phone: (888) 272-2484
Web site: http://www.hisoftware.com
E-mail: sales@hisoftware.com
Product: Hi-State

Company: Mach5 Software
Address: 13612 Pine Villa Lane
Ft. Myers, FL 33912
Phone: (877) 405-6224
Fax: (941) 432-0743

Web site: http://www.mach5.com
E-mail: sales@mach5.com
Product: FastStats

Company: MyComputer.com
Address: 1358 West Business Park Drive
Orem, UT 84058
Phone: (801) 722-7000
Fax: (801) 722-7001
Web site: http://www.mycomputer.com
E-mail: info@mycomputer.com
Product: SuperStats

Company: NetGenesis Corp
Address: One Alewife Center
Cambridge, MA 02140
Phone: (800) 982-6351
Web site: http://www.netgenesis.com
Product: NetGenesis

Company: Sane Solutions
Address: 35 Belver Avenue
Suite 230
North Kingstown, RI 02852
Phone: (800) 407-3570
Web site: http://www.sane.com
E-mail: sales@sane.com
Product: Net Tracker

Company: SurfReport Inc.
Address: 114 Horatio Street
Suite 405
New York, NY 10014
Phone: (645) 314-9272
Web site: http://www.surfreport.com
E-mail: surfreport@rcn.com
Product: ProxyReport

Company: WhiteCross Systems Inc.
Address: 388 Market Street,
Suite 1450
San Francisco, CA 94111

Phone: (415) 249-0115
Web site: http://www.whitecross.com
E-mail: sales@whitecross.com
Product: WebAnalytics

Animation Tools

Company: Adobe Systems Inc.
Address: 345 Park Avenue
San Jose, CA 95110
Phone: (408) 536-6000
Web site: http://www.adobe.com
E-mail: info@adobe.com
Product: LiveMotion

Company: Alchemy Mindwords Inc.
Address: PO Box 500
Beeton, Ontario
Canada
Phone: (800) 263-1138
Web site: http://www.mindworkshop.com
E-mail: alchemy@mindworkshop.com
Product: GIF Construction Set

Company: Beatware Inc.
Address: 1179 Woodside Road
Suite 200
Redwood City, CA 94061
Phone: (650) 556-7900
Web site: http://www.beatware.com
E-mail: info@beatware.com
Product: eZ-Motion

Company: Extensis
Address: 1800 SW First Avenue
Suite 500
Portland, OR 97201
Phone: (503) 274-2020
Web site: http://www.extensis.com
Product: PhotoAnimator

Company: Jasc Software
Address: 7905 Fuller Road

Eden Prairie, MN 55344
Phone: (800) 622-2793
Web site: http://www.jasc.com
Product: Animation Shop

Company: Macromedia Inc.
Address: 600 Townsend Street
San Francisco, CA 94103
Web site: http://www.macromedia.com
E-mail: buy@macromedia.com
Product: Shockwave; Flash; Fireworks

Company: ParaGraph
Address: 1960 Zanker Road
San Jose, CA 95112
Web site: http://www.paragraph.com
E-mail: info@paragraph.com
Product: Morphink 99

Company: PeakSoft Corporation
Address: 114 West Magnolia Street
Suite 447
Bellingham, WA 98225
Phone: (360) 392-3912
Web site: http://www.peaksoft.com
E-mail: info@peaksoft.com
Product: JetEffects

Company: Right to Left Software Inc.
Address: 3324 Yonge Street
Toronto, Ontario
Canda
Phone: (416) 489-7440
Web site: http://www.rtlsoft.com
E-mail: info@rtlsoft.com
Product: Animagic GIF Animator

Company: Ulead Systems Inc.
Address: 970 West 190th Street
Suite 520
Torrance, CA 90502
Phone: (310) 523-9393

Web site: http://www.ulead.com
E-mail: info@ulead.com
Product: Ulead GIF Animator

Application Servers

Company: Bluestone Software
Address: 300 Stevens Drive
Philadelphia, PA 19113
Phone: (610) 915-5000
Fax: (610) 915-5012
Web site: http://www.bluestone.com/products/sapphire
E-mail: info@bluestone.com
Product: Sapphire

Company: GemStone Systems Inc.
Address: 20575 NW von Neumann Drive
Beaverton, OR 97006
Phone: (800) 243-9369
Web site: http://www.gemstone.com/
Email: info@gemstone.com
Product: VisualWave Internet Application Server

Company: IBM Corp.
Address: 13860 Diplomat Drive
Dallas, TX 75234
Phone: (800) 288-9584
Web site: http://www.ibm.com/
E-mail: prgsvc@us.ibm.com
Product: WebSphere Application Server

Company: iPlanet (a Sun/Netscape Alliance)
Address: 901 San Antonio Road
Palo Alto, CA 94303
Phone: (650) 254-1900
Web site: http://www.iplanet.com/
E-mail: sales@iplanet.com
Product: iPlanet Application Server

Company: Lotus Development Corp.
Address: 55 Cambridge Parkway
Cambridge, MA 02142

Phone: (617) 577-8500
Web site: http://www.lotus.com
E-mail: info@lotus.com
Product: Domino Application Server

Company: Lutris Technologies
Address: 1200 Pacific Avenue
Suite 300
Santa Cruz, CA 95060
Phone: (831) 471-9753
Web site: http://www.lutris.com/
E-mail: sales@lutris.com
Product: Lutris Enhydra

Company: Microsoft Corp.
Address: One Microsoft Way
Redmond, WA 98052-6399
Phone: (425) 936-4400 (International)
Web site: http://www.microsoft.com
E-mail: info@microsoft.com
Product: Internet Information Server

Company: Oracle Corp.
Address: 500 Oracle Parkway
Redwood Shores, CA 94065
Phone: (650) 506-7000
Web site: http://www.oracle.com/
E-mail: web-mkt1@us.oracle.com
Product: Oracle9i Application Server

Company: Sybase Inc.
Address: 6475 Christie Avenue
Emeryville, CA 94608
Phone: (800) 8-SYBASE
Web site: http://www.sybase.com/products/applicationservers/easerver/
Product: EAServer

Audio

Company: The DSP Group Inc.
Address: 3120 Scott Boulevard

Santa Clara, CA 95054
Phone: (408) 986-4300
Fax: (408) 986-4323
Web site: http://www.dspg.com/
E-mail: support@dspg.com
Product: TrueSpeech

Company: Liquid Audio Inc.
Address : 2221 Broadway
Redwood City, CA 94063
Phone: (650) 549-2000
Fax: (650) 549-2099
Web site: http://www.liquidaudio.com/
Email: webmaster@liquidaudio.com
Product: Liquid Music System

Company: RealNetworks
Address: PO Box 91123
Seattle, WA 98111-9223
Phone: (206) 674-2700
Web site: http://www.realnetworks.com
E-mail: sales@real.com
Products: RealSystem Producer Plus; RealSystem Server; SoundForge XP

Company: Sonic Foundry Inc.
Address: 1617 Sherman Avenue
Madison, WI 53704
Phone: (800) 577-6642
Web site: http://www.sonicfoundry.com
E-mail: sales@sonicfoundry.com
Product: Sound Forge

Company: Telos Systems
Address: 2101 Superior Avenue
Cleveland, OH 44114
Phone: (216) 241-7225
Fax: (216) 241-4103
Web site: http://www.audioactive.com
E-mail: info@telos-systems.com
Product: Audioactive Production Studio

Company Name: Voxware Inc.
Address: Lawrenceville Office Park

PO Box 5363
Princeton, NJ 08543
Phone: (609) 514-4100
Fax: (609) 514-4101
Web site: http://www.voxware.com
E-mail: vox@voxware.com
Product: VoiceLogistics Suite

Chat

Company Name: iChat Inc.
Address: 5001 South Miami Boulevard
Suite 118
Durham, NC 27703
Phone: (919) 767-2727
Fax: (919) 767-2900
Web site: http://www.ichat.com
E-mail: sales@ichat.com
Product: ROOMS; boards, pager

Content Management

Company: BroadVision Inc.
Address: 585 Broadway
Redwood City, CA 94063
Phone: (650) 261-5100
Web site: http://www.broadvision.com
Product: One-to-One Publishing

Company: eBT
Address: 299 Promenade Street
Providence, RI 02908
Phone: (401) 752-4400
Web site: http://www.ebt.com
E-mail: info@ebt.com
Product: Engenda is an XML-enabled content management and workflow automation
solution created to support ongoing Internet, Intranet, and Extranet requirements.

Company: Eprise Corp.
Address: 200 Crossing Boulevard
Framingham, MA 01702
Phone: (508) 661-5200

Web site: http://www.eprise.com
Product: Participant Server

Company: IBM Corp.
Address: New Orchard Road
Armonk, NY 10504
Phone: (914) 499-1900
Web site: http://www.ibm.com
Product: Content Manager

Company: Interwoven Inc.
Address: 1195 West Fremont Avenue
Sunnyvale, CA 94087-3825
Phone: (408) 774-2000
Web site: http://www.interwoven.com
Product: TeamSite

Company: IntraNet Solutions Inc.
Address: 7777 Golden Triangle Drive
Eden Prairie, MN 55344
Phone: (952) 903-2000
Web site: http://www.intranetsolutions.com
Product: Xpedio Content Server

Company: NCompass Labs Inc.
Address: Hudson House
321 Water Street
Vancouver, BC
Canada V6B 1B8
Phone: (877) 606-0950
Web site: http://www.ncompasslabs.com
Product: Resolution

Company: OpenMarket Inc.
Address: One Wayside Road
Bington, MA 01803
Phone: (781) 359-3000
Web site: http://www.openmarket.com
Product: Content Centre and Content Server

Company: Rational Software Corp.
Address: 18880 Homestead Road

Cupertino, CA 95014
Phone: (408) 863-9900
Web site: http://www.rational.com
E-mail: info@rational.com
Product: Rational Suite ContentStudio

Company Name: Vignette Inc.
Address: 901 South MoPac Expressway
Building 3
Austin, TX 78746
Phone: (512) 741-4300
Fax: (512) 741-4500
Web site: http://www.vignette.com
E-mail: usinfo@vignette.com
Product: Content Manager Generator; StoryServer

Database Modeling

Company: Embarcadero Technologies
Address: 425 Market Street
Suite 425
San Francisco, CA 94105
Phone: (415) 834-3131
Web site: http://www.embarcadero.com
E-mail: sales@embarcadero.com
Product: ER/Studio is a data-modeling application for logical and physical database design and construction.

Data Conversion Services

Company: Data Conversion Laboratory
Address: 184-13 Horace Harding Expressway
Fresh Meadows, NY 11365
Phone: (718) 357-8700
Web site: http://www.dclab.com

Digital Cameras

Company: Eastman Kodak Co.
Address: 343 State Street
Rochester, NY 14650
Phone: (800) 235-6325

Web site: http://www.kodak.com/
Product: Kodak DC 280 Zoom

Company: Nikon Inc.
Address: 1300 Walt Whitman Road
Melville, NY 11747
Phone: (516) 547-4200
Web site: http://www.nikonusa.com/
Product: Nikon Coolpix 990

Company: Ricoh Co.
Address: 5 Dedrick Place
West Caldwell, NJ 07006
Phone: (201) 882-2000
Web site: http://www.ricoh-usa.com/
E-mail: cust_support@ricohcpg.com
Product: RDC-5300

Company: Xir Link Inc.
Address: 2210 O'Toole Avenue
San Jose, CA 95131
Phone: (408) 324-2100
Web site: http://www.xirlink.com/
Product: Xirlink IBM PC Camera Pro Max

Digital Rights Management

Company: Reciprocal Inc.
Address: 330 Madison Avenue
19th Floor
New York, NY 10017
Phone: (212) 983-8200
Web site: http://www.reciprocal.com

E-Commerce Customer Management

Company: Art Technology Group
Address: 25 First Street, 2nd Floor
Cambridge, MA 02141
Phone: (617) 386-1000
Fax: (617) 386-1111
Web site: http://www.atg.com

E-mail: info@atg.com
Product: ATG Dynamo e-Business Platform

E-Commerce Stores

Company: Open Market's ShopSite
Address: 5252 North Edgewood Drive
Suite 275
Provo, UT 84604
Phone: (801) 705-4100; (888) 373-4347
Fax: 801-705-4184
Web site: http://www.shopsite.com
E-mail: info@shopsite.com
Product: ShopSite Store-Building Solution

Company: SpaceWorks
Address: 51 Monroe Street
Rockville, MD 20850
Phone: (301) 251-4136; (800) S-SPACE-S
Fax: (301) 738-9284
Web site: http://www.spaceworks.com
E-mail: info@spaceworks.com
Product: Web BusinessManager Suite

Globalization of Web Sites

Company: Lionbridge Multilingual Content Management
Address: 492 Old Connecticut Path
Framingham, MA 01701
Phone: (508) 620-3900
Fax: (508) 620-3999
Web site: http://www.lionbridge.com
E-mail: info@lionbridge.com
Product: Localization and translation services, localizing into over 22 different languages.

Graphic Optimization

Company: NetMechanic Inc.
Address: 2905 Westcorp Boulevard
Suite 112
Huntsville, AL 35805

Phone: (256) 533-0076
Web site: http://www.netmechanic.com
E-mail: sales@netmechanic.com
Product: GIFBot is a free tool designed to optimize load times by reducing the size of Web graphics up to 90 percent.

Graphic Tools

Company: Adobe Systems Inc.
Address: 345 Park Avenue
San Jose, CA 95110
Phone: (408) 536-6000
Web site: http://www.adobe.com
E-mail: info@adobe.com
Product: PhotoShop

Company: Pegasus Imaging Corp.
Address: 4522 Spruce Street
Suite 200
Tampa, FL 33607
Phone: (800) 875-7009
Web site: http://www.jpegwizard.com
E-mail: sales@jpgwizard.com
Product: Images Asap; JPEG Wizard

Company: Wacom Technology Corp.
Address: 1311 SE Cardinal Court
Vancouver, WA 98683
Phone: (800) 922-9348
Web site: http://www.wacom.com
E-mail: sales@wacom.com
Product: Studio Artist; GRAPHIRE Power Suit; Pen Tools; Deep Paint

HTML Development and Maintenance Tools

Company: Macromedia
Address: 600 Townsend Street
San Francisco, CA 94103
Web site: http://www.macromedia.com
E-mail: info@macromedia.com
Product: DreamWeaver

Company: Microsoft Corp.
Address: One Microsoft Way
Redmond, WA 98052-6399
Phone: (425) 936-4400 (International)
Web site: http://www.microsoft.com
E-mail: info@microsoft.com
Product: FrontPage; Internet Assistant

Company: NetMechanic Inc.
Address: 2905 Westcorp Bouldevard
Suite 112
Huntsville, AL 35805
Phone: (256) 533-0076
Web site: http://www.netmechanic.com
E-mail: sales@netmechanic.com
Product: HTML Toolbox 2.0; Browser Photo is an easy-to-use tool offering Web site builders an inexpensive alternative to preview their Web pages on all major browsers in order to correct display differences.

Company: SoftQuad Software Inc.
Address: 161 Eglinton Avenue East
Suite 400
Toronto, Ontario
Canada
Phone: (416) 544-9000
Web site: http://www.hotmetalpro.com
E-mail: hotmotel-order@softquad.com
Product: HotMeTal Pro

Company: Sybase Inc.
Address: 6475 Christie Avenue
Emeryville, CA 94608
Phone: (800) 8-SYBASE
Web site: http://www.sybase.com/products/internetappdevttools/powerbuilder
Product: PowerBuilder 8

Company: WebAuthor.com LLC
Address: 1900 West Commercial Boulevard
Suite 100
Ft. Lauderdale, FL 33309
Phone: (954) 257-4900

Web site: http://www.webauthor.com
E-mail: info@webauthor.com
Product: Web Author

Industry/Market Research

Company: Fuji-Keizai U.S.A. Inc.
Address: 141 East 55 Street
Suite 3F
New York, NY 10022
Phone: (212) 371-4773
Web site: http://www.fuji-keizai.com

Java Development

Company: Allaire Corp.
Address: 275 Grove Street
Newton, MA 02466
Phone: (617) 219-2000
Web site: http://www.allaire.com
E-mail: info@allaire.com
Product: JRun; Kawa

Company: Borland Software Corp.
Address: 100 Enterprise Way
Scotts Valley, CA 95066
Phone: (831) 431-1000
Web site: http://www.borland.com/jbuilder
E-mail: customer-server@borland.com
Product: JBuilder

Company: Computer Associates
Address: One Computer Associates Plaza
Islandia, NH 11749
Phone: (972) 801-6644
Web site: www.ca.com/products/cool/cooljoe.htm
E-mail: info@ca.com
Product: COOL:Joe

Company: Diamond Edge
Address: 184 South 300 West
Lindon, UT 84042

Phone: (801) 785-8473
Web site: http://www.diamondedge.com
E-mail: sales@diamondedge.com
Product: Applet Desinger 3.0

Company: Microsoft Corp.
Address: One Microsoft Way
Redmond, WA 98052-6399
Phone: (425) 936-4400 (International)
Web site: http://www.microsoft.com/
E-mail: info@microsoft.com
Product: Visual J++

Company: Modelworks Software
Address: 14612 NE 169 Street
Woodonville, WA 98072
Phone: (425) 488-5686
Web site: http://www.modelworks.com
E-mail: support@modelworks.com
Product: JpadPro

Company: Oracle Corporation
Address: 500 Oracle Parkway
Redwood Shores CA 94065
Phone: (800) ORACLE-1
Web site: http://www.oracle.com/tools/jdeveloper
E-mail: info@oracle.com
Product: Oracle JDeveloper

Company: RegNet
Address: 675 Southpointe Court
Suite 250
Colorado Springs, CO 80906
Phone: (719) 576-0123
Web site: http://www.reg.net
E-mail: info@reg.net
Product: JavaSpy

Company: Sun Microsystems
Address: Mountain View, CA
Phone: (415) 960-1300
Web site: http://www.sun.com

E-mail: info@sun.com
Product: Forte for Java

Company: Sybase
Address: 6475 Christie Avenue
Emeryville, CA 94068
Phone: (800) 8SYBASE
Web site: http://www.sybase.com
E-mail: info@sybase.com
Product: PowerJ

Company: Tower Technology Corp.
Address: 505 East Huntland Drive
Suite 530
Austin, TX 78752
Phone: (512) 452-9455; (800) 285-5124
Web site: http://www.towerj.com
E-mail: sales@towerj.com
Product: TowerJ product line of Java performance solutions. Tower's performance training courses teach Java engineers how to increase application scalability and improve response times. Tower's Java Performance Assessment and Optimization services

Company: WebGain
Address: 5425 Stevens Creek Boulevard
Santa Clara, CA 95051
Phone: (888) 822-3409
Web site: http://www.webgain.com
E-mail: sales@webgain.com
Product: WebGain Studio; VisualCafe

Online Payments

Company: BillPoint
Address: San Jose, California
Web site: http://www.billpoint.com
E-mail: info@billpoint.com
Product: Billpoint (take credit cards using Billpoints service)

Company: CyberCash Inc.
Address: 2100 Reston Parkway
Reston, VA 20191
Phone: (703) 620-4200
Fax: (703) 620-4215

Web site: http://www.cybercash.com
E-mail: info@cybercash.com
Product: CashRegister; B2B Payment Services; WebAuthorize; FraudPatrol; ICVER-IFY; PCAUTHORIZE

Company: PayPal
Address: PO Box 50185
Palo Alto, CA 94303
Web site: http://www.paypal.com
E-mail: service@paypal.com
Product: Secure online payment

Product Development Portal

Company: Mesa Systems International Inc.
Address: 1600 Division Road
Suite 1
East West Warwick, RI 02893
Phone: (401) 886-9494
Web site: http://www.mesasys.com
E-mail: info@mesasys.com
Product: MesaVista

Search Engine Submission and Optimization

Company: NetMechanic Inc.
Address: 2905 Westcorp Boulevard
Suite 112
Huntsville, AL 35805
Phone: (256) 533-0076
Web site: http://www.netmechanic.com
E-mail: sales@netmechanic.com
Product: Search Engine Starter Stand-Alone; Search Engine Power Pack

Server Monitoring

Company: NetMechanic, Inc.
Address: 2905 Westcorp Boulevard
Suite 112
Huntsville, AL 35805
Phone: (256) 533-0076
Web site: http://www.netmechanic.com

E-mail: sales@netmechanic.com
Product: Server Check Pro

Video

Company: Adobe Systems
Address: 345 Park Avenue
San Jose, CA 95110
Phone: (408) 536-6000
Fax: (408) 537-6000
Web site: http://www.adobe.com/
E-mail: support@adobe.com
Product: Adobe Premiere

Company: Digigami Inc.
Address: 906 10th Avenue
San Diego, CA 92101
Phone: (619) 231-2600
Fax: (619) 231-2273
Web site: http://www.digigami.com/
E-mail: info@digigami.com
Product: Movie Screamer

Company: Microsoft Corp.
Address: One Microsoft Way
Redmond, WA 98052-6399
Phone: (425) 936-4400 (International)
Web site: http://www.microsoft.com/
E-mail: info@microsoft.com
Product: NetShow; Windows Media Player

Company: Pinnacle Systems Inc.
Address: 7340 Shadeland Station
Indianapolis, IN 46256
Phone: (217) 576-7728
Web site: http://www.pinnaclesys.com/
E-mail: info@pinnaclesys.com
Product: CINE WAVE

Company: RealNetworks
Address: PO Box 91123
Seattle, WA 98111-9223
Phone: (206) 674-2700

Web site: http://www.realnetworks.com
E-mail: sales@real.com
Products: RealSystem Producer Plus; RealSystem Server; Studio Solution for RealVideo; VideoFramer; RealVideo Creation Kit; Xing Streamworks

Company: Terran Interactive
Address: 15951 Los Gatos Boulevard
Suite 1
Los Gatos, CA 95032
Phone: (800) 572-3487
Fax: (408) 356-0373
Web site: http://www.terran.com/
E-mail: info@terran.com
Product: WiredStream

Company: Wacom Technology Corp.
Address: 1311 SE Cardinal Court
Vancouver, WA 98683
Phone: (800) 922-9348
Web site: http://www.wacom.com
E-mail: sales@wacom.com
Product: Commotion DV

Web Application Development Tools

Company: Hamilton Technologies Inc.
Address: 17 Inman Street
Cambridge, MA 02139
Phone: (617) 492-0058
Fax: (617) 492-1727
Web site: http://world.std.com/~hti
E-mail: sales@htius.com
Product: 001

Company: Interwoven Inc.
Address: 1195 West Fremont Avenue
Sunnyvale, CA 94087
Phone: (408) 774-2000
Fax: (408) 774-2002
Web site: http://www.interwoven.com
E-mail: info@interwoven.com
Product: TeamSite; ExpoSite

Company: Speedware Corp.
Address: 9999 Cavendish Boulevard
St. Laurent, Quebec
H4M 2X5 Canada
Phone: (514) 747-7007
Fax: (514) 747-3380
Web site: http://www.speedware.com
E-mail: info@speedware.com
Products: Visual Speedware; Speedware Autobahn; MobileDev

Company: Sybase Inc.
Address: 6475 Christie Avenue
Emeryville, CA 94608
Phone: (800) 8-SYBASE
Web site: http://www.sybasecom/products/internetappdevttools/powerbuilder
Product: PowerBuilder 8

Web/ASP Hosting

Company: AveHost.com
Address: 5 Pembroke Way
2nd Floor
Palisades Park, NJ 07650
Phone: (888) 430-1600
Web site: http://www.avehost.com
E-mail: info@avehost.com
Product: Web hosting

Company: Trellix Corp.
Address: 300 Baker Avenue
Concord, MA 01742
Phone: (978) 318-7200
Fax: (978) 318-7294
Web site: http://www.trellix.com
Product: Trellix Web Express; Trellix Web

Web Design and Consulting

Company: The Marant Group
Address: 3200 North Hayden Road
Suite 300

Scottsdale, AZ 85251
Phone: (480) 663-6279
Fax: (480) 663-6629
Web site: http://www.marantgroup.com
E-mail: info@marantgroup.com

Company: OnePoint
Address: PO Box 241
Wernersville, PA 19565-0241
Phone: (610) 927-3990
Web site: http://www.onepointonline.net
E-mail: OnePoint@mail.com

Wireless Application Development Tools

Company: Aether Systems
Address: 11460 Cronridge Drive
Owings Mills, MD 21117
Phone: (410) 654-6400; (888) 812-6767
Web site: http://www.aethersystems.com
Product: Aether's ScoutBuilder for the Palm OS platform

Company: AvidWireless
Address: 7750 North MacArthur Boulevard
#120 PMB 340
Irving, TX 75063-7519
Phone: (972) 401-3655; (888) 772-4570
Web site: http://www.avidwireless.com
E-mail: info@avidwireless.com
Product: AVIDRapidTools

Company: Broadbeam Corp.
Address: 100 College Road West
Princeton, NJ 08540-5052
Phone: (609) 734-0300
Web site: http://www.broadbeam.com
E-mail: info@broadbeam.com
Product: The Broadbeam Developer Suite

Company: BSQUARE
Address: 3150 139th Place SE
Bellevue, WA 98005

Phone: (425) 519-5900; (888) 820-4500
Web site: http://www.bsquare.com
E-mail: sales@bsquare.com
Product: WinDK Extension for Bluetooth

Company: Extended Systems
Address: 5777 North Meeker Avenue
Boise, ID 83713
Phone: (208) 322-7800; (800) 235-7576
Web site: http://www.extendedsystems.com
E-mail: info@extendsys.com
Product: XTNDConnect Blue SDK for Windows

Company: Metrowerks.com
Address: 9801 Metric Boulevard
Austin, TX 78758
Phone: (512) 997-4700; (800) 377-35416
Web site: http://www.metrowerks.com
E-mail: info@metrowerks.com
Product: CodeWarrior

Company: Nokia
Address: Nokia Mobile Internet Applications
Finland
Phone: (877) 997-9199
Web site: http://www.forum.nokia.com/
E-mail: info.ipnetworking.Americas@nokia.com
Product: Nokia Wap Toolkit

Company: OracleMobile Inc.
Phone: (650) 506-4300
Web site: http://www.oraclemobile.com
E-mail: info@oraclemobile.com
Product: OracleMobile Online Studio

Company: River Run Software Group
Address: 9 Greenwich Office Park
Greenwich, CT 06831
Phone: (203) 861-0096
Web site: http://www.riverrun.com
E-mail: webmaster@riverrun.com

Product: River Run AppsBuilder
Company: SpeedWare
Address: 9999 Cavendish Boulevard
Suite 100
St. Laurent, Quebec
Canada
Phone: (514) 747-7007
Web site: http://mobiledev.speedware.com
E-mail: info@speedware.com
Product: Mobile Dev

Company: WaveLink Corp.
Address: 11332 NE 122nd Way
Suite 300
Kirkland, WA 98034-6936
Phone: (425) 823-0111; (888) 697-WAVE
Web site: http://www.wavelink.com
E-mail: info@wavelink.com
Product: WaveLink Studio

Wireless Content Publishing

Company: AirMedia
Address: 11 East 26 Street
16th Floor
New York, NY 10010
Phone: (212) 843-0000
Web site: http://www.airmedia.com
E-mail: info@airmedia.com
Product: Airmedia mobile content publishing and selling system

Wireless Systems Integrators

Company: WaveDev.com
Address: Bermuda
Phone: (441) 232-3070
Web site: http://www.wavedev.com
E-mail: marketing@wavedev.com
Product: Development and consulting services to integrate wireless applications into existing enterprise or Web systems.

XML Tools

Company: Apache Software Foundation
Address: 1901 Munsey Drive
Forest Hill, MD 21050
Phone: (410) 803-2258
Web site: http://xml.apache.org
E-mail: apache@apache.org
Product: Xerces Java Parser

Company: IBM Corp.
Address: Armonk, NY
Phone: (425) 882-8080
Web site: http://www.alphaworks.ibm.com/formula/xml
Product: XML for Java

Company: Oracle Corporation
Address: 500 Oracle Parkway
Redwood Shores, CA 94065
Phone: (800) ORACLE1
Web site: http://www.oracle.com
Product: Oracle's XML Parser

Links of Interest

Web Developer Sites of Interest

Browsers, Viewers, and HTML Preparation Resources
http://www.utoronto.ca/webdocs/HTMLdocs/intro_tools.html

CGI Programming OpenFAQ
http://www.boutell.com/openfaq/cgi

CNet Feature on GIF89a Animation
http://www.cnet.com/Content/Features/Techno/Gif89

CSS Validation Service
http://jigsaw.w3.org/css-validator/

Free Web Resources
http://www.thefreesite.com

HTML Developer's JumpStation
http://oneworld.wa.com/htmldev/devpage/dev-page.html

List of Web Hosting Services
http://www.webhosters.com

Review of Hosting Services
http://www.hostreview.com

The Transparent/Interlaced GIF Resource Page
http://www.best.com/~adamb/GIFpage.html

The Web Developer's Virtual Library
http://www.stars.com/Vlib

W3C HTML/XHTML Validation Service
http://validator.w3.org

Yahoo World Wide Web Resources Index
http://www.yahoo.com/Computers_and_Internet/Internet/World_Wide_Web/

ZDNet Developer's Resources
http://www.zdnet.com/devhead/

Web Development Software

Adobe PageMill HTML Editor
http://www.adobe.com/prodindex/pagemill

BBEdit Text and HTML Editors for Mac
http://web.barebones.com/products/bbedit/litevfull.html

HomeSite HTML Editor
http://www.allaire.com/products/HOMESITE

Hot Dog HTML Editor and Hot Dog Express
http://www.sausage.com

InContext Spider: HTML Editor
http://www.incontext.com/SPinfo.html

Macromedia Dreamweaver
http://www.macromedia.com/software/dreamweaver

SoftQuad HotMetal Pro: HTML Editor
http://www.sq.com

Graphics Packages

Graphics Links
http://www.dcs.ed.ac.uk/home/mxr/gfx/utils-hi.html

HTML Paint Brush Web Page Color Chooser
http://members.xoom.com/mattp/htmlpb.htm

LView Pro Graphic Editing Software
http://www.lview.com

Mapedit
http://www.boutell.com/mapedit

Paint Shop Pro Graphic Editing Software
http://www.jasc.com/psp.html

Reptile Background Generation Utility
http://www.sausage.com/reptile/reptile.html

Perl

CGI, Perl, and TCL Coding Page
http://www.zdnet.com/devhead/filters/cgiperltcl

Free Perl Code
http://www.freeperlcode.com

Free Perl Scripts
http://www.scrubtheweb.com/abs/cgi/index.html

The Perl Institute
http://www.perl.org

The Perl Journal
http://tpj.com

The Perl Language Home Page
http://language.perl.com

Perl Resource Center
http://index.thescripts.com/Perl_Scripts

Java

Free Java Applets
http://www.scrubtheweb.com/abs/cgi/index.html

Gamelan: A Directory and Registry of Java Resources
http://www.gamelan.com

Java FAQ Archives
http://www.net.com/java/faq

More Free Applets
http://www.applets.freeserve.co.uk

The Official Sun Java Site
http://java.sun.com

Yahoo! Java Resources
http://dir.yahoo.com/Computers_and_Internet/Programming_Languages/Java

Your Ultimate Java Software Directory
http://www.jfind.com

JavaScript

Free JavaScript Scripts
http://javascript.internet.com

JavaScript FAQs
http://www.irt.org/script/faq.htm

One of the Better Freebie Sites
http://www.javascriptwizard.com

Yahoo! JavaScript Resources
http://dir.yahoo.com/Computers_and_Internet/Programming_Languages/JavaScript

ActiveX

Microsoft ActiveX Site
http://www.microsoft.com/com/activex.asp

VRML

The VRML Consortium
http://www.vrml.org

The VRML Repository: Resource for VRML Information
http://www.sdsc.edu/vrml

Reading Matter

BizReport.com
http://www.bizreport.com

CIO Magazine
http://www.cio.com

CNet News.com
http://www.news.com

E-Commerce Alert
http://www.zdjournals.com/eca

E-Commerce Guide
http://ecommerce.internet.com

E-Commerce Times
http://www.ecommercetimes.com

E-Commerce Weekly
http://www.eweekly.com

Edupage—Technology Industry News Summarization
http://listserv.educause.edu/cgi-bin/wa.exe?SUBED1=edupage&A=1

Fast Company
http://www.fastcompany.com

IDG Net
http://www.idg.net

Information Week Magazine
http://www.informationweek.com

InfoWorld Newspaper
http://www.infoworld.com

Red Herring
http://www.redherring.com

Slashdot (for Nerds)
http://www.slashdot.org

Techweb
http://www.techweb.com

The Standard (Internet related)
http://www.thestandard.com

Wired Magazine News
http://www.wired.com

ZDNet e-Business
http://www.zdnet.com/enterprise/e-business

Index

A
ActionScript, Flash, 131
active server pages (ASP)
   ASP+, 436
   database-Internet connectivity, 435–437
   functions of, 205, 436
ActiveWatch, 454
adaptive algorithms, 518
ADK 2.0, VoiceXML development tool, 282
Adobe Acrobat, for PDF files, 58–60, 151
advertising. *See* marketing
affiliate program
   links to sites, 100
   operation of, 99–100
aggregator services, licensing arrangements, 188
ahead-of-time (AOT) native compilation, Java, 506–508
Akamai, 197
Alchemy Mindworks, 29
alignment
   CSS property, 726–728
   JavaScript property, 726–728
AllFreeClipArt, 20
Alpha channel, 136
amazon.com
   affiliate program, 99–100
   branch stores, 91–92
   confirmation of order, 87, 88
   marketing expense, 85
   one-click patent, 162
   storage/shipping facilities, 87–88
ambient sounds, 138, 141

analysis stage. *See* Web site analysis
animation, 28–32
   and browser, 29
   development tools, 29, 738–739
   Flash, 55, 124–133
   Shockwave, 54–55
   steps in, 30–31
anti-aliasing, 136
Apache, and mod_Perl, 262
applets
   communication with server, 460–463
   Java, 77, 78
application hosting
   capability requirements, 487
   development tools, 756
   e-mail handling, 494
   information sources on, 497
   minimum requirements, 487–488
   networks/hardware support, 492–493
   and network topology, 493–494
   and operating system, 489–491
   privacy, 496
   and programming language, 491–492
   reseller program, 496–497
   security, 494–495
   shared hosting, 488
application servers, development tools, 740–741
Application Service Provider. *See* ASP (Application Service Provider)
archiving content, 194
arrays, Perl, 260